Financial Accounting Theory

european
edition

LANCHESTER
Gosford Str

Financial Accounting Theory

european edition

Craig Deegan
Jeffrey Unerman

The **McGraw·Hill** Companies

London Boston Burr Ridge, IL Dubuque, IA Madison, WI New York San Francisco
St. Louis Bangkok Bogotá Caracas Kuala Lumpur Lisbon Madrid Mexico City
Milan Montreal New Delhi Santiago Seoul Singapore Sydney Taipei Toronto

Financial Accounting Theory
Craig Deegan & Jeffrey Unerman
ISBN-13 9780077108960
ISBN-10 0-07-710896-5

Published by McGraw-Hill Education
Shoppenhangers Road
Maidenhead
Berkshire
SL6 2QL
Telephone: 44 (0) 1628 502 500
Fax: 44 (0) 1628 770 224
Website: www.mcgraw-hill.co.uk

British Library Cataloguing in Publication Data
A catalogue record for this book is available from the British Library

Library of Congress Cataloging in Publication Data
The Library of Congress data for this book has been applied for from the Library of Congress

Acquisitions Editor: Mark Kavanagh
Senior Development Editor: Natalie Jacobs
Marketing Manager: Marca Wosoba
Production Editor: James Bishop

Dedication

From Craig: My efforts are dedicated to my beautiful young daughter, Cassandra Joy Deegan.

From Jeffrey: This book is dedicated to Terry and Alan Unerman – a most loving, devoted and very special couple.

Brief table of contents

Detailed table of contents

Preface

This book has been written to provide readers with a balanced discussion of different theories of financial accounting. Various theories for and against regulation of financial accounting are critically discussed and various theoretical perspectives, including those provided by positive accounting theory, political economy theory, stakeholder theory, institutional theory and legitimacy theory, are introduced to explain different types of voluntary reporting decisions. The book also analyses and evaluates the development of various normative theories of accounting, including various approaches developed to account for changing prices, and different normative perspectives about the accountability of business entities, as well as various conceptual framework projects. It also emphasizes the role of a number of factors in explaining both international differences in accounting and recent institutional efforts towards international harmonizing of accounting.

In addition to providing explanations for why or how organizations should disclose particular items of financial information, the book investigates research that explores how or whether people at an aggregate and individual level demand or react to particular disclosures. Reflecting the growing relevance of social and environmental reporting issues to students, government, industry and the accounting profession, social and environmental reporting issues are discussed in depth. The book also provides an insight into the role of financial accounting from the perspective of a group of researchers who are often described as working from a critical perspective.

Being divided into 12 chapters sequenced in a logical order, this book can provide the entire core material required for a course on financial accounting theory. Alternatively, the book can be used as a key text for more general courses which include coverage of aspects of financial accounting theory. All of the material within the book could realistically be covered in the average 10 to 12 week university term, with chapters being studied in the sequence in which they are presented. Because it provides a balanced perspective of alternative and sometimes conflicting theories of financial accounting, it also provides a sound basis for readers contemplating further research in different areas of financial accounting.

In writing this book, a style has been adopted that enables students at both the undergraduate and postgraduate level to gain a sound understanding of financial accounting theory. Each chapter incorporates research from throughout the world, hence the book is of relevance to financial accounting theory students internationally. Much of the explanatory material has been drawn from European practical examples – thus making the text even more accessible and relevant to students in Europe. To assist in the learning process, each chapter provides learning objectives, chapter summaries and end-of-chapter discussion questions. Throughout the book readers are encouraged to critically evaluate and challenge the various views presented. To give the various perspectives a 'real world' feel, many chapters use recent articles from different newspapers, directly relating to the issues under consideration.

In the five years since Craig Deegan wrote the Australian edition of this book, it has proved very popular among both students and lecturers throughout Europe. In addition to the academic coverage of the book, readers have praised the accessible and engaging style in which it was written. This new European edition retains the features of the Australian edition that students and lecturers found so appealing and distinctive, such as use of straightforward explanations, frequent practical examples, and illustrations using newspaper articles. With many illustrations drawn from European business and accounting situations, we believe this European edition will be even more appealing, accessible and relevant to readers in Europe than the earlier Australian edition. We have also taken the opportunity of updating the text to reflect the sometimes significant developments in accounting theory in the past five years.

Craig Deegan and Jeffrey Unerman

About the Authors
Craig Deegan

Craig Deegan BCom (University of NSW), MCom (Hons) (University of NSW), PhD (University of Queensland) is Professor of Accounting and Director of Research and Development within the School of Accounting and Law at RMIT University, Melbourne, Australia. Craig has taught at both undergraduate and postgraduate levels at universities in Australia for more than two decades and has presented lectures internationally, including within the United Kingdom, United States, South Africa, France, China, Singapore, Hong Kong, Malaysia, South Korea and New Zealand. Prior to working within the university sector Craig worked as a chartered accountant in practice. He is a Fellow of the Institute of Chartered Accountants in Australia.

Craig's research has tended to focus on various social and environmental accountability and financial accounting issues and has been published in a number of leading international accounting journals, including: *Accounting, Organizations and Society; Accounting and Business Research; Accounting, Auditing and Accountability Journal; British Accounting Review* and *The International Journal of Accounting*.

Jeffrey Unerman

Jeffrey Unerman BA (CNAA), MSc (London), PhD (Sheffield), ACA, ILTM is Professor of Accounting and Corporate Accountability in the School of Management at Royal Holloway, which is one of the larger colleges of the University of London. He has taught at both undergraduate and postgraduate levels at universities in the UK since 1992. During this time he has also addressed audiences internationally in Ireland, France, Spain, Sweden, the Czech Republic, Lithuania, Belarus, the USA and Australia. Before joining the academic sector, he qualified as a chartered accountant (he is a member of the Institute of Chartered Accountants in England and Wales) and worked both in practice and commerce.

His research, which has been published in a range of international academic journals – including *Accounting, Organizations and Society, Accounting, Auditing and Accountability Journal, Critical Perspectives on Accounting, The European Accounting Review* and *Accounting Forum* – focuses on issues of accountability both for social and environmental performance and for the management of intellectual capital. He has worked on several research projects with other academics in the UK, Ireland, the Netherlands and Australia, and is a member of the Research Committee of the ACCA.

Guided tour

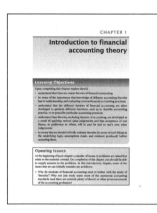

Learning Objectives

Each chapter opens with a set of learning objectives, summarising what students should learn from each chapter.

Opening issue

This section introduces the chapter by providing a topical debate issue for students to consider while they progress through the chapter.

Exhibits

To give the various perspectives covered a 'real-world' feel many chapters include recent articles from a variety of newspapers, directly relating to the issues under consideration.

Chapter summary

This briefly reviews and reinforces the main topics students will have covered in each chapter to ensure they have acquired a solid understanding of the key topics.

Questions

This end-of-chapter feature is the perfect way to practice the techniques students have been taught and apply the methodology to real-world situations.

Technology to enhance learning and teaching

Online Learning Centre (OLC)

After completing each chapter, log on to the supporting Online Learning Centre website. Take advantage of the study tools offered to reinforce the material you have read in the text, and to develop your knowledge of financial accounting theory in a fun and effective way.

Resources for students include:

◆ Weblinks

Also available for lecturers:

◆ Solutions Manual
◆ PowerPoint Slides
◆ Group Assignments

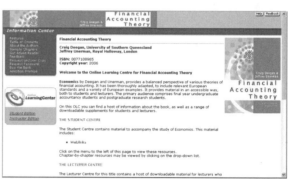

Visit **www.mcgraw-hill.co.uk/textbooks/deegan** today

For lecturers

Primis Content Centre

If you need to supplement your course with additional cases or content, create a personalised e-Book for your students. Visit **www.primiscontentcenter.com** or e-mail **primis_euro@mcgraw-hill.com** for more information.

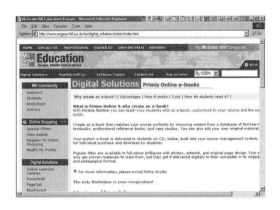

For students

Study skills

We publish guides to help you study, research, pass exams and write essays, all the way through your university studies.

Visit **www.openup.co.uk/ss/** to see the full selection and get £2 discount by entering promotional code **study** when buying online!

Computing skills

If you'd like to brush up on your computing skills, we have a range of titles covering MS Office applications such as Word, Excel, PowerPoint, Access and more.

Get a £2 discount off these titles by entering the promotional code **app** when ordering online at **www.mcgraw-hill.co.uk/app**

Acknowledgements

Authors' Acknowledgments

Many people must be thanked for helping us write this book. Professor Rob Gray from the University of St. Andrews is to be thanked for very useful and insightful advice provided in the initial development of this book and, through his Centre for Social and Environmental Accounting Research, for generously providing a great deal of useful research material. We also thank Professor David Owen from the University of Nottingham for his incisive advice and encouragement throughout the writing of both editions of this book. Dr Julie Cotter from the University of Southern Queensland is also to be thanked for her views about how the book should be structured and for her assistance in the writing of Chapter 10. In relation to development of the original Australian edition, we also thank Professor Reg Mathews (Charles Sturt University), Brian Millanta (Macquarie University), Colin Dolley (Edith Cowan University), Dean Ardern (La Trobe University), Natalie Gallery (University of Sydney), for providing critical comments in relation to a number of the chapters, and Tanya Ziebell (University of Queensland) for unearthing some difficult-to-find research papers.

In developing this European edition, we are very grateful for the helpful, perceptive and constructive comments – and for their strong encouragement – provided by Professor Brendan O'Dwyer (University of Amsterdam), Professor Richard Laughlin (King's College, University of London), Alan Murray (University of Sheffield) and, as noted above, Professor David Owen (University of Nottingham). We are also especially grateful to Franco Zappettini for his encouragement, patience and support, and to our colleagues at Royal Holloway and RMIT for their ongoing support, particularly John Ahwere-Bafo at Royal Holloway for his work on the companion website. Lastly, we thank the staff at McGraw-Hill for supporting this project. Particular thanks go to Mark Kavanagh, Natalie Jacobs and Deborah Hey in the UK and to Luisa Cecotti and Valerie Reed in Australia.

We hope readers continue to find this European edition interesting, informative and enjoyable to read, and we welcome constructive feedback.

Publisher's Acknowledgments

Our thanks go to the following reviewers for their comments at various stages in the text's development:

Patrick Devlin   – Caledonian Business School
Reggy Hooghiemstra – Erasmus University, Rotterdam
George Iatridis   – University of Manchester
Carolyn Isaaks   – Nottingham Trent University
Chris Knoops   – Erasmus University, Rotterdam
Alan Murray   – Sheffield University Management School
David Owen   – University of Nottingham
Margaret Woods   – University of Nottingham

Thanks to companies and organisations who granted us permission to reproduce material in the text. Every effort has been made to trace and acknowledge copyright and to obtain permissions to reproduce material in the text. The publishers would be pleased to make arrangements to clear permission with any copyright holders it has not been possible to contact.

CHAPTER 1

Introduction to financial accounting theory

Learning Objectives

Upon completing this chapter readers should:

◆ understand that there are many theories of financial accounting;

◆ be aware of the importance that knowledge of different accounting theories has in understanding and evaluating various financial accounting practices;

◆ understand that the different theories of financial accounting are often developed to perform different functions, such as to describe accounting practice, or to prescribe particular accounting practices;

◆ understand that theories, including theories of accounting, are developed as a result of applying various value judgements and that acceptance of one theory, in preference to others, will in part be tied to one's own value judgements;

◆ be aware that we should critically evaluate theories (in terms of such things as the underlying logic, assumptions made, and evidence produced) before accepting them.

Opening issues

At the beginning of each chapter a number of issues or problems are raised that relate to the material covered. On completion of the chapter you should be able to supply answers to the problems. In this introductory chapter, some of the issues that we can initially consider are as follows:

◆ Why do students of financial accounting need to bother with the study of 'theories'? Why not just study some more of the numerous accounting standards (and there are certainly plenty of them!) or other pronouncements of the accounting profession?

◆ Why would (or perhaps 'should') accounting practitioners and accounting regulators consider various theories of accounting?

◆ Do all 'theories of accounting' seek to fulfil the same role, and if there are alternative theories to explain or guide particular practice, how does somebody select one theory in preference to another?

No specific answers are provided for each chapter's opening issues. Rather, as a result of reading the respective chapters, readers should be able to provide their own answers to the particular issues. You might like to consider providing an answer to the opening issues before reading the material provided in the chapters, and then, on completing the chapter, revisit the opening issues and see whether you might change your opinions as a result of being exposed to particular points of view.

What is a theory?

In this book we consider various theories of financial accounting. Perhaps, therefore, we should start by considering what we mean by a 'theory'. There are various perspectives of what constitutes a theory. The Oxford English Dictionary provides various definitions, including:

> A scheme or system of ideas or statements held as an explanation or account of a group of facts or phenomena.

The accounting researcher Hendriksen (1970, p. 1) defines a theory as:

> A coherent set of hypothetical, conceptual and pragmatic principles forming the general framework of reference for a field of inquiry.

The definition provided by Hendriksen is very similar to the US Financial Accounting Standards Board's definition of their Conceptual Framework Project (which in itself is deemed to be a *normative* theory of accounting), which is defined as 'a coherent system of interrelated objectives and fundamentals that can lead to consistent standards' (FASB, 1976).

What the above definitions imply is that a theory should be based on logical (systematic and coherent) reasoning. As we will see, some accounting theories are developed on the basis of past observations (empirically based) of which some are further developed to make predictions about likely occurrences (and sometimes also to provide explanations of why the events occur). That is, particular theories may be generated and subsequently supported by undertaking numerous observations of the actual phenomena in question. Such empirically based theories are said to be based on inductive reasoning and are often labelled 'scientific', as, like many theories in the 'sciences', they are based on observation. Alternatively, other accounting theories which we also consider do not seek to provide explanations or predictions of particular phenomena, but rather, *prescribe* what *should* be done (as opposed to describing or predicting what *is* done) in particular circumstances. Llewelyn (2003) points out that the term 'theory' in accounting not only applies to 'grand theories' which seek to tell us about broad generalizable issues (like the theory of gravity in physics), but also applies to any framework which helps us make sense of aspects of the (social) world in which we live, and which helps provide a structure to understand our (social) experiences. We stress that different theories of accounting often have different objectives.

Because accounting is a human activity (you cannot have 'accounting' without accountants), theories of financial accounting (and there are many) will consider such things as people's behaviour and/or people's needs as regards financial accounting information, or the reasons why people within organizations might elect to supply particular information to particular stakeholder groups. For example, we consider, among others, theories which:

* *prescribe* how, based upon a particular perspective of the role of accounting, assets *should* be valued for external reporting purposes (we consider such pre-scriptive or normative theories in Chapters 5 and 6);
* *predict* that managers paid bonuses on the basis of measures such as profits will seek to adopt those accounting methods that lead to an increase in reported profits (we consider such descriptive or positive theories in Chapter 7);
* seek to *explain* how an individual's cultural background will impact on the types of accounting information that the individual seeks to provide to people outside the organization (we consider such a theory in Chapter 4);
* *prescribe* the accounting information that should be provided to particular classes of stakeholders on the basis of their perceived information needs (such theories are often referred to as decision usefulness theories, and we discuss them in Chapter 5);
* *predict* that the relative power of a particular stakeholder group (with 'power' often being defined in terms of the group's control over scarce resources) will determine whether that group receives the accounting information it desires (which derives from a branch of stakeholder theory, discussed in Chapter 8);
* *predict* that organizations seek to be perceived by the community as *legitimate* and that accounting information can be used as one means to bring legitimacy to the organization (which derives from legitimacy theory, considered in Chapter 8).

Why it is important for accounting students to study accounting theory

As a student of financial accounting you will be required to learn how to construct and read financial statements prepared in conformity with various accounting standards and other professional and statutory requirements. In your working life (whether or not you choose to specialize in accounting) you could be involved in such activities as analysing financial statements for the purposes of making particular decisions, compiling financial statements for others to read, or generating accounting guidance or rules for others to follow. The better you understand the accounting practices underlying these various activities, the more effective you are likely to be in performing these activities – and therefore the better equipped you are likely to be to succeed in your chosen career.

Given that accounting theories aim to provide a coherent and systematic framework for investigating, understanding and/or developing various accounting practices, the evaluation of individual accounting practices is likely to be much more effective where the person evaluating these practices has a thorough grasp of accounting theory. Although we believe that all students of accounting (like students in any subject) should always have been interested in critically evaluating the phenomena they have studied, we recognize that, in the past, many students have been content with simply learning how to apply various accounting practices without questioning the basis of these practices.

However, in the wake of a growing number of high-profile accounting failures (such as Enron and WorldCom in the USA, Ahold in the Netherlands, Parmalat in Italy, Shell in the Netherlands and the UK, and Addeco in Switzerland), it has never been more important for accountants to thoroughly understand and be able to critique the accounting practices which they use. Without such a theoretically informed understanding, it is difficult to evaluate the suitability of current accounting practices, to develop improved accounting practices where current practices are unsuitable for changed business situations, and to defend the reputation of accounting where accounting practices are wrongly blamed for causing companies to fail. This is a key reason why it is important for you to study and understand accounting theories.

As a result of studying various theories of financial accounting in this book, you will be exposed to various issues including:

 ♦ how the various elements of accounting should be measured;
 ♦ what motivates organizations to provide certain types of accounting information;
 ♦ what motivates individuals to support and perhaps lobby regulators for some accounting methods in preference to others;

- what the implications for particular types of organizations and their stakeholders are if one method of accounting is chosen or mandated in preference to other methods;
- how and why the capital markets react to particular accounting information;
- whether there is a 'true measure' of income.

Accounting plays a very important and pervasive role within society. To simply learn the various rules of financial accounting (as embodied within accounting standards and the like) without considering the implications that accounting information can have would seem illogical and, following the high profile accounting failures at Enron and other organizations, potentially dangerous. Many significant decisions are made on the basis of information that accountants provide (or in some circumstances, elect not to provide), so accountants are often regarded as being very powerful and influential people. The information generated by accountants enables others to make important decisions, for example: should they support the organization? Is the organization earning sufficient 'profits'? Is it earning excessive 'profits'? Is the organization fulfilling its social responsibilities by investing in community support programmes and recycling initiatives and if so, how much? In considering profits, is profitability a valid measure of organizational success? Further, if the accountant/accounting profession emphasizes particular attributes of organizational performance (for example, profitability) does this in turn impact on what society perceives as the legitimate goals of business?[1] As a result of considering various theories of financial accounting, we provide some answers to the above important issues.

At a broader level, an understanding of accounting theories can be crucial to the reputation and future of the accounting profession. Unerman and O'Dwyer (2004) have argued that the recent rise in high-profile accounting failures has raised the level of awareness among non-accountants of some of the significant impacts which accounting has on their lives. These events have also led to a substantial reduction in the level of trust which many non-accountants place in financial accounts and in accountants. If we are to effectively rebuild this trust, and the reputation of accountants, it is now more crucial than ever that we develop the capacity to critically evaluate accounting practices and to refine these practices as the business environment rapidly changes. The insights from a varied range of accounting theories are essential to this process of continual improvement in financial accounting practices.

A brief overview of theories of accounting

There are many theories of financial accounting. That is, there is no universally accepted theory of financial accounting or, indeed, any universally agreed perspective of how accounting theories should be developed. In part this is because different researchers have different perspectives of the role of accounting theory and/or what the central objective, role and scope of financial accounting should be. For example, some researchers believe that the principal role of accounting theory should be to *explain* and *predict* particular accounting-related phenomena (for example, to explain why some accountants adopt one particular accounting method, while others elect to adopt an alternative approach), while other researchers believe that the role of accounting theory is to *prescribe* (as opposed to *describe*) particular approaches to accounting (for example, based on a perspective of the role of accounting, there is a theory that prescribes that assets *should* be valued on the basis of market values rather than historical costs).

Inductive accounting theories

Early development of accounting theory relied on the process of induction, that is, the development of ideas or theories through observation. From approximately the 1920s to the 1960s, theories of accounting were predominantly developed on the basis of observation of what accountants actually did in practice. Common practices were then codified in the form of doctrines or conventions of accounting (for example, the doctrine of conservatism). Notable theorists at this time included Paton (1922); Hatfield (1927); Paton and Littleton (1940); and Canning (1929). Henderson, Peirson and Brown (1992, p. 61) describe the approaches adopted by these theorists as follows:

> Careful observation of accounting practice revealed patterns of consistent behaviour. For example, it could be observed that accountants tended to be very prudent in measuring both revenues and expenses. Where judgement was necessary it was observed that accountants usually underestimated revenues and overstated expenses. The result was a conservative measure of profit. Similarly, it could be observed that accountants behaved as if the value of money, which was the unit of account, remained constant. These observations of accounting practice led to the formulation of a number of hypotheses such as 'that where judgement is needed, a conservative procedure is adopted' and 'that it is assumed that the value of money remains constant'. These hypotheses were confirmed by many observations of the behaviour of accountants.

While there was a general shift towards prescriptive research in the 1960s, some research of an inductive nature still occurs. Research based on the inductive approach has been subject to many criticisms. For example, Gray, Owen and Maunders (1987, p. 66) state:

> Studying extant practice is a study of 'what is' and, by definition, does not study 'what is not' or 'what should be'. It therefore concentrates on the status quo, is reactionary in attitude, and cannot provide a basis upon which current practice may be evaluated or from which future improvements may be deduced.

In generating theories of accounting based upon what accountants actually do, it is assumed (often implicitly) that what is done by the majority of accountants is the most appropriate practice. In adopting such a perspective there is, in a sense, a perspective of *accounting Darwinism* – a view that accounting practice has evolved, and the fittest, or perhaps 'best', practices have survived. Prescriptions or advice are provided to others on the basis of what most accountants do – the 'logic' being that the majority of accountants must be doing the most appropriate thing. What do you think of the logic of such an argument?

As a specific example of this inductive approach to theory development we can consider the work of Grady (1965). His research was commissioned by the American Institute of Certified Public Accountants (AICPA) and was undertaken at a time when there was a great deal of prescriptive (as opposed to descriptive) research being undertaken. Interestingly, in 1961 and 1962 the Accounting Research Division of the AICPA had already commissioned prescriptive studies by Moonitz (1961) and Sprouse and Moonitz (1962) which proposed that accounting measurement systems be changed from historical cost to a system based on current values. However, before the release of these research works, the AICPA released a statement saying that 'while these studies are a valuable contribution to accounting principles, they are too radically different from generally accepted principles for acceptance at this time' (Statement by the Accounting Principles Board, AICPA, April, 1962).

History shows that rarely have regulatory bodies accepted suggestions for significant changes to accounting practice. This is an interesting issue considered more fully in Chapter 6 when we discuss conceptual framework projects. However, it is useful to consider at this point a statement made in the US by Miller and Reading (1986, p. 64):

> The mere discovery of a problem is not sufficient to assure that the FASB will undertake its solution ... . There must be a suitably high likelihood that the Board can resolve the issues in a manner that will be acceptable to the constituency – without some prior sense of the likelihood that the Board members will be able to reach a consensus, it is generally not advisable to undertake a formal project.

Grady's (1965) work formed the basis of APB Statement No. 4, 'Basic Concepts and Accounting Principles Underlying the Financial Statements of Business Enterprises'. In effect, APB Statement No. 4 simply reflected the generally accepted accounting principles of the time. It was therefore not controversial and had a high probability of being acceptable to the AICPA's constituency (Miller and Reading, 1986).

While some accounting researchers continued to adopt an inductive approach, a different approach became popular in the 1960s and 1970s. This approach sought to *prescribe* particular accounting procedures, and as such was not driven by existing practices. At this time there tended to be widespread inflation throughout various countries of the world and much of the research and the related theories sought to explain the limitations of historical cost accounting and to provide improved approaches (based upon particular value judgements held by the researchers) for asset valuation in times of rapidly rising prices.

Predictive accounting theories

In the mid- to late 1970s there were further changes in the focus of accounting research and theory development. At this time a great deal of accounting research had the major aim of *explaining* and *predicting* accounting practice, rather than *prescribing* particular approaches. This was another movement by many accounting researchers away from descriptive research – this time towards predictive research. Nevertheless, there are many researchers who still undertake descriptive research.

In reading accounting research you will see that much research is labelled either *positive research* or *normative research*. Research that seeks to predict and explain particular phenomena (as opposed to prescribing particular activity) is classified as *positive research* and the associated theories are referred to as *positive theories*. Henderson, Peirson and Brown (1992, p. 326) provide a useful description of positive theories. They state:

> A positive theory begins with some assumption(s) and, through logical deduction, enables some prediction(s) to be made about the way things will be. If the prediction is sufficiently accurate when tested against observations of reality, then the story is regarded as having provided an explanation of why things are as they are. For example, in climatology, a positive theory of rainfall may yield a prediction that, if certain conditions are met, then heavy rainfall will be observed. In economics, a positive theory of prices may yield a prediction that, if certain conditions are met, then rapidly rising prices will be observed. Similarly, a positive theory of accounting may yield a prediction that, if certain conditions are met, then particular accounting practices will be observed.

As noted above, positive theories are typically based on observation. Empirically (observation) based theories can continue to be tested and perhaps refined through further observation, perhaps in different institutional or geographical settings, and a great deal of published research is undertaken to see if particular results can be replicated in different settings, thereby increasing the generalizability of the theory in question. Apart from providing the basis for predicting future actions or effects, positive accounting research often goes to the next step of attempting to provide explanations for the phenomena in question.

In Chapter 7 we consider a positive theory of accounting principally developed by Watts and Zimmerman (relying upon the works of others, such as Jensen and Meckling (1976) and Gordon (1964)). Their positive theory of accounting, which they called *Positive Accounting Theory*, seeks to predict and explain why managers (and/or accountants) elect to adopt particular accounting methods in preference to others.[2]

Chapter 7 demonstrates that the development of Positive Accounting Theory relied in great part on work undertaken in the field of economics, and central to the development of Positive Accounting Theory was the acceptance of the economics-based 'rational economic person assumption'. That is, an assumption was made that accountants (and, in fact, all individuals) are primarily motivated by self-interest (tied to wealth maximization), and that the particular accounting method selected (where alternatives are available) will be dependent upon certain considerations:

◆ whether the accountant is rewarded in terms of accounting-based bonus systems (for example, whether they receive a bonus tied to reported profits);

◆ whether the organization they work for is close to breaching negotiated accounting-based debt covenants (such as a debt-to-asset constraint);

◆ whether the organization that employs them is subject to political scrutiny from various external groups, such as government, employee groups or environmental groups (with that scrutiny being focused on the organization's reported profits).

The assumption of self-interest challenges the view that accountants will predominantly be objective when determining which accounting methods should be used to record particular transactions and events (objectivity is a qualitative characteristic promoted within various conceptual frameworks of accounting, as we see in Chapter 6).

Positive theories of accounting do not seek to tell us that what is being done in practice is the most efficient or equitable process. For example, while we have a (positive) theory of accounting, developed to predict which accounting methods most accountants will use in particular circumstances (Positive Accounting Theory), this theory will not tell us anything about the efficiency of what is being done. As Watts and Zimmerman (1986, p. 7) state:

> It [Positive Accounting Theory] is concerned with explaining [accounting] practice. It is designed to explain and predict which firms will and which firms will not use a particular [accounting method] ... but it says nothing as to which method a firm should use.

As we will see shortly, the practice of electing not to advise others as to what should be done in particular circumstances has been the subject of criticism of positive accounting research.

Prescriptive (normative) accounting theories

While positive theories tend to be based on empirical observation, there are other theories based not upon observation but rather on what the researcher believes *should* occur in particular circumstances. For example, in Chapter 5 we discuss a theory of accounting developed by Raymond Chambers. His theory of accounting, called *continuously contemporary accounting*, describes how financial accounting *should* be undertaken. That is, his theory is prescriptive. Central to his theory is a view that the most useful information about an organization's assets for the purposes of economic decision making is information about their 'current cash equivalents' – a measure tied to their current net market values. As such, it prescribes that assets *should* be valued on the basis of their net market values.

Theories that prescribe (as opposed to describe) particular actions are called normative theories as they are based on the norms (or values or beliefs) held by the researchers proposing the theories (they are also often referred to as prescriptive theories). The dichotomy of positive and normative theories is one often used to categorize accounting theories and it is adopted in this book.

As noted above, normative theories of accounting are not necessarily based on observation and therefore cannot (or should not) be evaluated on whether they reflect actual accounting practice. In fact they may suggest radical changes to current practice. For example, for a number of decades, Chambers had been advocating the valuation of assets on a basis related to their net market values – a prescription that challenged the widespread use of historical cost accounting (it is interesting to note, however, that the use of market values for asset valuation has gained popularity in some countries in recent years). Other researchers concerned about the social and environmental implications of business (see, for example, Gray and Bebbington, 2001; Gray, *et al.*, 1996; Mathews, 1993) have developed theories that prescribe significant changes to traditional financial accounting practice (Chapter 9 of this book considers such theories). The conceptual framework of accounting that we discuss in Chapter 6 is an example of a normative theory of accounting. Relying upon various assumptions about the types or attributes of information useful for decision making, it provides guidance on how assets, liabilities, expenses, revenues and equity should be defined, when they should be recognized, and ultimately how they should be measured. As we see in later chapters, normative theories can be further subdivided. For example, we can classify some normative theories as 'true income theories' and other theories as 'decision usefulness theories'. The true income theories make certain assumptions about the role of accounting and then seek to provide a single 'best measure' of profits (for example, see Lee, 1974).[3]

Decision usefulness theories ascribe a particular type of information for particular classes of users on the basis of assumed decision-making needs. According to Bebbington, Gray and Laughlin (2001, p. 418) the decision usefulness approach can be considered to have two branches, the *decision-makers emphasis*, and the *decision-models emphasis*. The decision-makers emphasis relies on undertaking research that seeks to ask them what information they want.[4] Once that is determined, this knowledge is used to prescribe what information should be supplied to the users of financial statements. Much of this research is questionnaire-based. This branch of research tends to be fairly disjointed as different studies typically address different types of information, with limited linkages between them.

Another variant of the decision-makers emphasis, which we explore in Chapter 10, is security price research. Briefly, security price research works on the assumption that if the capital market responds to information (as evidenced through price changes that occur around the time of the release of particular information) the information must be useful.[5] This forms the basis for subsequent prescriptions about the types of information that should be provided to users of financial statements. It also has been used to determine whether particular mandatory reporting requirements (such as the introduction of new accounting standards) were necessary or effective, the rationale being that if a new accounting standard does not evoke a market reaction, then it is questionable whether the new requirement is useful or necessary in providing information to the stock market or investors. Research that evaluates information on the basis of whether it evokes a market reaction, or whether stakeholders indicate that it is useful to them, ignores the possibility that there could be information that is 'better' than that provided or sought. There is also a broader philosophical issue of whether what they 'want' is actually what they 'need'. These broader issues are explored throughout this book.

On the other hand, proponents of the *decision-models emphasis* develop models based upon the researchers' perceptions of what is necessary for efficient decision making. Information prescriptions follow (for example, that information should be provided about the market value of the reporting entity's assets). This branch of research typically assumes that classes of stakeholders have identical information needs. Unlike the decision-makers emphasis, the decision-models emphasis does not ask the decision makers what information they want but, instead, concentrates on the types of information considered useful for decision making. As Wolk and Tearney (1997, p. 39) indicate, a premise underlying this research is that decision makers may need to be taught how to use this information if they are unfamiliar with it.

Evaluating theories of accounting

In the process of studying accounting, students will typically be exposed to numerous theories of accounting, and accompanying research and argument which attempts to either support or reject the particular theories in question. In undertaking this study students should consider the merit of the argument and the research methods employed. What many students find interesting is that many researchers seem to adopt one theory of accounting and thereafter adopt various strategies (including overt condemnation of alternative theories) in an endeavour to support their own research and theoretical perspective. In some respects, the attitudes of some researchers are akin to those of the disciples of particular religions. (In fact, Chambers (1993) refers to advocates of Positive Accounting Theory as belonging to the 'PA Cult'.) In Deegan (1997) a series of quotes are provided from the works of various high profile researchers which are opposed to Watts and Zimmerman's *positive theory of accounting*. In providing arguments against the validity of Positive Accounting Theory, the opponents used such terms and descriptions as:

◆ it is a dead philosophical movement (Christenson, 1983, p. 7);

◆ it has provided no accomplishments (Sterling, 1990, p. 97);

- it is marred by oversights, inconsistencies and paradoxes (Chambers, 1993, p. 1);
- it is imperiously dictatorial (Sterling, 1990, p. 121);
- it is empty and commonplace (Sterling, 1990, p. 130);
- it is akin to a cottage industry (Sterling, 1990, p. 132);
- it is responsible for turning back the clock of research 1000 years (Chambers, 1993, p. 22);
- it suffers from logical incoherence (Williams, 1989, p. 459); and
- it is a wasted effort (Sterling, 1990, p. 132).

The quoted criticisms clearly indicate the degree of emotion that a particular theory (Positive Accounting Theory) has stimulated among its critics, particularly those who see the role of accounting theory as providing prescription, rather than description. Students of financial accounting theory will find it interesting to ponder why some people are so angered by such a theory – after all, it is just a theory (isn't it?). Many proponents of Positive Accounting Theory have also tended to be very critical of normative theorists.

In explaining or describing why a certain 'camp' of researchers might try to denigrate the credibility of alternative research paradigms (consistent with Kuhn (1962), a paradigm can be defined as an approach to knowledge advancement that adopts particular theoretical assumptions, research goals and research methods) it is relevant to consider one of the various views about how knowledge advances.[6] Kuhn (1962) explained how knowledge, or science, develops: scientific progress is not evolutionary, but rather, revolutionary. His view is that knowledge advances when one theory is replaced by another as particular researchers attack the credibility of an existing paradigm and advance an alternative, promoted as being superior, thereby potentially bringing the existing paradigm into 'crisis'. As knowledge develops, the new paradigm may be replaced by a further research perspective, or a prior paradigm may be resurrected. In discussing the process of how researchers switch from one research perspective to another, Kuhn likens it to one of 'religious conversion'.[7] While the perspective provided by Kuhn does appear to have some relevance to explaining developments in the advancement of accounting theory, so far no accounting theory has ever been successful in overthrowing all other alternatives. There have been, and apparently will continue to be, advocates of various alternative theories of accounting – many of which are discussed.

Returning to our brief review of financial accounting theories, we have stated previously that positive theories of accounting do not seek to prescribe. Some critics of this perspective have argued that the decision not to prescribe could alienate academic accountants from their counterparts within the profession. As Howieson (1996, p. 31) states:

> ... an unwillingness to tackle policy issues is arguably an abrogation of academics' duty to serve the community which supports them. Among other activities, practitioners are

concerned on a day-to-day basis with the question of which accounting policies they should choose. Traditionally, academics have acted as commentators and reformers on such normative issues. By concentrating on positive questions, they risk neglecting one of their important roles in the community.

Counter to this view, many proponents of Positive Accounting Theory have, at different times, tried to undermine normative research because it was not based on observation (observation based research was deemed to be 'scientific', and 'scientific research' was considered to be akin to 'good research'), but rather was based on personal opinion about what *should* happen. Positive Accounting theorists often argue that in undertaking research they do not want to impose their own views on others as this is 'unscientific', but rather they prefer to provide information about the expected implications of particular actions (for example, the selection of a particular accounting method) and thereafter let people decide for themselves what they should do (for example, they may provide evidence to support a prediction that organizations that are close to breaching accounting-based debt covenants will adopt accounting methods that increase the firm's reported profits and assets).

However, as a number of accounting academics have quite rightly pointed out, and as we should remember when reading this book, selecting a theory to adopt for research (such as public interest theory, capture theory, legitimacy theory, stakeholder theory or Positive Accounting Theory) is based on a value judgement; what to research is based on a value judgement; believing that all individual action is driven by self-interest, as the Positive Accounting theorists do, is a value judgement; and so on. Hence, no research, whether utilizing Positive Accounting Theory or otherwise, is value free and it would arguably be quite wrong to assert that it is value free. As Gray, Owen and Maunders (1987, p. 66) state:

> In common with all forms of empirical investigation we must recognise that all perception is theory-laden. That is, our preconceptions about the world significantly colour what we observe and which aspects of particular events we focus upon. Thus accountants are more likely to view the world through accounting frameworks and conventions.

Watts and Zimmerman (1990, p. 146) did modify their original stance in relation to the objectivity of their research and conceded that value judgements do play a part in positive research just as they do in normative research. As they stated:

> Positive theories are value laden. Tinker *et al.* (1982, p. 167) argue that all research is value laden and not socially neutral. Specifically, 'Realism operating in the clothes of positive theory claims theoretical supremacy because it is born of fact, not values' (p. 172). We concede the importance of values in determining research: both the researcher's and user's preferences affect the process.
>
> Competition among theories to meet users' demand constrains the extent to which researcher values influence research design. Positive theories are 'If ... then' propositions that are both predictive and explanatory. Researchers choose the topics to investigate, the methods to use, and the assumptions to make. Researchers' preferences and

expected pay-offs (publications and citations) affect the choice of topics, methods and assumptions. In this sense, all research, including positive research, is 'value laden'.

The position taken in this book is that theories of accounting, of necessity, are abstractions of reality, and the choice of one theory in preference to another is based on particular value judgements. Some of us may prefer particular theories to others because they more closely reflect how we believe people do, or should, act. We cannot really expect to provide perfect explanations or predictions of human behaviour, nor can we expect to assess perfectly what types of information the users of financial statements actually need – our perceptions of information needs will most probably be different from your views about information needs. There is a role for prescription if it is based on logical argument and there is a role for research that provides predictions if the research methods employed to provide the predictions are assessed as valid.

Can we prove a theory?

While this book does not intend to provide an in-depth insight into the development of scientific thought, one interesting issue that often arises with students is whether a theory can actually be 'proved'. In this book we consider various theories – a number of which provide alternative explanations for the same events. In the next section of this chapter we will consider how to evaluate a theory in terms of logic and evidence, but before we consider such evaluation, we should perhaps consider the issue of whether we can prove a theory.

One's view about whether we can prove a theory as correct depends upon how one views the development of scientific thought. When it comes to accounting theories – which might, for example, consider how people react to particular accounting numbers, or might consider why accountants would choose particular accounting methods in preference to others – we need to again appreciate that financial accounting is a human activity (we cannot have accounting without accountants) and that common sense would dictate that not all people will react in a similar way to accounting numbers. Hence, logic might indicate that a theory of financial accounting (and therefore a theory that describes human behaviour in relation to accounting numbers) would not provide perfect predictions of behaviour in all cases (and in this explanation we are talking about positive theories – theories that seek to explain and predict particular phenomena).

If the theories of financial accounting were developed to explain and predict peoples' actions and reactions to financial accounting information (that is, they are positive theories) then we might consider that if a theory provides sound predictions the majority of the time then the theory is still of use, albeit that its predictions are not 'perfect'. That is, we would evaluate it on the basis of the correspondence between the prediction of behaviours provided by the theory and the subsequent behaviour, and we might accept that a theory is useful although it does not provide accurate predictions in all cases. That is, an 'acceptable' theory might nevertheless admit exceptions.[8] It should also be appreciated that while we might use observations to 'support' a theory, it would generally be inadvisable to state that we have proved a theory on the basis of observations. There is always the possibility that one further observation might be made that is inconsistent with our theory's predictions.

In relation to the issue of whether we can 'prove' a theory (or not) it is useful to refer to insights provided by a group of theorists known as 'falsificationists' – the major leader of which is considered to be Karl Popper.[9]

Popper, and the falsificationists, consider that knowledge develops through trial and error. For example, a researcher might develop hypotheses from a theory.[10] To develop scientific knowledge, the falsificationists believe that these hypotheses must be of a form that allows them to be rejected if the evidence is not supportive of the hypotheses. For example, a hypothesis of the following form would be deemed to be falsifiable:

> *H1: Managers that receive bonuses based on accounting profits will adopt income-increasing accounting methods.*

According to Popper and other falsificationists, knowledge develops as a result of continual refinement of a theory. When particular hypotheses are deemed to be false through lack of empirical support, the pre-existing theories will be refined (or abandoned). The refined theories will be accepted until a related hypothesis is deemed to be false (falsified) at which time the theory will be further refined. Chalmers (1982, p. 38) provides a useful overview of falsificationism. He states:

> The falsificationist freely admits that observation is guided by and presupposes theory. He is also happy to abandon any claims implying that theories can be established as true or probably true in the light of observational evidence. Theories are construed as speculative and tentative conjectures or guesses freely created by the human intellect in an attempt to overcome problems encountered by previous theories and to give an adequate account of the behaviour of some aspects of the world or universe. Once proposed, speculative theories are to be rigorously and ruthlessly tested by observation and experiment. Theories that fail to stand up to observational and experimental tests must be eliminated and replaced by further speculative conjectures. Science progresses by trial and error, by conjectures and refutations. Only the fittest theories survive. While it can never be legitimately said of a theory that it is true, it can hopefully be said that it is the best available, that it is better than anything that has come before.

We can contrast Popper's view regarding how theories are developed with the views adopted by the inductivists considered earlier in this chapter. The inductivists construct theories based on typically long periods of careful observation. We will not pursue this discussion any further in terms of how theories develop, but consistent with some of the above discussion we would caution readers about making any claims to 'proving' a theory. It is always safer to say that our evidence 'supports' a theory but that it is also possible that we might embrace an alternative theoretical perspective at a future time should better explanations for a particular phenomenon become available.

Evaluating theories – considerations of logic and evidence

Throughout this book we discuss various theories of financial accounting. Where appropriate, we also undertake an evaluation of the theories. We consider such issues as whether the argument supporting the theories is (or at least appears to be) logical and/or plausible in terms of the central assumptions (if any) that are being made. If possible the argument or theory should be broken down into its main premises to see if the argument, in simplified form, appears logical. What we emphasize is that we/you must question the theories that we/you are exposed to – not simply accept them. Acceptance of a theory and its associated hypotheses (as indicated previously, hypotheses can be described as predictions typically expressed in the form of a relationship between one or more variables) must be tied to whether we accept the logic of the argument, the underlying assumptions, and any supporting evidence provided.

Evaluating logical deduction

As an example of logical deduction, consider the following simplistic non-accounting related argument (reflecting the biases of one of the authors – it refers to surfing). It shows that although the argument may be logical (if we accept the premises), if it can be shown that one of the premises is untrue or in doubt, then the conclusions or predictions may be rejected. Where we have a number of premises and a conclusion we often refer to this as a syllogism.

- All surfers over the age of 35 ride longboards.
- Jack is a surfer over the age of 35.
- Jack therefore rides a longboard.

If we accept the above premises, we might accept the conclusion. It is logical. To determine the logic of the argument we do not need to understand what is a 'surfer' or what is a 'longboard'. That is, we do not need to refer to 'real-world' observations. We could have deconstructed the argument to the form:

- All As ride a B.
- C is an A.
- Therefore C rides a B.

An argument is logical to the extent that *if* the premises on which it is based are true, *then* the conclusion will be true. That is, the argument (even if logical) will only provide a true account of the real world if the premises on which it is based are true. Referring to the above syllogism, evidence gathered through observation will show that the first premise does not always hold. There are surfers over 35 who do not ride longboards. Hence we reject the conclusion on the basis of observation, not on the basis of logic. Therefore we had two considerations. If the argument seeks to provide an account of real world phenomena we must consider the logic of the premises and the correspondence between the premises and actual observation. However, it should be remembered that not all theories or arguments seek to correspond with real-world phenomena – for example, some normative theories of accounting promote radical changes to existing practices. For many normative theories we might consider only the logic of the argument and whether we are prepared to accept the premises on which the argument is based.

Returning to the subject of the syllogism provided above, we could have argued alternatively that:

- A lot of surfers over 35 ride longboards.
- Jack is a surfer over 35.
- Therefore Jack rides a longboard.

The above is not a logical argument. The first premise has admitted alternatives and hence the conclusion, which does not admit alternatives, does not follow. We can dismiss the argument on the basis of a logical flaw without actually seeking any evidence to support the premises.

Evaluating underlying assumptions

In Chapter 7 we review in greater depth Positive Accounting Theory as developed by such researchers as Jensen and Meckling (1976) and Watts and Zimmerman (1978). As noted earlier, their positive theory of accounting has a number of central assumptions, including an assumption that all people are *opportunistic* and will adopt particular strategies to the extent that such strategies lead to an increase in the personal wealth of those parties making the decisions. Wealth accumulation is assumed to be at the centre of all decisions. The theory does not incorporate considerations of morality, loyalty, social responsibility and the like.

If we were to accept the economics-based assumption or premise of researchers such as Watts and Zimmerman that:

- self-interest tied to wealth maximization motivates *all* decisions by individuals,

plus *if* we accept the following premises (which we might confirm through direct observation or through research undertaken by others) that:

- manager X is paid on the basis of reported profits (for example, he/she is given a bonus of 5 per cent of profits); and
- accounting method Y is an available method of accounting that will increase reported profits relative to other methods,

then we might accept a prediction that, all other things being equal:

◆ manager X will adopt accounting method Y.

The above argument appears logical. Whether manager X is paid on the basis of reported profits and whether accounting method Y will increase reported profits are matters that can be confirmed though observation. But if the premises are both logical and true then the conclusion will be true.

　The above argument may be logical but we might only accept it if we accept the critical assumption of *wealth maximization.* If we do not accept the central assumption, then we may reject the prediction. What is being emphasized here is that you need to consider whether you are prepared to accept the logic *and* the assumptions upon which the arguments are based. If not, then we may reject the theory and the associated predictions. For example, in Gray, Owen and Adams (1996) the authors explicitly state that they reject the central assumptions of Positive Accounting Theory (although by their own admission it has 'some useful insights') and that they will not use it as a means of explaining or describing the practice of corporate social responsibility reporting. (Corporate social reporting is a topic covered in Chapter 9 of this book.) As they state (p. 75):

> There is little doubt that these theories have provided some useful insights into the way in which they model the world. There is equally little doubt that some company management and many gambling investors may act in line with these theories. It is also the case that some authors have found the form of analysis employed in these theories useful for explaining corporate social reporting; but apart from the limitations which must arise from a pristine liberal economic perspective on the world and the profound philosophical limitations of the approach, the approach cannot offer any justification why we might accept the description of the world as a desirable one. It is a morally bankrupt view of the world in general and accounting in particular. Its (usual) exclusion of corporate social reporting is therefore actually attractive as an argument for corporate social reporting.

In Chapter 6 we discuss the conceptual framework project, which is considered to be a normative theory of accounting (applying a decision usefulness perspective). This framework provides a view about the objective of general purpose financial reporting (to provide information that is useful for economics-based decisions) and the qualitative characteristics that financial information should possess. It also provides definitions of the elements of accounting (assets, liabilities, revenues, expenses, equity) and prescribes recognition criteria for each of the elements. It is based on a central premise that the objective of financial accounting is to provide information that allows users of general purpose financial reports to make and evaluate decisions about the allocation of scarce resources. If we were not to accept this central premise then we could reject the guidance provided by the framework, even though it could be considered to be logically structured.

While the in-depth study of logic and a critique of argument are beyond the scope of this book, interested readers should consider studying books or articles that concentrate on the development of logical argument.[11] Thouless (1974) describes various approaches to identifying logical flaws in arguments and he also identifies 38 'dishonest tricks in argument' that some writers use to support their argument. Some of the 'tricks' he refers to are:

- the use of emotionally toned words;
- making a statement in which 'all' is implied but 'some' is true;
- evasion of a sound refutation of an argument by use of a sophisticated formula;
- diversion to another question, to a side issue, or by irrelevant objection;
- the use of an argument of logically unsound form;
- change in the meaning of a term during the course of an argument;
- suggestion by repeated affirmation;
- prestige by false credentials;
- the appeal to mere authority; and
- argument by mere analogy.

When reading documents written to support particular ideas or theories, we must also be vigilant to ensure that our acceptance of a theory has not, in a sense, been coerced through the use of colourful or emotive language, or an incorrect appeal to authority. We referred to some earlier quotes from critics of Positive Accounting Theory – some of which were very emotive. Quite often (but not always) emotive or colourful language is introduced to support an otherwise weak argument. Where emotive or colourful language has been used, we should perhaps consider whether we would take the same position in terms of accepting the author's arguments if that author had used relatively neutral language. Thouless (1974, p. 24) provides some advice in this regard. He suggests:

> The practical exercise which I recommend is one that I have already performed on some passages in which truth seemed to be obscured by emotional thinking. I suggest that readers should copy out controversial passages from newspapers, books, or speeches which contain emotionally coloured words. They should then underline all the emotional words, afterwards rewriting the passages with the emotional words replaced by neutral ones. Examine the passage then in its new form in which it merely states facts without indicating the writer's emotional attitude towards them, and see whether it is still good evidence for the proposition it is trying to prove. If it is, the passage is a piece of straight thinking in which emotionally coloured words have been introduced merely as an ornament. If not, it is crooked thinking, because the conclusion depends not on the factual meaning of the passage but on the emotions roused by the words.

Universal applicability of theories

While we must always consider the logic of an argument and the various assumptions that have been made, what we also must remember is that theories, particularly those in the social sciences, are by nature, abstractions of reality. We cannot really expect particular theories about human behaviour to apply all the time. People (thankfully) are different and to expect theories or models of human behaviour to have perfect predictive ability would be naive. If a number of theories are available to describe a particular phenomenon, then considering more than one theory may provide a more rounded perspective. Difficulties will arise if the theories provide diametrically opposite predictions or explanations – in such cases a choice of theory must generally be made.

For those theories that attempt to predict and explain accounting practice (positive theories of accounting) it is common practice to empirically test the theories in various settings and for various types of decisions – but what if the particular theories do not seem to hold in all settings? Should the theories be abandoned? Returning to an issue we considered previously in this chapter, can we accept a theory that admits exceptions? Certainly, readings of various accounting research journals will show that many studies that adopt Positive Accounting Theory as the theoretical basis of the argument fail to generate findings consistent with the theory (however, many do). According to Christenson (1983, p. 18), an outspoken critic of Positive Accounting Theory:

> We are told, for example, that 'we can only expect a positive theory to hold on average' [Watts and Zimmerman, 1978, p. 127, n. 37]. We are also advised 'to remember that as in all empirical theories we are concerned with general trends' [Watts and Zimmerman, 1978, pp. 288–289], where 'general' is used in the weak sense of 'true or applicable in most instances but not all' rather than in the strong sense of 'relating to, concerned with, or applicable to every member of a class' [American Heritage Dictionary, 1969, p. 548] ... A law that admits exceptions has no significance, and knowledge of it is not of the slightest use. By arguing that their theories admit exceptions, Watts and Zimmerman condemn them as insignificant and useless.

Christenson uses the fact that Positive Accounting Theory is not always supported in practice to reject it.[12] However, as stressed previously, as a study of people (accountants, not 'accounting'), it is very hard to see how any model or theory could ever fully explain human action. In fact, ability to do so would constitute a very dehumanizing view of people. Hence, the failure of a particular study to support a theory might not in itself provide a basis for rejecting a theory as 'useless and insignificant'. From another perspective, the failure to support the theory may have been due to the data being inappropriately collected or because the data did not provide a sound correspondence with the theoretical variables involved. However, if the theory in question continuously fails to be supported, then its acceptance will obviously be threatened. At this point we could speculate whether in fact there are any theories pertaining to human activities that always hold.

Generalizing theories from the testing of samples

In developing and testing accounting theories many accounting researchers use methods borrowed from the pure sciences (such as physics and chemistry) which assume that the phenomena being studied will behave in the same way in all similar situations. As we will see when reading accounting (and other) research, these researchers believe that it is possible to develop generalizable accounting theories and therefore that the results they derive from particular samples of observations can be generalized to the broader population of the phenomenon in question. Other researchers hold the opposite view – that it is not possible to make any valid generalizations in social sciences as we are dealing with human activity, and human behaviour is variable from person to person. These researchers will develop theories of a fundamentally different nature to those developed by researchers who believe that it is possible to generalize in accounting theory, and these theories will tend to deal with specific localized situations. Between these two extremes, there are other researchers (such as Laughlin, 1995, 2004) who believe that it is possible to make some very broad generalizations in developing social science theories, but the way these broad generalizations apply to specific situations will vary according to the specific individual factors applicable to each situation. Researchers holding this view regarding the way the world works may use some very broad theories to help understand some aspects of the phenomena they are studying, but are ready to amend and adapt these broad generalizations in light of specific evidence from each individual study.

While a comprehensive review of research methods is beyond the scope of this book, if researchers are attempting to generalize the findings of their studies (based on particular samples) to a larger population, we need to consider the data on which the generalization is based.[13] For example, if we are going to generalize our findings from a sample (we typically cannot test the whole population), then we must consider how the sample was chosen. For example, if we have a prediction that all companies will adopt a particular accounting method in times of inflation and we test this prediction against the 10 largest companies listed on the stock exchange in a period of inflation, then common sense should dictate that the findings really should not be considered generalizable. Can we really be confident about what small companies will do? Hence, throughout your readings of various research studies you should consider not only how the argument is developed, but also how it is tested. If there are flaws in how the testing has been done, we may question or reject the significance of the findings. We must evaluate whether the data collected really represent valid measures of the theoretical variables in question.

As noted previously, for normative theories it is usually not appropriate to test them empirically. If researchers are arguing that accountants should provide particular types of accounting information, or if other researchers are providing a view that organizations have a social responsibility to consider the needs of all stakeholders, then this does not mean that what they are prescribing actually exists in practice. For example, if Chambers' model of accounting prescribes that all assets should be valued at their net market value, and we go out and find that accountants predominantly value their assets on the basis of historical cost, we should not reject Chambers' theory as he was *prescribing*, not *predicting* or *describing*. We should always keep in mind what the researchers are attempting to achieve. Our acceptance of Chambers' theory is dependent upon whether we accept the logic of the argument as well as the assumptions made by Chambers, including the assumption that the central role of accounting should be to provide information about an entity's ability to adapt to changing circumstances (which he argues is best reflected by measures of assets that are tied to their net market values), and the assumption that firms should exist primarily to increase the wealth of the owners.

Outline of this book

In a book of this size we cannot expect to cover all the theories of financial accounting. We nevertheless cover those theories that have tended to gain widespread acceptance by various sectors of the accounting community.

In Chapter 2 we provide an overview of various financial reporting decisions that entities typically face, emphasizing that some reporting pertaining to particular transactions and events is regulated, while some is unregulated. We emphasize that financial accountants typically make many professional judgements throughout the accounting process, and we discuss the qualitative attribute of objectivity, but emphasize that considerations (other than the pursuit of objectivity) may sometimes influence accounting method selection and disclosure practices.

Chapter 3 provides an overview of various arguments for and against the regulation of financial reporting, with an overview of various perspectives on the *costs* and *benefits* of regulating financial reporting. The chapter explores why some accounting approaches and/or methods are adopted by regulators and/or the profession, while others are not. The political process involved in the setting of accounting standards is highlighted.

Chapter 4 explores the international harmonization of accounting requirements. Recently, moves have been made to harmonize accounting requirements internationally. The European Union is at the forefront of such moves. This chapter considers some potential costs and benefits of this process. Particular consideration is given to issues of *culture* and how *cultural differences* have typically been proposed as a reason to explain international differences in accounting requirements. International harmonization ignores this research and assumes that all countries (with different cultures) can simply adopt the same accounting practices.

Chapter 5 gives an overview of various normative (or prescriptive) theories of accounting that have been advanced to deal with various accounting issues associated with periods of rising prices (inflation). The chapter considers such issues as whether there is a *true measure* of income. Conceptual frameworks as normative theories of accounting are considered in Chapter 6. Applying material covered in

Chapter 3, Chapters 5 and 6 also consider why various normative theories of accounting did not gain favour with the accounting profession or the accounting standard-setters.

Chapters 7 and 8 show that while much financial reporting is regulated, organizations still have some scope for voluntarily selecting between alternative accounting methods for particular types of transactions. The treatment of many transactions and the disclosure of many/most issues associated with various social and environmental events relating to an organization is unregulated. Chapters 7 and 8 consider some theoretical perspectives (including Positive Accounting Theory, legitimacy theory, stakeholder theory, political economy theory and institutional theory) about what drives the various unregulated/voluntary reporting decisions.

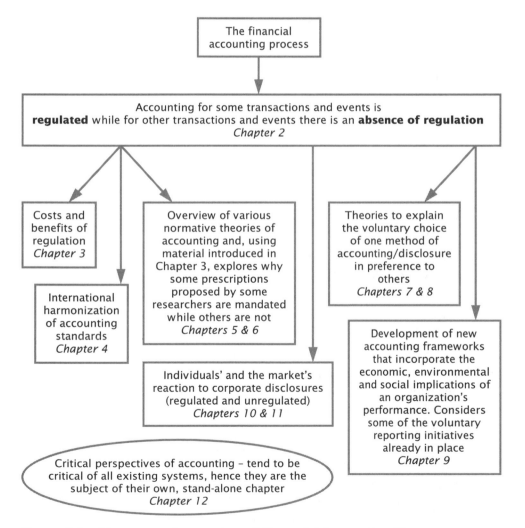

Figure 1.1   Diagrammatic overview of *Financial Accounting Theory*

Chapter 9 considers the development and use of extended systems of accounting that incorporate the economic, social and environmental performance of an organization. The relationship between accounting and sustainable development is explored. This chapter includes a consideration of the limitations of traditional financial accounting, with particular focus on its inability to incorporate social and environmental issues. Issues associated with stakeholder *rights to know* are also explored.

Chapters 10 and 11 consider how individuals and capital markets react to various corporate disclosures. These chapters consider the various theories that have been used to test whether the market is actually using particular types of disclosures, as well as theories that indicate how individuals use accounting information. The chapters also consider who should be deemed to be the users of various types of disclosures.

The concluding chapter, Chapter 12, provides an overview of various critical perspectives of accounting – perspectives that tend to criticize the entire system of accounting as it stands (accounting practice is anthropocentric, masculine, etc.) arguing that accounting tends to support current social systems, which favour those with economic power, but marginalize the interests of parties who lack control of necessary resources.

In summary, the balance of this book can be presented diagrammatically, as in Figure 1.1.

Questions

1.1   What is the difference between a positive theory of accounting and a normative theory of accounting?

1.2   Why would it not be appropriate to reject a normative theory of accounting because its prescriptions could not be confirmed through empirical observation?

1.3   Is the study of financial accounting theory a waste of time for accounting students? Explain your answer.

1.4   In the 1960s a number of accounting researchers concentrated on developing theories of accounting based on observing and documenting the behaviour of practising accountants. Do you think that such research is useful in improving the practice of financial accounting? Explain your answer.

1.5   Explain the meaning of the following paragraph and evaluate the logic of the perspective described:

> In generating theories of accounting that are based upon what accountants actually do, it is assumed (often implicitly) that what is done by the majority of accountants is the most appropriate practice. In adopting such a perspective there is, in a sense, a perspective of accounting Darwinism – a view that

accounting practice has evolved, and the fittest, or perhaps 'best', practices have survived. Prescriptions or advice are provided to others on the basis of what most accountants do – the logic being that the majority of accountants must be doing the most appropriate thing.

1.6 This chapter explains that in 1961 and 1962 the Accounting Research Division of the American Institute of Certified Public Accountants commissioned studies by Moonitz, and by Sprouse and Moonitz, respectively. These studies proposed that accounting measurement systems be changed from historical cost to a system based on current values. However, before the release of these studies, the AICPA released a statement saying that 'while these studies are a valuable contribution to accounting principles, they are too radically different from generally accepted principles for acceptance at this time' (Statement by the Accounting Principles Board, AICPA, April 1962). Explain why if something is 'radically different' (though it might be logically sound) this difference in itself might be enough to stop regulators embracing a particular approach to accounting.

1.7 Read the following quotation from Miller and Reading (1986). If constituency support is necessary before particular accounting approaches become embodied in accounting standards, does this have implications for the 'neutrality' and 'representational faithfulness' (qualitative characteristics that exist in various conceptual framework projects around the world) of reports generated in accordance with accounting standards?

> The mere discovery of a problem is not sufficient to assure that the FASB will undertake its solution ... There must be a suitably high likelihood that the Board can resolve the issues in a manner that will be acceptable to the constituency – without some prior sense of the likelihood that the Board members will be able to reach a consensus, it is generally not advisable to undertake a formal project (Miller and Reading, 1986, p. 64).

1.8 As Watts and Zimmerman (1986, p. 7) state, Positive Accounting Theory is concerned with explaining accounting practice. It is designed to explain and predict which firms will, and which firms will not, use a particular accounting method, but says nothing as to which method a firm should use. Do you think that this represents an 'abrogation of the academics' duty to serve the community that supports them'?

1.9 This chapter describes two branches of 'decision usefulness' theories. Briefly identify and explain what they are.

1.10 Briefly explain the *revolutionary perspective* of knowledge advancement proposed by Kuhn (1962).

1.11 In your opinion, can accounting research be 'value free'? Explain your answer.

1.12   Assume that you have been asked to evaluate a particular theory of accounting. What factors would you consider before making a judgement that the theory appears 'sound'?

1.13   If you were trying to convince another party to support your theory about a particular facet of financial accounting, would you be inclined to use emotive or colourful language? Why, or why not?

1.14   What do we mean when we say that 'theories are abstractions of reality'? Do you agree that theories of accounting are necessarily abstractions of reality?

1.15   Would you reject as 'insignificant and useless' a positive theory of accounting on the basis that in a particular research study the results derived failed to support the hypotheses and the related theory? Explain your answer.

1.16   If a researcher tested a theory on a particular sample of companies, what considerations would you examine before you would agree with the researcher that the results can be generalized to the larger population of companies?

Notes

1   In Chapters 2 and 3 we consider some research (for example, Hines, 1988) which suggests that accountants and accounting do not necessarily provide an unbiased account of reality, but rather, create reality. If the accounting profession emphasizes a measure (such as profitability) as being a measure of success and legitimacy, then in turn, profitable companies will be considered successful and legitimate. If something other than profitability had been supported as a valid measure, then this may not have been the case.

2   It should be noted at this point that Positive Accounting Theory is one of several positive theories of accounting (other positive theories that relate to accounting would include legitimacy theory and certain branches of stakeholder theory). We will refer to the general class of theories that attempt to explain and predict accounting practice in lower case (that is, as positive theories of accounting) and we will refer to Watts and Zimmerman's positive theory of accounting as Positive Accounting Theory (that is, in upper case).

3   Much of the work undertaken in developing 'true income theories' relies upon the work of Hicks (1946). Hicks defined 'income' as the maximum amount that can be consumed by a person or an organization in a particular period without depleting the wealth that existed for that person or organization at the start of the period.

4   For example, in recent years a number of research studies have asked a number of different stakeholder groups what types of environmental performance information the stakeholders considered to be useful to their various decision-making processes.

5   Based on the efficient markets hypothesis that the stock market instantaneously reacts, through price adjustments (changes), to all relevant publicly available information.

6   A similar definition of a paradigm is provided by Wolk and Tearney (1997, p. 47). They define a paradigm as a shared problem-solving view among members of a science or discipline.

7   Kuhn's 'revolutionary' perspective about the development of knowledge is a theory, and as with financial accounting theories, there are alternative views of how knowledge develops and advances. Although a review of the various perspectives of the development of science is beyond the scope of this book,

interested readers are referred to Popper (1959), Lakatos and Musgrove (1974), Feyerabend (1975), and Chalmers (1982).

8 The degree to which we might consider a theory to be acceptable will perhaps depend upon the costs or implications associated with the theory 'getting it wrong' in a particular circumstance. For example, if the theory related to medicine and the theory was wrong only 10 per cent of the time – thereby causing deaths in 10 per cent of the patients – then such a theory might not be acceptable. In accounting we might tolerate higher levels of inconsistency between theory predictions and related outcomes.

9 One of the first detailed descriptions of falsificationism appeared in Karl Popper (1968).

10 Simply stated, a hypothesis can be defined as a proposition typically derived from theory which can be tested for causality or association using empirical data.

11 A good book in this regard is entitled *Straight and Crooked Thinking*, written by Robert H. Thouless (1974). Sterling (1970) is also useful.

12 Where a proposition is not supported in a particular instance, many of us have probably heard the phrase 'the exception proves the rule' being applied. Such a statement implies that we cannot accept a rule or proposition unless we find some evidence that appears to refute it. This clearly is illogical argument. As emphasized above, we must always guard against accepting arguments that are not logically sound.

13 Entire books are dedicated to research methods. Interested readers may refer to: Humphrey and Lee (eds), (2004); Collis and Hussey (2003); Bryman (2004); Ghauri and Gronhaug (2002).

References

Bebbington, J., Gray, R., & Laughlin, R. (2001) *Financial Accounting: Practice and Principles*, London: International Thomson Business Press.

Bryman, A. (2004) *Social Research Methods*, 2nd edn, Oxford: Oxford University Press.

Canning, J. B. (1929) *The Economics of Accountancy: A Critical Analysis of Accounting Theory*, New York: Ronald Press.

Chalmers, A. F. (1982) *What is this Thing called Science?* 2nd edn, Brisbane, Australia: University of Queensland Press.

Chambers, R. J. (1993) 'Positive accounting theory and the PA cult', *ABACUS*, **29** (1), pp. 1–26.

Christenson, C. (1983) 'The methodology of positive accounting', *The Accounting Review*, **58** (January), pp. 1–22.

Collis, J. & Hussey, R. (2003) *Business Research*, London: Palgrave Macmillan.

Deegan, C. (1997) 'Varied perceptions of positive accounting theory: A useful tool for explanation and prediction, or a body of vacuous, insidious and discredited thoughts?', *Accounting Forum*, **20** (5), pp. 63–73.

FASB (1976) 'Scope and implications of the conceptual framework project', Financial Accounting Standards Board.

Feyerabend, P. (1975) *Against Method: Outline of an Anarchic Theory of Knowledge*, London: New Left Books.

Ghauri, P. & Gronhaug, K. (2002) *Research Methods in Business Studies: A Practical Guide*, Harlow: FT Prentice Hall.

Gordon, M. J. (1964) 'Postulates, principles, and research in accounting', *The Accounting Review*, **39** (April), pp. 251–63.

Grady, P. (1965) 'An inventory of generally accepted accounting principles for business enterprises', *Accounting Research Study No. 7*, New York: AICPA.

Gray, R. & Bebbington, J. (2001) *Accounting for the Environment*, London: Sage Publications Ltd.

Gray, R., Owen, D. & Adams, C. (1996) *Accounting and Accountability: Changes and Challenges in Corporate Social and Environmental Reporting*, London: Prentice-Hall.

Gray, R., Owen, D. & Maunders, K. T. (1987) *Corporate Social Reporting: Accounting and Accountability*, Hemel Hempstead: Prentice-Hall.

Hatfield, H. R. (1927) *Accounting, its Principles and Problems*, New York: D. Appleton & Co.

Henderson, S., Peirson, G. & Brown, R. (1992) *Financial Accounting Theory: Its Nature and Development*, 2nd edn, Melbourne: Longman Cheshire.

Hendriksen, E. (1970) *Accounting Theory*, Illinois: Richard D. Irwin.

Hicks, J. R. (1946) *Value and Capital*, Oxford: Oxford University Press.

Hines, R. (1988) 'Financial accounting: In communicating reality, we construct reality', *Accounting Organizations and Society*, **13** (3), pp. 251–62.

Howieson, B. (1996) 'Whither financial accounting research: A modern-day bo-peep?', *Australian Accounting Review*, **6** (1), pp. 29–36.

Humphrey, C. & Lee, B. (eds) (2004) *The Real Life Guide to Accounting Research: A Behind-the-scenes View of Using Qualitative Research Methods*, Kidlington, Oxford: Elsevier.

Jensen, M. C. & Meckling, W. H. (1976) 'Theory of the firm: Managerial behavior, agency costs and ownership structure', *Journal of Financial Economics*, **3** (October), pp. 305–60.

Kuhn, T. S. (1962) *The Structure of Scientific Revolutions*, Illinois: University of Chicago Press.

Lakatos, I. & Musgrove, A. (1974) *Criticism and the Growth of Knowledge*, Cambridge: Cambridge University Press.

Laughlin, R. (1995) 'Empirical research in accounting: Alternative approaches and a case for "middle-range" thinking', *Accounting, Auditing & Accountability Journal*, **8** (1), pp. 63–87.

Laughlin, R. (2004) 'Putting the record straight: A critique of "methodology choices and the construction of facts: Some implications from the sociology of knowledge"', *Critical Perspectives on Accounting*, **15** (2), pp. 261–77.

Lee, T. A. (1974) 'Enterprise income–survival or decline and fall?', *Accounting and Business Research*, **15**, pp. 178–92.

Llewelyn, S. (2003) 'What counts as "theory" in qualitative management and accounting research?', *Accounting, Auditing & Accountability Journal*, **16** (4), pp. 662–708.

Mathews, M. R. (1993) *Socially Responsible Accounting*, London: Chapman and Hall.

Miller, P. B. W. & Reading, R. (1986) *The FASB: The People, the Process, and the Politics*, Illinois: Irwin.

Moonitz, M. (1961) 'The basic postulates of accounting', *Accounting Research Study No. 1*, New York: AICPA.

Paton, W. A. (1922) *Accounting Theory*, Kansas: Scholars Book Co, reprinted 1973.

Paton, W. A. & Littleton, A. C. (1940) *An Introduction to Corporate Accounting Standards*, USA: American Accounting Association.

Popper, K. R. (1968) *The Logic of Scientific Discovery*, 2nd edn, London: Hutchinson.

Popper, K. R. (1959) *The Logic of Scientific Discovery*, London: Hutchinson.

Sprouse, R. & Moonitz, M. (1962) 'A tentative set of broad accounting principles for business enterprises', *Accounting Research Study No. 3*, New York: American Institute of Certified Public Accountants.

Sterling, R. R. (1970) *Theory of the Measurement of Enterprise Income*, USA: University of Kansas Press.

Sterling, R. R. (1990) 'Positive accounting: An assessment', *ABACUS*, **26** (2), pp. 97–135.

Thouless, R. H. (1974) *Straight and Crooked Thinking*, London: Pan Books.

Tinker, A. M., Merino, B. D. & Neimark, M. D. (1982) 'The normative origins of positive theories: Ideology and accounting thought', *Accounting Organizations and Society*, **7** (2), pp. 167–200.

Unerman, J. & O'Dwyer, B. (2004) 'Enron, WorldCom, Andersen *et al.*: A challenge to modernity', *Critical Perspectives on Accounting*, **15** (6–7), pp. 971–93.

Watts, R. & Zimmerman, J. (1978) 'Towards a positive theory of the determination of accounting standards', *Accounting Review*, **53** (1), pp. 112–34.

Watts, R. L. & Zimmerman, J. L. (1986) *Positive Accounting Theory*, Englewood Cliffs, New Jersey: Prentice-Hall Inc.

Watts, R. L. & Zimmerman, J. L. (1990) 'Positive accounting theory: A ten year perspective', *The Accounting Review*, **65** (1), pp. 259–85.

Williams, P. F. (1989) 'The logic of positive accounting research', *Accounting Organizations and Society*, **14** (5/6), pp. 455–68.

Wolk, H. I. & Tearney, M. G. (1997) *Accounting Theory: A Conceptual and Institutional Approach*, Cincinnati, Ohio: International Thomson Publishing.

CHAPTER 2

The financial reporting environment

Learning Objectives

Upon completing this chapter readers should:

- have a broad understanding of the history of the accounting profession and of accounting regulation;
- be aware of some of the arguments for and against the existence of accounting regulation;
- be aware of some of the theoretical perspectives used to explain the existence of regulation;
- be aware of how and why various groups within society try to influence the accounting standard-setting process;
- acknowledge that many accounting decisions are based on professional opinions and have an awareness of some of the theories used to explain what influences the accountant to choose one accounting method in preference to another;
- be aware of some of the arguments advanced to support a view that the accountant can be considered to be a powerful member of society.

Opening issues

(a) Through such mechanisms as conceptual framework programmes, accounting professions throughout the world promote a view that accounting reports, when prepared properly, will be objective and will faithfully represent the underlying transactions and events of the reporting entity. Is it in the interests of the accounting profession to promote this view of objectivity and neutrality, and if so, why?

(b) Further, because of the economic and social impacts of many accounting decisions (for example, decisions that involve choosing one method of accounting in preference to another), and because accounting standard-setters take such economic and social impacts into account when developing new accounting standards, standard-setters themselves are not developing accounting standards that can subsequently enable a reliable account of organizational performance to be provided. Do you agree or disagree with this view, and why?

Introduction

Financial accounting is a process involving the collection and processing of financial information to assist in the making of various decisions by many parties external to the organization. These parties are diverse and include present and potential investors, lenders, suppliers, employees, customers, governments, the local community, parties performing a review or oversight function, and the media. Financial accounting deals with the provision of information to parties not involved in the day-to-day running of the organization. As there are many parties external to the firm, with potentially vastly different information demands and needs, it is not possible to generate a single report which will satisfy the specific needs of all parties (reports that meet specific information needs are often referred to as special-purpose reports). As such, the process of financial accounting leads to the generation of reports deemed to be general purpose financial reports.[1]

Financial accounting tends to be heavily regulated in most countries, with many accounting standards and other regulations governing how particular transactions and events are to be recognized, measured and disclosed. The reports generated, such as the balance sheet, profit and loss account (or income statement), statement of cash flows, operating and financial review, and supporting notes, are directly impacted by the various accounting regulations in place. When existing accounting regulations change, or new accounting regulations are implemented, this will typically have an impact on the various numbers (such as particular revenues, expenses, assets and liabilities) included in the reports provided to the public.

Ideally, users of financial reports should have a sound working knowledge of the various accounting standards and other regulations because, arguably, without such a knowledge it can be difficult (or perhaps near impossible) to interpret what the reports are actually reflecting. For example, 'profit' is the outcome of applying particular accounting rules and conventions, many of which are contained within accounting standards. As these rules change (as they frequently do), the same series of transactions will lead to different measures of 'profits' and net assets. Such a situation leads to an obvious question: should readers of financial reports be expected to understand financial accounting? The answer is yes, even though many users of financial statements (including many company directors and financial analysts) have a very poor working knowledge of accounting.

Throughout the world, various professional accounting bodies have stated specifically that users of financial reports do need to have some level of knowledge of financial accounting if they are to understand financial reports properly. For example, the International Accounting Standards Board's conceptual framework (IASC, 1989, paragraph 25) states that:

> ... users are assumed to have a reasonable knowledge of business and economic activities and accounting and a willingness to study the information with reasonable diligence.[2]

If we are to review an annual report of a company listed on a stock exchange, we will soon realize just how confusing such a document would be to readers with a limited knowledge of accounting (and, as became clear in the aftermath of the collapse of Enron, many people with formal qualifications in accounting also have trouble interpreting the accounting reports of companies which have more complex financial structures and engage in more complex financial transactions). Unfortunately, many readers of financial statements have tended to consider figures such as 'profits' or 'assets' as being 'hard' objective numbers which are not subject to various professional judgements. Hence, although such users may not understand some of the descriptions of accounting methods used, they may believe that they understand what 'profits' and 'net assets' mean. As we know, however, the accounting results (or numbers) will be heavily dependent upon the particular accounting methods chosen, as well as upon various professional judgements made. Depending upon who compiles the accounting reports, measures of profits and net assets can vary greatly.[3]

A review of annual reports will indicate that many companies provide summary 'highlight' statements at the beginning of the reports. Often, multi-year summaries are given of such figures as profits, return on assets, earnings per share, dividend yield, and net asset backing per share. By highlighting particular information, management could be deemed to be helping the less accounting-literate readers to focus on the important results. However, a downside of this is that management itself is selecting the information to be highlighted (that is, such disclosures are voluntary) and as a result, a large amount of otherwise important information may be overlooked.

Financial accounting can be contrasted with management accounting. Management accounting focuses on providing information for decision making by parties who work within an organization (that is, for internal as opposed to external users) and it is largely unregulated. While we will find that most countries have a multitude of financial accounting standards which are often given the force of law, the same cannot be said for management accounting. Because management accounting relates to the provision of information for parties within the organization, the view taken is that there is no need to protect their information needs or rights. It is the information rights of outsiders who are not involved in the day-to-day management of an entity that must be protected. Because financial reports are often used as a source of information for parties contemplating transferring resources to an organization, it is arguably important that certain rules be put in place to govern how the information should be compiled. That is (adopting a pro-regulation perspective), to protect the interests of parties external to a firm, some regulation relating to accounting information is required. We now briefly consider the history of accounting practice and its associated regulation.[4]

An overview of the development and regulation of accounting practice

This section examines the development of accounting regulations in jurisdictions where the primary role of financial accounts has been to aid investment decisions made by external investors in developed capital markets. As we will see in Chapter 4, the primary role of financial accounting in many European countries has historically been different to this capital market based role. However, with increasing globaliz-ation of business and capital markets, the role of financial accounting by large companies in all European countries is now primarily focused on the provision of information to capital markets, and regulations developed over a long period of time in capital market dominated economies (with large numbers of external share-holders) now apply to most large European Union (EU) companies.

While the practice of financial accounting can be traced back many hundreds of years, the regulation of financial accounting in most capital market dominated economies (such as the USA, UK, Ireland, Australia, Canada) generally com-menced in the twentieth century. In part this lack of regulation in the early days may have been due to the fact that until recent centuries there was a limited separation between the ownership and management of business entities and, as such, most systems of accounting were designed to provide information to the owner/manager. In the last century there was an increase in the degree of separation between ownership and management in many countries, and with this increased separation came an increased tendency to regulate accounting disclosures.

Reliance on double entry bookkeeping

Early systems of double entry bookkeeping and accounting, similar to the system we use today, have been traced back to thirteenth- and fourteenth-century Northern Italy. One of the earliest surviving descriptions of a system of double entry accounting is by the Franciscan monk Luca Pacioli as part of his most famous work entitled *Summa de Arithmetica, Geometrica, Proportioni et Proportionalita*, published in Venice in 1494. A review of this work (there are translated versions) indicates that our current system of double entry accounting is very similar to that developed many hundreds of years ago. Even in the days of Pacioli there were debits and credits, with debits going on the left, credits on the right.[5] There were also journals and ledgers. Reflecting on the origins of double entry accounting, Hendriksen and Van Breda (1992, p. 36) state:

> Debits, credits, journal entries, ledgers, accounts, trial balances, balance sheets and income statements all date back to the Renaissance. Accounting, therefore, can claim as noble a lineage as many of the liberal arts.[6] Accounting students can take pride in their heritage. Part of this heritage is a rich vocabulary, almost all of which dates back to this period and much of which is fascinating in its origin.

Debits and credits, which as we now know originated a number of centuries ago, have, over the ages, proved to be the bane of many an accounting student. So, did we really need them? Why couldn't we have simply used positive and negative numbers? For example, if we were to pay wages, why couldn't we have simply put a positive number under the wages column and a negative number under the cash column? The simple answer to this appears to be that negative numbers were not really used in mathematics until the seventeenth century. Hence, the t account was devised to solve this problem with increases being on one side, and decreases on the other. But why keep the t-account, now that we accept the existence of negative numbers? Pondering this issue, Hendriksen and Van Breda (1992, p. 51) comment:

> Textbook writers still explain how debits are found on the left and credits on the right and teach students the subtraction-by-opposition technique that was made obsolete in arithmetic three centuries ago. Programmers then faithfully seek to reflect these medieval ideas on the modern computer screen.

As we will see in subsequent chapters, there are many criticisms of our financial accounting systems. For example, there is an increasing trend towards the view that financial accounting should reflect the various social and environmental consequences of a reporting entity's existence. Unfortunately, however, our 'dated' double entry system has a general inability to take such consequences into account – but we will cover more of this in later chapters, particularly in Chapter 9.

Early development of professional bodies

While accounting and accountants have existed for hundreds of years, it was not until the nineteenth century that accountants within the United Kingdom and the United States banded together to form professional associations. According to Goldberg (1949), a Society of Accountants was formed in Edinburgh in 1854, later to be followed by a number of other bodies, including the Institute of Chartered Accountants in England and Wales (ICAEW), which was established in 1880. According to Mathews and Perera (1996, p. 16), from the early years, the ICAEW was very concerned about the reputation of its members and as a result set conditions for admission, including general education examinations, five years of articles served with a member of the institute, and intermediate and final examinations in a range of subjects.

Within the United States the American Association of Public Accountants was formed in 1887 (Goldberg, 1949). This association went on to form the basis of the American Institute of Certified Public Accountants (AICPA). While members of these bodies were often called upon to perform audits in particular circumstances, and while companies were generally required to prepare accounting reports subject to various company laws and stock exchange requirements,[7] there was a general absence of regulation about what the reports should disclose or how the accounting numbers should be compiled.[8]

Early codification of accounting rules

In the early part of the twentieth century there was limited work undertaken to codify particular accounting principles or rules. Basically, accountants used those rules of which they were aware and which they (hopefully) believed were most appropriate to the particular circumstances. There was very limited uniformity between the accounting methods adopted by different organizations, thereby creating obvious comparability problems. Around the 1920s a number of people undertook research that sought to observe practice and to identify commonly accepted accounting conventions. That is, they sought to describe 'what was', rather than assuming a normative position with regards to 'what should be'. By simply describing current practice, the researchers gave themselves limited possibility for actually improving accounting procedures. As Mathews and Perera (1996, p. 20) state:

> This led to a practice-theory-practice cycle and tended to retard the progress of accounting, because there was no value judgement exercised in respect of the practices which were observed. In other words, there was no opportunity to examine critically what was being practised before the next generation of accountants were prepared in the same manner.

Early researchers who provided detailed descriptions of existing conventions of accounting included Paton (1922); Paton and Littleton (1940); Sanders, Hatfield and Moore (1938); and Gilman (1939). These studies described such things as the doctrines of conservatism, concepts of materiality, consistency, the entity assumption, and the matching principle.

A great deal of the early work undertaken to establish particular accounting rules and doctrines was undertaken in the United States. In 1930 the accounting profession within the United States cooperated with the New York Stock Exchange (NYSE) to develop a list of broadly used accounting principles. According to Zeff (1972), this publication is one of the most important documents in the history of accounting regulation and set the foundation for the codification and acceptance of generally accepted accounting principles. The NYSE requested the accounting profession to compile the document as it was concerned that many companies were using a variety of (typically undisclosed) accounting methods.[9]

Development of disclosure regulations

Within the United States it was not until 1934 that specific disclosures of financial information were required by organizations seeking to trade their securities. The Securities Exchange Act of 1934, as administered by the Securities Exchange Commission (SEC), stipulated the disclosure of specific financial information. The SEC was given authority to stipulate accounting principles and reporting practices. However, it allowed the accounting profession to take charge of this activity as long as it could clearly indicate that it would perform such duties diligently. In an effort to convince the SEC that it could identify acceptable accounting practices, the American Institute of Accountants (one of the predecessors of the AICPA) released, in 1938, a study by Sanders, Hatfield and Moore entitled *A Statement of Accounting Principles.*

In 1938 the SEC stated (within Accounting Series Release No. 4) that it would only accept financial statements prepared in accordance with the generally accepted accounting principles of the accounting profession – thereby giving a great deal of power to the profession. In part, ASR No. 4 stated:

> In cases where financial statements filed with the Commission ... are prepared in accordance with accounting principles for which there is no substantial authoritative support, such financial statements will be presumed to be misleading or inaccurate despite disclosures contained in the certificate of the accountant or in footnotes to the statements provided the matters are material. In cases where there is a difference of opinion between the Commission and the registrant as to proper principles of accounting to be followed, disclosure will be accepted in lieu of correction of the financial statements themselves, only if the points involved are such that there is substantial authoritative support for the practices followed by the registrant and the position of the Commission has not previously been expressed in rules, regulations, or other releases of the Commission, including the published opinion of its chief accountant.

While the above statement does indicate that the SEC was to allow the accounting profession to determine acceptable practice, many considered that the SEC was also warning the accounting profession that it must take an authoritative lead in developing accounting standards, otherwise the SEC would take over the role (Zeff, 1972). From 1939 the Committee on Accounting Procedure, a committee of the accounting profession, began issuing statements on accounting principles, and between 1938 and 1939 it released 12 Accounting Research Bulletins (Zeff, 1972).

Development by the accounting profession of mandatory accounting standards is a relatively recent phenomenon. In the United Kingdom it was not until 1970, when the Accounting Standards Steering Committee was established (later to become the Accounting Standards Committee and then the Accounting Standards Board), that UK accountants had to conform with professionally developed mandatory accounting standards. Prior to this time the ICAEW had released a series of 'recommendations' to members. In the United States, although there had been Accounting Research Bulletins (released by the Committee on Accounting

Procedure, formed in 1938), and Opinions (released by the Accounting Principles Board, formed in 1959), these Bulletins and Opinions were not mandatory. Rather they indicated perceived best practice. There tended to be many corporate departures from these Bulletins and Opinions and as a result, in 1965 a rule (Rule 203 of the AICPA) was introduced that required departures from principles published in APB Opinions to be disclosed in footnotes to financial statements. From 1 July 1973 the APB was replaced by the Financial Accounting Standards Board (FASB), which has subsequently released many accounting standards that are mandatory.

As noted at the beginning of this section, and as will be explored in greater depth in Chapter 4, financial accounting practices (and therefore the regulation of financial accounts) in many European countries was not primarily focused on the provision of information to aid investment decisions by external shareholders in capital markets. Regulation of accounting through professionally developed standards is therefore an even more recent phenomenon in large parts of Europe than it is, for example, in the UK, Ireland or the Netherlands. However, regulation through accounting standards of the consolidated financial statements of all companies whose shares are traded on any stock exchange in the EU became compulsory from 1 January 2005. A further significant change in the accounting regulatory frameworks of many countries occurred following several high profile accounting and audit failures in the USA in 2001 and 2002 (such as Enron and WorldCom). Although, as Unerman and O'Dwyer (2004) point out, these were not the first large scale accounting failures to occur since the inception of regulation through professional accounting standards, they were much larger than previous failures and occurred at a time of sharply falling stock markets. Private investors who were already losing confidence in stock markets due to their financial losses on falling share prices now perceived accounting failures as contributing to even larger losses. In this climate, politicians came under pressure to make accounting regulation more rigorous, and they passed legislation (such as the US Sarbanes-Oxley Act of 2002) to give greater legal force to many existing and new regulations.

The rationale for regulating financial accounting practice

As indicated above, even though financial reports have been in existence for hundreds of years, the regulation of accounting in economies dominated by capital markets (with large numbers of external investors) is a fairly recent phenomenon. Early moves for regulation of accounting were introduced in the United States around the 1930s and followed events such as the Wall Street stock market crash of 1929. Rightly or wrongly it was argued that problems inherent to accounting led to many poor and uninformed investment decisions (Boer, 1994, Ray, 1960), and this fuelled the public desire for information generated by companies to be subject to greater regulation.

In most countries with developed capital markets and large numbers of external investors, there are a multitude of accounting regulations covering a broad cross-section of issues – but do we really need all this regulation? As we will see in the next chapter, there are two broad schools of thought on this issue. There are parties who argue that regulation is necessary, with reasons including:

* markets for information are not efficient and without regulation a sub-optimal amount of information will be produced;

* while proponents of the 'free-market' approach may argue that the capital market *on average* is efficient, such *on average* arguments ignore the rights of individual investors, some of whom can lose their savings as a result of relying upon unregulated disclosures;

* those who demand information can often do so due to power over scarce resources. Parties with limited power (limited resources) will generally be unable to secure information about an organization, even though that organization may impact on their lives;

* investors need protection from fraudulent organizations that may produce misleading information, which due to information asymmetries, cannot be known to be fraudulent when used (such as apparently occurred at WorldCom in the USA and Parmalat in Italy);

* regulation leads to uniform methods being adopted by different entities, thus enhancing comparability.

Others argue that regulation is not necessary, particularly to the extent that it currently exists. Some of the reasons cited include:

* accounting information is like any other good, and people (financial statement users) will be prepared to pay for it to the extent that it has use. This will lead to an optimal supply of information by entities;[10, 11]

* capital markets require information, and any organization that fails to provide information will be punished by the market – an absence of information will be deemed to imply bad news;[12]

* because users of financial information typically do not bear its cost of production, regulation will lead to oversupply of information (at a cost to the producing firms) as users will tend to overstate the need for the information;

* regulation typically restricts the accounting methods that may be used. This means that some organizations will be prohibited from using accounting methods which they believe best reflect their particular performance and position. This is considered to impact on the efficiency with which the firm can inform the markets about its operations.

When regulation is introduced, there are various theories available to describe who benefits from such regulation. There is the *public interest theory* of regulation which proposes that regulation be introduced to protect the public. This protection may be required as a result of inefficient markets. Public interest theory assumes that the regulatory body (usually government) is a neutral arbiter of the 'public interest' and does not let its own self-interest impact on its rule-making processes. According to Scott (2003, p. 448), following public interest theory, the regulator 'does its best to regulate so as to maximize social welfare. Consequently, regulation is thought of as a trade-off between the costs of regulation and its social benefits in the form of improved operation of markets'.

A contrary perspective of regulation is provided by *capture theory* which argues that although regulation is often introduced to protect the public, the regulatory mechanisms are often subsequently controlled (captured) so as to protect the interests of particular self-interested groups within society, typically those whose activities are most affected by the regulation. That is, the 'regulated' tend to capture the 'regulator'. Posner (1974, p. 342) argues that 'the original purposes of the regulatory program are later thwarted through the efforts of the interest group'. Empirical evidence of a regulator making individual decisions which favour the groups that it regulates is not sufficient to demonstrate regulatory capture (as each of these decisions might be regarded as the most appropriate in the circumstances). Rather, most of the regulator's whole programme of regulation needs to work in the interests of the regulated, and usually against the interests of those who the regulator is intended to protect. This implies that accounting regulations can have a different impact on different people or groups, and there is evidence (discussed in the next chapter) showing that specific accounting regulations do have social and/or economic consequences which vary between different groups.

Both public interest theories and capture theories of regulation assert that initially regulation is put in place to protect the public (capture theory simply asserts that the regulated will then subsequently attempt to control the regulatory process). Another view, which is often referred to as *private interest theory* (or *economic interest group theory*), is proposed by researchers such as Stigler (1971) and Peltzman (1976). This theory relaxes the assumption that regulations are initially put in place to protect the public interest, as well as the assumption that government regulators are neutral arbiters not driven by self-interest. Stigler (1971) proposes that governments are made up of individuals who are self-interested and will introduce regulations more likely to lead to their re-election. In deciding upon particular regulation they will consider the impacts upon key voters, as well as on election campaign finances. Individuals with an interest in particular legislation are deemed more likely to get their preferred legislation if they can form themselves into large organized groups with strong cohesive voting power. These theories of regulation (public interest theory, capture theory and private interest theory), as well as others, are further considered in Chapter 3.

If we are to accept the need for accounting regulation, a further issue to consider is who should be responsible for the regulation – should it be in the hands of the private sector (such as the accounting profession), or in the hands of government?[13] Can private sector regulators be expected to put in place regulations that are always in the public interest, or will they seek to put in place rules that favour their own constituency? Advocates of private sector accounting standard-setting would argue that the accounting profession is best able to develop accounting standards because of its superior knowledge of accounting, and because of the greater likelihood that its rules and regulations would be accepted by the business community. Proponents of public sector accounting standard-setting argue that government has greater enforcement powers, hence the rules of government are more likely to be followed. It might also be less responsive to pressures exerted by business, and more likely to consider overall public interest.

What we demonstrate in subsequent chapters is that the regulation of accounting (or indeed an absence of regulation) can have many economic and social consequences. As such, the accounting standard-setting process is typically considered to be a very political process, with various interested parties lobbying the standard-setters.

The role of professional judgement in financial accounting

As we know from studying accounting, the process involved in generating accounts depends upon many professional judgements. While the accounting treatment of many transactions and events is regulated, a great deal of accounting treatment pertaining to other transactions and events is unregulated. Even when particular regulations are in place, for example, that buildings must be depreciated, there is still scope to select the useful life of the building and the residual value. Many such judgements must be made – should an item be capitalized or expensed? This in turn will depend upon crucial assessments as to whether the expenditure is likely to generate future economic benefits.

At the core of the accounting process is an expectation that accountants should be objective and free from bias when performing their duties. The information being generated should *represent faithfully* the underlying transactions and events and it should be *neutral* and *complete* (IASC, 1989, paragraphs 33, 36 and 38).[14] However, can we really accept that accounting can be 'neutral' or objective? Throughout the world, several national accounting standard-setters have explicitly considered the economic and social implications of possible accounting standards prior to their introduction (the consideration of economic and social consequences is referred to in some countries' conceptual framework projects). In these countries, if the economic or social implications of a particular accounting standard have been deemed to be significantly negative, then it is likely that the introduction of the standard would have been abandoned – even though the particular standard may have been deemed to more accurately reflect particular transactions or events. While it is difficult to criticize a process that considers potential impacts on others, it is nevertheless difficult to accept that accounting standards are neutral or unbiased. In a sense the acceptance of the need to consider economic and social consequences as part of the standard-setting process has created a dilemma for standard-setters. According to Zeff (1978, p. 62):

> The board (FASB) is thus faced with a dilemma which requires a delicate balancing of accounting and non-accounting variables. Although its decisions should rest – and be seen to rest – chiefly on accounting considerations, it must also study – and be seen to study – the possible adverse economic and social consequences of its proposed actions ... What is abundantly clear is that we have entered an era in which economic and social consequences may no longer be ignored as a substantive issue in the setting of accounting standards. The profession must respond to the changing tenor of the times while continuing to perform its essential role in the areas in which it possesses undoubted expertise.

However, this willingness to take into account the possible wider social and economic consequences in developing accounting standards has reduced in several countries in recent years. For example, in the UK in 2001 and 2002, many large companies blamed (possibly unfairly) the rules in a controversial new accounting standard on pension costs for their decisions to withdraw elements of their pension schemes from many employees. This can be considered to have been a significant negative social consequence from the new accounting standard for these employees, but the UK accounting regulator refused to change the accounting standard (despite considerable political pressure).

In Chapters 7 and 8 we consider various theoretical perspectives proposed as explanations for why particular accounting methods may be implemented by a reporting entity (remember, the accounting treatment of many transactions and events is not subject to accounting standards). Consistent with a perspective of objectivity is a view that organizations are best served by selecting accounting methods that best reflect their underlying performance. This is referred to as an 'efficiency perspective' (derived from Positive Accounting Theory). The efficiency perspective asserts that different organizational characteristics explain why different firms adopt different accounting methods (Jensen and Meckling, 1976). For example, firms that have different patterns of use in relation to a particular type of asset will be predicted to adopt different amortization policies. Advocates of the efficiency perspective argue that firms should be allowed to choose those accounting methods that best reflect their performance, and that accounting regulations that restrict the set of available accounting techniques will be costly. For example, if a new accounting standard is released that bans a particular accounting method being used by a reporting entity, then this will lead to inefficiencies as the resulting financial statements may no longer provide the best reflection of the performance of the organization. It would be argued that management is best able to select which accounting methods are appropriate in given circumstances, and government or other bodies should not intervene in the standard-setting process. This perspective, however, does not consider that some financial statement pre-parers may be less than objective (that is, like Enron, WorldCom or Parmalat, they may be *creative*) when preparing the financial reports. The efficiency perspective also dismisses the comparability benefits that may arise if standard-setters reduce the available set of accounting methods.

An alternative perspective to explain why particular accounting methods are selected (and which is also derived from Positive Accounting Theory) is the 'oppor-tunistic perspective'. This perspective does not assume that those responsible for selecting accounting methods will be objective. Rather, it assumes that they will be driven by self-interest (Watts and Zimmerman, 1978). This perspective provides an explanation of the practice of *creative accounting*, which is defined as an approach to accounting wherein objectivity is not employed, but rather, refers to a situation where those responsible for the preparation of accounts select accounting methods that provide the result desired by the preparers. As an example, an organization might, like Enron, opportunistically elect to structure certain transactions in a manner designed to remove specific assets and related liabilities from its balance sheet (a technique known as *off balance sheet funding*) not because these assets and liabilities do not 'belong' to the organization, but perhaps because this off balance sheet funding has the effect of reducing the reported debt to equity (capital gearing) ratio at a time when the organization is close to breaching particular accounting-based agreements negotiated with external parties, such as loan agreements which have a stipulated minimum allowable debt to equity ratio, below which particular assets of the reporting entity may be seized.

Apart from the efficiency and opportunistic perspectives, there are a number of other theoretical perspectives proposed to explain why an entity may select par-ticular accounting and disclosure policies (other perspectives include legitimacy theory, political economy theory and stakeholder theory). Chapter 8 further explores the alternative perspectives. However, what is being emphasized at this point is that, although there is much accounting regulation in place (and there are various theories to explain the existence of regulation), there are also many accounting decisions that are unregulated (giving rise to various theories to explain the choice of particular accounting methods from the set of available alternatives).

How powerful is the accountant?

Accountants are often the butt of many a cruel joke. They are often portrayed as small, weak individuals with poor social skills. For example, consider the depictions of accountants in various movies and television programmes. In the (in)famous Monty Python 'Lion Tamer' sketch, in which John Cleese is cast as a recruitment consultant who interviews Michael Palin (who plays Mr Anchovy the accountant and aspiring lion tamer), Cleese describes the accountant as:

> An extremely dull fellow, unimaginative, timid, lacking in initiative, spineless, easily dominated ... Whereas in most professions these would be considerable drawbacks, in accountancy they are a positive boon. [15]

Most of us would also probably remember such characters as Louis Tully, the 'nerd' accountant in *Ghostbusters* and Leo Getz the bumbling accountant in *Lethal Weapon 2* and *3*. These are only two of many poor depictions that movies make of accountants. While accountants may be the subject of such (poorly informed and unpleasant) depictions and taunts, we can rest in the knowledge that we accountants are indeed very powerful individuals. The assertion that accountants are *powerful* (which is obviously flattering to students of accounting) is based on a number of perspectives, as follows:

◆ The output of the accounting process (for example, *profits* or *net asset backing per share*) impacts on many decisions such as whether to invest in or lend funds to an entity, whether to lobby for increased wages based on profitability, whether to place an entity into technical default for failure to comply with previously agreed accounting-based restrictions, whether to lobby government for intervention because of excessive *profits*, and so on. That is, many transfers of funds (and therefore wealth) arise as a result of reports generated by accountants through the accounting process. Because accounting is heavily reliant on professional judgement, the judgement of the accountant can directly impact on various parties' wealth.

◆ There is also a perspective that accountants, in providing objective information to interested parties, can in a sense provide or transfer to them a source of 'power' to drive changes to corporations' behaviour. As Gray (1992, p. 404) states:

> ... power can be exercised in some degree by all ... external parties. For that power to be exercised there is a basic need for information (as an essential element of the participatory democratic process ...) and this information will be an extension of that currently available. That is, the widest possible range of participants must be emancipated and enabled through the manifestation of existing but unfulfilled rights to information.

◆ By emphasizing particular performance attributes (such as profits), accountants can tend to give legitimacy to organizations that otherwise may not be deemed to be legitimate.

Further reflecting on the above points, we can consider the work of Hines (1988, 1991). Hines (1991, p. 313) stresses a perspective that 'financial accounting practices are implicated in the construction and reproduction of the social world'. What she is arguing is that by emphasizing measures such as profits (which ignores many negative social and environmental impacts) accounting can cause people to support organizations that may not otherwise be supported. By holding profitability out as some ideal in terms of performance, profitable companies are considered to be *good* companies.

Consider Exhibit 2.1. The newspaper report emphasizes the profits (and cost reduction measures) of British American Tobacco (BAT). If underlying profits increase, this is typically portrayed as a sign of sound management. The earning of profits tends to be seen as consistent with a notion of legitimacy – profits are reported and emphasized as some form of objective measure of performance. But as we know, and what the media typically neglects to note, is that the measure of profits really depends on the assumptions and judgements made by the particular team of accountants involved. As can be seen from Exhibit 2.1, no mention is made of the accounting methods employed by BAT. This is typical of media coverage given to corporate performance, with accounting results (for example, profits) being apparently promoted as hard, objective calculations. Financial accounting can engender such views because it is promoted (through such media as conceptual frameworks) as being objective and reliable and having the capacity to accurately reflect underlying facts.[16] As Hines (1991, p. 315) states in relation to conceptual framework projects:

> It appears that the ontological assumption underpinning the CF is that the relationship between financial accounting and economic reality is a unidirectional, reflecting or faithfully reproducing relationship: economic reality exists objectively, inter-subjectively, concretely and independently of financial accounting practices; financial accounting reflects, mirrors, represents or measures this pre-existent reality.

What also should be appreciated is that the measures of profit calculated for BAT (and also other organizations) ignore many social and environmental externalities caused by the reporting entity. In the case of a cigarette manufacturer such as BAT there is scientific evidence that their product causes major adverse social (and related economic) consequences. Accounting, however, ignores these externalities. Furthermore, the factory closures mentioned in the newspaper report were portrayed in the (positive) terms of cost savings, ignoring the negative social impact (externalities) of the closures on the workers employed in these factories or the communities where the factories were located.

A counter view to the above perspective (that accounting is *objective* and provides an accurate reflection of a pre-existent reality) is the view adopted by Hines that accountants can, in a sense, create different realities, depending upon the particular

Exhibit 2.1 Profits as an indicator of organizational performance

BAT takes £50m China write-down

Lisa Urquhart

British American Tobacco has taken a £50m write-down on the money it spent trying to get agreement to build a factory in China.

The group is in a stand-off with the Chinese state tobacco monopoly over whether it has agreement to build a factory.

Paul Adams, chief executive, said the decision did not reduce BAT's determination to break into the world's biggest cigarette market. 'We continue to have our discussions with the Chinese government and we continue to make slow progress.'

BAT also raised the prospect of factory closures across its 65 sites worldwide to reduce costs. Supply-chain savings have reached £120m over the last two years as the group has closed factories and moved production.

Analysts also welcomed the news that the group had stepped up its overhead cost saving targets from £200m to £320m by 2007 after finding itself ahead of schedule.

The emphasis on cost savings helped Jan du Plessis, chairman, to predict future earnings per share growth in high single figures. Underlying earnings per share rose 10 per cent in 2004, ahead of expectations.

But he once again ruled out a large acquisition to aid growth. 'We are comfortable that our strategy can deliver organic growth, we don't need to do any large acquisitions to add growth,' he said. There has long been speculation that BAT might bid for rival Gallaher.

The group reported 2004 pre-tax profit up 20 per cent to £1.87bn. Underlying operating profit rose 2 per cent to £2.83bn, in line with forecasts.

Group volumes, including make-your-own cigarettes, increased 8 per cent to £853bn cigarettes in the year, helped by the merger of its US business with RJ Reynolds.

The price war and duty increases continued to be felt in Canada, where profit from Imperial Tobacco Canada fell by £122m, or 36 per cent, to £342m. Despite some recovery in prices, the group predicted further profit and volume falls in Canada for 2005.

The contribution from BAT's €2.3bn (£1.6bn) purchase of Ente Tabacchi Italiani went some way to offset the Canadian performance as European profit rose by £190m to £726m.

The proposed final dividend of 29.2p (27p) gives a total of 41.9p (38.8p) on earnings per share that almost doubled from 26.93p to 52.2p. This was helped by a share buy-back. BAT promised to pay half its future earnings in dividends.

Financial Times, 2 March 2005, p. 24

judgements taken, the accounting standards available, and so on. That is, accounting does not objectively reflect a particular reality – it creates it. This view is also supported by Handel (1982, p. 36) who states:

> Things may exist independently of our accounts, but they have no human existence until they become accountable. Things may not exist, but they may take on human significance by becoming accountable ... . Accounts define reality and at the same time they are that reality ... . The processes by which accounts are offered and accepted are the fundamental social process ... . Accounts do not more or less accurately describe things. Instead they establish what is accountable in the setting in which they occur. Whether they are accurate or inaccurate by some other standards, accounts define reality for a situation in the sense that people act on the basis of what is accountable in the situation of their action. The account provides a basis for action, a definition of what is real, and it is acted on so long as it remains accountable.

While one team of accountants may make various accounting assumptions and judgements which lead to a profit being reported, it is possible that another team of accountants may make different assumptions and judgements which lead to the same organization (with the same transactions and events) reporting a loss. Recording a loss may generate many negative reactions from various stakeholder groups (for example, from shareholders, the media and analysts) and may cause real negative cash flow consequences for the reporting entity. Hines (1991, p. 20) further reflects on the power of the accounting profession. She states:

> If, say, auditors qualify their report with respect to the going-concern assumption, and/or insist that a corporation's financial statements be prepared on the basis of liquidation values, this in itself may precipitate the failure of a company which may otherwise have traded out of its difficulties.

Another point to be made (which is related to the above point), and one which we consider further in Chapter 3, is that few, if any, accounting standards are introduced without some form of economic and social impact (which as we know from previous discussion in this chapter is considered by many accounting standard-setters). As an example, we can consider the various arguments that were raised over the implementation of International Accounting Standard (IAS) 39 (Financial Instruments: Recognition and Measurement) by several EU countries. Many European banks argued that implementation of IAS 39 would require them to value certain financial assets and liabilities in a manner which would not reflect the underlying economic reality of many financial transactions, and this would result in unrepresentative and highly volatile profit or loss figures and substantially weakened balance sheets. It was further argued that these weakened balance sheets and highly volatile reported profits would impact on market perceptions of banks' creditworthiness, thus increasing their cost of capital. Banks in some European countries successfully lobbied their own governments to actively support the banks in seeking to change certain requirements of IAS 39. As we will see in Chapter 4, as part of the EU regulatory process the EU established the Accounting Regulatory Committee (ARC) whose task is to scrutinize all international accounting standards and recommend whether they should be enforced in the EU. Successful lobbying by banks in Italy, Spain, Belgium and France led to these countries' members of the ARC voting against EU adoption of IAS 39 in July 2004, apparently because of its potential negative economic impact.

Because of these wider social and economic impacts, perspectives of accounting as being neutral in its effects are now widely dismissed (Zeff, 1978). Many national standard-setting bodies throughout the world explicitly state in their various documents (which often form part of their respective conceptual frameworks) that economic and social implications of particular pronouncements must be considered prior to the introduction of new accounting rules. As Zeff (1978, p. 60) states:

> The issue of economic consequences has, therefore, changed from one having only procedural implications for the standard-setting process to one which is now firmly a part of the standard-setters' substantive policy framework.

The IASB, which has now effectively taken over the accounting standard-setting process in many countries (including all members of the EU), does not have such a formal requirement to consider the broader social and economic implications of their accounting rules. However, members of both the IASB and its supervisory body (the International Accounting Standards Committee Foundation) must be aware that, in practice, if they develop too many accounting standards which have widespread negative social and/or economic impacts in many nations, the governments of these nations are likely to reduce or withdraw their support for continued use of International Financial Reporting Standards in their nations.

Hence we are left with a view that while the notion of objectivity and neutrality is promoted within various conceptual frameworks (perhaps, as Hines suggests, as a means of constructing a perceived legitimacy for the accounting profession), various factors such as the possible economic and social implications, and the potential influences of management self-interest (culminating in some form of *creative accounting*) can lead us to question such claims of objectivity. This chapter has also promoted a view that accountants do have quite a degree of *power* – many decisions with real economic and social implications are made on the basis of accounting information. Whether accounting information is like any other good that can be freely traded in the marketplace, or whether it should be subject to regulation, is an issue that we further investigate in the next chapter.

Chapter summary

In this chapter we explored how the output of the financial accounting process is used in many different decisions by parties both within, and outside, an organization. Because the financial accounting process provides information to parties external to the organization who otherwise would not have information, and because this information is often used as the basis for many decisions, it is generally accepted that it is necessary to regulate the practice of financial accounting.

Financial accounting practices are heavily regulated. However, in countries dominated by strong capital markets (with large numbers of external investors), the history of financial accounting regulation is relatively recent and there was a general absence of such regulation prior to the twentieth century. In the early parts of the twentieth century, accounting research often involved documenting commonly used accounting practices. This research led to the development and acceptance of broad principles of accounting that all accountants were expected to follow. Over time, broad principles gave way to the development of specific accounting standards. Accounting standards began to be released by various accounting professional bodies throughout the world around the 1970s and standard-setting activity has tended to increase since then. Financial accounting practices throughout the world today are generally regulated by a large number of accounting standards.

The act of regulating accounting practices through the continual release of new and revised accounting standards has led to various arguments for and against regulation. The arguments range from the belief that there is no need to regulate accounting practices (the 'free-market' approach) to a view that regulation is necessary to protect the interests of those parties with a stake in a reporting entity. Arguments against regulation often rely upon the view that the output of the financial accounting system should be treated like any other good, and if the market is left to operate freely, optimal amounts of accounting information will be produced. Introducing regulation leads to an oversupply of accounting information and can cause organizations to use accounting methods that do not efficiently reflect their actual operations, financial position, and financial performance. As we see in subsequent chapters, such 'free-market' arguments are challenged by many people.

This chapter has also briefly considered various theories about who is likely to benefit from regulation once it is introduced (Chapter 3 extends much of this discussion). We considered public interest theory which proposes that regulation is introduced to protect the public and when putting regulation in place, regulators seek to maximize the overall welfare of the community (which obviously requires trade-offs of particular costs and benefits). Another theory that we considered was capture theory which proposes that while regulation might initially be introduced for the public's benefit, ultimately the group that is regulated will gain control of the regulation process. That is, they will eventually 'capture' the regulatory process. We also considered private interest theories of regulation, which propose that the regulators introduce regulation that best serves the regulators' own private interests. That is, regulators are motivated not by the public interest, but by their own self-interest. For example, politicians will introduce regulation likely to generate enough support to ensure their re-election.

We also considered issues associated with the 'power' of accountants. Arguments were advanced to support a view that accountants hold a very powerful role within society (which stands in contrast to how they are often portrayed in the media). Accountants provide information that is used in many decisions and they are able to highlight or downplay particular facets of an organization's performance.

Questions

2.1 Do you consider that users of financial reports should have a sound working knowledge of the various accounting standards in use? Explain your answer.

2.2 Do you believe that the media portray accounting numbers, such as profits, as some sort of 'hard' and objective performance indicator? Why do you think they might do this, and if they do, what are some of the implications that might arise as a result of this approach?

2.3 Briefly outline some arguments in favour of regulating the practice of financial accounting.

2.4 Briefly outline some arguments in favour of eliminating the regulation pertaining to financial accounting.

2.5 As this chapter indicates, Stigler (1971) proposes a theory (*private interest theory*) in which it is proposed that regulatory bodies (including accounting standard-setters) are made up of individuals who are self-interested, and these individuals will introduce regulation that best serves their own self-interest. Under this perspective, the view that regulators act in the public interest is rejected. From your experience, do you think that this is an acceptable assumption? Assuming that you reject this central assumption, would this have implications for whether you would be prepared to accept any predictions generated by the private interest theory?

2.6 Because accounting standard-setters throughout the world typically consider the potential economic and social consequences of potential accounting standards when developing accounting standards, it has been argued that reports developed in accordance with the accounting standards cannot be considered neutral or unbiased. Do you agree with this perspective? Is this perspective consistent with the qualitative attributes typically promoted in accounting conceptual framework projects?

2.7 Hines (1991) promotes a view that it is in the interest of the accounting profession to publicly promote a view that the information they generate is 'objective'. Why do you think this is the case?

2.8 Solomons (1978, p. 69) quotes the American Accounting Association: 'Every policy choice represents a trade-off among differing individual preferences, and possibly among alternative consequences, regardless of whether the policy-makers see it that way or not. In this sense, accounting policy choices can never be neutral. There is someone who is granted his preference, and someone who is not.'
Required: Evaluate the above statement.

2.9 While it is difficult to criticize a process that considers potential impacts on others, at the same time it is difficult to accept that accounting standards are neutral or unbiased.
Required: Evaluate the above statement.

2.10 Hines (1991, p. 313) stresses a view that 'financial accounting practices are implicated in the construction and reproduction of the social world'.
Required: What does Hines mean in the above statement? Do you agree or disagree with her, and why?

2.11 Why might accountants be construed as being powerful individuals?

Notes

1 In its Preface to International Financial Reporting Standards (IASB, 2002, paragraph 10), The International Accounting Standards Board defines 'general purpose financial statements' as reports 'directed towards the common information needs of a wide range of users'.

2 Within the United States conceptual framework project, reference is made to the 'informed reader' who should have sufficient knowledge of accounting to be able to appropriately interpret financial statements compiled in accordance with generally accepted accounting principles.

3 Yet all the various financial statements may be deemed to be *true and fair* – which implies that accountants are able to provide different versions of the 'truth'.

4 Although we are focusing on financial accounting in this text, a similar argument can be made in favour of the regulation of social and environmental reporting. Corporations generate many social and environmental impacts which can affect a variety of stakeholders. Such stakeholders arguably have a right to know about the social and environmental implications of an organization's operations. Such information

could then provide the basis for decisions about whether the stakeholders will support the organization's operations.

5 According to Hendriksen and Van Breda (1992, p. 36), our use of the word debit can be traced back to the word *debere* (which is shortened to dr). This is the Latin word for an obligation, and can be interpreted as meaning *to owe*. The word credit (abbreviated to cr) can be linked to the Latin word *credere* which means to believe or trust in someone.

6 Hatfield (1924) points out that Luca Pacioli (who was a prominent academic of his day) was a close friend of Leonardo da Vinci, and that da Vinci was one of the first people to buy a copy of *Summa de Arithmetica* and drew the illustrations for one of Pacioli's later books.

7 For example, within the United Kingdom the Joint Stock Companies Act 1844 required that companies produce a balance sheet and an auditor's report thereon for distribution to shareholders before its annual meeting. This requirement was removed in a 1862 Act, but reinstated in a 1900 Act. In 1929 a requirement to produce a profit and loss account was introduced.

8 In 1900 the New York Stock Exchange required companies applying for listing to prepare financial statements showing the results of their operations as well as details about their financial position. In 1926 the exchange further required that all listed companies provide their shareholders with an annual financial report in advance of the companies' annual general meetings. The report did not have to be audited.

9 Five of the identified principles subsequently formed the basis of Chapter 1 of Accounting Research Bulletin No. 43, as issued by the Committee on Accounting Procedure.

10 Advocates of a regulated approach would argue, however, that accounting information is a public good and, as a result, many individuals will obtain the information for free (this is often referred to as the 'free-rider' problem). Once this occurs, reliance on market-mechanism arguments tends to be flawed and the usual pricing mechanisms of a market cannot be expected to operate (Cooper and Keim, 1983).

11 This 'free-market' perspective is adopted by researchers who work within the agency theory paradigm. This paradigm is discussed in Chapter 7.

12 Accepting this perspective, and consistent with Akcrlof (1970), companies that fail to produce necessary information, particularly if the information is being produced by other entities, will be viewed as 'lemons', and these 'lemons' will find it more costly to attract funds than other ('non-lemon') entities.

13 In some countries, accounting regulation is in the hands of both private sector and public sector entities. As an example, within the EU, accounting regulations are developed by the International Accounting Standards Board (private sector) but have to be endorsed by the Accounting Regulatory Committee (public sector) before they are enforced for EU companies. In the United States, both the Financial Accounting Standards Board (private sector) and the SEC (public sector) have released accounting standards.

14 According to Hines (1991, p. 330) it is in the accounting profession's interest to publicly promote a perspective of objectivity. As she states, 'the very talk, predicated on an assumption of an objective world to which accountants have privileged access via their "measurement expertise", serves to construct a perceived legitimacy for the profession's power and autonomy'.

15 Smith and Briggs (1999) provide a more thorough overview of how accountants have been portrayed in movies and on television.

16 Authors such as Molotch and Boden (1985) provide a view that a form of social power is attributed to those people and professions able to 'trade on the objectivity assumption' (p. 281).

References

Akerlof, G. A. (1970) 'The market for "lemons": quality uncertainty and the market mechanism', *Quarterly Journal of Economics*, **84**, pp. 488–500.

Boer, G. (1994) 'Five modern management accounting myths', *Management Accounting* (January), pp. 22–27.

Cooper, K. & Keim, G. (1983) 'The economic rationale for the nature and extent of corporate financial disclosure regulation: A critical assessment', *Journal of Accounting and Public Policy*, **2**.

Gilman, S. (1939) *Accounting concepts of profits*, New York: Ronald Press.

Goldberg, L. (1949) 'The development of accounting', in Gibson, C. T., Meredith, C. G., & R., P. (eds) *Accounting Concepts Readings*, Melbourne: Cassell.

Gray, R. (1992) 'Accounting and environmentalism: An exploration of the challenge of gently accounting for accountability, transparency and sustainability', *Accounting Organizations and Society*, **17** (5), pp. 399–426.

Handel, W. (1982) *Ethnomethodology: How People Make Sense*, Hemel Hempstead: Prentice-Hall.

Hatfield, H. R. (1924) 'An historical defense of bookkeeping', *The Journal of Accountancy*, **37** (4), pp. 241–53.

Hendriksen, E. S. & Van Breda, M. F. (1992) *Accounting Theory*, 5th edn, Homewood: Irwin.

Hines, R. (1988) 'Financial accounting: In communicating reality, we construct reality', *Accounting Organizations and Society*, **13** (3), pp. 251–62.

Hines, R. (1991) 'The FASB's conceptual framework, financial accounting and the maintenance of the social world', *Accounting Organizations and Society*, **16** (4), pp. 313–51.

IASB (2002) 'Preface to International Financial Reporting Standards', London: International Accounting Standards Board.

IASC (1989) 'Framework for the preparation and presentation of financial statements', London: International Accounting Standards Committee.

Jensen, M. C. & Meckling, W. H. (1976) 'Theory of the firm: Managerial behavior, agency costs and ownership structure', *Journal of Financial Economics*, **3** (October), pp. 305–60.

Mathews, M. R. & Perera, M. H. B. (1996) *Accounting Theory and Development*, 3rd edn, Thomas Nelson.

Molotch, H. L. & Boden, D. (1985) 'Talking social structure: Discourse, domination and the Watergate hearings', *American Sociological Review*, pp. 477–86.

Paton, W. A. (1922) *Accounting Theory*, Kansas: Scholars Book Co, reprinted 1973.

Paton, W. A. & Littleton, A. C. (1940) *An Introduction to Corporate Accounting Standards*, USA: American Accounting Association.

Peltzman, S. (1976) 'Towards a more general theory of regulation', *Journal of Law and Economics* (August), pp. 211–40.

Posner, R. A. (1974) 'Theories of economic regulation', *Bell Journal of Economics and Management Science*, **5** (Autumn), pp. 335–58.

Ray, D. D. (1960) *Accounting and Business Fluctuations*, USA: University of Florida Press.

Sanders, T. H., Hatfield, H. R. & Moore, U. (1938) *A statement of accounting principles*, reprinted AAA 1959 edn, USA: American Institute of Accountants.

Scott, W. R. (2003) *Financial Accounting Theory*, 3rd edn, Toronto: Pearson Education Canada Inc.

Smith, M. & Briggs, S. (1999) 'From beancounter to action hero', *Charter*, **70** (1), pp. 36–39.

Solomons, D. (1978) 'The politicisation of accounting', *Journal of Accountancy*, **146** (5), pp. 65–72.

Stigler, G. J. (1971) 'The theory of economic regulation', *Bell Journal of Economics and Management Science* (Spring), pp. 2–21.

Unerman, J. & O'Dwyer, B. (2004) 'Enron, WorldCom, Andersen *et al.*: A challenge to modernity', *Critical Perspectives on Accounting*, **15** (6–7), pp. 971–93.

Watts, R. & Zimmerman, J. (1978) 'Towards a positive theory of the determination of accounting standards', *Accounting Review*, **53** (1), pp. 112–34.

Zeff, S. A. (1972) *Forging Accounting Principles in Five Countries*, Champaign, Illinois: Stipes Publishing Co.

Zeff, S. A. (1978) 'The rise of economic consequences', *Journal of Accountancy*, **146** (6), pp. 56–63.

CHAPTER 3

The regulation of financial accounting

Learning Objectives

Upon completing this chapter readers should:

- understand some of the various theoretical arguments that have been proposed in favour of reducing the extent of regulation of financial accounting;
- understand some of the various theoretical arguments for regulating the practice of financial accounting;
- understand various theoretical perspectives that describe who is likely to gain the greatest advantage from the implementation of accounting regulation;
- understand that accounting standard-setting is a very political process which seeks the views of a broad cross-section of account users;
- understand the relevance to the accounting standard-setting process of potential economic and social impacts arising from accounting regulations.

Opening issues

(a) Throughout the world in recent years a number of industries have been deregulated, for example, the banking industry, the telecommunications industry and the airline industry. There were numerous similar calls for a reduction in accounting regulations prior to the widely publicized accounting 'scandals' at Enron and other large companies in recent years (these calls used such terminology as *accounting standard overload*) – but what could some of the implications have been if financial accounting was deregulated?

> (b) If financial accounting were to be deregulated, what incentives or mechanisms might operate to cause an organization to produce publicly available financial statements? Would these mechanisms operate to ensure that an optimal amount of reliable information is produced? What is the 'optimal' amount of information?

Introduction

In Chapter 2 we briefly considered a number of theories to explain the existence of accounting regulation. This chapter extends that discussion. While financial accounting is quite heavily regulated in many countries, with this level of regulation generally increasing in the aftermath of recent high profile accounting failures at Enron, Parmalat and other companies, it is nevertheless interesting to consider arguments for and against the continued existence of regulation. It is also interesting to consider various theories that explain what drives the imposition of regulation. By considering such theories we will be better placed to understand why some of the various accounting prescriptions become formal regulations, while others do not. Perhaps some proposed accounting regulations did not have the support of parties that have influence (or power) over the regulatory process. At issue here is whether issues of 'power' should be allowed to impact on the implementation of regulations, including accounting regulations. Is it realistic to expect that the interests of various affected parties will not impact on the final regulations? We will see that the accounting standard-setting process is a very political process. While some proposed requirements might appear technically sound and logical, we will see that this is not sufficient for them to be mandated. What often seems to be important is whether various parts of the constituency who might be affected either socially or economically by the regulations are in favour of them.

In considering accounting regulations, we examine arguments for reducing or eliminating regulation, many of which propose that accounting information should be treated like any other good and that forces of *demand* and *supply* should be allowed to determine the optimal amount of information to be produced. Proponents of this 'free-market' approach (that is, proponents of the view that the provision of accounting information should be based on the laws of supply and demand rather than on regulation) have at times relied on the work of the famous eighteenth-century economist, Adam Smith, and his much cited notion of the 'invisible hand'. However, we will see that he actually proposed the need for regulation to support the interests of those individuals who would otherwise be disadvantaged by the functioning of unregulated market systems.

We also consider a number of perspectives that explain why regulation might be necessary. We review the *public interest theory of regulation*. While public interest theory provides an explanation of why regulation is necessary to protect the rights of the public, there are other theories (for example, *capture theory* and *private interest theory*) which we consider that provide explanations of why regulations might be put in place that actually serve the interests of some groups at the expense of others (rather than serving the 'public interest'). This chapter also considers how perceptions about the economic and social consequences of potential accounting requirements affect the decisions of standard-setters and whether, in the light of regulators considering economic and social consequences, we can really say that financial accounting can ever be expected to have qualitative characteristics such as *neutrality* and *representational faithfulness*.

The 'free market' perspective

As indicated in Chapter 2, a fundamental assumption underlying a 'free market' perspective to accounting regulation is that accounting information should be treated like other goods, and demand and supply forces should be allowed to operate so as to generate an optimal supply of information about an entity. A number of arguments have been used in support of this perspective. One such argument, based on the work of authors such as Jensen and Meckling (1976), Watts and Zimmerman (1978), Smith and Warner (1979), and Smith and Watts (1982) is that, even in the absence of regulation, there are private economics-based incentives for the organization to provide credible information about its operations and performance to certain parties outside the organization, otherwise the costs of the organization's operations will rise.

The basis of this view is that in the absence of information about the organization's operations, other parties, including the owners of the firm (shareholders) who are not involved in the management of the organization, will assume that the managers might be operating the business for their own benefit.[1] That is, the managers will operate the business for their own personal gain, rather than with the aim of maximizing the value of the organization (there is assumed to be a lack of alignment of goals between the external owners and the managers).[2] It is further assumed that potential 'external' shareholders will expect the managers to be opportunistic, and in the absence of safeguards will reduce the amount they will pay for the shares. Likewise, under this economics-based perspective of 'rationality' (self-interest), potential lenders (such as banks and bondholders) are assumed to expect managers to undertake opportunistic actions with the funds the lenders might advance, and therefore in the absence of safeguards the lenders will charge the organization a higher price for their funds.[3] That is, the lenders will 'price-protect' – such that the higher the perceived risk, the higher is the demanded return.

The expectations noted above (which are based on the rather pessimistic assumption that all parties will assume that others will work in their own self-interest unless constrained to do otherwise) will have the effect of increasing the operating costs of the organization – the cost of attracting capital will increase and this will have negative implications for the value of the organization.[4] In situations where managers have large investments in their organization's shares (i.e. where they are a type of 'internal' shareholder), it will be in the interests of the managers to maximize the value of the firm – as they will often gain more economically from an increase in the value of their investment than they would gain in direct 'spoils' from opportunistic behaviour.

To achieve this maximization of share value, managers will voluntarily enter into contracts with shareholders and lenders which make a clear commitment that certain management strategies, such as those that might be against the interests of the shareholders and lenders, will not be undertaken. For example, management might make an agreement with bondholders that they will keep future debt levels below a certain percentage of total assets (the view being that, all things being equal, the lower the ratio of debt to assets, the lower is the risk that the organization will default on paying the bondholders). To further safeguard the bondholders' assets, the organization might agree to ensure that profits will cover interest expense by a specified number of times (referred to as an interest coverage clause). In relation to concerns that the manager might 'shirk' (which might be of particular concern to shareholders, given that shareholders will share in any profits generated by the actions of the managers) the organization might require managers to be rewarded on the basis of a bonus tied to profits, so the higher the profit (which is in the interests of shareholders and lenders), the higher will be the rewards paid to managers. Most private corporations will give their managers (particularly the more senior managers) some form of profit share (Deegan, 1997) as well as being involved in negotiated agreements with lenders (such as debt to asset constraints and interest coverage requirements).

What should be obvious from the brief discussion above is that such contractual arrangements are tied to accounting numbers. Hence the argument by some advocates of the 'free market' perspective is that in the absence of regulation there will be private incentives to produce accounting information. That is, proponents of this view (based on agency theory, which is more fully discussed in Chapter 7) assert that there will (naturally) be conflicts between external owners and internal managers, and the costs of these potential conflicts will be mitigated through the process of private contracting and associated financial reporting.[5] Organizations that do not produce information will be penalized by higher costs of capital, and this will damage the financial interests of those managers who own shares in their organization.

Further, depending upon the parties involved and the types of assets in place, the organization will be best placed to determine what information should be produced to increase the confidence of external stakeholders (thereby decreasing the organization's cost of attracting capital). Imposing regulation that restricts the available set of accounting methods (for example, banning a particular method of depreciation or amortization which was previously used by some organizations) will decrease the efficiency with which negotiated contracts will reduce agency costs.[6]

Given the theoretical economics-based assumption that managers will act in their own self-interest, there will also be a contractual demand to have the accounting reports audited by an external party. Such an activity will increase the perceived reliability of the data, and this in turn is expected to reduce the perceived risk of the external stakeholders, thus further decreasing the organization's cost of capital (Francis and Wilson, 1988; Watts, 1977; Watts and Zimmerman, 1983). That is, financial statement audits can also be expected to be undertaken, even in the absence of regulation, and evidence indicates that many organizations did have their financial statements audited prior to any legislative requirements to do so (Morris, 1984).[7]

Hence, if we accept the above arguments, we can propose that in the presence of a limited number of contracting parties then, perhaps, reducing regulation might seem reasonable given the view that various items of financial information (as negotiated between the various parties) will be provided. Further, such information will be expected to be subject, where deemed necessary by the contracting parties, to an audit by an independent third party. However, in the presence of a multitude of different parties this argument seems to break down. As Scott (2003, p. 416) states:

> Unfortunately, while direct contracting for information production may be fine in principle, it will not always work in practice .... In many cases there are simply too many parties for contracts to be feasible. If the firm manager were to attempt to negotiate a contract for information production with every potential investor, the negotiation costs alone would be prohibitive. In addition, to the extent that different investors want different information, the firm's cost of information production would also be prohibitive. If, as an alternative, the manager attempted to negotiate a single contract with all investors, these investors would have to agree on what information they wanted. Again, given the disparate information needs of different investors, this process would be extremely time-consuming and costly, if indeed, it was possible at all. Hence, the contracting approach only seems feasible when there are few parties involved.

Market-related incentives

While the above arguments are based on a private contracting perspective, there are further arguments for reducing or eliminating accounting regulation which are based on various market-related incentives, principally tied to the 'market for managers' and the 'market for corporate takeovers'. The 'market for managers' argument (see Fama, 1980) relies upon an assumption of an efficient market for managers and that managers' previous performance will impact upon how much remuneration they command in future periods, either from their current employer, or elsewhere. Adopting this perspective, it is assumed that, even in the absence of contractual requirements, managers will be encouraged to adopt strategies to maximize the value of their organization (which provides a favourable view of their own performance) and these strategies would include providing an optimal amount of financial accounting information. However, arguments such as this are based on assumptions that the managerial labour market operates efficiently, and that information about past managerial performance will not only be known by other prospective employers, but will also be fully impounded in future salaries. It also assumes that the capital market is efficient when determining the value of the organization and that effective managerial strategies will be reflected in positive share price movements. In reality, these assumptions will clearly not always be met. Markets will not always be efficient. The arguments can also break down if the managers involved are approaching retirement, in which case future market prices for their services in the 'market for managers' may be irrelevant.

The 'market for corporate takeovers' argument works on the assumption that an underperforming organization will be taken over by another entity that will subsequently replace the existing management team. With such a perceived threat, managers would be motivated to maximize firm value to minimize the likelihood that outsiders could seize control of the organization at low cost. The 'market for corporate takeovers' and the 'market for managers' arguments assume that information will be produced to minimize the organization's cost of capital and thereby increase the value of the organisation. Therefore, the arguments assume that management will know the *marginal costs* and *marginal benefits* involved in providing information, and in accordance with economic theories about the production of other goods, management will provide information to the point where the marginal cost equals the marginal benefit. Clearly, working out the marginal costs and marginal benefits of information production would be difficult, and to assume that the majority of corporate managers have the expertise to determine such costs and benefits is again, perhaps, somewhat unrealistic.

There is also a perspective that even in the absence of regulation, organizations would still be motivated to disclose both good and bad news about their financial position and performance. Such a perspective is often referred to as the 'market for lemons' perspective (Akerlof, 1970), the view being that in the absence of disclosure the capital market will assume that the organization is a 'lemon'.[8] That is, *no information* is viewed in the same light as *bad information*. Hence, even though the firm may be worried about disclosing bad news, the market may make an assessment that silence implies that the organization has very bad news to disclose (otherwise, they would disclose it). This 'market for lemons' perspective provides an incentive for managers to release information in the absence of regulation, as failure to do so will have implications for the manager's wealth (perhaps in the form of current lower remuneration and a decreased value in the market for managers). That is, 'non-lemon owners have an incentive to communicate' (Spence, 1974, p. 93).

Drawing upon arguments such as those adopted in the 'lemons' argument above and applying them to preliminary profit announcements, Skinner (1994, p. 39) states:

> Managers may incur reputational costs if they fail to disclose bad news in a timely manner. Money managers, stockholders, security analysts, and other investors dislike adverse earnings surprises, and may impose costs on firms whose managers are less than candid about potential earnings problems. For example, money managers may choose not to hold the stocks of firms whose managers have a reputation for withholding bad news and analysts may choose not to follow these firms' stocks .... Articles in the financial press suggest that professional money managers, security analysts, and other investors impose costs on firms when their managers appear to delay bad news disclosures. These articles claim that firms whose managers acquire a reputation for failing to disclose bad news are less likely to be followed by analysts and money managers, thus reducing the price and/or liquidity of their firms' stocks.

Reviewing previous studies, Skinner (p. 44) notes that there is evidence that managers disclose both good and bad news forecasts voluntarily. These findings are supported by his own empirical research which shows that when firms are performing well, managers make 'good news disclosures' to distinguish their firms from those doing less well, and when firms are not doing so well, managers make pre-emptive bad news disclosures consistent with 'reputational-effects' arguments (p. 58).

Arguments that the market will penalize organizations for failure to disclose information (which may or may not be bad) of course assumes that the market knows that the manager has particular information to disclose. As has been seen with the many apparently unforeseen accounting failures in recent years (such as Enron, WorldCom and Parmalat), this expectation might not always be so realistic, as the market will not always know that there is information available to disclose. That is, in the presence of information asymmetry the manager might know of some bad news, but the market might not expect any information disclosures at that time. However, if it does subsequently come to light that news was available that was not disclosed, then we could perhaps expect the market to react (and in the presence of regulation, we could expect regulators to react, as failure to disclose information in a timely manner may be in contravention of particular laws in that jurisdiction). Also, at certain times, withholding information (particularly of a proprietary nature) could be in the interests of the organization. For example, the organization may not want to disclose information about certain market opportunities for fear of competitors utilizing such information.

So, in summary to this point, there are various arguments or mechanisms in favour of reducing accounting regulation (including private contracting, markets for managers, and markets for corporate takeovers), as even in the absence of regulation, firms will have incentives to make disclosures. We now consider some arguments in favour of the alternative of regulating financial accounting practice.

The 'pro-regulation' perspective

In the above discussion we have considered a number of reasons proffered in favour of reducing or eliminating regulation. One of the most simple arguments is that if somebody really desired information about an organization, they would be prepared to pay for it (perhaps in the form of reducing their required rate of return) and the forces of supply and demand should operate to ensure an optimal amount of information is produced. Another perspective was that if information is not produced, there will be greater uncertainty about the performance of the entity and this will translate into increased costs for the organization. With this in mind, organizations would, it is argued, elect to produce information to reduce costs. However, arguments in favour of a 'free market' rely upon users paying for the goods or services that are being produced and consumed. Such arguments can break down when we consider the consumption of 'free' or 'public' goods.

Accounting information is a public good – once available, people can use it without paying and can pass it on to others. Parties who use goods or services without incurring some of the associated production costs are referred to as 'free-riders'. In the presence of free-riders, true demand is understated because people know they can obtain the goods or services without paying for them. Few people will then have an incentive to pay for the goods or services, as they know that they themselves might be able to act as free-riders. This dilemma in turn is argued to provide a lack of incentive for producers of the particular good or service, which in turn leads to an underproduction of information. As Cooper and Keim (1983, p. 190) state:

> Market failure occurs in the case of a public good because, since other individuals (without paying) can receive the good, the price system cannot function. Public goods lack the exclusion attribute, i.e. the price system cannot function properly if it is not possible to exclude nonpurchasers (those who will not pay the asked price) from consuming the good in question.

To alleviate this underproduction, regulation is argued to be necessary to reduce the impacts of market failure.[9] In specific relation to the production of information, Demski and Feltham (1976, p. 209) state:

> Unlike pretzels and automobiles, [information] is not necessarily destroyed or even altered through private consumption by one individual ... . This characteristic may induce market failure. In particular, if those who do not pay for information cannot be excluded from using it and if the information is valuable to these 'free riders', then information is a public good. That is, under these circumstances, production of information by any single individuals or firm will costlessly make that information available to all ... . Hence, a more collective approach to production may be desirable.

However, as we often come to expect, there are counter-arguments to the perspective that the supply of 'free goods' should be regulated. Some economists argue that free goods are often overproduced as a result of regulation. The argument is that segments of the public (the users of the good or service), knowing that they do not have to pay for the free good, will overstate their need for the good or service. This argument could perhaps be applied to investment analysts. They will typically be a main user of accounting information. If they lobby for additional regulation which requires further disclosure, they will tend to receive a disproportionate amount of the benefits relative to the costs of producing this further information. When considering the consumption of free goods it is argued by some that non-users effectively subsidize the consumers of the public good as, like other parties, the non-users pay towards the production of the good without benefiting from its consumption. The result of concerted lobbying by particular parties, such as analysts, could in turn lead to the existence of what has been termed an *accounting standards overload* which creates a cost for companies in terms of compliance. However, if we do not regulate, then in the presence of the 'free-riders' we could arguably have an underproduction of accounting information. Clearly, this is not an easy thing to balance and we can start to understand the difficult position in which regulators find themselves.

Regulators often use the 'level playing field' argument to justify putting regulations in place. From a financial accounting perspective, this means that everybody should (on the basis of fairness) have access to the same information. This is the basis of laws that prohibit insider trading, which rely upon an acceptance of the view that there will not be, or perhaps should not be, transfers of wealth between parties simply because one party has access to information which others do not.[10] Putting in place greater disclosure regulations will increase the confidence of external stakeholders that they are playing on a 'level playing field'. If this helps build or sustain confidence in the capital markets, then it is often deemed to be in 'the public interest'. However, we will always be left with the issue as to what is the socially 'right' level of information. Arguably, such a question cannot be answered with any level of certainty.

Many theories which argue in favour of free-market approaches to accounting regulation rely upon the work of the famous eighteenth-century economist, Adam Smith (1937), as a basis for supporting their free market approach. Adam Smith has become famous for his notion of the 'invisible hand'. The 'invisible hand', which was mentioned only once in his five-book treatise, appears in Book Four of the *Wealth of Nations*, referring to the distribution of capital in society: 'the annual revenue ... is always equal to the whole product of its industry ... as every individual attempts to employ his [her] capital ... every individual necessarily endeavors the capital as great as he can ... he intends only his own industry ... his own gain ... led by an invisible hand by it.'[11]

Subsequent free market exponents have drawn on the notion of the 'invisible hand' to promote a belief 'in market omnipotence', arguing against state involvement because it 'disturbs the spontaneous order and the spontaneous society' (Lehman, 1991, p. xi). That is, without regulatory involvement there is a view that somehow, as if by an 'invisible hand', productive resources will, as a result of individuals pursuing their own self-interests, find their way to their most productive uses. Some writers actually went to the next step by arguing that leaving activities to be controlled by market mechanisms will actually protect market participants. For example, Milton Friedman (1962, p. 82) states:

> The central feature of the market organisation of economic activity is that it prevents one person from interfering with another in respect of most of its activities. The consumer is protected from coercion by the seller because of the presence of other sellers with whom he can deal. The seller is protected from coercion by the consumer because of other consumers to whom he can sell.

These views ignore market failures (such as unequal access to information) and uneven distributions of power. Smith was concerned with particular problems which occur in monopolistic situations where prices for needed goods might be driven up by suppliers. According to Collison (2003, p. 864):

> Smith ... was against legislation that protected the strong and the privileged either by conferring monopoly powers over consumers, or by worsening the already weak position of employees. He did not counsel against steps taken to protect the weak and was not against regulation *per se.*

Therefore Smith did not advocate that there should be no regulatory intervention. He was aware of the problems that might arise in an unregulated free market, and while it is rarely mentioned by the advocates of the 'free market', Smith actually wrote of the need for the government to be involved in the 'public interest' to protect the more vulnerable. As Lehman (1991, p. x) states:

> Among the passages revealing Smith's concern for harmful unintended consequences [of the free-market approach] are those appearing in Book V, Chapter 1, where Smith writes that in the progress of the division of labour, the progress of the great body of people will be the man [or woman] who spends much time doing a few simple operations, with no invention, with no tender sentiment, incapable of judging, incapable of defending the country in war. In every society, the great body of people will fall this way, 'unless the government takes some pains to prevent it'.

This view is also supported by Collison (2003, p. 863) who states:

> Adam Smith himself was well aware that conditions in the world he inhabited did not conform to the competitive ideal: he was not opposed to government action in pursuit of general welfare; indeed he favoured it, and was acutely conscious of the danger of undue power in the hands of the capitalist class.

So if we accept that Smith's work has been misrepresented as a treatise in favour of the 'free market' (as a number of authors suggest), why has it been misrepresented? Collison (2003) argues that it is in the interests of many businesses that regulatory interference (such as minimum wage controls) be reduced. As such, he provides a view that many businesses used the work of acclaimed economists (such as Smith) as a form of 'propaganda' to support their arguments for reduced regulation. [12] This perspective is consistent with the economic interest theory of regulation, which we consider later in this chapter.

While we have provided only a fairly brief overview of the free market versus regulation arguments, it should be stressed that this is an argument that is ongoing in respect of many activities and industries, with various vested interests putting forward many different and often conflicting arguments for or against regulation. It is an argument that is often the subject of heated debate within many university economics and accounting departments throughout the world. What do you think? Should financial accounting be regulated, and if so, how much regulation should be put in place?

As an example of another, post-Enron, perspective on the 'regulate or not to regulate' debate, consider Exhibit 3.1, which argues that regulation can introduce inefficiencies into the market. It questions whether an increasing amount of accounting regulation has been effective in protecting investors.

Public interest theory

According to Posner (1974, p. 335) public interest theory 'holds that regulation is supplied in response to the demand of the public for the correction of inefficient or inequitable market practices'. That is, regulation is initially put in place to benefit society as a whole, rather than particular vested interests, and the regulatory body is considered to represent the interests of the society in which it operates, rather than the private interests of the regulators. [13] The enactment of legislation is considered a balancing act between the social benefits and the social costs of the regulation. Applying this argument to financial accounting, and accepting the existence of a capitalist economy, society needs confidence that capital markets efficiently direct (or allocate) resources to productive assets. Regulation is deemed to be an instrument to create such confidence.

Many people are critical of this fairly simplistic perspective of why regulation is introduced (for example, Peltzman, 1976; Posner, 1974; Stigler, 1971). Posner (1974) questions the 'assumptions that economic markets are extremely fragile and apt to operate very inefficiently (or inequitably) if left alone; the other that government regulation is virtually costless' (p. 336). Posner also criticizes arguments that legislation is typically initially put in place for 'the public good' but only fails to achieve its aims due to government ineptitude, mismanagement, or lack of funds. As he states (p. 337):

> [There is] a good deal of evidence that the socially undesirable results of regulation are frequently desired by groups influential in the enactment of the legislation setting up the regulatory scheme .... Sometimes the regulatory statute itself reveals an unmistakable

---

Exhibit 3.1 Perspectives about the regulation of accounting

Future Enrons Will Result From Over Regulation of Accountancy says IEA Study

Referring to the recent Enron and WorldCom scandals, David Myddelton, Professor of Finance and Accounting at Cranfield Business School, says that such events are more likely, not less likely, to occur in the future as a result of increased regulation of accounting. The UK and EU are increasingly following the failed approach of the US in prescribing in detail how companies produce accounts.

'In nine years the volume of accounting regulation has increased by 150 per cent, from an already high level, at a huge cost to companies, without any corresponding benefit,' says Myddelton in [his book] *Unshackling Accountants*. Sometimes regulators impose standards that are wrong and even dangerous.

Myddelton is highly critical of new regulations, such as the International Standards, being imposed by professional bodies, by international organisations and by government regulators. He suggests that radical new approaches to accounting are not generally accepted by the profession and are likely to lead to greater risk of financial and accounting scandals.

At the very least, increasingly prescriptive approaches to accounting lull users into a false sense of security and prevent auditors and accountants from using their judgement to ensure that accounts provide a reasonable picture of a company's financial situation. Users of accounts should understand that they come with 'health warnings' attached and interpret accounts with caution. Increasing the regulation of accounting shifts responsibility away from users and gives them a false sense of security. It also prevents the evolution of new and better accounting practices to deal with a changing world.

Reprinted with kind permission of the Institute of Economic Affairs, London, 25 June 2004. The full text of the monograph is available in hard copy form or electronically from www.iea.org.uk.

purpose of altering the operation of markets in directions inexplicable on public interest grounds .... . The evidence that has been offered to show mismanagement by the regulatory body is surprisingly weak. Much of it is consistent with the rival theory that the typical regulatory agency operates with reasonable efficiency to attain deliberately inefficient or inequitable goals set by the legislature that created it.

Proponents of the economics-based assumption of 'self-interest' would argue against accepting that any legislation was put in place by particular parties because they genuinely believed that it was in the public interest. Rather, they consider that legislators will only put in place legislation because it might increase their own wealth (perhaps through increasing their likelihood of being re-elected), and people will only lobby for particular legislation if it is in their own self-interest. Obviously, as with most theoretical assumptions, this self-interest assumption is one that (hopefully!) will not always hold. We consider the private interest group theory of regulation later in this chapter. In the following discussion we consider the regulatory capture theory of regulation. Unlike the private interest group theory of regulation, capture theory admits the possibility that regulation might initially be put in place for the public interest. However, it argues that the regulation will ultimately become controlled by those parties who it was supposed to control.

Capture theory

Under this perspective the regulated party seeks to take charge of (capture) the regulator with the intention that the rules subsequently released (post-capture) will be advantageous to those parties subject to the requirements. Mitnick (1980, p. 95 as reproduced in Walker, 1987, p. 281) provides a useful description:

> Capture is said to occur if the regulated interest controls the regulation and the regulated agency; or if the regulated parties succeed in coordinating the regulatory body's activities with their activities so that their private interest is satisfied; or if the regulated party somehow manages to neutralise or ensure non-performance (or mediocre performance) by the regulating body; or if in a subtle process of interaction with the regulators the regulated party succeeds (perhaps not even deliberately) in co-opting the regulators into seeing things from their own perspective and thus giving them the regulation they want; or if, quite independently of the formal or conscious desires of either the regulators or the regulated parties, the basic structure of the reward system leads neither venal nor incompetent regulators inevitably to a community of interests with the regulated party.

While the introduction of regulation can, in many cases, be explained in terms of protecting the 'public interest', it is argued that it is difficult for a regulator to remain independent of those being regulated, as continuity over a period of time often depends on satisfying the expectations of the regulated.

At various times and in various jurisdictions it has been argued that the large accounting firms have captured the accounting standard-setting process. This was of such concern in the United States that in 1977 the United States Congress investigated whether the (then) Big Eight accounting firms had 'captured' the standard-setting process (Metcalf Inquiry). Walker (1987) argued that the Australian Accounting Standards Review Board was apparently 'captured' by the accounting profession. He cites a variety of evidence in support of this argument, concluding that within two years of its formation:

> the profession had managed to influence the procedures, the priorities and the output of the Board. It was controlling both the regulations and the regulatory agency; it had

> managed to achieve coordination of [its] activities; and it appears to have influenced new appointments so that virtually all members of the Board might reasonably be expected to have some community of interests with the professional associations. (p. 282)

Proponents of capture theory typically argue that regulation is usually introduced, or regulatory bodies are established, to protect the public interest. For example, new regulatory systems and regimes are often established in response to high profile accounting failures where members of the public are perceived to have suffered a financial loss, and where it is argued that new regulations will help prevent a repeat of the accounting failures. This happened with the establishment of the Securities Exchange Commission in the USA in the early 1930s, which was formed in response to the Wall Street Crash of 1929; with the establishment of the UK Accounting Standards Steering Committee in the early 1970s following negative publicity over accounting failures at some large UK companies in the late 1960s; with the establishment of the Accounting Standards Board in the UK in 1990 following further large scale accounting failures in the late 1980s; and with many tighter accounting and corporate governance regulations being imposed in many countries following the accounting failures at Enron, WorldCom, Parmalat and other companies in the early 2000s.

While the resultant regulatory bodies are often portrayed as 'objective' and 'independent', in the past their members have predominantly been professional accountants and finance directors (the preparers of accounts whom these regulatory bodies are meant to be regulating!), which Walker (1987) argues is an important component of regulatory capture.

However, in recent years there has been a movement towards ensuring greater independence of accounting regulators. For example, the 14 members of the International Accounting Standards Board (IASB) all have to work full time and exclusively for the Board, and are required to sever their ties with previous employers. They are also appointed by a board of trustees, who represent a broad cross-section of interests, and who have all agreed that they will act in the public (not their own private) interest. While this may help in giving an image of detached and impartial objectivity to the IASB standard-setting process (which is discussed in the next chapter), it should be remembered that the members of the IASB are still mostly professionally qualified accountants, whose views are bound to be conditioned to a certain extent by their previous experiences and training. In these circumstances, how independent and impartial do you think the accounting standard-setting process can be?

As we appreciate from reading previous chapters in this book, while a particular theory, such as capture theory, may be embraced by some researchers, there will be others who oppose such theories. Posner (1974), an advocate of the economic (private-interests) theory of regulation (which we will look at next), argues against a regular sequence wherein the original purposes of a regulatory programme are subsequently thwarted though the efforts of the regulated group.

No reason is suggested as to why the regulated industry should be the only interest group to influence an agency. Customers of the regulated firm have an obvious interest in the outcome of the regulatory process – why may they not be able to 'capture' the agency as effectively as the regulated firms, or more so? No reason is suggested as to why industries are able to capture only existing agencies – never to procure the creation of an agency that will promote their interests – or why an industry strong enough to capture an agency set up to tame it could not prevent the creation of the agency in the first place. (p. 340)

A key component underlying all the above perspectives on regulatory capture is that different groups will have different interests, and accounting regulations will have an impact on these social and/or economic interests. If particular groups did not perceive a potential threat (or opportunity) from a regulator to their specific social or economic interests, why would they devote resources to attempting to capture their regulator? The remainder of this chapter discusses perspectives on the impact of these private interests on the regulatory process.

Economic and social impacts of accounting regulation

Before examining various theories which address the influence of private interests on the accounting regulatory process, it is necessary to establish whether accounting regulations can and do have a social and/or economic impact on the interests of preparers or users of accounts. Although many people might argue that accounting regulations just affect how underlying economic transactions and events are reflected in the accounts, without any impact on the nature or shape of this underlying economic reality, there is a considerable body of evidence which demonstrates that accounting regulations have real social and economic consequences for many organizations and people.

For example, one of the first new accounting standards issued by the IASB deals with the accounting treatment of share options (IFRS 2). Although many companies use large numbers of share options as part of their management remuneration and incentive plans, most companies simply ignored share options they had issued when calculating their annual profit before this accounting standard became effective in January 2005. The justification for this former practice was that when executives exercised the share options, and the company issued new shares to these executives at below market value, this did not cost the company itself anything – despite it diluting the value of existing shareholders' investments. However, the IASB view was that by granting valuable share options to employees, companies were able to pay these employees a lower amount of money than if they had not been granted share options. As the company receives valuable services from employees in exchange for these options, which would have been recorded as an expense if they had been paid for in money, under IFRS 2 the fair value of share options now has to be recognized as an expense in the profit and loss account. This new accounting treatment does not have any direct impact on cash flows, as companies that continue to offer the same employee share option and remuneration packages as before will still pay their employees the same amount of money as they did before. All that IFRS 2 requires is recognition in the accounts of an expense that exists but was previously not recognized.

Although implementation of IFRS 2 should have no direct impact on underlying cash flows, during the development of IFRS 2 it was extensively argued that it would have many indirect negative economic and social consequences for many people. As some companies would now be required to recognize a potentially large share option expense each year, some people maintained that these companies would be less likely to use share options as part of their pay and rewards packages. If valuable share options are an effective way to incentivize managers, and help align their self-interests with those of shareholders, a reduction in the use of this form of incentive could lead to less motivated executives (or a less motivated workforce overall if share options were granted to many employees). This could lead to a reduction in underlying company performance, simply because IFRS 2 changed the manner in which a specific item was reflected in the accounts. Therefore, while it was argued that IFRS 2 (in common with most, if not all, other accounting standards) should not lead to any direct changes in underlying business performance or cash flows, its indirect economic consequences could be potentially large and negative.

A more extensive indirect impact of new accounting regulations on employees' social and economic interests seems to have occurred with the implementation of a new UK accounting standard on pension liabilities in the early 2000s. This new standard introduced considerable volatility into the accounting measurement of pension fund assets and liabilities for a type of company pension scheme known as a defined benefit, or final salary, scheme. Many investment experts maintain that this type of pension is usually more generous, and less risky, to employees than the common alternative forms of pension provision. As briefly mentioned in Chapter 2, many companies claimed that the increased volatility in accounting numbers (but not in the underlying economic performance of a pension fund) arising from the introduction of this new accounting standard contributed to their decisions to close their final salary pension schemes, and switch new (and sometimes existing) employees to less advantageous pension schemes. This clearly had a negative impact on the social and economic interests of many employees, who are now likely to receive reduced pensions when they retire. However, it is possible that these companies might have closed their final salary schemes in any event (as they were becoming ever more expensive to fund), and just used the new accounting standard as a convenient excuse to hide the real motives for closure of these schemes.

There are many other examples of accounting standards which have potential indirect economic and social impacts. Indeed, some might argue that all accounting regulations will have an impact on managerial decisions (as managers will seek to manage their business so as to optimize their reported accounting numbers), and the resulting changes in managerial decisions will have a social and/or economic impact on those affected by the decisions. Several academic studies, which are discussed in the next section, have illustrated how the potential economic consequences for particular organizations have motivated these organizations to lobby regulators. This lobbying attempts to shape the regulations in a manner which will maximize the positive, or minimize the negative, likely economic consequences from the new accounting regulations for the lobbying organizations.

Lobbying and the economic interest group theory of regulation

The economic interest group theory of regulation (or as it is sometimes called, the private interest theory of regulation) assumes that groups will form to protect particular economic interests. Different groups, with incompatible or mutually exclusive interests and objectives, are viewed as often being in conflict with each other and each will lobby government or other regulators to put in place legislation that economically benefits them (at the expense of the others). As an example, consumers might lobby government for price protection, or producers lobby for tariff protection. This theoretical perspective adopts no notion of *public interest* – rather, private interests are considered to dominate the legislative process.[14]

In relation to financial accounting, particular industry groups may lobby the regulator (the accounting standard-setter) to accept or reject a particular accounting standard. For example, Hope and Gray (1982) show how a small number of aerospace companies were successful, during a consultation process, in changing the detailed requirements of a UK accounting standard on research and development in favour of their (private) interests. This was despite the overwhelming majority of participants in the consultation process not sharing the objections which had been made to the original proposals by the aerospace companies. These original proposals required all research and development expenditure to be charged as an expense in the year in which it had been incurred. The aerospace companies successfully argued that in certain circumstances they should be allowed to treat development expenditure as a form of capital expenditure, and charge it as an expense in future years by matching it against the income which it eventually generated. Although the impact on reported profits over the life of a project would be nil (the accounting treatment simply allowed a deferral of the expenditure between years), this accounting treatment resulted in higher net assets being reported in the balance sheet each year during a project than would have been the case if the development expenditure had been charged against profits in the year it was incurred. At the time, the prices which these aerospace companies could charge the UK government for large defence contracts was based upon a percentage return on net assets. Clearly, the higher the reported net assets in any particular year, the more a company could charge the government for a contract, so it was clearly in the private interests of these aerospace companies that the accounting standard permitted deferral of development expenditure.

A more recent example of successful lobbying of an accounting regulator by an industry group, apparently seeking outcomes which were in the industry's own interests, has been lobbying by some banks against the revised provisions of International Accounting Standard (IAS) 39. As discussed briefly in Chapter 2, banks in several European countries argued that some of the provisions of IAS 39 would result in their accounts showing significant volatility which did not reflect the underlying economic reality, and this could be damaging to a bank's standing. The IASB made some limited changes in response to the banks' concerns, but refused to substantially change IAS 39. As we will see in the next chapter, from 1 January 2005 IASs (and their new form of International Financial Reporting Standards (IFRS)) became the accounting regulations that must be followed by all companies which have their shares traded on any stock exchange in the European Union. However, as part of the EU accounting regulatory process, for any account-ing regulation to be mandated for use by EU companies it has to be endorsed first by the European Commission. The endorsement of each IAS/IFRS follows advice from a newly established Accounting Regulatory Committee (ARC) which has one member from each of the 25 EU member states. At a meeting of the ARC in July 2004, four member states voted against full EU endorsement of IAS 39 and a further six states abstained, principally objecting to the elements of IAS 39 which banks in their countries had lobbied against. The 15 states who voted in favour of full endorsement of IAS 39 were insufficient to form the two-thirds majority of the ARC required for approval by the EU of an IAS.[15]

Watts and Zimmerman (1978) reviewed the lobbying behaviour of United States corporations in relation to a proposal for the introduction of general price level accounting – a method of accounting that, in periods of inflation, would lead to a reduction in reported profits. They demonstrated that large politically sensitive firms favoured the proposed method of accounting, which led to reduced profits. This was counter to normal expectations that companies generally would prefer to show higher rather than lower earnings. It was explained on the (self-interest) basis that it was the larger firms which could be subject to negative public sentiment (and pressures for regulation of their prices) if their profits were widely seen to be abnormally high, and they might therefore be seen more favourably if they reported lower profits. Hence, by reporting lower profits, there was less likely to be negative wealth implications for the organiz-ations (perhaps in the form of government intervention, consumer boycotts or claims for higher wages).

Accounting firms also make submissions as part of the accounting standard-setting process. If we are to embrace the interest group theory of regulation, we would argue that these submissions can be explained as efforts to protect the interests of professional accountants. Perhaps auditors favour rules that reduce the risk involved in an audit, as more standardization and less judgement reduces the risk of an audit, and therefore the potential for costly law suits. Evidence in Deegan, Morris and Stokes (1990) also supports the view that audit firms are relatively more likely to lobby in favour of particular accounting methods if those methods are already in use by a number of their clients. Analysts also frequently lobby regulators for increased disclosure, perhaps because they can use the information in their job, but pay only a very small amount for it (other non-users will effectively subsidize the costs of the information – part of the free-rider issue discussed earlier in this chapter).

Under the economic interest group theory of regulation, the regulator itself is an interest group – a group that is motivated to embrace strategies to ensure re-election, or to ensure the maintenance of its position of power or privilege within the community. For example, Broadbent and Laughlin (2002) argue that in the UK lobbying surrounding the development of accounting regulations applicable to governmental accounting for projects involving private sector provision of public services (known as Private Finance Initiative projects, or Public Private Partnerships), various regulatory bodies adopted positions which could be interpreted as seeking to defend or enhance their standing with the groups who appoint them and give them legitimacy. We should remember that regulatory bodies can be very powerful. The regulatory body, typically government controlled or influenced, has a resource (potential regulation) that can increase or decrease the wealth of various sectors of the constituency. As Stigler (1971, p. 3) states:

> The state – the machinery and power of the state – is a potential resource or threat to every industry in society …. Regulation may be actively sought by an industry, or it may be thrust upon it … as a rule, regulation is acquired by the industry and is designed and operated primarily for its benefit …. We propose the general hypothesis: every industry or occupation that has enough political power to utilise the state will seek to control entry.

Under this 'economic interest' perspective of regulation, rather than regulation initially being put in place for the *public interest* (as is initially assumed within capture theory and also in public interest theory), it is proposed that regulation is put in place to serve the *private interests* of particular parties, including politicians who seek re-election. According to Posner (1974, p. 343), economic interest theories of regulation insist that economic regulation serves the private interests of politically effective groups. Further, Stigler (1971, p. 12) states:

> The industry which seeks regulation must be prepared to pay with the two things a party needs: votes and resources. The resources may be provided by campaign contributions, contributed services (the businessman heads a fund-raising committee), and more indirect methods such as the employment of party workers. The votes in support of the

measure are rallied, and the votes in opposition are dispersed, by expensive programs to educate (or uneducate) members of the industry and other concerned industries ... . The smallest industries are therefore effectively precluded from the political process unless they have some special advantage such as geographical concentration in a sparsely settled political subdivision.[16]

Under the economic interest theory of regulation, the regulation itself is considered to be a *commodity* subject to the economic principles of supply and demand. According to Posner (1974, p. 344):

> Since the coercive power of government can be used to give valuable benefits to parti- cular individuals or groups, economic regulation – the expression of that power in the economic sphere – can be viewed as a product whose allocation is governed by laws of supply and demand ... . There are a fair number of case studies – of trucking, airlines, railroads, and many other industries – that support the view that economic regulation is better explained as a product supplied to interest groups than as an expression of the social interest in efficiency or justice.

The above position is consistent with that adopted by Peltzman (1976). He states (p. 212):

> The essential commodity being transacted in the political market is a transfer of wealth, with constituents on the demand side and their political representatives on the supply side. Viewed in this way, the market here, as elsewhere, will distribute more of the good to those whose effective demand is the highest ... . I begin with the assumption that what is basically at stake in the regulatory process is a transfer of wealth.

The idea being promoted by the advocates of economic interest group theories of regulation is that if a particular group (perhaps a minority) does not have sufficient power (which might be proxied by numbers of controlled votes, or by the potential funds available to support an election campaign) then that group will not be able to effectively lobby for regulation that might protect its various interests. This view is compatible with some of the arguments used by a number of critical theorists, who often contend that the legislation supporting our social system (including corpo- ration law and accounting standards) acts to protect and maintain the position of those with power (capital) and suppresses the ability of others (those without financial wealth) to exert a great deal of influence within society. For example, in a review of the United States Securities Acts of 1933 and 1934, Merino and Neimark (1982, p. 49) conclude that:

> The security acts were designed to maintain the ideological, social and economic status quo while restoring confidence in the existing system and its institutions.

They further state (p. 51) that the establishment of the Securities Acts:

> ... may have further contributed to the virtual absence of any serious attempts to ensure corporate accountability by broadening the set of transactions for which corporations are to be held accountable.

We consider the works of some critical theorists in greater depth in Chapter 13.

Accounting regulation as an output of a political process

If we accept that accounting standard-setting is a political process, then the view that financial accounting should be *objective*, *neutral* and *apolitical* (as espoused internationally within various conceptual framework projects) is something that can be easily challenged. As we saw in the previous section, because financial accounting affects the distribution of wealth within society it consequently will be political.[17]

Standard-setting bodies typically encourage various affected parties to make submissions on draft versions of proposed accounting standards. This is deemed to be part of the normal 'due process'.[18] If the views of various parts of the constituency are not considered, the implication might be that the very existence of the regulatory body could be challenged. As Gerboth (1973, p. 497) states:

> When a decision making process depends for its success on the public confidence, the critical issues are not technical; they are political ... . In the face of conflict between competing interests, rationality as well as prudence lies not in seeking final answers, but rather in compromise – essentially a political process.

In the earlier example of objections made by banks in some EU countries to certain detailed provisions of IAS 39, failure of the IASB to compromise or concede to the wishes of these banks, and willingness of certain EU governments to fight the banks' case, led to a confrontation between two regulators – the EU and the IASB. At the time, this confrontation was seen as potentially highly damaging to both regulators. If the EU endorsed a revised EU regulation on accounting for financial instruments which had important (although possibly only small) differences from IAS 39, then rules underlying the accounts of EU companies would be different from the rules underlying the accounts of non-EU companies, and this would frustrate the objectives of international accounting harmonization (which we discuss in the next chapter). A common accounting regulation required both sides to compromise.

An obstacle to reaching compromise between two powerful (and sometimes apparently intransigent) international regulatory bodies is that, as we discussed earlier in this chapter, accounting standards (and therefore financial accounting reports themselves) are the result of various social and economic considerations.[19] Hence they are very much tied to the values, norms and expectations of the society in which the standards are developed. Therefore, it is arguably very questionable whether financial accounting can ever claim to be *neutral* or *objective* (Hines, 1988, 1991). While it is frequently argued within conceptual frameworks that proposed disclosures should be useful for decision making, this in itself is not enough. The proposed requirements must be acceptable to various parts of the constituency, and the benefits to be derived from the proposals must, it is argued, exceed the costs that might arise. Obviously determining these costs and benefits is very problematic and this is an area where academic advice and academic research is often used. According to Beaver (1973, p. 56):

> ... without a knowledge of consequences ... it is inconceivable that a policy-making body ... will be able to select optimal accounting standards.

May and Sundem (1976) take the argument further. They argue that:

> If the social welfare impact of accounting policy decisions were ignored, the basis for the existence of a regulatory body would disappear (p. 750).

Any consideration of possible economic consequences necessarily involves a trade-off between the various consequences. For example, if neutrality/representational faithfulness is sacrificed to reduce potential negative impacts on some parties (for example, preparers who might have otherwise been required to disclose proprietary information, or to amend their accounting policies with the implication that they will default on existing debt contracts) this may have negative consequences for users seeking to make decisions on the basis of information provided.

While it is accepted that accounting standards are developed having regard to social and economic consequences, it is also a requirement in many jurisdictions – including all EU member states – that corporate financial statements be 'true and fair'. But can we really say they are *true* when the standards are determined depending upon various economic and social consequences? Perhaps it is easier to say they are *fair*. 'Truth' itself is obviously a difficult concept to define and this might explain why in some jurisdictions it was decided that *true and fair* was achieved if financial reports simply complied with relevant accounting regulations and generally accepted accounting practice.

As another issue to consider, would it be reasonable to assume that users of financial reports generally know that accounting reports are the outcome of various political pressures, or would they expect that the reports are objective and accurate reflections of an organization's performance and financial position? There could in fact be an accounting report *expectations gap* in this regard, although there is limited evidence of this.[20] According to Solomons (1978, p. 71), 'It is perfectly proper for measurements to be selected with particular political ends if it is made clear to users of the measurement what is being done'. However, is it realistic or practical to assume that users of financial statements would be able or prepared to accept that financial accounting necessarily needs to accommodate political considerations? Further, could or would users rely upon financial statements if they had such knowledge? Would there be a reduction of confidence in capital markets?

The argument that economic consequences need to be taken into account before new rules are introduced (or existing rules are changed) also assumes that in the first instance (before any amendments are to be made) there was some sort of equity that did not need addressing or rebalancing. As Collett (1995, p. 27) states:

> The claim that all affected parties such as the preparers of reports are entitled to have their interest taken into account in deciding on a standard, and not only dependent users, assumes that the position immediately prior to implementing the standard was equitable. If, however, users were being misled prior to the standard – for example, because certain liabilities were being kept off the balance sheet – then the argument that the interests of preparers of reports were being neglected in the standard-setting process would lose its force.

This was the case at Enron, where substantial liabilities were hidden from users of the financial accounts through complex financial arrangements which resulted in these liabilities 'being kept off the balance sheet'. As Unerman and O'Dwyer (2004) explain, the false image portrayed by Enron's accounts led many people, including Enron's employees, to lose money which they probably would not have invested if they had been aware of the true extent of Enron's liabilities. The senior executives ultimately responsible for preparing Enron's accounts appear to have provided misleading information, which resulted in economic resources of external parties being allocated in a highly inefficient manner – but a manner which might have been perceived at the time by Enron's senior executives as being in their own personal interests. Clearly, the absence of adequate regulation had very real and significant economic consequences in this case, which demonstrates that regulation might be needed in some instances to protect the interests of less powerful stakeholders.

As a further related issue for readers to consider, is it appropriate for regulators to consider the views of financial statement preparers when developing accounting standards, given that accounting standards are put in place to limit what preparers are allowed to do, that is, to regulate their behaviour in the *public interest*? As we can hopefully see, regulating accounting practice requires many difficult assessments.

Chapter summary

In this chapter we considered various arguments that either supported or opposed the regulation of financial accounting. We saw that advocates of the 'free market' (anti-regulation) approach argue that there are private economic incentives for organizations to produce accounting information voluntarily, and imposing accounting regulation leads to costly inefficiencies. To support their argument for a reduction in financial accounting regulation, the 'free market' advocates rely upon such mechanisms as private contracting (to reduce agency costs), the market for managers, and the market for takeovers.

Advocates of the 'pro-regulation' perspective argue that accounting information should not be treated like other goods, as being a 'public good' it is unrealistic to rely upon the forces of supply and demand. Because users of financial information can obtain the information at zero cost (they can be 'free-riders') producers will tend to produce a lower amount of information than might be socially optimal (which in itself is obviously difficult to determine). Further, there is a view that the stakeholders of an organization have a right to various information about an entity, and regulation is typically needed to ensure that this obligation is adhered to by all reporting entities. Regulation itself is often introduced on the basis that it is in the 'public interest' to do so – the view being that regulators balance the costs of the regulation against the economic and social benefits that the legislation will bring. Clearly, assessments of costs and benefits are difficult to undertake and will almost always be subject to critical comment.

There are alternative views as to why regulation is put in place in the first place. There is one perspective (referred to above) that legislation is put in place for the *public interest* by regulators who are working for the interests of the constituency (public interest theory). Public interest theory does not assume that individuals are primarily driven by their own self-interest. However, an assumption of self-interest is made by other researchers who argue in favour of an economic interest theory of regulation. They argue that *all* action by *all* individuals can be traced back to self-interest in which all people will be seeking to increase their own economic wealth.[21] Under this perspective, regulators will be seeking votes and election funding/support, and will tend to provide the legislation to groups who can pay for it.

Capture theory provides another perspective of the development of regulation. It argues that while regulation might initially be put in place for well-intentioned reasons (for example, in the 'public interest'), the regulated party will, over time, tend to gain control of (or capture) the regulator so that the regulation will ultimately favour those parties that the regulation was initially intended to control.

In this chapter we have also considered how perceptions about potential economic and social consequences impact on the development of accounting standards. In the light of this we have questioned whether financial accounting reports can really be considered as neutral, objective and representationally faithful.

Questions

3.1 As this chapter indicates, some people argue that the extent of regulation relating to financial accounting is excessive and should be reduced.

    (a) What arguments do these people use to support this view?

    (b) How would you rate the arguments in terms of their logic?

3.2 What is the basis of the 'lemons' argument?

3.3 What is meant by saying that financial accounting information is a 'public good'?

3.4 Is regulation more likely to be required in respect of *public goods* than other goods? Why?

3.5 Why would an 'accounting standards overload' occur?

3.6 Can regulatory intervention be explained on fairness or equity grounds? If so, what is the basis of this argument?

3.7 Read and evaluate the following paragraph extracted from Cooper and Keim (1983, p. 202):

> It should also be noted that the nature and degree of the effect of disclosure requirements (and other aspects of security regulation) on public confidence in the financial markets is unknown. Investors who have never read a prospectus or even thumbed through a 10-K report may have a great deal more confidence in the capital markets because the SEC and its regulations are an integral aspect of the financial system. The salutary effect of such enhancement of the perceived integrity and credibility of the investment process is to reduce the cost of capital for all firms, and the magnitude of this effect may be quite significant.

3.8 Private contractual incentives will assist in ensuring that even in the absence of regulation, organizations will provide such information as is demanded by its respective stakeholders. Evaluate this argument.

3.9 Why would the managerial labour market motivate the manager to voluntarily provide information to outside parties?

3.10 A newspaper article entitled 'Hannes "knew of TNT valuation"' (*The Australian*, 18 June 1999, p. 24) reported a case involving a person who was before the courts on a charge of insider trading. In part, the article stated:

> Macquarie Bank executive director Simon Hannes learnt of the value the bank had placed on TNT shares three months before the transport giant was subject to a takeover bid by Dutch company KPN, a jury heard yesterday.
>
> The Crown has alleged that Mr Hannes, using the alias Mark Booth, used that confidential information to make a $2 million profit trading in TNT options at the time of the October 1996 takeover offer. Macquarie was advising TNT on the bid and the Downing Centre District Court jury has previously heard Mr Hannes claimed to have had only a general knowledge of a possible transaction involving TNT. Mr Hannes, 39, has pleaded not guilty to one charge of insider

trading and two of structuring bank withdrawals to avoid reporting requirements.

Required:

(a) Which of the theoretical perspectives of regulation reviewed in this chapter might best explain the existence of laws that prohibit insider trading?

(b) How would advocates of a 'free market' approach justify the removal of legislation pertaining to insider trading?

3.11 What assumptions are made about the motivations of the regulators in:

(a) the public interest theory of regulation?

(b) the capture theory of regulation?

(c) the economic interest theory of regulation?

3.12 Is it realistic to assume, in accordance with 'public interest theory', that regulators will not be driven by their own self-interest when designing regulations?

3.13 Is it in the 'public interest' for regulators to be driven by their own self-interest?

3.14 Identify and evaluate the key negative economic and social consequences which might potentially arise from an accounting standard with which you are familiar.

3.15 Under the economic interest theory of regulation, what factors will determine whether a particular interest group is able to secure legislation that directly favours that group above all others?

3.16 What do we mean when we say that financial accounting standards are the outcome of a political process? Why is the process political?

3.17 Is the fact that accounting standard-setters consider the economic and social consequences of accounting standards consistent with a view that accounting reports, if compiled in accordance with accounting standards and other generally accepted accounting principles, will be neutral and objective?

3.18 If an accounting standard-setter deems that a particular accounting standard is likely to adversely impact some preparers of financial statements, what do you think it should do?

Notes

1 The costs that arise from the perspective of the owner when the owner (or principal) appoints a manager (the agent) would include costs associated with the agent shirking (being idle) or consuming excessive perquisites (using the organization's funds for the manager's private purposes). These are called agency costs. Agency costs can be defined as costs that arise as a result of the delegation of decision making from one party to another party (the agency relationship). They are more fully considered in Chapter 7 when we consider agency theory. Another agency cost that might arise when decision making is delegated to the agent could include the costs associated with the manager using information that is not available to the owners, for the manager's personal gain. Smith and Watts (1982) provide an overview of the conflicts of interest that arise between managers and owners.

2 What should be appreciated at this point is that these arguments are based on a central assumption that individuals will act in their own self-interest, which, in itself, is a cornerstone of many economic theories. If an individual acts with self-interest with the intention of maximizing personal wealth, this is typically referred to as being 'economically rational'. 'Economic rationality' is a theoretical assumption, and, as might be expected, is an assumption that is challenged by advocates of alternative views about what drives or motivates human behaviour.

3 In considering the relationship between managers and lenders, actions that would be detrimental to the interests of lenders would include managers paying excessive dividends; taking on additional and possibly excessive levels of debt; and using the advanced funds for risky ventures, thereby reducing the probability of repayment. Smith and Warner (1979) provide an overview of some of the conflicts of interest that arise between managers and lenders.

4 This is based on the assumption that the value of an organization is the present value of its expected future net cash flows. A higher cost of capital will result in a decreased net present value of future cash flows.

5 This is consistent with the usual notion of 'stewardship' wherein management is expected to provide an account of how it has utilized the funds that have been provided.

6 It has also been argued that certain mandated disclosures will be costly to the organization if they enable competitors to take advantage of certain proprietary information. Hakansson (1977) used this argument to explain costs that would be imposed as a result of mandating segmental disclosures.

7 As Cooper and Keim (1983, p. 199) indicate, to be an effective strategy, 'the auditor must be perceived to be truly independent and the accounting methods employed and the statements' prescribed content must be sufficiently well-defined'. Public perceptions of auditor independence were damaged as a results of revelations in 2002 of Andersen's role in both designing and auditing complex accounting transactions at Enron (Unerman and O'Dwyer, 2004)

8 Something is a 'lemon' if it initially appears or is assumed (due to insufficient information) to be of a quality comparable to other products, but later turns out to be inferior. Acquiring the 'lemon' will be the result of information asymmetry in favour of the seller.

9 Scott (1997, p. 329) defines market failure as 'an inability of market forces to produce a socially 'right' amount of information, that is, to produce information to the point where its marginal cost to society equals its marginal benefit'.

10 There is also a view (Ronen, 1977) that extensive insider trading will erode investor confidence such that market efficiency will be impaired.

11 This quote is reproduced from Lehman (1991).

12 Other authors (such as Carey, 1997) have argued that many larger businesses were able to influence academics (through the provision of funding) to support particular views. The results of the academic research studies were then provided to government to substantiate or support particular positions.

13 This perspective would not be accepted by advocates of the 'rational economic person' assumption as they would argue that all activities, including the activities of regulators and politicians, are primarily motivated by a desire to maximize personal wealth rather than any notion of *public interest*.

14 As Posner (1974) states, 'the economic theory of regulation is committed to the strong assumptions of economic theory generally, notably that people seek to advance their self-interest and do so rationally'.

15 In recent years, environmental groups have also lobbied government to introduce a requirement for companies to report various items of social and environmental information. Such submissions could perhaps prove a problem for advocates of the view that lobbying behaviour will be dictated by private concerns about wealth maximization (the rational economic person assumption). Perhaps (and we are clutching at straws here!) to maintain support for their 'self-interest' view of the world, proponents of the economic interest theory of regulation might argue that the submissions are made by officers of the environmental lobby group in an endeavour to increase their probability of reappointment.

16 As an example, Stigler (1971, p. 8) refers to the railroad industry. 'The railroad industry took early cognizance of this emerging competitor, and one of the methods by which trucking was combated was state regulation. By the early 1930s all states regulated the dimensions and weight of trucks.'

17 For example, whether dividends are paid to shareholders will be dependent upon whether there are reported profits. Further, whether a company incurs the costs associated with defaulting on an accounting-based debt agreement may be dependent upon the accounting methods it is permitted to apply.

18 Due process can be defined as a process wherein the regulator involves those parties likely to be affected by the proposed regulation in the discussions leading to the regulation – it provides an opportunity to 'be heard'.

19 At this point we will not pursue the perspective adopted by the economic interest group theory of regulation. If we had persisted with this perspective, we would argue that the standard-setters would support those submissions which best served the standard-setters' self-interest.

20 Liggio (1974) and Deegan and Rankin (1999) provide definitions of the expectations gap. An expectations gap is considered to exist when there is a difference between the expectations users have with regard to particular attributes of information, and the expectations preparers believe users have in regard to that information.

21 There are, of course, many researchers who oppose this (rather cynical) view of human behaviour (authors, such as Gray *et al.*, 1996, refer to this perspective as being 'morally bankrupt'). We consider some of these alternative perspectives in Chapters 8 and 9.

References

Akerlof, G. A. (1970) 'The market for 'lemons': quality uncertainty and the market mechanism', *Quarterly Journal of Economics*, **84**, pp. 488–500.

Beaver, W. H. (1973) 'What should be the FASB's objectives?' *The Journal of Accountancy*, **136**, pp. 49–56.

Broadbent, J. & Laughlin, R. (2002) 'Accounting choices: Technical and political trade-offs and the UK's private finance initiative', *Accounting, Auditing & Accountability Journal*, **15** (5), pp. 622–54.

Carey, A. (1997) *Taking the Risk out of Democracy: Corporate Propaganda versus Freedom and Liberty*, USA: University of Illinois Press.

Collett, P. (1995) 'Standard setting and economic consequences: An ethical issue', *ABACUS*, **31** (1), pp. 18–30.

Collison, D. J. (2003) 'Corporate propaganda: Its implications for accounting and accountability', *Accounting, Auditing & Accountability Journal*, **16** (5), pp. 853–86.

Cooper, K. & Keim, G. (1983) 'The economic rationale for the nature and extent of corporate financial disclosure regulation: A critical assessment', *Journal of Accounting and Public Policy*, **2**.

Deegan, C. (1997) 'The design of efficient management remuneration contracts: A consideration of specific human capital investments', *Accounting and Finance*, **37** (1), pp. 1–40.

Deegan, C., Morris, R., & Stokes, D. (1990) 'Audit firm lobbying on proposed accounting disclosure requirements', *Australian Journal of Management*, **15** (2), pp. 261–80.

Deegan, C. & Rankin, M. (1999) 'The environmental reporting expectations gap: Australian evidence', *British Accounting Review*, **31** (3).

Demski, J. & Feltham, G. (1976) *Cost Determination: A Conceptual Approach*, USA: The Iowa State University Press.

Fama, E. (1980) 'Agency problems and the theory of the firm', *Journal of Political Economy*, **88**, pp. 288–307.

Francis, J. R. & Wilson, E. R. (1988) 'Auditor changes: A joint test of theories relating to agency costs and auditor differentiation', *The Accounting Review*, **63** (4), pp. 663–82.

Friedman, M. (1962) *Capitalism and Freedom*, Chicago: University of Chicago Press.

Gerboth, D. L. (1973) 'Research, intuition, and politics in accounting inquiry', *The Accounting Review* (July).

Gray, R., Owen, D., & Adams, C. (1996) *Accounting and Accountability: Changes and Challenges in Corporate Social and Environmental Reporting*, London: Prentice-Hall.

Hakansson, N. H. (1977) 'Interim disclosure and public forecasts: An economic analysis and framework for choice', *The Accounting Review* (April), pp. 396–416.

Hines, R. (1988) 'Financial accounting: In communicating reality, we construct reality', *Accounting Organizations and Society*, **13** (3), pp. 251–62.

Hines, R. (1991) 'The FASB's conceptual framework, financial accounting and the maintenance of the social world', *Accounting Organizations and Society*, **16** (4), pp. 313–51.

Hope, T. & Gray, R. (1982) 'Power and policy making: The development of an R & D standard', *Journal of Business Finance and Accounting*, **9** (4), pp. 531–58.

Jensen, M. C. & Meckling, W. H. (1976) 'Theory of the firm: Managerial behavior, agency costs and ownership structure', *Journal of Financial Economics*, **3** (October), pp. 305–60.

Lehman, C. (1991) 'Editorial: The invisible Adam Smith', *Advances in Public Interest Accounting*, **4**, pp. ix–xiv.

Liggio, C. D. (1974) 'The expectations gap: the accountants' Waterloo', *Journal of Contemporary Business*, **3** (No 3), pp. 27–44.

May, R. G. & Sundem, G. L. (1976) 'Research for accounting policy: An overview', *The Accounting Review*, **51** (4), pp. 747–63.

Merino, B. & Neimark, M. (1982) 'Disclosure regulation and public policy: A socio-historical appraisal', *Journal of Accounting and Public Policy*, **1**, pp. 33–57.

Mitnick, B. M. (1980) *The Political Economy of Regulation*, USA: Columbia University Press.

Morris, R. (1984) 'Corporate disclosure in a substantially unregulated environment', *ABACUS* (June), pp. 52–86.

Peltzman, S. (1976) 'Towards a more general theory of regulation', *Journal of Law and Economics* (August), pp. 211–40.

Posner, R. A. (1974) 'Theories of economic regulation', *Bell Journal of Economics and Management Science*, **5** (Autumn), pp. 335–58.

Ronen, J. (1977) 'The effect of insider trading rules on information generation and disclosure by corporations', *The Accounting Review*, **52**, pp. 438–49.

Scott, W. R. (1997) *Financial Accounting Theory*, New Jersey: Prentice-Hall.

Scott, W. R. (2003) *Financial Accounting Theory*, 3rd ed, Toronto: Pearson Education Canada Inc.

Skinner, D. J. (1994) 'Why firms voluntarily disclose bad news', *Journal of Accounting Research*, **32** (No. 1), pp. 38–60.

Smith, A. (1937) *The Wealth of Nations*, originally published in 1776, edn New York: Modern Library.

Smith, C. W. & Warner, J. B. (1979) 'On financial contracting: An analysis of bond covenants', *Journal of Financial Economics* (June), pp. 117–61.

Smith, C. W. & Watts, R. (1982) 'Incentive and tax effects of executive compensation plans', *Australian Journal of Management* (December), pp. 139–57.

Solomons, D. (1978) 'The politicisation of accounting', *Journal of Accountancy*, **146** (5), pp. 65–72.

Spence, A. (1974) *Market Signalling: Information Transfer in Hiring and Related Screening Processes*, USA: Harvard University Press.

Stigler, G. J. (1971) 'The theory of economic regulation', *Bell Journal of Economics and Management Science* (Spring), pp. 2–21.

Unerman, J. & O'Dwyer, B. (2004) 'Enron, WorldCom, Andersen *et al.*: A challenge to modernity', *Critical Perspectives on Accounting*, **15** (6–7), pp. 971–93.

Walker, R. G. (1987) 'Australia's ASRB: A case study of political activity and regulatory capture', *Accounting and Business Research*, **17** (67), pp. 269–86.

Watts, R. L. (1977) 'Corporate financial statements: A product of the market and political processes', *Australian Journal of Management* (April), pp. 53–75.

Watts, R. & Zimmerman, J. (1978) 'Towards a positive theory of the determination of accounting standards', *Accounting Review*, **53** (1), pp. 112–34.

Watts, R. L. & Zimmerman, J. L. (1983) 'Agency problems: Auditing and the theory of the firm: Some evidence', *Journal of Law and Economics*, **26** (October), pp. 613–34.

CHAPTER 4

International accounting

Learning Objectives

Upon completing this chapter readers should:

- appreciate that there are important differences between the accounting policies and practices adopted in different countries;

- understand various theoretical explanations about why countries adopt particular accounting practices in preference to others;

- be able to explain what is meant by the term harmonization (or standardization) of accounting;

- be able to identify and explain some of the perceived benefits of, and obstacles to, harmonizing or standardizing accounting practices on an international scale; and

- understand the key factors which are leading to greater international harmonization of accounting – especially within the European Union.

Opening issues

Since the start of 2005, accounting standards issued by the International Accounting Standards Board (IASB) have been the accounting rules which must be used by most large companies in all EU countries. Do you believe that this is the best avenue for EU accounting regulation to follow (rather than having different rules in each member state, or a common set of accounting rules developed specifically by EU regulators separate from the accounting rules in other parts of the world)? What disadvantages do you think arise from EU adoption of these international standards?

Introduction

In the previous chapters we considered how regulation can shape the practice of financial reporting. We learned that various factors can influence the actions of regulators (for example, their own perceptions about what is in the 'public interest', or about the economic implications of newly proposed accounting standards), and that various theoretical perspectives can be applied when making a judgement about the factors that will be more likely to impact on a regulator's ultimate decision to support or oppose particular financial accounting requirements. We saw how differences in, or changes to, accounting regulations can result in different accounting 'numbers' being reported for a given underlying transaction or event, and how these differences in reported accounting results can lead to both positive and negative social and economic consequences. Clearly, therefore, any differences in accounting regulations between different countries are likely to result in the accounting outcomes reported from a specific set of transactions and/or events varying from country to country.

In this chapter we consider theoretical explanations regarding why accounting regulations and practices vary between different countries, including the impact various cultural and institutional factors might have on the shape of accounting. We also explore some theoretical insights into reasons for, and the potential success of, attempts to reduce international differences in accounting regulation. To provide context for the latter area, we examine recent developments in accounting harmonization within the EU.

Evidence of international differences in accounting

Before we explore some key theoretical reasons which have been used to explain why accounting practices vary between countries, it would be useful to establish whether such differences actually exist. Evidence of these international differences would be provided if a given set of transactions or events produced different accounting results in different countries. Differences in the underlying economic performance of companies from different countries are not evidence of accounting differences – they are just indicators that the economic climate varies from country to country. Therefore, for example, if a French steel manufacturer which produced and sold all of its steel in France *reported* a different pattern of profits compared to an Italian steel company (which produced and sold all of its steel in Italy), this could be the result of different economic and market conditions between France and Italy. The differences in the reported results could also be partially due to differences in accounting rules, but unless we knew all of the underlying transactions and events, it would not be possible for us (as external users of accounts) to tell how much of the difference in reported profits was due to differences in the underlying economic performance, and how much was due to differences between French and Italian accounting rules.

Instead, an effective way to establish whether there are international differences in accounting, which impact directly on reported accounting results, is to compare the results reported in different countries from an identical set of underlying economic transactions and events. Given that each company will have a unique set of transactions and events each year, this comparison cannot effectively be undertaken by comparing the results of different companies located in different countries. The comparison can, however, be undertaken by looking at the results of a single company (or group of companies) which produces separate financial accounts in accordance with the regulations of more than one country.

In recent years there have been a number of large multinational corporations which have raised finance through the stock exchanges of more than one country (for example by selling shares through the Frankfurt, London and New York stock exchanges – where their shares continue to be listed). To support its sale of shares and continued listing on any stock exchange, a company has to produce financial accounts which have been drawn up in accordance with accounting regulations acceptable to that stock exchange. Historically, this has usually been the national accounting regulations of the country where the stock exchange is located. Therefore, when a multinational corporation has its shares traded on stock exchanges in more than one country, it has usually had to produce more than one version of its accounts – with a separate set of results drawn up in accordance with the national accounting regulations of each nation where its shares are traded.[1] Clearly, as these different accounts are based on the same set of underlying economic transactions and events (all the economic activities of the particular multinational for that particular year), any differences in the reported results between the different versions of the accounts should be due solely to international differences in accounting regulations.

Nobes and Parker (2004, p. 4) have undertaken a comparison of the results of a small number of European-based multinationals who report their results in accordance with both their home nation accounting rules and US accounting rules. This shows, for example, that the underlying economic transactions and events of the Anglo–Swedish drug company AstraZeneca in the year 2000 produced a profit of £9,521 million when reported under UK accounting rules, but the same set of transactions produced a reported profit of £29,707 million under US accounting rules – a difference of 212 per cent in reported profits from an identical set of underlying transactions and events! Extending this analysis to a more recent period, the 2003 annual report of AstraZeneca (p. 116) shows that profits under UK accounting rules of $3,036 million became profits of $2,268 million when calculated in accordance with US accounting rules – this time a difference of 25 per cent compared to the UK rules. In its balance sheet, AstraZeneca's shareholders' equity at 31 December 2003 was $13,178 million when reported in accordance with UK accounting rules, but this became $33,654 million when calculated in accordance with US accounting rules, a difference of 155 per cent. Although percentage differences of this size might be unusual, examination of the accounts of almost any company which reports its results in accordance with more than one set of accounting regulations will show some differences both between the profits reported under each set of regulations and between the net assets reported under each set of regulations.

A further dramatic example of the existence of differences between the accounting rules of different countries was provided by Enron. As Unerman and O'Dwyer (2004) explain, in the aftermath of the collapse of Enron many accounting regulators, practitioners and politicians in European countries claimed that the accounting practices which enabled Enron to 'hide' vast liabilities by keeping them off their US balance sheet would not have been effective in Europe. In the UK this explanation highlighted the differences between the UK and US approaches to accounting regulation, and argued that under UK accounting regulations these liabilities would not have been treated as off-balance sheet, thus potentially producing significant differences between Enron's balance sheet under UK and US accounting practices.

Having demonstrated that differences do exist in practice between the accounting regulations of different countries, we will now proceed to explore some of the key theoretical reasons which have been provided to explain the existence of these differences.

Explanations of differences in accounting practices employed in different countries

Authors such as Perera (1989) have argued that accounting practices within particular countries evolve to suit the circumstances of a particular society, at a particular time. While there is a large variation in accounting systems adopted in different countries, it has been commonly accepted that there are two main models of financial accounting which have evolved within economically developed countries: the Anglo-American model and the continental European model (Mueller, 1967; Nobes, 1984).[2] The Anglo-American model is characterized by a system of accounting that is strongly influenced by professional accounting bodies rather than government, emphasizes the importance of capital markets (the entities within the countries that use this model of accounting are typically very reliant on public sources of equity and debt finance), and relies upon terms such as 'true and fair' or 'presents fairly', which in turn are based upon considerations of economic substance over and above legal form (legal form being bound by legislation).

The continental European model of accounting, on the other hand, typically is characterized by relatively small input from the accounting profession, little reliance upon qualitative requirements such as true and fair, and stronger reliance upon government. The accounting methods tend to be heavily associated with the tax rules in place, and the information tends to be of a nature to protect the interest of creditors, rather than investors *per se* (the entities within countries that use the continental European model have historically tended to obtain most of their long-term funds from family sources, governments or lenders, often banks).

Over time, numerous reasons have been given for differences in the accounting methods of different countries. Mueller (1968) suggests that such differences might be caused by differences in the underlying laws of the country, the political systems in place (for example, a capitalistic/free market system versus a centralized/communistic system), or their level of development from an economic perspective. As Mueller (1968, p. 95) explains:

> In society, accounting performs a service function. This function is put in jeopardy unless accounting remains, above all, practically useful. Thus, it must respond to the ever-changing needs of society and must reflect the social, political, legal and economic conditions within which it operates. Its meaningfulness depends on its ability to mirror these conditions.

Other reasons such as tax systems, level of education, and level of economic development have also been suggested to explain differences in accounting practices (Doupnik and Salter, 1995). At present there is no single clear theory that explains international differences in accounting practices. Many different causes have been suggested. Nobes (1998) reviewed the literature and confirmed that numerous reasons have been proposed to explain the differences. These are summarized in Table 4.1.

According to Nobes, many of the factors in Table 4.1 are interrelated. A number are deemed to be 'institutional', and a number relate to the broader notion of *culture*. We will now consider individually some of the factors identified in Table 4.1. Firstly we will examine the impact which, it has been claimed by some academics, cultural factors (including religious influences) could have on shaping accounting practices. We will then consider how institutional factors, such as different legal and financing systems, might also have caused accounting practices to vary between countries.

Culture

Culture is a broad concept that would be expected to impact on legal systems, tax systems, the way businesses are formed and financed, and so on. For many years culture has been used in the psychology, anthropology and sociology literatures as the basis for explaining differences in social systems (Hofstede, 1980). In recent

Table 4.1 Reasons proposed for international accounting differences

1.	Nature of business ownership and financing system
2.	Colonial inheritance
3.	Invasions
4.	Taxation
5.	Inflation
6.	Level of education
7.	Age and size of accountancy profession
8.	Stage of economic development
9.	Legal systems
10.	Culture
11.	History
12.	Geography
13.	Language
14.	Influence of theory
15.	Political systems, social climate
16.	Religion
17.	Accidents

Source: Nobes (1998, p. 163)

decades it has also been used to try to explain international differences in accounting systems. One of the earlier papers to consider the impact of culture on accounting was Violet (1983) who argued that accounting is a 'socio-technical activity' that involved interaction between both human and non-human resources. Because the two interact, Violet claims that accounting cannot be considered culture-free. Relating accounting to culture, Violet (1983, p. 8) claims:

> Accounting is a social institution established by most cultures to report and explain certain social phenomena occurring in economic transactions. As a social institution, accounting has integrated certain cultural customs and elements within the constraints of cultural postulates. Accounting cannot be isolated and analyzed as an independent component of a culture. It is, like mankind and other social institutions, a product of culture and contributes to the evolution of the culture which employs it. Since accounting is culturally determined, other cultural customs, beliefs, and institutions influence it.

Takatera and Yamamoto (1987) have defined culture as 'an expression of norms, values and customs which reflect typical behavioural characteristics'. Hofstede (1980, p. 25) has defined culture as 'the collective programming of the mind which distinguishes the members of one human group from another'. It describes a system of societal or collectively held values (Gray, 1988, p. 4) rather than values held at an individual level. 'Values' are deemed to determine behaviour. Gray (1988, p. 4) explains that the term 'culture' is typically reserved for societies as a whole, or nations, whereas 'subculture' is used for the level of an organization, profession (such as the accounting profession) or family. It is expected that different subcultures within a particular society will share common characteristics. In the discussion that follows we consider the work of Professor Sid Gray in some depth. This work is generally acknowledged as constituting some of the most rigorous research into accounting's relationship to, and to some extent dependence on, national culture.

Gray (1988, p. 5) argues that 'a methodological framework incorporating culture may be used to explain and predict international differences in accounting systems and patterns of accounting development internationally'. Any consideration of culture necessarily requires difficult choices as to aspects of culture that are important to the issue under consideration, and in turn, how one goes about measuring the relevant cultural attributes. As Perera (1989, p. 43) states, 'the study of culture is characterized by a unique problem arising from the inexhaustible nature of its components'.[3] Gray used the work of Hofstede (1980, 1983). Gray (1988, p. 5) explains:

> Hofstede's (1980, 1983) research was aimed at detecting the structural elements of culture and particularly those which most strongly affect known behaviour in work situations in organizations and institutions. In what is probably one of the most extensive cross-cultural studies ever conducted, psychologists collected data about 'values' from the employees of a multinational corporation located in more than fifty countries. Subsequent statistical analysis and reasoning revealed four underlying societal value dimensions along which countries could be positioned. These dimensions, with substantial support from prior work in the field, were labeled Individualism, Power Distance, Uncertainty Avoidance, and Masculinity. Such dimensions were perceived to represent a common structure in cultural systems. It was also shown how countries could be grouped into culture areas, on the basis of their scores on the four dimensions.

Gray argues that the value systems of accountants will be derived and related to societal values (which are reflected by Hofstede's cultural dimensions of Individualism, Power Distance, Uncertainty Avoidance and Masculinity).[4] These social values, which are also held by accountants (which Gray terms the accounting subculture), will in turn, it is believed, impact on the development of the respective accounting systems at the national level. Therefore, at this point we can perhaps start to question whether accounting systems can be developed in a 'one-size-fits-all' perspective – an approach which, in some respects, the IASB appears to have adopted (we return to this point later in the chapter). However, while it is argued that there should be some association between various value systems and accounting systems, over time, many events would typically have occurred that confound this possible relationship. For example, in relation to developing countries, Baydoun and Willett (1995, p. 72) state:

> It is quite possible that had accounting systems evolved independently in developing countries they would have a rather different form from any we now witness in present day Europe. However, most accounting systems used in developing countries have been directly imported from the West through a variety of channels: by colonialism in the past; and through Western multinational companies, the influence of local professional associations (usually founded originally by Western counterpart organizations) and aid and loan agencies from the industrialised countries.

Returning to the work of Hofstede, the four societal value dimensions identified by Hofstede can be summarized as follows (quoted from Hofstede, 1984):

Individualism versus Collectivism

Individualism stands for a preference for a loosely knit social framework in society wherein individuals are supposed to take care of themselves and their immediate families only. Its opposite, Collectivism, stands for a preference for a tightly knit social framework in which individuals can expect their relatives, clan, or other in-group to look after them in exchange for unquestioning loyalty (it will be clear that the word 'collectivism' is not used here to describe any particular social system). The fundamental issue addressed by this dimension is the degree of interdependence a society maintains among individuals. It relates to people's self concept: 'I' or 'we'.

With regard to the cultural dimension of *Individualism versus Collectivism* it is interesting to note that a great deal of economic theory is based on the notion of *self-interest* and the *rational economic person* (one who undertakes action to maximize personal wealth at the expense of others). This is very much based in the *Individualism dimension*. In a culture that exhibited *Collectivism* it is expected that members of the society would look after each other and issues of loyalty would exist.[5]

Large versus Small Power Distance

Power Distance is the extent to which the members of a society accept that power in institutions and organisations is distributed unequally. This affects the behaviour of the less powerful as well as of the more powerful members of society. People in Large Power Distance societies accept a hierarchical order in which everybody has a place, which needs no further justification. People in Small Power Distance societies strive for power equalisation and demand justification for power inequities. The fundamental issue addressed by this dimension is how a society handles inequalities among people when they occur. This has obvious consequences for the way people build their institutions and organisations.

Strong versus Weak Uncertainty Avoidance

Uncertainty Avoidance is the degree to which the members of a society feel uncomfortable with uncertainty and ambiguity. This feeling leads them to beliefs promising certainty and to sustaining institutions protecting conformity. Strong Uncertainty

Avoidance societies maintain rigid codes of belief and behaviour and are intolerant towards deviant persons and ideas. Weak Uncertainty Avoidance societies maintain a more relaxed atmosphere in which practice counts more than principles and deviance is more easily tolerated. The fundamental issue addressed by this dimension is how a society reacts to the fact that time only runs one way and that the future is unknown: whether it tries to control the future or to let it happen. Like Power Distance, Uncertainty Avoidance has consequences for the way people build their institutions and organisations.

Masculinity versus **Femininity**

Masculinity stands for a preference in society for achievement, heroism, assertiveness, and material success. Its opposite, Femininity, stands for a preference for relationships, modesty, caring for the weak, and the quality of life. The fundamental issue addressed by this dimension is the way in which a society allocates social (as opposed to biological) roles to the sexes.

Again, as stated earlier, when countries are given scores on the four value dimensions, a number of countries can be clustered together, reflecting that they have similar cultural values.[6] Having considered Hofstede's value dimensions, the next step for Gray was to relate them to the values that he perceived to be in place within the accounting subculture. Gray developed four accounting values that were deemed to relate to the accounting subculture with the intention that the accounting values would then be directly linked to Hofstede's four societal values (which we discussed above). Gray's four accounting values were defined as follows (1988, p. 8):

Professionalism versus **Statutory Control**

A preference for the existence of individual professional judgement and the maintenance of professional self-regulation, as opposed to compliance with prescriptive legal requirements and statutory control.

Uniformity versus **Flexibility**

A preference for the enforcement of uniform accounting practices between companies and the consistent use of such practices over time, as opposed to flexibility in accordance with the perceived circumstances of individual companies.

Conservatism versus **Optimism**

A preference for a cautious approach to measurement so as to cope with the uncertainty of future events, as opposed to a more optimistic, laissez-faire, risk-taking approach.

Secrecy versus **Transparency**

A preference for confidentiality and the restriction of disclosure of information about the business only to those who are closely involved with its management and financing, as opposed to a more transparent, open and publicly accountable approach.

Gray (1988) then developed a number of hypotheses relating Hofstede's four societal cultural dimensions to each one of his own four accounting values.[7] The hypotheses were as follows:

H1: The higher a country ranks in terms of *Individualism* and the lower it ranks in terms of *Uncertainty Avoidance* and *Power Distance*, then the more likely it is to rank highly in terms of *Professionalism*.

The basis for the above hypothesis was that a preference for applying judgement (for example, determining whether something is *true and fair*) rather than strict rules is more likely where people tend to be individualistic; where people arc relatively more comfortable with people using their own judgement, rather than conforming to rigid codes of rules; and where different people are allowed to make judgements rather than relying on strict rules 'from above' (lower Power Distance).

Gray's second hypothesis was:

H2: The higher a country ranks in terms of *Uncertainty Avoidance* and *Power Distance* and the lower it ranks in terms of *Individualism*, then the more likely it is to rank highly in terms of *Uniformity*.

The basis for the second hypothesis is that communities that prefer to avoid uncertainty prefer more rigid codes of behaviour and greater conformity. A desire for uniformity is also deemed to be consistent with a preference for Collectivism (as opposed to Individualism) and an acceptance of a relatively more Power Distance society in which laws are more likely to be accepted.

Gray's third hypothesis was:

H3: The higher a country ranks in terms of *Uncertainty Avoidance* and the lower it ranks in terms of *Individualism* and *Masculinity*, then the more likely it is to rank highly in terms of *Conservatism*.

As noted previously, Conservatism implies that accountants favour notions such as prudence (which traditionally means that profits and assets are calculated in a conservative manner with a tendency towards understatement rather than over-statement). The basis for the third hypothesis is that communities that have strong Uncertainty Avoidance characteristics tend to prefer a more cautious approach to cope with existing uncertainties. On the other hand, Conservatism is expected to be associated with communities that care less about individual achievement. Communities that tend to demonstrate masculine tendencies emphasize achieve-ment – hence the expectation that lower levels of Masculinity will lead to higher preferences for conservative accounting principles. A more highly Masculine community would be deemed to prefer to use methods of accounting that lead to higher levels of performance being reported.

Gray's fourth hypothesis is:

H4: The higher a country ranks in terms of *Uncertainty Avoidance* and *Power Distance* and the lower it ranks in terms of *Individualism* and *Masculinity*, then the more likely it is to rank highly in terms of *Secrecy*.

The basis for the fourth hypothesis is that communities that have a higher preference for Uncertainty Avoidance prefer not to disclose too much information because this could lead to conflict, competition and security problems. Also, communities that accept higher Power Distance would accept restricted information, as this acts to preserve power inequalities. Also, a community that prefers a collective approach, as opposed to an individualistic approach, would prefer to keep information disclosures to a minimum to protect those close to the firm and to reflect limited concern for those external to the organization. A more *Masculine* community would be expected to provide more information about its financial position and performance to enable comparisons of the level of performance of different entities. (Masculine communities would be deemed to be more concerned with issues such as ranking the performance of one entity against another.) However, as a caveat to the general position that more Masculine communities disclose more accounting information, Gray (1988, p. 11) argues that 'a significant but less important link with masculinity also seems likely to the extent that more caring societies, where more emphasis is given to the quality of life, people and the environment, will tend to be more open, especially as regards socially related information'.[8] Table 4.2 summarizes the hypothesized relationships between Gray's accounting values and Hofstede's cultural values.

Gray (1988) further hypothesized that relationships can be established between accounting values and the *authority* and *enforcement* of accounting systems (the extent to which they are determined and enforced by statutory control or professional means), and the *measurement* and *disclosure* characteristics of the accounting systems. According to Gray (1988, p. 12):

> Accounting value systems most relevant to the professional or statutory authority for accounting systems and their enforcement would seem to be the professionalism and uniformity dimensions, in that they are concerned with regulation and the extent of enforcement and conformity .... Accounting values most relevant to the measurement

Table 4.2 Summary of the hypothesized relationships between Gray's accounting values and Hofstede's cultural values

| Cultural values (from Hofstede) | Accounting values (from Gray) | | | |
	Professionalism	Uniformity	Conservatism	Secrecy
Power Distance	–	+	?	+
Uncertainty Avoidance	–	+	+	+
Individualism	+	–	–	–
Masculinity	?	?	–	–

Note: '+' indicates a positive relationship; '–' indicates a negative relationship; and '?' indicates that the direction of the relationship is unclear.

practices used and the extent of information disclosed are self-evidently the conservatism and the secrecy dimensions.

Gray's linkage between societal values, accounting values and accounting practice can be summarized, as in Figure 4.1 (as summarized in Fechner and Kilgore, 1994, p. 269). Perera (1989, p. 47) provides additional discussion in respect of the relationships summarised in Figure 4.1. He states:

> The higher the degree of professionalism the greater the degree of professional self-regulation and the lower the need for government intervention. The degree of uniformity preferred in an accounting sub-culture would have an effect on the manner in which the accounting system is applied. The higher the degree of uniformity the lower the extent of professional judgement and the stronger the force applying accounting rules and procedures. The amount of conservatism preferred in an accounting sub-culture would influence the measurement practices used. The higher the degree of conservatism the stronger the ties with traditional measurement practices. The degree of secrecy preferred in an accounting sub-culture would influence the extent of the information disclosed in accounting reports. The higher the degree of secrecy, the lower the extent of disclosure.

One objective of Gray's research was to explain how differences between countries in respect of their culture may impede any moves towards international harmonization of accounting standards. While some of the above material might appear a little confusing (perhaps not), it does represent quite an intellectual body of research, which is attempting to relate a fairly difficult-to-measure construct, culture, to differences in values of the accounting subculture, and ultimately to differences in the systems of accounting employed. While we might not be able to remember all the hypothesized relationships described above, what is important is that we appreciate how researchers have attempted to link cultural measures to accounting practice.

A number of other authors have also used Hofstede's cultural dimensions.[9] Zarzeski (1996) provides evidence that supports a view that entities located in countries classified as relatively more Individualistic and Masculine and relatively

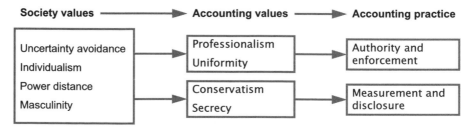

Figure 4.1 Gray's hypothesized relationships between society values, accounting values and accounting practice (from Fechner and Kilgore, 1994, p. 269)

less in terms of Uncertainty Avoidance provide greater levels of disclosure. Zarzeski also considered issues associated with international profile and found that those entities with a relatively higher international profile tend to be less secretive than other entities. Further, entities from continental European countries, such as France and Germany, which have historically tended to rely more heavily on debt financing than, say, Anglo-American companies, have lower levels of disclosure than Anglo-American companies. In relation to the issue of secrecy, Zarzeski shows that local enterprises are more likely to disclose information commensurate with the secrecy of their culture than are international enterprises. In explaining this she states (p. 20):

> The global market is just a different 'culture' than the one the firm faces at home. When a firm does business in the global market, it is operating in a different 'culture' and therefore may need to have different 'practices'. Higher levels of financial disclosures may be necessary for international survival because disclosure of quality operations should result in lower resource costs. When enterprises from more secretive countries perceive economic gain from increasing their financial disclosures, cultural borrowing may occur. The culture being borrowed will be a 'global market culture,' rather than a specific country culture.

Perera (1989) considered both Hofstede's cultural dimensions and Gray's accounting subcultural value dimensions and uses them to explain apparent differences in the accounting practices adopted in continental European countries and Anglo-American countries. According to Perera (p. 51), many countries in continental Europe are characterized by relatively high levels of uncertainty avoidance where rules or 'social codes' tend to shape behaviour, while the opposite applies in Anglo-American countries:

> The presence of these rules satisfied people's emotional needs for order and predictability in society, and people feel uncomfortable in situations where there are no rules. Therefore, in general, one can expect more formalization and institutionalization of procedures in strong uncertainty avoidance societies than in weak uncertainty avoidance countries.
>
> There is a preference for the existence of individual professional judgement, the maintenance of professional self-regulation, and flexibility in accordance with the perceived circumstances of individual companies in the accounting sub-culture of Anglo-American countries, whereas there is a preference for compliance with prescriptive legal requirements and statutory control, the maintenance of uniform accounting practices between companies, and the consistent application of such practices over time in the accounting sub-cultures of Continental Europe. Also, there is more support in the latter group for a prudent and cautious approach to income measurement to cope with the uncertainty of future events and the confidentiality of the information by restricting disclosures to only those involved with the management and financing of the organization.

These characteristics, in turn, tend to influence the degree of disclosure expected in the respective accounting systems or practices. For example, in France and West Germany, where the level of professionalism is relatively low and the preference for conservatism and secrecy is relatively high, the combined effect on the degree of disclosure will be negative. On the other hand, the collectivist or anti-individualist values of the society require business enterprises to be accountable to society by way of providing information. Therefore, it becomes necessary for the Government to intervene and prescribe certain disclosure requirements, including those in regard to social accounting. Furthermore, this situation is not likely to be rejected by the accounting profession, because here is a preference for compliance with prescriptive legal regulation and statutory control in the accounting sub-culture. By comparison, in the United States and U.K., although the relatively high level of professionalism and low level of preference for conservatism and secrecy tend to have a positive combined effect on the degree of disclosure in accounting practices, the individualistic values of the society are more concerned with the provision of information to shareholders or investors than those issues involving accountability to society at large.

Baydoun and Willett (1995) used the Hofstede–Gray theory to investigate the use of the French United Accounting System (which was ranked lowly in terms of Professionalism and highly in terms of Uniformity as well as being considered as quite conservative) in Lebanon. According to Baydoun and Willett, following World War I the Allied Supreme Council granted France a mandatory authority over Lebanon. Lebanon was a French colony until 1943 and French troops remained there until 1946. Strong trading relations between France and Lebanon continued to exist and in 1983 the French Government sponsored the transfer of the French Uniform Accounting System (UAS) to Lebanon. What was of interest is whether the French system was actually suited to the Lebanon cultural environment. Baydoun and Willett provided evidence to suggest that Lebanon and France ranked in a relatively similar manner in terms of Power Distance and Individualism. However, Lebanon was considered to rank lower in terms of Uncertainty Avoidance and higher in terms of Masculinity. On this basis (and we can refer back to Table 4.2), Baydoun and Willett (p. 81) conclude that 'it would appear that Lebanon's requirements are for less Uniformity, Conservatism and Secrecy in financial reporting practices'.[10] They further state (p. 87):

> Assuming that cultural relevance is or should be a factor in determining the form of financial statements, we would expect Lebanese financial statements to be less uniform across time and between entities, to contain more market value information and provide more items of disaggregated information. Normal publication dates should be relatively flexible and there should be less call for conservative valuation rules such as lower of cost and market. It would appear that these and other similar prescriptions cannot be tested directly at present. Since 1983 all Lebanese firms have been required to follow UAS and this system has not yet been modified to accommodate any cultural differences between France and Lebanon .... However, our analysis suggests that modifications along the lines described above either will or should take place in Lebanese accounting in the future.

Religion

A great deal of the culture-based research, particularly that based on the work of Hofstede and Gray, tends to lead to countries being grouped together in terms of both community and accounting subculture – this is perceived as providing guidance in the harmonization process and, particularly, in identifying limits therein. That is, a feature of the work of Gray is that it relies on indigenous characteristics which are confined within the boundaries of the countries under review. In subsequent work, Hamid, Craig and Clarke (1993) considered the influence of one cultural input or factor, *religion*, on accounting practices. As they indicate, religion transcends national boundaries. They consider how Islamic cultures, which exist in numerous countries, have typically failed to embrace 'Western' accounting practices and they reflect upon how issues of religion had previously occupied minimal space in the accounting literature. They state (p. 134):

> The existing literature dealing with the interaction of business activity and Islam needs extending to capture the particular effects which compliance with Islamic beliefs have on the structure of business and finance within an Islamic framework. In particular, the incompatibility of many Western accounting practices with Islamic principles requires explanation. For jurisprudential Islamic law influences the conduct of businesses in a manner not accommodated automatically by Anglo-American accounting practice. And many Western accounting practices draw upon assumptions which conflict with the tenets of Islam … . There seems to be little understanding that, unlike the Western tradition, fundamental business ethics flow automatically from the practices of the religion, rather than from the codes (mainly of etiquette) devised and imposed upon members by professional associations.

Hamid, Craig and Clarke (1993) point out that the Islamic tradition does have notions of stewardship – but to God rather than to suppliers of equity or debt capital. That is, Muslims believe that they hold assets not for themselves, but in trust for God. There are also other fundamental differences – for example, Islam precludes debt financing and prohibits the payment of interest, and this prohibition has significant implications for processes aimed at the international harmonization of accounting standards, particularly:

> … in-so-far as harmonisation is perceived necessary to entail implementation of many standard Western accounting procedures in which interest calculations are integral. Many past and present Western standards entail discounting procedures involving a time value of money concept, which is not admitted by Islam. (p. 144)[11]

Hence, Hamid, Craig and Clarke (1993) appear to provide a logical argument that religion can have a major impact on the accounting system chosen. Religion can potentially affect how people do business and how they make decisions. As will be seen in Chapter 6, the conceptual framework projects developed in countries such as the USA, Australia, Canada, the UK and New Zealand (which, interestingly, have all been grouped together by Hofstede), and by the IASB's predecessor (the International Accounting Standards Committee, or IASC), are based on the underlying objective that financial report users require financial information as the basis for making *rational economic decisions*. Such rational economic decisions also take into account the time value of money, which necessarily requires considerations of appropriate interest or discount rates. In some societies, such as Islamic states, this may not be a relevant objective. Further, any claims that particular frameworks of accounting are superior to others should only be made after considering the environments in which the frameworks are to be utilized.

Having examined several theories which seek to explain international accounting differences in terms of broad cultural (including religious) influences, we will now move on to explore five of the more concrete institutional factors which some theorists believe influence the shape of accounting practices in any nation at any point in time. As you may appreciate when reading the following sections, these institutional factors are both interrelated and can be linked to the broader cultural influences we have just examined. A useful exercise to help develop your understanding of both the cultural and institutional factors is for you to attempt, while reading the following sections, to associate (in a broad way) the institutional factors we discuss with cultural influences.

Legal systems

The first institutional factor we will examine is the legal systems operating in different countries. These can be divided into two broad categories: common law and Roman law systems. In common law systems, there have historically been relatively few prescriptive statutory laws dealing with many areas of life. Instead, the body of law has been developed by judges applying both the limited amount of statutory law and the outcomes of previous judicial decisions to the facts of a specific case. Each judgement then becomes a legal precedent for future cases. Conversely, in Roman law systems, parliamentary (statutory) law tends to be very detailed and covers most aspects of daily life. The implications of this for accounting is that in common law countries we would expect to find relatively few detailed accounting laws guiding accounting practices, and therefore historically the development of accounting practices would have been left much more to the professional judgement of accountants (and auditors). With Roman law systems, in contrast, we would expect to find a body of codified accounting laws prescribing in detail how each type of transaction or event should be treated in the accounts. In this type of system there was therefore much less need or scope for the use of professional judgement in preparing accounts or developing accounting practices.

As Nobes and Parker (2004) explain, the common law system was developed in England after the Norman Conquest of 1066, whereas the Roman law system was developed in continental European countries. Countries where the development of legal systems and practices was heavily influenced by England tend to have common law systems. These countries include England and Wales, Ireland, India, the USA, Canada, Australia and New Zealand. Conversely, most continental European countries, along with countries whose legal systems were developed under the influence of these countries, tend to have Roman law systems. Such countries include most members of the EU (other than England, Wales and Ireland) and many countries in other parts of the world which were former colonies of continental European nations.[12]

Therefore, in the EU, we would expect England, Wales, Ireland and (partially) Scotland historically to have had relatively few codified accounting laws, with the development of accounting practices being left to the professional judgement of accountants. In the remainder of the EU we would expect accounting practice historically to have been developed through detailed codified accounting laws (or legally recognized regulations) with relatively little input from professional accountants.

Business ownership and financing system

A second key institutional factor which researchers have demonstrated has an impact on the shape of a nation's accounting practices is the business ownership and financing system. Similarly to legal systems, this factor can be broadly divided into two distinct types – this time referred to as 'outsider' and 'insider' systems.

In 'outsider' systems, external shareholders (that is, those who are not involved in the management of the company) are a significant source of finance for much business activity. As these external shareholders will not be involved in the detailed management of the company, and will therefore not have access to the company's detailed management accounting information, they will need to be provided with separate financial accounting information to help them make their investment decisions. They may invest in the shares of a number of companies, and need a basis to evaluate the performance of any company – for example by comparing it to the performance of other companies. To help ensure an effective and efficient allocation of finance to different companies in this type of outsider-financed system, it is important for external investors (and potential investors) to be provided with financial accounting information which reflects the underlying economic performance of a business in a fair, balanced and unbiased manner. Thus, given the significance of outsider finance, financial accounting will have developed historically with a primary aim of providing this fair, balanced and unbiased information to external shareholders – a process which requires rather extensive use of professional judgement (Nobes, 1998), for example to handle regular developments or innovations in business practices which cannot easily have been foreseen when writing accounting codes or legislation.

Conversely, in 'insider' systems of finance, provision of finance by external shareholders is much less significant. Instead, there has either been a dominance of family-owned businesses, and/or the dominant providers of long-term finance have historically been either banks or governments (Zysman, 1983). With family-owned businesses, the owners will tend to have access to the detailed internal management accounting information of the business, so there is no obvious need for financial accounts to provide information to aid investment decision-making by shareholders.

In some countries (such as Germany) where banks have historically been the dominant source of long-term finance for large companies, banks and companies have tended to develop long-term supportive relationships. These involve banks having a representative on the supervisory board of companies to whom they are major lenders, and these representatives are provided with the detailed management accounting information available to all members of the supervisory board. As is the case with family-owned businesses, given that the predominant providers of finance are effectively 'insiders' to the business and have access to detailed management information, there will have been little pressure for financial accounting to have developed to provide information to aid external investment decisions in these countries (Nobes, 1998).

Nobes and Parker (2004) explain that in systems where governments provide a significant amount of long-term business finance, government representatives will often become directors of the state-funded companies, and will thus have access to the inside management information. Thus, a characteristic shared by all countries in which insider systems of finance predominate is that the primary role of accounting has historically not been to provide fair, balanced and unbiased information to help outside investors make efficient and effective investment decisions. Thus, financial accounting in these countries has developed to fulfil a different role than in outsider-financed countries. One such role, which we will explore in the next section, is the provision of information to calculate taxation liabilities.

Countries which have historically been dominated by insider systems of finance have also tended to be countries with Roman law systems, while outsider-financed countries usually have common law systems (La Porta *et al.*, 1997). Thus, most continental European countries (with the exception of the Netherlands which has a Roman law system but a large amount of outsider finance) have historically relied on insider forms of finance, with the result that financial accounting in these nations did not develop to serve the needs of investment decisions in capital markets. Conversely, the UK and Ireland (and, importantly, the US among other non-European states) have relied to a much greater extent on outsider forms of finance, with a primary role of accounting historically being to service the information needs of capital markets with fair, balanced and unbiased information.[13]

As an example of empirical research linking financing systems with differences in accounting practices, Pratt and Behr (1987) compared the standard-setting processes adopted in the US and Switzerland. Differences in the standards and processes adopted were explained by differences in 'size, complexity, and diversity of capital transactions, the wide distribution of ownership, and the opportunistic nature of the capital market participants'.

Before leaving our discussion of the impact of different financing systems on the shape of accounting practices, we should emphasize that with the increasing scale of globalized businesses, multinational corporations based in any country are increasingly relying on financing from more than one nation. The funding needs of many of these companies in countries which have traditionally relied upon insider forms of finance have grown beyond the funding capacity of these insider sources of finance, with several companies now increasingly also relying upon outsider finance – from shareholders in both their home country and in other nations. Thus, the information requirements associated with outsider-financed systems are now becoming applicable to many large companies in continental European countries (Nobes and Parker, 2004).

Taxation systems

As we saw in the previous subsection, in countries with predominantly outsider systems of finance, financial accounting practices historically developed to provide a fair, balanced and unbiased representation of the underlying economic performance of a business to help improve the effectiveness of investment allocation decisions by external shareholders. Such a system requires that accounting reflects some sort of economic reality with, for example, each business selecting depreciation methods that most closely reflect the manner in which it uses its fixed assets.

Conversely, in countries with largely insider systems of finance, this pressure for accounts to have developed to reflect fairly some form of underlying economic reality is not present. Rather, accounts have developed for different purposes, and one important purpose is the calculation of tax (Nobes and Parker, 2004). In most continental European countries which have traditionally relied heavily on insider forms of finance, for a company to claim an allowance for tax, this allowance must be included in its financial accounts. For example, if a company wishes to reduce its tax liability by taking advantage of the maximum permitted taxable depreciation allowances, it has to include these tax depreciation allowances in its financial accounts. These tax depreciation allowances will be determined by taxation law, and will not necessarily bear any relationship to the amount of the fixed assets which have actually been used in any particular year. The financial accounting results will therefore be substantially affected and determined by the provisions of taxation law in many continental European countries which have historically relied upon insider systems of finance.

In outsider-financed countries, the tax accounts have historically been separate from the financial accounts. Thus, if a company wishes to claim the maximum tax depreciation allowances permitted by taxation law in these countries, this will not affect the calculation of its reported profits in its financial accounts. These financial accounts can therefore include a fair depreciation charge reflecting the utilization of assets without affecting the company's ability to claim the maximum tax depreciation allowances in its tax accounts, and the provisions of taxation law have not therefore exerted much influence on the financial accounts.

Given that (with the notable European exception of the Netherlands) there has tended to be a high correlation between insider-financed systems and Roman law countries (La Porta *et al.*, 1997), this has resulted in the detailed provisions of taxation law effectively becoming a large part of the detailed accounting regulations in many continental European countries which have codified Roman law systems. A further institutional factor which tends to be differentiated between, and also reinforces the distinction between, Roman law insider-financed countries and common law outsider-financed systems is the strength of the accounting profession.

Strength of the accounting profession

Nobes and Parker (2004) explain that the strength of the accounting profession in any country has historically both been determined by, and helped to reinforce, the influence on financial accounting systems of the institutional factors we have discussed above. In a common law country which has a predominantly outsider system of long-term finance and where tax law has had little influence on financial accounting, there will have been relatively few statutory laws determining the contents of accounts. The primary purpose of these accounts will have been to provide a fair, balanced and unbiased representation of the underlying economic performance of the business, and this will have required the exercise of professional judgement to cope with each different situation. Thus, in these countries, there will have historically been demand for a large number of accountants who are able to apply professional judgement to determine the most suitable way of reflecting unique sets of transactions and events in financial accounting reports of many companies. This need for accountants who are able to, and have scope to, exercise professional judgement has led to the development of large and strong accounting professions in countries such as the UK, Ireland, the USA and Australia. Strong accounting professions have then been effective in lobbying governments to ensure that accounting regulatory systems give scope for the exercise of professional judgement, thus possibly reinforcing the strength and influence of the accounting profession.

Conversely, in Roman law countries which have largely insider systems of finance and where compliance with the details of tax laws exerts a substantial influence on the shape of financial accounts, there will have been little need or scope for the use of professional judgement when drawing up financial accounting statements. There has therefore been much less impetus for the development of accounting professions than in outsider-financed common law systems. The accounting professions in many continental European countries have therefore historically been smaller and weaker (in terms of influence) than their counterparts in the UK, Ireland or the USA. Nobes and Parker (2004) argue that these weaker accounting professions have had an impact in reinforcing accounting practices which require little exercise of professional judgement in these countries, because the effective implementation of flexible, judgemental accounting practices requires a reasonably large accounting profession which is comfortable with (and has sufficient experience of) applying professional judgements to complex accounting issues.

Accidents of history

As indicated at the beginning of this section, accounting systems tend to be regarded as following either an Anglo-American or a continental European model. The cultural and institutional differences we have discussed so far in this chapter support this view, with countries following the Anglo-American model tending to have common law systems, outsider financing, little influence of taxation law on financial accounting, and a strong accounting profession accustomed to exercising a considerable amount of professional judgement – with the opposite applying in countries following the continental European model. If we accept that these influences are significant in shaping a nation's accounting practices, we should expect accounting practices in countries with Anglo-American systems to be broadly similar. However, this is not consistent with the evidence presented in the first section of this chapter when, for example, we saw that both the reported profits and the net assets of the multinational pharmaceutical company AstraZeneca were significantly different when calculated in accordance with UK accounting rules than when calculated in accordance with US rules. If the cultural and institutional influences we have examined so far in this chapter, and which are broadly similar between the UK and the USA, are significant in shaping accounting practices, then there must be an important additional influencing factor which varies between the UK and the USA.

Nobes and Parker (2004) point to the importance of the additional factor of accidents of history, whose influence will be restricted to the accounting systems of the individual countries affected by the accidents. For example, following the Wall Street Crash of 1929, the US established Securities Exchange legislation aimed at investor protection, while there was no such development at the time in the UK. This legislation included certain accounting requirements, which have been delegated to private sector accounting standard-setting bodies, and which have produced a detailed set of US accounting rules (as we would expect to see in a Roman law country). In contrast, following a series of high profile accounting failures in the UK in the late 1980s, the UK has established a more principles-based systems of accounting regulation since the early 1990s. As Unerman and O'Dwyer (2004) highlight, in the aftermath of accounting failures at Enron in 2001, it was claimed by many in the UK that these different regulatory systems would have prevented Enron using in the UK the creative accounting techniques it followed in the USA. Going back to the case of AstraZeneca, studying the reconciliation provided in the financial accounts between the results calculated using UK and US accounting rules, it is apparent that a substantial difference between the two sets of accounting regulations (in the case of this company) arises from differences between the US and the UK accounting treatment of mergers and acquisitions (including the calculation of goodwill). Different pressures in the UK (possibly including different lobbying efforts by interested parties in each country) resulted in UK and US accounting rules for mergers and acquisitions being somewhat different, although for reasons we explore when discussing the IASB towards the end of this chapter, these differences are likely to reduce substantially from 2005.

In summarizing this chapter so far, we can see that a number of reasons, including culture, religion (which is a subset of culture) and institutional factors (which we could also imagine would be influenced by culture), have been advanced to explain the accounting systems in place in each country. This discussion has by no means been exhaustive in identifying the many factors proposed to explain international differences in accounting systems, but nevertheless, the referenced research indicates that one general approach to accounting, such as that used in the UK, Ireland, the Netherlands, the USA, Australia, New Zealand or Canada, may suit a particular environment, but not others. Therefore, it is probably somewhat naive to claim that there is any one 'best' system of accounting. Despite this, there have been extensive efforts over several decades to reduce the differences between accounting systems in different countries. Before we discuss some of these efforts, termed international harmonization or standardization of accounting, we will now consider theoretical reasons which have been proposed to explain why international harmonization or standardization is important, and reasons why this harmonization or standardization might not be desirable or effective.

Reasons for harmonization and standardization

Nobes and Parker (2004, p. 77) distinguish between 'harmonization' and 'standardization' of accounting. They define 'harmonization' as:

> a process of increasing the compatibility of accounting practices by setting bounds to their degree of variation

'Standardization' of accounting is explained as a term which 'appears to imply the imposition of a more rigid and narrow set of rules [than harmonization]' (p. 77).

Therefore, harmonization appears to allow more flexibility than standardization, but as Nobes and Parker (2004) point out, the two terms have more recently been used almost synonymously in international accounting. We will therefore use the two terms interchangeably in this chapter.

Nobes and Parker (2004) explain that the reasons for increased international standardization of financial accounting are similar to the reasons for standardizing financial accounting within any individual country. With increased globalization, these reasons have gained importance in terms of international standardization. Thus, for example, if investors are increasingly investing in companies from a variety of countries, and these investors use financial accounts as an important source of information upon which to base their investment decisions, it is important for them to both understand the financial accounts and have a reasonable basis to compare the financial accounting numbers of companies from different countries. Just as is the case domestically (see the arguments in Chapters 2 and 3) both understandability and interpretation of financial accounting information should be more effective if all accounts are compiled using the same set of underlying assumptions – or accounting rules. If a single international investor has to understand numerous different sets of accounting assumptions and regulations, then the task of making efficient and effective international investment decisions is complicated considerably.

If the long-term finance needs of a multinational company are too great for the providers of finance in a single country, then it may need to raise finance on the stock exchanges of more than one country. For reasons of domestic investor protection, the stock exchange regulators in any country are likely to be reluctant to permit a company's shares to be traded on their exchange if that company does not produce financial accounts which are readily comparable with the accounts of all other companies whose shares are traded on that exchange – that is, accounts which have been prepared using comparable assumptions (or rules). Where, as in the case of AstraZeneca, companies have to produce financial accounting results in accordance with the accounting rules of each of the stock exchanges where its shares are traded, its accounting procedures would be considerably simplified if there was a single set of internationally recognized accounting rules which were acceptable to all the stock exchanges where its shares are traded. As these are likely to have to be very similar to the accounting rules used by all other companies whose shares are traded on each of the stock exchanges, it makes sense to utilize a single set of international accounting rules and regulations for all companies listed on any stock exchange – even where companies' shares are traded only on their domestic stock exchange.

A further reason for international standardization of accounting provided by Nobes and Parker (2004) is that it will facilitate greater flexibility and efficiency in use of staff by multinational firms of accountants and auditors, as different accounting regulations in different countries act as a barrier to the transfer of staff between counties.

Obstacles to harmonization and standardization of accounting

So it seems that there are strong reasons for accounting to be standardized internationally. However, as this has not happened there must be forces preventing the complete international standardization of accounting. Some theoretical explanations have been advanced to clarify these obstacles to harmonization.

One key obstacle to international harmonization or standardization is the cultural and institutional differences which we saw caused financial accounting to vary in the first place. As argued earlier, if these causal factors continue to vary between countries, then it is difficult to see how a single set of accounting rules will be appropriate or suitable for all countries. That is, as accounting varies between different countries for good reasons, a key impediment to international standardization is the fact that these good reasons continue to exist. As an example of this obstacle to harmonization, Perera (1989, p. 52) considers the potential success of transferring accounting skills from Anglo-American countries to developing countries. He notes:

> The skill so transferred from Anglo-American countries may not work because they are culturally irrelevant or dysfunctional in the receiving countries' context.

Perera (1989) also argues that international accounting standards themselves are strongly influenced by Anglo-American accounting models and, as such, these international standards tend to reflect the circumstances and patterns of thinking in a particular group of countries. He argues that these standards are likely to encounter problems of relevance in countries where different environments from those found in Anglo-American countries exist. Thus, for example, if the majority of German companies continue to rely on 'insider' forms of finance, and Germany continues to use a Roman law system, its existing codified accounting regulations will probably be more appropriate for most German companies than the imposition of a form of Anglo-American accounting system.[14] Nobes and Parker (2004) suggest that in such circumstances, it might be more appropriate to have a dual system, where all companies in each country are required to prepare financial accounts in accordance with their historically developed domestic system, and companies which raise funds internationally can prepare an additional set of accounts (probably only the consolidated or group accounts) in accordance with Anglo-American style international accounting rules.

A further obstacle to harmonization has been explained by Nobes and Parker (2004) as the lack of a developed accounting profession in some countries. Thus, as discussed earlier, in countries where strong accounting professions have not developed there are likely to be initial problems in implementing international accounting regulations based on the Anglo-American professional judgement model. Furthermore, some countries might have nationalistic difficulties in being seen to implement a system of international accounting standards which are regarded as being closely aligned to the Anglo-American systems.

A final potential significant obstacle to international standardization is that, as we saw in Chapters 2 and 3, accounting regulations can and do have economic consequences (Nobes and Parker, 2004). Governments of individual countries may be unwilling to give control over a process which has real economic consequences to an international body over which they have little influence. We saw how this can impact on the process of international standardization in Chapter 3, when we examined the recent difficulties which have been experienced with the refusal of some EU countries to fully endorse the provisions of the revised IAS 39, partly because of the potential negative economic impact these provisions might have on banks in their countries.

Processes and institutions of international accounting standardization

Examination of the processes and institutions of international harmonization and standardization of accounting is much more closely related to accounting practice than to accounting theory, and might therefore be considered to be outside the scope of a book such as this on accounting theory. However, given the importance of recent developments in harmonization and standardization of accounting, both in the EU and globally, a basic knowledge of the current processes of international accounting harmonization, especially as they affect accounting regulations in the EU, should help in understanding several of the empirical examples we use in this book. The final section of this chapter will therefore briefly examine these processes and institutions of harmonization and standardization.

The International Accounting Standards Board

The main institution involved in international standardization of financial accounting is the International Accounting Standards Board (IASB), and its predecessor the International Accounting Standards Committee (IASC). The IASC was established in 1973 with the objectives of:

> formulating and publishing in the public interest accounting standards to be observed in the presentation of financial statements and promoting their worldwide acceptance and observance; and working generally for the improvement and harmonisation of regulations, accounting standards and procedures relating to the presentation of financial statements. (IASC, 1998, p. 6)

Its approach to accounting regulation essentially followed the Anglo-American model, but initially many of the International Accounting Standards (IASs) it published permitted a wide range of accounting options. As such, they were not particularly effective at standardizing accounting practices internationally, as different companies (or countries) could use substantially different accounting policies while all being able to state that they complied with the single set of IAS regulations. Therefore compliance with IAS did not ensure or enhance the comparability or understandability of financial accounts – a key purpose of accounting regulation – and was not accepted by stock exchanges as a basis of the preparation of financial accounts to support a listing on their exchange.

In the late 1980s the International Organization of Securities Commissions (IOSCO), a body representing government securities regulators worldwide, recognized that to foster a greater number of multinationals raising funding from stock exchanges in more than one country, it would be useful to have a single set of rigorous international accounting standards – compliance with which would be acceptable to any stock exchange regulated by an IOSCO member. This would then reduce costs of companies that had to produce a different set of financial accounting results for each of the countries in which their shares were listed. However, for IAS to be acceptable for this purpose, they would have to be much more effective at standardizing accounting practice, and would therefore need to permit a much narrower set of accounting practices.

Accordingly, the IASC then embarked on a comparability and improvements project to reduce the range of permitted options in IASs, and make them acceptable to IOSCO (Purvis *et al.*, 1991). This project culminated in the publication of a revised core set of IASs by 1999, which was then accepted by IOSCO members – with the important exception of the US Securities Exchange Commission. After this endorsement by IOSCO, any company which drew up its accounts in accordance with the revised IASs could use this single set of IAS-based accounts to support its listing on any stock exchange regulated by any IOSCO member anywhere in the world – with the exception of the USA.

After completion of the core of this comparability and improvements project, the IASC was replaced in 2001 by the IASB, which adopted all existing IASs and from 2001 has published new regulations in the form of International Financial Reporting Standards (IFRS).[15] The IASB has a structure which is seen to be considerably more independent and rigorous than the former IASC, and comprises 14 full-time members who have to sever their connections with other organizations (including previous employers). They are appointed by a board of '19 trustees, who have promised to operate in the public interest' (Nobes and Parker, 2004, p. 102). A two-thirds majority of the 14 members of the IASB is all that is needed to approve an IFRS (or a revised IAS), and this is regarded as a mechanism likely to ensure that the IASB can develop rigorous regulations which deal with contentious issues, especially where the resultant accounting standard might be unpopular among many companies. Initial membership of the IASB was dominated by accountants from Anglo-American type accounting nations, and this could reinforce its tendency to develop Anglo-American style accounting regulations.

Despite these reforms to the IASB, IFRSs/IASs have still not been accepted by the US Securities Exchange Commission as an adequate basis for the preparation of accounts to support a listing on a US stock exchange. However, the IASB and the US standard-setter (the Financial Accounting Standards Board) have been working to reduce the differences between international standards and US accounting standards (Nobes and Parker, 2004).

The European Union and international accounting harmonization

A key reason why the EU became involved in accounting regulation at the EU level (rather than leaving this entirely to individual member states) is that a founding principle of the EU was freedom of movement within the EU of people, goods and capital. As we saw earlier in this chapter, differing accounting principles in different countries acts as an impediment to investors understanding and comparing the financial accounts of companies in these different countries, and thereby acts as an impediment to them freely investing their capital in companies from different EU member states (an inhibition to the free movement of capital). The approach towards harmonization of accounting in the European Union has historically differed from the IASC/IASB approach. This should be of little surprise, given that most countries in the EU, by definition, follow a continental European system of accounting rather than the Anglo-American model of the IASC/IASB, so the EU approach to accounting harmonization has historically been through legislation. This EU legislation has been primarily in the form of EU directives on company law, which have to be agreed on by the EU and then implemented in the domestic legislation of each EU member state. This is a very lengthy process, and during the 1990s the EU recognized that it was far too inflexible to respond to the requirements of a dynamic business environment where financial accounting practices need to quickly adapt to rapidly changing business practices – especially for companies which rely on 'outsider' forms of finance (which include an increasing number of the largest companies in many continental European nations).

Following proposals made in 2000, the EU agreed in 2002 that from 1 January 2005 all companies whose shares were traded on any stock exchange in the EU would have to compile their consolidated accounts in accordance with IASs/IFRSs.[16] This was seen as a method of both ensuring accounting rules were flexible enough to suit the needs of a dynamic business environment, and ensuring that the financial accounts of EU-listed companies maintained international credibility. Further details regarding the EU adoption of IASs/IFRSs are shown in Exhibit 4.1, which reproduces a press release issued by the European Commission when this route for accounting regulation was formally adopted in 2002.

Having read Exhibit 4.1, it appears that the views being embraced in favour of the adoption of IAS/IFRS are based on various beliefs about the information people

---

Exhibit 4.1 EU adoption of IASs/IFRSs

Agreement on International Accounting Standards will help investors and boost business in EU

The European Commission has welcomed the Council's adoption, in a single reading, of the Regulation requiring listed companies, including banks and insurance companies, to prepare their consolidated accounts in accordance with International Accounting Standards (IAS) from 2005 onwards (see IP/01/200 and MEMO/01/40). The Regulation will help eliminate barriers to cross-border trading in securities by ensuring that company accounts throughout the EU are more reliable and transparent and that they can be more easily compared. This will in turn increase market efficiency and reduce the cost of raising capital for companies, ultimately improving competitiveness and helping boost growth. The IAS Regulation was proposed by the Commission in February 2001. It is a key measure in the Financial Services Action Plan, on which significant progress has been made in the last few weeks (see IP/02/796). Unlike Directives, EU Regulations have the force of law without requiring transposition into national legislation. Member States have the option of extending the requirements of this Regulation to unlisted companies and to the production of individual accounts. Although the Commission put forward the IAS proposal long before the Enron affair, this is one of a series of measures which will help to protect the EU from such problems – others include the Commission's recent Recommendation on Auditor Independence (see IP/02/723) and its proposal to amend the Accounting Directives (see IP/02/799).

Internal Market Commissioner Frits Bolkestein said: 'I am delighted that the IAS Regulation has been adopted in a single reading and am grateful for the positive attitude of both the Parliament and the Council. I believe IAS are the best standards that exist. Applying them throughout the EU will put an end to the current Tower of Babel in financial reporting. It will help protect us against malpractice. It will mean investors and other stakeholders will be able to compare like with like. It will help European firms to compete on equal terms when raising capital on world markets. What is more, during my recent visit to the US, I saw hopeful signs that the US will now work with us towards full convergence of our accounting standards.'

To ensure appropriate political oversight, the Regulation establishes a new EU mechanism to assess IAS adopted by the International Accounting Standards Board (IASB), the international accounting standard-setting organisation based in London, to give them legal endorsement for use within the EU. The Accounting Regulatory Committee chaired by the

Commission and composed of representatives of the Member States, will decide whether to endorse IAS on the basis of Commission proposals.

In its task, the Commission will be helped by EFRAG, the European Financial Reporting Advisory Group, a group composed of accounting experts from the private sector in several Member States.

EFRAG provides technical expertise concerning the use of IAS within the European legal environment and participates actively in the international accounting standard setting process. The Commission invites all parties interested in financial reporting to contribute actively to the work of EFRAG. The Commission recently proposed amendments to the Accounting Directives which would complement the IAS Regulation by allowing Member States which do not apply IAS to all companies to move towards similar, high quality financial reporting (see IP/02/799).

'Agreement on international accounting standards will help investors and boost business in the EU', European Commission, 7 June 2002

need in making various decisions (which can be tied back to decision usefulness theories – some of which we consider in Chapters 5 and 6); beliefs about how individuals and capital markets react to accounting information (which can be tied back into behavioural and capital markets research – the topics of Chapters 10 and 11); and a view that the adoption of IAS/IFRS is in the public interest, rather than being driven by the private interests of particular constituents (and we considered public interest theories and private interest theories in Chapter 3). There also appears to be a view that new accounting methods will be embraced in a similar manner across various countries (which perhaps disregards some of the literature discussed in this chapter – for example, that religion, culture or taxation systems influence the usefulness of various alternative accounting approaches). It would be hoped that accounting regulators making important decisions in relation to matters such as accounting, as well as commentators that report on actual and proposed accounting changes, should be familiar with the research being undertaken within the academic community – some of which might question the logic or efficacy of various proposals for reform to accounting. Unfortunately this will not always be the case. Accounting researchers must make an effort to ensure that accounting regulators are aware of the relevance of the research being undertaken.

Despite the European Commission's enthusiasm for the adoption of IASs/IFRSs, there were concerns that, for both legal and political reasons, the EU could not be seen to endorse in advance regulations which could be developed at any time in the future by an international body not under the control of the EU (Nobes and Parker, 2004). That is, the EU were unwilling to give a blanket approval covering all future IFRSs (which would apply to many EU companies) without considering the details of these IFRSs. Therefore, as can be seen in Exhibit 4.1, the EU established a mechanism whereby each IAS/IFRS would have to be endorsed separately by the EU before becoming mandatory for listed companies in the EU. This endorsement process involves an 11-member committee entitled the European Financial Reporting Advisory Group (EFRAG), with members drawn from preparers and users of accounts, commenting on each IAS/IFRS to a new EU Accounting Regulatory Committee (ARC). This ARC has a member from each EU state, and votes on whether to recommend approval of the IAS/IFRS to the EU commission, with a two-thirds majority of the 25 members of the ARC required to recommend approval of any IAS/IFRS. As we saw in Chapter 3, this mechanism was used in 2004 to block recommendation of full EU endorsement of IAS 39 (on financial instruments) by governments who argued that aspects of IAS 39 were unrealistic and would have potentially significant negative economic consequences on banks in their nations. It will be interesting to see whether this action by the EU will damage the movement towards international harmonization and standardization of accounting, as was argued by some commentators at the time.

In a separate and earlier initiative by the EU related to changes in accounting practice at an international level, in 1992 the EU released a document entitled 'Towards Sustainability' as part of its Fifth Action Programme. In this document, which suggested quite radical changes to the practice of accounting on a worldwide basis, one of the suggestions of the programme was for the accounting profession to take a role in implementing costing systems that internalize many environmental costs which were previously ignored. Specifically, the EU called for a 'redefinition of accounting concepts, rules, conventions and methodology so as to ensure that the consumption and use of environmental resources are accounted for as part of the full cost of production and reflected in market prices' (European Commission, 1992, Vol. II, Section 7.4, p. 67).

Chapter summary

In this chapter we identified and considered international differences in accounting practices and we have seen that numerous reasons (generated from different theoretical perspectives) have been advanced to explain such differences (including differences in culture, religions as a subset of culture, legal systems, financing systems, taxation systems, the strength of the accounting profession and accidents of history). Much of the existing research into comparative international accounting questions whether it is appropriate to expect that we will ever have one system of accounting adopted uniformly throughout the world (which has been stated as a long-term objective of the IASB).

While many researchers question the relevance of 'Western style' accounting standards across all countries, efforts by a number of international organizations are nevertheless continuing to encourage quite culturally-disparate countries to adopt IASs/IFRSs. This implies that the members of some international organizations are either unaware of the literature, or alternatively, choose to reject it as irrelevant. As efforts by a number of countries, in particular members of the EU, continue in relation to the domestic implementation of international standards, it is to be expected that this debate will continue.

Questions

4.1 In the context of financial accounting, what is harmonization and/or standardization?

4.2 Identify some factors that might be expected to explain why different countries use different systems of accounting.

4.3 After considering the Hofstede–Gray model, briefly explain the hypothesized link between society values, accounting values and accounting practice.

4.4 Any efforts towards standardizing accounting practices on an international basis implies a belief that a 'one-size-fits-all' approach is appropriate. Is this naive?

4.5 While it is often argued that within particular countries there should be some association between various value systems and accounting systems, it is also argued (for example, by Baydoun and Willett, 1995) that over time many events would typically have occurred that confound this expected relationship. What type of events might confound the expected relationship?

4.6 Baydoun and Willett (1995, p. 72) identify a number of problems in testing the Hofstede–Gray theory. They emphasize that many accounting systems are imported from other countries with possibly different cultures. As they state: 'Due to the interference in what would otherwise have been the natural evolution of financial information requirements, there are no uncontaminated examples of modern accounting practices in developing countries. Consequently great care has to be taken in using data from developing countries to draw inferences about relevance on the basis of the Hofstede–Gray framework.' Explain the point of view being provided by Baydoun and Willett. Do you believe that they are correct?

4.7 As noted in this chapter, Hamid, Craig and Clarke (1993) provide an argument that religion can have a major impact on the accounting system chosen by particular countries and that before 'Western' methods of accounting are exported to particular countries, it must be determined whether particular religious beliefs will make the 'Western' accounting policies irrelevant. Provide an explanation of their argument.

4.8 Nobes (1998) suggests that for countries that have organizations that rely relatively heavily upon equity markets, as opposed to other sources of finance, there will be a greater propensity for such organizations to make public disclosures of information. Evaluate this argument.

4.9 In the early 1990s, US Financial Accounting Standards Board's chairman Dennis Beresford claimed that the US accounting and reporting system was regarded by many as 'the most comprehensive and sophisticated system in the world'. Evaluate this statement. How do you think its validity might have changed in the aftermath of accounting failures at Enron, WorldCom and Andersen in 2001/02? Do you think that the US system would be regarded as sophisticated in all cultural contexts?

4.10 Do you think it is realistic to expect that one day there will be internationally uniform accounting standards? What factors would work for or against achieving this aim?

4.11 Evaluate how reasonable it is to assume that inflow of foreign investment into EU member states would have been restricted if the EU had not made compliance with IAS/IFRS compulsory for all EU listed companies from 2005.

4.12 Explain possible barriers to harmonization or standardization of financial accounting across all EU member states. Given these barriers, do you think that the EU has been naive in embracing the harmonization process?

4.13 The IASC (1998, p. 50) stated: 'many developing and newly industrialized countries are using International Accounting Standards as their national requirements, or as the basis for their national requirements. These countries have a growing need for relevant and reliable financial information to meet the requirements both of domestic users and of international providers of the capital that they need.' Do you think that IASs/IFRSs will provide 'relevant and reliable information' that meets the needs of all financial statement users in all countries?

Notes

1 As we will see later in this chapter, many stock exchanges now accept accounts drawn up in accordance with International Financial Reporting Standards/ International Accounting Standards. If a company has its shares traded on stock exchanges in more than one country, but all these stock exchanges accept accounts drawn up using these international standards, then the company may only have to produce one version of its accounts which will be accepted by all of the stock exchanges where its shares are traded.

2 For example, France, Italy, Spain and Germany are often presented as examples of the Continental European group, while countries such as the US, UK, Ireland, the Netherlands, Canada, Australia and New Zealand are often presented as examples of the Anglo-American group.

3 Perera (1989, p. 43) further states that 'it is essential, therefore, that in analyzing the impact of culture upon the behaviour of the members of any particular subculture, a researcher must select the cultural components or dimensions most pertinent to the particular facet of cultural behaviour being studied'. This is clearly not a straightforward task.

4 Hofstede's theory, while being applied to accounting issues, is from the cross-cultural psychology literature and was of itself not directly concerned with accounting.

5 Positive Accounting Theory, a theory developed by Watts and Zimmerman (and which we discuss in depth in Chapter 7), attempts to explain and predict managers' selection of accounting methods. In developing their theory, Watts and Zimmerman assume that individuals will *always* act in their own self-interest. Such an assumption would be invalid in a community which embraces a Collectivist perspective. In a similar vein, Hamid, Craig and Clarke (1993) suggest that finance theories developed in Western cultures will not apply in Islamic cultures. According to Hamid, Craig and Clarke (1993), the Islamic principles do not allow the payment of interest. They argue (p. 146) therefore that 'much of Western finance theory, in particular the capital asset pricing model, which draws upon interest-dependent explanations of risk, cannot be part of the (Islamic) accounting and finance package'.

6 For example, of the many groups, one group with similar scores on each of the four societal values comprises Australia, Canada, Ireland, New Zealand, UK and USA. Another group is Denmark, Finland, Netherlands, Norway and Sweden, while another group comprises Indonesia, Pakistan, Taiwan and Thailand. The view is that people within these various groupings of countries share a similar culture and therefore share similar *norms* and *value systems*.

7 Although Gray (1988) developed four hypotheses, he did not test them empirically. To test them, as others have subsequently done, one must determine whether an accounting system scores high or low in a particular country on the four dimensions developed by Gray.

8 Socially related information would relate to such issues as health and safety issues, employee education and training, charitable donations, support of community projects and environmental performance. A more feminine (less masculine) society would tend to consider these issues more important. Hence while femininity might be associated with less financial disclosure, it is assumed to be associated with greater social disclosure.

9 Baydoun and Willett (1995, p. 72) identify a number of problems in testing the Hofstede–Gray theory. They emphasize that many accounting systems are imported from other countries with possibly different cultures. As they state: 'Due to the interference in what would otherwise have been the natural evolution of financial information requirements there are no uncontaminated examples of modern accounting practices in developing countries. Consequently great care has to be taken in using data from developing countries to draw inferences about relevance on the basis of the Hofstede–Gray framework.'

10 In undertaking their work, Baydoun and Willett were, in a number of respects, critical of Gray's work. For example, they state (p. 82) that 'all of Gray's accounting values are defined in terms of preferences for particular courses of action, rather than in terms of apparent attributes of financial statements, such as the qualitative characteristics described in the FASB's conceptual framework project'. Also they state that Gray's theory does not clearly indicate what forms of financial statements might be preferred.

11 For example, notions of discounting are found in 'Western' accounting standards dealing with employee benefits, lease capitalization, impairment of assets and general insurers.

12 Nobes and Parker (2004) point out that a very small number of countries (such as

Scotland, South Africa and Israel) have developed legal systems which incorporate aspects of both common and Roman law.

13 As we will see in the final chapter, many critical accounting theorists strongly disagree that accounting information is fair, balanced or unbiased.

14 In a similar way, the imposition of a detailed, codified accounting system would not be appropriate for the UK or Ireland, where the 'outsider' system of finance requires financial accounts to provide fair and balanced information reflecting some form of underlying economic reality.

15 For issues covered by an existing IAS which has been updated by the IASB, the revised regulation has usually retained its old IAS number and title rather than becoming an IFRS.

16 For a small number of companies, the deadline was 2007 instead of 2005.

References

Baydoun, N. & Willett, R. (1995) 'Cultural relevance of Western accounting systems to developing countries', *ABACUS*, **31** (1), pp. 67–92.

Doupnik, T. S. & Salter, S. B. (1995) 'External environment, culture, and accounting practice: A preliminary test of a general model of international accounting development', *The International Journal of Accounting*, **30** (3), pp. 189–207.

European Commission (1992) 'Towards sustainability: A community programme of policy and action in relation to the environment and sustainable development', Brussels: European Commission.

Fechner, H. H. E. & Kilgore, A. (1994) 'The influence of cultural factors on accounting practice', *The International Journal of Accounting*, **29**, pp. 265–77.

Gray, S. J. (1988) 'Towards a theory of cultural influence on the development of accounting systems internationally', *ABACUS*, **24** (1), pp. 1–15.

Hamid, S., Craig, R., & Clarke, F. (1993) 'Religion: A confounding cultural element in the international harmonization of accounting?' *ABACUS*, **29** (2), pp. 131–48.

Hofstede, G. (1980) *Culture's Consequences: International Differences in Work-related Values*, Beverley Hills, CA: Sage Publications.

Hofstede, G. (1983) 'Dimensions of national cultures in fifty countries and three regions', in Derogowski, J. B., Dziuraweic, S. & Annis, R. (eds) *Expiscations in Cross-Cultural Psychology*, Lisse, Netherlands: Swets and Zeitlinger.

Hofstede, G. (1984) 'Cultural dimensions in management and planning', *Asia Pacific Journal of Management* (January).

IASC (1998) 'Shaping IASC for the future', London: International Accounting Standards Committee.

La Porta, R., Lopez-de-Silanes, F., Shleifer, A., & Vishny, R. W. (1997) 'Legal determinants of external finance', *Journal of Finance*, **52** (3), pp. 1131–50.

Mueller, G. G. (1967) *International Accounting*, New York: Macmillan.

Mueller, G. G. (1968) 'Accounting principles generally accepted in the United States versus those generally accepted elsewhere', *The International Journal of Accounting Education and Research*, **3** (2), pp. 91–103.

Nobes, C. (1984) *International Classification of Financial Reporting*, London: Croom Helm.

Nobes, C. (1998) 'Towards a general model of the reasons for international differences in financial reporting', *ABACUS*, **34** (2).

Nobes, C. & Parker, R. (2004) *Comparative International Accounting*, Harlow: Pearson Education Limited.

Perera, H. (1989) 'Towards a framework to analyze the impact of culture on accounting', *The International Journal of Accounting*, **24** (1), pp. 42–56.

Pratt, J. & Behr, G. (1987) 'Environmental factors, transaction costs, and external reporting: A cross national comparison',

The International Journal of Accounting Education and Research (Spring).

Purvis, S. E. C., Gernon, H., & Diamond, M. A. (1991) 'The IASC and its comparability project', *Accounting Horizons*, **5** (2), pp. 25–44.

Takatera, S. & Yamamoto, M. (1987) 'The cultural significance of accounting in Japan', *Seminar on Accounting and Culture*, European Institute for Advanced Studies in Management, Brussels.

Unerman, J. & O'Dwyer, B. (2004) 'Basking in Enron's reflexive goriness: Mixed messages from the UK profession's reaction', *Paper presented at Asia Pacific Interdisciplinary Research on Accounting Conference*, Singapore.

Violet, W. J. (1983) 'The development of international accounting standards: An anthropological perspective', *The International Journal of Accounting Education and Research*, **18** (2), pp. 1–12.

Zarzeski, M. T. (1996) 'Spontaneous harmonization effects of culture and market forces on accounting disclosure practices', *Accounting Horizons*, **10** (1), pp. 18–37.

Zysman, J. (1983) *Government, Markets and Growth: Financial Systems and the Politics of Change*, USA: Cornell University Press.

CHAPTER 5

Normative theories of accounting 1: The case of accounting for changing prices

Learning Objectives

Upon completing this chapter readers should:

◆ be aware of some particular limitations of historical cost accounting in terms of its ability to cope with various issues associated with changing prices;

◆ be aware of a number of alternative methods of accounting that have been developed to address problems associated with changing prices;

◆ be able to identify some of the strengths and weaknesses of the various alternative accounting methods;

◆ understand that the calculation of income under a particular method of accounting will depend on the perspective of capital maintenance that has been adopted.

Opening issues

Various asset valuation approaches are often adopted in the financial statements of large corporations. Fixed assets acquired (or perhaps revalued) in different years will simply be added together to give a total euro value, even though the various costs or valuations might provide little reflection of the current values of the respective assets.

Issues to consider:

(a) What are some of the criticisms that can be made in relation to the practice of accounting, wherein we add together, without adjustment, assets that have been acquired or valued in different years, when the purchasing power of the euro was conceivably quite different?

(b) What are some of the alternative methods of accounting (alternatives to historical cost accounting) that have been advanced to cope with the issue of changing prices, and what acceptance have these alternatives received from the accounting profession?
(c) What are some of the strengths and weaknesses of the various alternatives to historical cost?

Introduction

In Chapter 3 we considered various theoretical explanations about why regulation might be put in place. Perspectives derived from *public interest theory*, *capture theory* and the *economic interest theory of regulation* did not attempt to explain what form of regulation was most optimal or efficient. Rather, by adopting certain theoretical assumptions about individual behaviour and motivations, these theories attempted to explain which parties were most likely to attempt to, perhaps successfully, impact on the regulatory process.

In this chapter we consider a number of *normative theories* of accounting. Based upon particular judgements about the types of information people *need* (which could be different to what they *want*) the various normative theories provide prescriptions about how the process of financial accounting *should* be undertaken.[1]

Across time, numerous normative theories of accounting have been developed by a number of well-respected academics. However, they have typically failed to be embraced by the accounting profession, or to be mandated within financial accounting regulations. Relying in part on material introduced in Chapter 3, we consider why some proposed methods of accounting are ultimately accepted by the profession and/or accounting standard-setters, while many are rejected. We question whether the rejection is related to the *merit* of their arguments (or lack thereof), or due to the *political nature* of the standard-setting process wherein various vested interests and economic implications are considered. In this chapter we specifically consider various prescriptive theories of accounting that were advanced by various people on the basis that historical cost accounting has too many shortcomings, particularly in times of rising prices. Some of these shortcomings were summarized by the IASC in IAS 29:

> In a hyperinflationary economy, reporting of operating results and financial position in the local currency without restatement is not useful. Money loses purchasing power at such a rate that comparison of amounts from transactions and other events that have occurred at different times, even within the same accounting period, is misleading.

Limitations of historical cost accounting in times of rising prices

Over time, criticisms of historical cost accounting have been raised by a number of notable scholars, particularly in relation to its ability to provide useful information in times of rising prices.[2] For example, criticisms were raised by Sweeney (1964, originally published 1936), MacNeal (1970, originally published 1939), Canning (1929) and Paton (1922) in the 1920s and 1930s. From the 1950s the levels of criticism increased, with notable academics (such as Chambers, Sterling, Edwards and Bell) prescribing different models of accounting that they considered provided more useful information than was available under conventional historical cost accounting. Such work continued through to the early 1980s, but declined thereafter as levels of inflation throughout the world began to drop. Nevertheless, the debate continues.[3]

Historical cost accounting assumes that money holds a constant purchasing power. As Elliot (1986, p. 33) states:

> An implicit and troublesome assumption in the historical cost model is that the monetary unit is fixed and constant over time. However, there are three components of the modern economy that make this assumption less valid than it was at the time the model was developed.[4]
>
> One component is specific price-level changes, occasioned by such things as technological advances and shifts in consumer preferences; the second component is general price-level changes (inflation); and the third component is the fluctuation in exchange rates for currencies. Thus, the book value of a company, as reported in its financial statements, only coincidentally reflects the current value of assets.

Again it is emphasized that under our current accounting standards, many assets can or must be measured at historical cost (for example, inventory (or stock) must be measured at cost – or net realizable value if it is lower, and property, plant and equipment can be valued at cost where an entity has adopted the 'cost model' pursuant to IAS 16). While there was much criticism of historical cost accounting during the high inflation periods of the 1970s and 1980s, there were also many who supported historical cost accounting. The method of accounting predominantly used today is still based on historical cost accounting (although the conceptual frameworks we discuss in the next chapter, and some recent accounting standards, have introduced elements of current value – or fair value – measurements). Hence the accounting profession and reporting entities have tended to maintain the support for this historical cost approach.[5] The very fact that historical cost accounting has continued to be applied by business entities has been used by a number of academics to support its continued use (which in a sense is a form of *accounting-Darwinism* perspective – the view that those things that are most efficient and effective will survive over time). For example, Mautz (1973) states:

> Accounting is what it is today not so much because of the desire of accountants as because of the influence of businessmen. If those who make management and investment decisions had not found financial reports based on historical cost useful over the years, changes in accounting would long since have been made. [6, 7]

It has been argued (for example, Chambers, 1966) that historical cost accounting information suffers from problems of irrelevance in times of rising prices. That is, it is questioned whether it is useful to be informed that something cost a particular amount many years ago when its current value (as perhaps reflected by its replacement cost, or current market value) might be considerably different. It has also been argued that there is a real problem of additivity. At issue is whether it is really logical to add together assets acquired in different periods when those assets were acquired with euros of different purchasing power. [8]

In a number of countries, organizations are permitted to revalue their noncurrent assets. What often happens, however, is that different assets are revalued in different periods (with the euro having different purchasing power in each period), yet the revalued assets might all be added together, along with assets that have continued to be valued at cost, for the purposes of balance sheet disclosure. [9]

There is also an argument that methods of accounting that do not take account of changing prices, such as historical cost accounting, can tend to overstate profits in times of rising prices, and that distribution to shareholders of historical cost profits can actually lead to an erosion of operating capacity. For example, assume that a company commenced operations at the beginning of the year 2007 with €100,000 in stock (or inventory) made up of 20,000 units at €5.00 each. If at the end of the year all the stock had been sold, there were assets (cash) of €120,000, and throughout the year there had been no contributions from owners, no borrowings, and no distributions to owners, then profit under an historical cost system would be €20,000. If the entire profit of €20,000 was distributed to owners in the form of dividends, then the financial capital would be the same as it was at the beginning of the year. Financial capital would remain intact. [10]

However, if prices had increased throughout the period, then the actual operating capacity of the entity may not have remained intact. Let us assume that the company referred to above wishes to acquire another 20,000 units of stock after it has paid €20,000 in dividends, but finds that the financial year-end replacement cost has increased to €5.40 per unit. The company will only be able to acquire 18,518 units with the €100,000 it still has available. By distributing its total historical cost profit of €20,000, with no adjustments being made for rising prices, the company's ability to acquire goods and services has fallen from one period to the next. Some advocates of alternative approaches to accounting would prescribe that the profit of the period is more accurately recorded as €120,000 less 20,000 units at

€5.40 per unit which then equals €12,000. That is, if €12,000 is distributed to owners in dividends, the company can still buy the same amount of stock (20,000 units) as it had at the beginning of the period – its purchasing power remains intact.[11]

In relation to the treatment of changing prices we can usefully, and briefly, consider IAS 41 'Agriculture'. IAS 41 provides the measurement rules for biological assets (for example, for grape vines or cattle). The accounting standard requires that changes in the fair value of biological assets from period to period be treated as part of the period's profit or loss. In the development of the accounting standard there were arguments by some researchers (Roberts *et al.*, 1995) that the increases in fair value associated with changing prices should be differentiated from changes in fair value that are due to physical changes (for example, changes in the size or number of the biological assets). The argument was that only the physical changes should be treated as part of profit or loss. Although IAS 41 treats the total change in fair value as part of income it is interesting to note that IAS 41 'encourages' disclosures which differentiate between changes in fair values which are based upon price changes and those based upon physical changes. As paragraph 51 of IAS 41 states:

> The fair value less estimated point-of sale costs of a biological asset can change due to both physical changes and price changes in the market. Separate disclosure of physical and price changes is useful in appraising current period performance and future prospects, particularly when there is a production cycle of more than one year. In such cases, an entity is encouraged to disclose, by group or otherwise, the amount of the change in fair value less estimated point-of-sales costs included in profit or loss due to physical changes and due to price changes. This information is generally less useful when the production cycle is less than one year (for example, when raising chickens or growing cereal crops).

In relation to the above disclosure guidance it is interesting to consider why the regulators considered that financial statement users would benefit from separate disclosure of price changes and physical changes in relation to agricultural assets when similar suggestions are not provided within other accounting standards relating to other categories of assets.

Returning to the use of historical cost in general, it has also been argued that historical cost accounting distorts the current year's operating results by including in the current year's income holding gains that actually accrued in previous periods.[12] For example, some assets may have been acquired at a very low cost in a previous period (and perhaps in anticipation of future price increases pertaining to the assets), yet under historical cost accounting, the gains attributable to such actions will only be recognized in the subsequent periods when the assets are ultimately sold.

There is a generally accepted view that dividends should only be paid from income (and this is enshrined within the corporations laws of many countries).

However, one central issue relates to how we measure income. There are various definitions of income. One famous definition was provided by Hicks (1946), that is, that income is the maximum amount that can be consumed during a period while still expecting to be as well off at the end of the period as at the beginning of the period. Any consideration of 'well-offness' relies upon a notion of capital maintenance – but which one? Different notions will provide different perspectives of income.

There are a number of perspectives of capital maintenance. One version of capital maintenance is based on maintaining financial capital intact, and this is the position taken in historical cost accounting. Under historical cost accounting, dividends should normally only be paid to the extent that the payment will not erode financial capital, as illustrated in the previous example where €20,000 is distributed to owners in the form of dividends and no adjustment is made to take account of changes in prices and the related impact on the purchasing power of the entity.

Another perspective of capital maintenance is one that aims at maintaining purchasing power intact.[13] Under this perspective, historical cost accounts are adjusted for changes in the purchasing power of the euro (typically by use of the price index) which, in times of rising prices, will lead to a reduction in income relative to the income calculated under historical cost accounting. As an example, under general price level adjustment accounting (which we will consider more fully later in this chapter) the historical cost of an item is adjusted by multiplying it by the chosen price index at the end of the current period, divided by the price index at the time the asset was acquired. For example, if some land, which was sold for €1,200,000, was initially acquired for €1,000,000 when the price index was 100, and the price index at the end of the current period is 118 (reflecting an increase in prices of 18 per cent), then the adjusted cost would be €1,180,000. The adjusted profit would be €20,000 (compared to an historical cost profit of €200,000).[14] What should be realized is that under this approach to accounting where adjustments are made by way of a general price index, the value of €1,180,000 will not necessarily (except due to chance) reflect the current market value of the land. Various assets will be adjusted using the same general price index.

Use of actual current values (as opposed to adjustments to historical cost using price indices) is made under another approach to accounting which seeks to provide a measure of profits which, if distributed, maintains physical operating capital intact. This approach to accounting (which could be referred to as current cost accounting) relies upon the use of current values, which could be based on present values, entry prices (for example, replacement costs) or exit prices.

Reflective of the attention that the impact of inflation was having on financial statements, Exhibit 5.1 reproduces an article that appeared in *Accountancy* in January 1974 (a period of high inflation – and a time when debate in this area of accounting was widespread). The impact of high levels of inflation continued into the early 1980s in many western nations and its continued impact on accounting information is reflected in Exhibit 5.2, which reproduces a further *Accountancy* article, this time from 1980.

In the discussion that follows we consider a number of different approaches to undertaking financial accounting in times of rising prices. This discussion is by no means exhaustive but does give some insight into some of the various models that have been prescribed by various parties. [15]

Exhibit 5.1 An insight into some professional initiatives in the area of accounting for changing prices

---

C. P. P. accounting – an end or a beginning? ... There are two methods of inflation accounting, current purchasing power accounting and replacement cost accounting, and the relative merits of the two were elaborated and discussed throughout [a] day-long conference, organized and jointly sponsored by the English Institute [of Chartered Accountants] and the *Financial Times*. After an introduction by the chairman, Sir Ronald Leach CBE FCA (also chairman of the Accounting Standards Steering Committee), in which he outlined the compromise reached between the Government and the Institute on the production of a provisional [accounting] standard for inflation accounting, Chris Westwick presented his case for the use of CPP accounting. Current purchasing power accounting involves substitution of the current pound in the accounts, whereas replacement cost accounting utilises revaluation of the company's assets on the basis of their replacement cost. Mr Westwick felt CPP accounting would provide more information to the shareholder, being concerned with the maintenance of the shareholders' capital rather than the maintenance of physical assets (as in the RCA method), and therefore would be the more suitable technique to employ. He said that RCA placed too much importance on the business of the company, and not enough on making money for shareholders, also tending to ignore the gain on long-term money.

The second speaker was R. S. Allen, a director of J. A. Scrimgeour and a council member of the society of investment analysts; he likened CPP accounting to Esperanto – conceived in idealism but not practicable; he was, needless to say, putting the other point of view. Mr Allen favoured the RCA method as something within the shareholder's grasp, but also acceptable to management and appropriate, since inflation increases the value of assets.

Accountancy, January 1974, p. 6.

Exhibit 5.2 The need for accounting for changing prices

... as the president of the Institute [of Chartered Accountants in England and Wales], David Richards FCA, made clear at the annual dinner of the Nottingham Society of Chartered Accountants on 14 March ... [that] useful as it may be, 'historic cost accounting has an unfortunate tranquillising side-effect in not a few boardrooms. The historic cost figures often look good – on paper – and they tend to induce a boardroom euphoria. It is only when these figures are adjusted for the effects of a diminishing pound that the more realistic picture of past performance of the company begins to emerge.'

Arguably, current cost accounting, and a general awareness of the effects of inflation, are, if anything, more important to the small organization than to the large. After the best part of a decade of high-level inflation, there is little excuse for the medium to large company being unaware of the problem, or lacking trained accounting staff to highlight it.

Accountancy, April 1980, p. 1.

Current purchasing power accounting

Current purchasing power accounting (or, as it is also called, general purchasing power accounting; general price level accounting; or constant dollar/euro accounting) can be traced to the early works of such authors as Sweeney (1964, but originally published in 1936) and has since been favoured by a number of other researchers. Current purchasing power accounting (CPPA) has also, at various times, been supported by professional accounting bodies throughout the world (but more in the form of supplementary disclosures to accompany financial statements prepared under historical cost accounting principles). CPPA was developed on the basis of a view that in times of rising prices, if an entity were to distribute unadjusted profits based on historical costs, the result could be a reduction in the real value of an entity – that is, in real terms the entity could risk distributing part of its capital.

In considering the development of accounting for changing prices, the majority of research initially related to restating historical costs to account for changing prices by using historical cost accounts as the basis, but restating the accounts by use of particular price indices. This is the approach we consider in this section of the chapter. The literature then tended to move towards current cost accounting (which we consider later in this chapter), which changed the basis of measurement to current values as opposed to restated historical values. Consistent with this trend, the accounting profession initially tended to favour price-level-adjusted accounts (using indices), but then tended to switch to current cost accounting which required the entity to find the current values of the individual assets held by the reporting entity.[16,17]

CPPA, with its reliance on the use of indices, is generally accepted as being easier and less costly to apply than methods that rely upon current valuations of particular assets.[18] It was initially considered by some people that it would be too costly and perhaps unnecessary to attempt to find current values for all the individual assets. Rather than considering the price changes of specific goods and services, it was suggested on practical grounds that price indices be used.

Calculating indices

When applying general price level accounting, a price index must be applied. A price index is a weighted average of the current prices of goods and services relative to a weighted average of prices in a prior period, often referred to as a base period. Price indices may be broad or narrow – they may relate to changes in prices of particular assets within a particular industry (a specific price index), or they might be based on a broad cross-section of goods and services that are consumed (a general price index, such as the Consumer Price Index (CPI) in the UK).

But which price indices should be used? Should we use changes in a general price index (for example, as reflected in the UK by the CPI) or should we use an index that is more closely tied to the acquisition of production-related resources? There is no clear answer. From the shareholders' perspective the CPI may more accurately reflect their buying pattern – but prices will not change by the same amount for shareholders in different locations. Further, not everybody will have the same consumption patterns as is assumed when constructing a particular index. The choice of an index can be very subjective. Where CPPA has been recommended by particular professional bodies, CPI-type indices have been suggested.

Because CPPA relies upon the use of price indices, it is useful to consider how such indices are constructed. To explain one common way that indices may be constructed we can consider the following example which is consistent with how the UK CPI is determined. Let us assume that there are three types of commodities (A, B and C) that are consumed in the following base year quantities and at the following prices:

Year	Commodity A Price €	Quantity	Commodity B Price €	Quantity	Commodity C Price €	Quantity
Base year (2007)	10.00	100	15.00	200	20.00	250
2008	12.00		15.50		21.20	

From the above data we can see that prices have increased. The price index in the base year is frequently given a value of 100 and it is also frequently assumed that consumption quantities thereafter remain the same, such that the price index at the end of year 2008 would be calculated as:

$$100 \times \frac{(12.00 \times 100) + (15.50 \times 200) + (21.20 \times 250)}{(10.00 \times 100) + (15.00 \times 200) + (20.00 \times 250)}$$
$$= 106.67100$$

From the above calculations we can see that the prices within this particular 'bundle' of goods have been calculated as rising on average by 6.67 per cent from the year 2007 to the year 2008. The reciprocal of the price index represents the change in general purchasing power across the period. For example, if the index increased from 100 to 106.67, as in the above example, the purchasing power of the euro would be 93.75 per cent (100/106.67) of what it was previously. That is, the purchasing power of the euro has decreased.

Performing current purchase power adjustments

When applying CPPA, all adjustments are done at the end of the period, with the adjustments being applied to accounts prepared under the historical cost convention. When considering changes in the value of assets as a result of changes in the purchasing power of money (due to inflation) it is necessary to consider monetary assets and non-monetary assets separately. Monetary assets are those assets that remain fixed in terms of their monetary value, for example, cash and claims to a specified amount of cash (such as trade debtors and investments that are redeemable for a set amount of cash). These assets will not change their monetary value as a result of inflation. For example, if we are holding €10 in cash and there is rapid inflation, we will still be holding €10 in cash, but the asset's purchasing power will have decreased over time.

Non-monetary assets can be defined as those assets whose monetary equivalents will change over time as a result of inflation, and would include such things as plant and equipment and stock (or inventory). For example, stock may cost €100 at the beginning of the year, but the same stock could cost, say, €110 at the end of the year due to inflation. Relative to monetary assets, the purchasing power of non-monetary assets is assumed to remain relatively constant as a result of inflation.

Most liabilities are fixed in monetary terms (there is an obligation to pay a pre-specified amount of cash at a particular time in the future independent of the change in the purchasing power of the particular currency) and hence liabilities would typically be considered as monetary items (monetary liabilities). Non-monetary liabilities, on the other hand, although less common, would include obligations to transfer goods and services in the future, items which could change in terms of their monetary equivalents.

Net monetary assets would be defined as monetary assets less monetary liabilities. In times of inflation, holders of monetary assets will lose in real terms as a result of holding the monetary assets, as the assets will have less purchasing power at the end of the period relative to what they had at the beginning of the period (and the greater the level of general price increases, the greater the losses). Conversely, holders of monetary liabilities will gain, given that the amount they have to repay at the end of the period will be worth less (in terms of purchasing power) than it was at the beginning of the period.

Let us consider an example to demonstrate how gains and losses might be calculated on monetary items (and under CPPA, gains and losses will relate to net monetary assets rather than net non-monetary assets). Let us assume that an organization holds the following assets and liabilities at the beginning of the financial year:

	€
Current assets	
Cash	6,000
Stock	9,000
	15,000
Non-current assets	
Land	10,000
Total assets	25,000
Liabilities	
Bank loan	5,000
Owners' equity	20,000

Let us also assume that the general level of prices has increased 5 per cent since the beginning of the year and let us make a further simplifying assumption (which will be relaxed later) that the company did not trade during the year and that the same assets and liabilities were in place at the end of the year as at the beginning. Assuming that general prices, perhaps as reflected by changes in the CPI, have increased by 5 per cent, then the CPI-adjusted values would be:

	Unadjusted €	Price adjustment factor	Adjusted €
Current assets			
Cash	6,000		6,000
Stock	9,000	0.05	9,450
	15,000		15,450
Non-current assets			
Land	10,000	0.05	10,500
Total assets	25,000		25,950
Liabilities			
Bank loan	5,000		5,000
Owners' equity	20,000		20,950

Again, monetary items are not adjusted by the change in the particular price index because they will retain the same monetary value regardless of inflation. Under CPPA there is an assumption that the organization has not gained or lost in terms of the purchasing power attributed to the non-monetary assets, but rather, it will gain or lose in terms of purchasing power changes attributable to its holdings of the net monetary assets. In the above example, to be as 'well off' at the end of the period the entity would need €21,000 in net assets (which equals €20,000 × 1.05) to have the same purchasing power as it had one year earlier (given the general increase in prices of 5 per cent). In terms of end-of-year euros, in the above illustration the entity is €50 worse off in adjusted terms (it only has net assets with an adjusted value of €20,950, which does not have the same purchasing power as €20,000 did at the beginning of the period). As indicated above, this €50 loss relates to the holdings of net monetary assets and not to the holding of non-monetary assets, and is calculated as the balance of cash, less the balance of the bank loan, multiplied by the general price level increase. That is, (€6,000 – €5,000) × 0.05. If the monetary liabilities had exceeded the monetary assets throughout the period, a purchasing power gain would have been recorded. If the amount of monetary assets held was the same as the amount of monetary liabilities held, then no gain or loss would result.

Again, it is stressed that under current purchasing power accounting, no change in the purchasing power of the entity is assumed to arise as a result of holding non-monetary assets. Under general price level accounting, non-monetary assets are restated to current purchasing power and no gain or loss is recognized. Purchasing power losses arise only as a result of holding net monetary assets. As noted at paragraph 7 of Provisional Statement of Standard Accounting Practice 7 (PSSAP 7), issued in the UK in 1974:

> Holders of non-monetary assets are assumed neither to gain nor to lose purchasing power by reason only of inflation as changes in the prices of these assets will tend to compensate for any changes in the purchasing power of the pound.

An important issue to consider is how the purchasing power gains and losses should be treated for income purposes. Should they be treated as part of the period's profit or loss, or should they be transferred directly to a reserve? Generally, where this method of accounting has been recommended it has been advised that the gain or loss should be included in income. Such recommendations are found in the US Accounting Research Bulletin No. 6 (issued in 1961), the Accounting Principles Board (APB) statement No. 3 (issued in 1969 by the American Institute of Certified Public Accountants (AICPA)); in the Financial Accounting Standards Board's (FASB) Exposure Draft entitled 'Financial Reporting in Units of General Purchasing Power'; and within Provisional Statement of Accounting Practice No. 7 issued by the Accounting Standards Steering Committee (UK) in 1974.

As a further example of calculating gains or losses in purchasing power pertaining to monetary items, let us assume four quarters with the following CPI index figures:

At the beginning of the year	120
At the end of the first quarter	125
At the end of the second quarter	130
At the end of the third quarter	132
At the end of the fourth quarter	135

Let us also assume the following movements in net monetary assets (total monetary assets less total monetary liabilities):

Opening net monetary assets		100,000
Inflows:		
First quarter net inflow	20,000	
Second quarter net inflow	24,000	
Total inflows		44,000
Outflows:		
Third quarter net outflow	(17,000)	
Fourth quarter net outflow	(13,000)	
Total outflows		(30,000)
Closing net monetary assets		114,000

In terms of year-end purchasing power euros, the purchasing power gain or loss can be calculated as:

	Unadjusted euros		Price index		Adjusted euros
Opening net monetary assets	100,000	×	135/120	=	112,500
Inflows:					
First quarter net inflow	20,000	×	135/125	=	21,600
Second quarter net inflow	24,000	×	135/130	=	24,923
Outflows:					
Third quarter net outflow	(17,000)	×	135/132	=	(17,386)
Fourth quarter net outflow	(13,000)	×	135/135	=	(13,000)
Net monetary assets adjusted for changes in purchasing power					128,637

What the above calculation reflects is that to have the same purchasing power as when the particular transactions took place, then in terms of end-of-period euros, €128,637 in net monetary assets would need to be on hand at year end.[19] The actual balance on hand however is €114,000. Hence, there is a purchasing power loss of

€14,637 which under CPPA would be treated as an expense in the profit and loss account.

Let us now consider a more realistic example of CPPA adjustments. We will restate the financial statements to reflect purchasing power as at the end of the current financial year. Let us assume that the entity commenced operation on 1 January 2007 and the unadjusted balance sheet is as follows:

CPP plc balance sheet as at 1 January 2007

Current assets		
Cash	10,000	
Stock	25,000	35,000
Non-current assets		
Plant and equipment	90,000	
Land	75,000	165,000
Total assets		200,000
Current liabilities		
Bank overdraft	10,000	
Non-current liabilities		
Bank loan	10,000	
Total liabilities		20,000
Net assets		180,000
Represented by:		
Shareholders' funds		
Paid-up capital		180,000

As a result of its operations for the year, CPP plc had the historical cost income statement (profit and loss account) and balance sheet at year end as shown below:

CPP plc income statement for year ended 31 December 2007

Sales revenue		200,000
Less:		
Cost of goods sold		
Opening stock	25,000	
Purchases	110,000	
	135,000	
Closing stock	35,000	100,000
Gross profit		100,000
Other expenses		
Administrative expenses	9,000	
Interest expense	1,000	
Depreciation	9,000	19,000

Operating profit before tax		81,000
Tax		26,000
Operating profit after tax		55,000
Opening retained earnings		0
Dividends proposed		15,000
Closing retained earnings		40,000

CPP plc balance sheet as at 31 December 2007

Current assets		
Cash	100,000	
Trade debtors	20,000	
Stock	35,000	155,000
Non-current assets		
Plant and equipment	90,000	
Accumulated depreciation	(9,000)	
Land	75,000	156,000
Total assets		311,000
Current liabilities		
Bank overdraft	10,000	
Trade creditors	30,000	
Tax payable	26,000	
Provision for dividends	15,000	
	81,000	
Non-current liabilities		
Bank loan	10,000	
Total liabilities		91,000
Net assets		220,000
Represented by:		
Shareholders' funds		
Paid-up capital		180,000
Retained earnings		40,000
		220,000

As we have already stated, under CPPA, gains or losses only occur as a result of holding net monetary assets. To determine the gain or loss, we must consider the movements in the net monetary assets. For example, if the organization sold stock during the year, this will ultimately impact on cash. However, over time, the cash will be worth less in terms of its ability to acquire goods and services, hence there will be a purchasing power loss on the cash that was received during the year. Conversely, expenses will decrease cash during the year. In times of rising prices, more cash would be required to pay for the expense, hence in a sense we gain in relation to those expenses that were incurred earlier in the year (the logic being that if the expenses were incurred later in the year, more cash would have been required).

We must identify changes in net monetary assets from the beginning of the period until the end of the period.

Movement in net monetary assets from 1 January 2007 to 31 December 2007

	1 January 2007	31 December 2007
Monetary assets		
Cash	10,000	100,000
Trade debtors		20,000
	10,000	120,000
Less:		
Monetary liabilities		
Bank overdraft	10,000	10,000
Trade creditors		30,000
Tax payable		26,000
Provision for dividends		15,000
Bank loan	10,000	10,000
Net monetary assets	(10,000)	29,000

To determine any adjustments in CPP we must identify the reasons for the change in net monetary assets.

Reconciliation of opening and closing net monetary assets

Opening net monetary assets	(10,000)
Sales	200,000
Purchase of goods	(110,000)
Payment of interest	(1,000)
Payment of administrative expenses	(9,000)
Tax expense	(26,000)
Dividends	(15,000)
Closing net monetary assets	29,000

What we need to determine is whether, had all the transactions taken place at year end, the company would have had to transfer the same amount, measured in monetary terms, as it actually did. Any payments to outside parties throughout the period would have required a greater payment at the end of the period if the same items were to be transferred. Any receipts during the year will, however, be worth less in purchasing power.

To adjust for changes in purchasing power we need to have details about how prices have changed during the period, and we also need to know when the actual changes took place. We make the following assumptions:

* the interest expense and administrative expenses were incurred uniformly throughout the year;
* the tax liability did not arise until year end;
* the dividends were declared at the end of the year;
* the stock on hand at year end was acquired in the last quarter of the year;
* purchases of goods occurred uniformly throughout the year;
* sales occurred uniformly throughout the year.

We also assume that the price level index at the beginning of the year was 130. Subsequent indices were as follows:

31 December 2007	140
Average for the year	135
Average for first quarter	132
Average for second quarter	135
Average for third quarter	137
Average for fourth quarter	139

Rather than using price indices as at the particular dates of transactions (which would generally not be available) it is common to use averages for a particular period.

	Unadjusted	Index	Adjusted
Opening net monetary assets	(10,000)	140/130	(10,769)
Sales	200,000	140/135	207,407
Purchase of goods	(110,000)	140/135	(114,074)
Payment of interest	(1,000)	140/135	(1,037)
Payment of administrative expenses	(9,000)	140/135	(9,333)
Tax expense	(26,000)	140/140	(26,000)
Dividends	(15,000)	140/140	(15,000)
Closing net monetary assets	29,000		31,194

The difference between €29,000 and the amount of €31,194 represents a loss of €2,194. It is considered to be a loss, because to have the same purchasing power at year end as when the entity held the particular net monetary assets, the entity would need the adjusted amount of €31,194, rather than the actual amount of €29,000.

Price level adjusted income statement for year ended 31 December 2007

Sales revenue	200,000	140/135	207,407
Less:			
Cost of goods sold			
Opening stock	25,000	140/130	26,923
Purchases	110,000	140/135	114,074
	135,000		140,997
Closing stock	35,000	140/139	35,252
	100,000		105,745
Gross profit	100,000		101,662
Other expenses			
Administrative expenses	9,000	140/135	9,333
Interest expense	1,000	140/135	1,037
Depreciation	9,000	140/130	9,692
	19,000		20,062
Operating profit before tax	81,000		81,600
Tax	26,000	140/140	26,000
Operating profit after tax	55,000		55,600
Loss on purchasing power			2,194
			53,406
Opening retained earnings	0		0
Dividends proposed	15,000	140/140	15,000
Closing retained earnings	40,000		38,406

Price level adjusted balance sheet as at 31 December 2007

Current assets			
Cash	100,000		100,000
Trade debtors	20,000		20,000
Stock	35,000	140/139	35,252
Total current assets	155,000		155,252
Non-current assets			
Plant and equipment	90,000	140/130	96,923
Accumulated depreciation	(9,000)	140/130	(9,692)
Land	75,000	140/130	80,769
Total non-current assets	156,000		168,000
Total assets	311,000		323,252

Current liabilities

Bank overdraft	10,000		10,000
Trade creditors	30,000		30,000
Tax payable	26,000		26,000
Provision for dividends	15,000		15,000
Non-current liabilities			
Bank loan	10,000		10,000
Total liabilities	91,000		91,000
Net assets	220,000		232,252
Represented by:			
Shareholders' funds			
Paid-up capital	180,000	140/130	193,846
Retained earnings	40,000		38,406
	220,000		232,252

From the above balance sheet we can again emphasize that the non-monetary items are translated into euros of year-end purchasing power, whereas the monetary items are already stated in current purchasing power euros, and hence no changes are made to the reported balances of monetary assets.

One main strength of CPPA is its ease of application. The method relies on data that would already be available under historical cost accounting and does not require the reporting entity to incur the cost or effort involved in collecting data about the current values of the various non-monetary assets. CPI data would also be readily available. However, and as indicated previously, movements in the prices of goods and services included in a general price index might not be reflective of price movements involved in the goods and services involved in different industries. That is, different industries may be impacted differently by inflation.

Another possible limitation is that the information generated under CPPA might actually be confusing to users. They might consider that the adjusted amounts reflect the specific value of specific assets (and this is a criticism that can also be made of historical cost information). However, as the same index is used for all assets, this will rarely be the case. Another potential limitation that we consider at the end of the chapter is that various studies (which have looked at such things as movements in share prices around the time of disclosure of CPPA information) have failed to find much support for the view that the data generated under CPPA are relevant for decision making (the information when released caused little if any share price reaction).

Following the initial acceptance of CPPA in some countries in the 1970s, there was a move towards methods of accounting that used actual current values. We will now consider such approaches.

Current cost accounting

Current cost accounting (CCA) is one of the various alternatives to historical cost accounting that has tended to gain the most acceptance. Notable advocates of this approach have included Paton (1922), and Edwards and Bell (1961). Such authors decided to reject historical cost accounting and current purchasing power accounting in favour of a method that considered actual valuations. As we will see, unlike historical cost accounting, CCA differentiates between profits from trading, and those gains that result from holding an asset.

Holding gains can be considered as realized or unrealized. If a financial capital maintenance perspective is adopted with respect to the recognition of income, then holding gains or losses can be treated as income. Alternatively they can be treated as capital adjustments if a physical capital maintenance approach is adopted.[20] Some versions of CCA, such as that proposed by Edwards and Bell (1961), adopt a physical capital maintenance approach to income recognition. In this approach, which determines valuations on the basis of replacement costs,[21] operating income represents realized revenues, less the replacement cost of the assets in question. It is considered that this generates a measure of income which represents the maximum amount that can be distributed, while maintaining operating capacity intact. For example, assume that an entity acquired 150 items of stock at a cost of €10.00 each and sold 100 of the items for €15 each when the replacement cost to the entity was €12 each. We will also assume that the replacement cost of the 50 remaining items of stock at year end was €14. Under the Edwards and Bell approach the operating profit that would be available for dividends would be €300 which is $100 \times (€15 - €12)$. There would be a realized holding gain on the goods that were sold, which would amount to $100 \times (€12 - €10)$, or €200, and there would be an unrealized holding gain in relation to closing stock of $50 \times (€14 - €10)$, or €200. Neither the realized nor the unrealized holding gain would be considered to be available for dividend distribution.[22]

In undertaking current cost accounting, adjustments are usually made at year end using the historical cost accounts as the basis of adjustments. If we adopt the Edwards and Bell approach to profit calculation, operating profit is derived after ensuring that the operating capacity of the organization is maintained intact. Edwards and Bell believe operating profit is best calculated by using replacement costs.[23, 24] As noted above, in calculating operating profit, gains that accrue from holding an asset (holding gains) are excluded and are not made available for dividends – although they are included when calculating what is referred to as business profit. For example, if an entity acquired goods for €20 and sold them for €30, then business profit would be €10, meaning that €10 could be distributed and still leave financial capital intact. But if at the time the goods were sold their replacement cost to the entity was €23, then €3 would be considered a holding gain, and to maintain physical operating capacity, only €7 could be distributed – current cost operating profit would be €7. No adjustment is made to sales revenue.

In relation to non-current assets, for the purposes of determining current cost operating profit, depreciation is based on the replacement cost of the asset. For example, if an item of machinery was acquired in 2006 for €100,000 and had a projected life of 10 years and no salvage value, then assuming the straight-line method of depreciation is used, its depreciation expense under historical cost accounting would be €10,000 per year. If at the end of 2007 its replacement cost had increased to €120,000, then under current cost accounting a further €2,000 would be deducted to determine current cost operating profit. However, this €2,000 would be treated as a realized cost saving (because historical cost profits would have been lower if the entity had not already acquired the asset) and would be recognized in business profit (it would be added back below operating profit) and the other €18,000 would be treated as an unrealized cost saving and would also be included in business profit. As with CPPA, no restatement of monetary assets is required as they are already recorded in current euros and hence in terms of end-of-period purchasing power euros.

As an example of one version of CCA (consistent with the Edwards and Bell proposals) let us consider the following example. CCA plc's balance sheet at the commencement of the year is provided below. This is assumed to be the first year of CCA plc's operations.

CCA plc balance sheet as at 1 January 2007

Current assets		
Cash	10,000	
Stock	25,000	35,000
Non-current assets		
Plant and equipment	90,000	
Land	75,000	165,000
Total assets		200,000
Current liabilities		
Bank overdraft	10,000	
Non-current liabilities		
Bank loan	10,000	
Total liabilities		20,000
Net assets		180,000
Represented by:		
Shareholders' funds		
Paid-up capital		180,000

The unadjusted income statement and balance sheet for CCA plc after one year's operations are provided below.

CCA plc income statement for year ended 31 December 2007

Sales revenue		200,000
Less:		
Cost of goods sold		
Opening stock	25,000	
Purchases	110,000	
	135,000	
Closing stock	35,000	100,000
Gross profit		100,000
Other expenses		
Administrative expenses	9,000	
Interest expense	1,000	
Depreciation	9,000	19,000
Operating profit before tax		81,000
Tax		26,000
Operating profit after tax		55,000
Opening retained earnings		0
Dividends proposed		15,000
Closing retained earnings		40,000

CCA plc balance sheet as at 31 December 2007

Current assets		
Cash	100,000	
Trade debtors	20,000	
Stock	35,000	155,000
Non-current assets		
Plant and equipment	90,000	
Accumulated depreciation	(9,000)	
Land	75,000	156,000
Total assets		311,000
Current liabilities		
Bank overdraft	10,000	
Trade creditors	30,000	
Tax payable	26,000	
Provision for dividends	15,000	
	81,000	

Non-current liabilities

Bank loan	10,000	
Total liabilities		91,000
Net assets		220,000

Represented by:
Shareholders' funds

Paid-up capital		180,000
Retained earnings		40,000
		220,000

We will assume that the stock on hand at year end comprised 3,500 units that cost €10 per unit. The replacement cost at year end was €11.00 per unit. We will also assume that the replacement cost of the units actually sold during the year was €105,000 (as opposed to the historical cost of €100,000) and that the year-end replacement cost of the plant and equipment increased to €115,000.

CCA plc income statement for year ended 31 December 2007
Adjusted by application of current cost accounting

Sales revenue		200,000
Less:		
Cost of goods sold		105,000
		95,000
Other expenses		
Administrative expenses	9,000	
Interest expense	1,000	
Tax	26,000	
Depreciation (€115,000 × 1/10)	11,500	47,500
Current cost operating profit		47,500
Realized savings		
Savings related to stock actually sold		5,000
Savings related to depreciation actually incurred		
[(115,000 − 90,000) × 1/10]		2,500
Historical cost profit		55,000
Unrealized savings		
Gains on holding stock – yet to be realized		3,500
Gains on holding plant and machinery – not yet realized		
through the process of depreciation [(115,000 − 90,000) × 9/10)]		22,500
Business profit		81,000
Opening retained earnings		0
Dividends proposed		15,000
Closing retained earnings		66,000

CCA plc balance sheet as at 31 December 2007
Adjusted by application of current cost accounting

Current assets		
Cash	100,000	
Trade debtors	20,000	
Stock (3,500 × €11.00)	38,500	158,500
Non-current assets		
Plant and equipment	115,000	
Accumulated depreciation	(11,500)	
Land	75,000	178,500
Total assets		337,000
Current liabilities		
Bank overdraft	10,000	
Trade creditors	30,000	
Tax payable	26,000	
Provision for dividends	15,000	
	81,000	
Non-current liabilities		
Bank loan	10,000	
Total liabilities		91,000
Net assets		246,000
Represented by:		
Shareholders' funds		
Paid-up capital		180,000
Retained earnings		66,000
		246,000

Consistent with the CCA model prescribed by Edwards and Bell, all non-monetary assets have to be adjusted to their respective replacement costs. Unlike historical cost accounting, there is no need for stock cost flow assumptions (such as last-in-first-out; first-in-first-out; weighted average). Business profit shows how the entity has gained in financial terms from the increase in cost of its resources – something typically ignored by historical cost accounting. In the above illustration, and consistent with a number of versions of CCA, no adjustments have been made for changes in the purchasing power of net monetary assets (in contrast with CPPA).[25]

The current cost operating profit before holding gains and losses, and the realized holding gains, are both tied to the notion of realization, and hence the sum of the two equates to historical cost profit.

Differentiating operating profit from holding gains and losses (both realized and unrealized) has been claimed to enhance the usefulness of the information being provided. Holding gains are deemed to be different to trading income as they are due to market-wide movements, most of which are beyond the control of management. Edwards and Bell (1961, p. 73) state:

> These two kinds of gains are often the result of quite different decisions. The business firm usually has considerable freedom in deciding what quantities of assets to hold over time at any or all stages of the production process and what quantity of assets to commit to the production process itself ... . The difference between the forces motivating the business firm to make profit by one means rather than by another and the difference between the events on which the two methods of making profit depend require that the two kinds of gain be separated if the two types of decisions involved are to be meaningfully evaluated.

As with CPPA, the CCA model described above has been identified as having a number of strengths and weaknesses. Some of the criticisms relate to its reliance on replacement values. The CCA model we have just described uses replacement values, but what is the rationale for replacement cost? Perhaps it is a reflection of the 'real' value of the particular asset. If the market is prepared to pay the replacement cost, and if we assume economic rationality, then the amount paid must be a reflection of the returns it is expected to generate. However, it might not be worth that amount (the replacement cost) to all firms – some firms might not elect to replace a given asset if they have an option. Further, past costs are sunk costs and if the entity were required to acquire new plant, it might find it more efficient and less costly to acquire different types of assets. If they do buy it, then this might reflect that it is actually worth much more. Further, replacement cost does not reflect what it would be worth if the firm decided to sell it.

As was indicated previously, it has been argued that separating holding gains and losses from other results provides a better insight into management performance, as such gains and losses are due to impacts generated outside the organization – however, this can be criticized on the basis that acquiring assets in advance of price movements might also be part of efficient operations.

Another potential limitation of CCA is that it is often difficult to determine replacement costs. The approach also suffers from the criticism that allocating replacement cost via depreciation is still arbitrary, just as it is with historical cost accounting.

An advantage of CCA is better comparability of various entities' performance, as one entity's profits are not higher simply because they bought assets years earlier and therefore would have generated lower depreciation under historical cost accounting.

Chambers, an advocate of current cost accounting based on exit values, was particularly critical of the Edwards and Bell model of accounting. He states (1995, p. 82) that:

> In the context of judgement of the past and decision making for the future, the products of current value accounting of the Edwards and Bell variety are irrelevant and misleading.

We now consider the alternative accounting model prescribed by Chambers and a number of others – a model that relies upon the use of *exit values*.

Exit price accounting: the case of Chambers' continuously contemporary accounting

Exit price accounting has been proposed by researchers such as MacNeal (1970), Sterling (1970) and Chambers (1955). It is a form of current cost accounting which is based on valuing assets at their net selling prices (exit prices) at the balance sheet date and on the basis of orderly sales. Chambers coined the term current cash equivalent to refer to the cash that an entity would expect to receive through the orderly sale of an asset, and he had the view that information about current cash equivalents was fundamental to effective decision making. He labelled his method of accounting continuously contemporary accounting, or CoCoA.

Although he generated some much cited research throughout the 1950s (such as Chambers, 1955) a great deal of his work culminated in 1966 in the publication of *Accounting, Evaluation and Economic Behavior*. This document stressed that the key information for economic decision making relates to capacity to adapt – a function of current cash equivalents. The statement of financial position (balance sheet) is considered to be the prime financial statement and should show the net selling prices of the entity's assets. Profit would directly relate to changes in adaptive capital, with adaptive capital reflected by the total exit values of the entity's assets.

As indicated previously in this chapter, how one calculates income is based, in part, on how one defines wealth. According to Sterling, an advocate of exit price accounting, (1970, p. 189).

> The present [selling] price is the proper and correct valuation coefficient for the measurement of wealth at a point in time and income is the difference between dated wealths so calculated.

Consistent with the views of Sterling, Chambers (1966, p. 91) states:

> At any *present time*, all past prices are simply a matter of history. Only present prices have any bearing on the choice of an action. The price of a good ten years ago has no more relation to this question than the hypothetical price 20 years hence. As individual prices may change even over an interval when the purchasing power of money does not, and as the general purchasing power of money may change even though some individual prices do not, no useful inference may be drawn from past prices which has a necessary bearing on present capacity to operate in a market. Every measurement of a financial property for the purpose of choosing a course of action – to buy, to hold, to sell – is a measurement at a point in time, in the circumstances of the time, and in the units of currency at that time, even if the measurement process itself takes some time.
>
> Excluding all past prices, there are two prices which could be used to measure the monetary equivalent of any non-monetary good in possession: the buying price and the

selling price. But the buying price, or replace price, does not indicate capacity, on the basis of present holdings, to go into a market with cash for the purpose of adapting oneself to contemporary conditions, whereas the selling price does. We propose, therefore, that the single financial property which is uniformly relevant at a point of time for all possible future actions in markets is the market selling price or realizable price of any goods held. Realizable price may be described as *current cash equivalent*. What men wish to know, for the purpose of adaptation, is the numerosity of the money tokens which could be substituted for particular objects and for collections of objects if money is required beyond the amount which one already holds. [26]

We can see that Chambers has made a judgement about what people need in terms of information. Like authors such as Edwards and Bell, and unlike some of the earlier work which documented existing accounting practices to identify particular principles and postulates (descriptive research),[27] Chambers set out to develop what he considered was a superior model of accounting – a model that represented quite a dramatic change from existing practice. We call this prescriptive or normative research. The research typically highlighted the limitations of historical cost accounting and then proposed an alternative on the basis that it would enable better decision making. Chambers adopts a decision usefulness approach and within this approach he adopts a decision models perspective.[28]

The Chambers' approach is focused on new opportunities – the ability or capacity of the entity to adapt to changing circumstances and the most important item of information to evaluate future decisions is, according to Chambers, current cash equivalents. Chambers makes an assumption about the objective of accounting – to guide future actions. Capacity to adapt is the key and the capacity to adapt to changing circumstances is dependent upon the current cash equivalents of the assets on hand. The higher the current market value of the entity's assets the greater is the ability of the organization to adapt to changing circumstances.

As stated previously, in the Chambers' model, profit is directly tied to the increase (or decrease) in the current net selling prices of the entity's assets. No distinction is drawn between realized and unrealized gains. Unlike some other models of accounting, all gains are treated as part of profit. Profit is that amount that can be distributed, while maintaining the entity's adaptive ability (adaptive capital). CoCoA abandons notions of realization in terms of recognizing revenue, and hence, revenue recognition points' change relative to historical cost accounting. Rather than relying on sales, revenues are recognized at such points as production or purchase.

Unlike the Edwards and Bell approach to current cost accounting, within CoCoA there is an adjustment to take account of changes in general purchasing power, which is referred to as a capital maintenance adjustment. The capital maintenance adjustment also forms part of the period's income, with a corresponding credit to a capital maintenance reserve (which forms part of owners' equity). In determining the capital maintenance adjustment, the opening residual equity of the entity (that is, the net assets) is multiplied by the proportionate change in the general price index from the beginning of the period to the end of the financial period. As an example, if opening residual equity was €5,000,000 and the price index increased from 140 to 148, then the capital maintenance adjustment (in the case of increasing prices, an expense) would be calculated as €5,000,000 × 8/140 = €285,714. According to Chambers (1995, p. 86):

> Deduction of that amount, a capital maintenance or inflation adjustment, from the nominal difference between opening and closing capitals, would give the net increment in purchasing power, the real income, of a period. The inflation adjustment would automatically cover gains and losses in purchasing power from net holdings of money and money's worth. Net real income would then be the algebraic sum of (a) net realized revenues based on consummated transactions, or net cash flows, (b) the aggregate of price variation adjustments, the unrealized changes in value of assets on hand at balance date, and (c) the inflation adjustment. The amount of the inflation adjustment would be added proportionately to the opening balances of contributed capital and undivided surplus, giving closing amounts in units of up to date purchasing power.

We can now summarize some of the above points by referring to Exhibit 5.3 below, which is a reproduction of an article that appeared in *The Australian Financial Review* (10 May 1973). It reported some of Chambers' concerns with regards to historical cost accounting.

Exhibit 5.3 Some views of Professor Raymond Chambers

Where company reports fail – Prof Chambers

Financial reports of companies generally failed to give a fair idea of their financial positions and profits, Professor R. J. Chambers, professor of accounting at the University of Sydney, said last night.

He called for amplification of the law on company reporting to ensure that balance sheets recognize changes in the prices of specific assets and profit and loss accounts reflect changes in the general purchasing power of money.

The accounting rules used were so different in effect that comparisons between companies were often quite misleading.

These rules had been debated for years among accountants but never yet had accountants settled on rules which gave consistent and up-to-date information year by year.

Addressing the university's Pacioli Society, Professor Chambers outlined specific amendments to the Companies Acts which are contained in his new book, 'Securities and Obscurities'.

Professor Chambers' amendment to the laws governing balance sheet reporting was that no balance sheet should be deemed to give a true and fair view of the state of affairs of a company unless the amounts shown for the several assets were the best possible approximations of the net selling prices in the ordinary course of business.

Debts receivable should be the best possible approximations to the amounts expected at the date of the balance sheet to be receivable or recoverable.

On the profit and loss account, Professor Chambers urged that it be deemed to give a true and fair view only if the profit or loss was calculated so as to include changes during the year in the net selling prices of assets and the effects during the year of changes in the purchasing power of the unit of account as specified in the Schedule of the Act.

Professor Chambers said thousands of shareholders had lost millions of dollars on security investments made on the basis of out-of-date information or on fictions which were reported as facts.

The Australian Financial Review, 10 May 1973, p. 30.

As a simple illustration of CoCoA, consider the following information. Assume that Cocoa plc had the following balance sheets as at 30 June 2007, one compiled using historical cost accounting and the other using CoCoA.

Cocoa plc Historical cost balance sheet as at 30 June 2007		Cocoa plc CoCoA balance sheet as at 30 June 2007	
Assets		**Assets**	
Cash	6,000	Cash	6,000
Stock	10,000	Stock	16,000
Plant and equipment	24,000	Plant and equipment	28,000
Total assets	40,000	**Total assets**	50,000
Liabilities		**Liabilities**	
Bank loan	10,000	Bank loan	10,000
Net assets	30,000	**Net assets**	40,000
Represented by: **Shareholders' funds**		Represented by: **Shareholders' funds**	
Paid-up capital	10,000	Paid-up capital	10,000
Retained earnings	20,000	Retained earnings	22,000
		Capital maintenance reserve	8,000
	30,000		40,000

We assume that in the financial year ending on 30 June 2008, all the opening stock was sold for €16,000 and the same quantity of stock was reacquired at a cost of €11,000 (and which had a retail price of €18,000). There were salaries of €2,000 and historical cost depreciation was based on 5 per cent of book value of plant and equipment. Prices rose generally throughout the period by 10 per cent and the net market value of the plant and equipment was assessed as €29,000.

The income determined for the year ended 30 June 2008 under both historical cost accounting and CoCoA can be calculated as follows:

Cocoa plc **Historical cost profit and loss statement for year ended 30 June 2008**		Cocoa plc **CoCoA profit and loss statement for year ended 30 June 2008**	
Sales	16,000	Sale price of stock	18,000
Cost of goods sold	(10,000)	Cost of stock	11,000
Gross margin	6,000	**Trading income**	7,000
Salaries expense	(2,000)	Salaries expense	(2,000)
Depreciation	(1,200)	Increase in exit value of plant	1,000
		Capital maintenance adjustment (40,000 × 0.10)	(4,000)
Net profit	2,800	**Net profit**	2,000
Opening retained earnings	20,000	Opening retained earnings	22,000
Closing retained earnings	22,800	**Closing retained earnings**	24,000

Cocoa plc **Historical cost balance sheet as at 30 June 2008**		Cocoa plc **CoCoA balance sheet as at 30 June 2008**	
Assets		**Assets**	
Cash	9,000	Cash	9,000
Stock	11,000	Stock	18,000
Plant and equipment (net)	22,800	Plant and equipment	29,000
Total assets	42,800	**Total assets**	56,000
Liabilities		**Liabilities**	
Bank loan	10,000	Bank loan	10,000
Net assets	32,800	**Net assets**	46,000
Represented by: **Shareholders' funds**		Represented by: **Shareholders' funds**	
Paid-up capital	10,000	Paid-up capital	10,000
Retained earnings	22,800	Retained earnings	24,000
		Capital maintenance reserve	12,000
	32,800		46,000

What must be remembered is that under CoCoA, when the stock recorded above is sold for €18,000, no profit or loss will be recognized. Such gain was recognized when the stock was purchased, with the gain being the difference between the expected retail price (net of related expenses) and the cost to Cocoa Ltd. Hence, it is again emphasized, CoCoA involves a fundamental shift in revenue recognition principles compared to historical cost accounting.

As with other methods of accounting, a number of strengths and weaknesses have been associated with CoCoA. Considering the strengths, advocates of CoCoA have argued that by using one method of valuation for all assets (exit value) the resulting numbers can logically be added together (this is often referred to as 'additivity').[29] When CoCoA is adopted there is also no need for arbitrary cost allocations for depreciation as depreciation will be based on movements in exit price.

Considering possible limitations, CoCoA has never gained widespread acceptance, despite being supported by a small number of widely respected academics (there was more support for replacement costs). Also, if CoCoA was implemented it would involve a fundamental and major shift in financial accounting (for example, including major shifts in revenue recognition points and major adjustments to asset valuations) and this in itself could lead to many unacceptable social and environmental consequences.

The relevance of exit prices has also been questioned, particularly if we do not expect to sell assets (just as we questioned the relevance of replacement costs if we do not expect to replace the asset). Further, under CoCoA, assets of a specialized nature (such as a blast furnace) are considered to have no value because they cannot be separately disposed of. This is an assertion that is often challenged because it ignores the 'value in use' of an asset.[30] Further, is it appropriate to value all assets on the basis of their exit values if the entity is considered to be a going concern? Determination of exit values can also be expected to introduce a degree of subjectivity into the accounts (relative to historical cost), particularly if the assets are unique.

CoCoA also requires assets to be valued separately with regard to their current cash equivalents, rather than as a bundle of assets. Hence, CoCoA would not recognize goodwill as an asset because it cannot be sold separately. Evidence shows that the value of assets sold together can be very different to the total amount that would be received if they were sold individually (Larson and Schattke, 1966).

Just as Chambers was critical of the Edwards and Bell model, Edwards and Bell were also critical of the Chambers approach. For example, Edwards (1975, p. 238) states:

> I am not convinced of the merit of adopting, as a normal basis for asset valuation in the going concern, exit prices in buyer markets. These are unusual values suitable for unusual situations. I would not object in principle to keeping track of such exit prices at all times and, as Solomons (1966) has suggested, substituting them for entry values when

they are the lesser of the two and the firm has taken a definite decision not to replace the asset, or even the function it performs.

The demand for price adjusted accounting information

One research method often used to assess the usefulness of particular disclosures is to look for a stock market reaction around the time of the release of the information, the rationale being that if share prices react to the disclosures, then such disclosures must have information content. That is, the information impacts on the decisions made by individuals participating in the capital market. A number of studies have looked at the stock market reaction to current cost and CPPA information. Results are inconclusive, with studies such as Ro (1980, 1981), Beaver, Christie and Griffin (1980), Gheyara and Boatsman (1980), Beaver and Landsman (1987), Murdoch (1986), Schaefer (1984), Dyckman (1969), Morris (1975), and Peterson (1975) finding limited evidence of any price changes around the time of disclosure of current cost information. (However Lobo and Song (1989) and Bublitz, Freka and McKeown (1985) provide limited evidence that there is information content in current cost disclosures.)

While the majority of share price studies show little or no reaction to price adjusted accounting information, it is possible that the failure to find a significant share price reaction might have been due to limitations in the research methods used. For example, there could have been other information released around the time of the release of the CCA/CPPA information. However, with the weight of research that indicates little or no reaction by the share market, we are probably on safe ground to believe that the market does not value such information when disclosed within the annual report. Of course there are a number of issues in why the capital market might not react to such information. Perhaps individuals or organizations are able to obtain this information from sources other than corporate annual reports, and hence, as the market is already aware of the information, no reaction would then be expected when the annual reports are released.

Apart from analysing share price reactions, another way to investigate the apparent usefulness of particular information is to undertake surveys. Surveys of managers (for example Ferguson and Wines, 1986) have indicated limited corporate support for current cost accounting, with managers citing such issues as the expense, limited benefits from disclosure, and lack of agreement as to the appropriate approach.

In the United States, and in relation to the relevance of FASB Statement No. 33 (which required a mixture of CCA and CPPA information), Elliot (1986, p. 33) states:

> FASB Statement No. 33 requires the disclosure of value information on one or two bases, either price level adjusted or current cost. Surveys taken since this rule became effective

suggest that users do not find the information helpful, don't use it, and they say it doesn't tell them anything they didn't already know. Preparers of the information complain that it is a nuisance to assemble.

Given the above results, we can perhaps say that, in general, there is limited evidence to support the view that the methods used to account for changing prices have been deemed to be successful in providing information of relevance to financial statement users. This is an interesting outcome, particularly given that many organizations over time have elected to provide CCA/CPPA information in their annual reports even when there was no requirement to do so, and also given that many organizations have actively lobbied for or against the particular methods of accounting. Adopting the method for disclosure purposes, or lobbying for it, implies that corporate management, at least, considered that the information was relevant and likely to impact on behaviour – a view at odds with some of the surveys and share price studies reported earlier.

In relation to research that has attempted to analyse the motivations underlying the corporate adoption of alternative accounting methods, an influential paper was Watts and Zimmerman (1978). That paper is generally considered to be one of the most important papers in the development of Positive Accounting Theory (which we consider in Chapter 7). The authors investigated the lobbying positions taken by corporate managers with respect to the FASB's 1974 Discussion Memorandum on general price level accounting (current purchasing power accounting). As we know from material presented in this chapter, if general price level accounting were introduced, then in times of rising prices, reported profits would be reduced relative to profits reported under historical cost conventions. The reduction in profits would be due to such effects as higher depreciation, and purchasing power losses due to holding net monetary assets.

Watts and Zimmerman (1978) proposed that the political process was a major factor in explaining which corporate managers were more likely to favour or oppose the introduction of general price level accounting. The political process itself is seen as a competition for wealth transfers. For example, some groups may lobby government to transfer wealth away from particular companies or industries (for example, through increased taxes, decreased tariff support, decreased subsidies, increases in award wages, more stringent licensing arrangements), and towards other organizations or groups otherwise considered to be poorly treated. Apart from government, groups such as consumer groups (perhaps through product boycotts), employee groups (through wage demands or strikes), community interest groups (through impeding operations or lobbying government), can act to transfer wealth away from organizations through political processes.

The perspective of Watts and Zimmerman was that entities deemed to be politically visible are more likely to favour methods of accounting that allow them to reduce their reported profits. High profitability itself was considered to be one attribute that could lead to the unwanted (and perhaps, costly) attention and scrutiny of particular corporations.

The corporate lobbying positions in the submissions made to the FASB are explained by Watts and Zimmerman on the basis of self-interest considerations (rather than any consideration of such issues as the 'public interest').[31] The study suggests that large firms (and large firms are considered to be more politically sensitive) favour general price level accounting because it enables them to report lower profits.[32, 33]

Other research has also shown that companies might support CCA for the political benefits it provides. In times of rising prices, the adoption of current cost accounting (as with general price level accounting) can lead to reduced profits. In a New Zealand study, Wong (1988) investigated the accounting practices of New Zealand companies between 1977 and 1981 and found that corporations that adopted CCA had higher effective tax rates and larger market concentration ratios than entities that did not adopt CCA, both variables being suggestive of political visibility. In a UK study, Sutton (1988) found that politically sensitive companies were more likely to lobby in favour of current cost accounting. Sutton investigated lobbying submissions made in the UK in relation to an exposure draft of a proposed accounting standard that recommended the disclosure of CCA information. Applying a Positive Accounting Theory perspective he found support for a view that organizations that considered they would benefit from the requirement tended to lobby in support of it. Those expected to benefit were:

- capital intensive firms because it was expected that the adoption of CCA would lead to decreased profits (due to higher depreciation) and this would be particularly beneficial if the method was accepted for the purposes of taxation; and
- politically sensitive firms, as it would allow them to show reduced profits.

Examining possible perceived political 'benefits' of inflation adjusted accounting information from a different perspective, Broadbent and Laughlin (2005) draw on debates in the UK in the 1970s to argue that the then British Government considered CPP as likely to produce undesirable economic impacts compared to CCA. The main issue was that the Government believed CPP accounts could foster divestment at a time when the UK economy needed investment. In support of their argument, Broadbent and Laughlin (2005) quote Bryer and Brignall (1985, p. 32) who state that in launching a governmental committee of enquiry to examine inflation accounting a government minister had commented that:

> inflation accounting ... involved issues much broader than pure accounting matters. The committee would 'take into account a broad range of issues including the implications for investment and efficiency; allocation of resources through the capital market; the need to restrain inflation in the UK'.[34]

Professional support for various approaches to accounting for changing prices

Over time, varying levels of support have been given to different approaches to accounting in times of rising prices. Current purchasing power accounting was generally favoured by accounting standard-setters from the 1960s to the mid-1970s, with a number of countries, including the USA, the UK, Canada, Australia, New Zealand, Ireland, Argentina, Chile and Mexico, issuing documents that supported the approach. For example, in the USA the American Institute of Certified Public Accountants (AICPA) supported general price-level restatement in Accounting Research Study No. 6 released in 1961. The Accounting Principles Board also supported the practice in Statement No. 3. Early in its existence, the FASB also issued an exposure draft supporting the use of general purchasing power – 'Financial Reporting in Units of General Purchasing Power' – which required CPPA to be disclosed as supplementary information.

From about 1975, preference tended to shift to current cost accounting. In 1976 the SEC released ASR 190 which required certain large organizations to provide supplementary information about 'the estimated current replacement cost of inventories and productive capacity at the end of the fiscal year for which a balance sheet is required and the approximate amount of cost of sales and depreciation based on replacement cost for the two most recent full fiscal years'. In Australia, a Statement of Accounting Practice (SAP 1) entitled Current Cost Accounting was issued in 1983. Although not mandatory, SAP 1 recommended that reporting entities provide supplementary current cost accounting information. In the United Kingdom, support for current cost accounting was demonstrated by the Sandilands Committee (a government committee) in 1975. In 1980 the Accounting Standards Committee (UK) issued SSAP 16 which required supplementary disclosure of current cost data (SSAP 16 was withdrawn in 1985).

In the late 1970s and early 1980s many accounting standard-setters issued recommendations that favoured disclosure based upon a mixture of current purchasing power accounting and current cost accounting. Such 'mixed' reporting recommendations were released in the USA, the UK, Canada, Australia, New Zealand, Ireland, West Germany and Mexico. For example, in 1979 the FASB released SFAS 33 which required a mixture of information, including:

◆ purchasing power gains and losses on net monetary assets;

◆ income determined on a current cost basis; and

◆ current costs of year-end stock and property plant and equipment.

Around the mid-1980s, generally a time of falling inflation, accounting professions worldwide tended to move away from issues associated with accounting in times of changing prices. It is an interesting exercise to consider why particular methods of accounting did not gain and maintain professional support. Perhaps it was because (as indicated in Broadbent and Laughlin, 2005) the profession, like a number of researchers, questioned the relevance of the information, particularly in times of lower inflation. If they did question the relevance of the information to various parties (such as the capital market) it would be difficult for them to support regulation from a 'public interest' perspective, given the costs that would be involved in implementing a new system of accounting.[35]

Even in the absence of concerns about the relevance of the information, standard-setters might have been concerned that a drastic change in our accounting conventions could cause widespread disruption and confusion in the capital markets and therefore might not be in the public interest. Although there have been numerous accounting controversies and disputes over time (for example, how to account for goodwill or research and development, or how to account for investments in associates), such controversies typically impact on only a small subset of accounts. Adopting a new model of accounting would have much more widespread effects, which again might not have been in the public interest.

It has also been speculated that the adoption of a new method of accounting could have consequences for the amount of taxation that the government ultimately collects from businesses. As Zeff and Dharan (1996, p. 632) state:

> Some governments fear that an accounting regimen of generally lower reported profits under current cost accounting (with physical capital maintenance) would lead to intensified pressure for a concomitant reform of corporate income tax law.

Throughout the 1970s and 1980s, many organizations opposed introduction of alternative methods of accounting (alternative to historical cost). Corporate opposition to various alternative methods of accounting could also be explained by the notion of self-interest as embraced within the economic interest theory of regulation. Under historical cost accounting, management has a mechanism available to manage its reported profitability. Holding gains might not be recognized for income purposes until such time as the assets are sold. For example, an organization might have acquired shares in another organization some years earlier. In periods in which reported profits are expected to be lower than management wants, management could elect to sell some of the shares to offset other losses. If alternative methods of accounting were introduced, this ability to manipulate reported results could be lost.[36] Hence such corporations might have lobbied government, the basis of the submissions being rooted in self-interest. Because there are typically corporate or business representatives on most standard-setting bodies, there is also the possibility that corporations/business interests were able to effectively capture the standard-setting process (Walker, 1987).

As we have already seen in this chapter, there is some evidence that accounting information adjusted to take account of changing prices might not be relevant to the decision-making processes of those parties involved in the capital market (as reflected by various share price studies) and hence the alternative models of accounting might not be favoured by analysts (accepting the private economic interest theory of regulation, analysts might have little to gain personally if the alternative methods of accounting were introduced).

Of course we will never know for sure why particular parties did not favour particular accounting models, but what we can see is that alternative explanations can be provided from public interest theory, capture theory, or the economic interest theory of regulation – theories that were discussed at greater length in earlier chapters.

Throughout the CCA/CPPA debates a number of key academics continued to promote their favoured methods of accounting (and some continued to do so through the 1990s). We can obviously speculate what drove them – was it the public interest, or was it self-interest? What do you think?

In concluding this chapter, we can see that the debate is far from settled as to which method of accounting is most appropriate in accounting for changing prices. While debate in this area has generally abated since the mid-1980s it is very possible that, if levels of inflation increase to their previously high levels, such debates will again be ignited. Various authors have developed accounting models that differ in many respects. Some of these differences are due to fundamental differences of opinion about the role of accounting and the sort of information necessary for effective decision making. Because information generated by systems of accounting based on the historical cost convention is used in many decisions, major change in accounting conventions would conceivably have widespread social and economic impacts. This in itself will restrict any major modifications/changes to our (somewhat outdated) accounting system. This perspective was reflected in the 1960s, and arguably the perspective is just as relevant now.

As an example of how the profession has typically been reluctant to implement major reforms, we can consider activities undertaken in 1961 and 1962 where the Accounting Research Division of the American Institute of Certified Public Accountants (AICPA) commissioned studies by Moonitz (1961), and by Sprouse and Moonitz (1962) respectively. In these documents the authors proposed that accounting measurement systems be changed from historical cost to a system based on current values. However, prior to the release of the Sprouse and Moonitz study the Accounting Principles Board of the AICPA stated in relation to the Moonitz, and Sprouse and Moonitz studies that 'while these studies are a valuable contribution to accounting principles, they are too radically different from generally accepted principles for acceptance at this time' (Statement by the Accounting Principles Board, AICPA, April 1962).

While this chapter has emphasized various issues and debates associated with how best to measure the financial performance of an entity in times when prices are changing, we must remember that financial performance is only one facet of the total performance of an entity. As we see in Chapter 9, there is much debate about how to measure and report information on the social and environmental performance of reporting entities. As with the debate we have considered in this chapter, the debates about the appropriate methodology and relevance of social and environmental information are far from settled. As has been emphasized, the practice of accounting generates a multitude of interesting debates.

Chapter summary

This chapter has explored different models of accounting that have been developed to provide financial information in periods of rising prices. These models have been developed because of the perceived limitations of historical cost accounting, particularly in times of rising prices. Critics of historical cost accounting suggest that because historical cost adopts a capital maintenance perspective which is tied to maintaining financial capital intact, it tends to overstate profits in periods of rising prices. Historical cost accounting adopts an assumption that the purchasing power of the entity's currency remains constant over time. Debate about the best model of accounting to use in periods of rising prices was vigorous in the 1960s through to the mid-1980s. During this time, inflation levels tended to be relatively high. Since this time, inflation levels internationally have tended to be low and the debate about which model to adopt to adjust for rising prices has tended to wane. Nevertheless, there has been a general movement by regulators such as the IASB towards the use of fair values in various accounting standards – although the adoption of fair value tends to be on a piecemeal basis as particular accounting standards are developed. With this said, however, there are still various assets that are measured on the basis of historical costs.[37]

A number of alternative models have been suggested. For example, current purchasing power accounting (CPPA) was one of the earlier models to be developed. CPPA was supported by a number of professional accounting bodies during the 1960s and 1970s, although support then tended to shift to current cost accounting. CPPA uses numbers generated by the historical cost accounting as the basis of the financial statements and at the end of each period, CPPA applies a price index, typically a general price index, to adjust the historical cost numbers. For balance sheet purposes, adjustments are made to non-monetary assets. Monetary items are not adjusted by the price index. However, although monetary items are not adjusted for disclosure purposes, holding monetary items will lead to gains or losses in purchasing power which are recognized in the period's profit or loss. No gains or losses are recorded in relation to holding non-monetary items. One of the advantages of using CPPA is that it is easy to apply. It simply uses the historical cost accounting numbers that are already available and applies a price index to these numbers. A disadvantage is that the adjusted prices may provide a poor reflection of the actual value of the items in question.

Another model of accounting that we considered was current cost accounting (CCA). It uses actual valuations of assets, typically based on replacement costs, and operating income is calculated after consideration of the replacement costs of the assets used in the production and sale cycle. Non-monetary assets are adjusted to take account of changes in replacement costs, and depreciation expenses are also adjusted on the basis of changes in replacement costs. While not in use today, CCA attracted support from professional accounting bodies in the early 1980s. Opponents of CCA argued that replacement costs have little relevance if an entity is not considering replacing an asset, and further, that replacement costs might not accurately reflect the current market values of the assets in question.

The final model of accounting considered was continuously contemporary accounting (CoCoA). One key objective of CoCoA was to provide information about an entity's capacity to adapt to changing circumstances, with profit being directly related to changes in adaptive capacity. Profit is calculated as the amount that can be distributed while maintaining the adaptive capital intact. CoCoA does not differentiate between realized and unrealized gains. In support of CoCoA, it requires only one type of valuation for all assets (based on exit prices). There is no need for arbitrary cost allocations, such as depreciation. Criticisms of CoCoA include the relevance of values based on exit (selling) prices if there is no intention of selling an item. Also, many people have challenged the perspective that if an asset cannot be sold separately, it has no value, for example, goodwill. It has also been argued that valuing items on the basis of sales prices can introduce an unacceptable degree of subjectivity into accounting, particularly if the items in question are quite specialized and rarely traded.

Questions

5.1   What assumptions, if any, does historical cost accounting make about the purchasing power of the currency?

5.2   List some of the criticisms that can be made of historical cost accounting when it is applied in times of rising prices.

5.3   As shown in this chapter, Mautz (1973) made the following statement:

> Accounting is what it is today not so much because of the desire of accountants as because of the influence of businessmen. If those who make management and investment decisions had not found financial reports based on historical cost useful over the years, changes in accounting would long since have been made.

Required: Evaluate the above statement.

5.4   What is the 'additivity' problem that Chambers refers to?

5.5   Explain the difference between income derived from the viewpoint of maintaining financial capital (as in historical cost accounting) and income derived from a system of ensuring that physical capital remains intact.

5.6   In current purchasing power accounting:
   (a)   Why is it necessary to consider monetary assets separately from non-monetary assets?
   (b)   Why does holding monetary assets lead to a purchasing power loss, but holding non-monetary assets does not lead to a purchasing power loss?

5.7   What is the basis of Chambers' argument against valuing assets on the basis of replacement costs?

5.8   If continuously contemporary accounting is adopted and an organization is involved with selling goods, when would the profit from the sale of goods be recognized? How does this compare with historical cost accounting?

5.9   What are holding gains, and how are holding gains treated if current cost accounting is applied? Do we need to differentiate between realized and unrealized holding gains?

5.10 What are some of the major strengths and weaknesses of historical cost accounting?

5.11 What are some of the major strengths and weaknesses of current purchasing power accounting?

5.12 What are some of the major strengths and weaknesses of current cost accounting (applying replacement costs)?

5.13 What are some of the major strengths and weaknesses of continuously contemporary accounting?

5.14 Evaluate the statement of Chambers (1995, p. 82) that 'in the context of judgement of the past and decision making for the future, the products of current value accounting of the Edwards and Bell variety are irrelevant and misleading. No budget can properly proceed except from an up-to-date statement of the amount of money's worth available to enter the budget period'.

5.15 Evaluate the statement of Edwards (1975, p. 238) that 'I am not convinced of the merit of adopting, as a normal basis for asset valuation in the going concern, exit prices in buyer markets. These are unusual values suitable for unusual situations. I would not object in principle to keeping track of such exit prices at all times and, as Solomons (1966) has suggested, substituting them for entry values when they are the lesser of the two and the firm has taken a definite decision not to replace the asset or even the function it performs'.

5.16 Despite the efforts of authors such as Chambers, Edwards and Bell, and Sterling, historical cost accounting has maintained its position of dominance in how we do financial accounting. Why do you think that historical cost accounting has remained the principal method of accounting?

5.17 As indicated in this chapter, various studies have provided support for a view that CCA/CPPA is of little relevance to users of financial statements. Nevertheless numerous organizations lobbied in support of the methods, as well as voluntarily providing such information in their annual reports. Why do you think this is so?

Notes

1 Positive theories, by contrast, attempt to explain and predict accounting practice without seeking to prescribe particular actions. Positive accounting theories are the subject of analysis in Chapter 7.

2 Across time, these criticisms appear to have been accepted by accounting regulators – at least on a piecemeal basis as various accounting standards have been released that require the application of fair values when measuring assets. For example, financial instruments (pursuant to IAS 39), property, plant and equipment (where the revaluation model has been adopted pursuant to IAS 16), some intangible assets (where there is an 'active market' pursuant to IAS 38), investment properties (pursuant to IAS 14), and biological assets (pursuant to IAS 41) are required to be valued at fair value.

3 For example, there is a great deal of debate about whether stock (inventory) measurement rules (which require inventory to be measured at the lower of costs and net realizable value pursuant to IAS 2) provide relevant information in situations where the market (fair) value of the inventory greatly exceeds its cost.

4 As indicated in Chapter 2, the historical cost method of accounting was documented as early as 1494 by the Franciscan monk Pacioli in his famous work *Summa de Arithmetica, Geometrica, Proportioni et Proportionalita.*

5 IAS 16 provides reporting entities with an option to adopt either the 'cost model' (measuring property, plant and equipment at historical cost) or the 'fair-value model' for measuring classes of property, plant and equipment. The 'fair-value' model requires the revaluation of the assets to their fair value (which in itself means that a modified version of historical cost accounting can be used), which is one way to take account of changing values. Basing revised depreciation on the revalued amounts is one limited way of accounting for the effects of changing prices.

6 However, because something continues to be used does not mean that there is nothing else that might not be better. This is a common error made by proponents of decision usefulness studies. Such studies attempt to provide either support for, or rejection of, something on the basis that particular respondents or users indicated that it would,

or would not, be useful for their particular purposes. Often there are things that might be more 'useful' – but they are unknown by the respondents. As Gray *et al.* (1996, p. 75) state: 'Decision usefulness purports to describe the central characteristics of accounting in general and financial statements in particular. To describe accounting as useful for decisions is no more illuminating than describing a screwdriver as being useful for digging a hole – it is better than nothing (and therefore "useful") but hardly what one might ideally like for such a task.'

7   Reflective of the lack of agreement in the area, Elliot (1986) adopts a contrary view. Still relying upon metaphors associated with evolution, Elliot (1986, p. 35) states: 'There is growing evidence in the market place ... that historical cost-basis information is of ever declining usefulness to the modern business world. The issue for the financial accounting profession is to move the accounting model toward greater relevance or face the fate of the dinosaur and the messenger pigeon.'

8   Again, under existing accounting standards, assets such as property, plant and equipment can be measured at fair value or at cost. IAS 16 gives reporting entities the choice between applying the fair value model or the cost model to the different classes of property, plant and equipment. Hence we are currently left with a situation where, even within a category of assets (for example, property, plant and equipment), some assets might be measured at cost while others might be measured at fair value.

9   In relation to property, plant and equipment IAS 16 requires that where revaluations to fair value are undertaken, the revaluations must be made with sufficient regularity to ensure that the carrying amount of each asset in the class does not differ materially from its fair value at the reporting date. Nevertheless, there will still be instances where some assets have not been revalued for three to five years but they will still be aggregated with assets that have been recently revalued.

10   While it might be considered that measuring stock (inventory) at fair value would provide relevant information, IAS 2 'Inventories' prohibits the revaluation of stock. Specifically, IAS 2 requires stock to be measured at the lower of cost and net realizable value.

11   In some countries, such as the USA, stock can be valued on the basis of the last-in-first-out (LIFO) method (this method is not allowed under IAS 2). The effect of employing LIFO is that the cost of goods sold will be determined on the basis of the latest cost, which in times of rising prices will be higher, thereby leading to a reduction in reported profits. This does provide some level of (although certainly not complete) protection against the possibility of eroding the real operating capacity of the organization.

12   Holding gains are those that arise while an asset is in the possession of the reporting entity.

13   Gray *et al.* (1996, p. 74) also provide yet another concept of capital maintenance – one that includes environmental capital. They state 'it is quite a simple matter to demonstrate that company "income" contains a significant element of capital distribution – in this case "environmental capital". An essential tenet of accounting is that income must allow for the maintenance of capital. Current organizational behaviour clearly does not maintain environmental capital and so overstates earnings. If diminution of environmental capital is factored into the income figure it seems likely that no company in the western world has actually made any kind of a profit for many years.' We will consider this issue further in Chapter 9.

14   Hence, if €20,000 is distributed as dividends, the entity would still be in a position to acquire the same land that it had at the beginning of the period (assuming that actual prices increased by the same amount as the particular price index used).

15   For example, we will not be considering one approach to determining income based on present values which did not have wide support, but would be consistent with Hicks' income definition (and which might be considered as a *true income* approach). A present value approach would determine the discounted present value of the firm's assets and liabilities and use this as the basis for the financial statements. Under such an approach the calculated value of assets will depend upon various expectations, such as

expectations about the cash flows the asset would return through its use in production (its value in use) or its current market value (value in exchange). Such an approach relies upon many assumptions and judgements, including the determination of the appropriate discount rate. Under a present value approach to accounting, profit would be determined as the amount that could be withdrawn, yet maintain the present value of the net assets intact from one period to the next.

16 Current values could be based on *entry* or *exit* prices. As we will see, there is much debate as to which 'current' value is most appropriate.

17 The professional support for the use of replacement costs appeared to heighten around the time of the 1976 release of ASR 190 within the United States.

18 However, many questions can be raised with regard to what the restated value actually represents after being multiplied by an index such as the general rate of inflation. This confusion is reflected in studies that question the relevance of information restated for changes in purchasing power.

19 For example, we can consider the initial net monetary asset balance of €100,000 at the beginning of the period. For illustration, we can assume that this was represented by cash of €100,000. Given the inflation which has caused general prices to rise from a base of 120 to 135, to have the same general purchasing power at the end of the period an amount of cash equal to €112,500 would need to be on hand. The difference between the required amount of €112,500 and the actual balance of €100,000 is treated as a purchasing power loss relating to holding the cash. Conversely, if the net monetary balance had been (€100,000), meaning that monetary liabilities exceeded monetary assets, then we would have gained, as the purchasing power of what we must pay has decreased over time.

20 In some countries non-current assets can be revalued upward by way of an increase in the asset account and an increase in a reserve, such as a revaluation reserve. This increment is typically not treated as income and therefore the treatment is consistent with a physical capital maintenance approach to income recognition (this approach is embodied within IAS 16 as it relates to property, plant and equipment, and within IAS 38 as it relates to intangible assets).

21 We will also see later in this chapter that there are approaches to current cost accounting that rely upon exit (sales) prices.

22 Comparing this approach to income calculations under historical cost accounting we see that if we add the current cost accounting operating profit of €300 and the realized holding gain of €200, then this will give the same total as we would have calculated for income under historical cost accounting.

23 In a sense, the Edwards and Bell approach represents a 'true income' approach to profit calculation. They believe that profit can only be correctly measured after considering the various asset replacement costs.

24 Those who favour a method of income calculation that requires a maintenance of financial capital (advocates of historical cost accounting) treat holding gains as income, while those who favour a maintenance of physical capital approach to income determination (such as Edwards and Bell) tend to exclude holding gains from income. A physical capital perspective was adopted by most countries in their professional releases pertaining to CCA.

25 Some variants of current cost accounting do include some purchasing power changes as part of the profit calculations. For example, if an entity issued €1 million of debt when the market required a rate of return of 6 per cent, but that required rate subsequently rises to 8 per cent, then the unrealized savings would include the difference between what the entity received for the debt and what they would receive at the new rate. This unrealized saving would benefit the organization throughout the loan as a result of the lower interest charges.

26 As quoted in Riahi-Belkaoui (2004, pp. 496–7).

27 As a specific example of the inductive (descriptive) approach to theory development we can consider the work of Grady (1965). This research was commissioned by the American Institute of Certified Public Accountants and documented the generally accepted conventions of accounting of the time.

28 As indicated in Chapter 1, decision useful-ness research can be considered to have two branches, these being the *decision-makers' emphasis*, and the *decision-models emphasis*. The *decision-makers' emphasis* relies upon undertaking research that seeks to ask deci-sion makers what information they want. Proponents of the *decision-models emphasis*, on the other hand, develop models based upon the researchers' perceptions about what is necessary for efficient decision making. Information prescriptions follow (for example, that information should be provided about the market value of the reporting entity's assets). This branch of research typically assumes that different classes of stakeholders have identical infor-mation needs. Unlike the decision-makers' emphasis, the decision-models emphasis does not ask the decision makers what infor-mation they want, but, instead, it concen-trates on what types of information are considered to be useful for decision making.

29 This can be contrasted with the current situation where it is common to find that various classes of assets are valued using a different approach (for example, for stock – lower of cost and net realizable value; for marketable securities – at fair value; for buildings – at cost or fair value; for debtors – at face value, less a provision for doubtful debts), yet they are simply added together to give a *total asset* amount.

30 In considering 'value in use', logically, if an asset's 'value in use' exceeds its market value, then it will be retained, otherwise it will be sold. 'Value in use' is defined in IAS 36 as the present value of the future cash flows expected to be derived from an asset. Hence the point might be that there has actually been a choice not to sell the assets that the entity has on hand (Solomons, 1966). Further, specialised assets might be of particular value to one entity, but not to any others.

31 As we discuss in Chapter 7, and as already discussed in earlier chapters, one of the central assumptions of Positive Accounting Theory is that all individual action is motivated by self-interest considerations, with that interest being directly tied to the goal of maximising an individual's own wealth.

32 Ball and Foster (1982), however, indicate that size can be a proxy for many things other than political sensitivity (such as industry membership).

33 Within the Watts and Zimmerman study many of the respondents were members of the oil industry and such industry members were also inclined to favour the introduction of general price level accounting. Consistent with the political cost hypothesis, 1974 (the time of the submissions) was a time of intense scrutiny of oil companies.

34 This quotation indicates the existence of broader perceived economic impacts of accounting regulation, as discussed in Chapter 3.

35 Broadbent and Laughlin (2005) argue that the conception of 'public interest' will vary both from person to person (or interest group to interest group) and will also change over time.

36 In recent years the discretion of manage-ment in relation to the measurement of equity investments has been reduced. IAS 39 stipulates a general requirement that such investments shall be measured at fair value.

37 For example, inventory and property, plant and equipment where the entity has elected to adopt the 'cost model'.

References

Ball, R. & Foster, G. (1982) 'Corporate finan-cial reporting: A methodological review of empirical research', *Studies on current research methodologies in accounting: A crit-ical evaluation – supplement to The Journal of Accounting Research*, **20** (Supplement), pp. 161–234.

Beaver, W., Christie, A., & Griffin, P. (1980) 'The information content of SEC ASR 190', *Journal of Accounting and Economics*, **2**.

Beaver, W. & Landsman, W. (1987) 'The incremental information content of FAS 33 disclosures', *research report*, Stamford: FASB.

Broadbent, J. & Laughlin, R. (2005) 'Government concerns and tensions in accounting standard setting: The case of accounting for the private finance initiative in the UK', *Accounting and Business Research*, **21** (1), pp. 75–97.

Bryer, R. & Brignall, S. (1985) 'The GAAP in inflation accounting debate', *Accountancy*, pp. 32–3.

Bublitz, B., Freka, T., & McKeown, J. (1985) 'Market association tests and FASB statement 33 disclosures: A re-examination', *Journal of Accounting Research* (Supplement), pp. 1–23.

Canning, J. B. (1929) *The Economics of Accountancy: A Critical Analysis of Accounting Theory*, New York: Ronald Press.

Chambers, R. J. (1955) 'Blueprint for a theory of accounting', *Accounting Research* (January), pp. 17–55.

Chambers, R. J. (1966) *Accounting, Evaluation and Economic Behavior*, Englewood Cliffs, N. J.: Prentice-Hall.

Chambers, R. J. (1995) 'An introduction to price variation and inflation accounting research', In Jones, S., Romana, C., & Ratnatunga, J. (eds) *Accounting Theory: A Contemporary Review*, Sydney: Harcourt Brace.

Dyckman, T. R. (1969) *Studies in Accounting Research No. 1: Investment Analysis and General Price Level Adjustments*, USA: American Accounting Association.

Edwards, E. (1975) 'The state of current value accounting', *Accounting Review*, **50** (2), pp. 235–45.

Edwards, E. O. & Bell, P. W. (1961) *The Theory and Measurement of Business Income*, Berkeley: University of California Press.

Elliot, R. K. (1986) 'Dinosaurs, passenger pigeons, and financial accountants', *World*, pp. 32–5, as reproduced in Zeff, S. A. & Dharan, B. G. (1996) *Readings and Notes on Financial Accounting*, 5th edn, New York: McGraw-Hill.

Ferguson, C. & Wines, G. (1986) 'Incidence of the use of current cost accounting in published annual financial statements', *Accounting Forum* (March).

Gheyara, K. & Boatsman, J. (1980) 'Market reaction to the 1976 replacement cost disclosures', *Journal of Accounting and Economics*, **2** (2), pp. 107–25.

Grady, P. (1965) 'An inventory of generally accepted accounting principles for business enterprises', *Accounting Research Study No. 7*, New York: AICPA.

Gray, R., Owen, D., & Adams, C. (1996) *Accounting and Accountability: Changes and Challenges in Corporate Social and Environmental Reporting*, London: Prentice-Hall.

Hicks, J. R. (1946) *Value and Capital*, Oxford: Oxford University Press.

Larson, K. & Schattke, R. (1966) 'Current cash equivalent, additivity and financial action', *Accounting Review*, **41** (4), pp. 634–41.

Lobo, G. & Song, I. (1989) 'The incremental information in SFAS 33 income disclosures over historical cost income and its cash and accrual components', *Accounting Review*, **64** (2), pp. 329–43.

MacNeal, K. (1970) *Truth in Accounting*, originally published in 1939 edn, Kansas: Scholars Book Company.

Mautz, R. K. (1973) 'A few words for historical cost', *Financial Executive* (January), pp. 23–7.

Moonitz, M. (1961) 'The basic postulates of accounting', *Accounting Research Study No. 1*, New York: AICPA.

Morris, R. C. (1975) 'Evidence of the impact of inflation on share prices', *Accounting and Business Research* (Spring), pp. 87–95.

Murdoch, B. (1986) 'The information content of FAS 33 returns on equity', *The Accounting Review*, **61** (2), pp. 273–87.

Paton, W. A. (1922) *Accounting Theory*, Kansas: Scholars Book Co, reprinted 1973.

Peterson, R. J. (1975) 'A portfolio analysis of general price-level restatement', *The Accounting Review*, **50** (3), pp. 525–32.

Riahi-Belkaoui, A. (2004) *Accounting Theory*, 5th edn. London: Thomson Learning.

Ro, B. T. (1980) 'The adjustment of security returns to the disclosure of replacement cost accounting information', *Journal of Accounting and Economics*, **2** (2), pp. 159–89.

Ro, B. T. (1981) 'The disclosure of replacement cost accounting data and its effect on transaction volumes', *Accounting Review*, **56** (1), pp. 70–84.

Roberts, D. L., Staunton, J. J., & Hagan, L. L. (1995) 'Accounting for self-generating and regenerating assets', *Discussion Paper No. 23*, Melbourne: Australian Accounting Research Foundation.

Schaefer, T. (1984) 'The information content of current cost income relative to dividends and historical cost income', *Journal of Accounting Research*, **22** (2), pp. 647–56.

Solomons, D. (1966) 'An overview of exit price accounting', *ABACUS* (December).

Sprouse, R. & Moonitz, M. (1962) 'A tentative set of broad accounting principles for business enterprises', *Accounting Research Study No. 3*, New York: American Institute of Certified Public Accountants.

Sterling, R. R. (1970) *Theory of the Measurement of Enterprise Income*, USA: University of Kansas Press.

Sutton, T. G. (1988) 'The proposed introduction of current cost accounting in the UK: Determinants of corporate preference', *Journal of Accounting and Economics*, **10** (2), pp. 127–49.

Sweeney, H. W. (1964) *Stabilised Accounting*, originally published in 1936; Holt Rinehart and Winston.

Walker, R. G. (1987) 'Australia's ASRB: A case study of political activity and regulatory capture', *Accounting and Business Research*, **17** (67), pp. 269–86.

Watts, R. & Zimmerman, J. (1978) 'Towards a positive theory of the determination of accounting standards', *Accounting Review*, **53** (1), pp. 112–34.

Wong, J. (1988) 'Economic incentives for the voluntary disclosure of current cost financial statements', *Journal of Accounting and Economics*, **10** (2), pp. 151–67.

Zeff, S. A. & Dharan, B. G. (1996) *Readings and Notes on Financial Accounting*, 5th edn, New York: McGraw-Hill.

CHAPTER 6

Normative theories of accounting 2: The case of conceptual framework projects

Learning Objectives

Upon completing this chapter readers should:

- understand the role that conceptual frameworks can play in the practice of financial reporting;
- be aware of the history of the development of the various existing conceptual framework projects;
- be able to identify, explain and critically evaluate the various building blocks that have been developed within various conceptual framework projects;
- be able to identify some of the perceived advantages and disadvantages that arise from the establishment and development of conceptual frameworks;
- be able to identify some factors, including political factors, that might help or hinder the development of conceptual framework projects;
- be able to explain which groups within society are likely to benefit from the establishment and development of conceptual framework projects.

Opening issues

For many years the practice of financial accounting lacked a generally accepted theory that clearly enunciated the objectives of financial reporting, the required qualitative characteristics of financial information, or provided clear guidance as to when and how to recognize and measure the various elements of accounting. In the absence of an accepted theory, accounting standards tended to be developed in a rather *ad hoc* manner with various inconsistencies between the various standards. For example, various accounting standards relating to different classes of assets used different recognition and measurement criteria. It has been argued that the development of a conceptual framework will lead to improved financial reporting, and this improved reporting will provide benefits to the various financial statement readers as it will enable them to make more informed resource allocation decisions. Do you agree with this argument, and what is the basis of your view?

Introduction

In Chapter 5 we considered a number of normative theories developed by some notable accounting academics to address various accounting issues associated with how financial accounting *should* be undertaken in the presence of changing prices (typically increasing prices associated with inflation). These theories included current purchasing power accounting, current cost accounting and continuously contemporary accounting (or exit price accounting). As revealed in Chapter 5, the various normative theories, which represented quite significant departures from existing accounting practice, failed to be embraced by professional accounting bodies and regulators throughout the world, and with the decline in levels of inflation within most countries, debate about the relative benefits of alternative approaches of accounting for changing prices has subsided in recent years.

While the various normative theories advanced to deal with changing prices did not ultimately gain the support of accounting professions, professional accounting bodies within countries such as the USA, the UK, Canada, Australia and New Zealand, as well as the International Accounting Standards Committee (IASC) (which subsequently became the International Accounting Standards Board (IASB)), have undertaken work to develop conceptual frameworks for accounting, which in themselves can be considered to constitute *normative theories of accounting*. In this chapter we consider what is meant by the term 'conceptual framework' and we consider why particular professional bodies thought there was a need to develop them. We see that there are numerous perceived advantages and disadvantages associated with conceptual frameworks and we consider certain arguments that have been advanced to suggest that conceptual frameworks play a part in *legitimizing* the existence of the accounting profession.

What is a conceptual framework of accounting?

There is no definitive view of what constitutes a 'conceptual framework'. The Financial Accounting Standards Board (FASB) in the USA, which developed one of the first conceptual frameworks in accounting, defined its conceptual framework as 'a coherent system of interrelated objectives and fundamentals that is expected to lead to consistent standards' (Statement of Financial Accounting Concepts No. 1: *Objectives of Financial Reporting by Business Enterprises, 1978*).

In Chapter 1 we provided a definition of 'theory' (from the Oxford English Dictionary) as 'A scheme or system of ideas or statements held as an explanation or account of a group of facts or phenomena'. This definition was similar to that provided by the accounting researcher Hendriksen (1970, p. 1). He defined a theory as 'a coherent set of hypothetical, conceptual and pragmatic principles forming the general framework of reference for a field of inquiry'. Looking at these definitions of theory and looking at the FASB's definition of its conceptual framework, it is reasonable to argue that the conceptual framework attempts to provide a theory of accounting, and one that appears quite structured. Because conceptual frameworks provide a great deal of *prescription* (that is, they prescribe certain actions, such as when to recognize an asset for financial statement purposes) they are considered to have *normative* characteristics. According to the FASB, the conceptual framework 'prescribes the nature, function and limits of financial accounting and reporting' (as stated in Statement of Financial Accounting Concepts No. 1: *Objectives of Financial Reporting by Business Enterprises*, 1978).

The view taken by people involved in developing conceptual frameworks tends to be that if the practice of financial reporting is to be developed logically and consistently (which might be important for creating public confidence in the practice of accounting) we first need to develop some consensus on important issues such as what we actually mean by *financial reporting* and what should be its scope; what organizational characteristics or attributes indicate that an entity should produce financial reports; what the *objective* of financial reporting is; what *qualitative characteristics* financial information should possess; what the elements of financial reporting are; what measurement rules should be employed in relation to the various elements of accounting; and so forth. It has been proposed that unless we have some agreement on fundamental issues, such as those mentioned above, accounting standards will be developed in a rather *ad hoc* or piecemeal manner with limited consistency between the various accounting standards developed over time. It is perhaps somewhat illogical to consider how to account for a particular item of expenditure if we have not agreed in the first place on what the *objective* of financial accounting actually is, or indeed on issues such as what an *asset* is or what a *liability* is. Nevertheless, for many years accounting standards were developed in many countries in the absence of conceptual frameworks.[1] This in itself led to a great deal of criticism. As Horngren (1981, p. 94) states:

> All regulatory bodies have been flayed because they have used piecemeal approaches, solving one accounting issue at a time. Observers have alleged that not enough tidy rationality has been used in the process of accounting policymaking. Again and again, critics have cited a need for a conceptual framework.

In developing a conceptual framework for accounting it is considered that there are a number of 'building blocks' that must be developed. The framework must be developed in a particular order, with some issues necessarily requiring agreement before work can move on to subsequent building blocks. Figure 6.1 provides an overview of the framework developed in the late 1980s by the International Accounting Standards Committee (IASC), and which was later adopted by the IASC's successor – the International Accounting Standards Board (IASB).

The IASC/IASB view of a conceptual framework in Figure 6.1 is also broadly consistent with the definitions in the conceptual frameworks developed by some individual countries, although the relative emphasis given to the different components tends to vary slightly from one framework to another.

As we can see, the first issue to be addressed is the definition of *financial reporting*. Unless there is some agreement on this it would be difficult to construct a framework for financial reporting. Having determined what financial reporting

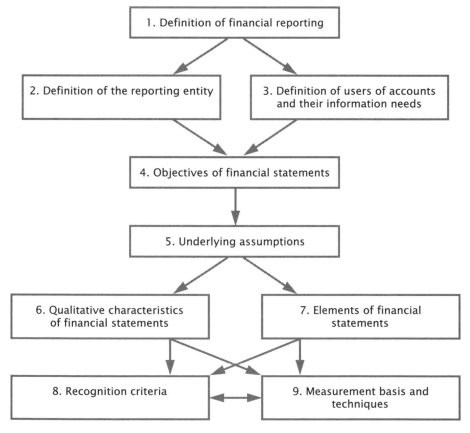

Figure 6.1 Components of a conceptual framework (based on the IASC/IASB framework)

means, attention is then turned to the *subject* of financial reporting, specifically which entities are required to produce general purpose financial reports,[2] and the likely characteristics of the users of these reports. Attention is then turned to the *objective* of financial reporting. As we will see shortly the objective of general purpose financial reporting is deemed to be:

> to provide information about the financial position, performance and changes in financial position of an entity that is useful to a wide range of users in making economic decisions. (paragraph 12 of the IASC *Framework for the Preparation and Presentation of Financial Statements*)

If it is accepted that this is the objective of financial reporting, the next step is to determine the basic underlying assumptions and qualitative characteristics of financial information necessary to allow users to make economic decisions. We address these issues later in this chapter.

Over time, it is to be expected that perspectives of the role of financial reporting will change. Consistent with this view, there is an expectation by many, including accounting standard-setters, that the development of conceptual frameworks will continue. They will evolve over time.

In the discussion that follows we consider the history of the development of conceptual frameworks in different countries. We see that conceptual frameworks are largely prescriptive, or normative in approach, for example, indicating how the elements of accounting (the elements being assets, liabilities, income, expenses and equity) are defined and when they *should* be recognized. However, we also see that in certain cases, because of apparent coercion by powerful interest groups, parts of certain conceptual frameworks became descriptive of current practice, with limited implications for changing existing accounting practices.

A brief overview of the history of the development of conceptual frameworks

A number of countries, such as the USA, the UK, Ireland, Canada, Australia and New Zealand have undertaken various activities directed to the development of a conceptual framework. The IASC also undertook work to develop a conceptual framework. There are many similarities (and some differences) between the various conceptual frameworks developed in the different jurisdictions.[3] It is arguable whether any standard-setter anywhere in the world has developed what could be construed as a complete conceptual framework.

One country particularly active in developing frameworks in relation to financial reporting was the United States. Initially, some of the work involved developing *prescriptive* theories of how accounting *should* be undertaken, while other research related to the development of *descriptive* theories of how accounting was generally performed. For example, in 1961 and 1962 the Accounting Research Division of the American Institute of Certified Public Accountants (AICPA) commissioned studies by Moonitz (1961) and Sprouse and Moonitz (1962). These theorists prescribed that accounting practice should move towards a system based on current values, rather than historical cost. This work was considered 'too radically different from generally accepted principles' (AICPA, 1962) and was abandoned by the profession. The AICPA then commissioned Grady to develop a theory of accounting. Grady (1965) was basically descriptive of existing practice, thereby being quite uncontroversial. His work led to the release of Accounting Principles Board (APB) Statement No. 4, *Basic Concepts and Accounting Principles Underlying the Financial Statements of Business Enterprises* in 1970. As it was not controversial and simply reflected generally accepted accounting principles of the time, APB Statement No. 4 had a high probability of being acceptable to the AICPA's constituency (Miller and Reading, 1986).

The Trueblood Report

Although APB Statement No. 4 did not cause great controversy, the accounting profession was under some criticism for the apparent lack of any real framework.[4] The generally accepted accounting principles of the time allowed for much diversity in accounting treatments and this was seen by many to be a problem. There was an absence of agreement on key issues about the role and objectives of financial reporting, appropriate definition, recognition and measurement rules for the elements of accounting, and so on. Responding to the criticism, the AICPA formed the Trueblood Committee (named after the committee chairman, Robert Trueblood) in 1971. It produced a report, The Trueblood Report (released in 1973 by the AICPA), which listed 12 objectives of accounting and 7 qualitative characteristics that financial information should possess (relevance and materiality; form and substance; reliability; freedom from bias; comparability; consistency; understandability).

Objective 1 of the report was that financial statements are to provide information useful for making economic decisions. That is, there was a focus on the information needs of financial statement users. This objective, which was carried forward to subsequent documents, indicated that decision usefulness (as opposed to concepts such as *stewardship*) was a primary objective of financial statements.[5] This can be contrasted with previous perspectives of the role of accounting. For example, Accounting Terminology Bulletin No. 1, issued in 1953 by the AICPA, made no reference to the information needs of users. It stated:

> Accounting is the art of recording, classifying and summarizing in a significant manner and in terms of money, transactions and events which are in part at least of a financial character, and interpreting the results thereof.

Objective 2 provided by the Trueblood Committee stated that financial statements are to primarily serve those users who have limited authority, ability or resources to obtain information and who rely on financial statements as the principal source of information about an organization's activities. This objective, which was also carried forward in subsequent work, was interesting in that it tended to be a departure from much research that was being carried on at the time. A great deal of research being undertaken in the late 1960s and thereafter had embraced the *efficient markets hypothesis* (discussed more fully in Chapter 10), that markets react quickly to impound the information content of publicly available information whenever that information first becomes publicly available. Researchers working with the efficient markets hypothesis considered that as long as the information was publicly available to somebody, then given an assumption of market efficiency, this information would quickly be dispersed among all interested users. The Trueblood Committee and subsequent committees responsible for development of conceptual frameworks within the United States and elsewhere did not appear to embrace this view of market efficiency.

The Trueblood Committee acknowledged that a variety of different valuation methods were used for different classes of assets and liabilities. This had been an issue that had concerned a number of researchers, such as Raymond Chambers (as indicated in Chapter 5). However, the Trueblood Committee noted that they considered different valuation rules were relevant for different classes of assets, thereby ignoring the 'additivity problem' raised by individuals such as Chambers. As we will see shortly, prescribing a particular valuation or measurement approach is an activity that those responsible for developing conceptual frameworks have been reluctant to undertake.

The Financial Accounting Standards Board

In 1974 the Accounting Principles Board within the United States was replaced by the Financial Accounting Standards Board (FASB). The FASB embarked on its conceptual framework project early in its existence and the first release, Statement of Financial Accounting Concepts (SFAC) No. 1: *Objectives of Financial Reporting by Business Enterprises*, occurred in 1978. This was followed by the release of five more SFACs, with the latest one, SFAC No. 6, being issued in 1985. The initial SFACs were quite normative. However, when SFAC No. 5: *Recognition and Measurement in Financial Statements of Business Enterprises*, was released in 1984, the FASB appeared to opt for an approach largely descriptive of current practice. Rather than prescribe a particular valuation approach the FASB described some of the various valuation approaches commonly used: historical cost; current cost (replacement cost); current market value (exit value); net realizable value (amount gained from sale, less costs associated with the sale); and the present (discounted) value of future cash flows. The failure to take the lead and prescribe a particular valuation approach was referred to as a 'cop-out' by Solomons (1986). This view was also embraced by a number of others. For example, Nussbaumer (1992, p. 238) states:

> ... the issuance of SFAC 5 (December 1984) marked the greatest disappointment of the FASB's project for the conceptual framework. It did nothing more than describe present

practice; it was not prescriptive at all. The recognition and measurement issues, which the FASB promised to deal with in SFAC 5, were not settled, and the measurement issue was sidestepped. ... If the FASB cannot reach an agreement when there are only seven members, it is unlikely that the profession as a whole will come to agreement on these issues either. The FASB should provide leadership to the profession on these issues and not compromise them for the sake of expediency.

In a similar vein, Miller (1990) argued that the FASB conceptual framework in accounting initially provided much needed reform to accounting. For example, SFAC No. 1 explicitly put financial report users' needs at the forefront of consideration. However, when SFAC No. 5 was released, 'momentum was lost when FASB did not have sufficient political will to face down the counter-reformation and endorse expanded use of current values in the recognition and measurement phase of the project' (Miller, 1990, p. 32). Interestingly, since SFAC 5 was released there has been very limited activity in the FASB conceptual framework project. SFAC 6 was released in 1985, but this was primarily a replacement of an early statement (SFAC 3). No further SFACs have been released. It would appear that measurement issues represented a real stumbling block for the project. Had the FASB supported one valuation method over and above others, this would have been a dramatic departure from current accounting practice and may not have been palatable to its constituents. Although this is conjecture, perhaps the FASB went as far as it could politically. We consider this issue in more depth later in this chapter.

The (UK) Corporate Report

If we turn our attention to other conceptual framework projects we see that their degree of progression has also been slow. In the UK an early move towards developing guidance in relation to the objectives and the identification of the users of financial statements, as well as the methods to be used in financial reporting, was provided by *The Corporate Report* – a discussion paper released in 1976 by the Accounting Standards Steering Committee of the Institute of Chartered Accountants in England and Wales. As we see in subsequent discussion in this chapter, *The Corporate Report* was particularly concerned with addressing the *rights* of the community in terms of their access to financial information about the entities operating in their community. The view taken was that if the community gives an organization permission to operate, then that organisation has an *accountability* to the community and this accountability includes an obligation to provide information about its financial performance. This perspective of financial statement users was broader than that adopted in frameworks being developed in other countries and involved groups that did not have a direct financial interest in the organization, but were nevertheless impacted by its ongoing operations.

The Corporate Report was also part of a UK Government Green Paper on law reform. The report ultimately did not become enshrined in law and its contents were generally not accepted by the accounting profession. In 1991 the ASB embarked on a project to develop a conceptual framework, largely consistent with the main principles underlying the FASB and IASC frameworks, and thereby abandoned the broader notions of *users' rights* raised in *The Corporate Report*.

Development of conceptual frameworks in other nations

Other countries such as Australia, Canada and New Zealand have devoted resources to the development of a conceptual framework. In Australia, work on the conceptual framework started in the 1980s with the first Statement of Accounting Concept being issued in 1990. The Australian conceptual framework had a number of similarities to the FASB project and, as with the FASB, prescribing a particular measurement principle was a major stumbling block[6]. In Canada, initial efforts were incorporated in a document entitled *Corporate Reporting: Its Future Evolution*, which was released in 1980. This report was written by Edward Stamp (1980) and became known as *The Stamp Report*. This report appeared to rely heavily on *The Corporate Report* and like *The Corporate Report*, was not embraced by the accounting profession. Subsequently, further work was undertaken towards developing a conceptual framework with a number of similarities to the FASB project. In 1990 the Accounting Research and Standards Board in New Zealand also commenced some work related to a conceptual framework. It has many similarities to other frameworks developed in other countries.

At the international level, the IASC published a conceptual framework in 1989, entitled *Framework for the Preparation and Presentation of Financial Statements*, which is also similar in many respects to the conceptual frameworks developed in the above countries. Given the new centrality of International Accounting Standards/International Financial Reporting Standards in European and global financial reporting (particularly since January 2005), some argue that the IASB needs a more up-to-date conceptual framework to guide their accounting standard setting process. Exhibit 6.1 provides an example of these arguments.

What the above information demonstrates is that a number of countries have devoted resources to the development of a conceptual framework. What also is apparent is that those responsible for the frameworks have either been reluctant to promote significant changes from accounting practice (which obviously limits their ability to generate significant changes in financial reporting), or where frameworks have suggested significant changes, such changes have not been embraced by the accounting professions and many of their constituents. The reasons for this are provided in the discussion that follows.

Building blocks of a conceptual framework

In this section we consider some of the guidance that has already been produced in existing conceptual framework projects. We consider issues such as definition of a reporting entity; perceived users of financial statements; the objectives of general

---

Exhibit 6.1 Example of arguments for an updated IASB conceptual framework

Which way forward?

By David Bence and Nadine Fry (from Bristol Business School)

... If the IASB's movement towards the worldwide adoption of IFRSs is to be successful, the establishment of a more coherent international conceptual framework is necessary. This is particularly important given the IASB's principles-based, as opposed to rules-based, approach to standard-setting, and the political interest in accounting regulation.

However, the IASB has no plans to re-issue its 1989 Framework; although this would appear to be the most logical place to start if the IASB is to ensure that its output is theoretically sound. As a result of ignoring the need to harmonise conceptual frameworks, inconsistent standards are being developed.

... So far, harmonisation has only arisen at the standards level with the convergence of national and international standards. Discrepancies still arise between conceptual frameworks and standards at both the national and international level.

Although the IASB has stated that it will be guided by the Framework in its review of existing IFRSs and the development of future standards, there is much evidence to suggest the reverse is true and that many conceptual issues are being inherently decided in the development of new standards.

Accountancy, November 2004, p. 88.

---

purpose financial reporting; the qualitative characteristics that general purpose financial reports should possess; the elements of financial statements; and discussions of possible approaches to recognition and measurement of the elements of financial statements.

Definition of the reporting entity

One key issue in any discussion about financial reporting is what characteristics of an entity provide an indication of an apparent need for it to produce general purpose financial reports. The term *general purpose financial reports* refers to financial reports that comply with accounting standards and other generally accepted accounting principles and are released by reporting entities to satisfy the information demands of a varied cross-section of users. They can be contrasted with special purpose financial reports, which are provided to meet the information demands of a particular user, or group of users. As stated earlier, the guidance that we consider in this chapter relates to general purpose financial reports.

Some researchers, such as Walker (2003), have been critical of the practicality of conceptual frameworks directed at general purpose financial statements, as a single set (or framework) of accounting concepts is unlikely to be able to address the diversity of information needs from a heterogeneous range of different stakeholders.

Clearly, not all entities should be expected to produce general purpose financial reports. For example, there would be limited benefits in requiring a small owner/manager to prepare general purpose financial reports (which comply with the numerous accounting standards) for, say, a small corner shop. There would be few external users with a significant stake or interest in the organization. Limited guidance is provided by some conceptual frameworks regarding the types of entities to whose financial reports the conceptual framework is relevant. For example, paragraph 8 of the IASC *Framework for the Preparation and Presentation of Financial Statements*, which has now been adopted as the IASB framework, states that:

> The *Framework* applies to the financial statements of all commercial, industrial and business reporting entities, whether in the public or private sectors. A reporting entity is an entity for which there are users who rely on the financial statements as their major source of financial information about the entity.

Consistent with the discussion above, general purpose financial reports are considered in the IASB framework (paragraph 6) to be statements which 'are directed towards the common information needs of a wide range of users'.

Users of financial reports

If conceptual frameworks are designed to meet the 'information needs of a wide range of users', to be effective it is necessary for them to identify these potential users and their main information needs. The definition of users provided in the IASB Framework encompasses investors, employees, lenders, suppliers, customers, government agencies and the public, and is thereby broader than that used by the FASB in the USA. In the FASB's SFAC 1 the main focus of financial reports is present and potential investors and other users (with either a direct financial interest, or somehow related to those with a financial interest, for example, stockbrokers, analysts, lawyers, or regulatory bodies). Within SFAC 1 there appears to be limited consideration of the public being a legitimate user of financial reports. However, in the IASB framework, even though a range of users (along with the nature of their likely information needs) are identified, it is concluded that accounting information designed to meet the information needs of investors will usually also meet the needs of the other user groups identified. This claim is justified on the basis that 'investors are providers of risk capital to the entity' (paragraph 10), but the framework does not explain why information designed to be useful to providers of risk capital is also likely to be useful to the other types of stakeholders in most circumstances.

The issue as to which groups should be considered to be legitimate users of financial information about an organization is an argument that has attracted a great deal of debate. There are many, such as the authors of *The Corporate Report*, who hold that all groups impacted by an organization's operations have *rights* to information about the reporting entity, including financial information, regardless of whether they are contemplating resource allocation decisions.

Indeed, many would question whether the need for information to enable 'resource allocation decisions' is the only or dominant issue to consider in determining whether an organization has a public obligation to provide information about its performance.[7]

In considering the issue of the level of expertise expected of financial report readers, it has generally been accepted that readers are expected to have some proficiency in financial accounting. As a result, accounting standards are developed on this basis. The FASB conceptual framework refers to the 'informed reader'. In the IASB framework, paragraph 25 explains that:

> ... users are assumed to have a reasonable knowledge of business and economic activities and accounting and a willingness to study the information with reasonable diligence.

In considering the required qualitative characteristics financial information should possess (for example, relevance, understandability), some assumptions about the ability of report users are required. It would appear that those responsible for developing conceptual frameworks have accepted that individuals without any expertise in accounting are not the intended audience of reporting entities' financial reports (even though such people may have a considerable amount of their own wealth invested). Having established the audience for general purpose financial statements, we now consider the objectives of such statements aimed at these users.

Objectives of general purpose financial reporting

Over time, a number of objectives have been attributed to information provided within financial statements.[8] A traditionally cited objective was to enable outsiders to assess the *stewardship* of management. That is, whether the resources entrusted to management have been used for their intended or appropriate purposes. It is generally accepted that historical cost accounting enables management to effectively report on the stewardship of the resources provided to the reporting entity.

Another objective of financial reporting, and one that has become a commonly accepted goal of financial reporting, is to assist in report users' economic decision making. That is, in recent times, less emphasis has been placed on the stewardship function of financial reports. For example, the FASB notes in SFAC 1 that a major objective of financial reporting is that it:

> ... should provide information that is useful to present and potential investors and creditors and other users in making rational investment, credit and similar decisions.

This objective refers to 'rational' decisions. It is commonly accepted in the economics and accounting literature that a 'rational decision' is one that maximizes expected utility, with this utility typically considered to be related to the maximization of wealth. The FASB framework emphasizes the information needs of those who have a financial stake in the reporting entity. For example, the above objective refers to the needs of present and potential investors and creditors. It also refers to the needs of 'others', but the 'others' are also explained in terms of having financial interests in the reporting entity.

This focus on the information needs of financial report users has also been embraced in other conceptual frameworks. For example, in the IASB framework the objective of financial reporting is 'to provide information about the financial position, performance, and changes in financial position of an enterprise that is useful to a wide range of users in making economic decisions' (paragraph 12).[9]

The IASB framework then explains that economic decisions should be based on an assessment of an enterprise's future cash flows, indicating that the main objective of general purpose financial statements is to assist stakeholders in judging likely future cash flows. Moving towards a system of reporting a range of cash flow forecasts would clearly be a significant change to existing accounting practices which focus on reporting (some of) the effects of past transactions and events. However, the IASB framework then explains that:

> Users are better able to evaluate this ability to generate cash and cash equivalents if they are provided with information that focuses on the financial position, performance and changes in financial position of an entity. (paragraph 15)

Therefore, while the objective of financial statements is to aid economic decisions which will be based on an evaluation of future cash flows, the IASB framework argues that this objective of enabling stakeholders to evaluate cash flows will be effectively addressed through the information contained in balance sheets, profit and loss accounts (income statements) and cash flow/funds flow statements. Thus, there is no need for a radical change in the types of main financial statements which are needed if the objective of the financial statements as a whole (i.e. the annual report and accounts) is to provide information that is useful for making economic decisions.

Once we move towards this notion of *decision usefulness*, an objective embraced within all conceptual framework projects, we might question whether historical cost information (which arguably is useful for assessing stewardship) is useful for financial report users' decisions, such as whether to invest in, or lend funds to, an organization. Arguably, such decisions could be more effectively made if information on current market values was made available.[10]

Apart from *stewardship* and *decision usefulness*, another commonly cited objective of financial reporting is to enable reporting entities to demonstrate *accountability* between the entity and those parties to which the entity is deemed to be accountable. Gray *et al.* (1996, p. 38) provide a definition of accountability: 'the duty to provide an account or reckoning of those actions for which one is held responsible.' Issues that arise here are *to whom* is a reporting entity accountable, and *for what*? There are a multitude of opinions on this. Within the FASB project it would appear that those responsible for developing a framework considered that there is a duty to provide an account of the entity's financial performance to those parties who have a direct financial stake in the reporting entity. Emphasis seems to be placed on economic efficiencies. This can be contrasted with the guidance provided by *The Corporate Report* (UK) which argues that society effectively allows organizations to exist as long as they accept certain responsibilities, one being that they are accountable for their actions to society generally, rather than solely to those that have a financial stake in the entity. *The Corporate Report* makes the following statement at paragraph 25:

> The public's right to information arises not from a direct financial or human relationship with the reporting entity but from the general role played in our society by economic entities. Such organisations, which exist with the general consent of the community, are afforded special legal and operational privileges; they compete for resources of manpower, materials and energy and they make use of community owned assets such as roads and harbours.

Although *The Corporate Report* emphasized an accountability perspective of financial reporting, it was generally not accepted, and the UK position (through the ASB's subsequent conceptual framework project) was basically one of acceptance of the *decision-makers' emphasis* with prime consideration being given to the needs of those with a financial interest or stake in the organization.

Before moving on to consider some of the suggested *qualitative characteristics* of financial information, for the sake of completeness we will briefly mention the underlying assumptions set out as a separate section in the IASB's framework, but not given such prominence in most other conceptual framework projects. These underlying assumptions are simply that for financial statements to meet the objectives of providing information for economic decision making, they should be prepared on the accrual and going concern basis.

Qualitative characteristics of financial reports

If it is accepted that financial information should be useful for economic decision making, as conceptual frameworks indicate, then a subsequent issue to consider (or in terms of the terminology used earlier, a subsequent 'building block' to consider) is the *qualitative characteristics* (attributes or qualities) that financial information should have if it is to be *useful* for such decisions (implying that an absence of such qualities would mean that the central objectives of general purpose financial reports would not be met).

Conceptual frameworks have dedicated a great deal of their material to discussing qualitative characteristics of financial information. The primary qualitative characteristics have been identified in the IASB framework as *understandability, relevance, reliability,* and *comparability.* In the IASB framework, information is considered to be *understandable* if it is likely to be understood by users with some business and accounting knowledge (as discussed earlier in this chapter). However, this does not mean that complex information which is relevant to economic decision making should be omitted from the financial statements just because it might not be understood by some users. Given that conceptual frameworks have been developed primarily to guide accounting standard-setters in the setting of accounting rules (rather than as a set of rules to which entities must refer when compiling their financial statements), this qualitative characteristic of *understandability* is perhaps best seen as a requirement (or challenge) for standard-setters to ensure that the accounting standards they develop for dealing with complex areas produce accounting disclosures which are understandable (irrespective of the complexity of the underlying transactions or events). Based on your knowledge of accounting practice, how successful do you think accounting standard-setters have been in this task?

Under the IASB framework, information is regarded as *relevant* if it:

> ... influences the economic decisions of users by helping them evaluate past, present or future events or confirming, or correcting, their past evaluations. (paragraph 26)

There are two main aspects to relevance – for information to be relevant it should have both *predictive value* and *feedback (or confirmatory) value,* the latter referring to the information's utility in confirming or correcting earlier expectations.

Closely tied to the notion of *relevance* is the notion of *materiality.* This is embodied in various conceptual framework projects. For example, paragraph 30 of the IASB framework states that an item is material if:

> ... its omission or misstatement could influence the economic decisions of users taken on the basis of the financial statements. ... Materiality provides a cut-off point rather than being a primary qualitative characteristic which information must have if it is to be useful.

Considerations of materiality provide the basis for restricting the amount of information provided to levels that are comprehensible to financial statement users. It would arguably be poor practice to provide hundreds of pages of potentially relevant and reliable information to report readers – this would only result in an overload of information. Nevertheless, materiality is a heavily judgemental issue and at times we could expect that it might actually be used as a justification for failing to disclose some information that might be deemed to be potentially harmful to the reporting entity.

Turning to another primary qualitative characteristic, something is deemed to be *reliable* if it 'is free from material bias and error and can be depended upon by users to represent faithfully' the underlying items it claims to represent (IASB framework, paragraph 31) Within the United States, SFAC 2 defines reliability as 'the quality of information that assures that information is reasonably free from error and bias and faithfully represents what it purports to represent'. SFAC 2 notes that reliability is a function of *representational faithfulness, verifiability* and *neutrality.* According to SFAC 2, representational faithfulness refers to the 'correspondence or agreement between a measure or description and the phenomenon that it purports to represent'. Verifiability is defined in SFAC 2 as 'the ability through consensus among measurers to ensure that information represents what it purports to represent, or that the chosen method of measurement has been used without error or bias'. *Neutrality* implies that the information was not constructed or compiled to generate a predetermined result. In addition to freedom from bias and material error, the IASB framework assesses reliability in terms of *faithful representation, substance over form, neutrality, prudence* and *completeness.* Where the economic substance of a transaction is inconsistent with its legal form, *substance over form* requires that the accounting represents the economic substance (or impact) of the transaction. *Prudence* in paragraph 37 of the IASB framework requires 'a degree of caution in the exercise of judgement needed in making the estimates required under conditions of uncertainty', but this does not extend to 'excessive provisions, the deliberate understatement of assets or income, or the deliberate overstatement of liabilities or expenses' as this would conflict with the requirement of neutrality.

Introducing notions of *prudence* with the associated notions of *neutrality* and *representational faithfulness* has implications for how financial accounting has traditionally been practised. Traditionally, accountants adopted the doctrine of conservatism or prudence. In practice, this meant that asset values should never have been shown at amounts in excess of their realizable values (but they could be understated), and liabilities should never have been understated (although it was generally acceptable for liabilities to be overstated). That is, there was traditionally a bias towards undervaluing the *net assets* of an entity. It would appear that such a doctrine is not consistent with the qualitative characteristic of 'freedom from bias', as financial statements should, arguably, not be biased in one direction or another. In more recent conceptual framework projects (such as the UK ASB's *Statement of Principles*), and recently developed accounting standards in many jurisdictions, the requirement of prudence has been 'softened' in favour of a greater focus on neutrality and representational faithfulness.

The final primary qualitative characteristic in the IASB framework is *comparability*. To facilitate the comparison of accounts of different entities (and for a single entity over a period of time), methods of measurement and disclosure must be consistent – but should be changed if no longer relevant to an entity's circumstances.

Drawing on a studies by Loftus (2003) and Booth (2003), Wells (2003) argues that a key role of a conceptual framework should be to produce consistent accounting standards which lead to comparable accounting information between different entities, as without such comparability it is difficult for users to evaluate accounting information.

Desirable characteristics such as consistency thus imply that there are advantages in restricting the number of accounting methods that can be used by reporting entities. However, other academics have argued that any actions which result in a reduction in the accounting methods that can be used by reporting entities lead potentially to reductions in the efficiency with which organizations operate (Watts and Zimmerman, 1986). For example, management might elect to use a particular accounting method because it believes that for their particular and perhaps unique circumstances the specific method of accounting best reflects their underlying performance. Restricting the use of the specific method can result in a reduction in how efficiently external parties can monitor the performance of the entity, and this in itself has been assumed to lead to increased costs for the reporting entity (this 'efficiency perspective', which has been applied in Positive Accounting Theory, is explored in Chapter 7).

If it is assumed, consistent with the *efficiency perspective* briefly mentioned above, that firms adopt particular accounting methods because the methods best reflect the underlying economic performance of the entity, then it is argued by some theorists that the regulation of financial accounting imposes unwarranted costs on reporting entities. For example, if a new accounting standard is released that bans an accounting method being used by particular organizations, this will lead to inefficiencies, as the resulting financial statements will no longer provide the best reflection of the performance of the organization. Many theorists would argue that management is best able to select appropriate accounting methods in given circumstances, and government and/or others should not intervene.

Returning to the specific requirements of the IASB's framework, it is considered important for information to possess each of the four primary qualitative characteristics if it is to be useful in aiding economic decision making. However, it appears that the IASB framework gives greater prominence to *reliability* and *relevance* than to *understandability* or *comparability*. In balancing *relevance* and *reliability*, paragraph 32 notes: 'Information might be relevant but so unreliable in nature or representation that its recognition may be potentially misleading.'

Another consideration that needs to be addressed when deciding whether to disclose particular information is thus the potential constraints on producing relevant and reliable information. The IASB framework discusses two such constraints, being: *timeliness*, and *balancing costs and benefits*. In relation to the former, paragraph 43 recognizes that for much accounting information there will be a trade-off between being able to produce information quickly (and thereby enhancing the *relevance* of the information) and measuring this information accurately (and therefore *reliably*), as the production of accurate information often requires corroboration which occurs sometime later. In these circumstances, it is a judgemental matter regarding how to balance *relevance* and *reliability* (that is, how long to wait against the extent of reliability required).

With the other major constraint, consideration of costs and benefits of disclosure is a highly subjective activity and requires decisions about many issues. Paragraph 44 of the IASB framework requires that 'the benefits derived from information should exceed the cost of providing it'. But from whose perspective are we to consider costs and benefits? Are costs and benefits attributable to some user groups more or less important than others, and so on. Any analysis of costs and benefits is highly judgemental and open to critical comment.

Can financial statements provide neutral and unbiased accounts of an entity's performance and position?

A review of existing conceptual frameworks, as reflected by some of the material provided above, indicates that they provide a perspective that accounting can, if performed properly, provide an *objective* (*neutral* and *representationally faithful*) view of the performance and position of a reporting entity. Reflecting on this apparent perspective, Hines (1991, p. 314) states:

> ... it appears that the ontological assumption underpinning the Conceptual Framework is that the relationship between financial accounting and economic reality is a uni-directional, reflecting or faithfully reproducing relationship: economic reality exists objectively, intersubjectively, concretely and independently of financial accounting practices; financial accounting reflects, mirrors, represents or measures the pre-existent reality.

In fact, the role of a well-functioning system of accounting has been compared with that of cartography. That is, just as an area can be objectively 'mapped', some have argued that so can the financial position and performance of an organization (Solomons, 1978). But as we would appreciate, the practice of accounting is heavily based on professional judgement. As we will see in the sub-section dealing with recognition, the elements of financial accounting are, in some jurisdictions and in the IASB framework, explicitly tied to assessments of probabilities. Clearly there is a degree of subjectivity associated with such assessments.

Although conceptual frameworks argue for attributes such as *neutrality* and *representational faithfulness*, we should perhaps take time to question whether it is valid or realistic to believe that financial accounting provides an objective perspective of an entity's performance. In Chapter 3 we considered research that investigated the economic consequences of accounting regulations. It was argued that before an accounting standard-setting body releases new or amended reporting requirements, it attempts to consider the economic consequences that would follow from the decision. Even if a proposed accounting rule was considered the *best* way to account (however this is determined – which of course would be an issue provoking much debate), if this proposed accounting rule would lead to significant costs being imposed on particular parties (for example, preparers) then plans to require the approach could be abandoned by the standard-setters. Once a profession starts considering the *economic consequences* of particular accounting standards, it is difficult to perceive that the accounting standards, and therefore accounting, can really be considered objective or neutral.

Tied to issues associated with economic implications, there is a body of literature (Positive Accounting Theory, which we have already briefly discussed and which we consider in Chapter 7) that suggests that those responsible for preparing financial statements will be driven by self-interest to select accounting methods that lead to outcomes that provide favourable outcomes for their own personal wealth. That is, this literature predicts that managers and others involved in the accounting function will always put their self-interests ahead of those of others.[11] *If* we accept this body of literature, we would perhaps dismiss notions of objectivity or neutrality as being unrealistic. Self-interest perspectives are often used to explain the phenomenon of 'creative accounting' – a situation where those responsible for the preparation of financial reports select accounting methods that provide the most desired outcomes from their own perspective (such as apparently occurred at Enron).

Accounting standards and conceptual frameworks form the foundation of general-purpose financial reporting. As we have noted in earlier chapters, accounting standards and conceptual frameworks are developed through public consultation, which involves the release of exposure drafts and, subsequently, a review of the written submissions made by various interested parties, including both the preparers and users of the financial information. Consequently, the process leading to finalized accounting standards and conceptual frameworks can be considered to be political. The political solutions and compromises impact on the financial information being presented and that information is, therefore, an outcome of a political process – a process where parties with particular attributes (power) may be able to have a relatively greater impact on final reporting requirements than other parties. This can be considered to have implications for the objectivity or neutrality of the financial information being disclosed.[12]

Hines is one author who has written quite a deal of material on what she sees as the apparent 'myth' of accounting neutrality. Hines (1988) argues that parties involved in the practice and regulation of accounting impose their own judgements about what attributes of an entity's performance should be emphasized (for example, *profits* or *return on assets*), and also what attributes of an entity's operations (for example, expenditure on employee health and safety initiatives) are not important enough to emphasize or highlight separately. The accountant can determine, under the 'guise' of objectivity, which attributes of an entity's operations are important and which can be used as a means of comparing the performance of different organizations. For example, we are informed in the USA's SFAC No. 1 that reported earnings measure an *enterprise's performance* during a period (paragraph 45) – but clearly there are other perspectives of organizational performance (clearly some that would take a more social, as opposed to financial, form).[13] Hines emphasizes that in *communicating reality*, accountants simultaneously *construct reality*.

> If people take a definition or description of reality, for example, an organisational chart, or a budget, or a set of financial statements, to be reality, then they will act on the basis of it, and thereby perpetuate, and in so doing validate, that account of reality. Having acted on the basis of that definition of reality, and having thereby caused consequences to flow from that conception of reality, those same consequences will appear to social actors, in retrospect, to be proof that the definition of reality on which they based their actions was real ... . Decisions and actions based on that account predicate consequences, which, in retrospect, generally confirm the validity of the subsequent account. For example, say an investigator, or a newspaper report, suggested that a 'healthy' set of financial statements is not faithfully representational, and that a firm 'really' is in trouble. If this new definition of reality is accepted by, say, creditors, they may panic and precipitate the failure of the firm, or through the court, they may petition for a liquidation. A new definition of reality, if accepted, will be 'real in its consequences', because people will act on the basis of it. (Hines, 1991, p. 322)

Until accountants determine something is worthy of being the subject of the accounting system, then, in a sense, the issue or item does not exist. There is no transparency, and as such there is no perceived accountability in relation to the item. This perspective is adopted by Handel (1982, p. 36), who states:

> Things may exist independently of our accounts, but they have no human existence until they become accountable. Things may not exist, but they may take on human significance by becoming accountable ... . Accounts define reality and at the same time they are that reality ... . The processes by which accounts are offered and accepted are the fundamental social process ... . Accounts do not more or less accurately describe things. Instead they establish what is accountable in the setting in which they occur. Whether they are accurate or inaccurate by some other standards, accounts define reality for a situation in the sense that people act on the basis of what is accountable in the situation of their action. The account provides a basis for action, a definition of what is real, and it is acted on so long as it remains accountable.[14]

Hence, in concluding this sub-section of the chapter we can see that there are a number of arguments that suggest that characteristics such as neutrality, while playing a part in the development of conceptual frameworks, do not, and perhaps may never be expected to, reflect the underlying characteristics of financial reports.

As with much of the material presented in this book, whether we accept these arguments is a matter of personal opinion. As a concluding comment to challenge the belief in the objectivity or neutrality of accounting practice, we can reflect on the following statement of Baker and Bettner (1997, p. 293):

> Accounting's capacity to create and control social reality translates into empowerment for those who use it. Such power resides in organizations and institutions, where it is used to instill values, sustain legitimizing myths, mask conflict and promote self-perpetuating social orders. Throughout society, the influence of accounting permeates fundamental issues concerning wealth distribution, social justice, political ideology and environmental degradation. Contrary to public opinion, accounting is not a static reflection of economic reality, but rather is a highly partisan activity. [15]

Definition of the elements of financial reporting

Having considered perspectives on the required qualitative characteristics of financial information, the next building block we can consider is how the elements of financial reporting are defined. The definitions provided within conceptual frameworks indicate the characteristics or attributes that are required before an item can be considered as belonging to a particular class of element (for example, before it can be considered to be an *asset*). Recognition criteria (which we consider in the next sub-section of this chapter), on the other hand, are employed to determine whether the item can actually be included within the financial reports (i.e. whether a particular transaction or event should be recognized as affecting the accounts).

Alternative approaches have been adopted in defining the elements of financial reporting. In the United States, 10 elements of financial reporting are identified in SFAC 3, and subsequently in SFAC 6. [16] These elements are assets, liabilities, equity, investments, distributions, comprehensive income, revenues, expenses, gains, and losses. The IASB's 1989 framework identifies five elements, split into two broad groups. The first group are elements relating to *financial position*, comprising the elements of: *assets, liabilities* and *equity*. The second group are elements relating to *performance* and comprise *income* and *expenses*. In the UK, the elements defined in the ASB's 1999 framework were somewhere between the US and the IASB frameworks, being: *assets, liabilities, ownership interest, gains, losses, contributions from owners*, and *distributions to owners*.

In the FASB conceptual framework, rather than simply having a single element entitled *income* (or *gains* in the ASB's framework), two elements are provided, *revenues* and *gains*, where revenues relate to the 'ongoing major or central operations' of the entity, while gains relate to 'peripheral or incidental transactions'. Clearly the FASB classification system requires some judgement to be made about whether an item does or does not relate to the central operations of the entity. Such differentiation admits the possibility that managers might opportunistically manipulate whether items are treated as part of the ongoing operations of the entity, or whether they are treated as peripheral or incidental.

Approaches to determining profits

There are different approaches that can be applied to determining profits (revenues less expenses). Two such approaches are commonly referred to as the *asset/liability approach*, and the *revenue/expense approach*. The asset/liability approach links profit to changes that have occurred in the assets and liabilities of the reporting entity, whereas the revenue/expense approach tends to rely on concepts such as the matching principle, which is very much focused on actual transactions and which gives limited consideration to changes in the values of assets and liabilities.

In the asset/liability approach, the principal consideration in determining how to account for any transaction (or other event) is to determine what impact this transaction or event has had on increasing or decreasing assets or liabilities. The amount of the impact of any transaction or event which has not affected the value of assets or liabilities is effectively treated as a gain or loss (income or expense). This approach therefore treats the balance sheet as the primary financial statement, and anything which does not belong in the balance sheet is put through the profit and loss account (or income statement). For example, where an entity incurs expenditure, the decision process regarding how to treat this expenditure in the accounts is firstly to ask: has this expenditure given rise to a new asset (or an increase in the value of an existing asset)? Where all of the expenditure is deemed to have created an asset, all of the expenditure will be reflected in the balance sheet as an increase in the book value of assets and there will be no immediate impact on the profit and loss account. In situations where it is deemed that the value of an asset created (in accordance with the definition of assets discussed below) is lower than the expenditure incurred, the balance sheet increase in book value of assets will be the value of the asset created, and the difference between this value of the asset created and the amount of the expenditure incurred will be reflected in the profit and loss account as an expense. Thus, if an entity incurs €1,000 expenditure on purchasing goods for resale, but by the date these goods are received by the entity their realizable value has fallen to €800, then €800 of this expenditure will be reflected in the balance sheet as an asset and the balance of the transaction (€200) will be reflected as a loss (or expense) in the profit and loss account.

Conversely, the revenue/expense approach treats the profit and loss account as the principal financial statement, with the first consideration for any transaction or event being how much of this transaction or event can (and should) be treated as income or expenses in accordance with the accruals and prudence concepts. Any amount not treated as income or expenditure is then placed in the balance sheet as an asset or liability – with assets broadly representing the amount of expenditure which has not yet been consumed at the balance sheet date (and the amount of income which has not yet been received in cash), while liabilities represent expenditure which has been consumed in advance of payment (and income received in advance). Thus, in the example at the end of the last paragraph, the decision process would be: how much of the €1,000 expenditure should be treated as an expense immediately? – the €200 which is unlikely to be recovered in future sales. The balance of €800 would then be placed in the balance sheet as an asset representing the amount of expenditure which has yet to be matched against income (or consumed by selling the goods).

As in the above simplified example, for many transactions and events the asset/liability approach will produce the same accounting results as the revenue/expense approach, but the decision processes in arriving at this result are fundamentally different. However, for many more complex transactions and events, the two approaches will result in different accounting treatments. Most conceptual framework projects adopt the asset/liability approach. Within these frameworks the definitions of elements of financial statements must thus start with definitions of assets and liabilities, as the definitions of all other elements flow from these definitions of assets and liabilities.

Definition of assets

In the IASB framework, paragraph 49(a) defines an asset as:

> ... a resource controlled by the entity as a result of past events and from which future economic benefits are expected to flow to the entity.

This definition, which is similar to that adopted by FASB, identifies three key characteristics:

* there must be an expected future economic benefit;
* the reporting entity must control the resource giving rise to these future economic benefits; and
* the transaction or other event giving rise to the reporting entity's control over the future economic benefits must have occurred.

The IASB framework makes clear that the future economic benefits can be distinguished from the source of the benefit – a particular object or right. The definition refers to the benefit and not the source. Thus whether an object or right is disclosed as an asset will be dependent upon the likely economic benefits flowing from it. In the absence of the benefits, the object should not be disclosed as an asset. As paragraph 59 of the framework states:

> There is a close association between incurring expenditure and generating assets but the two do not necessarily coincide. Hence, when an entity incurs expenditure, this may provide evidence that future economic benefits were sought but is not conclusive proof that an item satisfying the definition of an asset has been obtained.

Conceptual frameworks do not require that an item must have a value in exchange before it can be recognized as an *asset*. The economic benefits may result from its ongoing use within the organization. This approach can be contrasted with the model of accounting proposed by Raymond Chambers: *continuously contemporary accounting* (which we considered in Chapter 5). Under Chambers' approach to accounting, if an asset does not have a current market value (value in exchange) then it is to be excluded from the financial statements.

The characteristic of *control* relates to the capacity of a reporting entity to benefit from the asset and to deny or regulate the access of others to the benefit. The capacity to control would normally stem from legal rights. However, legal enforceability is not a prerequisite for establishing the existence of control. Hence, it is important to realize that control, and not legal ownership, is required before an asset can be shown within the body of an entity's balance sheet. Frequently, controlled assets are owned but this is not always the case. As paragraph 57 of the framework states:

> In determining the existence of an asset, the right of ownership is not essential; thus, for example, property held on a lease is an asset if the entity controls the benefits which are expected to flow from the property. Although the capacity of an entity to control benefits is usually the result of legal rights, an item may nonetheless satisfy the definition of an asset even where there is no legal control.

Definition of liabilities

Paragraph 49(b) of the IASB framework defines a liability as:

> ... a present obligation of the entity arising from past events, the settlement of which is expected to result in an outflow from the entity of resources embodying economic benefits.

This definition is also very similar to the definition provided in other conceptual frameworks and, as with the definition of assets, there are three key characteristics:

- there must be an expected future disposition or transfer of economic benefits to other entities;
- it must be a present obligation; and
- a past transaction or other event must have created the obligation.

In considering the requirement that it be a present obligation, paragraph 60 of the IASB framework requires the inclusion not only of legally enforceable obligations but also those arising 'from normal business practice, custom and a desire to maintain good business relations or act in an equitable manner'.

Requiring liability recognition to be dependent upon there being a present obligation to other entities has implications for the disclosure of various provision accounts, such as a provision for maintenance. Generally accepted accounting practice in some countries has required such amounts to be disclosed as a liability, even though it does not involve an obligation to an external party. This issue is partially addressed in paragraph 64 of the IASB framework. It states:

> ... when a provision involves a present obligation and satisfies the rest of the definition, it is a liability even if the amount has to be estimated. Examples include provisions for payments to be made under existing warranties and provisions to cover pension obligations

Thus, the IASB framework requires estimated (and therefore uncertain) present obligations, which have resulted from past events and are likely to result in an outflow of economic resources, to be treated as liabilities. In more recent conceptual frameworks (such as the ASB's UK and Irish framework and the Australian Accounting Standards Board's framework – both of which have now effectively been superseded with the older IASB framework given the adoption of IASs/IFRSs in both the EU and Australia from 2005) there tends to be an explicit restriction in the use of uncommitted provisions. For example, paragraph 60 of the Australian *Statement of Accounting Concepts No. 4* states:

> Some entities that carry out overhauls, repairs and renewals relating to major items of property, plant and equipment regularly 'provide' in their financial reports for such work to be undertaken in the future, with concomitant recognition of an expense. These provisions do not satisfy the definition of liabilities, because the entity does not have a present obligation to an external party ... . Also, some entities create 'provisions' for uninsured future losses (sometimes known as 'self-insurance provisions') for the purpose of retaining funds in the entity to meet losses which may arise in the future. In these situations, the entity does not have an obligation to an external party. [17]

Definition of equity

Paragraph 49(c) of the IASB framework defines equity as 'the residual interest in the assets of the entity after deducting all its liabilities'. This definition is essentially the same as that provided by the FASB and the ASB. The residual interest is a claim or right to the net assets of the reporting entity. As a residual interest, it ranks after liabilities in terms of a claim against the assets of a reporting entity. Consistent with the *asset/liability approach* to determining profits (discussed earlier in this section), the definition of equity is directly a function of the definitions of assets and liabilities. Profit or loss, income and expenses are then calculated in terms of changes in equity (i.e. changes in net assets).

Definition of income

Consistent with the *asset/liability approach*, the definition of income (and expenses) provided in the IASB framework is dependent upon the definitions given to assets and liabilities. Paragraph 70(a) defines income as:

> ... increases in economic benefits during the accounting period in the form of inflows or enhancements of assets or decreases of liabilities that result in increases in equity, other than those relating to contributions from equity participants.

This definition is broadly consistent with that provided by the FASB, except that the FASB definition in SFAC 3 and 6 restricts revenues to the transaction or events that relate to the 'ongoing major or central operations' of the entity. Income can therefore be considered as relating to transactions or events that cause an increase in the net assets of the reporting entity, other than owner contributions. Strictly speaking, applying the definition of income, increases in the market values of all assets could be treated as income. However, this is not always the case.

Within the IASB approach, revenues can be recognized from normal trading relations, as well as from non-reciprocal transfers such as grants, donations, bequests, or where liabilities are forgiven.

The IASB framework further subdivides income into revenues and gains. Pursuant to the IASB framework, 'revenue' arises in the course of the ordinary activities of an entity and is referred to by a variety of different names including sales, fees, interest, dividends, royalties and rent. 'Gains' represent other items that meet the definition of income and may, or may not, arise in the course of the ordinary activities of an enterprise. Gains include, for example, those arising on the disposal of non-current assets. There will be a degree of professional judgement involved in determining whether a component of income should be classified as revenue, or as a gain. Conceptually, it is not clear why the IASB framework subdivides income into revenues and gains and there is minimal justification provided for this subdivision within the framework.

Definition of expenses

As with income, the definition of expenses is dependent upon the definitions of assets and liabilities. Paragraph 70(b) of the IASB framework defines expenses as:

> ... decreases in economic benefits during the accounting period in the form of outflows
> or depletions of assets or incurrences of liabilities that result in decreases in equity, other
> than those relating to distributions to equity participants.

There is no reference within the IASB framework to traditional notions of 'matching' expenses with related revenues. The definition provided by the FASB in SFAC 3 and 6 is also similar, but restricts expenses to transactions or events relating to 'ongoing major or central operations'.[18] Expenses may therefore be considered as transactions or events that cause reductions in the net assets or equity of the reporting entity, other than those caused by distributions to the owners. They include losses (reductions in net assets) caused by events which are not under the control of an entity – such as the uninsured element of losses caused by fires or floods, or losses caused by unhedged changes in foreign exchange rates.

Reviewing the above definition of expenses (which we know is a direct function of the definitions given to assets and liabilities) we can see that if a resource is used up or damaged by an entity, but that entity does not *control* the resource – that is, it is not an *asset* of the entity – then to the extent that no liabilities or fines are imposed, no expenses will be recorded by the entity. For example, if an entity pollutes the environment but incurs no related fines, then no expense will be acknowledged, and reported profits will not be impacted, no matter how much pollution was emitted or how much damage was done to resources that are shared with others (and hence, not controlled by the reporting entity). This has been seen as a limitation of financial accounting and a number of experimental approaches have been adopted by a number of entities to recognize the externalities their operations can generate, but which would normally be ignored by traditional systems of accounting, including those proposed by the various conceptual framework projects. (Issues related to this point are examined in Chapter 9.)

The IASB framework does not have a separate definition of profits or income, but rather, only defines income and expenses as elements of performance. Profit is a presentational issue and is represented as the difference between the two elements, income and expenses.

Recognition of the elements of financial reporting

Having considered definitions of financial reporting, the next building block we can consider is the recognition criteria for these elements. Recognition criteria are employed to determine whether an item can actually be included within any of the elements of the financial reports. Issues of recognition are tied to issues of measurement, which we consider in the next sub-section of this chapter, as an item cannot be recognized if it cannot be reliably measured.

Paragraph 83 of the IASB framework specifies that:

> An item that meets the definition of an element should be recognised if:
> (a) it is probable that any future economic benefit associated with the item will flow to or from the entity; and
> (b) the item has a cost or value that can be measured with reliability.

Thus, recognition is dependent upon the degree of probability that a future flow of economic benefits will arise which can be reliably measured. Obviously, considerations of *probability* can be very subjective, such that different people in different organizations might make different probability assessments for similar items. This will have implications for issues such as comparability – a qualitative characteristic of financial reporting. The IASB framework provides relatively little guidance in judging probability, other than stating (in paragraph 85) that:

> Assessments of the degree of uncertainty attaching to the flow of future economic benefits are made on the basis of the evidence available when the financial statements are prepared.

Other paragraphs in the IASB framework also mention that recognition depends upon materiality, and that given the interconnectedness of the definitions of the various elements, recognition of a transaction or event in respect of one element requires recognition in all elements related to that transaction or event. For example, if an event occurs which leads to the recognition that the value of a fixed asset has decreased (for example, depreciation) then the impact of this event on both assets and expenses must be recognized.

As noted above, issues of recognition are often regarded as standing side-by-side with issues of measurements. For example, Sterling (1985) argues that it is illogical to discuss how or when to recognize an element of accounting if we are not sure what measurement characteristics are to be recognized in relation to assets. What do you think of Sterling's argument that considering recognition issues in advance of measurement issues is akin to 'putting the cart before the horse'?

Measurement principles

Conceptual frameworks have tended to provide very limited prescription in relation to measurement issues. Assets and liabilities are often (and certainly in practice under IAS/IFRS) measured in a variety of ways depending upon the particular class of assets or liabilities being considered, and given the way assets and liabilities are defined this has direct implications for reported profits. For example, liabilities are frequently recorded at present value, face value or on some other basis. In relation to assets, there are various ways these are measured – on the basis of historical costs, market values, current replacement costs, current selling prices and so forth.

Issues associated with measurement appeared to represent a stumbling block in the development of the FASB conceptual framework. While the FASB framework was initially promoted as being prescriptive, when SFAC 5 was issued in 1984 the FASB appeared to side-step the difficult measurement issues, and rather, the statement provided a description of various approaches to measuring the elements of accounting. SFAC 5 simply notes that there are generally accepted to be five alternative measurement bases applied in practice: historical cost, current replacement cost, current market value, net realizable value, and present value. As noted previously in this chapter, such a descriptive approach was generally considered to represent a 'cop-out' on behalf of the FASB (Solomons, 1986). The IASB framework explicitly recognizes the same variety of acceptable measurement bases as the FASB framework, with the exception of current market value (which could be regarded as comprising elements of current replacement cost and net realizable (sale) value).

Benefits associated with having a conceptual framework

Conceptual frameworks are costly to develop and open to many forms of political interference. In some respects their degree of progress, while initially promising, has in recent years been rather slow and disappointing. Is it worth continuing with these frameworks? In this section we consider some perceived advantages that have been advanced by standard-setting bodies as being likely to follow from the development of a conceptual framework (we will also consider some criticisms). These include the following.

(a) Accounting standards should be more consistent and logical because they are developed from an orderly set of concepts. The view is that in the absence of a coherent the ~~~~ ~~~ nent of accounting standards could be somewhat

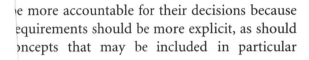

e more accountable for their decisions because equirements should be more explicit, as should oncepts that may be included in particular

n between the standard-setters and their con- because the conceptual underpinnings of pro- uld be more apparent when the standard-setters Preparers and auditors will have a better under- rting/auditing. There is also a perspective that should alleviate some of the political pressure when accounting standards are developed – the n a sense, provide a defence against political

standards should be more economical because guide the standard-setters in their decision

er a particular issue, there might be a reduced ccounting standards. d the effect of emphasizing the 'decision use- rather than simply just restricting concern to p.

tages of conceptual frameworks, as with all bbying processes and political actions, there disadvantaged relative to others.

Perhaps some smaller organizations feel that they are overburdened by reporting requirements because analysts have been able to convince regulators that particular information was necessary for an efficiently functioning economy.

Another criticism raised in terms of conceptual framework projects relates to their focus. Being principally economic in focus, general purpose financial reports typically ignore transactions or events that have not involved market transactions or an exchange of property rights. That is, transactions or events that cannot be linked to a 'market price' are not recognized. For example, a great deal of recent literature has been critical of traditional financial accounting for its failure to recognize the environmental externalities caused by business entities (see Deegan and Rankin, 1997, Gray and Bebbington, 2001, Gray *et al.*, 1996, Rubenstein, 1992).

Following on from the above point, it has been argued that by focusing on economic performance, this, in itself, further reinforces the importance of economic performance relative to various levels of social performance. Several writers such as Hines (1988) and Gray and Bebbington (2001) have argued that the accounting profession can play a large part in influencing the forms of social conduct acceptable to the broader community. As has been indicated previously, accounting can both reflect and construct social expectations. For example, if profits and associated financial data are promoted as the best measure of organizational success, it could be argued that dominant consideration – by both the organization and the community – will only be given to activities that impact on this measure. If accountants were encouraged to embrace other types of performance indicators, including those that relate to environmental and other social performance, this may conceivably filter through to broadening people's expectations about organizational performance. Nevertheless, at the present time, profitability, as indicated by the output of the accounting system, is typically used as a guide to the success of the organization.

Another criticism of conceptual frameworks is that they simply represent a codification of existing practice (Dean and Clarke, 2003, Hines, 1989), putting in place a series of documents that describe existing practice, rather than prescribing an 'ideal' or logically derived approach to accounting. Hines (1989) also argues that accounting regulations, as generated by the accounting regulators, are no more than the residual of a political process and as such do not represent any form of *ideal* model.

It has also been argued that conceptual frameworks have a more important objective from the perspective of the accounting standard-setters and one that does not provide benefits to financial statement users. Hines (1989) provides evidence that conceptual framework projects were actually initiated at times when professions were under threat – that they are 'a strategic manoeuvre for providing legitimacy to standard-setting boards during periods of competition or threatened government intervention' (1989, p. 89).

In supporting her case, Hines referred to the work undertaken in Canada. The Canadian Institute of Chartered Accountants (CICA) had done very little throughout the 1980s in relation to its conceptual framework project. It had commenced the development of a framework in about 1980, a period Hines claimed was 'a time of pressures for reform and criticisms of accounting standard-setting in Canada' (Hines, 1989, p. 88). However, interest 'waned' until another Canadian professional accounting body, the Certified General Accountants Association, through its

Accounting Standards Authority of Canada, began developing a conceptual framework in 1986. This was deemed to represent a threat to CICA 'who were motivated into action'. Solomons (1983) also provides an argument that conceptual frameworks are a defence against political interference by other interest groups.

Conceptual frameworks as a means of legitimizing standard-setting bodies

While accounting standard-setters have promoted the benefits of conceptual frameworks, some of which have been discussed above, a number of writers (including Hines and Solomons, as identified above) have suggested that conceptual frameworks are created primarily to provide benefits to the parties that actually develop or commission the frameworks. It has been argued that they have been used as devices to help ensure the ongoing existence of the accounting profession by 'boosting' their public standing (Dopuch and Sunder, 1980, p. 17). As Hines (1989, p. 74) suggests:

> One of the main obstacles against which accountants have continually had to struggle in the professionalism quest has been the threat of an apparent absence of a formal body of accounting knowledge, and that creating the perception of possessing such knowledge has been an important part of creating and reproducing their social identity as a profession .... Viewing these attempts (at establishing conceptual frameworks) as claims to accounting knowledge, which are used as a political resource in reducing the threat of government intervention and competing with other groups, in order to maintain and increase professionalism and social mobility seems to explain these projects better than viewing them from a technical/functional perspective.

It is argued that conceptual frameworks provide a means of increasing the ability of a profession to self-regulate, thereby countering the possibility that government intervention will occur. Hines (1991, p. 328) states:

> CFs presume, legitimise and reproduce the assumption of an objective world and as such they play a part in constituting the social world .... CFs provide social legitimacy to the accounting profession.
>
> Since the objectivity assumption is the central premise of our society ... a fundamental form of social power accrues to those who are able to trade on the objectivity assumption. Legitimacy is achieved by tapping into this central proposition because accounts generated around this proposition are perceived as 'normal'. It is perhaps not surprising or anomalous then that CF projects continue to be undertaken which rely on information qualities such as 'representational faithfulness', 'neutrality', 'reliability', etc., which presume a concrete, objective world, even though past CFs have not succeeded in generating Accounting Standards which achieve these qualities. The very talk, predicated on the assumption of an objective world to which accountants have privileged access via their 'measurement expertise', serves to construct a perceived legitimacy for the profession's power and autonomy.

If we accept the argument of Hines, we would perhaps reject notions that the accounting profession was attempting to uncover any *truths* or *ideals*, and rather, we would consider that the development of conceptual frameworks was a political action to ensure the survival of the profession. Reflecting on the role of conceptual frameworks in assisting a professional accounting body to survive, Horngren (1981, p. 87) notes:

> The useful life of the FASB is not going to rest on issues of technical competence. The pivotal issue will be the ability of the board to resolve conflicts among the various constituencies in a manner perceived to be acceptable to the ultimate constituent, the 800-pound gorilla in the form of the federal government, particularly the SEC (of course, the federal gorilla is also subject to pressure from its constituents). The ability will be manifested in the FASB's decisions, appointments and conceptual framework. So the conceptual framework is desirable if the survival of the FASB is considered to be desirable. That is, the framework is likely to help provide power to the board. After all, the board has no coercive power. Instead, the board must really rely on power by persuasion.

Chapter summary

In this chapter we have considered the development of conceptual frameworks. We have seen that conceptual frameworks are made up of a number of building blocks that cover issues of central importance to the financial reporting process. From a technical or functional perspective it has been argued by accounting standard-setters that the development of a conceptual framework will lead to improvements in financial reporting practices, which will in turn lead to reports that are deemed more useful for the economic decisions made by the report users. With a well-formulated conceptual framework there is an expectation that information will be generated that is of more relevance to report users, as well as being more reliable. The use of a logically derived conceptual framework will also lead to the development of accounting standards which are consistent with each other. Further, there is a view that conceptual frameworks will allow constituents to understand more fully how and why particular accounting standards require specific approaches to be adopted, and will provide preparers with guidance when no specific accounting standards exist.

In considering the success of conceptual frameworks there are numerous authors who suggest that the frameworks have been a failure and have questioned whether such work should continue (Dopuch and Sunder, 1980). It has appeared that issues such as those relating to measurement have been very real stumbling blocks for the ongoing development of conceptual frameworks. The progress, or in some cases the lack of it, emphasizes the political nature of the accounting standard-setting process and shows that where constituents do not support particular approaches, the standard-setters will quite often abandon particular endeavours.

While we can question the technical accomplishments of conceptual frameworks, some authors have suggested that technical advances were not the goal of the standard-setters. Rather, they have suggested that conceptual frameworks are actually established to bolster the ongoing existence and position of accountants in society. As Hines (1989, p. 79) states:

> Since professional powers, professional prestige and financial rewards are legitimised in society by being assumed to be founded on a formal body of knowledge unique to the profession, the possibility of the loss of this mystique poses a threat to the successful advancement or social reproduction of the profession. The phenomenon of the proliferation of conceptual framework projects in the UK, USA, Canada and Australia is better understood as a response to such a threat than in the functional/technical terms in which the CFs have been articulated and discussed.

Whether we accept that conceptual frameworks are developed to improve the practice of accounting, or that such frameworks are primarily created to assist those within the accounting profession, is obviously a matter of personal opinion. Having read this chapter you should be better informed to make a judgement.

Questions

6.1 What is a conceptual framework of accounting?

6.2 Do you consider that we need conceptual frameworks? Explain your answer.

6.3 What advantages or benefits have been advanced by standard-setters to support the development of conceptual framework projects? Do you agree that in practice such benefits will be achieved?

6.4 Conceptual framework projects identify a number of qualitative criteria that financial information should possess if it is to be useful for economic decision making. Two such attributes include neutrality and representational faithfulness. Do you believe that financial information can, in reality, be neutral and representationally faithful? Explain your answer.

6.5 The two main qualitative characteristics that financial information should possess have been identified as relevance and reliability. Is one more important than the other, or are they equally important?

6.6 What are some possible objectives of general purpose financial reporting? Which objective appears to have been embraced within existing conceptual framework projects?

6.7 Which groups within society are likely to benefit from the development of a conceptual framework of accounting?

6.8 Would you consider that conceptual frameworks have been successful in achieving their stated objectives? Why, or why not?

6.9 Conceptual frameworks have yet to provide prescription in relation to measurement issues. Why do you think this is the case?

6.10 Hines (1989, p. 89) argues that conceptual frameworks are 'a strategic manoeuvre for providing legitimacy to standard-setting boards during periods of competition or threatened government intervention'. Explain the basis of her argument and consider whether the history of the development of conceptual frameworks supports her position.

6.11 *The Corporate Report* (UK) referred to the 'public's right to information'. How does this differ from the perspectives adopted in other conceptual framework projects?

6.12 Hines (1991) states that 'in communicating reality, accountants simultaneously create reality'. What does she mean?

6.13 In this chapter we discussed how accounting standard-setters typically find it difficult to get support for newly developed requirements if those requirements represent major changes from existing practice. Why do you think this is the case and do you think the potential lack of support would influence the strategies adopted by accounting standard-setters?

Notes

1 For example, the UK's Accounting Standards Board initiated a conceptual framework development project in 1991. However, recommendations related to the practice of accounting first started being released in the 1940s, followed some years later by accounting standards. By the time the UK's conceptual framework (entitled *The Statement of Principles*) was issued in 1999, there were already many accounting standards in place. Reflective of the lack of agreement in many key areas of financial reporting, there was a degree of inconsistency between the various accounting standards.

2 Conceptual frameworks of accounting relate to general purpose financial reporting (which meets the needs of a multitude of user groups, many of which have information needs in common) as opposed to special purpose financial reports (special purpose financial reports are specifically designed to meet the information needs of a specific user or group). We consider definitions of general purpose financial reporting in more depth later in this chapter.

3 This raises issues associated with the possible duplication of effort and whether it might have been more cost-efficient for the various countries to pool their resources and develop one unified conceptual framework. However as Kenneth Most states in Staunton (1984, p. 87) when comparing the Australian and USA conceptual frameworks, 'a conceptual framework differs from a straight-jacket; one size does not fit all. The kind of doctrinaire thinkers who have dominated the standard-setting process in this country (United States) are not subject to the same economic, sociological, and professional influences that would affect Australians faced with a similar task'.

Consistent with this view, Chapter 4 considered how issues such as *culture* are used to explain differences between the rules released by standard-setters in different countries.

4   In relation to APB Statement No. 4, Peasnell (1982, p. 245) notes that 'at best it was a defensive, descriptive document'.

5   This focus on decision users' needs was also embraced in the earlier document, *A Statement of Basic Accounting Theory*, issued by the American Accounting Association in 1966. It was also embraced in APB Statement No. 4 released in 1970.

6   Since 2005 Australia has embraced the IASB conceptual framework. This move was based upon the view that as Australia elected to adopt IASs/IFRSs from 2005 – many of which represented significant changes from Australian accounting standards – then it also had to embrace the IASB framework given that IAS, and more recently, IFRS are developed based, at least in part, on the contents of the IASB framework. This was an interesting move given that many commentators considered that the IASB framework was deficient relative to the Australian conceptual framework, which amongst other things provided extensive guidance in relation to identifying and classifying an entity as a reporting entity as well as providing extensive discussion of the objectives of general purpose financial reporting (Deegan, 2005).

7   We consider this issue further in Chapter 9.

8   In an FASB Discussion Memorandum released in 1974, the FASB defines an objective as 'something toward which effort is directed, an aim, or end of action, a goal'. It is perhaps questionable whether information itself can have objectives. Certainly, users of information can have objectives which can be achieved (or not) as a result of using information. Nevertheless, it is common for accounting standard-setters to talk about the objectives of financial information, and as such, we maintain this convention.

9   The more traditional stewardship role of financial statements is explicitly recognized as an additional objective in the IASB framework, where paragraph 14 states: 'Financial statements also show the results of the stewardship of management, or the accountability of management for the resources entrusted to it'.

10   Within Chambers' model of accounting, continuously contemporary accounting, which is covered in Chapter 5, one objective of financial accounting is to provide information about the *adaptive capacity* of an entity. Historical cost information does not help meet this objective. It is interesting to note that although the IASB framework does not really address measurement issues, many recently released accounting standards require assets to be valued on the basis of fair values, and also various liabilities to be valued on the basis of present values. In effect accounting regulators appear to be side-stepping the use of the conceptual framework as the foundation of developing the measurement principles of general purpose financial reporting and instead are using the ongoing release of new accounting standards as the means of bringing major change to accounting measurement principles. Such an approach seems to be inconsistent with the reasons why conceptual frameworks are established.

11   One example that is often provided by proponents of Positive Accounting Theory is managers being provided with a bonus tied to the output of the accounting system, for example, to profits. It would be argued in such a case that managers will have incentives to increase reported profits, rather than be objective.

12   Hines (1989, p. 80) argues that many individuals not involved in the standard-setting process would be very surprised to find out just how political the development of accounting standards actually is. She states 'an accounting outsider might find it remarkable that accounting knowledge should be articulated not only by professional accountants, but also by accounting information users – much like doctors and patients collaborating on the development of medical knowledge'.

13   And of course financial 'performance' is very much tied to the judgements about which particular accounting methods should be employed, over how many years an asset should be amortized, and so forth. Further, because accounting rules can change over

time, this in itself can lead to a change in reported profits and hence a change in apparent 'performance'.

14 As quoted in Hines (1991).

15 The view that the practice of accounting provides the means of maintaining existing positions of power and wealth by a favoured 'elite' is further investigated in Chapter 12 which considers the works of a body of theorists who are labelled *critical theorists*.

16 SFAC 3 was superseded by SFAC 6. SFAC 3 related to business enterprises. SFAC 6 includes non-business entities.

17 Within Australia, SAC 4 was replaced in 2005 by the IASB framework.

18 The definition of expenses provided in SFAC 3 and 6 is 'outflows or other using up of the assets of the entity or incurrences of liabilities of an entity (or a combination of both) during a period that result from delivering or producing goods, rendering services, or carrying out other activities that constitute the entity's ongoing major or central operations'.

References

Accounting Standards Steering Committee (1975) 'The Corporate Report', London: Institute of Chartered Accountants in England & Wales.

AICPA (1973) 'Report of study group on objectives of financial statements', *The Trueblood Report*, New York: American Institute of Certified Public Accountants.

Baker, C. & Bettner, M. (1997) 'Interpretive and critical research in accounting: A commentary on its absence from mainstream accounting research', *Critical Perspectives on Accounting*, **8** (1), pp. 293–310.

Booth, B. (2003) 'The conceptual framework as a coherent system for the development of accounting standards', *ABACUS*, **39** (3), pp. 310–24.

Chambers, R. J. (1966) *Accounting, Evaluation and Economic Behavior*, Englewood Cliffs, N.J.: Prentice-Hall.

Dean, G. W. & Clarke, F. L. (2003) 'An evolving conceptual framework?' *ABACUS*, **39** (3), pp. 279–97.

Deegan, C. (2005) *Australian Financial Accounting*, 4th edn, Sydney: McGraw-Hill Book Company.

Deegan, C. M. & Rankin, M. (1997) 'The materiality of environmental information to users of accounting reports', *Accounting, Auditing and Accountability Journal*, **10** (4), pp. 562–83.

Dopuch, N. & Sunder, S. (1980) 'FASB's statements on objectives and elements of financial accounting: A review', *The Accounting Review*, **55** (1), pp. 1–21.

Grady, P. (1965) 'An inventory of generally accepted accounting principles for business enterprises', *Accounting Research Study No. 7*, New York: AICPA.

Gray, R. & Bebbington, J. (2001) *Accounting for the Environment*, London: Sage Publications Ltd.

Gray, R., Owen, D., & Adams, C. (1996) *Accounting and Accountability: Changes and Challenges in Corporate Social and Environmental Reporting*, London: Prentice-Hall.

Handel, W. (1982) *Ethnomethodology: How People Make Sense*, Hemel Hempstead: Prentice-Hall.

Hendriksen, E. (1970) *Accounting Theory*, Illinois: Richard D. Irwin.

Hines, R. (1988) 'Financial accounting: In communicating reality, we construct reality', *Accounting Organizations and Society*, **13** (3), pp. 251–62.

Hines, R. (1989) 'Financial accounting knowledge, conceptual framework projects and the social construction of the accounting profession', *Accounting, Auditing and Accountability Journal*, **2** (2), pp. 72–92.

Hines, R. (1991) 'The FASB's conceptual framework, financial accounting and the maintenance of the social world', *Accounting Organizations and Society*, **16** (4), pp. 313–31.

Horngren, C. T. (1981) 'Uses and limitations of a conceptual framework', *Journal of Accountancy*, **151** (4), pp. 86–95.

International Accounting Standards Committee (1989) *Framework for the Preparation and Presentation of Financial Statements*, International Accounting Standards Committee, London.

Loftus, J. A. (2003) 'The CF and accounting standards: The persistence of discrepancies', *ABACUS*, **39** (3), pp. 298–309.

Miller, P. B. W. (1990) 'The conceptual framework as reformation and counter-reformation', *Accounting Horizons* (June), pp. 23–32.

Miller, P. B. W. & Reading, R. (1986) *The FASB: The People, the Process, and the Politics*, Illinois: Irwin.

Moonitz, M. (1961) 'The basic postulates of accounting', *Accounting Research Study No. 1*, New York: AICPA.

Nussbaumer, N. (1992) 'Does the FASB's conceptual framework help solve real accounting issues?' *Journal of Accounting Education*, **10** (1), pp. 235–42.

Peasnell, K. V. (1982) 'The function of a conceptual framework for corporate financial reporting', *Accounting and Business Research*, **12** (4), pp. 243–56.

Rubenstein, D. B. (1992) 'Bridging the gap between green accounting and black ink', *Accounting Organizations and Society*, **17** (5), pp. 501–8.

Solomons, D. (1978) 'The politicization of accounting', *Journal of Accountancy*, **146** (5), pp. 65–72.

Solomons, D. (1983) 'The political implications of accounting and accounting standard setting', *Accounting and Business Research*, **13** (56), pp. 107–18.

Solomons, D. (1986) 'The FASB's conceptual framework: An evaluation', *Journal of Accountancy*, **161** (6), pp. 114–24.

Sprouse, R. & Moonitz, M. (1962) 'A tentative set of broad accounting principles for business enterprises', *Accounting Research Study No. 3*, New York: American Institute of Certified Public Accountants.

Stamp, E. (1980) *Corporate Reporting: Its Future Evolution*, Toronto: Canadian Institute of Chartered Accountants.

Staunton, J. (1984) 'Why a conceptual framework of accounting?' *Accounting Forum*, **7** (2), pp. 85–90.

Sterling, R. R. (1985) 'An essay on recognition', Sydney: The University of Sydney Accounting Research Centre.

Walker, R. G. (2003) 'Objectives of financial reporting', *ABACUS*, **39** (3), pp. 340–55.

Watts, R. L. & Zimmerman, J. L. (1986) *Positive Accounting Theory*, Englewood Cliffs, New Jersey: Prentice-Hall Inc.

Wells, M. (2003) 'Forum: The accounting conceptual framework', *ABACUS*, **39** (3), pp. 273–8.

Positive Accounting Theory

Opening issues

Corporate management often expends considerable time and effort making submissions to accounting regulators on proposed introductions of, or amendments to, mandated accounting requirements. For example, as we discussed in Chapter 3, elements of the revised IAS 39 (which required market valuations for financial instruments) were opposed by many banks in Europe. The banks argued that these elements of IAS 39 failed to take account of the underlying economic realities of the manner in which these banks operated, and would result in financial statements which would not reflect the underlying economic reality. Executives of many banks lobbied against the introduction of these elements of IAS 39. What would have motivated such opposition?

Positive Accounting Theory defined

As indicated in Chapter 1, a *positive theory* is a theory that seeks to explain and predict particular phenomena. According to Watts (1995, p. 334), the use of the term *positive research* was popularized in economics by Friedman (1953) and was used to distinguish research which sought to *explain* and *predict* (which is positive research), from research which aimed to provide *prescription* (prescriptive research is often labelled *normative* research). Positive Accounting Theory, the topic discussed in this chapter and the theory popularized by Watts and Zimmerman, is one of several positive theories of accounting.[1] As indicated in Chapter 1, we will refer to the general class of theories that attempt to explain and predict accounting practice in lower case (that is, as positive theories of accounting), and will refer to Watts and Zimmerman's particular positive theory of accounting as Positive Accounting Theory (that is, in upper case). Hence, while it might be confusing, we must remember that Watts and Zimmerman's Positive Accounting Theory is an example of *one* particular positive theory of accounting. This confusion might not have arisen had Watts and Zimmerman elected to adopt an alternative name (or 'trademark') for their particular theory. According to Watts and Zimmerman (1990, p. 148):

> We adopted the label 'positive' from economics where it was used to distinguish research aimed at explanation and prediction from research whose objective was prescription. Given the connotation already attached to the term in economics we thought it would be useful in distinguishing accounting research aimed at understanding accounting from research directed at generating prescriptions ... . The phrase 'positive' created a trademark and like all trademarks it conveys information. 'Coke', 'Kodak', 'Levi's' convey information.

As Watts and Zimmerman (1986, p. 7) state, Positive Accounting Theory:

> ... is concerned with explaining accounting practice. It is designed to explain and predict which firms will and which firms will not use a particular method ... but it says nothing as to which method a firm should use.[2]

Positive theories can be contrasted with normative theories. In Chapters 5 and 6 we considered different normative theories of accounting. Normative theories prescribe how a particular practice *should* be undertaken and this prescription might be a significant departure from existing practice. A normative theory is generated as a result of the particular theorist applying some norm, standard or objective against which actual practice should strive to achieve. For example, in Chapter 5 we considered Chambers' theory of accounting, which he labelled *continuously contemporary accounting*. Under this theory Chambers prescribes that *all* assets *should* be measured at net market value and that such information is more useful for informed decision making than information based on historical costs, and which, according to Chambers, may actually be misleading. Chambers made a judgement about the role of accounting (to provide information about an entity's *capacity to adapt* to changing circumstances) and as a result of this judgement he prescribed particular accounting practice.

Returning our focus to Positive Accounting Theory, we see in this chapter that Positive Accounting Theory focuses on the relationships between the various individuals involved in providing resources to an organization and how accounting is used to assist in the functioning of these relationships. Examples are the relationships between the owners (as suppliers of equity capital) and the managers (as suppliers of managerial labour), or between the managers and the firm's debt providers (that is, the creditors). Many relationships involve the delegation of decision making from one party (the principal) to another party (the agent) – this is referred to as an agency relationship. When decision-making authority is delegated, this can lead to some loss of efficiency and consequent costs. For example, if the owner (principal) delegates decision-making authority to a manager (agent) it is possible that the manager may not work as hard as would the owner, given that the manager might not share directly in the results of the organization. Any potential loss of profits brought about by the manager underperforming is considered to be a cost that results from the decision-making delegation within this agency relationship – an agency cost. The agency costs that arise as a result of delegating decision-making authority from the owner to the manager are referred to in Positive Accounting Theory as *agency costs of equity*.

Positive Accounting Theory, as developed by Watts and Zimmerman and others, is based on the central economics-based assumption that all individuals' action is driven by *self-interest* and that individuals will always act in an opportunistic manner to the extent that the actions will increase their wealth. Notions of loyalty, morality and the like are not incorporated in the theory (as they typically are not incorporated in other accounting or economic theories). Given an assumption that self-interest drives all individual actions, Positive Accounting Theory predicts that organizations will seek to put in place mechanisms that align the interests of the managers of the firm (the agents) with the interests of the owners of the firm (the principals). As we see later in this chapter, some of these methods of aligning interests will be based on the output of the accounting system (such as providing the manager with a share of the organization's *profits*). Where such accounting-based 'alignment mechanisms' are in place, there will be a need for financial statements to be produced. Managers are predicted to 'bond' themselves to prepare these financial statements.[3] This is costly in itself, and in Positive Accounting Theory would be referred to as a 'bonding cost'. If we assume that managers (agents) will be responsible for preparing the financial statements, then Positive Accounting Theory also would predict that there would be a demand for those statements to be audited or monitored, otherwise agents would, assuming self-interest, try to overstate profits, thereby increasing their absolute share of profits. In

Positive Accounting Theory, the cost of undertaking an audit is referred to as a 'monitoring cost'.

To address the agency problems that arise within an organization, there may be various bonding and monitoring costs incurred. If it was assumed, contrary to the assumptions of Positive Accounting Theory, that individuals always worked for the benefit of their employers, then there would not be such a demand for such activities – other than perhaps to review the efficiency with which the manager was operating the business. As Positive Accounting Theory assumes that not all opportunistic actions of agents can be controlled by contractual arrangements or otherwise, there will always be some residual costs associated with appointing an agent.

Having provided this introductory overview of Positive Accounting Theory we now turn to the origins and development of Positive Accounting Theory. We return to the issue of how accounting can be used to reduce conflicts within the firm later in this chapter. The following discussion shows that Positive Accounting Theory developed out of the economics literature and was heavily reliant on assumptions about the efficiency of markets (from the efficient markets hypothesis); on research which considered the reactions of capital markets to accounting information (which was developed from models such as the capital assets pricing model); and on the role of contractual arrangements in minimizing conflicts within an organization (from agency theory).

The origins and development of Positive Accounting Theory

Positive research in accounting started coming to prominence around the mid-1960s and appeared to become the dominant research paradigm in the 1970s and 1980s. Prior to this time the dominant type of accounting research was normative accounting research – research that sought to provide prescription based on the theorists' perspective of the underlying objective of accounting. High profile normative researchers of this time included Sterling, Edwards and Bell, and Chambers and the focus of much of the research at this time was how to undertake accounting in times of rising prices.[4] Such normative research did not rely on examining existing practice – that is, it did not tend to be empirical.

Watts (1995, p. 299) provides an insight into the trends in accounting research that occurred from the 1950s to the 1970s. As evidence of the trends, and relying on the works of Dyckman and Zeff (1984), he documents the number of publications accepted by two dominant academic accounting journals – *The Accounting Review* and the *Journal of Accounting Research*.[5] He states:

> The introduction of positive research into accounting in the mid-1960s represented a paradigm shift. Prior to that time, the most common type of paper published in the leading

English language academic journal of the time (The Accounting Review) was normative (like the works of Edwards and Bell, Chambers and Sterling). In the period 1956–1963, 365 of Accounting Review articles were of this type. These papers use assumptions about phenomena and objectives to deduce their prescriptions. They do not use systematic evidence and/or advance hypotheses for formal testing. Only 3% of the articles published in Accounting Review in 1956–1963 were empirical and most were not designed to test hypotheses. Virtually none of the papers in this time period were attempts to explain current accounting using mathematical modelling or less formal techniques. Today, almost all papers in Accounting Review are in the positive tradition and the same is true of most other leading academic journals (all of which started in 1963 or later). [6]

In reflecting on what caused the shift in paradigm from normative to positive research, Watts (1995, p. 299) argues that:

> The paradigm shift is associated with changes in US business schools in the late 1950s and early 1960s. Reports on business education commissioned by the Ford Foundation and the Carnegie Corporation of New York were catalysts for those changes ... . Hypothesis forming and testing were viewed as essential for good research.

It is also argued that around the mid-1960s and through the 1970s, computing facilities improved markedly, such that it became increasingly practical to undertake large-scale statistical analysis – an approach used within the positive research paradigm. As Watts and Zimmerman (1986, p. 339) state:

> Computers and large machine-readable data bases (CRSP and Compustat) became available in the 1960s. And, partially in response to the lowered cost of empirical work, finance and economic positive theories became available for accounting researchers' use. This led to the development of positive accounting research and to researchers trained in the methodology of positive theory. [7]

Watts considers that one paper which was crucial to the acceptance of the positive research paradigm was Ball and Brown (1968). According to Watts (1995, p. 303), the publication of this paper in *Journal of Accounting Research* caused widespread interest in accounting-related capital market research (research which seeks to explain and predict share price reaction to the public release of accounting information), and led to ever-increasing numbers of papers being published in the area (we will consider this paper shortly). Reflecting on the subsequent shift in publications towards positive research, Watts (1995, p. 303) states:

> Empirical papers as a proportion of papers published in Journal of Accounting Research rose from 13 per cent in 1967 to 31 per cent in 1968 and to 60 per cent by 1972. Normative papers in Journal of Accounting Research fell from 24 per cent in 1967 to seven per cent in 1968 and by 1972 to zero. Accounting Review followed suit and stopped publishing normative papers. The empirical papers in the capital markets area were in the positivist tradition. The normativists challenged the evidence and its interpretation, but did not supply their own counter-evidence. They did not have the training nor likely the desire to compete in this dimension.

Role of the efficient market hypothesis

One development from the 1960s that was crucial to the development of Positive Accounting Theory was the work of theorists such as Fama, particularly work that related to the development of the efficient markets hypothesis (EMH). The EMH is based on the assumption that capital markets react in an efficient and unbiased manner to publicly available information.[8] The perspective taken is that security prices reflect the information content of publicly available information and this information is not restricted to accounting disclosures. The capital market is considered to be highly competitive, and as a result, newly released public information is expected to be quickly impounded into share prices. As Watts and Zimmerman (1986, p. 6) state:

> Underlying the EMH is competition for information. Competition drives investors and financial analysts to obtain information on the firm from many sources outside the firm's accounting reports and even outside the firm itself. For example, analysts obtain weekly production data on automobile firms and interview management. Analysts also interview competitors about a corporation's sales and creditors about the corporation's credit standing.

If accounting results are released by an organization, and these results were already anticipated by the market (perhaps as a result of interim announcements), then the expectation is that the price of the security will not react to the release of the accounting results. Consistent with traditional finance theory, the price of a security is determined on the basis of beliefs about the present value of future cash flows pertaining to that security and when these beliefs change (as a result of particular information becoming available) the expectation is that the security's price will also change.[9]

Because share prices are expected to reflect information from various sources (as the information relates to predicting future cash flows), there was a view that management cannot manipulate share prices by changing accounting methods in an opportunistic manner. If the change in accounting method does not signal a change in cash flows, then early proponents of the EMH would argue that the capital market will not react. Further, because there are many sources of data used by the capital market, if managers make less than truthful disclosures, which are not corroborated or contradict other available information, then, assuming that the market is efficient, the market will question the integrity of the managers. Consequently the market will tend to pay less attention to subsequent accounting disclosures made by such managers. Watts and Zimmerman (1986) rely upon this perspective to argue against the need for extensive accounting regulation. Because accounting information is only one source of information, because markets are assumed to be efficient in evaluating information, and because of the existence of other potentially non-corroboratory evidence, there is believed to be limited benefit in imposing accounting regulation.

Share price reactions to unexpected earnings announcements

Researchers such as Ball and Brown (1968) and Beaver (1968) sought to empirically investigate stock market reactions to accounting earnings announcements. Utilizing monthly information about earnings announcements in the Wall Street Journal and information about share returns, Ball and Brown investigated whether unexpected changes in accounting earnings lead to abnormal returns on an organization's securities. Relying upon the EMH, Ball and Brown proposed that if the earnings announcements were useful to the capital market (there was *new* or *unexpected* information in the announcement), then share prices would adjust to reflect the new information. As they stated (1968, p. 159):

> If security prices do in fact adjust rapidly to new information as it becomes available, then changes in security prices will reflect the flow of information to the market. An observed revision of stock prices associated with the release of the income report would thus provide evidence that the information reflected in income numbers is useful.

Hence Ball and Brown needed to determine whether the earnings announcement contained any information that was unexpected and therefore potentially 'useful'. Using statistical modelling they calculated an estimate of what was the *expected earnings* of the entity in the absence of the earnings announcement. They also needed a model to estimate what the market return from holding the entity's securities would have been in the absence of the information. That is, they needed to be able to determine what *normal* returns would have been on the securities so that they could then determine whether any *abnormal* returns arose (which would have been assumed to relate to the information disclosure).

In determining what normal returns would have been, had there been no unexpected information in the earnings announcement, reliance is placed on the market model which is derived from the capital assets pricing model (CAPM).[10] These models are more fully discussed in Chapter 10. Briefly, on the basis of past information, the CAPM provides an indication of the expected rate of return on securities by applying a linear model.[11] The expected return on a particular stock is calculated by considering the risk-free rate of return (for example, the return from holding government bonds), plus a risk/return component which is based on how the returns on the particular security have fluctuated historically relative to the movements in the overall (diversified) stock market. The difference between the expected return and the actual return constitutes the abnormal return. The results of the Ball and Brown study were generally supportive of the view that if earnings announcements provided unexpected information, the capital market reacted to the information, the reaction taking the form of abnormal returns on the entity's securities.

By indicating that earnings announcements (mainly based on historical cost accounting) were impacting share prices, Ball and Brown provided evidence that they considered was consistent with a view that historical cost information was useful to the market.[12] This was in direct conflict with various normative theorists (such as Chambers) who had argued that historical cost information is rather useless and misleading.[13] The capital market apparently thought otherwise (if we accept that the change in share price reflected the *usefulness* of the accounting information).[14] In this respect, Watts and Zimmerman (1986, p. 161) state:

> Some critics charge that, because earnings are calculated using several different methods of valuation (e.g. historical cost, current cost, and market value), the earnings numbers are meaningless and stock prices based on those numbers do not discriminate between efficient and less efficient firms. Given the EMH, evidence is inconsistent with this criticism. Positive stock price changes are associated with positive unexpected earnings and negative stock prices with negative unexpected earnings. Therefore, since the stock price is an unbiased estimate of value, earnings changes are measures of value changes.

Throughout the 1970s and subsequent years, many other studies were published that documented the relationship between accounting earnings and security returns (and a number of these are considered in Chapter 10). However, while supportive of the EMH, the literature was unable to explain *why* particular accounting methods might have been selected in the first place. That is, the research provided no hypotheses to *predict* and *explain* accounting choices – rather the existing research simply considered the market's reaction to the ultimate disclosures.

Use of agency theory to help explain and predict managerial choice of accounting policies

Much of the research based on EMH assumed that there were zero contracting and information costs, as well as assuming that the capital market could efficiently 'undo' the implications of management selecting different accounting methods.[15] For example, if an entity elected to switch its inventory cost flow assumptions and this led to an increase in reported income, then the market was assumed to be able to 'see through' this change, and to the extent that there were no apparent cash flow implications (for example, through changing taxes), there would be no share price reaction. Hence, if the particular accounting method had no direct taxation implications, and assuming that markets were efficient and able to understand the effects of using alternative accounting methods, there was an inability to explain why one method of accounting was selected by management in preference to another. As Watts and Zimmerman (1990, p. 132) state:

> An important reason that the information perspective (e.g. Ball and Brown, 1968) failed to generate hypotheses explaining and predicting accounting choice is that in the finance theory underlying the empirical studies, accounting choice per se could not affect firm value. Information is costless and there are no transaction costs in the CAPM frameworks. Hence if accounting methods do not affect taxes they do not affect firm value. In that situation there is no basis for predicting and explaining accounting choice. Accounting is irrelevant.

Yet, evidence indicated that corporate managers expended considerable resources lobbying regulators in regard to particular accounting methods. To such individuals, the choice of accounting method *did* matter. Further, there was evidence (for example, Kaplan and Roll, 1972) that firms within an entire industry often elected to switch accounting methods at a particular time.

A key to explaining managers' choice of particular accounting methods came from agency theory. Agency theory provided a necessary explanation of why the selection of particular accounting methods might matter, and hence was an important facet in the development of Positive Accounting Theory. Agency theory focused on the relationships between principals and agents (for example, the relationship between shareholders and corporate managers), a relationship which, due to various information asymmetries, created much uncertainty. Agency theory accepted that transaction costs and information costs exist.

Jensen and Meckling (1976) was a key paper in the development of agency theory and was a paper that Watts and Zimmerman greatly relied upon when developing Positive Accounting Theory. Jensen and Meckling defined the agency relationship (1976, p. 308) as:

> A contract under which one or more (principals) engage another person (the agent) to perform some service on their behalf which involves delegating some decision-making authority to the agent. [16]

Relying upon traditional economics literature (including accepting assumptions such as that all individuals are driven by desires to maximize their own wealth) Jensen and Meckling considered the relationships and conflicts between agents and principals and how efficient markets and various contractual mechanisms can assist in minimizing the cost to the firm of these potential conflicts.

Within agency theory, a well-functioning firm was considered to be one that minimizes its agency costs (those costs inherent in the principal/agent relationship). As indicated earlier in this chapter, if there is no mechanism to make an agent pay, then that agent (or manager) will, it is assumed, have an incentive to consume many perquisites, as well as to use confidential information for personal gain at the expense of the principals (the owners). It is the incentive problems that are at the heart of agency theory, As Lambert (2001) states:

> Agency theory models are constructed based on the philosophy that it is important to examine incentive problems and their 'resolution' in an economic setting in which the potential incentive problem actually exists. Typical reasons for conflicts of interest include (i) effort aversion by the agent, (ii) the agent can divert resources for his private consumption or use, (iii) differential time horizons, e.g., the agent is less concerned about the future period effects of his current period actions because he does not expect to be with the firm or the agent is concerned about how his actions will affect others' assessments of his skill, which will affect compensation in the future, or (iv) differential risk aversion on the part of the agent.

It is assumed within agency theory that principals will assume that the agent (like the principal and, indeed, all individuals) will be driven by self-interest, and therefore the principals will anticipate that the manager, unless restricted from doing otherwise, will undertake self-serving activities that could be detrimental to the economic welfare of the principals. In the absence of any contractual mechanisms to restrict the agents' potentially opportunistic behaviour, the principal will pay the agent a lower salary in anticipation of the opportunistic actions.[17] This lower salary will compensate the owners for the adverse actions of the managers (this is referred to as *price protection*). Hence, the perspective is that it is the agents who, on average, pay for the principals' expectations of their opportunistic behaviour. The agents are therefore assumed to have an incentive to enter into contractual arrangements that appear to be able to reduce their ability to undertake actions detrimental to the interests of the principals. Consistent with this, Watts and Zimmerman (1986, p. 184) state:

> This (perspective) provides the prime insight in the Jensen and Meckling analysis: the agent, not the principal, has the incentive to contract for monitoring. The outside shareholders do not care if monitoring (often involving accounting and auditing) is conducted. Competition in the capital markets leads to price protection and ensures that outside investors earn a normal return. Owner-managers (the agents) have the incentive to offer guarantees to limit their consumption of perks, for owner-managers receive all the gains …. With competition and rational expectations, owner-managers who have incentives to take value reducing actions (opportunistic actions) such as over-consuming perks, shirking, or stealing when they sell outside shares, bear the costs of those dysfunctional actions. Hence they have incentives to contract to limit those actions and to have their actions monitored. The incentive is reduced (but not eliminated) by price protection in managerial labour markets.[18]

That is, if it is assumed that managers would prefer higher salaries, then there will be an incentive for them to agree to enter into contractual arrangements that minimize their ability to undertake activities that might be detrimental to the interests of the owners (many of these contractual arrangements will be tied to accounting numbers). The managers (agents) will have incentives to provide information to demonstrate that they are not acting in a manner detrimental to the owners (principals).[19]

In reflecting upon why many accounting researchers embraced agency theory as part of their research, Lambert (2001, p. 4) states:

> The primary feature of agency theory that has made it attractive to accounting researchers is that it allows us to explicitly incorporate conflicts of interest, incentive problems, and mechanisms for controlling incentive problems into our models. This is important because much of the motivation for accounting and auditing has to do with the control of incentive problems. For example, the reason we insist on having an 'independent' auditor is that we do not believe we can trust managers to issue truthful reports on their own. Similarly, much of the motivation for focusing on objective and verifiable information and for conservatism in financial reporting lies with incentive problems. At the most fundamental level, agency theory is used in accounting research to address two

questions: (i) how do features of information, accounting, and compensation systems affect (reduce or make worse) incentive problems and (ii) how does the existence of incentive problems affect the design and structure of information, accounting, and compensation systems?

Agency theory and the firm as a contractual mechanism

In the agency theory literature, the firm itself is considered to be a *nexus of contracts* and these contracts are put in place with the intention of ensuring that all parties, acting in their own self-interest, are at the same time motivated towards maximizing the value of the organization. The view of the firm as a nexus of contracts is consistent with Smith and Watts' (1983) definition of a corporation. They define the corporation as:

> ... a set of contracts among various parties who have a claim to a common output. These parties include stockholders, bondholders, managers, employees, suppliers and customers. The bounds of the corporation are defined by the set of rights under the contracts. The corporation has an indefinite life and the set of contracts which comprise the corporation evolves over time. (p. 3)

Agency theory does not assume that individuals will ever act other than in self-interest, and the key to a well-functioning organization is to put in place mechanisms that ensure that actions that benefit the individual also benefit the organization.[20] Apart from internal mechanisms (for example, compensation contracts with managers that pay managers a bonus tied to accounting profits), there will be other market-wide mechanisms that are also assumed to constrain the opportunistic actions of the managers. As Bushman and Smith (2001, p. 238) state:

> Corporate control mechanisms are the means by which managers are disciplined to act in the investors' interest. Control mechanisms include both internal mechanisms, such as managerial incentive plans, director monitoring, and the internal labor market, and external mechanisms, such as outside shareholder or debtholder monitoring, the market for corporate control, competition in the product market, the external managerial labor market, and securities laws that protect outside investors against expropriation by corporate insiders.

As indicated above, agency theory provides an explanation for the existence of the firm. The establishment of the firm is seen as an alternative and efficient way to produce or supply goods and services relative to dealing with 'the market' by way of a series of separate transactions. As Emanuel *et al.* (2003, p. 151) state:

> The firm is an alternative to the market when the costs of using the market become excessive. When a firm replaces the market, authority substitutes for the price mechanism in determining how decisions are made .... Accounting, together with employment contracts, compensation arrangements, debt contracts and the board of directors including its audit and compensation committees comprise a package of structures that have evolved to govern the firm. These institutional devices become the

firm's efficient contracting technology. As accounting is part of that contracting technology, the accounting controls and systems and board structures that evolve and get implemented are efficient and the accounting methods that are used in calculating the numbers in the contractual arrangements are, likewise, efficient.

In explaining the existence of firms from an agency theory perspective, reliance is often placed on the early work of Ronald Coase. As Emanuel *et al.* (2003, p. 152) state:

> Coase (1937) suggests that the firm is an alternative form of organisation for managing the very same transactions [that otherwise could be made with market participants]. For example, a firm could make its raw materials as opposed to acquiring them through the market. Coase indicates that firms exist because there are costs of using the pricing mechanism. Examples of these costs are the costs of discovering what the relevant prices are, the costs of determining quality, and the costs of negotiating and concluding a separate contract for each exchange transaction. Further, there are costs associated with drawing up a long-term contract because, due to uncertainty (i.e., where knowledge of future possible states of the world and all involved relationships are incomplete) and bounded rationality (i.e., the limitations of humans to make economic decisions because of their limited ability to receive, store, retrieve, and process information), complete contracting is not feasible (Williamson, 1975, 1985, 1988, 1996). Coase suggests that economies of scale in long-term contracting are what cause activity to be organised in firms … . The Coasian and Williamson analysis suggests that firms exist because they are contracting-cost-efficient. Economic Darwinism ensures that competition will weed out inefficient structures and ill-designed organisations. Over the long-term, the institutional structure that survives is the firm's efficient contracting technology. As accounting is part of that contracting technology, the accounting controls and systems that the firm uses and the accounting methods that are used to reduce conflicts of interests between parties to the firm and that align with the firm's value-increasing activities are, likewise, efficient. In respect of the accounting methods, Watts and Zimmerman (1990, p. 134) describe these procedures as efficient accounting choices because they 'are the result of a similar economic equilibrium'.

Apart from the effects of various contractual arrangements within 'the firm', the literature of the 1970s also proposed that various markets, such as the *market for corporate control* and the *market for managers*, provided incentives for managers to work in the interests of the owners (Fama, 1980).[21]

The view that agents have incentives to provide information to show they are working to the benefit of the owners (from agency theory), and the view that markets were efficient, were used as a basis for arguments against the regulation of accounting. Agents are deemed to have incentives to provide information that best reflects the underlying performance of the entity. Failure to do so will have negative implications for their reputation and hence will negatively impact on the total amount of income they can receive from within the organization, or elsewhere. Referring to the work of Fama, Watts and Zimmerman (1986, p. 192) argue:

> Fama (1980) suggests that information on managers' opportunistic value-reducing behavior eventually becomes known and affects their reputation. As a consequence, if

managers consume a large quantity of perks (e.g., shirks), it eventually becomes known and they acquire a reputation. Such managers are expected to over-consume perks in the future, and their future compensation is reduced. Hence, even if managers' compensation is not adjusted in the period in which they over-consume, they still bear a cost for that over-consumption – the present value of the reductions in their future compensation. This effect is mitigated if the manager is close to retirement and does not have any deferred compensation (i.e., compensation paid after retirement).

Emergence of Positive Accounting Theory from prior research and theories

By the mid- to late 1970s, theory had therefore been developed that proposed that markets were efficient and that contractual arrangements were used as a basis for controlling the efforts of self-interested agents. The existence of firms was also explained on the basis of the firms' efficiency in terms of reducing transaction costs. This research provided the necessary basis for the development of Positive Accounting Theory. Positive Accounting Theory emphasized the role of accounting in reducing the agency costs of an organization. It is also emphasized that efficiently written contracts, with many being tied to the output of the accounting system, were a crucial component of an efficient corporate governance structure.

One of the first papers to document how considerations of contracting costs,[22] as well as how considerations of the political process, impacted on the choice of accounting methods was Watts (1977), which did not attract great attention. However, in the subsequent year, Watts and Zimmerman (1978) was published and this paper has become accepted as the key paper in the development and acceptance of Positive Accounting Theory. It attempted to explain the lobbying positions taken by corporate managers in relation to the FASB's 1974 Discussion Memorandum on general price level adjustments (GPLA). According to Watts and Zimmerman (1978, p. 113):

> In this paper, we assume that individuals act to maximize their own utility. In doing so they are resourceful and innovative. The obvious implication of this assumption is that management lobbies on accounting standards based on its own self-interest.

As indicated in Chapter 5, general price level accounting, through the use of a general price index, makes adjustments to historical cost profits to take into account the effects of changing prices. In times of inflation this typically has the effect of decreasing income, as well as increasing assets. Watts and Zimmerman considered how particular organizational attributes might affect whether the managers of an organization supported, or opposed, a particular accounting requirement. Among the factors considered, two were the possibility that managers were paid bonuses tied to reported profits (the management compensation hypothesis), and the possibility that the organization was subject to high levels of political scrutiny (the political cost hypothesis). In relation to the issue of political scrutiny and the associated costs, Watts and Zimmerman (1978, p. 115) state:

> To counter potential government intrusions, corporations employ a number of devices, such as social responsibility campaigns in the media, government lobbying and selection of accounting procedures to minimize reported earnings. By avoiding the attention that 'high' profits draw because of the public's association of high reported profits and monopoly rents, management can reduce the likelihood of adverse political actions and, thereby, reduce its expected costs (including the legal costs the firm would incur opposing the political actions). Included in political costs are the costs labor unions impose through increased demands generated by large reported profits. The magnitude of the political costs is highly dependent on firm size.

The results of Watts and Zimmerman (1978) did not provide support for the management compensation hypothesis.[23] This was probably due to the fact that the discussion memorandum required GPLA disclosures to be provided as a supplement to the financial statements and did not require the financial statements themselves to be altered (and the bonus plans were expected to be tied to the numbers presented in the financial statements). However, significant findings were presented in relation to the political cost hypothesis.[24] More specifically, larger firms (who were deemed to be subject to higher political scrutiny) tended to support the Discussion Memorandum – an approach which would indicate (in times of rising prices) that the profits of the firm, adjusted for the effects of inflation, were lower than were otherwise reported.[25] The view of Watts and Zimmerman was that, by presenting lower adjusted profits, these firms would attract less political attention and hence there would be less likelihood that parties would attempt to transfer wealth away from the firm (perhaps in the form of calls for increased taxes, for less tariff protection, for higher wages, etc.). In concluding their paper, Watts and Zimmerman (1978, p. 131) state:

> The single most important factor explaining managerial voting behavior on General Price Level Accounting is firm size (after controlling for the direction of change in earnings). The larger firms, ceteris paribus, are more likely to favour GPLA if earnings decline. This finding is consistent with our government intervention argument since the larger firms are more likely to be subjected to government interference and, hence, have more to lose than smaller organisations.

Following the work of Watts and Zimmerman (1978), research in the area of Positive Accounting Theory flourished. Much of this research sought to address some of the limitations inherent in Watts and Zimmerman's work. For example, subsequent research acknowledged that reported profits are impacted by many different accounting choices (rather than just the one choice, such as the choice to use GPLA), some of which may be income increasing, while others are income decreasing (thereby potentially offsetting each other). Zmijewski and Hagerman (1981) was an early paper that considered this issue and they undertook research in an endeavour to predict managements' choice in relation to four accounting methods choices, these relating to how to account for depreciation, stock (or inventory), investment tax credits and past pension costs.

In 1990 Watts and Zimmerman published an article in *The Accounting Review* that considered 10 years of development of Positive Accounting Theory ('Positive Accounting Theory: A Ten Year Perspective'). They identified three key hypotheses that had become frequently used in the Positive Accounting Theory literature to explain and predict whether an organization would support or oppose a particular accounting method. These hypotheses can be called the management compensation hypothesis (or bonus plan hypothesis), the debt hypothesis (or debt/equity hypothesis) and the political cost hypothesis. Watts and Zimmerman (1990) explain these hypotheses as follows:

> The bonus plan hypothesis is that managers of firms with bonus plans [tied to reported income] are more likely to use accounting methods that increase current period reported income. Such selection will presumably increase the present value of bonuses if the compensation committee of the board of directors does not adjust for the method chosen. The choice studies to date find results generally consistent with the bonus plan hypothesis. (1990, p. 138)

Hence, all things being equal, this hypothesis predicts that if a manager is rewarded in terms of a measure of performance such as accounting profits, that manager will attempt to increase profits to the extent that this leads to an increase in his or her bonus. Turning our attention to the 'debt hypothesis', they state:

> The debt/equity hypothesis predicts [that] the higher the firm's debt/equity ratio, the more likely managers use accounting methods that increase income. The higher the debt/equity ratio, the closer (i.e. tighter) the firm is to the constraints in the debt covenants. The tighter the covenant constraint, the greater [is] the probability of a covenant violation and of incurring costs from technical default. Managers exercising discretion by choosing income increasing accounting methods relax debt constraints and reduce the costs of technical default. (1990, p. 139)

Hence, all things being equal, if a firm has entered into agreements with lenders, and these agreements involve accounting-based debt covenants (such as stipulating a maximum allowable debt/equity or debt/asset constraint) then managers have an incentive to adopt accounting methods that relax the potential impacts of the constraints (such as adopting accounting methods that increase reported income and assets). Turning our attention to the third hypothesis of their study – the 'political costs hypothesis' – Watts and Zimmerman state:

> The political cost hypothesis predicts [that] large firms rather than small firms are more likely to use accounting choices that reduce reported profits. Size is a proxy variable for political attention. Underlying this hypothesis is the assumption that it is costly for individuals to become informed about whether accounting profits really represent monopoly profits and to 'contract' with others in the political process to enact laws and

regulations that enhance their welfare. Thus rational individuals are less than fully informed. The political process is no different from the market process in that respect. Given the cost of information and monitoring, managers have incentive to exercise discretion over accounting profits and the parties in the political process settle for a rational amount of ex post opportunism. (1990, p. 139)

Hence, all things being equal, if managers consider that they are under a deal of political scrutiny, this could motivate them to adopt accounting methods that reduce reported income, and thereby reduce the possibility that people will argue that the organization is exploiting other parties.

Researchers using the above three hypotheses (the management bonus hypothesis, the debt/equity hypothesis, and the political cost hypothesis), and there have been many such researchers, often adopted the perspective that managers (or agents) will act opportunistically when selecting particular accounting methods (for example, managers will select particular accounting methods because the choice will lead to an increase in profit and therefore to an increase in *their* bonus). Watts and Zimmerman (1978) was mainly grounded in the *opportunistic perspective*. However, a deal of the subsequent Positive Accounting Theory research also adopted an *efficiency perspective*. This perspective proposes that managers will elect to use a particular accounting method because the method most efficiently provides a record of how the organization performed. For example, the manager might have selected a particular depreciation method, not because it will lead to an increase in his or her bonus (the opportunistic perspective), but because the method most correctly reflects the use of the underlying asset. The following discussion considers the *opportunistic* and *efficiency* perspectives of Positive Accounting Theory. In practice it is often difficult to determine whether opportunistic or efficiency considerations drove the managers' choice of a particular method – and this has been one limitation of much of this research.

Opportunistic and efficiency perspectives

As noted above, research that applies Positive Accounting Theory typically adopts either an *efficiency perspective* or an *opportunistic perspective*. Within the efficiency perspective, researchers explain how various contracting mechanisms can be put in place to minimize the agency costs of the firm, that is, the costs associated with assigning decision-making authority to the agent. The efficiency perspective is often referred to as an *ex ante* perspective – *ex ante* meaning before the fact – as it considers what mechanisms are put in place up front, with the objective of minimizing future agency and contracting costs. For example, many organizations throughout the world voluntarily prepared publicly available financial statements before there was any regulatory requirement to do so. These financial statements were also frequently subjected to an audit, even when there was also no regulatory requirement to do so (Morris, 1984).[26] Researchers such as Jensen and Meckling (1976) argue that the practice of providing audited financial statements leads to real cost savings as it enables organizations to attract funds at lower cost. As a result of the audit, external parties have more reliable information about the resources and obligations of the organization, which therefore enables the organization to attract funds at a lower cost than would otherwise be possible, thereby increasing the value of the organization.

Within this efficiency (*ex ante*) perspective of Positive Accounting Theory it is also argued that the accounting practices adopted by firms are often explained on the basis that such methods best reflect the underlying financial performance of the entity. Different organizational characteristics are used to explain why different firms adopt different accounting methods. For example, the selection of a particular asset depreciation rule from among alternative approaches is explained on the basis that it best reflects the underlying use of the asset. Firms that have different patterns of use in relation to an asset will be predicted to adopt different depreciation or amortization policies. That is, organizations will differ in the nature of their business, and these differences will in turn lead to differences in the accounting methods (as well as their other policies) being adopted. By providing measures of performance that best reflect the underlying performance of the firm it is argued that investors and other parties will not need to gather additional information from other sources. This will consequently lead to cost savings.

As an illustration of research that adopts an efficiency perspective, Whittred (1987) sought to explain why firms voluntarily prepared publicly available consolidated financial statements in a period when there was no regulation that required them to do so. He found that when companies borrowed funds, security for debt often took the form of guarantees provided by other entities within the group of organizations. Consolidated financial statements were described as being a more efficient means of providing information about the group's ability to borrow and repay debts than providing lenders with separate financial statements for each entity in the group.[27]

If it is assumed, consistent with the efficiency perspective, that firms adopt particular accounting methods because the methods best reflect the underlying economic performance of the entity, then it is argued by Positive Accounting theorists that the regulation of financial accounting imposes unwarranted costs on reporting entities. For example, if a new accounting standard is released that bans an accounting method being used by particular organizations, this will lead to inefficiencies, as the resulting financial statements will no longer provide the best reflection of the performance of the organization. Many Positive Accounting theorists would argue that management is best able to select appropriate accounting methods in given circumstances, and government should not intervene in the process.[28]

The *opportunistic perspective* of Positive Accounting Theory, on the other hand, takes as given the negotiated contractual arrangements of the firm (some of which are discussed later in this chapter) and seeks to explain and predict certain opportunistic behaviours that will subsequently occur. Initially, the particular contractual arrangements might have been negotiated because they were considered to be most efficient in aligning the interests of the various individuals within the firm. However, it is not possible or efficient to write complete contracts that provide guidance on all accounting methods to be used in all circumstances – hence there will always be some scope for managers to be opportunistic.

The opportunistic perspective is often referred to as an *ex post* perspective – *ex post* meaning after the fact – because it considers opportunistic actions that could be undertaken once various contractual arrangements have been put in place. For example, in an endeavour to minimize agency costs (an efficiency perspective), a contractual arrangement might be negotiated that provides the managers with a bonus based on the profits generated by the entity. Once it is in place, the manager could elect to adopt particular accounting methods that increase accounting profits, and therefore the size of the bonus (an opportunistic perspective). Managers might elect to adopt a particular asset depreciation method that increases income, even though it might not reflect the actual use of the asset.

It is assumed within Positive Accounting Theory that managers will opportunistically select particular accounting methods whenever they believe that this will lead to an increase in their personal wealth. Positive Accounting Theory also assumes that principals would predict a manager to be opportunistic. With this in mind, principals often stipulate the accounting methods to be used for particular purposes. For example, a bonus plan agreement may stipulate that a particular depreciation or amortization method such as straight-line amortization be adopted to calculate income for the determination of the bonus.

However, as noted previously, it is assumed to be too costly to stipulate in advance all accounting rules to be used in all circumstances. Hence Positive Accounting Theory proposes that there will always be scope for agents to opportunistically select particular accounting methods in preference to others.

Across time there have been many reported cases of organizations that have been found to have overstated their reported earnings and assets. For example, consider Exhibit 7.1 which relates to the overstatement of profits at a large Dutch supermarket group. The opportunistic perspective provided by Positive Accounting Theory provides some possible reasons for the overstatement of reported assets and earnings. Perhaps the entities inflated their earnings and assets in an attempt to circumvent restrictions that had been put in place by lenders – for example, lenders might have stipulated debt-to-asset constraints or minimum earnings requirements (perhaps in the form of negotiated interest-coverage clauses in a debt agreement). As the level of debt increases, the tendency towards opportunistic overstatement of assets and income would be expected to increase (if we accept the arguments pro-

---

Exhibit 7.1

Dutch supermarket admits £317m error

AccountancyAge.com

Ahold, the Dutch-based supermarket giant, has admitted that it overstated its profits by at least $500m (£317m).

As a consequence, the company said its chief executive and chief financial officer would be leaving, while an investigation into its US food distribution division has begun.

It has also postponed its annual results, which were meant to have been announced on 5 March.

The news sent shock waves through the market as Ahold's share price tumbled 40%.

The trouble is believed to be centred around US Foodservice, Ahold's distribution service, over the way it accounted for income.

The company is already saddled with massive debt problems fuelled by an aggressive acquisition strategy, which has made merging different accounting practices together difficult.

Accountancy Age, 24 February 2003

---

vided by Positive Accounting Theory). The extent of the opportunistic accounting activities often only becomes evident following corporate failure, at which time the extent of asset overstatement will be highlighted.

The following discussion addresses the various contractual arrangements that may exist between owners and managers, and between debtholders and managers, particularly those contractual arrangements based on the output of the accounting system. Again, these contractual arrangements are initially assumed to be put in place to reduce the agency costs of the firm (the efficiency perspective). However, it is assumed by Positive Accounting theorists that once the arrangements are in place, parties will, if they can, adopt manipulative strategies to generate the greatest economic benefits to themselves (the opportunistic perspective). The following material also considers the political process and how firms might use accounting to minimize the costs of potential political scrutiny.

Whilst some researchers tend to utilize either the *efficiency* or *opportunistic* perspectives of Positive Accounting Theory to explain particular accounting choices, it should be noted that in reality it is often difficult to firmly conclude that an accounting choice was driven solely by an efficiency or an opportunistic motivation. As Fields *et al.* (2001) state:

> Unconstrained accounting choice is likely to impose costs on financial statement users because preparers are likely to have incentives to convey self-serving information.

For example, managers may choose accounting methods in self-interested attempts to increase the stock [share] price prior to the expiration of stock options they hold. On the other hand, the same accounting choices may be motivated by managers' objective assessment that the current stock price is undervalued (relative to their private information). In practice, it is difficult to distinguish between the two situations, but it is the presence of such mixed motives that makes the study of accounting choice interesting.

Owner/manager contracting

If the manager owned the firm, then that manager would bear the costs associated with their own perquisite consumption. Perquisite consumption could include consumption of the firm's resources for private purposes (for example, the manager may acquire an overly expensive company car, acquire overly luxurious offices, stay in overly expensive hotel accommodation) or the excessive generation and use of idle time. As the percentage ownership held by the manager decreases, that manager begins to bear less of the cost of his/her own perquisite consumption. The costs begin to be absorbed by the owners of the firm.

As noted previously, Positive Accounting Theory adopts as a central assumption that all action by individuals is driven by self-interest, and that the major interest of individuals is to maximize their own wealth. Such an assumption is often referred to as the 'rational economic person' assumption. If all individuals are assumed to act in their own self-interest, then owners would expect the managers (their agents) to undertake activities that may not always be in the interest of the owners (the principals). Further, because of their position within the firm, the managers will have access to information not available to the principals (this problem is frequently referred to as 'information asymmetry') and this may further increase the managers' ability to undertake actions beneficial to themselves at the expense of the owners. The costs of the divergent behaviour that arises as a result of the agency relationship (that is, the relationship between the principal and the agent appointed to perform duties on behalf of the principal) are, as indicated previously, referred to as agency costs (Jensen and Meckling, 1976).

It is assumed in Positive Accounting Theory that the principals hold expectations that their agents will undertake activities that may be disadvantageous to the value of the firm, and the principals will price this into the amounts they are prepared to pay the manager. That is, in the absence of controls to reduce the ability of the manager to act opportunistically, the principals expect such actions, and as a result, will pay the manager a lower salary. This lower salary compensates the principals for the expected opportunistic behaviour of the agents. The manager will therefore bear some of the costs of the potential opportunistic behaviours (the agency costs) that they may, or may not, undertake. If it is expected that managers would derive greater satisfaction from additional salary than from the perquisites that they will be predicted to consume, then managers may be better off if they are able to contractually commit themselves not to consume perquisites. That is, they contractually commit or bond themselves to reducing their set of available actions (some of which would not be beneficial to owners). Of course, the owners of the firm would need to ensure that any contractual commitments can be monitored for compliance before agreeing to increase the amounts paid to the managers. In a market where individuals are perfectly informed it could be assumed that managers would ultimately bear the costs associated with the bonding and monitoring mechanisms (Jensen and Meckling, 1976). However, markets are typically not perfectly informed.

Managers may be rewarded on a fixed basis (that is, a set salary independent of performance), on the basis of the results achieved, or on a combination of the two. If the manager was rewarded purely on a fixed basis, then assuming self-interest, that manager would not want to take great risks as he/she would not share in any potential gains. There would also be limited incentives for the manager to adopt strategies that increase the value of the firm (unlike equity owners whose share of the firm may increase in value). Like debtholders, managers with a fixed claim would want to protect their fixed income stream. Apart from rejecting risky projects, which may be beneficial to those with equity in the firm, the manager with a fixed income stream may also be reluctant to take on optimal levels of debt, as the claims of the debtholders would compete with the manager's own fixed income claim.

Assuming that self-interest drives the actions of the managers, it may be necessary to put in place remuneration schemes that reward the managers in a way that is, at least in part, tied to the performance of the firm. This will be in the interest of the manager as that manager will potentially receive greater rewards and will not have to bear the costs of the perceived opportunistic behaviours (which may not have been undertaken anyway). If the performance of the firm improves, the rewards paid to the manager correspondingly increase. Bonus schemes tied to the performance of the firm will be put in place to align the interests of the owners and the managers. If the firm performs well, both parties will benefit.

Bonus schemes generally

It is common practice for managers to be rewarded in line with the profits of the firm, sales of the firm, or return on assets, that is, for their remuneration to be based on the output of the accounting system. Table 7.1 describes some of the accounting-based remuneration plans found to have been used in Australia. It is also common for managers to be rewarded in line with the market price of the firm's shares. This may be through holding an equity interest in the firm, or perhaps by receiving a cash bonus explicitly tied to movements in the market value of the firm's securities.

Table 7.1 Accounting performance measures used within Australia as a basis for rewarding managers

- Percentage of after-tax profits of the last year
- Percentage of after-tax profits after adjustment for dividends paid
- Percentage of pre-tax profits of the last year
- Percentage of division's profit for the last year
- Percentage of division's sales for the last year
- Percentage of the last year's accounting rate of return on assets
- Percentage of previous year's division's sales, plus percentage of firm's after-tax profits
- Percentage of previous year's division's sales plus percentage of division's pre-tax profits
- Percentage of previous 2 years' division's sales, plus percentage of last 2 years' division's pre-tax profit
- Percentage of previous year's firm's sales, plus a percentage of firm's after-tax profit
- Average of pre-tax profit for the last 2 years
- Average of pre-tax profit for the last 3 years
- Percentage of the last 6 months' profit after tax

Source: Deegan (1997)

Accounting-based bonus schemes

As indicated above, the use of accounting-based bonus schemes is quite common. In considering their use within the US, Bushman and Smith (2001, p. 250) state:

> The extensive and explicit use of accounting numbers in top executive compensation plans at publicly traded firms in the U.S. is well documented. Murphy (1998) reports data from a survey conducted by Towers Perrin in 1996–1997. The survey contains detailed information on the annual bonus plans for 177 publicly traded U.S. companies. Murphy reports that 161 of the 177 sample firms explicitly use at least one measure of accounting profits in their annual bonus plans. Of the 68 companies in the survey that use a single performance measure in their annual bonus plan, 65 use a measure of accounting profits. While the accounting measure used is often the dollar value of profits, Murphy also reports common use of profits on a per-share basis, as a margin, return, or expressed as a growth rate. Ittner et al. (1997), using proxy statements and proprietary survey data, collect detailed performance measure information for the annual bonus plans of 317 U.S. firms for the 1993–1994 time period. The firms are drawn from 48 different two-digit SIC codes. Ittner et al. document that 312 of the 317 firms report using at least one financial measure in their annual plans. Earnings per share, net income and operating income are the most common financial measure, each being used by more than a quarter of the sample.

Given that the amounts paid to the manager may be directly tied to accounting numbers (such as profits/sales/assets), any changes in the accounting methods being used by the organization will affect the bonuses paid (unless the bonuses have been explicitly tied to the accounting numbers that would be derived from the use of the accounting methods in place when the bonus schemes were originally negotiated). Such a change may occur as a result of a new accounting standard being issued. For example, IAS 38 permits some development (but not research) expenditure to be capitalized as an intangible asset in certain circumstances. Consider the consequences if a new rule was issued that required all research *and* development expenditure to be written off. With such a change, profits for some firms which previously capitalized development expenditure could decline, and the bonuses paid to managers may also change. If it is accepted, consistent with classical finance theory, that the value of the firm is a function of the future cash flows of the firm, then the value of the organization may change (perhaps because less expenditure will be incurred in relation to development). Hence, once we consider the contractual arrangements within a firm, Positive Accounting theorists would argue that we can start to appreciate that a change in accounting method can lead to a change in cash flows, and hence a change in the value of the organization. This perspective is contrary to the views of early proponents of the EMH who argued that changes in accounting methods would not impact on share prices unless they had direct implications for expenses such as taxation.

As a recent case in point we can speculate on how the adoption of IAS 38 'Intangibles' in some countries (and amongst other things this standard requires that all research expenditure must be expensed as incurred) will impact upon the research and development activities of various organizations. For example, subject to certain requirements, listed companies in France and some Scandinavian countries could, prior to 2005, capitalize research expenditure. With the adoption of IFRS from 2005 this is no longer permitted and all research expenditure must be expensed as incurred (subject to certain requirements, development expenditure can be capitalized). As a result there might be some expectation that the accounting standard will affect the amount of research being conducted by some firms in those countries. With specific reference to the 'bonus hypothesis', there could be an expectation that if a manager is being paid a bonus tied to accounting profits, and given the 'harsh' treatment required in relation to research expenditure, the existence of a management bonus may motivate managers to reduce the level of research expenditure thereby increasing the size of their bonus. Such a strategy of reducing research expenditure might be even greater the closer the manager is to retirement – the reason for this being that the time-lag between the research expenditure and the subsequent economic benefits might be longer than the period until the manager retires (we will return to this 'horizon problem' shortly). Through the related impacts upon cash flows, such a change in research activity in turn can be expected to affect the value of the reporting entities' equity.

Of course it is possible that the bonus may be based on the 'old' accounting rules in place at the time the remuneration contract was negotiated (perhaps through a clause in the management compensation contract) such that a change in generally accepted accounting principles will not impact on the bonus, but this will not always be the case. Contracts that rely on accounting numbers may rely on 'floating' generally accepted accounting principles. This would suggest that should an accounting rule change, and should it affect an item used within a contract made by the firm, the value of the firm (through changes in related cash flows) might consequently change. Positive Accounting Theory would suggest that if a change in accounting policy had no impact on the cash flows of the firm, then a firm would be indifferent to the change.

In explaining the use of accounting-based bonus schemes, Emanuel *et al.* (2003, p. 155) state:

> Accounting earnings are often used to calculate the manager's payoff (Smith and Watts, 1982; Healy, 1985; Sloan, 1993) because it is a more efficient measure of the manager's performance than other measures such as stock prices and realised cash flows. There are two reasons for this. First, stock prices are influenced more by market factors that are outside the control of management and, hence, are less effective in isolating that part of performance that results from the manager's actions (Sloan, 1993). Secondly, realised cash flows do not take into account the manager's actions at the time those actions are put in place to increase the value of the firm. Hence, realised cash flows do not provide a timely measure of the effect of the manager's actions on firm performance, especially when performance is measured over short intervals (Dechow, 1994). Further, accounting earnings possess a variety of desirable characteristics that other performance measures do not have, including objectivity, reliability, verifiability and conservatism (Watts and Zimmerman, 1986, pp. 205–207). Since accounting earnings are efficient in measuring firm performance, they play an important role in determining the reward and punishment of performance. We observe the existence of earnings-based bonus plans that provide an efficient means of aligning the manager's and shareholders' interests so that the manager does not participate in activities that are opportunistic, because such actions detract from firm value maximization. To the extent that earnings are a good measure of future cash flows and all things else are constant, higher earnings lead to higher firm value and more compensation to the manager. Besides compensation, accounting performance measures affect other rewards and punishments of the firm's employees, such as continued employment and promotion (Blackwell *et al.*, 1994).

Incentives to manipulate accounting numbers

In considering the costs of implementing incentive schemes based on accounting output, there is a possibility that rewarding managers on the basis of accounting profits may induce them to manipulate the related accounting numbers to improve their apparent performance and, importantly, their related rewards (the opportunistic perspective). That is, accounting profits may not always provide an unbiased measure of firm performance or value. Healy (1985) provides an illustration of when managers may choose to manipulate accounting numbers opportunistically due to the presence of accounting-based bonus schemes. He found that when schemes existed that rewarded managers after a pre-specified level of earnings had been reached, the managers would adopt accounting methods consistent with maximizing that bonus. In situations where the profits were not expected to reach the minimum level required by the plan, the managers appeared to adopt strategies that further reduced income in that period (frequently referred to as 'taking a bath'), but would lead to higher income in subsequent periods – periods when the profits may be above the required threshold. As an example, the manager may write off an asset in one period, when a bonus was not going to be earned anyway, such that there would be nothing further to depreciate in future periods when profit-related bonuses may be paid.[29]

Investment strategies that maximize the present value of the firm's resources will not necessarily produce uniform periodic cash flows or accounting profits. It is possible that some strategies may generate minimal accounting returns in early years, yet still represent the best alternatives available to the firm. Rewarding management on the basis of accounting profits may discourage them from adopting such strategies. That is, it may encourage management to adopt a short-term, as opposed to long-term, focus.

In Lewellen, Loderer and Martin (1987) it was shown that US managers approaching retirement were less likely to undertake research and development expenditure if their rewards were based on accounting-based performance measures, such as profits. This was explained on the basis that all research and development had to be written off as incurred, in the US, and hence incurring research and development would lead directly to a reduction in profits. Although the research and development expenditure would be expected to lead to benefits in subsequent years, the retiring managers might not have been there to share in the gains. That is, the employment horizon of the manager is short relative to the 'horizon' relating to the continuation of the organization (which might be assumed to be infinite). This difference in 'horizons' is often referred to as an 'horizon problem'. Hence the *self-interested manager* who was rewarded on the basis of accounting profits was predicted not to undertake research and development in the periods close to the point of retirement because the manager would not share in any associated gains. This may, of course, have been detrimental to the ongoing operations (and value) of the business. In such a case it would have been advisable from an *efficiency perspective* for an organization that incurred research and development expenditure to take retiring managers off a profit-share bonus scheme, or alternatively, to calculate 'profits' for the purpose of the plan after adjusting for research and development expenditures. Alternatively, managers approaching retirement could have been rewarded in terms of market-based schemes that are tied to the long-term performance of the organization. Such schemes are addressed below.

Market-based bonus schemes

Firms involved in mining, or high technology research and development, may have accounting earnings that fluctuate greatly. Successful strategies may be put in place that will not provide accounting earnings for a number of periods. In such industries, Positive Accounting theorists may argue that it is more appropriate to reward the manager in terms of the market value of the firm's securities, which are assumed to be influenced by expectations about the net present value of expected future cash flows. This may be done either by basing a cash bonus on any increases in share prices, or by providing the manager with shares, or options to shares in the firm. If the value of the firm's shares increases, both the manager and the owners will benefit (their interests will be aligned). Importantly, the manager will be given an incentive to increase the value of the firm. In a survey of Australian managers, Deegan (1997) provides evidence that 21 per cent of the managers surveyed held shares in their employer.

As already indicated in this chapter, offering managers incentives that are tied to accounting profits might have the adverse effect of inducing them to undertake actions that are not in the interests of shareholders. This might particularly be the case in relation to expenditure on research and development. As already explained, within the US, all research and development is required to be expensed as incurred, and hence there is an immediate downward impact on profits when a firm undertakes research and development.[30] Apart from the initial impacts on profits, there is also evidence that capital markets frequently do not put a great amount of value on research and development expenditure because of the many uncertainties inherent in such expenditure (Kothari *et al.*, 2002; Lev and Sougiannis, 1996) – that is, the market is considered to undervalue the benefits attributable to research and development. In relation to the personal motivations of chief executive officers (CEOs) in the US, Cheng (2004, p. 307) states:

> CEOs consider the benefits and costs of R&D spending, and [consistent with the maintained assumption of self-interest] they invest in R&D only when the expected personal benefits dominate the personal costs. Their expected costs of R&D spending include the negative impact of R&D spending on short-term accounting and stock performance, since these measures affect CEO compensation and job security (Dechow and Skinner, 2000; Murphy, 1999). The negative impact of R&D spending on current accounting earnings is due to the fact that R&D spending is typically immediately expensed under US GAAP. Therefore, CEOs who want to boost current accounting earnings have incentives to reduce R&D spending (e.g., Baber et al., 1991; Dechow and Sloan 1991). In addition, CEOs may consider R&D investments as less desirable than other investments in terms of the impact of the investments on short-term stock prices [because of the tendency of capital markets to undervalue R&D expenditures]. Relative to other investments, R&D projects are associated with higher information asymmetry between managers and shareholders (e.g., Clinch, 1991) and greater uncertainty of the future benefits (e.g., Chan et al., 2001; Kothari et al., 2002). As a result, current stock prices

likely do not fully reflect the future benefits of R&D spending (Lev and Sougiannis 1996). Therefore, CEOs concerned with short-term stock prices may reduce R&D spending to increase other investment with benefits more fully (or better) reflected in current stock prices.

The above impacts are heightened as the manager approaches retirement. As Cheng (2004, p. 308) states:

> CEOs are concerned with short-term accounting and stock performance, and these concerns generate incentives for CEOs to reduce R&D spending. Such incentives become stronger when CEOs approach retirements or face earnings shortfalls (Baber *et al.* 1991; Dechow and Sloan 1991). As the CEO approaches retirement, it is less likely for the CEO to benefit from current R&D investments. Meanwhile, the CEO's career concern diminishes, and the CEO becomes more short-term oriented (Gibbons and Murphy 1992) due to weakened concern about the discipline from the managerial labor markets. Likewise, when facing deteriorating economic performance, the CEO is more concerned with the expected personal costs of R&D spending, since poor performance may trigger such results as job termination and corporate takeover, which may disentitle the CEO to the future of current R&D spending. Thus CEOs have incentives to reduce R&D spending in order to reverse a poor performance, especially if an expected shortfall is small and thus more easily reversed.

Given that there would conceivably be incentives for senior management to reduce spending on research and development (particularly if they are offered bonuses tied to accounting profit) it is perhaps predictable that additional contractual agreements might be put in place to reduce this motivation to reduce research and development. One approach would be to have those responsible who are responsible for determining senior management salaries (often done by way of a compensation committee that is established within the organization and on which non-managerial directors often serve) to specifically adjust management salaries in such a way that the salary is directly tied to research and development activity. As Cheng (2004, p. 308) states:

> When CEO incentives to reduce R&D spending become stronger, compensation committees may adjust CEO compensation arrangements to mitigate such incentives. This adjustment should affect CEO's consideration of the expected personal benefits and expected personal costs of R&D spending in favour of R&D expenditures. One possible adjustment is to establish a greater positive association between changes in R&D spending and changes in CEO compensation. Such a greater association makes increasing R&D spending more beneficial to the CEO, and reducing R&D spending more costly to the CEO.

The results of Cheng (2004) indicate that compensation committees do often establish a link between changes in R&D spending and changes in CEOs' total compensation. Further, the compensation being offered to the retiring managers is often by way of the provision of share options. Granting share options to the managers also increases the longer-term focus of managers thereby further motivating the CEOs to embrace appropriate levels of research and development activity.[31]

In considering the use of share options, and as with accounting-based bonus schemes, there are also problems associated with the manager being rewarded in ways that are influenced by share price movements. First, the share price will be affected not only by factors controlled by the manager, but also by outside, market-wide factors. That is, share prices may provide a 'noisy' measure of management performance – 'noisy' in the sense that they are not only affected by the actions of management but also are largely affected by general market movements over which the manager has no control. Further, only the senior managers would be likely to have a significant effect on the cash flows of the firm, and hence the value of the firm's securities. Therefore, market-related incentives may only be appropriate for senior management. Offering shares to lower level management may be demotivational as their own individual actions would have little likelihood (relative to senior management) to impact on share prices, and therefore, their personal wealth. Consistent with this, it is often more common for senior managers, relative to other employees, to hold shares in their employer. Within the Deegan (1997) sample, 35 per cent of the senior management, 16 per cent of the middle management, and 6 per cent of the lower management held shares in their employer.

Reflecting the way executives often share in the performance of an organization, Exhibit 7.2 shows how Barclays (along with other large companies) rewards its chief executives by way of a scheme tied to the market value of the organization's securities. It would be expected that rewarding the executives in the manner outlined should align the interests of the executives (agents) with those of the shareholders (principals) – a view consistent with agency theory and Positive Accounting Theory. It would be expected that such schemes would be restricted to senior management as they have the greatest ability to have an impact on share prices. However, as Exhibit 7.3 shows, there has been considerable criticism from shareholders in recent years of the size of executive share option schemes. From the perspective of Positive Accounting Theory this might indicate that shareholders believe the size of some such schemes now potentially dilutes the value of shareholders' existing shares (through the issue of new shares at a substantial discount to future market values) by so much that the agency benefits of these share options are outweighed by their cost to existing shareholders.

In general it is argued that the likelihood of accounting-based or market-based performance measures or reward schemes being put in place will, in part, be driven by considerations of the relative 'noise' of market-based versus accounting-based performance measures. The relative reliance upon accounting- or market-based measures may potentially be determined on the basis of the relative sensitivity of either measure to general market (largely uncontrollable) factors. Sloan (1993)

Exhibit 7.2 An example of the use of market-based incentives

Barclays boss set for £9m bonanza

Heather Connon, investments editor

Barclays Bank chief executive Matt Barrett has been awarded share options that could eventually earn him £9 million profit despite plunging profits and cuts in his fellow directors' pay.

He was given options over 7.8 million shares last year, and the profit could be realised if Barclays' shares just recover to last year's peak of 632p.

The award, buried in the small print of the bank's annual report, confirms warnings by remuneration experts that option awards are reaching unprecedented levels as firms try to reprise those of the stock market boom.

It is more than three times the 2.2 million shares Barrett had under option at the start of the year and more than 24 times the 320,000 shares awarded to board colleagues such as finance director John Varley and Chris Lendrum. The options can be exercised between March 2005 and 2012, if the bank meets targets for total returns to shareholders.

Barrett is already one of the highest-paid bankers in Britain, despite taking a pay cut following the 6 per cent drop in Barclays' profits last year. In 2002, he earned £1.7m.

A bank spokeswoman said it would have to turn in a 'fantastic performance' for him to get the full entitlement. Measured by return to shareholders, it would have to be first among 12 rival banks over three years. If it comes second, his award falls to 5.9 million shares and, at seventh place or lower, he gets none.

The scheme gives Barrett twice his salary, bonus, pension contributions and other benefits if Barclays is taken over. But one shareholder said: 'If we achieve what he needs to get the award, we would be quite happy.'

Corporate governance experts say the deal confirms a trend towards high levels of options. This is partly because awards are usually based on a multiple of salary – 37 times in Barrett's case – which are rising sharply, and partly because share prices are low so more shares are needed to achieve a set value.

If shares recover strongly, the awards could be costly. Manifest, the agency that votes by proxy for big investors at annual meetings, believes options were granted over more than 70 million shares last year.

Copyright Guardian Newspapers Limited, Sunday 30 March 2003

Exhibit 7.3 An example of shareholder resistance to the use of market-based incentives

Shares offer to mmO2 chief alarms City investors

Jill Treanor

Big City investors are warning that they will not tolerate share-related pay deals for company chairmen because they fear the latters' independence could be compromised.

Their objection appears to have been prompted by a new-style package for the incoming chairman of mmO2, David Arculus, who stands to receive shares in the telecoms company if it achieves share price targets in three years' time.

Remuneration consultants who devise pay packets for top executives said they had received a letter from the Association of British Insurers expressing the concerns of investors about 'geared share incentive awards'. They believe the letter is a sign that investors are turning their attention to the way chairmen's pay is structured.

The investor body, whose members control a quarter of the stock market, told the consultants: 'Incentives geared to either performance or share price may impair the ability of chairmen to provide objective oversight, given the possible impact on their remuneration of short-term price movements and the structure of performance targets.'

The ABI refused to comment on the letter. Pay consultants said it expressed investors' views that they 'do not regard it as appropriate for chairmen to be in receipt of geared share incentive awards'.

Investors would prefer chairmen to receive shares at current prices and hold them during their period of office, according to the letter.

Consultants who have received the letter said the ABI had said share incentive schemes should be used for chairmen only in 'highly exceptional' circumstances, for a specific reason and justified to shareholders in advance.

Remuneration consultants compete to win head-hunting commissions and may feel the complaints inhibit attempts at innovative incentive schemes.

In the letter, the investors said that they 'do not wish to make remuneration considerations a deterrent to the attraction of talent'.

A spokesman for mmO2 said the aim of the deal for Mr Arculus, who will relinquish chairmanship of water company Severn Trent at the end of the year, was to 'align his interests with those of shareholders'.

Peter Montagnon, head of investment affairs at the ABI, said investors were keen to 'forestall confrontation' with companies. The ABI's investment committee plans to incorporate new guidance into its remuneration guidelines in the autumn.

indicates that CEO salary and bonus compensation appears to be relatively more aligned with accounting earnings in those firms where:

* share returns are relatively more sensitive to general market movements (relatively noisy);
* earnings have a high association with the firm-specific movement in the firm's share values;
* earnings have a less positive (more negative) association with market-wide movements in equity values.

Whilst the above arguments have discussed how or why managers might work in the interests of owners if they are offered rewards that are tied to the value of the shares of the organization (and therefore become owners themselves), there is also an argument that if managers are provided with an equity interest in the organization then this will have other positive impacts in terms of encouraging the managers to increase the level of disclosure. Without an equity interest in the organization, managers might be motivated to withhold information from shareholders and other interested stakeholders. As Nagar *et al.* (2003, p. 284) state:

> Managers avoid disclosing private information because such disclosure reduces their private control benefits. For instance, a lack of information disclosure limits the ability of capital and labour markets to effectively monitor and discipline managers (Shleifer and Vishny, 1989). The disclosure agency problem can thus be regarded as a fundamental agency problem underlying other agency problems. Practitioners also echo the view that managers exhibit an inherent tendency to withhold information from investors, even in the 'high disclosure' environmental of US capital markets. A panellist at the recent STERN Stewart Executive Roundtable states, '... all things equal, the managers of most companies would rather not disclose things if they don't have to. They don't want you to see exactly what they're doing; to see the little bets they are taking' (Stern Stewart, 2001, p. 37).

In relation to the concern that managers might be motivated to restrict disclosure, Nagar *et al.* (2003) suggest that providing managers with equity interests in the organization will act to reduce the 'non-disclosure tendency'. Specifically, they state (p. 284):

> Stock [share] price-based incentives elicit both good news and bad news disclosures from managers. Managers have incentives to release good news and bad news because it boosts stock price. On the other hand, the potential negative investor interpretation of silence (Verrecchia, 1983; Milgrom, 1981), and litigation costs (which reduce the value of the managers' ownership interest) are incentives to release bad news. Therefore, we argue that managerial stock price-based incentives, both as periodic compensation and aggregate shareholdings, help align long-run managerial and investor disclosure preferences and mitigate disclosure agency problems .... Our basic premise is that stock price-based incentives are contractual mechanisms that align managerial disclosure preferences with those of shareholders.

The results of Nagar *et al.*'s study are consistent with their expectations. Their results show that offering managers equity based share price-based incentives increases the managers' propensity to disclose information. Specifically they found that firm disclosures, measured both by the frequency of earnings forecasts and analysts' ratings of the firms' disclosures, increase as the proportion of CEO compensation tied to the share prices, and the value of CEO shareholdings, increase.

In considering the use of share-based versus accounting-based bonus schemes, accounting-based rewards have the advantage that the accounting results may be based on subunit or divisional performance, but one would need to ensure that individuals do not focus on their division at the expense of the organization as a whole.

Positive Accounting Theory assumes that if a manager is rewarded on the basis of accounting numbers (for example, on the basis of a share of profits) then the manager will have an incentive to manipulate the accounting numbers. Given such an assumption, the value of audited financial statements becomes apparent. Rewarding managers in terms of accounting numbers (a strategy aimed at aligning the interests of owners and managers) may not be appropriate if management was solely responsible for compiling those numbers. The auditor will act to arbitrate on the reasonableness of the accounting methods adopted. However, it must be remembered that there will always be scope for opportunism.

The above arguments concentrate on how management's rewards will be directly impacted as particular accounting methods are chosen. Management might also be rewarded in other indirect ways as a result of electing to use particular accounting methods. For example, DeAngelo (1988) provided evidence that when individuals face a contest for their positions as managers of an organization they will, prior to the contest, adopt accounting methods that lead to an increase in reported profits (and the increased reported earnings could not be associated with any apparent increase in cash flows) thereby bolstering their case for re-election. DeAngelo also showed that where the existing managers were nevertheless unsuccessful in retaining their positions within the organization, the newly appointed managers were inclined to recognize many expenses as soon as they took office (that is, 'take a bath') in a bid to highlight the 'poor state of affairs' they had inherited. Such strategies as those described above would be consistent with the opportunistic perspective applied within Positive Accounting Theory. The view that incoming chief executive officers may 'take a bath' was also confirmed by Wells (2002). Using Australian data Wells (p. 191) states:

> There is support for the view that incoming CEOs take an 'earnings bath' in the year of the CEO change .... Tests of earnings management yield evidence of income decreasing earnings management in the year of the CEO change, with the strongest results for CEO changes categorised as 'non-routine'. In this setting, the incoming CEO is typically not associated with past decisions, implicit criticism of which may be embodied in down-

wards earnings management. Moreover, the outgoing CEO is unable to constrain such behaviour. This highlights an important corporate governance issue, namely the effect of the CEO succession process in constraining the opportunities for incoming management to undertake earnings management in the period subsequent to the CEO change.

Having considered the contractual relationship between managers and principals, and how accounting can be used as a means of reducing the costs associated with potential conflict, we can now consider the relationship between debtholders and managers. We will see that accounting can be used to restrict the implications of this conflict and thereby enable an organization to attract funds at a lower cost than might otherwise be possible.

Debt contracting

When a party lends funds to another organization the recipient of the funds may undertake activities that reduce or even eliminate the probability that the funds will be repaid. These costs that relate to the divergent behaviour of the borrower are referred to in Positive Accounting Theory as the *agency costs of debt* and under Positive Accounting Theory, lenders will anticipate divergent behaviour. For example, the recipient of the funds may pay excessive dividends, leaving few assets in the organization to service the debt. Alternatively, the organization may take on additional and perhaps excessive levels of debt. The new debtholders would then compete with the original debtholder for repayment.

Further, the firm may also invest in very high-risk projects. This strategy would also not be beneficial to the debtholders. They have a fixed claim and hence if the project generates high profits they will receive no greater return, unlike the owners, who will share in the increased value of the firm. If the project fails, which is more likely with a risky project, the debtholders may receive nothing. The debtholders therefore do not share in any 'upside' (the profits), but suffer the consequences of any significant losses (the 'downside').

In the absence of safeguards that protect the interests of debtholders, the holders of debt will assume that management will take actions – such as those described above – that might not always be in the debtholders' interest, and as a result, it is assumed that they will require the firm to pay higher costs of interest to compensate the debtholders for the high risk exposure (Smith and Warner, 1979).

If the firm agrees not to pay excessive dividends, not to take on high levels of debt, and not to invest in projects of an excessively risky nature, then it is assumed that the firm will be able to attract debt capital at a lower cost than would otherwise be possible. To the extent that the benefits of lower interest costs exceed the costs that may be associated with restricting how management can use the available funds, management will elect to sign agreements that restrict their subsequent actions. Evidence on debt contracts is provided by Cotter (1998), who found (in an

Australian-based study) that:

> Leverage covenants are frequently used in bank loan contracts, with leverage most frequently measured as the ratio of total liabilities to total tangible assets. In addition, prior charges covenants that restrict the amount of secured debt owed to other lenders are typically included in the term loan agreements of larger firms, and are defined as a percentage of total tangible assets. (p. 187)

Where covenants restrict the total level of debt that may be issued, this is assumed to lead to a reduction in the risk to existing debtholders. This is further assumed to translate to lower interest rates being charged by the 'protected' debtholders. Cotter (1998) found that the definition of assets commonly used within debt agreements allowed for assets to be revalued. However, for the purposes of the debt restriction, some banks restricted the frequency of revaluations to once every two or three years, while others tended to exclude revaluations undertaken by directors of the firm. These restrictions lessened the ability of firms to loosen debt constraints by revaluing assets. Cotter (1998) also found that apart from debt to assets constraints, interest coverage and current ratio clauses were frequently used in debt agreements. These clauses typically required that the ratio of net profit, with interest and tax added back, to interest expense be at least a minimum number of times. In the Cotter study, the number of times which interest had to be covered ranged from one-and-a-half to four times. The current ratio clauses reviewed by Cotter required that current assets had to be between one and two times the size of current liabilities, depending upon the size and industry of the borrowing firm.

As with management compensation contracts, Positive Accounting Theory assumes that the existence of debt contracts (which are initially put in place as a mechanism to reduce the agency costs of debt and can be explained from an *efficiency perspective*) provides management with a subsequent (*ex post*) incentive to manipulate accounting numbers, with the incentive to manipulate the numbers increasing as the accounting-based constraint approaches violation. As Watts (1995, p. 323) states:

> Early studies of debt contract-motivated choice test whether firms with higher leverage (gearing) are more likely to use earnings-increasing accounting methods to avoid default (leverage hypothesis). The underlying assumptions are that the higher the firm's leverage the less [is the] slack in debt covenants and the more likely the firm is to have changed accounting methods to have avoided default. This change is usually interpreted as opportunistic since technical default generates wealth transfers to creditors but it could also be efficient to the extent that it avoids real default and the deadweight loss associated with bankruptcy.

For example, if the firm contractually agreed that the ratio, debt to total tangible assets, should be kept below a certain figure, then if that figure was likely to be exceeded (causing a technical default of the loan agreement), management may have an incentive to either inflate assets or deflate liabilities. This is consistent with the results reported in Christie (1990) and Watts and Zimmerman (1990). To the extent that such an action was not objective, management would obviously be acting opportunistically and not to the benefit of individuals holding debt claims against the firm. Debt agreements typically require financial statements to be audited.

Other research to consider how management might manipulate accounting numbers in the presence of debt agreements includes that undertaken by DeFond and Jiambalvo (1994) and Sweeney (1994). Both of these studies investigated the behaviour of managers of firms known to have defaulted on accounting-related debt covenants. DeFond and Jiambalvo (1994) provided evidence that the managers manipulated accounting accruals in the years before and the year after violation of the agreement. Similarly, Sweeney (1994) found that as a firm approaches violation of a debt agreement, managers have a greater propensity to adopt income-increasing strategies, relative to firms that are not approaching technical default of accounting-based debt covenants. The income-increasing accounting strategies included changing key assumptions when calculating pension liabilities and adopting LIFO (last-in-first-out) cost flow assumptions for inventory.

Sweeney (1994) also showed that managers with an incentive to manipulate accounting earnings might also strategically determine when they will first adopt a new accounting requirement. When new accounting standards are issued there is typically a transition period (which could be a number of years) in which organizations can voluntarily opt to implement a new accounting requirement. After the transitional period the use of the new requirement becomes mandatory. Sweeney showed that organizations that defaulted on their debt agreements tended to adopt income-increasing requirements early, and deferred the adoption of accounting methods that would lead to a reduction in reported earnings.

Debt contracts occasionally restrict the accounting techniques that may be used by the firm, hence requiring adjustments to published accounting numbers. For example, and as stated above, Cotter (1998) showed that bank loan contracts sometimes did not allow the component related to asset revaluations to be included in the definition of 'assets' for the purpose of calculating ratios, such as 'debt to assets' restrictions. These revaluations were, however, permitted for external reporting purposes. Therefore, loan agreements sometimes require the revaluation component (or other accounting adjustments that are allowed by accounting standards) to be removed from the published accounting numbers prior to the calculation of any restrictive covenants included within the debt contract.

Within accounting, management usually has available a number of alternative ways to account for particular items. Hence management has at its disposal numerous ways to minimize the effects of existing accounting-based restrictions. Therefore, it may appear optimal for debtholders to stipulate in advance *all* accounting methods that management must use. However, and as noted previously, it would be too costly, and for practical purposes impossible, to write 'complete' contracts up front. As a consequence, management will always have some discretionary ability, which may enable them to loosen the effects of debtholder-negotiated restrictions. The role of external auditors (if appointed) would be to arbitrate on the reasonableness of the accounting methods chosen.

Apart from using debt covenants (such as debt to asset constraints), which may or may not be breached, another contractual mechanism which is becoming increasingly used is something known as 'performance pricing'. As Beatty and Weber (2003, p. 120) state:

> Performance pricing is a relatively new feature in bank debt contracts that explicitly makes the interest rate charged on a bank loan a function of the borrower's current creditworthiness. Asquith et al. (2002) document that performance-pricing features typically measure the borrower's creditworthiness using financial ratios such as debt to earnings before interest, taxes, depreciation and amortisation (EBITDA), leverage and interest coverage. That is, the interest rate charged in the contract does not remain fixed over the length of the loan, but varies inversely with changes in measures of financial performance. Compared to covenants under which accounting information affects loan rates only when the borrower violates a single threshold, performance pricing creates a more continuous and direct link between accounting information and interest rates. Thus, performance pricing likely gives managers additional incentives to make income-increasing accounting method changes.

Beatty and Weber (2003) explore whether the existence of accounting-based performance pricing increases borrowers' tendencies to adopt income increasing accounting method changes.

Beatty and Weber also note that debt contracts often prohibit borrowers from using voluntary accounting method changes to affect contract calculations. Hence they expect that borrowers who change their accounting methods are more likely to make income increasing changes if their debt contracts allow the changes to affect contract calculations.

Whilst we have previously argued in this chapter that borrowers would typically agree to various contractual restrictions (including restrictions on the accounting methods they are permitted to use) in an effort to reduce the interest costs and other borrowing costs that they are required to pay, Beatty and Weber (2003) also suggest that some borrowers might actually agree to pay higher costs of interest in return for being allowed greater flexibility in choosing accounting methods. That is, if we accept that restrictions placed on borrowers (which have the effect of reducing the ability of the borrower to transfer wealth away from the lenders and thereby potentially reduce the agency costs of debt) lead to a reduction in cost, then conversely we could speculate that in some circumstances some managers might be prepared to pay for increased flexibility – that is, there could be a value in having the ability to select alternative accounting measures – and managers might be prepared to pay for this flexibility.

In discussing their results, Beattie and Weber found that 75 borrowers from their sample of 125 US borrowing corporations had at least one contract that allowed voluntary accounting method changes to affect contract calculations. Predictably, they found that such firms are more likely to adopt income increasing accounting methods than other firms that have debt contract that do not allow debt covenants to be calculated by use of new accounting methods. Further, they found that the likelihood that such firms will adopt income increasing methods increases as the cost of technical violation of debt contracts increases. In relation to the existence of accounting-based performance pricing, their results show that borrowers that change their accounting methods are more likely to make income increasing accounting changes if their debt contracts include accounting-based performance pricing.

Having discussed how managers might have incentives to adopt income increasing accounting methods, we can now briefly consider the role of independent auditors. In relation to auditors, and following discussion so far provided in this chapter, there would arguably be a particular demand for financial statement auditing (that is, monitoring by external parties) when:

♦ management is rewarded on the basis of numbers generated by the accounting system (and therefore has an incentive to adopt increasing accounting numbers to increase personal financial rewards); and

♦ when the firm has borrowed funds, and accounting-based covenants are in place to protect the investments of the debtholders.

Consistent with the above, it could also be argued that as the managers' share of equity in the business decreases, and as the proportion of debt to total assets increases, there will be a corresponding increase in the demand for auditing. In this respect, Ettredge *et al.* (1994) show that organizations that voluntarily elect to have interim financial statements audited tend to have greater leverage, and lower management shareholding in the firm.

In the discussion that follows we will consider how expectations about the *political process* can also impact on managers' choice of accounting methods.

Political costs

As indicated previously in this chapter, firms (particularly larger ones) are sometimes under scrutiny by various groups, for example, by government, employee groups, consumer groups, environmental lobby groups, and so on. For example, the size of a firm is often used as an indication of market power and this in itself can attract the attention of regulatory bodies such as the Competition Commission (in the UK) or the Federal Trade Commission (in the US).

Government and interest groups may publicly promote the view that a particular organization (typically large) is generating excessive profits and not paying its 'fair share' to other segments of the community (for example, the wages it is paying are too low, its product prices are too high, its financial commitment to environmental and community initiatives is too low, its tax payments are too low, and so on). Watts and Zimmerman (1978, 1986) highlight the highly publicized claims about US oil companies made by consumers, unions and government within the US in the period of the late 1970s. The claims were that oil companies were making excessive reported profits and were in effect exploiting the nation. It is considered that such claims may have led to the imposition of additional taxes in the form of 'excess profits' taxes.

Consistent with the early work of Watts and Zimmerman (1978), it has been argued that to reduce the possibility of adverse political attention and the associated costs of this attention (for example, the costs associated with increased taxes, increased wage claims, or product boycotts), politically sensitive firms (typically large firms) should adopt accounting methods that lead to a reduction in reported profits.[32] However, the view that lower reported profits will lead to lower political scrutiny (and ultimately to lower wealth transfers away from the firm) assumes that parties involved in the political process are unable or not prepared to 'unravel' the implications of the managers' various accounting choices. That is, managers can somehow *fool* those involved in the political process by simply adopting one method of accounting (income decreasing) in preference to another. In this regard, Fields *et al.* (2001, p. 260) state:

> In order for earnings management to be successful the perceived frictions must exist and at least some users of accounting information must be unable or unwilling to unravel completely the effects of the earnings management … . Political cost-based motivations implicitly assume that users of accounting information (e.g. trade unions or government agencies) may be unable to undo completely the effects of earnings management.

But why would it be the case that external parties can potentially be 'fooled' by management as a result of management's choices of alternative accounting methods when elsewhere it has been assumed (consistent with the EMH) that individuals within other markets, such as the capital market, can efficiently unravel managements' choices of accounting methods?

In relation to political costs, and from an economic perspective, there is a view that in political markets there is limited expected 'pay-off' that can result from the actions of individuals (Downs, 1957). For example, if an individual seeks to know the real reasons why government elected to adopt a particular action from among many possible actions, then gathering such information would be costly. Yet that individual's vote would have very little likelihood of affecting the existence of the government. Hence, individuals will elect to remain *rationally uninformed*. However, should particular interest groups form, then such information costs can be shared and the ability to investigate government actions can increase. A similar perspective is taken with groups other than government, for example, representatives of labour unions, consumer bodies and so on. Officials of these bodies represent a diverse group of people, with the individual constituents again having limited incentive to be fully informed about the activities of the office-bearers.

Because Positive Accounting Theory assumes that *all* actions by *all* individuals (including officials of interest groups, politicians and so on) are driven by self-interest, representatives of interest groups are predicted to adopt strategies that maximize their own welfare in the knowledge that their constituents will have limited motivation to be fully informed about their activities.

With the above arguments in mind, we can consider the actions of politicians. Because politicians know that highly profitable companies could be unpopular with a large number of their constituency, the politicians could 'win' votes by taking actions against such companies. However, Watts and Zimmerman (1979) argue that politicians will claim that the actions they have taken were in the 'public interest' as obviously they need to disguise the fact that such actions best served the politicians' own interests. As Watts and Zimmerman (1979, p. 283) argue:

> In recent years economists have questioned whether the public interest assumption is consistent with observed phenomena. They have proposed an alternative assumption – that individuals involved in the political process act in their own self-interest (the self-interest assumption). This assumption yields implications which are more consistent with observed phenomena than those based on the public interest assumption.

To justify their own actions, politicians may simply rely on the reported profits of companies to provide an *excuse* for their actions, knowing that individual constituents are unlikely to face the cost of investigating the politicians' motives, or the cost of investigating how the corporation's profits were determined (that is, whether the profit resulted because a particular accounting method was used in a less than objective manner). To reduce the *excuses* of politicians, potentially politically sensitive firms are predicted to anticipate politicians' actions and therefore managements of politically vulnerable firms have an incentive to reduce their reported profits. As Watts and Zimmerman (1979, p. 281) state:

> Government commissions often use the contents of financial statements in the regulatory process (rate setting, anti-trust, etc.). Further, Congress often bases legislative actions on these statements. This, in turn, provides management with incentives to select accounting procedures which either reduce the costs they bear or increase the benefits they receive as a result of the actions of government regulators and legislators.

Interestingly, when the media reports a company's profitability it seldom gives any attention to the accounting methods used to calculate the profit. In a sense, profit is held out as some form of objective measure of organizational performance (much like governments might rely on profits to support a particular action). Media reports of high corporate profitability can potentially trigger political costs for a firm. In the discussion above we discussed how representatives of interest groups might use profits as a justification for particular actions. In this respect we can consider Exhibit 7.4 below. The article refers to the high profits of banks in the UK and links these profits to 'excessive' levels of consumer debt in the UK, with associated negative potential social outcomes. It also notes trade union comments that the high levels of profit have not been passed on in any real extent to the employees. In a sense, the reported accounting profits could be used as an excuse to push for greater regulation of bank lending practices, higher wages, and 'windfall' taxes. These factors could be costly for the UK banks. Perhaps if reported profits were not so high, there would be less chance that demands for increased consumer regulation, higher wages or 'windfall' taxes would be made. As Watts and Zimmerman (1978, p. 115) state:

> By avoiding the attention that high profits draw because of monopoly rents, management can reduce the likelihood of adverse political actions and, thereby, reduce its expected costs (including the legal costs the firm would incur opposing the political actions). Included in political costs are the costs labour unions impose through increased demands generated by large reported profits.

Exhibit 7.4 Profits as a consideration in the political process

Bank's profit to top £6bn

Heather Stewart

Royal Bank of Scotland, which owns NatWest, is likely to announce record profits of more than £6bn this week, stoking concerns that the big four high street banks are cashing in on Britain's debt-laden households.

The Consumers' Association last night accused the four – Royal Bank of Scotland, Lloyds TSB, Barclays and HSBC – of exploiting their 'stranglehold' on the high street, as RBS prepared to announce that it clocked up pretax profits of £300 for each of its 20 million customers in 2003.

... Mick McAteer, principal policy adviser at the Consumers' Association, said: 'We have always been concerned that [banks] exploit the stranglehold they have on the high street. They use the current account as a powerful platform to sell other, higher margin products. Customers think, what the hell, they're all as bad as each other, but we don't think the big four are taking their social responsibilities seriously.'

He added that, in general, the high street banks tend to offer worse value for money – and worse service – than their online counterparts.

Vincent Cable, the Liberal Democrats' Treasury spokesman, said record profits at the banks were the 'mirror-image' of growing amounts of

Exhibit 7.4 (*continued*)

household debt. 'At the end of the day, the banks will save themselves – they have people's houses as security. The people who will suffer if there's a downturn are the customers.'

The Lib Dems are calling for Treasury-imposed limits on mortgage lending, and cigarette-style 'health warnings' on financial advertisements.

A scathing report by the cross-party Treasury select committee of back-bench MPs in December accused the banks of 'lending and marketing practices which can lead users to sleepwalk into financial disaster'.

... A spokeswoman for RBS said: 'As a bank we are very much focused on delivering superior value for our shareholders. We have to look after our people, our customers and our shareholders.'

She added that around 10 per cent of profits was returned to the staff through a profit-sharing scheme; and RBS has promised not to relocate jobs abroad to lower-cost economies, as some of its competitors have done.

However, unions representing RBS's workers complained that despite the bumper profits, around 25,000 of its workers are being offered below-inflation pay rises.

'What happens when the downturn comes?' said Dai Davies, director of communications at Unifi. 'We like our members to work for profitable companies – but come on, let's have a bit of equity.'

Record profits at the banks could reignite calls for a windfall tax on the industry, like that imposed on the privatised utilities by Labour when it came to power. But a Treasury spokesman would not say whether that was an option the chancellor was considering. 'It's not something anyone's put to me,' he said.

Numerous studies have considered how particular accounting methods can be used in an endeavour to decrease political costs. We have already considered the work of Watts and Zimmerman. Other research has been undertaken by Jones (1991) who, in a US study, considered the behaviour of 23 domestic firms from five industries that were the subject of government import-related investigations over the period from 1980 to 1985. These government investigations by the International Trade Commission sought to determine whether the domestic firms were under threat from foreign competition. Where this threat is deemed to be unfair, the government can grant relief by devices such as tariff protection. In making its decision the government relies upon a number of factors, including economic measures such as profits and sales. The results of the study show that in the year of the investigations the sample companies selected accounting strategies that led to a decrease in reported profits. Such behaviour was not evidenced in the year before or the year after the government investigation (perhaps indicating that the politicians are fairly 'short sighted' when undertaking investigations).

In a UK study, Sutton (1988) found that politically sensitive companies were also more likely to lobby in favour of current cost accounting.[33] In a New Zealand study, Wong (1988) investigated the practice of New Zealand companies between 1977 and 1981 and found that those that adopted current cost accounting (which had the effect of reducing reported profits) had higher effective tax rates and larger market concentration ratios than other firms. Effective tax rates and market concentration rates were both used as a measure of political sensitivity.

Apart from adopting income-reducing accounting techniques, authors such as Ness and Mirza (1991) have argued that particular voluntary social disclosures in an organization's annual report can be explained as an effort to reduce the political costs of the disclosing entities. Ness and Mirza (1991) studied the environmental disclosure practices of a number of UK companies. They considered that companies in the oil industry had developed particularly poor reputations for their environmental practices and that such a reputation could be used by various interest groups to transfer wealth away from the firm (and presumably away from the managers). Such wealth transfers might be generated if certain groups lobbied government to impose particular taxes (perhaps related to their environmental performance), or perhaps if particular employee groups took actions to insist that the companies put in place strategies to improve their environmental performance and reputation. Ness and Mirza argued that if firms voluntarily provide environmental disclosures (typically of a positive or self-laudatory nature) then this may lead to a reduction in future wealth transfers away from the firm. They found, consistent with their expectations, that oil companies provided greater environmental disclosures within their annual reports than did companies operating in other industries. They argued that this was the case as oil companies had more potentially adverse wealth transfers at stake.

To this point, we have shown that Positive Accounting Theory indicates that the selection of particular and alternative accounting methods may impact on the cash flows associated with debt contracts, the cash flows associated with management compensation plans, and the political costs of the firm. Positive Accounting Theory indicates that these impacts can be used to explain why firms elect to use particular accounting methods in preference to others. Positive Accounting Theory also indicates that the use of particular accounting methods may have opposing effects. For example, if a firm was to adopt a policy that increased income (for example, it may capitalize an item, rather than expensing it as incurred), then this may reduce the probability of violating a debt constraint. However, it may increase the political visibility of the firm due to the higher profits. Managers are assumed to select the accounting methods that best balance the conflicting effects (and also that maximize their own wealth).

We have demonstrated in this chapter that Positive Accounting Theory became the dominant theory used by accounting researchers in the 1970s.[34] It represented a challenge to many normative theorists and conflicted with the views of many established researchers. Many individuals openly criticized Positive Accounting Theory. In the concluding section of this chapter we now consider some of these criticisms.

Some criticisms of Positive Accounting Theory

One widespread criticism of Positive Accounting Theory is that it does not provide *prescription* and therefore does not provide a means of improving accounting practice. It is argued that simply explaining and predicting accounting practice is not enough. Using a medical analogy, Sterling (1990, p. 130) states:

> Positive Accounting Theory cannot rise above giving the same answers because it restricts itself to the descriptive questions. If it ever asked how to solve a problem or correct an error (both of which require going beyond a description to an evaluation of the situation), then it might go on to different questions and obtain different answers after the previous problem was solved. If we had restricted the medical question to the description of the smallpox virus, for example, precluding prescriptions to be vaccinated, we would need more and more descriptive studies as the virus population increased and mutations appeared. Luckily Edward Jenner was naughtily normative, which allowed him to discover how cowpox could be used as a vaccine so smallpox was eventually eliminated, which made room for different questions on the medical agenda.

Howieson (1996, p. 31) provides a view that by failing to provide prescription, Positive Accounting theorists may alienate themselves from practising accountants. As he states:

> ... an unwillingness to tackle policy issues is arguably an abrogation of academics' duty to serve the community which supports them. Among other activities, practitioners are concerned on a day-to-day basis with the question of which accounting policies they should choose. Traditionally, academics have acted as commentators and reformers on such normative issues. By concentrating on positive questions, they risk neglecting one of their important roles in the community.

A second criticism of Positive Accounting Theory is that it is not *value free*, as it asserts. If we are to look at various research that has adopted Positive Accounting Theory, we will see a general absence of prescription (that is, there is no guidance as to what people *should* do – rather it explains or predicts what they *will* do). This is normally justified by Positive Accounting theorists by saying that they do not want to impose their views on others, but rather would prefer to provide information about the expected implications of particular actions and let people decide for themselves what they should do (for example, they may provide evidence to support a prediction that organizations close to breaching accounting-based debt covenants will adopt accounting methods that increase the firm's reported profits and assets). However, as a number of accounting academics have pointed out, selecting a theory to adopt for research (such as Positive Accounting Theory) is based on a value judgement; what to research is based on a value judgement; believing that all individual action is driven by self-interest is a value judgement; and so on.[35] Also, Watts and Zimmerman appear to have taken a normative position when they identify the objective of accounting research. According to them, 'the objective of accounting theory is to explain and predict accounting practice' (1986, p. 2). Clearly, there are many other views about the role of accounting theory. Hence, no research, whether conducted under Positive Accounting Theory or otherwise, is value free.

Following from the above points, a third criticism of Positive Accounting Theory relates to the fundamental assumption that *all action* is driven by a desire to maximize one's wealth. To many researchers such an assumption represents a far too negative and simplistic perspective of humankind. In this respect, Gray *et al.* (1996, p. 75) state that Positive Accounting Theory promotes 'a morally bankrupt view of the world'. Given that everybody is deemed to act in their own self-interest, the perspective of self-interest has also been applied to the research efforts of academics. For example, Watts and Zimmerman (1990, p. 146) argue that:

> Researchers choose the topics to investigate, the methods to use, and the assumptions to make. Researchers' preferences and expected payoffs (publications and citations) affect their choice of topic, methods, and assumptions.

Many academics would challenge this view and would argue that they undertake their research because of real personal interest in an issue. Another implication of the self-interest issue is that incorporation of this self-interest assumption into the teaching of undergraduate students (as has been done in many universities throughout the world) has the possible implication that students think that when they subsequently have to make decisions in the workplace, it is both acceptable and predictable for them to place their own interests above those of others. It is perhaps questionable whether such a philosophy is in the interests of the broader community. Nevertheless, while assuming that all action is driven by a desire to maximize one's own wealth is not an overly kind assumption about human nature, such an assumption has been the cornerstone of many past and existing theories used within the discipline of economics (and this is not a justification).

Another criticism of Positive Accounting Theory is that since its general inception in the 1970s the issues being addressed have not shown great development. Since the early days of Watts and Zimmerman (1978) there have been three key hypotheses: the debt hypothesis (which proposes that organizations close to breaching accounting-based debt covenants will select accounting methods that lead to an increase in profits and assets); the bonus hypothesis (which proposes that managers on accounting-based bonus schemes will select accounting methods that lead to an increase in profits); and the political cost hypothesis (which proposes that firms subject to political scrutiny will adopt accounting methods that reduce reported income). A review of the recent Positive Accounting Theory literature indicates that these hypotheses continue to be tested in different environments and in relation to different accounting policy issues – even after the passing of almost 30 years since Watts and Zimmerman (1978). In this respect, Sterling (1990, p. 130) posed the following question:

> What are the potential accomplishments [of Positive Accounting Theory]? I forecast more of the same: twenty years from now we will have been inundated with research reports that managers and others tend to manipulate accounting numerals when it is to their advantage to do so.

In commenting on the perceived lack of development of Positive Accounting Theory Fields *et al.* (2001, p. 301) state:

> Fundamentally, we believe it is necessary to step back from the current research agenda, and to develop the 'infrastructure' surrounding the field. In a sense, the accounting choice field has been a victim of its own perceived success, and has outrun the development of theories, statistical techniques and research design that are necessary to support it. We therefore are calling for a return to work in these basic areas, before the field is able to advance further.

Also much of the research within Positive Accounting Theory considers individual accounting choices (for example, whether an entity will revalue a particular class of non-current assets) when in practice, the organization will have a vast number of accounting choices, many of which might have opposing effects on financial performance and position. That is, whilst researchers might be studying whether an entity elects to adopt an accounting method that increases income, at the same time the entity might also be adopting another (unresearched) accounting method that reduces income. Considering one accounting method choice from the portfolio of all the accounting choices being made within the firm provides a very incomplete picture. In this regard Fields *et al.* (2001, p. 288) state:

> Most of the work [in Positive Accounting Theory] examines the choice of a particular accounting method within the context of the goals driving the accounting choice, whereas managers may make multiple accounting method choices to accomplish a specific goal. As a result, examining only one choice at a time may obscure the overall effect obtained through a portfolio of choices

Fields *et al.* (2001, p. 290) further state:

> In addition to the problem of addressing multiple accounting choices, generally as reflected in accruals, there is also the issue of multiple, and potentially conflicting,

motivations for the accounting choices. Most of the work discussed focuses on a single motive for accounting choice decisions. For example, the compensation literature focuses on the question of whether managers use accounting discretion to maximize their compensation. Implicitly, the results suggest that managers' actions come at the expense of shareholders. But if this is so, why do compensation contracts allow discretion? One plausible answer is that managers' actions are not only anticipated, but also desirable from shareholders' perspective. For example, the same accounting choices that maximize managers' compensation may also decrease bond covenant violations or increase asset valuations. However, such motives are typically not included in the analysis. By focusing on one goal at a time, much of the literature misses the more interesting question of the interactions between and tradeoffs among goals. Moreover, it is not clear whether the conclusions are attributable to the specific motivation being analyzed; generally results consistent with one hypothesis are consistent with many. For example, what may appear to be an opportunistic choice of an earnings increasing accounting method choice (to benefit managers at the expense of other stakeholders in the firm), may be in fact a response to avoid a bond covenant violation (and thus benefits all other stakeholders at the expense of the creditors). Finally, with only few exceptions, research in the 1990s generally focuses on motives identified in the 1970s and 1980s. Typically the usual suspects are rounded up. However, we suspect that new insights may be gained by investigating additional motives. The problem of multiple conflicts can be viewed, in turn, as a special case of the familiar 'correlated omitted variable' problem in econometrics.

Another criticism is that the measurements or proxies being used within the literature are often far too simplistic. As Fields *et al.* (2001, p. 272) state:

> Most work investigating the debt hypothesis in the 1980s used crude proxies such as the leverage ratio for the proximity of the firm to violation of its debt covenants. However, Lys (1984) documents that because leverage is determined endogenously, it is a poor proxy for default risk, unless there is a control for the risk of the underlying assets. On the other hand, Duke and Hunt (1990) determine that the debt to equity ratio is a good proxy for the closeness to some covenant violations, including retained earnings, net tangible assets and working capital, but not for other covenants. In the 1990s researchers began studying firms that actually violated covenants in order to avoid the use of proxies.

A further criticism is that Positive Accounting Theory is scientifically flawed. It has been argued that as the hypotheses generated pursuant to Positive Accounting Theory (for example, the debt hypothesis, the bonus hypothesis and the political cost hypothesis) are frequently not supported (they are falsified), then scientifically Positive Accounting Theory should be rejected. Christenson (1983, p. 18) states:

> We are told, for example, that 'we can only expect a positive theory to hold on average' [Watts and Zimmerman, 1978, p. 127, n. 37]. We are also advised 'to remember that as in all empirical theories we are concerned with general trends' [Watts and Zimmerman, 1978, pp. 288–9], where 'general' is used in the weak sense of 'true or applicable in most instances but not all' rather than in the strong sense of 'relating to, concerned with, or applicable to every member of a class' [American Heritage Dictionary, 1969, p. 548] ... .

> A law that admits exceptions has no significance, and knowledge of it is not of the slightest use. By arguing that their theories admit exceptions, Watts and Zimmerman condemn them as insignificant and useless.

As a study of people, however, (accounting is a process undertaken by people and the accounting process itself cannot exist in the absence of accountants), it is hard to consider that any model or theory could ever fully explain human action. In fact, ability to do so would constitute a dehumanizing action. Are there any theories of human activity or choice processes that always hold? In defence of the fact that Positive Accounting Theory predictions do not always hold, Watts and Zimmerman (1990, p. 148) state:

> But accounting research using this methodology has produced useful predictions of how the world works. A methodology that yields useful results should not be abandoned purely because it may not predict all human behaviour. Do we discard something that works in some situations because it may not work in every circumstance?

Another criticism of Positive Accounting Theory is that the positive researchers believe that they can generate laws and principles expected to operate in different situations, and that there is one underlying 'truth' that can be determined by an independent, impartial observer who is not influenced by individual perceptions, idiosyncrasies or biases (Tinker *et al.*, 1982, p. 167). That is, the apparent perspective is that reality exists objectively, and one observer's view of that reality will be the same as all other people's views. This is referred to as the 'realist philosophy'. A number of researchers have challenged this philosophy (for example, Hines, 1988). They have argued that in undertaking large-scale empirical research, positive researchers ignore many organization-specific relationships and the information collected is only the information that the researchers consider relevant. A different person would possibly consider that other information is more relevant. Many researchers critical of the 'realist perspective' argue that more insights might be gained by undertaking in-depth case studies. Positive researchers would provide a counter-argument, however, that case study research is very specific to a particular time and place and therefore cannot be generalized to a broader population. Such arguments about research methodology abound in the literature with potentially very limited likelihood that researchers operating across different paradigms will ever agree on what constitutes valid research. As Watts and Zimmerman (1990, p. 149) concede when defending their research against numerous criticisms:

> To most researchers, debating methodology is a 'no win' situation because each side argues from a different paradigm with different rules and no common ground. Our reason for replying here is that some have mistaken our lack of response as tacit acceptance of the criticisms.

While the above criticisms do, arguably, have some merit, Positive Accounting Theory does continue to be used by many accounting researchers. Respected accounting research journals continue to publish Positive Accounting Theory research (although the numbers appear to be declining). A number of the leading accounting research schools throughout the world continue to teach it. What must be remembered is that all theories of accounting will have limitations. They are, of necessity, abstractions of the 'real world'. Whether individually we prefer one theory of accounting in preference to another will be dependent upon our assumptions about many of the issues raised within this chapter.

Chapter summary

A positive theory seeks to explain and predict particular phenomena. In this chapter we considered Positive Accounting Theory, a theory that seeks to explain and predict managers' choices of accounting methods. Positive Accounting Theory focuses on relationships between various individuals within and outside an organization and explains how financial accounting can be used to minimize the costly implications associated with each contracting party operating in his or her own self-interest. The economic perspective that all individual behaviour is motivated by self-interest is central to Positive Accounting Theory, and Positive Accounting Theory predicts that contractual arrangements will be put in place to align the interests of the various self-interested parties. Many of these contractual arrangements will use the output of the accounting system.

Positive Accounting Theory became a dominant research paradigm in the 1970s and 1980s and its development owed much to previous research work that had been undertaken, including work on the efficient markets hypothesis (EMH) and agency theory. The EMH provided evidence that capital markets reacted to new information but it provided little explanation for why managers might elect to use particular accounting methods in preference to others. Positive Accounting Theory was developed to fill this void.

Applying agency theory, Positive Accounting Theory focused on relationships between principals and agents. Positive Accounting Theory proposed that agents have incentives to enter various contracts. Firms themselves were considered as a nexus of contracts between many self-interested individuals. The contractual arrangements are initially put in place for efficiency reasons with well-developed contracts reducing the overall agency costs that could arise within the firm. Further, agents are predicted to adopt those accounting methods that most efficiently reflect their own performance. Regulation is considered to introduce unnecessary costs and inefficiencies into the contractual arrangements, particularly as it often acts to reduce the methods of accounting that would otherwise be adopted.

Early work within Positive Accounting Theory relied upon three central hypotheses: the bonus hypothesis, the debt hypothesis and the political cost hypothesis. The bonus hypothesis predicts that from an efficiency perspective many organizations will elect to provide their managers with bonuses tied to the performance of the firm, with these bonuses often being directly related to accounting numbers (for example, management might be rewarded with a share of profits). Offering performance-based rewards will motivate the self-interested manager to work also in the best interests of the owners. However, under the opportunistic perspective, Positive Accounting Theory predicts that once bonus schemes are in place, managers will, to the extent that they can get away with it, manipulate performance indicators such as profits to generate higher individual rewards.

The debt hypothesis predicts that to reduce the cost of attracting debt capital, firms will enter into contractual arrangements with lenders which reduce the likelihood that the managers can expropriate the wealth of the debtholders. Arranging such agreements prior to obtaining debt finance is deemed to be an efficient way to attract lower cost funds. However, once a debt contract is in place, the opportunistic perspective of Positive Accounting Theory predicts that firms, particularly those close to breaching debt covenants, will adopt accounting methods that act to minimize or loosen the effects of the debt constraint.

The political cost hypothesis explores the relationships between a firm and various outside parties who, although perhaps not having any direct contractual relationships, can nevertheless impose various types of wealth transfers away from the firm. It is argued that high profits can attract adverse and costly attention to the firm, and hence managers of politically vulnerable firms look for ways to reduce the level of political scrutiny. One way is to adopt accounting methods that lead to a reduction in reported profits. Most tests of the political cost hypothesis use size of the firm as a proxy for the existence of political scrutiny.

The chapter also provided a number of criticisms of Positive Accounting Theory. Included among the various criticisms was a challenge to the central Positive Accounting Theory assumption that *all* individual action is driven by self-interest.

Questions

7.1 Early positive research investigated evidence of share price changes as a result of the disclosure of accounting information. However, such research did not explain why particular accounting methods were selected in the first place. How did Positive Accounting Theory fill this void?

7.2 Explain the *management bonus hypothesis* and the *debt hypothesis* of Positive Accounting Theory.

7.3 If a manager is paid a percentage of profits, does this generate a motive to manipulate profits? Would this be anticipated by principals, and if so, how would principals react to this expectation?

7.4 What is an *agency relationship* and what is an *agency cost*? How can agency costs be reduced?

7.5 Explain the *political cost hypothesis* of Positive Accounting Theory.

7.6 Explain the *efficiency perspective* and the *opportunistic perspective* of Positive Accounting Theory. Why is one considered to be *ex post* and the other *ex ante*?

7.7 Organizations typically have a number of contractual arrangements with debtholders, with many covenants written to incorporate accounting numbers.
   (a) Why would an organization agree to enter into such agreements with debtholders?
   (b) On average, do debtholders gain from the existence of such agreements?

7.8 Positive Accounting theorists typically argue that managers can reduce political costs by simply adopting an accounting method that leads to a reduction in reported income. Does this imply anything about the perceived efficiency of those parties involved in the political process, and if so, what perception is held?

7.9 Positive Accounting Theory assumes that all individual action is driven by self-interest, with the self-interest being tied to wealth maximization.
   (a) Is this a useful and/or realistic assumption?
   (b) Adopting this assumption, why would politicians introduce particular regulations?
   (c) Why would researchers study particular issues?

7.10 What are some of the criticisms of Positive Accounting Theory? Do you agree with them? Why or why not?

7.11 Read Exhibit 7.5 (below), and, adopting a positive accounting perspective, consider the following issues:
   (a) If a new accounting standard impacts on profits, should this impact on the value of the firm, and if so, why?
   (b) Will the imposition of a particular accounting method have implications for the *efficiency* of the organization?

7.12 Applying Positive Accounting Theory, and after reading Exhibit 7.6 (below), answer the following questions:

(a) From an efficiency perspective, why could the introduction of new rules on share option accounting be costly for an organization?

(b) Why could the introduction of the new rules on share option accounting be costly for a manager?

(c) What would motivate the regulators to develop the new rules?

7.13 Read Exhibit 7.4 (earlier in the chapter) and explain why publicity such as this might be costly to an organization. How would Positive Accounting theorists expect the banks to react to such publicity?

Exhibit 7.5 The introduction of accounting regulation

Northern Rock takes IFRS stoning

Paul Grant

The furore surrounding financial instruments standard has moved into the heart of the City, as leading analysts predict Northern Rock's profits will be slashed by up to 10%. But the bank has hit back, claiming predictions are just a 'storm in a teacup'.

It seems that the arguments surrounding the most controversial of accounting standards, IAS 39, just won't stop. But now, the machinations taking place in the political arena have moved into the business world, with companies, investors and analysts all hotly debating exactly how the financial instruments standard will affect annual profits.

The first big example of a purely financial spat was sparked by the views of market watchers Credit Suisse First Boston. While a report from the investment bank said that the changes to accounting standards would boost the profits of banks such as HSBC and Alliance & Leicester, it said that the profits of Newcastle-based Northern Rock could be hit by as much as 10%. Accordingly it downgraded its advice on the bank from outperform to neutral and the share price of Northern Rock took an immediate hit of 20p.

In what looks like an attempt to head off some of the trouble caused by this report Northern Rock took the rather unusual step of issuing a pre-close statement just two months after its last trading update in which the specific issue of IFRS was tackled.

In this statement the bank said that the impact of IFRS on its accounts was still being determined, but rather than a 10% fall in profits it claimed its restated 2004 accounts would see a profit change of plus or minus 5%.

'We expect the impact from the implementation of all IFRS – including IAS 39 and other changes – will have no material impact when 2004's results are restated next year,' said chief executive Adam Applegarth. He went on to say that the issue was a 'storm in a teacup'.

Exhibit 7.5 (*continued*)

This may well be the first example of a split between market watchers and companies over the new accounting regime, but it won't be the last. Accountancy Age has already reported that a Big Four firm has had to call in lawyers over the interpretation of IFRS, and differences of opinion seem to be becoming more commonplace.

The war of words between Northern Rock and CSFB highlights the difficulties the changeover is likely to bring in the near future. But it also signals that the controversy that IAS 39 has caused – and continues to cause – may well mean big problems for analysts.

Last month ratings agency Fitch sent out a warning about the way derivatives are being accounted for. It said that the way companies are accounting for their derivatives transaction could bring problems in the future.

'The complexity of current derivative accounting standards and the low level of transparency create a new set of challenges for investors and analysts,' said the agency.

A study of 57 international companies found a significant lack of consensus over how these companies are applying the accounting rules for derivatives, which includes IAS 39 and SFAS 133 in the US.

'This does not bode well for the pending implementation of IFRS for most large European companies,' warned Fitch.

The potential for confusion over derivatives has been compounded by the European Commission's decision to adopt a version of IAS 39 different to that drawn up by the International Accounting Standards Board.

The carved-out version, which removes sections of the original standard to do with the hedging of core deposits and the fair value option, would not necessarily cause confusion by itself. But by allowing companies the option to use the full version of the standard, the market will be faced with companies using different standards in their accounts. The ability to truly compare results between competitors could be severely curtailed.

The situation with IAS 39 arrives at a time when the market is struggling to come to terms with the biggest change in accounting for a generation. The introduction of IFRS means that market watchers have to cope with major changes in how a company's performance is viewed.

With many companies well behind in their preparations for IFRS, informing the market on how the move will affect the result has come quite low down on the list of priorities. Similarly there is concern that analysts have yet to undertake the training needed to help them understand forthcoming changes.

While the markets may eventually settle down, over the next year or so, when companies are reporting under the new standards for the first time, there are likely to be some bumpy times ahead in the market.

Exhibit 7.5 (*continued*)

IFRS battles blow by blow

Round 1

French banks raise opposition to several key proposals in financial instruments standard IAS 39, claiming they are unworkable, and receive the backing of the European Commission. The IASB stands its ground and the EC adopts its own version of the standard.

Round 2

Accountancy Age learns that a Big Four firm has called upon lawyers to help in the interpretation of IFRS for a particular client. IASB chairman Sir David Tweedie tells the firm to 'get some backbone'.

Round 3

Credit Suisse First Boston says Northern Rock profits will be hit by up to 10% by the introduction of IFRS. Following a hit to the share price the bank issues a statement to the market that refutes these claims.

Accountancy Age, 9 December 2004

Exhibit 7.6 Introduction of accounting regulation for accounting for share options

Are you getting your fair shares?

Joanna Osborne, senior IFRS technical partner at KPMG

Last month, the IASB issued IFRS2 on share-based payment, which will affect UK-listed companies preparing their first group financial statements under IFRS and applies to share-based payments active at 1 January 2005.

In the UK, share-based payments are already required to be expensed under UITF17. But whereas this expense is the difference between the underlying share price at grant date and the employee contribution (intrinsic value), IFRS2 requires share-based payments to be expensed at fair value.

This, alongside other differences to current UK practice, will mean a significant increase in the frequency and amount of expenses recorded for share-based payments in company accounts from 2005.

Exhibit 7.6 (*continued*)

IFRS2 seeks to measure the fair value of services received from employees by reference to the fair value of a share option, multiplied by the number of options that ultimately vest. This measure will mean a greater hit on the accounts, as the fair value of an option will be recorded as higher than the intrinsic value of the share.

To understand this, compare two different employee packages, one comprising cash plus an option to acquire a share at today's price in three years' time, and one comprising ownership of the share itself.

In the first package you can earn interest on the cash for three years, although you don't receive the generally small amount from dividends that you would in the second package. The major bonus of this package is the one-way nature of the share option.

In effect it is a free bet on whether the share price will be higher than today's price in three years' time. If you hold an actual share you suffer a loss if the price goes down. If you have an option, you don't have to exercise it and suffer that loss – you still have the cash and subsequent interest. If the share price rises you gain with either package.

It is, however, complicated to determine the fair value of a share option at grant date because it involves predicting, among other things, future share price movements. But there are well-established and accessible mathematical techniques, for example the Black-Scholes and the binomial models, that are used by option traders to predict the future movements in share price and therefore to derive the fair value of an option.

... The long-awaited arrival of IFRS2 is going to make the means of payment of bonuses largely neutral in profit and loss account terms between cash and shares or share options. But a significant increase in the amount of expense recorded for share-based payments is inevitable.

Accountancy Age, 8 March 2004

Notes

1 Legitimacy theory and stakeholder theory, both covered in Chapter 8, are other examples of positive theories. For example, legitimacy theory predicts that in certain circumstances organizations will use positive or favourable disclosures in an effort to restore the *legitimacy* of an organization. These other positive theories are not grounded in classical economic theory, whereas Positive Accounting Theory is.

2 Similarly, in Chapter 8 we see that two other positive theories, stakeholder theory (the managerial version) and legitimacy theory, provide alternative explanations (alternative to Positive Accounting Theory) about what drives an organization to make particular disclosures. These theoretical perspectives also do not prescribe particular actions, or methods of disclosure.

3 From the Positive Accounting Theory perspective, *bonding* occurs when the agent gives a guarantee to undertake, or not to undertake, certain activities.

4 We considered the work of these theorists in Chapter 5. As indicated in Chapter 5 as well as in Chapter 1, researchers such as Sterling, Chambers and many others were particularly critical of positive research, and particularly of Positive Accounting Theory.

5 By relying on only two journals it could easily be argued, given that there are many other accounting journals, that the data may not be representative of all accounting research being undertaken. Further, evidence would indicate that the editors of these journals developed an extremely favourable disposition towards positive research, a disposition not necessarily shared by editors of other journals. Nevertheless, there was certainly a significant movement towards positive research in the 1960s and 1970s.

6 As we might imagine, there are many researchers who do not favour the positive research paradigm, and hence would challenge Watts' view that journals that publish positive research are *leading* academic journals.

7 Chapter 12 (which considers the views of the *critical theorists*) provides alternative views about why positive accounting flourished in the 1970s and 1980s. These theorists (for example Mouck, 1992, Tinker *et al.*, 1991) believe that many accounting researchers provide research results and perspectives that aim to legitimize and maintain particular political ideologies. As an example, in the late 1970s and in the 1980s, there were moves by particular governments around the world towards deregulation. This was particularly the case in the United States and the United Kingdom. Around this time researchers working within the Positive Accounting framework, and researchers who embraced the efficient markets hypothesis, came to prominence. The researchers typically took an anti-regulation stance, a stance that matched the views of the government of the time. Coincidentally, perhaps, the critical theorists show that such research, which supported calls for deregulation, tended to attract considerable government-sourced research funding, thereby providing further resources for the theory's development.

8 Research that subsequently tested the EMH predominantly adopted the assumption of *semi-strong form market efficiency*. Under the assumption of semi-strong form efficiency the market price of a firm's securities reflects all publicly available information. According to Watts and Zimmerman (1986, p. 19) the available evidence is generally consistent with the semi-strong form of EMH. Two other forms of market efficiency (with less empirical support) have also have been advanced. A *weak form* of market efficiency assumes that existing security prices simply reflect information about past prices and trading volumes. The *strong form* of market efficiency assumes that security prices reflect all information known to anyone at that point in time (including information which is not publicly available).

9 In studies that investigate the reaction of the capital market to earnings announcements, it is generally assumed that accounting earnings are highly correlated with cash flows, hence new information about accounting earnings is deemed to indicate new information about cash flows.

10 Share returns would generally be calculated by taking into account the change in price of the security during the period, as well as any dividends received during the period.

11 The development of the CAPM is generally credited to the works of Sharpe (1964) and Lintner (1965).

12 Much research has followed Ball and Brown (1968). For example, subsequent research has shown that the relationship between the information content in earnings announcements and changes in share prices tends to be more significant for small firms. That is, in general, larger firms' earnings announcements have relatively less information content (for example). This is consistent with the EMH and is explained by the fact that larger firms tend to have more information being circulated about them, as well as attracting more attention from such parties as security analysts. Hence, on average, earnings announcements for larger firms tend to be more anticipated, and hence already impounded in the share price prior to the earnings announcement.

13 Ball and Brown's results were also considered to be important because they emphasize that accounting numbers were not the sole (or predominant) source of information about an organization. This was in contrast to the views held by many normative theorists who considered that accounting data were the sole, or at least the most important, source of information about an organization, hence their concerns about getting the accounting numbers 'right'.

14 What should also be appreciated is that research such as that undertaken by Ball and Brown and subsequent researchers actually represents a joint test of the EMH, as well as the procedures used to estimate *expected returns* and *normal returns*. That is, failure to generate significant results (or indeed, success in generating significant results) may be due to misspecification problems in the calculation of expected earnings and normal returns, rather than problems with the hypothesis itself.

15 As shown later in this chapter, however, subsequent arguments were developed to support a contrary view that a change in accounting method may have cash flow consequences (and therefore, consequences for share prices). For example, the new accounting method may be considered to provide information more efficiently about the performance of the firm, and hence may enable the firm to attract more funds at lower cost (perhaps because investors consider the available information to be more reliable). Further, and as shown shortly, many contractual arrangements with associated cash flows (for example, there might be an agreement that the manager gets paid a percentage of profits) are tied to accounting numbers and hence changing those numbers can ultimately change cash flows (and hence, firm value).

16 This *contract* does not have to be a written contract. That is, it may simply constitute implicit terms about how the principal expects the manager to the behave.

17 Or if shares are being sold in a company, the shareholders will, in the absence of contractual restraints on the manager, pay a lower price for shares in the organization.

18 In this context, reference is made to the owner/manager to imply that the manager might have some ownership in the organization but does not own the entire organization.

19 These arguments about managers' opportunistic behaviour are 'on average' arguments. Principals would not know with certainty whether specific agents will adopt particular opportunistic strategies which are detrimental to the principals' economic welfare. Rather, the principals will assume, on average, that the agent will adopt such strategies, and the principal will price protect accordingly. Hence agents who do not commit to restrict the available set of actions will be penalized (in the form of lower salary) even though they individually may not ultimately elect to undertake actions detrimental to the principal.

20 As shown later in this chapter, one way to align the interests of the manager with those of the owners of the firm might be for the manager to be given a share of profits in the organization. Hence the manager would be motivated to increase profits (to increase his or her own wealth) and such self-interested activity will also provide benefits to the owners, who, all things being equal, will benefit from higher accounting earnings.

21 See Chapter 3 for an overview of the implications for managers of an efficiently functioning 'market for managers' and 'market for corporate takeovers'. In Chapter 3 we show that an assumption about efficiency in these markets provides a justification for some people to argue against regulating accounting disclosures.

22 Contracting costs are costs that arise as a result of 'contracting' or formulating an agreement with another party (for example a manager) wherein one party provides a particular service for a particular payment. The contracting costs include: the costs of finding the other party to the contract; negotiating the agreement; costs associated with monitoring that the agreement has been carried out in the manner expected; possible renegotiation costs; and so on.

23 Specifically, the prediction provided within Watts and Zimmerman (1978, p. 116) in relation to management compensation plans was that: 'a change in accounting standards which increase the firm's reported

earnings would, *ceteris paribus*, lead to greater incentive income. But this would reduce the firm's cashflows and share prices would fall. As long as per manager present value of the after tax incentive income is greater than the decline in each manager's portfolio, we expect management to favour such an accounting change.'

24 Political costs are costs that particular groups external to the organization may be able to impose on the organization as a result of particular political actions. The costs could include increased taxes, increased wage claims or product boycotts.

25 The prediction provided by Watts and Zimmerman (1978, p. 118) in relation to political costs was: 'that managers have greater incentives to choose accounting standards which report lower earnings (thereby increasing cash flows, firm value and their welfare) due to tax, political, and regulatory considerations than to choose accounting standards which report higher earnings and, thereby, increase their incentive compensation. However, this prediction is conditional upon the firm being regulated or subject to political pressure. In small (i.e., lower political costs) unregulated firms, we would expect that managers do have incentives to select accounting standards which report higher earnings, if the expected gain in incentive compensation is greater than the foregone expected tax consequences. Finally, we expect managers to also consider the accounting standard's impact on the firm's bookkeeping costs (and hence their own welfare).'

26 Benston (1969) provides evidence that all the firms listed on the New York Stock Exchange in 1926 published balance sheets when there was no direct requirement to do so. Further, 82 per cent were audited by a CPA when there was also no direct requirement to do so.

27 These results were also supported by Mian and Smith (1990). Using US data they found that the inclusion of financial subsidiaries in consolidated financial statements prior to Financial Accounting Standard 94 (which required the subsidiaries to be included within consolidated statements) was directly related to whether guarantees of debt were in existence between members of the group of companies. As Watts (1995, p. 332) indicates, the fact that two independent studies (Mian and Smith, 1990, Whittred, 1987) in different time periods and in different countries found the same results provides a stronger case that the efficiency perspective appears to explain this type of accounting choice.

28 In this regard we can consider IAS 38 'Intangibles'. This accounting standard requires all research expenditure to be expensed as incurred regardless of whether the expenditure is considered likely to lead to future economic benefits (IAS 38 does, however, allow development expenditure to be carried forward subject to certain stringent requirements). The requirement that all research be expensed as incurred is highly conservative and does not allow financial report readers to differentiate between entities that have undertaken valuable research (in terms of generating economic benefits) and those entities who have pursued failed research projects. For financial accounting purposes all research (good and bad) is to be treated the same. Arguably, this does not enhance the 'efficiency' of general purpose financial reports in terms of assessing the past and future economic performance of respective reporting entities.

29 Holthausen *et al.* (1995) utilized private data on firms' compensation plans to also investigate managers' behaviour in the presence of management compensation plans. Their results confirmed those of Healy (1985), except that they did not find any evidence to support the view that management will 'take a bath' when earnings are below the lower pre-set bound.

30 By contrast, IAS 36 'Intangible Assets' requires expenditure on research expenditure to be expensed as incurred, but does allow development expenditure to be capitalized to the extent that future economic benefits are deemed 'probable' and the cost can be measured reliably.

31 As a particular example of the use of share options, Cheng (2004, p. 321) refers to the options provided to the CEO of a large US corporation. According to Cheng 'the CEO of the company was scheduled to retire on April 1, 2000 at age 64. The compensation committee approved to grant 1,500,000

stock options to the CEO in 1997 in order to provide a stock option-based incentive to continue his contributions to the improvement of the share price through and beyond retirement, and half the options would not become exercisable until the CEO became 66'.

32 Difficulties with using firm size to proxy for political costs, including the likelihood that it can proxy for many other effects, such as industry membership, are discussed in Ball and Foster (1982).

33 While a number of studies considered in this chapter investigate the choice between alternative accounting methods, it should be noted that in recent years there has been an increased focus on studying the manipulation of accounting accruals. Relative to investigating the selection of particular accounting methods (for example, the use of straight line depreciation versus reducing balance depreciation), the study of the accruals is more difficult and requires the use of modelling techniques to identify discretionary (those controlled by management) and non-discretionary accruals (Jones, 1991). The use of accruals can also be explained from either an *efficiency* or *opportunistic* perspective (Guay *et al.*, 1996).

34 While its popularity is still high, many accounting schools are now actively promoting alternative theories.

35 In Chapter 12 we also see that some researchers argue that Positive Accounting theorists adopt a conservative right-wing ideology in promoting the virtues of markets, the rights of shareholders (the capitalist class), and so on.

References

Asquith, P., Beatty, A. & Weber, J. (2002) *Performance Pricing in Private Debt Contracts*, Working paper, Massachusetts Institute of Technology, Cambridge, MA.

Ball, R. & Brown, P. (1968) 'An empirical evaluation of accounting income numbers', *Journal of Accounting Research*, **6** (2), pp. 159–78.

Ball, R. & Foster, G. (1982) 'Corporate financial reporting: A methodological review of empirical research', *Studies on current research methodologies in accounting: A critical evaluation – supplement to The Journal of Accounting Research*, **20** (Supplement), pp. 161–234.

Beatty, A. & Weber, J. (2003) 'The effects of debt contracting on Voluntary Accounting Method Changes', *The Accounting Review*, **78**, pp. 119–42.

Beaver, W. (1968) 'The information content of annual earnings announcements', *Journal of Accounting Research*, **6** (Supplement), pp. 67–92.

Benston, G. J. (1969) 'The value of the SEC's accounting disclosure requirements', *The Accounting Review* (July), pp. 515–32.

Blackwell, D., Brickley, J. & Weisbach, M. (1994) 'Accounting information and internal performance evaluation: Evidence from Texas banks', *Journal of Accounting and Economics*, **17**, pp. 331–58.

Bushman, R. & Smith, A. (2001) 'Financial accounting information and corporate governance', *Journal of Accounting and Economics*, **32**, pp. 237–333.

Cheng, S. (2004) 'R&D expenditures and CEO compensation', *The Accounting Review*, **79**, pp. 305–28.

Christenson, C. (1983) 'The methodology of positive accounting', *The Accounting Review*, **58** (January), pp. 1–22.

Christie, A. (1990) 'Aggregation of test statistics: An evaluation of the evidence on contracting and size hypotheses', *Journal of Accounting and Economics*, **12**, pp. 15–36.

Clinch, G. (1991) 'Employee compensation and firms' research and development and activity', *Journal of Accounting Research*, **29**, pp. 59–78.

Coase, R. (1937) 'The nature of the firm', *Economica*, **4**, pp. 386–406.

Cotter, J. (1998) 'Asset revaluations and debt contracting', unpublished PhD thesis, University of Queensland, Australia.

DeAngelo, L. (1988) 'Managerial competition,

information costs, and corporate governance: The use of accounting performance measures in proxy contests', *Journal of Accounting and Economics*, **10** (January), pp. 3–36.

Dechow, P. (1994) 'Accounting earnings and cash flows as a measure of firm performance: The role of accounting accruals', *Journal of Accounting and Economics*, **18**, pp. 3–42.

Dechow, P. & Skinner, D. (2000) 'Earnings management: Reconciling the views of accounting academics, practitioners and regulators', *Accounting Horizons*, **14**, pp. 235–50.

Dechow, D. & Sloane, R. (1991) 'Executive incentives and horizon problems', *Journal of Accounting and Economics*, **14**, pp. 51–89.

Deegan, C. (1997) 'The design of efficient management remuneration contracts: A consideration of specific human capital investments', *Accounting and Finance*, **37** (1), pp. 1–40.

DeFond, M. & Jiambalvo, J. (1994) 'Debt covenant violation and manipulation of accruals', *Journal of Accounting and Economics*, **17**, pp. 145–76.

Downs, A. (1957) *An Economic Theory of Democracy*, New York: Harper and Row.

Duke, J. & Hunt, H. (1990) 'An empirical examination of debt covenant restrictions and accounting-related debt proxies', *Journal of Accounting and Economics*, **12**, pp. 45–64.

Dyckman, A. & Zeff, S. (1984) 'Two decades of the Journal of Accounting Research', *Journal of Accounting Research*, **22**, pp. 225–97.

Ettredge, M., Simon, D., Smith, D., & Stone, M. (1994) 'Why do companies purchase timely quarterly reviews?' *Journal of Accounting and Economics*, **18** (2), pp. 131–56.

Emanuel, D., Wong, J. & Wong, N. (2003) 'Efficient contracting and accounting', *Accounting and Finance*, **43**, pp. 149–66.

Fama, E. (1965) 'The behavior of stock market prices', *Journal of Business*, **38**, pp. 34–105.

Fama, E. (1980) 'Agency problems and the theory of the firm', *Journal of Political Economy*, **88**, pp. 288–307.

Fields, T., Lys, T., & Vincent, L. (2001) 'Empirical Research on Accounting Choice', *Journal of Accounting and Economics*, **31**, pp. 255–307.

Friedman, M. (1953) *The Methodology of Positive Economics, Essays in Positive Economics*, reprinted in 1966 by Phoenix Books edn, Chicago: University of Chicago Press.

Gibbons, R. & Murphy, K. (1992) 'Optimal incentive contracts in the presence of career concerns: Theory and evidence', *Journal of Political Economy*, **100**, pp. 468–505.

Gray, R., Owen, D., & Adams, C. (1996) *Accounting and Accountability: Changes and Challenges in Corporate Social and Environmental Reporting*, London: Prentice-Hall.

Guay, W. R., Kothari, S. P., & Watts, R. L. (1996) 'A market-based evaluation of discretionary accrual models', *Journal of Accounting Research*, **34** (Supplement), pp. 83–105.

Healy, P. M. (1985) 'The effect of bonus schemes on accounting decisions', *Journal of Accounting and Economics*, **7**, pp. 85–107.

Hines, R. (1988) 'Financial accounting: In communicating reality, we construct reality', *Accounting Organizations and Society*, **13** (3), pp. 251–62.

Holthausen, R. W., Larcker, D. F., & Sloan, R. G. (1995) 'Annual bonus schemes and the manipulation of earnings', *Journal of Accounting and Economics*, **19**.

Howieson, B. (1996) 'Whither financial accounting research: A modern-day bo-peep?' *Australian Accounting Review*, **6** (1), pp. 29–36.

Ittner, C., Larker, D. & Rajan, M. (1997) 'The choice of performance measures in annual bonus contracts', *The Accounting Review*, **72**, pp. 231–55.

Jensen, M. C. & Meckling, W. H. (1976) 'Theory of the firm: Managerial behavior, agency costs and ownership structure', *Journal of Financial Economics*, **3** (October), pp. 305–60.

Jones, J. (1991) 'Earnings management during import relief investigations', *Journal of Accounting Research*, **29**, pp. 193–228.

Kaplan, R. S. & Roll, R. (1972) 'Investor evaluation of accounting information: Some empirical evidence', *Journal of Business*, **45**, pp. 225–57.

Kothari, S. P., Laguerre, T., & Leone, A. (2002) 'Capitalizing versus expensing: Evidence on the uncertainty of future earnings from capital expenditure versus R&D outlay', *Review of Accounting Studies*, **7**, pp. 355–82.

Lambert, R. (2001) 'Contracting theory and accounting', *Journal of Accounting and Economics*, **32**, pp. 3–87.

Lev, B. & Sougiannis, T. (1996), 'The capitalization, amortization, and value relevance of R&D', *Journal of Accounting and Economics*, **21**, pp. 107–38.

Lewellen, R. A., Loderer, C., & Martin, K. (1987) 'Executive compensation and executive incentive problems', *Journal of Accounting and Economics*, **9**, pp. 287–310.

Lintner, J. (1965) 'The valuation of risk assets and the selection of risky investments in stock portfolios and capital budgets', *Review of Economics and Statistics*, **47**, pp. 13–37.

Lys, T. (1984) 'Mandated accounting changes and debt covenants: The case of oil and gas accounting', *Journal of Accounting and Economics*, **9**, pp. 39–66.

Mian, S. L. & Smith, C. W. (1990) 'Incentives for consolidated financial reporting', *Journal of Accounting and Economics*, **12**, pp. 141–71.

Milgrom, P. (1981) 'Good news and bad news: Representation theorems and applications', *Bell Journal of Economics*, **12**, pp. 380–91.

Morris, R. (1984) 'Corporate disclosure in a substantially unregulated environment', *ABACUS* (June), pp. 52–86.

Mouck, T. (1992) 'The rhetoric of science and the rhetoric of revolt in the story of positive accounting theory', *Accounting, Auditing and Accountability Journal*, pp. 35–56.

Murphy, K. (1999) 'Executive Compensation', in *Handbook of Labor Economics*, 3B North Holland, Amsterdam.

Nagar, V., Nanda, D. & Wysocki, P. (2003) 'Discretionary disclosure and stock-based incentives', *Journal of Accounting and Economics*, 34, pp. 283–309.

Ness, K. & Mirza, A. (1991) 'Corporate social disclosure: A note on a test of agency theory', *British Accounting Review*, **23**, pp. 211–17.

Sharpe, W. F. (1964) 'Capital asset prices: A review of market equilibrium under conditions of risk', *Journal of Finance*, **19**, pp. 425–42.

Shleifer, A. & Vishny, R. (1989) 'Management entrenchment: The case of manager-specific investments', *Journal of Accounting and Economics*, **25**, pp. 8–41.

Sloan, R. G. (1993) 'Accounting earnings and top executive compensation', *Journal of Accounting and Economics*, **16**, pp. 55–100.

Smith, C. W. & Warner, J. B. (1979) 'On financial contracting: An analysis of bond covenants', *Journal of Financial Economics* (June), pp. 117–61.

Smith, C. W. & Watts, R. L. (1982) 'Incentive and tax effects of executive compensation plans', *Australian Journal of Management*, **7**, pp. 139–57.

Smith, C. W. & Watts, R. L. (1983) 'The structure of executive contracts and the control of management', unpublished manuscript, University of Rochester.

Sterling, R. R. (1990) 'Positive accounting: An assessment', *ABACUS*, **26** (2), pp. 97–135.

Stern, S. (2001) 'Stern Stewart roundtable on capital structure and stock repurchase', *Journal of Applied Corporate Finance*, **14**, pp. 8–41.

Sutton, T. G. (1988) 'The proposed introduction of current cost accounting in the UK: Determinants of corporate performance', *Journal of Accounting and Economics*, **10**, pp. 127–49.

Sweeney, A. P. (1994) 'Debt-covenant violations and managers accounting responses',

Journal of Accounting and Economics, **17**, pp. 281–308.

Tinker, A., Lehman, C., & Neimark, M. (1991) 'Corporate social reporting: Falling down the hole in the middle of the road', *Accounting, Auditing and Accountability Journal*, **4** (1), pp. 28–54.

Tinker, A. M., Merino, B. D., & Neimark, M. D. (1982) 'The normative origins of positive theories: Ideology and accounting thought', *Accounting Organizations and Society*, **7** (2), pp. 167–200.

Verrecchia, R. (1983) 'Discretionary disclosure', *Journal of Accounting and Economics*, **5**, pp. 179–94.

Watts, R. L. (1977) 'Corporate financial statements: A product of the market and political processes', *Australian Journal of Management* (April), pp. 53–75.

Watts, R. L. (1995) 'Nature and origins of positive research in accounting', in Jones, S., Romano, C., & Ratnatunga, J. (eds), *Accounting Theory: A Contemporary Review*, Sydney: Harcourt Brace, pp. 295–353.

Watts, R. L. & Zimmerman, J. (1978) 'Towards a positive theory of the determination of accounting standards', *Accounting Review*, **53** (1), pp. 112–34.

Watts, R. L. & Zimmerman, J. L. (1979) 'The demand for and supply of accounting theories: The market for excuses', *The Accounting Review*, **54** (2), pp. 273–305.

Watts, R. L. & Zimmerman, J. L. (1986) *Positive Accounting Theory*, Englewood Cliffs, New Jersey: Prentice-Hall Inc.

Watts, R. L. & Zimmerman, J. L. (1990) 'Positive accounting theory: A ten year perspective', *The Accounting Review*, **65** (1), pp. 259–85.

Wells, P. (2002) 'Earnings management surrounding CEO changes', *Accounting and Finance*, **42**, pp. 169–93.

Whittred, G. (1987) 'The derived demand for consolidated financial reporting', *Journal of Accounting and Economics*, **9** (December), pp. 259–85.

Whittred, G. & Zimmer, I. (1986) 'Accounting information in the market for debt', *Accounting and Finance*, **28** (1), pp. 1–12.

Williamson, O. E. (1975) *Markets and Hierarchies: Analysis and Antitrust Implications*, New York: Free Press.

Williamson, O. E. (1985) *The Economic Institutions of Capitalism*, New York: Free Press.

Williamson, O. E. (1988) 'Corporate finance and corporate governance', *Journal of Finance*, **43**, pp. 567 91.

Williamson, O. E. (1996) *The Mechanisms of Governance*, New York: Oxford University Press.

Wong, J. (1988) 'Economic incentives for the voluntary disclosure of current cost financial statements', *Journal of Accounting and Economics*, **10** (2), pp. 151–67.

Zmijewski, M. & Hagerman, R. (1981) 'An income strategy approach to the positive theory of accounting standard setting/choice', *Journal of Accounting and Economics*, **3**, pp. 129–49.

CHAPTER 8

Unregulated corporate reporting decisions: Considerations of systems oriented theories

Learning Objectives

Upon completing this chapter readers should:

- understand how community or stakeholders' perceptions can influence the disclosure policies of an organization;
- understand how legitimacy theory, stakeholder theory and institutional theory can be applied to help explain why an entity might elect to make particular voluntary disclosures;
- understand what we mean by *organizational legitimacy* and how corporate disclosures within such places as annual reports and corporate websites can be used as a strategy to maintain or restore the legitimacy of an organization;
- understand how the respective *power* and information demands of particular stakeholder groups can influence corporate disclosure policies;
- understand the view that a successful organization is one that is able to balance or manage the demands (sometimes conflicting), including information demands, of different stakeholder groups.

Opening issues

In *The Guardian* newspaper on 30 July 2002 a headline read: ' "Big four" banks are damaging small businesses, say MPs'. The article was particularly critical of the four large UK high street banks, accusing them of anti-competitive behaviour resulting in damage for small UK businesses.

Would you expect these banks to react to such negative media publicity, and if so, why? Further, would you expect them to make any disclosures within their respective annual reports or corporate websites in relation to these 'high profile' accusations of damaging anti-competitive behaviour? What form would you expect these disclosures to take?

Introduction

In Chapter 7 we considered a number of theoretical arguments as to why corporate management might elect to voluntarily provide particular information to parties outside the organization. These arguments were grounded within *Positive Accounting Theory*. In this chapter we consider some alternative theoretical perspectives that address this issue. Specifically we consider *legitimacy theory, stakeholder theory* and *institutional theory*.

As has been stressed throughout this book, and particularly in Chapter 1, theories are abstractions of reality and hence particular theories cannot be expected to provide a full account or description of particular behaviour. Hence, it is sometimes useful to consider the perspectives provided by alternative theories. Different researchers might study the same phenomenon but elect to adopt alternative theoretical perspectives.[1] The choice of one theoretical perspective in preference to others will, at least in part, be due to particular value judgements of the authors involved. As O'Leary (1985, p. 88) states:

> Theorists' own values or ideological predispositions may be among the factors that determine which side of the argument they will adopt in respect of disputable connections of a theory with evidence.

Legitimacy theory, stakeholder theory and institutional theory are three theoretical perspectives that have been adopted by a number of researchers in recent years. These theories are sometimes referred to as 'systems oriented theories'. In accordance with Gray, Owen and Adams (1996, p. 45):

> ... a systems-oriented view of the organisation and society ... permits us to focus on the role of information and disclosure in the relationship(s) between organisations, the State, individuals and groups.

Within a *systems-based perspective*, the entity is assumed to be influenced by, and in turn to have influence upon, the society in which it operates. This is simplistically represented in Figure 8.1.

Within legitimacy theory, stakeholder theory and institutional theory, accounting disclosure policies are considered to constitute a strategy to influence the organization's relationships with the other parties with which it interacts. In recent times, stakeholder theory and legitimacy theory have been applied primarily to explain why organizations make certain social responsibility disclosures within their annual reports.[2] These theories could, however, also be applied to explain why companies adopt particular financial accounting techniques. We will mainly focus on these two theories in this chapter, but towards the end of the chapter will also briefly explore some insights from the more recent application of institutional theory to analysis of voluntary corporate reporting.

Figure 8.1 The organization viewed as part of a wider social system

Political economy theory

According to Gray, Owen and Adams (1996), legitimacy theory and stakeholder theory are both derived from a broader theory which has been called *political economy theory*. Institutional theory can also be linked to political economy theory. The 'political economy' itself has been defined by Gray, Owen and Adams (p. 47) as 'the social, political and economic framework within which human life takes place'. The perspective embraced is that *society*, *politics* and *economics* are inseparable, and economic issues cannot meaningfully be investigated in the absence of considerations about the political, social and institutional framework in which the economic activity takes place. It is argued that by considering the *political economy* a researcher is able to consider broader (societal) issues that impact on how an organization operates, and what information it elects to disclose. According to Guthrie and Parker (1990, p. 166):

> The political economy perspective perceives accounting reports as social, political, and economic documents. They serve as a tool for constructing, sustaining, and legitimising economic and political arrangements, institutions, and ideological themes which contribute to the corporation's private interests. Disclosures have the capacity to transmit social, political, and economic meanings for a pluralistic set of report recipients.

Guthrie and Parker (1990, p. 166) further state that corporate reports cannot be considered as neutral, unbiased (or representationally faithful) documents, as many professional accounting bodies might suggest, but rather are 'a product of the interchange between the corporation and its environment and attempt to mediate and accommodate a variety of sectional interests'.[3] This view is consistent with Burchell *et al.* (1980, p. 6) who suggest that accounting can 'not be seen as a mere assembly of calculative routines, it functions as a cohesive and influential mechanism for economic and social management'.

Political economy theory has been divided (perhaps somewhat simplistically, but nevertheless usefully) into two broad streams which Gray, Owen and Adams (1996, p. 47) have labelled 'classical' and 'bourgeois' political economy. Classical political economy is related to the works of philosophers such as Karl Marx, and explicitly places 'sectional (class) interests, structural conflict, inequity, and the role of the State at the heart of the analysis' (Gray *et al.*, 1996, p. 47). This can be contrasted with 'bourgeois' political economy theory which, according to Gray, Kouhy and Lavers (1995, p. 53), largely ignores these elements and, as a result, is content to perceive the world as essentially pluralistic.

Classical political economy tends to perceive accounting reports and disclosures as a means of maintaining the favoured position (for example the wealth and power) of those who control scarce resources (capital), and as a means of under-mining the position of those without scarce capital. It focuses on the structural conflicts within society.[4]

According to Cooper and Sherer (1984), the study of accounting should recognize *power* and *conflict* in society, and consequently should focus on the effects of accounting reports on the distribution of income, wealth and power in society. This is consistent with Lowe and Tinker (1977) who argue that the majority of accounting research is based on a *pluralist* conception of society.[5] According to Lowe and Tinker, this pluralistic view assumes (incorrectly, they argue) that power is widely diffused and that society is composed of many individuals whose pre-ferences are to predominate in social choices, and with no individual able to consistently influence that society (or the accounting function therein). Researchers such as Lowe and Tinker (1977) and Cooper and Sherer (1984) oppose such a view and provide a counter-perspective that the *pluralist* view ignores a great deal of evidence which suggests that the majority of people in society are controlled by a small but 'well-defined elite' – an elite that uses accounting (as well as other mechanisms) as a means of maintaining their position of dominance. We further consider the works of authors who take this view when we consider *critical accounting perspectives* in Chapter 12. We show that such researchers tend to be extremely critical of current accounting and reporting techniques.

According to Gray, Owen and Adams (1996), and as briefly noted above, *bourgeois political economy*, on the other hand, does not explicitly consider struc-tural conflicts and *class struggles* but rather 'tends to be concerned with interactions between groups in an essentially pluralistic world (for example, the negotiation between a company and an environmental pressure group, or between a local authority and the State)'. It is this branch of political economy theory from which *legitimacy theory* and *stakeholder theory* derive. Neither theory questions or studies the various class structures (and possible struggles) within society.[6] However, *institutional theory* can be applied within either a classical or a bourgeois conception of political economy. We now turn our attention to legitimacy theory.

Legitimacy theory

Legitimacy theory asserts that organizations continually seek to ensure that they are perceived as operating within the bounds and norms of their respective societies, that is, they attempt to ensure that their activities are perceived by outside parties as being 'legitimate'. These bounds and norms are not considered to be fixed, but change over time, thereby requiring organizations to be responsive to the ethical (or moral) environment in which they operate. Lindblom (1994) distinguishes between *legitimacy* which is considered to be a status or condition, and *legitimation* which she considers to be the process that leads to an organization being adjudged *legitimate*. According to Lindblom (p. 2), legitimacy is:

> ... a condition or status which exists when an entity's value system is congruent with the value system of the larger social system of which the entity is a part. When a disparity, actual or potential, exists between the two value systems, there is a threat to the entity's legitimacy.

Legitimacy, public expectations and the social contract

Legitimacy theory relies upon the notion that there is a 'social contract' between the organization in question and the society in which it operates. The 'social contract' is not easy to define, but the concept is used to represent the multitude of implicit and explicit expectations that society has about how the organization should conduct its operations.[7] It can be argued that traditionally, profit maximization *was* perceived to be the optimal measure of corporate performance (Abbott and Monsen, 1979; Heard and Bolce, 1981; Patten, 1991, 1992; Ramanathan, 1976). Under this notion, a firm's profits were viewed as an all-inclusive measure of *organizational legitimacy* (Ramanathan, 1976). However, public expectations have undergone significant change in recent decades. Heard and Bolce (1981) note the expansion of the advocacy movement in the United States during the 1960s and 1970s, and the significant increase in legislation related to social issues, including the environment and employees' health and safety, which was enacted in the United States within the same period. With heightened social expectations it is anticipated that successful business corporations will react and attend to the human, environmental and other social consequences of their activities (Heard and Bolce, 1981).

It has been argued that society increasingly expects business to ' ... make outlays to repair or prevent damage to the physical environment, to ensure the health and safety of consumers, employees, and those who reside in the communities where products are manufactured and wastes are dumped ... ' (Tinker and Neimark, 1987, p. 84). Consequently, companies with a poor social and environmental performance record may increasingly find it difficult to obtain the necessary resources and support to continue operations within a community that values a clean environment. Perhaps this was not the case a number of decades ago.

It is assumed that society allows the organization to continue operations to the extent that it generally meets their expectations. Legitimacy theory emphasizes that the organization must appear to consider the rights of the public at large, not merely those of its investors. Failure to comply with societal expectations (that is, comply with the terms of the 'social contract') may lead to sanctions being imposed by society, for example, in the form of legal restrictions imposed on an organization's operations, limited resources (for example, financial capital and labour) being provided, and/or reduced demand for its products (sometimes through organized consumer boycotts).

Consistent with legitimacy theory, organisations are not considered to have any inherent right to resources. *Legitimacy* (from society's perspective) and the right to operate go hand in hand. As Mathews (1993, p. 26) states:

> The social contract would exist between corporations (usually limited companies) and individual members of society. Society (as a collection of individuals) provides corporations with their legal standing and attributes and the authority to own and use natural resources and to hire employees. Organisations draw on community resources and output both goods and services and waste products to the general environment. The organisation has no inherent rights to these benefits, and in order to allow their existence, society would expect the benefits to exceed the costs to society.

The idea of a 'social contract' is not new, having been discussed by philosophers such as Thomas Hobbes (1588–1679), John Locke (1632–1704) and Jean-Jacques Rousseau (1712–1778). Shocker and Sethi (1974, p. 67) provide a good overview of the concept of a social contract:

> Any social institution – and business is no exception – operates in society via a social contract, expressed or implied, whereby its survival and growth are based on:
>
> 1 the delivery of some socially desirable ends to society in general, and
>
> 2 the distribution of economic, social, or political benefits to groups from which it derives its power.
>
> In a dynamic society, neither the sources of institutional power nor the needs for its services are permanent. Therefore, an institution must constantly meet the twin tests of legitimacy and relevance by demonstrating that society requires its services and that the groups benefiting from its rewards have society's approval.

As indicated above, and in Deegan and Rankin (1996, p. 54) and Deegan (2002, p. 293), in accordance with legitimacy theory if an organization cannot justify its continued operation, then in a sense the community may revoke its 'contract' to continue its operations. Again, as indicated earlier, this may occur through consumers reducing or eliminating the demand for the products of the business, factor suppliers eliminating the supply of labour and financial capital to the business, and/or constituents lobbying government for increased taxes, fines or laws to prohibit actions that do not conform with the expectations of the community. Given the potential costs associated with conducting operations deemed to be outside the terms of the 'social contract', Dowling and Pfeffer (1975) state that organizations will take various actions to ensure that their operations are perceived to be legitimate. That is, they will attempt to establish congruence between 'the social values associated with or implied by their activities and the norms of acceptable behavior in the larger social system of which they are a part' (Dowling and Pfeffer, 1975, p. 122).

Legitimacy and changing social expectations

As community expectations change, organizations must also adapt and change. That is, if society's expectations about performance change, then arguably an organization will need to show that what it is doing is also changing (or perhaps it will need to explicitly communicate and justify why its operations have *not* changed). In relation to the dynamics associated with changing expectations, Lindblom (1994, p. 3) states:

> Legitimacy is dynamic in that the relevant publics continuously evaluate corporate output, methods, and goals against an ever evolving expectation. The legitimacy gap will fluctuate without any changes in action on the part of the corporation. Indeed, as expectations of the relevant publics change the corporation must make changes or the legitimacy gap will grow as the level of conflict increases and the levels of positive and passive support decreases.[8]

The process of maintaining the congruence between society's expectations and its perceptions about how the organization is performing leads to what is known as organizational legitimacy (Dowling and Pfeffer, 1975). It is assumed that *effective* managers react swiftly to changes in community concerns and priorities.

Dowling and Pfeffer outline the means by which an organization may legitimate its activities (p. 127):

- The organization can adapt its output, goals and methods of operation to conform to prevailing definitions of legitimacy.

- The organization can attempt, through communication, to alter the definition of social legitimacy so that it conforms to the organization's present practices, output and values.

- The organization can attempt, through communication, to become identified with symbols, values or institutions that have a strong base of legitimacy.

Consistent with Dowling and Pfeffer's strategy of 'communication', Lindblom (1994) proposes that an organization can adopt a number of strategies where it perceives that its legitimacy is in question because its actions (or operations) are at variance with society's expectations and values. Lindblom (1994) identifies four courses of action (there is some overlap with Dowling and Pfeffer) that an organization can take to obtain, or maintain, legitimacy in these circumstances. The organization can:

1. seek to educate and inform its 'relevant publics' about (actual) changes in the organization's performance and activities which bring the activities and performance more into line with society's values and expectations;

2. seek to change the perceptions that 'relevant publics' have of the organization's performance and activities – but not change the organization's actual behaviour (while using disclosures in corporate reports to falsely indicate that the performance and activities have changed);

3. seek to manipulate perception by deflecting attention from the issue of concern onto other related issues through an appeal to, for example, emotive symbols, thus seeking to demonstrate how the organization has fulfilled social expectations in other areas of its activities; or

4. seek to change external expectations of its performance, possibly by demonstrating that specific societal expectations are unreasonable.

Use of accounting reports in legitimation strategies

According to Lindblom, and Dowling and Pfeffer, the public disclosure of information in such places as annual reports can be used by an organization to implement each of the above strategies. Certainly this is a perspective that many researchers of social responsibility reporting have adopted, as we show shortly. For example, a firm may provide information to counter or offset negative news which may be publicly available, or it may simply provide information to inform the interested parties about attributes of the organization that were previously unknown. In addition, organizations may draw attention to strengths, for instance environmental awards won, or safety initiatives that have been implemented, while sometimes neglecting or down-playing information concerning negative implications of their activities, such as pollution or workplace accidents.[9]

Consistent with the positions taken both by Dowling and Pfeffer and by Lindblom, Hurst (1970) suggests that one of the functions of accounting, and subsequently accounting reports, is to legitimate the existence of the corporation. Such views highlight the strategic nature of financial statements and other related disclosures.

Corporate views on the importance of the social contract

The view within legitimacy theory that organizations will be penalized if they do not operate in a manner consistent with community expectations (that is, in accordance with the social contract) is a view being embraced publicly by corporate managers in many European and other nations. This is reflected, for example, in some statements made by Total S.A. (the large French-based multinational oil company) in its stand-alone corporate social responsibility report of 2003. In the report the chairman and chief executive of Total, Thierry Desmarest, states (p. 2):

Civil society expects companies, especially the biggest ones, to manage the environmental impact of their operations and industrial risk, as well as to plan for and manage their direct and indirect social and societal impacts, wherever they are located. ... Clearly, companies have yet to win the battle for legitimacy in the eyes of the general public, particularly in continental Europe. ... It's perfectly natural that we are asked to report on our actions and assume the direct and indirect impact of our operations.

The 2000 Corporate Social Responsibility Report of the Anglo-Swedish-based pharmaceutical multinational AstraZeneca PLC contained the following statement (p. 4):

The objective of social sustainability is to provide a better quality of life for all members of society. In order to make our contribution to this objective we need to understand the changing expectations of society. Our social objectives can be more clearly identified by considering all of our stakeholders – employees, customers, shareholders and the wider community – and the impact, both positive and negative, that our operations could have on them.

In AstraZeneca's 2003 Corporate Responsibility Summary Report (p. 1), the chief executive (Sir Tom McKillop) continued this theme when he stated:

Our reputation is built on the trust and confidence of all our stakeholders and is one of AstraZeneca's most valuable assets. Along with our commitment to competitiveness and performance, we will continue to be led by our core values to achieve sustainable success. ... Stakeholder expectations are constantly evolving and we continuously monitor our internal and external environment for issues relating to our business that affect or concern society today. ... Corporate responsibility (CR) is not an optional extra – it must be integral to all that we do. Our strategy to include considerations of corporate responsibility across all our activities is beginning to take effect.

Consistent with legitimacy theory, the above statements reflect the view that organizations must adapt to community expectations if they are to be successful. This view is also reflected in the Finnish-based multinational mobile phone company Nokia's 2003 Corporate Responsibility Report, where the executive statement on page 5 states:

Understanding what different stakeholders expect from us as a company, is just as important as understanding customer needs for our products. Stakeholder engagement is the chance to listen to, and translate expectations into business value. It is an opportunity to discuss what responsibility lies with the different members of society. ... By stakeholders, we mean individuals and groups of people that influence or are influenced by our company. These include, but are not limited to, consumers and network operators, business associates and suppliers, employees, shareholders and investors, academia, the media, non-governmental organizations (NGOs), consumer associations, governments and authorities. ... Our aim is to make stakeholder dialogue part of everyday business, in order to have the best exchange of information and get the right information quickly to the people who can evaluate it and put it to good use. Throughout this report we identify some of the various stakeholders we consult in the daily operations of our business, not only relating to our corporate responsibility but the manner in which we report on our activities.

The above statements illustrate that the notions embodied within legitimacy theory are reflective of the public positions being taken by European corporate executives. Management appears to consider that meeting the expectations of the community in which it operates can protect or enhance profitability while failure to do so can be detrimental to ongoing operations and survival.

Legitimacy and reputation risk management

Managers have recently begun to use the notion of *reputation risk management* to articulate this need for their companies to be seen to be meeting society's expectations. This reduces issues of social and environmental responsibility to a financial issue, whereby a company's reputation is considered to be of considerable (if normally unquantified) value in generating future profits, and any damage to this reputation will therefore affect future profitability. A *reputation risk management* perspective on voluntary social and environmental disclosures in annual reports assumes that threats to corporate legitimacy can result in damage to the value of a company's reputation, and such risks to reputation need to be minimized through active management. The following three quotes from AstraZeneca PLC's 2003 Corporate Responsibility Summary Report together illustrate the importance of reputation risk management in corporate responsibility policies and practices:

> You can read regularly in the newspapers about companies that have lost value through failing to manage some aspects that affect their reputation. These aspects can be far more important to the market than decisions that directly affect a company's profits. (*Quote from the Chief Financial Officer, p. 6*)

> Failure to deliver our core values could seriously impact our reputation, which we recognise is an important driver of the Company's worth. (*p. 7*)

> AstraZeneca's Risk Advisory Group, led by our Chief Financial Officer, Jonathan Symonds, looks at the risks the Company faces and how they are being addressed. Increasingly we are integrating reputational risk, including CR [corporate responsibility], into our risk management processes and aim to ensure that managers build it into their everyday thinking. Appropriate tools are available in the form of a shared risk management philosophy, principles and a framework that all managers can use to reflect on behaviours, assess risks and positively shape their decision making. (*p. 7*)

Exhibit 8.1 both demonstrates the importance of this reputation risk management motive for voluntary (social and environmental) disclosures, and clearly links this motive to a need to demonstrate that companies are fulfilling societal expectations (as maintained within legitimacy theory)

Empirical tests of legitimacy theory

In recent years legitimacy theory has been used by numerous accounting researchers who have elected to study social and environmental reporting practices. A number of papers have identified specific types of social responsibility disclosures

Exhibit 8.1 Reputation risk management as a factor motivating voluntary social and environmental reporting

Many companies now report on the social and environmental impacts of their activities as a way of enhancing their reputation. But is this just window-dressing for business-as-usual?

After years of defending itself from charges of worker exploitation, Gap, the clothing retailer, last week made the shock confession that many of its 3,000 factories across the world fail to comply with minimum labour standards.

Such an admission would have been unthinkable a few years ago when Shell dumped an oil platform in the North Sea. But while this corporate confession – unlike its theological equivalent – does not instantly absolve Gap from its responsibilities, it does demonstrate the changing role of business in society.

Corporate social responsibility (CSR) is a growth industry among consultants and PR firms as high-profile multinational companies learn to manage the social and environmental concerns of campaigners and customers as just another aspect of reputational risk. As a result, many big corporations have accepted – albeit voluntarily – arguments about social and environmental reporting that once made them balk.

Social and environmental impact reports (not all glossy) are now de rigueur among FTSE 100 companies, and not just those operating in pilloried industries such as oil, mining and garments.

Over the last year, the connection between CSR and health has brought ethical and responsible concerns closer to the British consumer than ever before. Whether it is too much salt in ready meals or the button-popping 'go large' options at fast-food restaurants, food manufacturers and retailers are being dragged into the debate about what is responsible business at a time when obesity levels in Britain are soaring ...

Cadbury's Get Active campaign, which pledged to give free sports equipment to schools, is ... not called cause-related marketing for nothing. To get the equipment, the children had to collect vouchers – by buying Cadbury chocolate. Schools decided to boycott the scheme, and Cadbury received hostile press coverage.

It is not the only company that has tarnished its reputation when trying to appear socially responsible and boost sales. The reason, according to Tim Wright, last year's winner of the Guardian/Ashridge MBA essay competition, is that CSR is little more than window-dressing. Wright argued that it is often a 'cosmetic and calculated mechanism that simply disguises the reality of business as usual'.

Marc Lopatin, printed in *The Guardian*, 19 May 2004, p. 12

that have appeared within annual reports. The respective researchers have attempted to explain these disclosures on the basis that they form part of the portfolio of strategies undertaken by accountants and their managers to bring legitimacy to, or maintain the legitimacy of, their respective organizations. We now consider a number of such papers.

An early study that sought to link legitimacy theory to corporate social disclosure policies was conducted by Hogner (1982). This longitudinal study examined corporate social reporting in the annual reports of US Steel Corporation over a period of 80 years, commencing in 1901, the data being analysed for year to year variation. Hogner showed that the extent of social disclosures varied from year to year and he speculated that the variation could represent a response to society's changing expectations of corporate behaviour.

Patten (1992) focused on the change in the extent of environmental disclosures made by North American oil companies, other than just Exxon Oil Company, both before and after the *Exxon Valdez* major oil spill in Alaska in 1989. He argued that if the Alaskan oil spill resulted in a threat to the legitimacy of the whole petroleum industry, and not just to Exxon, then legitimacy theory would suggest that companies operating within that industry would respond by increasing the amount of environmental disclosures in their annual reports. Patten's results indicate that there were increased environmental disclosures by the petroleum companies for the post-1989 period, consistent with a legitimation perspective. This disclosure reaction took place across the industry, even though the incident itself was directly related to one oil company. He argued (p. 475):

> ... it appears that at least for environmental disclosures, threats to a firm's legitimacy do entice the firm to include more social responsibility information in its annual report.

Deegan and Rankin (1996) utilized legitimacy theory to try to explain systematic changes in corporate annual report environmental disclosure policies around the time of proven environmental prosecutions. The authors examined the environmental disclosure practices of a sample of Australian firms that were successfully prosecuted by environmental protection authorities (EPAs) for breaches of various environmental protection laws during the period 1990 to 1993 (any prosecutions by these agencies were reported in the EPAs' annual reports which were publicly available). The annual reports of a final sample of 20 firms, prosecuted a total of 78 times, were reviewed to ascertain the extent of the environmental disclosures. These annual reports were matched by industry and size to the annual reports of a control group of 20 firms that had not been prosecuted.

Of the 20 prosecuted firms, 18 provided environmental information in their annual report, but the disclosures were predominantly positive and qualitative. Only two organizations made any mention of the prosecutions. Deegan and Rankin found that prosecuted firms disclosed significantly more environmental information (of a favourable nature) in the year of prosecution than any other year in the sample period. Consistent with the view that companies increase disclosure to offset any effects of EPA prosecutions, the EPA-prosecuted firms also disclosed more environmental information, relative to non-prosecuted firms. The authors concluded that the public disclosure of proven environmental prosecutions has an impact on the disclosure policies of firms involved.

With the results of Patten (1992) and Deegan and Rankin (1996) in mind we can consider Exhibit 8.2, which documents concerns about the attitudes of

---

Exhibit 8.2 Negative media coverage of the pharmaceutical industry's product safety record

Drugs early-warning system 'not working'

Stephen Foley

THE UK'S biggest pharmaceutical companies have called on the Government to do more to ensure that doctors report side effects from new drugs, in an attempt to head off growing public concern about the side effects of block-buster drugs ...

Drug safety has become one of the central concerns of an inquiry into the influence of the pharmaceutical industry by the House of Commons Health Select Committee. The issue has been given added impetus since the inquiry began last summer by the withdrawal of Vioxx, the arthritis painkiller linked to heart attacks, and shrill criticism in the US of other drugs on the market ...

John Patterson – who was appointed to the board of AstraZeneca last month, charged with reviewing the company's approach to drug safety – rejected MPs suggestions that the drug industry is more concerned with finding new uses for existing drugs than with monitoring their safety. He said: 'We have a legal, moral and ethical duty to follow the safety of our products.'

The Select Committee, chaired by David Hinchcliffe, is hoping to publish recommendations from its inquiry by the end of March. Previous sessions have heard criticism of the drug industry for 'disease-mongering' to promote drugs such as antidepressants or pills for erectile dysfunction, and of other marketing practices.

However, the executives before the committee yesterday insisted that the 'checks and balances' on the industry were about right. They said patients were missing out because new medicines are slow to be adopted in the UK, where doctors are perceived as more conservative and where the National Health Service reviews new products for cost effectiveness before allowing them to be prescribed.

The Independent, Friday 14 January 2005

pharmaceutical companies towards product safety. Read the exhibit and then consider how legitimacy theory could be used to predict how companies in the industry might react to such publicity. Do you think that companies in the pharmaceutical industry would be deemed to have breached their 'social contract', and if so, do you think that they might use their annual reports in an attempt to reinstate their legitimacy?

In another study, Deegan and Gordon (1996) reviewed annual report environmental disclosures made by a sample of companies from 1980 to 1991. They investigated the objectivity of corporate environmental disclosure practices and trends in environmental disclosures over time. They also sought to determine if environmental disclosures were related to concerns held by environmental groups about particular industries' environmental performance. The results derived by the Deegan and Gordon (1996) study indicated, among other findings, that during the period covered by the study:

- increases in corporate environmental disclosures over time were positively associated with increases in the levels of environmental group membership;

- corporate environmental disclosures were overwhelmingly self-laudatory; and

- there was a positive correlation between the environmental sensitivity of the industry to which the corporation belonged and the level of corporate environmental disclosure.[10]

These results were deemed to be consistent with legitimacy theory.

Gray, Kouhy and Lavers (1995) performed a longitudinal review of UK corporate social and environmental disclosures for the period 1979 to 1991. In discussing the trends in corporate environmental disclosure policies, they made use of legitimacy theory with specific reference to the strategies suggested by Lindblom (1994), which we considered earlier in this chapter. After considering the extent and types of corporate disclosures, they stated (p. 65):

> The tone, orientation and focus of the environmental disclosures accord closely with Lindblom's first, second and third legitimation strategies. A significant minority of companies found it necessary to 'change their actual performance' with respect to environmental interactions (Lindblom's first strategy) and use corporate social reporting to inform their 'relevant publics' about this. Similarly, companies' environmental disclosure has also been an attempt, first, to change perceptions of environmental performance – to alter perceptions of whether certain industries were 'dirty' and 'irresponsible' (Lindblom's second strategy) and, second, as Lindblom notes, to distract attention from the central environmental issues (the third legitimation strategy). Increasingly, companies are being required to demonstrate a satisfactory performance within the environmental domain. Corporate social reporting would appear to be one of the mechanisms by which the organisations satisfy (and manipulate) that requirement.

In relation to trends found in regard to health and safety disclosures Gray, Kouhy and Lavers (1995, p. 65) stated:

> We are persuaded that companies were increasingly under pressure from various 'relevant publics' to improve their performance in the area of health and safety and employed corporate social reporting to manage this 'legitimacy gap'. That is, while the disclosure did not, as such, demonstrate improved health and safety records (lack of previous information makes such assessment impossible), it did paint a picture of increasing concern being given by companies to the matter of protecting and training their workforce. This disclosure then helped add to the image of a competent and concerned organisation which took its responsibilities in this field seriously. As such, health and safety disclosure appears to be a strong illustration of Lindblom's second legitimation strategy – 'changing perceptions'.

Deegan, Rankin and Voght (2000) also utilized legitimacy theory to explain how the social disclosures included within the annual reports of companies in selected industries changed around the time of major social incidents or disasters that could be directly related to their particular industry. The results of this study were consistent with legitimacy theory and showed that companies did appear to change their disclosure policies around the time of major company- and industry-related social events. The authors argued that 'the results highlight the strategic nature of voluntary social disclosures and are consistent with a view that management considers that annual report social disclosures are a useful device to reduce the effects upon a corporation of events that are perceived to be unfavourable to a corporation's image' (p. 127).

Deegan, Rankin and Tobin (2002) undertook a further longitudinal study examining disclosures on social and environmental issues in the annual reports of BHP, a large Australian company, over the period 1983 to 1997. This study demonstrated positive correlations between media attention for certain social and environmental issues (which was taken as a proxy for social concerns with these issues) and the volume of disclosures on these issues. However, in a UK-based study of the annual report disclosures of five companies over a 20-year period from 1975, Campbell, Craven and Shrives (2003) found that 'Those companies that would be (according to legitimacy theory) expected to disclose more (because of society's negative perceptions) do not always do so and those companies with a lesser apparent legitimacy gap sometimes disclose more' (p. 573).

Studies of legitimacy theory and financial disclosure

Applying legitimacy theory to financial (as opposed to social and environmental) disclosure practices, in a US study the choice of an accounting framework was deemed to be related to a desire to increase the legitimacy of an organization. Carpenter and Feroz (1992) argued that the State of New York's (government) decision to adopt generally accepted accounting procedures (GAAP) (as opposed to a method of accounting based on cash flows rather than accruals) was 'an attempt to regain legitimacy for the State's financial management practices' (p. 613). According to Carpenter and Feroz, New York State was in a financial crisis in 1975, with the result that many parties began to question the adequacy of the financial reporting practices of all the associated government units. To regain legitimacy the State elected to implement GAAP (accruals-based accounting). As Carpenter and Feroz (pp. 635, 637) state:

> The state of New York needed a symbol of legitimacy to demonstrate to the public and the credit markets that the state's finances were well managed. GAAP, as an institutionalized legitimated practice, serves this purpose. ... We argue that New York's decision to adopt GAAP was an attempt to regain legitimacy for the state's financial management practices. Challenges to the state's financial management practices, led by the state comptroller, contributed to confusion and concern in the municipal securities market. The confusion resulted in a lowered credit rating. To restore the credit rating, a symbol of legitimacy in financial management practices was needed.
>
> It is debatable whether GAAP was the solution for the state's financial management problem. Indeed, there is strong evidence that GAAP did not solve the state's financial management problems.
>
> New York needed a symbol of legitimacy that could be easily recognised by the public. In the realm of financial reporting, 'GAAP' is the recognised symbol of legitimacy.

 According to Carpenter and Feroz, few people would be likely to oppose a system that was 'generally accepted' – general acceptance provides an impression of legitimacy. As they state (p. 632):

> In discussing whether to use the term 'GAAP' instead of 'accrual' in promoting the accounting conversion efforts, panel members argued that no one could oppose a system that is generally accepted. The name implies that any other accounting principles are not accepted in the accounting profession. GAAP is also seemingly apolitical.

Studies investigating managerial attitudes in relation to legitimacy theory

As has been emphasized in this chapter, legitimacy theory proposes a relationship between corporate disclosures (and other corporate strategies) and community expectations, the view being that management reacts to community concerns and changes therein. But we are left with a question – how does management determine community expectations? There is evidence that management might rely on sources such as the media to determine community expectations. For example, Brown and Deegan (1999) investigated the relationship between the print media coverage given to various industries' environmental effects, and the levels of annual report environmental disclosures made by a sample of firms within those industries. The basis of the argument was that the media can be particularly effective in driving the community's concern about the environmental performance of particular organizations and where such concern is raised, organizations will respond by increasing the extent of disclosure of environmental information within the annual report.

Brown and Deegan used the extent of media coverage given to a particular issue as a measure (or proxy) of community concern. They made explicit reference to *media agenda setting theory*. Media agenda setting theory proposes a relationship between the relative emphasis given by the media to various topics, and the degree of salience these topics have for the general public (Ader, 1995, p. 300). [11] In terms of causality, increased media attention is believed to lead to increased community concern for a particular issue. The media are not seen as mirroring public priorities; rather, they are seen as shaping them. [12] The arguments provided in Brown and Deegan (1999) can be summarized as:

* management uses the annual report as a tool to legitimize the ongoing operations of the organization (from legitimacy theory);

* community concerns with the environmental performance of a specific firm in an industry will also impact on the disclosure strategies of firms across that industry (consistent with Patten, 1992, who adopted legitimacy theory); and

* the media are able to influence community perceptions about issues such as the environment (from media agenda setting theory).

The results in Brown and Deegan (1999) indicate that for the majority of the industries studied, higher levels of media attention (as determined by a review of a number of print media newspapers and journals) are significantly associated with higher levels of annual report environmental disclosures. A range of other studies have investigated managerial attitudes towards the role of corporate reporting in legitimation strategies. For example, Wilmshurst and Frost (2000) conducted a questionnaire survey among a sample of chief financial officers (CFOs) which asked these executives to rank the importance of various factors in environmental disclosure decisions. Wilmshurst and Frost then analysed environmental disclosures within the annual reports of the companies for whom their sample of CFOs worked, and found (p. 22) 'the influences of the competitor response to environmental issues and customer concerns to have predictive power'. This provided 'limited support for the applicability of legitimacy theory'.

O'Dwyer (2002) interviewed 29 senior executives from 27 large Irish companies and found that managerial motives for engaging in corporate social and environmental reporting were only sometimes consistent with a legitimacy theory explanation. This was despite many managers perceiving clear threats to their organizations' legitimacy in the eyes of a range of powerful stakeholders. O'Dwyer states (p. 416) that detailed and close questioning revealed:

> ... an overwhelming perception of CSD [corporate social disclosure] as an unsuccessful legitimation mechanism. Therefore, while CSD is sometimes perceived as being employed as part of a legitimacy process, its employment in this manner is ultimately viewed as failing to aid in securing a state of legitimacy for organisations. Furthermore, despite the predominant view [among senior managers] that CSD is incapable of facilitating the achievement of a state of legitimacy, research into the CSD practices

[of the companies interviewed] subsequent to the interviews ... reveals that many of the interviewees' companies continue to engage in some form of CSD. In conjunction with the interviewees' perspectives, this questions the pervasive explanatory power of legitimacy theory with respect to the motives for CSD when considering Irish context.

Conversely, in a different interview-based study which discussed a range of hypothetical situations with a sample of six managers, O'Donovan (2002) found support for legitimacy theory. Providing an alternative view on the role of senior managers in the motivation for social and environmental disclosures from a legitimacy theory perspective, Campbell (2000) found that a more persuasive factor than possible stakeholder concerns and expectations (in determination of the extent of social disclosure by Marks & Spencer in the UK) was the tenures of different chairmen – who Campbell argued could exert some personal influence on disclosure priorities.

Distinguishing legitimacy theory from Positive Accounting Theory

Some writers have suggested that the propositions generated by legitimacy theory (that annual report disclosure practices can be used in a strategic manner to manage an organization's relations with the community in which it operates) are very similar to the propositions generated by the political cost hypothesis which is developed through Positive Accounting Theory (which we discussed in Chapter 7).[13] While there are some similarities, legitimacy theory relies upon the central notion of an organization's 'social contract' with society and predicts that management will adopt particular strategies (including reporting strategies) in a bid to assure the society that the organization is complying with the society's values and norms (which are predicted to change over time). Unlike Positive Accounting Theory, legitimacy theory does not rely upon the economics-based assumption that *all* action is driven by individual self-interest (tied to wealth maximization) and it emphasizes how the organization is part of the social system in which it operates. Also, unlike Positive Accounting Theory, legitimacy theory makes no assumptions about the efficiency of markets, such as the capital market and the market for managers.

Stakeholder theory

We now turn to stakeholder theory. It has both an ethical (moral) or normative branch (which is also considered as prescriptive), and a positive (managerial) branch.[14] We first consider the ethical branch. We then consider the positive (managerial) branch, which explicitly considers various groups (of stakeholders) that exist in society, and how the expectations of particular stakeholder groups may have more (or less) impact on corporate strategies. This in turn has implications for how the stakeholders' expectations are considered or managed.

In the discussion that follows we see that there are many similarities between legitimacy theory and stakeholder theory, and as such, to treat them as two totally distinct theories would be incorrect. As Gray, Kouhy and Lavers (1995, p. 52) state:

> It seems to us that the essential problem in the literature arises from treating each as competing theories of reporting behaviour, when 'stakeholder theory' and 'legitimacy theory' are better seen as two (overlapping) perspectives of the issue which are set within a framework of assumptions about 'political economy'.

As Deegan (2002, p. 295) indicates, both theories conceptualize the organization as part of a broader social system wherein the organization impacts, and is impacted by, other groups within society. Whilst legitimacy theory discusses the expectations of society in general (as encapsulated within the 'social contract'), stakeholder theory provides a more refined resolution by referring to particular groups within society (stakeholder groups). Essentially, stakeholder theory accepts that because different stakeholder groups will have different views about how an organization should conduct its operations, there will be various social contracts 'negotiated' with different stakeholder groups, rather than one contract with society in general. Whilst implied within legitimacy theory, the managerial branch of stakeholder theory explicitly refers to issues of stakeholder power, and how a stakeholder's relative power impacts their ability to 'coerce' the organization into complying with the stakeholder's expectations.

Hence, as we have already stated above, this chapter treats legitimacy theory and stakeholder theory as largely overlapping theories that provide consistent but slightly different insights into the factors that motivate managerial behaviour (Gray et al., 1995, O'Donovan, 2002). Differences between the theories largely relate to issues of resolution, with stakeholder theory focusing on how an organization interacts with particular stakeholders, whilst legitimacy theory considers interactions with 'society' as a whole. A consideration of both theories is deemed to provide a fuller explanation of management's actions. As Gray, Kouhy and Lavers (1995, p. 67) state in relation to social disclosure-related research:

> The different theoretical perspectives need not be seen as competitors for explanation but as sources of interpretation of different factors at different levels of resolution. In this sense, legitimacy theory and stakeholder theory enrich, rather than compete for, our understandings of corporate social disclosure practices.

It should be noted however that some researchers (for example, Nasi et al., 1997, Suchman, 1995) maintain that the theories are more discrete in nature than this chapter, and some others, assume. For example, Nasi et al. (1997, p. 296) argue that although the perspectives 'are not precisely competing, each leads to a different general prediction regarding the likelihood and evolution of a corporate response in the face of a social issue'. They further state (p. 303) that:

> although the perspectives agree on the need and reality of issues management activities, they disagree on the nature of the issues management and on managerial motivation for the issues management.

The ethical branch of stakeholder theory

The moral (and normative) perspective of stakeholder theory argues that all stake-holders have the right to be treated fairly by an organization, and that issues of *stakeholder power* are not directly relevant. That is, the impact of the organization on the life experiences of a stakeholder should be what determines the organization's responsibilities to that stakeholder, rather than the extent of that stakeholder's (economic) power over the organization. As Hasnas (1998, p. 32) states:

> When viewed as a normative (ethical) theory, the stakeholder theory asserts that, regardless of whether stakeholder management leads to improved financial performance, managers should manage the business for the benefit of all stakeholders. It views the firm not as a mechanism for increasing the stockholders' financial returns, but as a vehicle for coordinating stakeholder interests, and sees management as having a fiduciary relationship not only to the stockholders, but to all stakeholders. According to the normative stakeholder theory, management must give equal consideration to the interests of all stakeholders and, when these interests conflict, manage the business so as to attain the optimal balance among them. This of course implies that there will be times when management is obliged to at least partially sacrifice the interests of the stockholders to those of the other stakeholders. Hence, in its normative form, the stakeholder theory does imply that business has true social responsibilities.

Within the ethical branch of stakeholder theory there is a view that stakeholders have intrinsic rights (for example, to safe working conditions, fair pay, etc.), and these rights should not be violated.[15] That is, each group of stakeholders merits consideration for its own sake and not merely because of its ability to further the interests of some other group, such as the shareholders (Donaldson and Preston, 1995, p. 66). As Stoney and Winstanley (2001, p. 608) explain, fundamental to the ethical branch of stakeholder theory is a:

> concern for the ethical treatment of stakeholders which may require that the economic motive of organizations – to be profitable – be tempered to take account of the moral role of organizations and their enormous social effects on people's lives

Obviously, a normative discussion of *stakeholder rights* requires some definition of *stakeholders*. One definition we can use is that provided by Freeman and Reed (1983, p. 91):

> Any identifiable group or individual who can affect the achievement of an organisation's objectives, or is affected by the achievement of an organisation's objectives.

Clearly, many people (or other organizations) can be classified as stakeholders if we apply the above definition (for example, shareholders, creditors, government, media, employees, employees' families, local communities, local charities, future generations, and so on). With this in mind, Clarkson (1995) sought to divide stakeholders into *primary* and *secondary* stakeholders. A primary stakeholder was defined as 'one without whose continuing participation the corporation cannot survive as a going concern' (p. 106). Secondary stakeholders were defined as 'those who influence or affect, or are influenced or affected by, the corporation, but they are not engaged in transactions with the corporation and are not essential for its survival' (p. 107). According to Clarkson, primary stakeholders are the ones that must primarily be considered by management, because for the organization to succeed in the long run it must be run for the benefit of all primary stakeholders. Clarkson's definition of primary stakeholders would be similar to the definition of stakeholders applied by many researchers working within a managerial perspective of stakeholder theory, but this focus on primary stakeholders would be challenged by proponents of the ethical branch of stakeholder theory – who would argue that all stakeholders have a right to be considered by management.

The broader ethical (and normative) perspective that all stakeholders (both *primary* and *secondary*) have certain minimum rights that must not be violated can be extended to a notion that all stakeholders also have a right to be provided with information about how the organization is impacting on them (perhaps through pollution, community sponsorship, provision of employment safety initiatives, etc.), even if they choose not to use the information, and even if they cannot directly have an impact on the survival of the organization (see, for example, O'Dwyer, 2005).

In considering the notion of *rights to information* we can briefly consider Gray, Owen and Adams' (1996) perspective of accountability as used within their *accountability model*. They define accountability (1996, p. 38) as:

> The duty to provide an account (by no means necessarily a financial account) or reckoning of those actions for which one is held responsible.

According to Gray, Owen and Adams, accountability involves two responsibilities or duties:

- the responsibility to undertake certain actions (or to refrain from taking actions); and
- the responsibility to provide an account of those actions.

Under their accountability model, reporting is assumed to be *responsibility* driven rather than *demand* driven. The view being projected is that people in society have a right to be informed about certain facets of the organization's operations.[16] By considering *rights*, it is argued that the model avoids the problem of considering users' *needs* and how such needs are established (Gray *et al.*, 1991). Applying the accountability model to corporate social reporting, Gray, Owen and Maunders (1991, p. 15) argue that:

> ... the role of corporate social reporting is to provide society-at-large (the principal) with information (accountability?) about the extent to which the organisation (the agent) has met the responsibilities imposed upon it (has it played by the rules of the game?).

That is, the role of a corporate report is to inform society about the extent to which actions for which an organization is deemed to be responsible have been fulfilled. Under the accountability model, the argument is that the principal (society) can elect to be entirely passive with regard to their demand for information.

Nevertheless the agent (the organization) is still required to provide an account – the passive, non-demanding principal is merely electing not to use the information directly. Gray, Owen and Maunders state (p. 6) that 'if the principal chooses to ignore the account, this is his prerogative and matters not to the agent who, nevertheless, must account'.

Hurst (1970) also emphasizes the importance of accountability. He states (p. 58) that 'an institution which wields practical power – which compels men's wills or behaviour – must be accountable for its purposes and its performance by criteria not in the control of the institution itself'. The need to demonstrate accountability has also been stressed by the Research and Policy Committee of the Committee for Economic Development (a US-based organization). The committee states (1974, p. 21) that 'the great growth of corporations in size, market power, and impact on society has naturally brought with it a commensurate growth in responsibility; in a democratic society, power sooner or later begets equivalent accountability'.

Gray, Owen and Adams (1996) make use of the concept of the social contract to theorize about the responsibilities of business (against which there is a perceived accountability). Under their perspective they also perceive the law as providing the explicit terms of the social contract, while other non-legislated societal expectations embody the implicit terms of the contract.

In considering the above normative perspectives of how organizations *should* behave with respect to their stakeholders (relating to intrinsic rights including rights to information) it should be noted that these perspectives pertain to how the respective researchers believe organizations *should* act, which is not necessarily going to be the same as how they actually *do* act.[17] Hence, the various perspectives cannot be validated by empirical observation – as might be the case if the researchers were providing descriptive or predictive (positive) theories about organizational behaviour. As Donaldson and Preston (1995, p. 67) state:

> In normative uses, the correspondence between the theory and the observed facts of corporate life is not a significant issue, nor is the association between stakeholder management and conventional performance measures a critical test. Instead a normative theory attempts to interpret the function of, and offer guidance about, the investor-owned corporation on the basis of some underlying moral or philosophical principles.

The managerial branch of stakeholder theory

We now turn to perspectives of stakeholder theory that attempt to explain when corporate management will be likely to attend to the expectations of particular (typically powerful) stakeholders. According to Gray, Owen and Adams (1996), this alternative perspective tends to be more 'organization-centred'. Gray, Owen and Adams (1996, p. 45) state:

> Here (under this perspective), the stakeholders are identified by the organisation of concern, by reference to the extent to which the organisation believes the interplay with

each group needs to be managed in order to further the interests of the organisation. (The interests of the organisation need not be restricted to conventional profit-seeking assumptions.) The more important the stakeholder to the organisation, the more effort will be exerted in managing the relationship. Information is a major element that can be employed by the organisation to manage (or manipulate) the stakeholder in order to gain their support and approval, or to distract their opposition and disapproval.

Unlike the ethical branch of stakeholder theory, such (organization-centred) theories can be, and are often, tested by way of empirical observation.

As we learned earlier, within legitimacy theory the audience of interest is typically defined as *the society*. Within a descriptive managerial branch of stakeholder theory the organization is also considered to be part of the wider social system, but this perspective of stakeholder theory specifically considers the different stakeholder groups within society and how they should best be managed if the organization is to survive (hence we call it a 'managerial' perspective of stakeholder theory).[18] Like legitimacy theory, it is considered that the expectations of the various stakeholder groups will impact on the operating and disclosure policies of the organization. The organization will not respond to all stakeholders equally (from a practical perspective, they probably cannot), but rather, will respond to those that are deemed to be 'powerful' (Bailey *et al.*, 2000; Buhr, 2002). Nasi *et al.* (1997) build on this perspective to suggest that the most powerful stakeholders will be attended to first. This is consistent with Wallace (1995, p. 87) who argues that 'the higher the group in the stakeholder hierarchy, the more clout they have and the more complex their requirements will be'.

A stakeholder's (for example, owner's, creditor's, or regulator's) power to influence corporate management is viewed as a function of the stakeholder's degree of control over resources required by the organization (Ullman, 1985). The more critical the stakeholder resources are to the continued viability and success of the organization, the greater the expectation that stakeholder demands will be addressed. A successful organization is considered to be one that satisfies the demands (sometimes conflicting) of the various powerful stakeholder groups.[19] In this respect Ullman (1985, p. 2) states:

> ... our position is that organisations survive to the extent that they are effective. Their effectiveness derives from the management of demands, particularly the demands of interest groups upon which the organisation depends.

Power in itself will be stakeholder-organization specific, but may be tied to such things as command of limited resources (finance, labour), access to influential media, ability to legislate against the company, or ability to influence the consumption of the organization's goods and services. The behaviour of various stakeholder groups is considered a constraint on the strategy that is developed by management to best match corporate resources with its environment.

Freeman (1984) discusses the dynamics of stakeholder influence on corporate decisions. A major role of corporate management is to assess the importance of meeting stakeholder demands in order to achieve the strategic objectives of the firm. Further, as Friedman and Miles (2002) also point out, the expectations and power relativities of the various stakeholder groups can change over time. Organizations must therefore continually adapt their operating and disclosure strategies. Roberts (1992, p. 598) states:

> A major role of corporate management is to assess the importance of meeting stakeholder demands in order to achieve the strategic objectives of the firm. As the level of stakeholder power increases, the importance of meeting stakeholder demands increases also.

If we accept the view that a 'good' management is one that can successfully attend to various and sometimes conflicting demands of various (important) stakeholder groups, then we might, consistent with Evan and Freeman (1988), actually redefine the purpose of the firm. According to Evan and Freeman (1988), 'the very purpose of the firm is, in our view, to serve as a vehicle for coordinating stakeholders. It is through the firm that each stakeholder group makes itself better off through voluntary exchanges' (p. 82).

As indicated above, as the level of *stakeholder power* increases, the importance of meeting stakeholder demands increases. Some of this demand may relate to the provision of information about the activities of the organization. According to a number of writers, for example Ullman (1985) and Friedman and Miles (2002), the greater the importance to the organization of the respective stakeholder's resources/support, the greater the probability that the particular stakeholder's expectations will be incorporated within the organization's operations. From this perspective, various activities undertaken by organizations, including public reporting, will be directly related to the expectations of particular stakeholder groups. Furthermore, organizations will have an incentive to disclose information about their various programmes and initiatives to the respective stakeholder groups to indicate clearly that they are conforming with those stakeholders' expectations. Organizations must necessarily balance the expectations of the various stakeholder groups. Unerman and Bennett (2004) are among others who argue that as these expectations and power relativities can change over time, organizations must continually adapt their operating and reporting behaviours accordingly.

Within the managerial perspective of stakeholder theory, information (including financial accounting information and information about the organization's social performance) 'is a major element that can be employed by the organization to manage (or manipulate) the stakeholder in order to gain their support and approval, or to distract their opposition and disapproval' (Gray *et al.*, 1996, p. 46). This is consistent with the legitimation strategies suggested by Lindblom (1994), as discussed earlier in this chapter. In relation to corporate social disclosures, Roberts

(1992, p. 599) states:

> ... social responsibility activities are useful in developing and maintaining satisfactory relationships with stockholders, creditors, and political bodies. Developing a corporate reputation as being socially responsible through performing and disclosing social responsibility activities is part of a strategy for managing stakeholder relationships. [20]

Empirical tests of stakeholder theory

Utilising stakeholder theory to test the ability of stakeholders to impact on corporate social responsibility disclosures, Roberts (1992) found that measures of stakeholder power and their related information needs could provide some explanation about levels and types of corporate social disclosures.

Neu, Warsame and Pedwell (1998) also found support for the view that particular stakeholder groups can be more effective than others in demanding social responsibility disclosures. They reviewed the annual reports of a number of publicly traded Canadian companies operating in environmentally sensitive industries for the period from 1982 to 1991. A measure of correlation was sought between increases and decreases in environmental disclosure and the concerns held by particular stakeholder groups. The results indicated that the companies were more responsive to the demands or concerns of financial stakeholders and government regulators than to the concerns of environmentalists. They considered that these results supported a perspective that where corporations face situations where stakeholders have conflicting interests or expectations, the corporations will elect to provide information of a legitimizing nature to those stakeholders deemed to be more important to the survival of the organization, while down-playing the needs or expectations of less 'important' stakeholders.

Stakeholder theory of the 'managerial' variety does not directly provide prescriptions about what information *should* be disclosed other than indicating that the provision of information, including information within an annual report, can, if thoughtfully considered, be useful to the continued operations of a business entity. Of course, if we accept this view of the world, we would still be left with the difficult problem of determining who are our most important (powerful) stakeholders, and what their respective information demands are. [21]

As we have noted, organizations typically have a multitude of stakeholders with differing expectations about how the organization should operate. Read Exhibits 8.3 and 8.4. Exhibit 8.3 is critical of banks in terms of the accessibility of bank credit for lone-parent families and the impact this has in 'forcing' lone-parent families to use very high interest non-bank forms of credit. Would lone-parents or the charity One Parent Families, in your view, be considered to be powerful stakeholders, such that their concerns would be met by the banks (adopting the managerial perspective of stakeholder theory)? How would this view be different if we were adopting a moral/ethical perspective of stakeholder theory?

Exhibit 8.3 Stakeholders' concern about an attribute of an organization's performance

Give lone parents credit, banks told: Charity report finds that discrimination by financial sector forces low-income families to use doorstep lenders

Phillip Inman

Single parents struggling with debts are ill-served by the banking industry, which punishes them with high interest rates on loans or refuses to offer credit at all, pushing them into the arms of doorstep lenders, the charity One Parent Families said yesterday.

Despite large government subsidies through the tax credit system, which have improved the finances of single parents over the past four years, banks and other lenders continue to discriminate against them and force them to pay more for credit.

Almost half (48 per cent) of single-parent families had been in arrears in the past year, compared with a quarter of two-parent families. Even those parents who choose to work often fail to rid themselves of short-term, costly debts. The incidence of debt among working lone parents is twice as high as among couples where one person is in work – 14 per cent compared to 7 per cent, according to the report.

The charity said a 32-page report, Personal Finance and One-Parent Families: The Facts, revealed the wide-ranging problems faced by lone parents, who were more likely to use overdrafts, credit cards and personal loans than couples with children.

... banks had to do more to make basic bank accounts easier to open. Like other low-income groups, single parents will often be shy of opening a current account, fearing excessive surcharges for unapproved overdrafts or bounced cheques.

Most high-street banks have developed stripped-down current accounts – known as basic bank accounts – following demands by the Treasury that they support measures to end financial exclusion among poorer households. But low-income groups have criticised banks for doing little to promote them.

Ms Simpson said the Treasury should consider setting a target for the number of basic accounts to be opened by 2006. She said ministers should consider ways to persuade mainstream banks to lend small sums at low cost, attracting single parents away from doorstep lenders that charge between 50 per cent and 190 per cent interest on loan products.

Exhibit 8.4 A further example of stakeholders' concern about aspects of business activities

---

Corporate social responsibility means business must look beyond profits to its suppliers, workers and the wider community it serves

Oliver Morgan

Ask people involved in business to describe corporate social responsibility and one word is almost guaranteed to come up – stakeholding.

While it largely disappeared from Labour Party parlance after the 1997 election, it has retained its use to describe how companies ought to look beyond the bottom line in managing their activities. Nowhere is this more true than when companies consider corporate social responsibility (CSR).

The Confederation of British Industry says: 'CSR requires business to acknowledge that its responsibilities extend beyond maximising profitability – and thus shareholder value – to meeting demands of other interest groups. Often referred to as stakeholders, these groups may be defined as those with which the company closely interacts – such as employees, suppliers and local communities – or more broadly to include national governments and societies as a whole.'

As this suggests, employees are a key element in this jigsaw. Stephanie Draper, author of the Industrial Society's study on CSR, Corporate Nirvana, says: 'Staff are a central part of this debate. If you are a socially responsible organisation, you will start with the way you treat your staff.'

People today are more discerning in the jobs they choose. Increasingly they like to work for organisations whose values they share. Also, a growing skills deficit in Britain means companies have to think of ways of attracting staff – and reflecting their values is an important way of doing this.

Coupled with this is the perception of the company with another powerful stakeholding group – consumers. As Draper says, if staff are treated well, they are more likely to treat customers well.

Companies have responded differently. Giants such as Shell and Unilever, for example, have made much of environmental and social issues in annual reports. Smaller businesses have been slower to respond.

Some large companies have introduced codes of conduct and community programmes. British Airways, for example, has a programme involving youth development, education, environment, heritage and tourism.

But, trade unions argue, volunteerism is not enough. David Coats of the TUC says many companies do not take workers seriously enough. 'Much of the CSR stuff companies do is little more than a smokescreen to avoid

Exhibit 8.4 (*continued*)

statutory legislation. Most corporate responsibility programmes do not involve workers' rights. These tend to be dealt with separately.'

Unions, however, believe workers' rights are central to the agenda. And through pressure on companies, but perhaps more importantly on the Government and the European Commission, there have been successes.

Draper identifies key points for employees, including staff being offered a living wage, good training and development opportunities, good communication, healthy work-life balances, family-friendly policies, health and safety and employee representation. On several issues, union lobbying has secured benefits in law – a minimum wage, the Employment Relations Act, which sets out union-recognition processes at work, and part-time and maternity pay regulations.

In terms of better information for workers, unions have campaigned for information and consultation rights, which have been boosted by the agreement of an EU directive.

On training, unions have pressed for a statutory levy on businesses – as occurs in many European countries. The CBI resists this move, but there is currently a three-way dialogue with the Government on introducing a training tax credit.

Nevertheless, unions remain sceptical as to how enthusiastic companies are about CSR.

They are similarly sceptical on broader issues, such as the environment and ensuring that workers outside the UK, who supply British companies, enjoy the same labour standards.

... There has ... been co-ordinated pressure on companies from both the ICFTU [International Confederation of Free Trade Unions] and international bodies covering specific industries such as UNI.

Its director of multinational enterprises, Jim Baker, says his organisation's efforts to impose a code of conduct on multinational companies following International Labour Organisation principles – such as no child or forced labour, recognition of unions, free collective bargaining and non-discrimination – began to change corporate behaviour in the Nineties.

One example was the sports-goods industry. Fifa incorporated the ICFTU code, and companies such as Nike have been pressurised into expressing support for it.

The challenge is expanding these agreements and policing the codes of practice. Baker says: 'The real difficulty comes when you look down the supply chain from these big companies.'

Copyright Guardian Newspapers Limited, 8 July 2001

Exhibit 8.4 relates to trade union scepticism of the social and environmental responsibility claims of many UK companies. After reading the exhibit we can again consider whether UK or European companies would construe trade unions as being powerful stakeholders, and if they are deemed to be so, we can also consider how or whether UK or European companies might make certain disclosures of information (perhaps what they are doing about protecting and enhancing workers' rights) to allay the concerns of the unions.

As a concluding issue it should be realized that in the above discussion we have separately considered the normative moral/ethical perspective of stakeholder theory as well as the managerial (power based) perspective of stakeholder theory. By discussing them separately it could be construed that management might either be ethically/morally aware or solely focused on the survival of the organization, whereas in practice there is likely to be a continuum of possible positions between these two absolute points. By separately considering the two perspectives we are thus only likely to get a partial view, as it is unlikely that the managers of any company will be at one or other of the absolute extremes of the continuum. Instead, the managers of many companies will arguably be driven by both ethical consider-ations and performance-based decisions – not one or the other. As Wicks (1996) argues, many people have embraced a conceptual framework in which ethical considerations and market considerations are seen as constituting a categorically and independent realism. Wicks argues that this view is unrealistic since it implies that people cannot introduce 'moral imaginations when they act in the market world'. In terms of future research in stakeholder theory, Rowley (1998) provides some interesting advice. He states:

> The blurring of normative and descriptive analysis is problematic for the field, however, dividing them into separate camps is equally hazardous. I believe that if our most challenging issues 10 years from now are to be different from today, we will need to collectively understand the complementary roles that normative and descriptive research play in our research questions. Like market and society we cannot think of one without the other (p. 2).

Again, we are left with a view that particular theories (of accounting) can provide us with only a partial view, and hence it is sometimes useful to consider the insights provided by different theoretical perspectives. One additional systems oriented theoretical perspective, which has only recently begun to be applied to an analysis of voluntary corporate reporting decisions, is *institutional theory*.

Institutional theory

Institutional theory has been developed within the management academic literature (more specifically, in organizational theory) since the late 1970s, by researchers such as Meyer and Rowan (1977); DiMaggio and Powell (1983); Powell and

DiMaggio (1991); and Zucker (1977, 1987). While it has become a major and powerful theoretical perspective within organizational analysis, it has also been adopted by some accounting researchers. Several management accounting researchers, such as Covaleski and Dirsmith (1988); Broadbent, Jacobs and Laughlin (2001); and Brignall and Modell (2000), have used institutional theory. It has also been used by some researchers who investigate aspects of audit, such as Rollins and Bremser (1997), and others who research aspects of the development and role of the accounting profession, such as Fogarty (1996). More directly related to financial accounting theory, Fogarty (1992) applied institutional theory to an analysis of the accounting standard-setting process. Dillard, Rigsby and Goodman (2004, p. 506) state that:

> Institutional theory is becoming one of the dominant theoretical perspectives in organization theory and is increasingly being applied in accounting research to study the practice of accounting in organizations.

A key reason why institutional theory is relevant to researchers who investigate voluntary corporate reporting practices is that it provides a complementary perspective, to both stakeholder theory and legitimacy theory, in understanding how organizations understand and respond to changing social and institutional pressures and expectations. Among other factors, it links organizational practices (such as accounting and corporate reporting) to the values of the society in which an organization operates, and to a need to maintain organizational legitimacy. Dillard, Rigsby and Goodman (2004, p. 507) explain that institutional theory:

> ... concerns the development of the taken for granted assumptions beliefs and values underlying organizational characteristics ... [with accounting-based studies] suggesting the importance of social culture and environment on the practice of accounting; the use of accounting practices as rationalizations in order to maintain appearances of legitimacy; and the possibilities of decoupling these rationalizing accounting practices from the actual technical and administrative processes

Institutional theory therefore provides an explanation of how mechanisms through which organizations may seek to align perceptions of their practices and characteristics with social and cultural values (in order to gain or retain legitimacy) become institutionalized in particular organizations. Such mechanisms could include those proposed by both stakeholder theory and/or legitimacy theory, but could conceivably also encompass a broader range of legitimating mechanisms. This is why these three theoretical perspectives should be seen as complementary rather than competing.

There are two main dimensions to institutional theory. The first of these is termed *isomorphism* while the second is termed *decoupling*. Both of these can be of central relevance to explaining voluntary corporate reporting practices. Dillard, Rigsby and Goodman (2004, p. 509) explain that 'Isomorphism refers to the adaptation of an institutional practice by an organisation'. As voluntary corporate reporting by an organization is an institutional practice of that reporting organization, the processes by which voluntary corporate reporting adapts and changes in that organization are isomorphic processes.

DiMaggio and Powell (1983) set out three different isomorphic processes (processes whereby institutional practices such as voluntary corporate reporting adapt and change). The first of these is *coercive isomorphism* where organizations will only change their institutional practices because of pressure from those stakeholders upon whom the organization is dependant. This form of isomorphism is clearly related to the managerial branch of stakeholder theory (discussed earlier) whereby a company will use 'voluntary' corporate reporting disclosures to address the economic, social, environmental and ethical values and concerns of those stakeholders who have the most power over the company. The company is therefore coerced (in this case usually informally) by its influential (or powerful) stakeholders into adopting particular voluntary reporting practices. Explaining this more directly in terms of the earlier definition of isomorphism, the company is coerced into adapting its existing voluntary corporate reporting practices (including the issues upon which they report) to bring these into line with the expectations and demands of its powerful stakeholders (while possibly ignoring the expectations of less powerful stakeholders).

The second isomorphic process specified by DiMaggio and Powell (1983) is *mimetic isomorphism*. This involves organizations seeking to emulate or improve upon the institutional practices of other organizations, often for reasons of competitive advantage in terms of legitimacy. As Unerman and Bennett (2004, p. 692) explain in the context of a study investigating stakeholder dialogue in corporate social reporting:

> Some institutional theory studies ... have demonstrated a tendency for a number of organisations within a particular sector to adopt similar new policies and procedures as those adopted by other leading organisations in their sector. This process, referred to as 'mimetic isomorphism', is explained as being the result of attempts by managers of each organisation to maintain or enhance external stakeholders' perceptions of the legitimacy of their organisation, because any organisation which failed (at a minimum) to follow innovative practices and procedures adopted by other organisations in the same sector would risk losing legitimacy in relation to the rest of the sector (Broadbent, *et al.*, 2001, Scott, 1995). Drawing upon these observations, in the absence of any legislative intervention prescribing detailed mechanisms of debate, a key motivating force for many managers to introduce mechanisms allowing for greater equity in the determination of corporate responsibilities would therefore be their desire to maintain, or enhance, their own competitive advantage. They would strive to achieve this by implementing stakeholder dialogue mechanisms which their economically powerful stakeholders were likely to perceive as more effective than those used by their competitors. It is unlikely that these managers would readily embrace mechanisms designed to facilitate widespread

> participation in the determination of corporate responsibilities unless their economically powerful stakeholders expected the interests of economically marginalized stakeholders to be taken into account in this manner, and these managers are only likely to implement the minimum procedures which they feel their economically powerful stakeholders would consider acceptable.

This argument links pressures for mimetic isomorphism with pressures underlying coercive isomorphism, as Unerman and Bennett (2004) maintain that without coercive pressure from stakeholders, in this case there would be unlikely to be pressure to mimic or surpass the social reporting practices (institutional practices) of other companies.

The final isomorphic process explained by DiMaggio and Powell (1983) is *normative isomorphism.* This relates to the pressures arising from group norms to adopt particular institutional practices. In the case of corporate reporting, the professional expectation that accountants will comply with accounting standards acts as a form of normative isomorphism for the organizations for whom accountants work to produce accounting reports (an institutional practice) which are shaped by accounting standards. In terms of voluntary reporting practices, normative isomorphic pressures could arise through less formal group influences from a range of both formal and informal groups to which managers belong – such as the culture and working practices developed within their workplace. These could produce collective managerial views in favour or against certain types of reporting practices, such as collective managerial views on the desirability or necessity of providing a range of stakeholders with social and environmental information through the medium of corporate reports.

Turning to the other dimension of institutional theory, *decoupling* implies that while managers might perceive a need for their organization to be seen to be adopting certain institutional practices, and might even institute formal processes aimed at implementing these practices, actual organizational practices can be very different to these formally sanctioned and publicly pronounced processes and practices. Thus, the actual practices can be decoupled from the institutionalized (apparent) practices. In terms of voluntary corporate reporting practices, this decoupling can be linked to some of the insights from legitimacy theory whereby social and environmental disclosures can be used to construct an organizational image very different from actual organizational social and environmental performance. Thus, the organizational image constructed through corporate reports might be one of social and environmental responsibility when the actual managerial imperative is maximization of profitability or shareholder value. As Dillard, Rigsby and Goodman (2004, p. 510) put it:

> In essence, institutionalized, rationalized elements are incorporated into the organization's formal management systems because they maintain appearances and thus confer legitimacy whether or not they directly facilitate economic efficiency.

Chapter summary

This chapter provides a number of perspectives about why management elects to make particular disclosures. Specifically, it reviews legitimacy theory, stakeholder theory and, briefly, the newly emergent (in a financial reporting context) institutional theory – three theories that can be classified as systems oriented theories. Systems oriented theories see the organization as being part of a broader social system.

Legitimacy theory, stakeholder theory and institutional theory are all linked to political economy theory wherein the political economy constitutes the social, political and economic framework within which human life takes place and social, political and economic issues are considered as inseparable. Political economy theory can be classified as either classical or bourgeois. Bourgeois political economy theory ignores various tensions within society and accepts the world as essentially pluralistic with no particular class dominating another. Legitimacy theory and stakeholder theory adopt the bourgeois perspective. Institutional theory can adopt either the bourgeois or classical perspective.

Legitimacy theory relies upon the notion of a social contract, which is an implied contract representing the norms and expectations of the community in which an organization operates. An organization is deemed to be legitimate to the extent that it complies with the terms of the social contract. Legitimacy and the right to operate are considered to go hand in hand. Accounting disclosures are considered to represent one way in which an organization can legitimize its ongoing operations. Where legitimacy is threatened, disclosures are one strategy to restore legitimacy. In practice, policies to maintain or restore corporate legitimacy are sometimes articulated in terms of reputation risk management.

Two different categories of stakeholder theory have been reviewed, these being the ethical (or normative) branch, and the managerial branch. The ethical branch of stakeholder theory discusses issues associated with rights to information, rights that should be met regardless of the power of the stakeholders involved. Within the ethical branch, disclosures are considered to be responsibility driven. The managerial branch of stakeholder theory, on the other hand, predicts that organizations will tend to satisfy the information demands of those stakeholders who are important to the organization's ongoing survival. Whether a particular stakeholder receives information will be dependent upon how powerful they are perceived to be, with power often considered in terms of the scarcity of the resources controlled by the respective stakeholders. The disclosure of information is considered to represent an important strategy in managing stakeholders.

Institutional theory provides a complementary, and partially overlapping, perspective to both legitimacy and stakeholder theories. It explains that managers will be subject to pressures to change, or adopt, certain voluntary corporate reporting practices. These pressures can be either coercive, mimetic or normative, and the resulting institutional image can sometimes be more apparent than real.

Questions

8.1   Explain the notion of a *social contract* and what relevance the social contract has with respect to the *legitimacy* of an organization.

8.2   What does the notion of legitimacy and social contract have to do with corporate disclosure policies?

8.3   How would corporate management determine the terms of the *social contract* (if this is indeed possible) and what would be the implications for a firm if it breached the terms of the contract?

8.4   If an organization's management considered that the organization might not have operated in accordance with community expectations (it broke the terms of the *social contract*), consistent with legitimacy theory, what actions would you expect management to undertake in the subsequent period?

8.5   If an organization was involved in a major accident or incident, would you expect them to use vehicles such as an annual report to try to explain the incident? If so, explain *how* and *why* they would use the annual report in this way.

8.6   Consistent with the material provided in this chapter, would you expect management to make disclosures in relation to real-world events, or alternatively, in relation to how they believed the community perceived the real-world events? Why?

8.7   This chapter divided stakeholder theory into the *ethical branch* and the *managerial branch*. Explain the differences between the managerial and ethical branches of stakeholder theory in terms of the alternative perspectives about when information will, or should, be produced by an organization.

8.8   Under the *managerial perspective* of stakeholder theory, when would we expect an organization to meet the information demands of a particular stakeholder group?

8.9 Read Exhibit 8.3 on p. 292, an article that relates to claimed financial exclusion of some sectors of society. After reading the exhibit:

(a) Apply the managerial perspective of stakeholder theory to explain whether management would care about the concerns of the charity One Parent Families.

(b) If we applied an ethical perspective of stakeholder theory, *should* they care?

(c) If society considered that the banks' policies were unreasonable, would you expect the banks to use their annual report to defend their position (legitimacy)?

8.10 Explain the concepts: coercive isomorphism; mimetic isomorphism; and normative isomorphism. How can these concepts be used to explain voluntary corporate reporting practices?

8.11 To what extent do stakeholder, legitimacy and institutional theories provide competing, mutually exclusive, explanations of voluntary corporate reporting practices?

Notes

1 For example, some researchers operating within the Positive Accounting Theory paradigm (e.g. Ness and Mirza, 1991) argue that the voluntary disclosure of social responsibility information can be explained as a strategy to reduce political costs. Social responsibility reporting has also been explained from a legitimacy theory perspective (e.g. Deegan *et al.*, 2002), and from a stakeholder theory perspective (e.g. Swift, 2001)

2 Social responsibility disclosures are considered more fully in Chapter 9. However, at this stage they can be defined as disclosures that provide information about the interaction of an organization with its physical and social environment, inclusive of community involvement, the natural environment, human resources, energy and product safety (Gray and Bebbington, 2001, Gray *et al.*, 1996).

3 As we would appreciate, various professional accounting bodies throughout the world have released documents (normally as part of a conceptual framework project) indicating that financial reporting should embrace the attributes of *neutrality* and *representational faithfulness*. Proponents of political economy theories would argue that there are a multitude of political and social issues that make such a perspective unrealistic.

4 For example, in considering the practice of social responsibility reporting, classical political economists would typically argue that the growth of environmental disclosure by companies since the late 1980s can be seen as an attempt to act *as if* in response to environmental groups while, *actually*, attempting to wrest the initiative and control of the environment agenda from these groups in order to permit capital to carry on doing what it does best – making money from capital (Gray *et al.*, 1996, p. 47).

5 A pluralistic perspective assumes (typically implicitly) that many classes of stakeholders have the power to influence various decisions by corporations, government and other entities. Accounting is not considered to be put in place to favour specific interests (sometimes referred to as 'elites'). By using 'society' as the topic of focus rather than *subgroups* within society, theories such as legitimacy theory ignore 'struggles and inequities within society' (Puxty, 1991).

6   Positive Accounting Theory, the focus of Chapter 7, also does not consider issues associated with inequities within society or the role of accounting in sustaining these inequities.

7   It can be argued that requirements imposed by the law reflect the explicit terms of the social contract, while uncodified community expectations (and these will be perceived to be different by different people) constitute the implicit terms of the social contract.

8   The 'legitimacy gap' refers to the difference between the society's (or a sub-group thereof) expectations relating to how an organization *should act*, and the perceptions of how they *do act*.

9   What is being stressed is that managing *legitimacy* is very much about managing the *perceptions* of others.

10 Environmental sensitivity was determined by use of a questionnaire to environmental lobby groups in which office bearers were required to rate industries (on a 0 to 5 scale) on the basis of whether the industry had been made the focus of action as a result of its environmental performance/implications.

11 For an explanation of media agenda setting theory see McCombs and Shaw (1972); Zucker (1978); Eyal, Winter and DeGeorge (1981); Blood (1981); Mayer (1980); McCombs (1981); Ader (1995).

12 An extreme, but somewhat interesting, view of the media's power of influence is provided by White (1973, p. 23). In relation to the US he states that 'the power of the press in America is a primordial one. It sets the agenda of public discussion; and this sweeping political power is unrestrained by any law. It determines what people will talk and think about – an authority that in other nations is reserved for tyrants, priests, parties and mandarins'.

13 As Chapter 7 indicates, Positive Accounting Theory proposes that managers are motivated to undertake actions that will maximize their own wealth. To the extent that mechanisms have been put in place to align the interests of the managers with the goals of maximizing the value of the organization, the manager will adopt those accounting and disclosure methods that minimize the wealth transfers away from the organization – wealth transfers that might be due to various political processes.

14 Stakeholder theory itself is a confusing term as many different researchers have stated that they have used stakeholder theory in their research. Yet when we look at the research we see that different theories with different aims and assumptions have been employed – yet they have all been labelled as *stakeholder theory*. As Hasnas (1998, p. 26) states, 'stakeholder theory is somewhat of a troublesome label because it is used to refer to both an empirical theory of management and a normative theory of business ethics, often without clearly distinguishing between the two'. More correctly, perhaps, we can think of the term stakeholder theory as an *umbrella term* that actually represents a number of alternative theories that address various issues associated with relationships with stakeholders, including considerations of the rights of stakeholders, the power of stakeholders, or the effective management of stakeholders.

15 We can contrast this perspective with that provided in Friedman (1962). He states: 'few trends could so thoroughly undermine the very foundation of our free society as the acceptance by corporate officials of a social responsibility other than to make as much money for their stockholders as possible. This is a fundamentally subversive doctrine' (p. 133).

16 Within the model they refer to society as the 'principal' and the organization (that owes the accountability) as the 'agent'. However, according to Gray, Owen and Maunders (1991, p. 17), their 'principal–agent model must be distinguished from "agency theory" or "economic principal–agent theory" as employed in, for example, Jensen and Meckling (1976), Ronen (1979), Fellingham and Newman (1979), Jensen (1983, 1993), Watts and Zimmerman (1986). Economic agency theory is grounded in neo-classical economics and takes its assumptions from it. Most significant among these are the assumptions about the single-minded greed of the principal and agent who are actively seeking to gain at the other's expense. The principal–agent model we are using makes no such assumptions and adopts no assumptions from economics, but rather

owes its genesis to jurisprudence (Macpherson, 1973)'.

17　Nevertheless, Donaldson and Preston (1995) argue that observation suggests that corporate decisions are frequently made on the basis of ethical considerations, even when doing so could not enhance corporate profit or shareholder gain. According to Donaldson and Preston, such behaviour is deemed to be not only appropriate, but desirable. They argue that corporate officials are not less morally obliged than any other citizens to take ethical considerations into account, and it would be unwise social policy to preclude them from doing so.

18　By comparison, Donaldson and Preston (1995) refer to the *instrumental perspective* of stakeholder theory in which the principal focus of interest is the proposition that corporations practising stakeholder management will be relatively successful in conventional performance terms. This is obviously similar to our 'managerial' perspective of stakeholder theory.

19　In considering the managerial perspective of stakeholder theory, Hasnas (1998, p. 32) states: 'when viewed as an empirical theory of management designed to prescribe a method for improving a business's performance, the stakeholder theory does not imply that business has any social responsibilities'.

20　Again, we find that most of the accounting-related studies that use stakeholder theory (as with legitimacy theory) have researched issues associated with social and environmental disclosures. While these theories could be applied to financial disclosures, most researchers of financial accounting practices have, at least to date, tended to use other theories, such as Positive Accounting Theory. Issues associated with firms' capital structures have been studied from a stakeholder theory perspective by Barton, Hill and Sundaram (1989) and Cornell and Shapiro (1987).

21　Again it is emphasized that this will not always be an easy exercise. For example, and for the purpose of illustration (perhaps at an extreme) we may find that a company has elected to provide an elderly woman who lives in a modest house nearby with a report that details when coal dust can be expected to be released from the company's furnaces so that she can ensure that no washing is left out at this time. At face value such a person may not appear to be a powerful stakeholder and we as outsiders might question why the company provides such disclosures. However, we may find that the woman has a daughter who is a popular high profile radio personality who will readily complain on air, at some cost to the company in terms of community support, each time her mother's washing is put out and is subsequently covered with coal ash. Through her connections the elderly woman is a powerful stakeholder, and to alleviate her problems, coal-dust release information is provided so that she can schedule her washing. In relation to this illustration it should be noted that an ethical/moral view of stakeholder information rights would perhaps be that this person has a right to information, regardless of the fact that her daughter works in the media.

References

Abbott, W. & Monsen, R. (1979) 'On the measurement of corporate social responsibility: Self-reported disclosures as a method of measuring corporate social involvement', *Academy of Management Journal*, **22** (3), pp. 501–15.

Adams, C. A. (2002) 'Internal organisational factors influencing corporate social and ethical reporting', *Accounting, Auditing & Accountability Journal*, **15** (2), pp. 223–50.

Ader, C. (1995) 'A longitudinal study of agenda setting for the issue of environmental pollution', *Journalism & Mass Communication Quarterly*, **72** (3), pp. 300–11.

Bailey, D., Harte, G. & Sugden, R. (2000) 'Corporate disclosure and the deregulation of international investment', *Accounting, Auditing & Accountability Journal*, **13** (2), pp. 197–218.

Barton, S., Hill, N. & Sundaram, S. (1989) 'An empirical test of stakeholder theory predictions of capital structure', *Financial Management* (Spring), pp. 36–44.

Blood, R. W. (1981) 'Unobtrusive issues and the agenda-setting role of the press', Unpublished Doctoral Dissertation, Syracuse University, New York.

Brignall, S. & Modell, S. (2000) 'An institutional perspective on performance measurement and management in the "New Public Sector"', *Management Accounting Research*, **11** (3), pp. 281–306.

Broadbent, J., Jacobs, K. & Laughlin, R. (2001) 'Organisational resistance strategies to unwanted accounting and finance changes: The case of general medical practice in the UK', *Accounting, Auditing & Accountability Journal*, **14** (5), pp. 565–86.

Brown, N. & Deegan, C. (1999) 'The public disclosure of environmental performance information – a dual test of media agenda setting theory and legitimacy theory', *Accounting and Business Research*, **29** (1), pp. 21–41.

Buhr, N. (2002) 'A structuration view on the initiation of environmental reports', *Critical Perspectives on Accounting*, **13** (1), pp. 17–38.

Burchell, S., Clubb, C., Hopwood, A., Hughes, J. & Naphapiet, J. (1980) 'The roles of accounting in organisations and society', *Accounting, Organizations & Society*, **5** (1), pp. 5–28.

Campbell, D., Craven, B. & Shrives, P. (2003) 'Voluntary social reporting in three FTSE sectors: A comment on perception and legitimacy', *Accounting, Auditing & Accountability Journal*, **16** (4), pp. 558–81.

Campbell, D. J. (2000) 'Legitimacy theory or managerial construction? Corporate social disclosure in Marks and Spencer Plc corporate reports, 1969–1997', *Accounting Forum*, **24** (1), pp. 80–100.

Carpenter, V. & Feroz, E. (1992) 'GAAP as a symbol of legitimacy: New York State's decision to adopt generally accepted accounting principles', *Accounting, Organizations and Society*, **17** (7), pp. 613–43.

Clarkson, M. (1995) 'A stakeholder framework for analyzing and evaluating corporate social performance', *Academy of Management review*, **20** (1), pp. 92–118.

Committee for Economic Development (1974) *Measuring Business Social Performance: The Corporate Social Audit*, New York: Committee for Economic Development.

Cooper, D. J. & Sherer, M. J. (1984) 'The value of corporate accounting reports – arguments for a political economy of accounting', *Accounting, Organizations and Society*, **9** (3/4), pp. 207–32.

Cornell, B. & Shapiro, A. (1987) 'Corporate stakeholders and corporate finance', *Financial Management* (Spring), pp. 5–14.

Covaleski, M. A. & Dirsmith, M. W. (1988) 'An institutional perspective on the rise, social transformation, and fall of a university budget category', *Administrative Science Quarterly*, **33**, pp. 562–87.

Deegan, C. (2002) 'The legitimising effect of social and environmental disclosures – a theoretical foundation', *Accounting, Auditing & Accountability Journal*, **15** (3), pp. 282–311.

Deegan, C. & Gordon, B. (1996) 'A study of the environmental disclosure practices of Australian corporations', *Accounting and Business Research*, **26** (3), pp. 187–99.

Deegan, C. & Rankin, M. (1996) 'Do Australian companies report environmental news objectively? An analysis of environmental disclosures by firms prosecuted successfully by the environmental protection authority', *Accounting, Auditing and Accountability Journal*, **9** (2), pp. 52–69.

Deegan, C., Rankin, M. & Tobin, J. (2002) 'An examination of the corporate social and environmental disclosures of BHP from 1983–1997', *Accounting, Auditing & Accountability Journal*, **15** (3), pp. 312–43.

Deegan, C., Rankin, M. & Voght, P. (2000) 'Firms' disclosure reactions to major social incidents: Australian evidence', *Accounting Forum*, **24** (1), pp. 101–30.

Dillard, J. F., Rigsby, J. T. & Goodman, C. (2004) 'The making and remaking of organization context: Duality and the institutionalization process', *Accounting, Auditing & Accountability Journal,* **17** (4), pp. 506–42.

DiMaggio, P. J. & Powell, W. W. (1983) 'The iron cage revisited: Institutional isomorphism and collective rationality in organizational fields', *American Sociological Review,* **48**, pp. 146–60.

Donaldson, T. & Preston, L. (1995) 'The stakeholder theory of the corporation – concepts, evidence, and implications', *Academy of Management Review,* **20** (1), pp. 65–92.

Dowling, J. & Pfeffer, J. (1975) 'Organisational legitimacy: Social values and organisational behavior', *Pacific Sociological Review,* **18** (1), pp. 122–36.

Evan, W. & Freeman, R. (1988) 'A stakeholder theory of the modern corporation: Kantian capitalism', in Beauchamp, T. & Bowie, N. (eds) *Ethical Theory and Business,* Englewood Cliffs, NJ, pp. 75–93.

Eyal, C. H., Winter, J. P. & DeGeorge, W. F. (1981) 'The concept of time frame in agenda setting', in Wilhoit, G. C. (ed.) *Mass Communication Yearbook,* Beverly Hills, CA: Sage Publications Inc.

Fellingham, J. & Newman, D. (1979) 'Monitoring decisions in an agency setting', *Journal of Business Finance and Accounting,* **6** (2), pp. 203–22.

Fogarty, T. J. (1992) 'Financial accounting standard setting as an institutionalized action field: Constraints, opportunities and dilemmas', *Journal of Accounting and Public Policy,* **11** (4), pp. 331–55.

Fogarty, T. J. (1996) 'The imagery and reality of peer review in the US: Insights from institutional theory', *Accounting, Organizations & Society,* **18**, pp. 243–67.

Freeman, R. (1984) *Strategic Management: A Stakeholder Approach,* Marshall, MA: Pitman.

Freeman, R. & Reed, D. (1983) 'Stockholders and stakeholders: A new perspective on corporate governance', *Californian Management Review,* **25** (2), pp. 88–106.

Friedman, A. & Miles, S. (2002) 'Developing stakeholder theory', *Journal of Management Studies,* **39** (1), pp. 1–21.

Friedman, M. (1962) *Capitalism and Freedom,* Chicago: University of Chicago Press.

Gray, R. & Bebbington, J. (2001) *Accounting for the Environment,* London: Sage Publications Ltd.

Gray, R., Kouhy, R. & Lavers, S. (1995) 'Corporate social and environmental reporting: A review of the literature and a longitudinal study of UK disclosure', *Accounting, Auditing and Accountability Journal,* **8** (2), pp. 47–77.

Gray, R., Owen, D. & Adams, C. (1996) *Accounting and Accountability: Changes and Challenges in Corporate Social and Environmental Reporting,* London: Prentice-Hall.

Gray, R., Owen, D. & Maunders, K. T. (1991) 'Accountability, corporate social reporting and the external social audits', *Advances in Public Interest Accounting,* **4**, pp. 1–21.

Guthrie, J. & Parker, L. (1990) 'Corporate social disclosure practice: A comparative international analysis', *Advances in Public Interest Accounting,* **3**, pp. 159–75.

Hasnas, J. (1998) 'The normative theories of business ethics: A guide for the perplexed', *Business Ethics Quarterly,* **8** (1), pp. 19–42.

Heard, J. & Bolce, W. (1981) 'The political significance of corporate social reporting in the United States of America', *Accounting, Organizations and Society,* **6** (3), pp. 247–54.

Hogner, R. H. (1982) 'Corporate social reporting: Eight decades of development at US steel', *Research in Corporate Performance and Policy,* **4**, pp. 243–50.

Hurst, J. W. (1970) *The Legitimacy of the Business Corporation in the Law of the United States 1780–1970,* Charlottesville: The University Press of Virginia.

Jensen, M. C. (1983) 'Organisation theory and methodology', *The Accounting Review,* **58** (April), pp. 319–39.

Jensen, M. C. (1993) 'The modern industrial revolution, exit and failure of internal control systems', *Journal of Finance,* pp. 831–80.

Jensen, M. C. & Meckling, W. H. (1976) 'Theory of the firm: Managerial behavior, agency costs and ownership structure', *Journal of Financial Economics*, **3** (October), pp. 305–60.

Lindblom, C. K. (1994) 'The implications of organisational legitimacy for corporate social performance and disclosure', *Critical Perspectives on Accounting Conference*, New York.

Lowe, E. A. & Tinker, A. (1977) 'Sighting the accounting problematic: Towards an intellectual emancipation of accounting', *Journal of Business Finance and Accounting*, **4** (3), pp. 263–76.

Macpherson, C. B. (1973) *Democratic Theory: Essays in Retrieval*, Oxford: Oxford University Press.

Mathews, M. R. (1993), *Socially Responsible Accounting*, London: Chapman and Hall.

Mayer, H. (1980) 'Power and the press', *Murdoch University News*, **7** (8).

McCombs, M. (1981) 'The agenda-setting approach', in Nimmo, D. & Sanders, K. (eds) *Handbook of Political Communication*, Beverly Hills, California: Sage.

McCombs, M. & Shaw, D. (1972) 'The agenda setting function of mass media', *Public Opinion Quarterly* (36), pp. 176–87.

Meyer, J. W. & Rowan, B. (1977) 'Institutionalized organizations: Formal structure as myth and ceremony', *American Journal of Sociology*, **83**, pp. 340–63.

Nasi, J., Nasi, S., Phillips, N. & Zyglidopoulos, S. (1997) 'The evolution of corporate social responsiveness – an exploratory study of Finnish and Canadian forestry companies', *Business & Society*, **38** (3), pp. 296–321.

Ness, K. & Mirza, A. (1991) 'Corporate social disclosure: A note on a test of agency theory', *British Accounting Review*, **23**, pp. 211–17.

Neu, D., Warsame, H. & Pedwell, K. (1998) 'Managing public impressions: Environmental disclosures in annual reports', *Accounting, Organizations and Society*, **25** (3), pp. 265–82.

O'Donovan, G. (2002) 'Environmental disclosures in the annual report: Extending the applicability and predictive power of legitimacy theory', *Accounting, Auditing & Accountability Journal*, **15** (3), pp. 344–71.

O'Dwyer, B. (2002) 'Managerial perceptions of corporate social disclosure: An Irish story', *Accounting, Auditing & Accountability Journal*, **15** (3), pp. 406–36.

O'Dwyer, B. (2005) 'Stakeholder democracy: Challenges and contributions from social accounting', *Business Ethics: A European Review*, **14** (1), pp. 28–41.

O'Leary, T. (1985) 'Observations on corporate financial reporting in the name of politics', *Accounting, Organizations and Society*, **10** (1), pp. 87–102.

Patten, D. M. (1991) 'Exposure, legitimacy and social disclosure', *Journal of Accounting and Public Policy*, **10**, pp. 297–308.

Patten, D. M. (1992) 'Intra-industry environmental disclosures in response to the Alaskan oil spill: A note on legitimacy theory', *Accounting, Organizations and Society*, **15** (5), pp. 471–5.

Powell, W. W. & DiMaggio, P. J. (eds) (1991) *The New Institutionalism in Organizational Analysis*, Chicago, Illinois: University of Chicago Press.

Puxty, A. (1991) 'Social accountability and universal pragmatics', *Advances in Public Interest Accounting*, **4**, pp. 35–46.

Ramanathan, K. V. (1976) 'Toward a theory of corporate social accounting', *The Accounting Review*, **21** (3), pp. 516–28.

Roberts, R. (1992) 'Determinants of corporate social responsibility disclosure: An application of stakeholder theory', *Accounting, Organizations and Society*, **17** (6), pp. 595–612.

Rollins, T. P. & Bremser, W. G. (1997) 'The SEC's enforcement actions against auditors: An auditor reputation and institutional theory perspective', *Critical Perspectives on Accounting*, **8** (3), pp. 191–206.

Ronen, J. (1979) 'The dual role of accounting: A financial economic perspective', in Bicksler, J. L. (ed.) *Handbook of Financial Economics*, North Holland.

Rowley, T. (1998) 'A normative justification for

stakeholder theory', *Business and Society*, **37** (1), pp. 105–07.

Scott, W. R. (1995) *Institutions and Organisations*, Thousand Oaks, CA: Sage Publications Inc.

Shocker, A. D. & Sethi, S. P. (1974) 'An approach to incorporating social preferences in developing corporate action strategies', in Sethi, S. P. (ed.) *The Unstable Ground: Corporate Social Policy in a Dynamic Society*, California: Melville, pp. 67–80.

Stoney, C. & Winstanley, D. (2001) 'Stakeholding: Confusion or utopia: Mapping the conceptual terrain', *Journal of Management Studies*, **38** (5), pp. 603–66.

Suchman, M. C. (1995) 'Managing legitimacy: Strategic and institutional approaches', *Academy of Management Review*, **20** (3), pp. 571–610.

Swift, T. (2001) 'Trust, reputation and corporate accountability to stakeholders', *Business Ethics: A European Review*, **10** (1), pp. 16–26.

Tinker, A. & Neimark, M. (1987) 'The role of annual reports in gender and class contradictions at General Motors: 1917–1976', *Accounting, Organizations and Society*, **12** (1), pp. 71–88.

Ullman, A. (1985) 'Data in search of a theory: A critical examination of the relationships among social performance, social disclosure, and economic performance of US firms', *Academy of Management review*, **10** (3), pp. 540–57.

Unerman, J. & Bennett, M. (2004) 'Increased stakeholder dialogue and the internet: towards greater corporate accountability or reinforcing capitalist hegemony?' *Accounting, Organizations and Society*, **29** (7), pp. 685–707.

Wallace, G. (1995) 'Balancing conflicting stakeholder requirements', *Journal for Quality and Participation*, **18** (2), pp. 84–98.

Watts, R. L. & Zimmerman, J. L. (1986) *Positive Accounting Theory*, Englewood Cliffs, New Jersey: Prentice-Hall Inc.

White, T. (1973) *The Making of the President 1972*, New York: Bantam Press.

Wicks, A. (1996) 'Overcoming the separation thesis: The need for a reconsideration of business and business research', *Business and Society*, **35** (1), pp. 89–118.

Wilmshurst, T. & Frost, G. (2000) 'Corporate environmental reporting: A test of legitimacy theory', *Accounting, Auditing & Accountability Journal*, **13** (1), pp. 10–26.

Zucker, H. G. (1978) 'The variable nature of news media influence', in Rubin, B. D. (ed.) *Communication Yearbook No. 2*, New Jersey, pp. 225–45.

Zucker, L. G. (1977) 'The role of institutionalization in cultural persistence', *American Sociological Review*, **42**, pp. 726–43.

Zucker, L. G. (1987) 'Institutional theories of organizations', *Annual Review of Sociology*, **13**, pp. 443–64.

CHAPTER 9

Extended systems of accounting: The incorporation of social and environmental factors within external reporting

Learning Objectives

Upon completing this chapter readers should:

- be aware of various perspectives on the responsibilities of business;
- be able to provide an explanation of the relationship between organizational responsibility and organizational accountability;
- be aware of various theoretical perspectives that can explain why organizations might voluntarily elect to provide publicly available information about their social and environmental performance;
- be aware of the theoretical underpinnings of some recent initiatives in social and environmental accounting;
- be able to explain the concept of *sustainable development* and be able to explain how organizations are reporting their progress towards the goal of sustainable development;
- be able to identify some of the limitations of traditional financial accounting in enabling users of reports to assess a reporting entity's social and environmental performance.

Opening issues

(a) Many companies throughout the world publish reports that discuss their economic, environmental and social performance. There are also numerous instances of companies publicly stating their commitment to sustainable development. For example, the 'Our approach to reporting' section of the oil multinational BP plc's Sustainability Report 2004 commenced with the following statement (p. 52):

> In the past 10 years, there has been a marked growth in the publication of corporate non-financial performance reports. This has been, in part, a response to calls for corporations to be more transparent in explaining the principles and management processes they apply to non-financial performance in their businesses.
>
> BP began publicly reporting its non-financial performance in 1991, when we produced our first group Health, Safety and Environment Report. In 1997, we produced our first global Community Report and the following year we combined these reports into an Environmental and Social Review. In 2004, we published our first integrated Sustainability Report, the third stage in the evolution of our reporting.

Moves towards sustainable development require organizations to explicitly consider various facets of their economic, social and environmental performance. But why would companies embrace *sustainability* as a corporate goal rather than simply aiming for increased and continued profitability? Furthermore, if an entity embraces *triple bottom line reporting* (reporting which provides information about economic, social and environmental performance) what does this imply about the perceived accountability of business?

(b) Many professional accounting bodies throughout the world are actively sponsoring research that looks at various social and environmental reporting issues. For example, in 2004 the Institute of Chartered Accountants in England and Wales produced a report entitled *Sustainability: the role of accountants* (ICAEW, 2004). Are social and environmental reporting issues really within the domain of professional accounting bodies? If not, who should be responsible for formulating social and environmental reporting guidelines?

(c) Consider your own opinions: what sort of social and environmental information do you think organizations should disclose, and to whom should they make the disclosures (who are the stakeholders)? Do you think your views about organizations' accountabilities would be the same as those of your fellow students? Just how subjective do you consider such assessments to be?

Introduction

The first seven chapters of this book focused on issues related to the role of externally published accounting information in providing information about the economic/financial performance of an entity. As we would appreciate from studying financial accounting, in most countries financial accounting is heavily regulated according to corporations laws and accounting standards. On the other hand there is a relative absence of requirements relating to the public disclosure of information about the social and environmental performance of an entity. Nevertheless, for a number of years many organizations throughout the world have been voluntarily providing public disclosures about the social and environmental impact of their operations.

In Chapter 8 we examined some issues related to accountability for these broader (non-financial) aspects of an organization's activities, by exploring theories which explain voluntary (unregulated) reporting practices. In this chapter we will develop our theoretical understanding of these issues by examining aspects of the rapidly growing body of research which investigates the social and environmental reporting practices that are being adopted by an increasingly large number of organizations.

These social and environmental reporting practices are often referred to as sustainability reporting, with the latter sometimes covering aspects of (the more traditional) financial/economic sustainability in addition to social and environmental sustainability. We will use the terms *sustainability reporting* and *social and environmental reporting* interchangeably in this chapter to mean the provision, to a range of stakeholders, of information about the performance of an entity with regard to its interaction with its physical and social environment, inclusive of information about an entity's support of employees, local and overseas communities, safety record, and use of natural resources.

Somewhat surprisingly, many students of accounting complete their accounting qualifications without ever considering issues associated with the *accountability of business*. But the practice of accounting which, at a fairly simplistic level, can be defined as the provision of information about the performance of an entity to a particular group of report readers, cannot be divorced from a consideration of the extent of an entity's responsibility and accountability. This linkage should always be considered. If we accept that an entity has a responsibility and accountability for its social and environmental performance, then as accountants we will accept a duty to provide an account of an organization's social and environmental performance. If we don't accept this, then we won't provide such an account.

Because this area of reporting is relatively new and continually evolving, it is a very exciting area for accountants to be involved in. We are starting to see new 'breeds' of accountants – *environmental accountants* and *social accountants* – who work alongside 'traditional' financial accountants.

Stages of sustainability reporting

There are various stages involved in the production of a social and environmental, or sustainability, report (see, for example, O'Dwyer, 2005, pp. 282–3). These stages should be undertaken sequentially, as the decisions to be taken at each stage (other than the first stage) depend upon the decisions taken in the previous stages. You will notice in the following discussion that the first three of these stages are similar, in broad terms, to the decisions required in the initial stages of financial accounting conceptual framework projects, which we examined in Chapter 6.

In sustainability reporting, the first stage is for an organization to decide upon its broad objectives for undertaking social and environmental reporting – in other words, the reasons **why** it wishes to produce a sustainability report. These are likely to be similar to its broad reasons for developing social and environmental responsibility policies and practices, with these policies and practices usually referred to as *corporate social responsibility* (or *CSR*). The broad objectives driving any particular organization to undertake CSR and sustainability reporting can range from an ethically motivated desire to ensure that the organization benefits, or does not negatively impact upon, society and the natural environment, through to an economically focused motive to use social and environmental reporting and CSR to protect or enhance financial shareholder value. We discussed aspects of this range of motives in Chapter 8, when we explored the ethical/moral (or normative) and the managerial branches of stakeholder theory. In this chapter we will add to these perspectives by introducing additional research studies that address the broad objectives (or motives) which seek to explain *why* organizations engage in social and environmental reporting.

Once an organization has determined why it wishes to publish social and environmental reports (or reports containing social and environmental information in addition to more traditional financial/economic information), the next (second) broad stage of the reporting process is to identify the stakeholders whose information needs the report should address – in other words, at **whom** the social and environmental reporting will be directed. Referring back to our discussion in Chapter 8 of the ethical/moral and the managerial branches of stakeholder theory, it should be clear that if a corporation's social and environmental reporting is motivated exclusively by managerial reasoning, then the stakeholders to whom that corporation's social and environmental reporting is aimed will be narrowly defined as those stakeholders who hold and exercise the greatest economic power over the corporation. Conversely, social and environmental reporting motivated by ethical/moral reasoning will seek to address the information needs of a broader range of stakeholders.

Having identified the stakeholders whose information needs their social and environmental reporting is intended to address, the third broad stage in the sustainability reporting process is for an organization to ascertain the information needs of these stakeholders – in other words, **what** issues the social and environmental reporting should address.[1] Identifying what issues an entity is held responsible and accountable for by its stakeholders involves dialogue between the organization and its identified target stakeholders. Several research studies have addressed aspects of this process of communication with stakeholders.

Once an organization has identified the objectives of the reporting process (*why* report); the stakeholders to be addressed by the reporting process (*who* is the report intended for); and the information requirements of these stakeholders (*for what* issues the entity is held responsible and accountable by its stakeholders – or *what* issues the report should cover), the final stage in the social and environmental reporting process is the production of a report (or more than one form of report) which addresses these issues (or stakeholders' information needs). This is a very broad stage which involves many more detailed stages regarding **how** the report(s) should be compiled. In this stage several elements of the social and environmental reporting process diverge considerably from the financial reporting processes embodied in financial accounting conceptual frameworks, although some issues (such as reliability of information) are important in both.

In this chapter we will structure our examination of sustainability reporting in accordance with the '*why* – *who* – *for what* – *how*' stages of social and environmental reporting explained above. We will begin with a detailed exploration of motives (or objectives, or the *why* question) for organizations in general, and business corporations specifically, to engage in CSR and sustainability reporting. We will then briefly discuss the second (*who*, or *to whom*) stage by presenting arguments that the range of stakeholders to be addressed by any organization's social and environmental reporting practices will flow directly from the philosophical reasons underlying why it has engaged in social and environmental reporting.

The subsequent section will then address the third (*for what*) stage by firstly considering research studies which have demonstrated that there is actually a demand from stakeholders for information on social or environmental issues (in other words, that the answer to the *for what* question is not simply '*responsible and accountable for nothing at all*'). Having established that stakeholders do demand and use some level of social and environmental information, this section will then examine theoretical perspectives on processes of stakeholder dialogue which can be used to identify the issues for which any particular entity's stakeholders hold it responsible and accountable, and therefore what issues should be addressed in its social and environmental reporting.

This section will then be followed by a section discussing research studies that have investigated a variety of issues and processes involved in the *how* stage – the production of social and environmental reports. Included in this discussion will be: an analysis of the limitations of conventional financial reporting processes and practices in capturing the social and environmental impacts of organizations (to demonstrate that fulfilling stakeholders' social and environmental information needs is likely to require processes and practices which are different to those of financial reporting); the proposition and limitations of *triple bottom line reporting* in providing suitable social and environmental reporting processes and practices; some of the requirements of recently developed social and environmental reporting guidelines; and issues of social and environmental audit. However, as this is an accounting theory book rather than a technical accounting practice text, we will restrict our discussion of these social and environmental reporting processes and practices to issues closely related to the development of theoretical perspectives on social and environmental reporting.

But before moving on to discuss the stages of social and environmental reporting, it will be helpful to provide some context to this discussion by briefly outlining the history of the development of social and environmental reporting.

Historical development of social and environmental reporting practices

We stated in the first paragraph of the introduction that 'for a number of years many organizations throughout the world have been voluntarily providing public disclosures about the social and environmental impact of their operations'. These practices have become widespread among companies in many countries since the early 1990s, when a number of large companies made considerable advances in reporting aspects of their environmental impact. Subsequently, from about the mid-1990s, reporting about aspects of the social impact of organizations' operations became an increasingly popular practice (ICAEW, 2004). Development of these practices in the early and mid-1990s tended to take the form of disclosures within the annual report (accompanying the annual financial accounts) about the environmental (and subsequently social) policies, practices and/or impact of the reporting organization.

As these reporting practices became more widespread, and social and environmental disclosures made by some organizations became extensive, some of the 'leading edge' reporting organizations began separating their detailed social and environmental disclosures from the annual report and accounts – by publishing a separate social and environmental report (while still providing a summary of these disclosures in their annual reports). These separate, stand-alone, sustainability reports were produced by some corporations from the early 1990s (as indicated in the quote from BP's Sustainability Report 2004 in the 'Opening issues' section at the beginning of this chapter). However, they have only become more common since the late 1990s. Although they are still produced by only a relatively small number of companies worldwide, they have become standard practice among many large multinationals in several industrial sectors and countries.

Since the late 1990s, many of these corporations have also made increasing use of the Internet to disseminate information about aspects of their social and environmental policies and performance. The Internet has also been used by a number of organizations to engage in dialogue with a variety of stakeholders about these social and environmental issues.

Although, as we have outlined in the previous paragraphs, social and environmental reporting practices have only become widespread in many countries since the early to mid-1990s, this does not tell the whole story of the development of these practices. Some studies have found and analysed voluntary non-financial disclosures in a variety of different forms of corporate reports for periods commencing long before the 1990s' development of social and environmental reporting practices, and have demonstrated that forms of social and environmental reporting have existed for many decades.

For example, Guthrie and Parker (1989) examined social disclosures in the Australian company Broken Hill Proprietary for a 100-year period from 1885; Unerman (2000a, 2000b) found evidence of social disclosures in a variety of reports produced annually by the Anglo-Dutch oil company Shell dating back to 1897 – with these disclosures becoming more prevalent from the 1950s; Hogner (1982) found evidence of social reporting practices at US Steel dating back to the 1905; Tinker and Neimark (1987, 1988) and Neimark (1992) analysed social-type disclosures in the accounts of the US company General Motors from 1916; and Adams and Harte (1998) and Adams and McPhail (2004) analysed forms of social reporting in UK banks and retailers from 1935. There have also been several studies examining social and environmental disclosures in company reports from the 1960s and 1970s – such as Buhr (1998) and Campbell (2000). There was also a reasonable amount of practitioner attention paid in the 1970s to the information needs of a broad range of stakeholders, as evidenced by reports such as the UK's 'Corporate Report' (Accounting Standards Steering Committee, 1975), although this interest largely faded in the 1980s. Thus the development of social and environmental reporting from the early 1990s might, more accurately, be considered a renaissance of non-financial reporting practices rather than a completely new phenomenon.

Having established that social and environmental reporting is not a new phenomenon, we will now turn to the question of what motivates organizations to engage in social and environmental reporting or, in other words, questions of *why* do they engage in these practices?

Objectives of the social and environmental reporting process – the *why* stage

We have already considered various (often overlapping) theories that can be applied to explain why organizations might elect to voluntarily provide information about their organizational strategies, including their social and environmental performance.[2] For example:

- In Chapter 8 we considered legitimacy theory and the associated notion of a *social contract*. Adopting this perspective we could argue that an entity would undertake certain social activities (and provide an account thereof) if management perceived that the particular activities were expected by the communities in which it operates. Failure to undertake the expected activities may result in the entity no longer being considered legitimate (it is perceived as breaching its *social contract*) and this in turn will impact on the support it receives from the community, and hence its survival.[3] Success is contingent upon complying with the social contract.

♦ In Chapter 8 we also considered stakeholder theory. We learned that one version of stakeholder theory (the *managerial/positive* version and **not** the *ethical/ normative* version) predicts that management is more likely to focus on the expectations of powerful stakeholders. Powerful stakeholders are those who control resources that are both scarce and essential to achievement of the organization's (or its managers') objectives. For most businesses, these powerful stakeholders will be those who have the greatest potential to influence the firm's ability to generate maximum financial returns (or profits) – in other words, those stakeholders with the most economic power and influence over the firm. Under this *managerial* stakeholder perspective, management would be expected to take on those economic, social and environmental activities expected by the powerful stakeholders, and to provide an account of those activities to these stakeholders.

♦ In Chapter 8 we further considered the accountability model developed by Gray, Owen and Adams (1996). Under this model, organizations have many responsibilities (at a minimum, as required by law but expanded by society's expectations that have not also been codified within the law), and with every organizational responsibility comes a set of rights for stakeholders, including rights to information from the organization to demonstrate its accountability in relation to the stakeholders' expectations. Obviously, determining responsibilities is not a straightforward exercise – different people will have different perspectives of the responsibilities of business, and hence the accountability of business.

♦ We also considered institutional theory in Chapter 8. This perspective assumes that the managers of an organization will develop or adopt new practices (such as corporate social responsibility and/or social and environmental reporting) because of a variety of institutional pressures. For example, other organizations developing new practices in these areas and managers being concerned that, if they do not emulate these other organizations, they will risk disapproval from some of their economically powerful stakeholders.

♦ A final perspective we considered briefly in Chapter 8 was reputation risk management. This perspective refines some of the above perspectives that assume the main managerial motivation for voluntary reporting is maximization of profits. With reputation risk management it is assumed that the reputation of any organization has an economic value, and managers will use voluntary reporting practices (such as sustainability reporting) to seek to protect and enhance the value and income-generating potential of the organisation's reputation among its economically powerful stakeholders.

♦ In Chapter 7 we considered Positive Accounting Theory. This theory predicts that all people are driven by self-interest.[4] As such, this theory predicts that particular social and environmental activities, and their related disclosure, would only occur if they had positive wealth implications for the management involved.

A further perspective on the motivations for managers to engage in corporate social responsibility, and sustainability reporting, has been provided by Unerman and O'Dwyer (2004). This perspective draws on the social theorists Anthony Giddens (1990, 1991, 1994) and Ulrich Beck (1992, 1994, 1999, 2000) to propose that, in a world where perceptions of future negative outcomes from industrial activity and consumption of products are prevalent, managers use social and environmental reporting as part of a strategy of attempting to convince their economically powerful stakeholders that their products and activities carry low (or negligible) risks to society, or to individuals within society. Unerman and O'Dwyer propose that these risk communication strategies are designed to counter the negative predictions of future outcomes (arising from a business's current activities) which are promoted by many activists from outside the business world, and also by competing businesses.

These various theoretical perspectives on the broad reasons why organizations might engage in voluntary social and environmental reporting practices are not mutually exclusive. Furthermore, as emphasized throughout this book, the acceptance of particular theories is, at least in part, tied to one's own value system.

To move from a broad to a deeper understanding of the possible range of objectives businesses might have for producing sustainability reports requires an understanding of the nature of business responsibilities.

What are the responsibilities of business?

Moves by many companies throughout the world to implement reporting mechanisms that provide information about the social and environmental performance of their entities implies that the management of these organizations consider that they have an accountability not only for their economic performance, but also for their social and environmental performance. While this is a view held by many individuals, it is not necessarily a view that is accepted universally (however, as we will see shortly, some quotes from corporate annual reports show that a number of organizations are publicly embracing sustainable development as a core business goal). Many people still consider that the major goal (and to some people, the *only* goal) of business entities is to generate profits for the benefit of shareholders, with higher profits being preferable to lower profits. This goal is commonly referred to as *maximizing shareholder value.*

How does an individual entity determine its responsibilities? This is clearly based on the personal judgement of the management involved, and is relevant in deciding any organization's objectives for its social and environmental reporting practices – because the perceived *responsibility* of business and its *accountability* go hand in hand. Adopting a definition provided by Gray, Owen and Adams (1996, p. 38) we can define accountability as:

> The duty to provide an account (by no means necessarily a financial account) or reckoning of those actions for which one is held responsible.

As indicated in Chapter 8, according to Gray, Owen and Adams accountability involves two responsibilities or duties, these being:

1 the responsibility to undertake certain actions (or to refrain from taking actions); and

2 the responsibility to provide an account of those actions.

Any discussion of social and environmental reporting necessarily, therefore, needs to consider what the responsibilities of organizations are, or are perceived to be. Are businesses responsible to their direct owners (shareholders) alone, or do they owe a duty to the wider community in which they operate? Certainly, many organizations are making public statements to the effect that they consider that they do have responsibilities to parties other than just their shareholders. For example, the opening statement in the 2004 annual review of Unilever (the Anglo-Dutch multinational) included the following comment:

> ... To succeed also requires, we believe, the highest standards of corporate behaviour towards everyone we work with, the communities we touch, and the environment on which we have an impact.
>
> This is our road to sustainable, profitable growth, creating long-term value for our shareholders, our people, and our business partners.

As another issue, is the responsibility of business restricted to current generations, or should the implications for future generations be factored into current management decisions? Sustainable development has been defined as 'development that meets the needs of the present world without compromising the ability of future generations to meet their own needs' (World Commission on Environment and Development, 1987, commonly referred to as 'The Brundtland Report' – which is discussed in more depth later in this chapter). If sustainability is embraced then, as this definition indicates, our current production patterns should not be such that they compromise the ability of future generations to satisfy their own needs. Such a view is being publicly acknowledged throughout the world by many organizations. For example, consider the following statement by the British telecommunications multinational BT Group in its 2004 Social and Environmental Report (p. 25):

> The concept of sustainable development has increasingly come to represent a new kind of world – where economic growth delivers a more just and inclusive society, at the same

time as preserving the natural environment and the world's non-renewable resources for future generations.

Such quotes reflect the public positions being promoted by many organizations. Whether these public positions actually dominate decision making within the firm is another issue – we clearly cannot be sure. Exhibit 9.1 provides a perspective of the responsibilities of business. Read the exhibit and consider whether you are inclined to agree with the perspective.

Exhibit 9.1 A perspective of the social responsibility of business

Profit with a conscience: corporate social responsibility is not only essential, it pays off too

By Gareth Chadwick

Corporate social responsibility (CSR) is nothing if not a mouthful. But the jargon disguises a very simple idea: that rather than being narrowly focused on the pursuit of profit at the expense of all else, businesses should behave responsibly in the course of their profit-making, taking into account their wider role and impact on society.

It is not a new idea. From philanthropic Victorian industrialists such as the Lever brothers [whose company is now part of Unilever], the Cadbury brothers and Titus Salt, to the Co-operative movement and recent innovators such as The Body Shop or Ben & Jerry's ice cream, businesses have tried to be forces for good in the community, not just exploiters of manpower. Ben & Jerry's, for example, contracted the Greystone Bakery in Yonkers, New York, to bake its brownies, a firm that used its profits to house the homeless and train them as bakers.

But whether it is building links with community groups, treating staff fairly and ethically, implementing waste minimisation policies or sourcing environmentally friendly suppliers, modern CSR, or CR (corporate responsibility) as it is often shortened to, has moved far beyond philanthropy.

Today, the case is focused on the practical, tangible benefits of businesses behaving in a more responsible way. 'Businesses are much more aware of the broader impact of what they do. They increasingly realise that it is a false economy not to consider the social aspect, including environmental issues. If you do ignore it, it will eventually come back and bite you and there are likely to be financial consequences in that,' says Erik Bichard of the National Centre for Business and Sustainability.

Clearly, there is still a strong moral case for businesses to try to have a beneficial impact on society. But that has always been the situation and with one or two high profile exceptions, there has been very little to show for it.

Exhibit 9.1 (*continued*)

But the business case has become harder to ignore. One issue is recruitment. An undergraduate survey in 2003 conducted across the world's 20 largest economies found that three in five undergraduates would choose to work for a company that could demonstrate its ethical values and positive impact on society, while in the UK 80 per cent said they were more likely to stay in their jobs if their employer adopted a responsible approach to the work-life balance.

A second benefit is in terms of the new ideas and innovation that a close connection with the community can engender. Businesses don't operate in isolation from the rest of society and a stronger link between the two facilitates a better understanding of the market, of who the customers are and how best to service their needs.

The third element is reputation and branding. Over 85 per cent of consumers have a more positive image of companies that are seen to be pursuing more responsible business practices and over half of European consumers say they are prepared to pay more for environmentally responsible products.

It is a figure which is borne out by the rapid growth in the market for fair trade products. Sales of fair trade products grew by more than 50 per cent in the UK in 2004, with shoppers spending £140m on them.

CSR can also provide a competitive edge for smaller companies. As consumer choice increasingly takes ethical considerations into account, so larger organisations are exercising similar discretion when sourcing suppliers.

The CSR element can be a key differentiator. Businesses want to work with other businesses that reflect their own values and attitudes – and those of their customers. 'If as a business you are behaving in a way which doesn't accord with the way your customers think you should be behaving, it can withdraw your license to operate. Look at Andersen. It was tainted by the actions of its client Enron and disowned by the market. It never recovered,' says Bichard.

... Professor Jeremy Moon is director of the International Centre for Corporate Social Responsibility at Nottingham University Business School 'CSR has had its up and downs. It was big in the USA in the late 1960s and early 1970s. It emerged in the UK in the early 1980s in the wake of riots, mass unemployment and social alienation, particularly in urban areas.

'But CSR is getting more institutionalised now, which suggests it will endure. There are business associations devoted to it. CSR guidance and reporting systems are built into general policies on accountability and governance. It is even increasingly an investment consideration.

Exhibit 9.1 (*continued*)

'A key phrase in understanding its development is: "It is not what you do with your profits, it is how you make your profits", how you actually do business at a day-to-day level.

'British companies are among the leading international companies in CSR, whether it is signing up to relevant business associations, reporting their social responsibility or engaging in detailed stakeholder relations. Whatever the drivers may be, it is evidence that British companies take CSR seriously and feel it is important to demonstrate that, not just domestically, but internationally.'

... Caroline Waters is director of people and policy at BT. 'Being socially responsible means treating your own employees responsibly. It is about sustainability. It's about the future and nature of business.

'Any successful business is about its people. By being a responsible business you're building trust-based relationships. It's a whole new kind of employment contract. A psychological contract with the individual which gives you huge voluntary contributions from them and really makes for a different kind of organisation.

'It makes basic business sense. Society – and that includes customers – is becoming more demanding and you have to respond to that. More and more people tell us that they make consumer decisions on the basis of whether they think a company behaves responsibly, and that includes its policy towards its employees and the role it takes in society.

'For a company that has had "It's good to talk" as its strap line, what we've really found is it's better to listen. So we regularly engage with our people trying to understand what their needs are and how we can work in the broader society to help create that environment.'

The Independent, 21 March 2005

An alternative view is that some organizational actions which can be interpreted as having a beneficial social and/or environmental impact may not have been motivated by any social or environmental considerations. In other words, actions motivated purely by short-term economic considerations may, sometimes, result in a social and/or environmental outcome which is welcomed by many in society. Georgakopoulos and Thomson (2005) provide an example of this in the decision of some Scottish fish farms to institute organic farming practices. They state (p. 50) that:

> The shift to organic production was unproblematic and relatively inexpensive. It was not a reaction to protest movements nor was organic salmon regarded as a safer, healthy, product. The decision was not subjected to systematic accounting evaluations. The shift

to organic production was driven by the prospect of higher market prices and securing sales in a climate of declining market prices and volumes for 'unorganic' salmon.

Support for a narrow view of business responsibilities

Over time, many high profile people have provided their views about the responsibility of business. At one extreme are the views of the famous economist, Milton Friedman. In his widely cited book, *Capitalism and Freedom*, Friedman (1962) rejects the view that corporate managers have any *moral obligations* beyond maximizing their profits. In relation to the view that organizations have *moral responsibilities* he notes (p. 133) that such a view:

> ... shows a fundamental misconception of the character and nature of a free economy. In such an economy, there is one and only one social responsibility of business, to use its resources and engage in activities designed to increase its profits as long as it stays within the rules of the game, which is to say, engages in open and free competition, without deception or fraud. [5]

This is not to say that people who support Friedman's position believe that this is an immoral position. Rather, they tend to argue that if the actions of all individuals (and businesses) are motivated solely by a self-interested desire to maximize personal wealth, then this will benefit all in society because (through the resulting economic growth) the wealth generated by the successful will 'trickle down' to the less successful. In this way, they argue, the conditions of all in society will be improved if all people in society actively pursue their own self-interest, with this being a morally desirable outcome. Indeed, this 'trickle down' theory is commonly repeated as a key moral justification for the capitalist system. The main problem with this moral justification for a narrow and exclusive focus on maximizing shareholder wealth (or shareholder value) is that there is little, if any, evidence to show that it occurs. As Gray (2005, pp. 6–7) states:

> It is disturbing ... to discover that there is no direct evidence to support this precarious construction. The view relies, for its empirical support, on the generalised argument that, for example, we are all better off than we have ever been; that we are all getting better off all the time; and that this increase in well-being has coincided with the triumph of international capitalism. Such arguments are, at best, contestable. Whilst for many in the West this statement has a superficial veracity, it ignores the growing gap between rich and poor ...

A considerable amount of economic evidence shows that not only is there lack of support for the existence of a generalized 'trickle down' effect, but the reverse may have occurred. For example, Hutton (1996, p. 172) provides evidence that in the largely free-market economic conditions of the UK in the 1980s, the real (inflation adjusted) incomes of the wealthiest tenth of the population rose by over 50 per cent, while the poorest 15 per cent of the population experienced a real-terms fall in their incomes.

Despite an apparent lack of empirical support for this 'moral' position underlying a narrow focus on shareholder value, we could be excused for thinking that many individuals working within the contemporary financial press hold the same view as Friedman. The financial press continues to praise companies for increased profitability and to criticize companies who are subject to falling profitability. They often do this with little or no regard to any social costs or social benefits being generated by the operations of the particular entities – costs and benefits not directly incorporated within reported profit.

Another point, considered more fully in Chapter 12, is that 'profits' provide a measure of possible future returns (dividends) to one stakeholder group – shareholders. In commending organizations for high profits we are, perhaps, putting the interests of the investors (the owners) above the interests of other stakeholders. It is not uncommon to see a report in the financial press that a particular company generated a sound profit *despite* increased wage costs. In such a context there is an implication that returns to one stakeholder (employees) are somehow bad, but gains to other stakeholders (the owners of capital) are good. As Collison (2003, p. 7) states:

> Financial description of the factors of production in the business media, and even in textbooks, makes clear that profit is an output to be maximised while recompense to labour is a cost to be minimised. Furthermore, a high cost of capital may be described as an exogenous constraint on business, rather than as an indication of the size of resource flows to providers of capital. *Financial Times* contributors are fond of words like 'ominous' to describe real wage rises: such words are not used to describe profit increases.

As we will see in Chapter 12, some accounting researchers whom we refer to as *critical theorists* would consider that our whole system of accounting acts to support the interests of those with power (often proxied by financial wealth), and to undermine others (such as employees). Promoting performance indicators such as 'profits' will, it is argued, maintain the 'favoured' position of those in command of financial resources.

Consider Exhibit 9.2, which provides details of how an organization 'axed' jobs in an endeavour to cut 'costs'. In the same way as our traditional systems of financial accounting ignore social costs, such media articles ignore the social costs that arise as a result of 'axing' employees and thereby making them unemployed.

Support for a broader view of business responsibilities

Returning to the earlier view (Friedman, 1962) that the maximization of profits (or shareholder value) is management's major priority, it should be noted that there is (as you might expect) a contrary view embraced by many researchers working in the area of corporate social reporting. This is that organizations, public or private, *earn* their right to operate within the community. This right, which we considered in Chapter 8, is provided by the society in which they exist, and not solely by those parties with a direct financial interest (such as the shareholders who

---

Exhibit 9.2 Example of media attention directed towards accounting profits to the exclusion of the consideration of 'other' costs

Lloyds TSB to shed 465 jobs in the south-west and Wales

Jane Croft

Lloyds TSB is cutting 465 administrative jobs in Wales and south-west England to reduce costs.

The move will involve the closure of five small processing centres in Swansea, Cardiff, Plymouth, Stockton and Taunton. Work, which includes contacting customers in arrears, will be moved to larger Lloyds TSB centres in Glasgow, Manchester, Chelmsford and Andover.

This is the third wave of job cuts in the banking sector during the past week as banks seek to bolster profits by reducing UK cost bases.

... Although banks have reported record profits over the past two years they are now facing a much tougher market as consumers rein back on credit card and mortgage borrowing.

This means banks must fight harder to win new business and as a result are cutting costs – particularly in areas such as administration and processing – to help sustain current levels of profits.

... HSBC last year cut 3,500 UK jobs because it believed its UK cost base was too high. It believes costs in the UK have been rising almost as fast as income. Between 2001 and 2003 HSBC's UK income grew by 9.8 per cent but costs rose by 8.4 per cent.

David Fleming, national officer for the finance sector of Amicus, said job losses were also due to the fact that banks, including HSBC and Lloyds TSB, were offshoring work to cheaper locations such as India. 'I think this trend will continue and we don't see an immediate end to it.'

Staff in India are paid as little as one-tenth the salaries of UK employees.

Financial Times, 12 May 2005, p. 4.

---

directly benefit from increasing profits) or by government. That is, business organizations themselves are artificial entities that society chooses to create (Donaldson, 1982). Donaldson notes that if society chooses to create organizations, they can also choose either not to create them or to create different entities. The view held is that organizations do not have an inherent right to resources. As Mathews (1993, p. 26) states:

> Society (as a collection of individuals) provides corporations with their legal standing and attributes and the authority to own and use natural resources and to hire employees.

> Organisations draw on community resources and output both goods and services and waste products in the general environment. The organisation has no inherent rights to these benefits and, in order to allow their existence, society would expect the benefits to exceed the costs to society.

Consequently, the corporation receives its permission to operate from society, and is ultimately accountable to society for how it operates and what it does (Benston, 1982).

If society (and not just shareholders) considers that increasing profits is the over-riding duty of organizations, then this factor alone may be sufficient (as Friedman argues) to ensure the business's survival. However, if society has greater expect-ations (such as that the organization must provide goods or services that are safe; that it must not exploit its employees; that it must not exploit its physical environ-ment; and so on) then it is arguable whether an organization that is preoccupied with profitability alone could maintain an existence.

Supporting this reasoning, a report based on a survey of chief executives from the Global Fortune 500 (the world's largest companies by revenue), which was pub-lished by the Judge Institute of Management at the University of Cambridge (Brady, 2003, p. 5), showed that:

> Despite recent financial scandals (Enron, WorldCom etc), [chief executives] predict that in the near future social credibility will be as important as financial credibility, and environmental credibility will only be marginally less important.

The survey also found (p. 12) that chief executives:

> appear to believe that six key elements will contribute most towards the preservation of a positive corporate reputation. Conversely, any neglect of these key elements could result in the formation of a negative reputation. Notably, these six key elements include both environmental and social credibility (rated as being individually important).

Furthermore, a study by Ernst and Young (2002) which involved interviews conducted with senior executives at 147 of the Global 1000 companies found (p. 5) that:

> Companies are increasingly acknowledging that corporate ethical, environmental and social behaviour can have a material impact on business value. The great majority of companies (79 per cent) forecast the importance of this issue to rise over the next five years as companies across a range of industry sectors recognise its relevance to their business. Research has found that a company's reputation in respect to issues pertaining to CSR is a factor in purchasing decisions for 70 per cent of all consumers.

Some senior executives have gone further than this, and have released statements which indicate they do not consider that pursuit of profits alone is an acceptable strategy. As the chief executive officer of Dutch multinational logistics company TPG (owner of, among other companies, the courier company TNT) stated in his introduction to TPG's Corporate Sustainability Report 2004 (p. 2):

> ... For us, sustainability is our ongoing search for opportunities to actively do good things and then report on our progress.
>
> More than anything else, we want TPG to be a well-respected and trusted entity that demonstrates accountability not only to customers and shareholders, but also to our employees and the world at large. Over the last two years we have integrated our sustainability initiatives and approaches to ensure that our policies and practices effectively reflect our vision.

More common, however, and consistent with the above studies from the University of Cambridge (Brady, 2003) and Ernst and Young (2002), are senior executives who justify their reasons for engaging in corporate social responsibility initiatives by reference to the necessity of these initiatives for long-term (sustainable) profits. As O'Dwyer (2003) points out, these justifications are often explained in terms of *win–win* outcomes, where it is claimed that what is beneficial for society and the environment is also beneficial for shareholder financial returns. For example, the chief executive's foreword to British Airways' Social and Environmental Report 2003/04 includes the following statement (p. 1):

> ... we have recognised that our sustainability as a business depends not only on improving financial performance but also on continuing to manage responsibly. Without the loyalty and support of our customers and employees, and the trust of the communities in which we operate, we will not prosper and succeed over the longer term. Our social and environmental performance is critical to earning this loyalty, support and trust.

Similar sentiments are reflected in the chief executive's introduction to the pharmaceutical multinational GlaxoSmithKline's (GSK) 2004 Corporate Responsibility Report (p. 4):

> Responsible business practices are also the key to a good reputation. In 2004, the pharmaceutical industry and GSK continued to come under public scrutiny on how medicines are developed, tested and marketed. To meet this challenge we must act with integrity and be open about our approach to these important issues. We took an important step this year with the launch of our Clinical Trial Register, providing public access to our product information.

The group chief executive of BP also used similar reasoning in his introduction to BP's Sustainability Report 2004 (p. 1):

> The road to sustainability begins with our fundamental purpose as an organization – to provide better goods and services in the form of light, heat, power and mobility to increasing numbers of people and thereby to deliver shareholder value on a long-term basis.
>
> To succeed, we need to do this in a way that is profitable, consistent and sustainable.
>
> To deliver profitable performance, we provide high-quality products in an effective way – maximizing revenues and minimizing costs.

> To deliver consistent performance, we fund controlled investment that supports long-term growth, balancing this with returns to shareholders and the interests of all who are affected by our work.
>
> To deliver sustainable performance, we require a combination of factors. Our investments must be for the long term. We have to attract and retain the best people. We must work with others towards a sustainable environment. And we must build trust through relationships based on 'mutual advantage' – relationships that bring benefits to everyone concerned.
>
> Along with standards such as those set out in our new code of conduct, the consideration of mutual advantage keeps our ambition within legitimate bounds and marks out the path we take towards creating value.

These reasons for corporations engaging in corporate social responsibility programmes are based on a perspective of sustainability where a balance is sought between three areas of sustainability: economic, social and environmental sustainability. Understanding this approach towards sustainability will help us understand the reasons given by many businesses for their engagement with corporate social responsibility and sustainability reporting. To help develop this understanding, we will now explore this *three strand model* of sustainability in the context of the more general development of ideas towards sustainability.

Developing notions of sustainability

Since the 1970s there has been much discussion in various forums about the implications of continued economic development for the environment, and relatedly, for human-kind. Sustainable development is not something that will be easily achieved and many consider that, at least at this stage, it is nothing more than an ideal.

A significant step in placing *sustainability* on the agenda of governments and businesses worldwide was a report initiated by the General Assembly of the United Nations. The report entitled *Our Common Future* was presented in 1987 by the World Commission of Environment and Development under the chairmanship of Gro Harlem Brundtland, the then Norwegian Prime Minister. This important document subsequently became known as The Brundtland Report. The brief of the report was to produce a global agenda for change in order to combat or alleviate the ongoing pressures on the global environment – pressures considered as being clearly unsustainable. It was generally accepted that business organizations must change the way they do business and they must learn to question traditionally held business goals and principles (perhaps with encouragement from governments). As previously stated, The Brundtland Report defined sustainable development as:

> ... development that meets the needs of the present world without compromising the ability of future generations to meet their own needs.

The Brundtland Report clearly identified that equity issues, and particularly issues associated with inter-generational equity, are central to the sustainability agenda.

That is, it is argued that globally we must ensure that our generation's consumption patterns do not negatively impact on future generations' quality of life. Specifically, we should be in a position to say that the planet that we leave our children is in as good a shape as the planet we inherited (and preferably in better shape). The move towards sustainability implies that something other than short-term self-interest should drive decision making (a normative position). It implies that wealth creation for current generations should not be held as *the* all-consuming pursuit, and that consumption and personal wealth creation by us (now), while perhaps being considered as economically 'rational' (using the definition often applied in the economics literature) is not necessarily rational from a global and inter-generational perspective.

There is evidence from a number of sources that, for many years, the ecological impact of human (including business) activities has exceeded the earth's capacity to absorb these impacts (see, for example, Venetoulis *et al.*, 2004). This evidence demonstrates that our current levels of consumption (and other activities) are achieved at the expense of a degraded biosphere in which our children, grand-children and great-grandchildren will have to live. If we continue to 'consume' the world's environmental resources at this level, a time is likely to come where the biosphere will have been degraded to the extent that it can no longer support human life in anywhere near the numbers currently living – clearly an unsustain-able position for nature, society and business profitability. As indicated in Exhibit 9.3, this view has now become the dominant view among the worldwide scientific community.

Exhibit 9.3 Sustainability views within the global scientific community

G8 scientists tell Bush: Act now 'or else ...'. Unprecedented warning as global warming worsens

Steve Connor, Science Editor

An unprecedented joint statement issued by the leading scientific academies of the world has called on the G8 governments to take urgent action to avert a global catastrophe caused by climate change.

The national academies of science for all the G8 countries, along with those of Brazil, India and China, have warned that governments must no longer procrastinate on what is widely seen as the greatest danger facing humanity. The statement, which has taken months to finalise, is all the more important as it is signed by Bruce Alberts, president of the US National Academy of Sciences, which has warned George Bush of the dangers of ignoring the threat posed by global warming. It was released on the day Tony Blair met Mr Bush in Washington for talks ahead of next month's G8 summit in Scotland.

Exhibit 9.3 (*continued*)

However, at a press conference last night for the two leaders, little progress appeared to have been made on persuading the US President to soften his opposition to the Kyoto treaty on limiting greenhouse gas emissions. When asked about climate change Mr Bush appeared to dodge a question about whether he accepted the problem was man-made. The Prime Minister also conceded the Americans were coming at the problem from a different direction, 'the need to secure energy supplies.'

Lord May of Oxford, the president of the Royal Society, Britain's national academy of sciences, lambasted President Bush yesterday for ignoring his own scientists by withdrawing from the Kyoto treaty.

'The current US policy on climate change is misguided. The Bush administration has consistently refused to accept advice from the US National Academy of Sciences ... Getting the US on board is critical because of the sheer amount of greenhouse gas emissions they are responsible for,' he said.

Between 1990 and 2002, the carbon dioxide emissions of the US increased by 13 per cent, which on their own were greater than the combined cut in emissions that will be achieved if all Kyoto countries hit their targets, he said.

'President Bush has an opportunity at Gleneagles to signal that his administration will no longer ignore the scientific evidence and act to cut emissions,' Lord May said. 'The G8 summit is an unprecedented moment in human history. Our leaders face a stark choice: "act now to tackle climate change or let future generations face the price of their inaction".

'Never before have we faced such a global threat. And if we do not begin effective action now it will be much harder to stop the runaway train as it continues to gather momentum,' he added.

The joint statement by the national science academies of the 11 countries does not mention Kyoto but it does refer repeatedly to the United Nations Framework on Climate Change that spawned the 1995 protocol to limit future greenhouse gas emissions, which the US has signed up to.

Climate change is real, global warming is occurring and there is strong evidence that man-made greenhouse gases are implicated in a potentially catastrophic increase in global temperatures, the statement says. 'It is likely that most of the warming in recent decades can be attributed to human activities. This warming has already led to changes in the Earth's climate.'

Human activities are causing levels of carbon dioxide in the atmosphere to rise to a point not reached for at least 420,000 years. Meanwhile average global temperatures rose by 0.6C in the 20th century and are projected to increase by between 1.4C and 5.8C by 2100.

Exhibit 9.3 (*continued*)

'The scientific understanding of climate change is now sufficiently clear to justify nations taking prompt action. It is vital that all nations identify cost-effective steps that they can take now to contribute to substantial and long-term reduction in net global greenhouse gas emissions,' the statement says.

In a veiled reference to President Bush's reluctance to accept climate change by claiming that the science is unclear, the academies emphasise that action is needed now to reduce the build-up of greenhouse gases.

'A lack of full scientific certainty about some aspects of climate change is not a reason for delaying an immediate response that will, at a reasonable cost, prevent dangerous anthropogenic [man-made] interference with the climate system,' the statement says. 'We urge all nations ... to take prompt action to reduce the causes of climate change, adapt to its impacts and ensure that the issue is included in all relevant national and international strategies.'

The national academies warn that even if greenhouse gas emissions can be stabilised at existing levels, the climate would continue to change as it slowly responds to the extra carbon dioxide added to the atmosphere. 'Further changes in climate are therefore unavoidable. Nations must prepare for them,' the statement says.

The Independent, 8 June 2005

Also implicit in the above definition of sustainability is a requirement that intra-generational equity issues be addressed – that is, the needs of all 'of the present world' inhabitants need to be met, which requires strategies to alleviate the poverty and starvation that currently besets the peoples of various countries. While from a moral perspective efforts should clearly be undertaken with a view to eradicating poverty and starvation (again, this is a normative assertion), from a broader perspective, communities cannot be expected to focus on local or global environmental issues (necessary for sustainability) if they are in desperate need of money (for example, if they are starving, can they really be expected to keep their forests intact when such forests provide a means of 'free' heating and income?). Decisions by particular impoverished nations, such as to remove significant tracts of rain-forest, can have significant global implications. Any vision of sustainability clearly needs to address poverty.

A further significant event that followed The Brundtland Report was the 1992 Earth Summit in Rio de Janeiro which was attended by government representatives from around the world as well as numerous social and environmental experts and non-government organizations. The Earth Summit again placed the issue of sustainable development at the forefront of international politics and business. Globally, the Summit attracted considerable media attention. An important outcome of the Earth Summit was Agenda 21, which was deemed to be an action plan for the 21st century and which placed sustainability as the core consideration for ongoing national and global development.

In the same year as the Earth Summit (1992) the European Union (EU) released a document entitled 'Towards sustainability' as part of its *Fifth Action Programme*. One of the suggestions of the programme was for the accounting profession to take a role in implementing costing systems that internalize many environmental costs. As we discuss later in this chapter, traditional financial accounting typically ignores social and environmental costs and benefits. Specifically the EU called for a 'redefinition of accounting concepts, rules, conventions and methodology so as to ensure that the consumption and use of environmental resources are accounted for as part of the full cost of production and reflected in market prices' (European Commission, 1992, Vol. II, Section 7.4, p. 67). The rationale for the EU's proposal was that if the prices reflected the 'full costs' of production, including environmental costs, then such costs would flow through the various production and consumption cycles, and as a result of the higher costs there would be an inclination towards more sustainable consumption patterns.[6]

In 2002 a follow up to the Rio de Janeiro Earth Summit was held in Johannesburg. One of the outcomes of this 2002 Earth Summit was the launch of a revised set of guidelines for the process of reporting the social and environmental impact of an organization's operations. These guidelines are known as the Sustainability Reporting Guidelines and were developed by a broad range of organizations under the auspices of the Global Reporting Initiative (GRI) between 1997 and their re-launch in 2002 (an initial version of these guidelines had been published in the year 2000, and a further revised version is due for publication in 2006). We will discuss these guidelines in more depth later in this chapter.

Business adoption of sustainable development ideas

Since the important early developments of notions of sustainability in the late 1980s/early 1990s, many governments, industry and professional associations, and non-government organizations have released various documents addressing the need for shifts towards sustainable development. Indeed, sustainability appears to have become a central part of the language of government and business worldwide, and the definition provided within The Brundtland Report has attracted widespread acceptance. As an example, consider the following comments by the chief executive officer of Nokia in its 2004 Environmental Report (p. 4):

> With leadership comes great responsibility. As the leading company in our industry, Nokia also strives to be a leader in environmental performance. Future generations are relying on us to protect and preserve the natural environment. We believe that everyone must do their part.

> Nokia promotes sustainable development by managing its operations in a responsible way. We take environmental aspects into account throughout the life cycles of all our products. Energy efficiency continues to be one of the key focus areas in continuously improving environmental performance. We have consistently reduced the energy intensity of our products while the total use of materials in mobile devices has been reduced to a fraction of what it was a few years ago.

The Dutch electronics multinational Philips states in its Sustainability Report 2004 (p. 1) that:

> We firmly believe that socially and environmentally responsible behavior contributes to sustained profitable growth and value creation. That's why we are embedding sustainability thinking and acting throughout the organization.
>
> Sustainability is built into our heritage, our values and our commitment to improve the quality of people's lives. We have long been integrating economic prosperity, environmental quality and social equity – balancing these sometimes-competing demands.

A more detailed explanation about a particular organization's commitment to sustainability is given in the following extract from the UK Co-operative Financial Services Group's Sustainability Report 2003 (p. 10):

> Co-operative Financial Services (CFS) recognises the need to develop its business in a sustainable manner – i.e. business development that meets the needs of the present without compromising the ability of future generations to meet their own needs.
>
> ... alongside 'profitability', which is absolutely vital to CFS' continued existence, 'balance' [between the needs of different stakeholders] is a key component of our pursuit of sustainability.
>
> We recognise that there are physical limits to the resources of the Earth (both in terms of generating materials and absorbing wastes), and that any business activity that exceeds these limits is, by definition, unsustainable in the long-term and will need to be reconstituted. Nature cannot withstand a progressive build-up of waste derived from the Earth's crust, nor can it withstand a progressive build-up of society's waste, particularly substances that it cannot degrade into harmless materials. In addition, the productive area of nature should not be diminished in terms of quality (diversity) or quantity (volume) and must be enabled to grow. These we recognise as the minimum conditions for ecological sustainability.

Adopting perspectives provided by several of the theories we explored in Chapter 8, we can further argue that if sustainability becomes part of the expectations held by society, then it must become a business goal. As the concept of sustainable development continues to become part of various communities' expectations, communities will expect to be provided with information about how organizations, governments and other entities have performed against the central requirements of sustainability.

Business sustainability and the 'triple bottom line'

As noted earlier, many organizations conceive of sustainability as comprising three strands: economic, social and environmental. This model is often referred to as the *triple bottom line* approach to sustainability, a term developed by John Elkington (1997). The financial performance, or profit, of a business is often colloquially referred to as the business's *bottom line*, so a focus solely on economic performance can be considered as a focus on the single bottom line (figure) of financial profitability. The *triple bottom line* broadens this performance evaluation of an organization from a narrow focus on the single bottom line of financial profit to an evaluation of the three 'bottom lines' of economic, social and environmental performance.

These three aspects of sustainability tend to converge over longer time horizons. In the short term, it is possible to generate profits while negatively impacting upon society and the environment. In the medium term, given that businesses operate within society, negative impacts on society caused by some business activities might lead to a breakdown in social functions which are necessary to continued business profitability. The argument here is that most businesses rely on the effective functioning of many social systems – such as physical infrastructure (transport systems, utilities and so on), well-ordered markets, and a respect for property rights (law and order). If any of these systems breaks down then future profitability will be threatened.

Although some businesses might evolve to address, and thereby profit from, breakdowns in some social systems, these are unlikely to address all the problems arising for many businesses from large-scale social breakdown and will add financial costs to many businesses who have to buy additional services from the market. For example, *if* a narrow focus on profit maximization by many businesses contributed to increased unemployment and poverty in many sections of society, and then *if* this led to a breakdown in law and order, then while some businesses could profit from supplying additional private security services to those with wealth who were threatened by the breakdown in law and order, many other businesses could suffer a negative economic outcome as their activities/markets might be negatively impacted through the breakdown in law and order, and they might have to pay for additional private security services.

We stress that this scenario is just one of many possible outcomes from a business focus on profit maximization, and many people would argue that other scenarios are more likely to occur. Nevertheless, it is a possible scenario, and highlights one (of many) possible ways in which a narrow focus on short-term profit maximization could contribute to a breakdown in social systems.[7] As this scenario demonstrates, in the medium term if a narrow focus on profit maximization leads to a breakdown in social systems, then this might be neither socially nor financially/economically sustainable.

In the longer term the argument for equating economic, social and environmental sustainability is very straightforward. This argument is that the economy (including business activities) and all social systems operate within the natural environment. As outlined earlier in this chapter, if business (and other human) activities contribute to the destruction of the biosphere, then there will be no humans left to run businesses, buy the products of businesses or operate social systems. In an extreme scenario, destruction of the environment leads to destruction of the human race, following which there would clearly be no profits or social systems. Thus, in the longer term, environmental sustainability is necessary for both social and economic sustainability, so attention to 'bottom line' performance (or minimizing impact) in respect of the environment is necessary to ensure a sustainable social and economic bottom line.

The implication of these arguments is similar to the implication of the intergenerational requirement of sustainability (which we discussed earlier) – it might be necessary to sacrifice some short-term economic profitability to ensure long-term sustainable economic profits within a sustainable social and ecological system.

Dillard, Brown and Marshall (2005, p. 81) explain that, in practice, an obstacle to this *triple bottom line* approach to sustainability is that 'social systems (i.e. humans and their intentionality) have come to dominate and exploit natural systems' – in particular economics- (profit-)based social systems are dominant. They argue that moves towards sustainability will therefore require an explicit reversal of this socially constructed dominance of the economic over the ecological.

Relating the concept of the *triple bottom line* more specifically to accounting, it has been argued by some (for example, Elkington, 1997) that as the more traditional financial accounting has focused on reporting economic performance, this role can or should expand to incorporate reporting on the other bottom lines of social and environmental (in addition to economic) performance. The notion of reporting against the three components (or 'bottom lines') of economic, environmental and social performance is thus clearly directly tied to the concept and goal of *sustainable development*. We will return to a more detailed discussion (and critique) of the concept of *triple bottom line reporting* in the 'how' section of this chapter.

In this section we have addressed the *why* stage of social and environmental reporting – which is the initial stage where companies decide upon their motivation for engaging in corporate social responsibility and sustainability reporting. Consistent with some of the insights we developed in Chapter 8, we have seen that these motivations can range from a desire to maximize financial returns for shareholders and/or managers by using social and environmental reporting as a tool to maintain and enhance the support of economically powerful stakeholders, through to a desire to discharge duties of accountability for the social and environmental impact the organization (potentially) has on a wide range of stakeholders. We explored notions of sustainability to explain that shareholder interests of profit maximization tend to converge with interests of social and environmental sustainability over longer time horizons. Thus, in the long term, companies aiming for sustainable financial profits need to ensure they (and other businesses) are also socially and environmentally sustainable. This can make it difficult in practice to discern the true motives for *why* a company's executives develop and implement corporate social responsibility programmes and policies, and engage in social and environmental reporting, where the reasons for sustainability are explained in terms both of a need to avoid negative impacts on society and the environment and as being necessary to ensure future profitability. For example, the introduction to the environment section of Tesco's Corporate Responsibility Report 2005 (p. 42) stated:

> We believe in sustainable growth – it is responsible, it is what our customers want and it makes sound business sense. If we take decisions that are unsustainable, we may harm the world we all live in. Similarly, if we fail to minimise our environmental impacts, we will be inefficient and increase our costs.

Having considered several perspectives regarding *why* organizations might be motivated to report on their social and environmental impacts, we will now turn to the second broad stage of the sustainability reporting process – identifying the stakeholders to whose information needs social and environmental reporting should be addressed.[8]

Identifying stakeholders – the *who* stage

The range of stakeholders whose needs and expectations are considered by an organization when determining its corporate social responsibility policies, and when compiling its social and environmental reports, will be directly related to its motives for adopting these policies and practices. For an organization whose managers are motivated exclusively by the maximization of shareholder financial value, and who therefore will only use social and environmental reporting to win or maintain the approval of economically powerful stakeholders, the stakeholders to be addressed by social and environmental reporting will usually only be these economically powerful stakeholders.

Identifying 'relevant' stakeholders in accordance with the managerial branch of stakeholder theory

As we discussed in Chapter 8, the precise groups of stakeholders who are able to exert the most economic power over an organization will vary from organization to organization, and may also vary within any one organization over time. An example of how the stakeholders with the most economic power can vary from one business organization to another business organization is provided by comparing a company selling a largely generic product (such as coffee or flour) in a competitive consumer market with a monopoly supplier of an essential product or service (such as a commercial corporation operating a national or regional electricity grid – the wires that transmit electricity from power stations to consumers). For the former type of company, consumers are likely to hold considerable economic power because they could easily switch to buying the products of competitors if the company did something of which they disapproved. Conversely, for the monopoly supplier of essential goods or services, consumers will have little direct economic power because, by definition, they will have no alternative sources of supply and are usually not able to stop consuming the essential product or service.

For example, there will not usually be more than one electricity grid in any location and while, in a privatized system such as the UK, consumers might have a choice regarding which electricity generator they purchase their power from, this electricity will be delivered to them using a single national or regional grid of electricity cables (which in England is owned and operated by a single company, and in Scotland is owned and operated by another commercial company). Thus, while UK consumers might have a reasonable degree of economic power over the commercial companies which generate electricity (because they can relatively easily switch to buying electricity from other generators), they will have little or no direct economic power over the commercial company operating the cables delivering electricity to their homes – because the same cables are used to deliver this power irrespective of the electricity generating company a consumer chooses to supply their electricity (in other words, all electricity generating stations and all consumers are attached to the same, single, grid of cables). In the case of a monopoly supplier (such as an operator of an electricity grid), the government regulator of the monopoly will usually have considerable economic power over the company, as the regulator will often have the ability to determine prices charged to consumers, required service levels and quality standards.

Thus, a managerial stakeholder perspective would predict that in the case of a monopoly supplier, accountability disclosures would be aimed at helping convince the regulator (probably in conjunction with considerable private communication between the monopoly and its regulator) that the monopoly has operated in accordance with the economic, social and environmental standards required by the regulator – and required by the politicians who appoint the regulator (it is through this political connection with the regulator that consumers could be considered to have some very indirect economic power over the regulated monopoly). So, from a managerial stakeholder perspective, the economically powerful stakeholders whose views and expectations will be taken into consideration in determining a corporation's social and environmental responsibilities, and the accountability duties allied to these responsibilities, will tend to vary from consumers (for companies selling generic products in competitive markets) to government regulators (for monopoly suppliers of essential products or services).

As an example of how the economically powerful stakeholders can vary over time for a single organization, we can consider changes in the macroeconomic environment within which companies must operate. For a company which requires a large number of semi-skilled employees and sells its products in reasonably competitive markets, consumers may have considerable economic power in times of economic recession but may lose some of this power in times of economic boom (when consumer demand grows faster than supply). Conversely, the semi-skilled workforce may become more economically powerful during an economic boom, if unemployment falls and a general shortage of semi-skilled workers arises. In this case, the economically powerful stakeholders whose views the company will seek to address in accordance with the managerial branch of stakeholder theory, may shift from the company's consumers to its employees.

A broader identification of stakeholders in accordance with the ethical branch of stakeholder theory

In contrast to this narrow focus on economically powerful stakeholders provided by the managerial branch of stakeholder theory, a much wider range of stakeholders will be considered if we follow the ethical branch of stakeholder theory. Organizations whose corporate social responsibility, and whose sustainability reporting, is motivated by broader ethical considerations of reducing the negative impact (or maximizing the positive impact) which the organization has on every person and entity affected by the organization's operations might consider as stakeholders to whom the organization was accountable: all humans from current and future generations upon whom their operations could have an impact (no matter how remote these people were from the organization); all animals living today and in the future upon whom the organization's operations could impact; and any other elements of nature potentially affected by the organization's operations.

This theoretical position, that ethically motivated organizations should take account of the views and needs of all stakeholders (present and future) upon whom their operations might potentially impact, represents a philosophical ideal rather than a practical and attainable aim. In practice, the operations of many organizations are likely to have some form of impact on many people, animals and other elements of nature, and to try to take account of all of these potential impacts, and to seek to communicate to all those potentially affected, would be an impossible task.

This impossibility arises partially because in our highly complex and interrelated world, many activities have the potential to lead to numerous unintended and unforeseeable consequences (Beck, 1992, 1999). Where these future consequences of current actions are unforeseeable, it is difficult to conceive of how an organization could take them into account when determining the stakeholders affected (now and in the future) by its current operations, and thereby the stakeholders to whom the organization is accountable today. This impossibility also partially arises because, when it comes to the communication element of accountability (which, after all, is what this chapter is about) it is not possible to effectively communicate today with many non-human elements of nature or with future generations.

Thus, even when an organization's corporate social responsibility and social and environmental reporting is motivated by ethical rather than managerial reasoning, the organization will always need to identify a subset from all of the stakeholders who might be affected by their operations. The social and environmental needs and expectations of this subset of stakeholders will then determine the social and environmental responsibilities and accountability of the organization, and the social and environmental reporting which addresses these accountability duties.

Identifying a 'priority' subset of stakeholders within the ethical branch of stakeholder theory

One way to identify this subset of stakeholders whose needs should determine the economic, social and environmental responsibilities and accountability of an organization is to recognize that some of the social and environmental impacts of any organizations' operations on some stakeholders will be larger than other impacts on other stakeholders. While the operations of any organization might have widespread social and environmental consequences, many of these (often indirect, unforeseen and unintended) consequences will have a relatively small impact on some stakeholders. But other impacts may have a significant impact on the lives of other stakeholders. For example, highly toxic pollution discharged by a factory may lead directly to the development of fatal diseases in many people living close to (or sometimes even far away from) the factory – and may adversely affect the health of these people irrespective of whether they work for the factory, have any direct economic power over the factory or derive any economic benefit from the operations of the factory.

Some theorists, such as Gray *et al.* (1997) and Unerman and Bennett (2004), argue that an ethical approach to identifying, from a large number of stakeholders, those stakeholders to whom an organization is responsible and accountable requires consideration of the views of those stakeholders upon whom an organization's operations have the most impact. These will not always be those stakeholders who are closest to the organization's operations in economic (or even in physical/ geographical) terms. This approach would require organizations to prioritize the views and interests of those stakeholders upon whose lives their operations were likely to have the largest impact.

The practical implications of this theoretical approach to stakeholder prioritiz-ation (in accordance with the ethical branch of stakeholder theory) is that organiz-ations whose corporate social responsibility, and social and environmental reporting, is motivated by a desire to minimize the negative social and environ-mental impact of its operations will prioritize stakeholders' needs according to the extent of the impacts which the organization's operations are likely to have on any stakeholder's life. In determining its policies and practices, the organization will then seek to minimize its negative impacts on as many of these stakeholders as possible – addressing the needs and expectations of those stakeholders upon whom its operations have a potentially larger impact in priority to the needs and expect-ations of stakeholders upon whom it is likely to have a lesser impact. However, O'Dwyer (2005) demonstrates how problematic this process of stakeholder prioritization can be in practice, as stakeholders who some would regard as highly dependant on the organization may, for reasons of expediency, be omitted from the prioritized subset of stakeholders defined and determined by the organization's managers.

Stakeholder identification in practice

As an example of how some organizations are defining their stakeholders in prac-tice, in the Sustainability Report 2003 of the Co-operative Financial Services (CFS) group in the UK (which includes the Co-operative Bank), the organization defines its main stakeholders rather broadly as shareholders, customers, staff, suppliers, society and the cooperative movement, and it explains how each of these groups is defined. It does not explicitly include the environment, stating that (p. 13):

> Unlike some organisations, CFS does not define 'The Environment' as a separate Partner. The relationship between business and the 'Natural World' is essentially non-negotiable (in contrast to the relationship with suppliers, staff, etc.). The activities of CFS and its Partners are ultimately governed by nature's limited capacity to generate resources and assimilate waste. For this reason, CFS assesses the degree to which value is delivered to each Partner in an ecologically sustainable (and socially responsible) manner.

Broader evidence regarding how organizations are defining, and prioritizing, their stakeholders is provided by Owen, Shaw and Cooper (2005). As part of a UK survey investigating managerial attitudes towards the provision of social and environ-mental information, they asked managers to rate the importance of a variety of different stakeholder groups as recipients of stand-alone sustainability reports, on a scale of 0 (not important) to 5 (very important). Shareholders were considered to be the most important audience for this information (mean importance of 3.95 out of 5) followed by: employees (3.83); environmental pressure groups (3.68); govern-mental regulators (3.58); local communities (3.48); customers (3.20); non-equity investors (2.80); and suppliers (2.65). This managerial ranking of important stakeholders can vary between different countries. For example, Adams (2002) shows that views regarding which stakeholders are the most important vary between a sample of UK and German managers.

In practice, whichever approach to stakeholder prioritization is taken by an organization – whether prioritizing stakeholders on the basis of those stakeholders most able to exert an influence on the organization's profits (or shareholder value), prioritizing stakeholders on the basis of those whose lives are most affected by the organization's activities, or a position somewhere on the continuum between these extreme positions – once the organization has identified the stakeholders whose social and environmental needs and expectations it will address, it then has to identify *what* are the information needs and expectations of these stakeholders. This takes us to the third stage of the '*why – who – for what – how*' process of social and environmental reporting.

Identifying stakeholder information needs and expectations – the *for what* stage

A useful starting point to begin addressing the question of '*for what social and environmental issues do stakeholders wish to hold organizations responsible and accountable?*' is to identify whether there is any demand among stakeholders for social and environmental information. If there is (or if there appears to be) no such demand, then the answer to the '*for what social and environmental issues do stakeholders hold organizations responsible and accountable?*' question could be '*stakeholders do not hold organizations responsible or accountable for any social or environmental issues*'. However, if there is a demand from stakeholders for social and environmental information, this can be taken to indicate that stakeholders hold organizations responsible and accountable at least for the issues upon which they demand such information.

This section of the chapter begins by discussing various studies which have examined whether, at a broad level, there appears to be demand from stakeholders for social and environmental reporting information provided by corporations. As these studies indicate that there is such a demand (because stakeholders appear to make use of social and environmental information), we can conclude that stakeholders do hold organizations responsible and accountable for some social and environmental issues. Having established this point, we then proceed to examine some theoretical perspectives regarding the mechanisms which individual organizations can use to identify the specific economic, social and environmental needs and expectations of their stakeholders, and thereby identify *what* types of information they should cover in their social and environmental reporting to meet the accountability demands of these stakeholders. As this is a book on accounting theory (rather than a textbook showing you how to practice accounting), we restrict our discussion in this section to theories regarding mechanisms which can be used by organizations to identify what issues their particular stakeholders will expect to be covered in a social and environmental report.

Stakeholder demands for, and reactions to, social and environmental information

Obviously, for any form of public reporting to be useful, there needs to be an external demand for, or a reaction to, the particular information being disclosed. As Deegan and Rankin (1997) point out, the ability to shape perceptions through annual report or social and environmental report disclosures is possible only if members of society actually use the reported information. Deegan and Rankin (1997) examined the issue of whether people actually use or rely upon the environmental performance information provided within annual reports, in other words whether the answer to the *accountable for what* question was, at least, *accountable for something*. They solicited, by way of a questionnaire survey, the views of shareholders; stockbrokers and research analysts; accounting academics; representatives of financial institutions; and a number of organizations performing a general review or oversight function regarding:

◆ the materiality of environmental issues to certain groups in society who use annual reports to gain information;

◆ whether environmental information is sought from annual reports; and

◆ how important environmental information is to the decision-making process compared to other social responsibility information and information about the organization's financial performance and position.

Deegan and Rankin (1997) found, at statistically significant levels, that shareholders and individuals within organizations with a review or oversight function – these included consumer associations, employee groups, industry associations and environmental groups – considered that environmental information was material to the particular decisions they undertook. In addition, shareholders, accounting academics and individuals from organizations with a review or oversight function were found to seek environmental information from the annual report to assist in making their various decisions. The annual report was perceived by the total group of respondents to be significantly more important (in the mid-1990s) than any other source of information concerning an organization's interaction with the environment. This study shows that various stakeholder groups within society *do* demand information about the social and environmental performance of organizations and thus, at a very broad level, there are issues for which stakeholders hold organizations responsible and accountable.

Also demonstrating that the answer to the *accountable for what* question is *accountable for something*, a number of more narrowly focused studies have addressed stock market reactions to the disclosure of social information. The underlying theory used in many of these studies is the *efficient-markets hypothesis*, which proposes that the information content of news announcements, if relevant to the marketplace, will be immediately and unbiasedly impounded within share prices. That is, if an item of information about an organization can be associated with a change in the share price of that organization, then it is assumed that the information is of importance to investors.

Ingram (1978) and Anderson and Frankle (1980) found that the market does react to social disclosure, with Ingram concluding the reaction to be a function of, among other things, the industry to which the organization belongs and the types of social disclosures being made.

Belkaoui (1976) and Jaggi and Freedman (1982) studied investors' reactions to pollution disclosures. Belkaoui observed a positive share-market reaction to firms that provided evidence of responsible pollution control procedures, compared to firms that could not demonstrate responsibility. He concluded that the results verified the existence of an 'ethical investor', that is an investor who responds to demonstrations of social concern and invests in corporations that are socially responsible.

Jaggi and Freedman (1982) studied the market impact of pollution disclosures made by firms operating within highly polluting industries. Consistent with Belkaoui's results, Jaggi and Freedman observed a positive share-market reaction to those firms that could demonstrate greater pollution controls.

The above studies examined the market's reaction to disclosures made by the organizations themselves. Shane and Spicer (1983) undertook a study which investigated the market's response to environmental performance information emanating from a source outside the firm, specifically that produced by the New York-based organization, the Council on Economic Priorities. They found that organizations identified as having low pollution-control performance rankings were more likely to have significant negative security returns on the day that the rankings were publicly released compared to organizations with higher pollution-control performance rankings. Shane and Spicer considered that the results were consistent with an assumption that the information released by the Council on Economic Priorities permitted investors to discriminate between organizations with different pollution-control performance records.

Similarly, Lorraine, Collison and Power (2004) examined share price reaction in the UK to 'publicity about fines for environmental pollution as well as commendations about good environmental achievements' (p. 7) over a $5\frac{1}{2}$ year period. They found that while there was little market reaction on the day fines or commendations were announced publicly, there was a significant impact on share prices within a week of these announcements. Furthermore, they found that:

> ... the share price response is mainly a function of the relative fine imposed on the firm; other explanatory variables such as environmental performance news or sector membership were unsuccessful in explaining variations in market responses. (p. 7)

Examining market reactions to negative environmental performance information from sources both inside and outside the firm, Freedman and Patten (2004) found that where corporations (in the US) published information in their annual reports about high levels of pollution emissions from their factories, the share price reaction was lower than for companies which were known to emit high levels of pollution but did not report this in their annual reports.

In further research, Blacconiere and Patten (1994) examined the market reaction to Union Carbide's chemical leak in India in 1984. Using a sample of 47 US firms, they observed a significant intra-industry market reaction to the event. However, firms with more extensive environmental disclosures in their annual reports before the disaster experienced a smaller negative reaction than those with less extensive disclosures.

From the evidence provided above, it would appear that investors *do* react to an organization's social responsibility disclosures, and therefore the broad answer to the *accountable for what* question is *accountable for some level of social responsibility practices and/or impacts.*

Furthermore, in recent years, banking and insurance institutions have become key users of social and environmental information, particularly about organizations' environmental performance. In some countries, banks will not provide funds to organizations unless information about their environmental policies and performance is provided. The reason for this, in part, would be that an organization that has demonstrated poor environmental performance is considered to be higher risk in terms of compliance with environmental laws and in terms of potential costs associated with rectifying environmental damage caused. Further, in some industries it is possible that collateral provided for loans (such as land) might be contaminated because of poor environmental management systems. Some analysts also evaluate the social and environmental performance of corporations as part of their investment analysis. For example, Solomon and Solomon (2005) demonstrate the growing importance of corporate environmental and social information for investment analysts.

Another increasing source of demand for corporate social and environmental information is the growing ethical investment market, and fund managers are also using their power to demand that corporations provide social and environmental performance information. According to Greene (2002):

> Funds managers are beginning to use their financial clout to impose environmental requirements on companies. Morley Fund Management, a major London-based asset

manager, recently announced it would begin requiring large UK companies to publish environment reports. Morley is the asset manager of CGNU plc, the UK's largest insurer and the world's sixth largest insurance group. It manages assets equivalent to 2.5 per cent of the UK stock market. With this kind of market influence, Morley's policy changes are sure to be felt by a significant number of companies.

Due to supply chain pressures, many organizations are also now demanding that suppliers provide them with details of their social and environmental performance prior to entering supply arrangements. Supply chain considerations have in the past negatively impacted a number of organizations, with corporations like Nike being prime examples.

In an international poll undertaken in 1999 by Environics (involving samples of 1,000 citizens in 23 countries) in collaboration with the Prince of Wales Business Leadership Forum in London and the Conference Board in New York, Environics undertook a corporate responsibility survey to determine global public opinion on the role of companies in society. Approximately 70 per cent of people expected corporations to be completely responsible for ensuring that their products and operations do not harm the environment. Surveys such as this show that the community generally is also starting to demand that corporations, as part of their 'community license to operate', produce environmental performance information.

Hence, whilst we have only referred to a very small proportion of the studies of demand for environmental performance information, it is very clear that there is a demand. For reasons discussed at the beginning of this section, this demand indicates that stakeholders do hold organizations responsible and accountable for some social and/or environmental issues. But identifying that stakeholders do use, and therefore that there is a demand for, social and environmental information, does not tell us precisely *for what* issues the stakeholders of a particular organization will hold that organization responsible and accountable. To identify these issues at the level of an individual organization requires the organization to enter into some form of dialogue with its stakeholders.

Identifying information needs through dialogue with stakeholders

As we saw in the *who* section earlier in this chapter, managers motivated to engage in corporate social responsibility (and sustainability reporting) for strategic economic reasons (following the managerial branch of stakeholder theory) will tend to identify relevant stakeholders as those who are able to exert the most influence over their company's ability to generate profits (or maximize shareholder value). Such managers will seek to convince these economically powerful stakeholders that their organization's policies and actions accord with the social, environmental, economic and ethical views and expectations of these stakeholders, with social and environmental reporting being one of the mechanisms that may be used to convince these stakeholders. For social and environmental reporting to be effectively used to convince these stakeholders that the organization has operated in accordance with their expectations, the organization will need to know and understand these expectations – which will define *what* information is provided in the organization's social and environmental reports.

Conversely, following the ethical branch of stakeholder theory, managers who seek to minimize their organization's negative impact on a wide range of stakeholders will need to know and understand how their organization is likely to impact upon the lives of a range of stakeholders. The attitudes and experiences of these stakeholders regarding actual and potential organizational impacts are an important element of developing this knowledge and understanding. With an awareness of these views and expectations, managers can then focus their social responsibility policies and actions accordingly, and direct their social and environmental reporting towards providing an account to these stakeholders regarding how the organization has acted in relation to these responsibilities.

Furthermore, ethical reasoning indicates that people should be allowed to participate in making decisions on issues and matters which are likely to affect their lives. Therefore, where managers are motivated by broader ethical considerations, they will actively encourage all those stakeholders who are (or might be) affected by the organization's activities to participate in decision making regarding these activities. To be able to participate in this manner, a wide range of stakeholders will need information about the impacts that the organization has (or is likely to have) upon them, and managers will need to provide this information. In this situation, the answer to the *accountable for what* question is clearly *accountable to all stakeholders for the impact that the organization's actions have (or may have) upon these stakeholders.*

In these cases, and for any position on the continuum between these cases, managers need to understand their relevant stakeholders' views, needs and expectations to determine *for what* economic, social and environmental issues they will provide an account. Ascertaining these views, needs and expectations is likely to be more straightforward where corporate social responsibility has been motivated by a strategic economic desire to maintain or increase the support of economically powerful (or influential) stakeholders, as many of these stakeholders will often be close to, and therefore relatively easily identifiable by, the organization. For many commercial organizations, these powerful stakeholders will often be located in developed nations (or will be part of wealthy elites in developing nations) and will be accessible through commercial mass media such as television/radio, newspaper articles and the Internet. They may even read annual financial reports!

However, for organizations whose social responsibility, and social and environmental reporting, is motivated by ethical reasoning to minimize the organization's impact on those most affected by its operations (and to allow these stakeholders to participate in decisions on issues which significantly affect their lives), ascertaining these stakeholders' views, needs and expectations is likely to be more problematic. Firstly, there is likely to be a broader range of stakeholders whose views need to be ascertained. Secondly, while many of the stakeholders who are significantly affected by an organization's activities (such as employees) might be close to the organization, many others (such as those affected indirectly but substantially by environmental damage caused by the organization's operations, or workers of subcontractors in remote parts of the world) are likely to be remote from the organization itself. Thirdly, as demonstrated by O'Dwyer (2005), some of the stakeholders who are considerably affected by an organization's operations might feel constrained by concerns about the consequences of 'upsetting' the organization if they express their 'true' feelings, in which case the organization can be regarded as being in a position of power which prevents open and honest dialogue with some stakeholders. Fourthly, Adams (2004, p. 736) reports that there is often a 'lack of stakeholder awareness of, and even concern for, corporate impacts', and this can reduce the capacity of some stakeholders to engage in dialogue with the organization. Finally if, following the reasoning discussed earlier in this chapter, we include future generations, non-humans and nature within our definition of stakeholders who are potentially significantly negatively affected by an organization's current operations, it is difficult to conceive of how any organization today could effectively engage in dialogue with these stakeholders to directly ascertain their views, needs and expectations regarding current organizational policies and practices.[9]

To overcome some (but not all) of these difficulties, organizations need to use a variety of channels of communication to engage in active (and not just reactive) dialogue with their stakeholders. For example, some companies have made use of the interactive communication facilities of the Internet to solicit the views of anyone worldwide regarding the social, environmental, ethical and economic responsibilities that should be applied to their organization. However, as Unerman and Bennett (2004) have contended, because access to the Internet is not available to all those potentially impacted by an organization's activities (particularly in many developing nations), Internet-based communication with stakeholders needs to be supplemented with other channels of communication that, between them, are accessible (and likely to be accessed by) a large proportion of the stakeholders upon whom an organization's operations might have an impact.

Such communications can include, for example, face-to-face meetings with a variety of stakeholders, questionnaire surveys, opinion polls, focus groups, and invitations to write to the company about specific issues. O'Dwyer (2005, p. 286) indicates that whatever channels of communication are used to engage stakeholders in dialogue, to be effective these communication channels need to be adapted to the 'cultural differences encountered' between different groups of stakeholders.

Identifying stakeholder information needs and expectations in practice

In addressing processes of stakeholder dialogue, in late 1999 the Institute of Social and Ethical Accountability (ISEA) launched a social and environmental accountability 'framework', AA1000, which places communication between the organization and its stakeholders at the core of social and environmental accountability practices. A central part of this framework, which has evolved since its launch, is guidance on the process of understanding stakeholders' information needs and expectations (in other words, understanding *for what* issues stakeholders consider the organization to be responsible and accountable). The ISEA website states:

> Launched in 1999, the AA1000 framework is designed to improve accountability and performance by **learning through stakeholder engagement**.
>
> It was developed to address the need for organisations to integrate their stakeholder engagement processes into daily activities. It has been used worldwide by leading businesses, non-profit organisations and public bodies.
>
> The Framework helps users to establish a systematic stakeholder engagement process that generates the **indicators, targets, and reporting systems** needed to ensure its effectiveness in overall organisational performance. (ISEA, 2005b, emphasis in original)

In reflecting on the benefits to companies from complying with AA1000, Simon Zadek, a representative of ISEA, states (as quoted in Environmental Accounting and Auditing Reporter, 2000, p. 2):

> There is an increasing body of evidence that organisations which listen to their stakeholders are more likely to be successful in the long term. AA1000's continuous cycle of consultation with stakeholders is designed to encourage transparency, clear goal-setting and the building of trust in relationships with people. Organisations which adhere to its principles and processes will be able to draw strength from association with this quality standard and, ultimately, can expect to achieve competitive advantage. Companies like Railtrack and Monsanto must wish, in retrospect, they had invested in these kinds of processes to help avoid billions being wiped off their market values. [10]

The following extract from the Sustainability Report 2004 (p. 20) of the Dutch electronics group Philips is an example of the importance accorded to understanding stakeholder needs and expectations by some companies, and gives examples of several channels of communication used to understand stakeholders' views, needs and expectations:

> At Philips we strive to balance the often-competing demands of various constituencies. To understand the needs of our stakeholders, we are continuing to strengthen our approach to stakeholder dialogue. By listening to our internal and external stakeholders, we gain the information we need to help us effectively manage issues of importance to them and to our business.
>
> ... The chart below illustrates some of the ways we engage stakeholders ...

Economic stakeholders

- Customers: (B2C) Surveys (trend related, customer satisfaction related, application research), complaint resolution, focus groups; (B2B) Advisory boards, co-R&D, co-strategy development.
- Employees: Employee engagement surveys, town hall meetings, People Performance management system, compliance management system, (local), ombudsman.
- Suppliers/business partners: Supplier days (local, global), co-R&D, industry membership (e.g.,WBCSD).
- Mainstream investors: Road shows, analyst (face to face) meetings, ratings.
- Social investors: Surveys.
- Financial service providers: Ongoing ad hoc involvement, financial ratings.

Social stakeholders

- Communities: Social investment activities focused on education and health, local networking.
- Local/national/international regulatory bodies: Local networking (business/community driven). Participation in advisory bodies, cooperation in community projects.
- Non-governmental organizations: Surveys, project development, ad hoc involvement.
- Academia: Co-R&D, exchange programs, local networking.
- Media: Local networking, surveys.

A further example is the following extract from The Shell Report 2004 (p. 6):

> Contributing to sustainable development for us means, above all, helping to meet the global energy challenge by responding to society's rapidly-growing need for energy and petrochemicals in environmentally and socially responsible ways. This starts with listening to our stakeholders, so that we understand society's changing expectations and learn to see our business through a wider lens. It then involves working with others to provide the innovative energy solutions needed to meet those expectations, as well as behaving honestly and being transparent about our successes and failures.

Negotiating a consensus among competing stakeholder needs and expectations

As indicated in the above quote from The Shell Report 2004, the expectations of stakeholders (or society) are likely to change over time. Lewis and Unerman (1999) have explained this in terms of social values (upon which stakeholder expectations of corporate behaviour are based) changing over time. These values can also differ at a single point in time between different groups within society. Therefore, to imply (as many corporate reports do – including the above quote from Shell) that there is a single set of societal expectations at a particular point in time appears somewhat unrealistic.

If there was such a single set of societal expectations at any point in time regarding standards of corporate behaviour, then ascertaining these needs would be a relatively straightforward task. All an organization would need to do would be to ascertain the values and expectations of one stakeholder regarding the organization's social, environmental and economic responsibilities (and the balance between these responsibilities) and the organization would then know the views of all stakeholders (as these would be identical between all stakeholders).

In practice, many organizations are faced with a variety of values and expectations held by different stakeholders, and often these values and expectations will be incompatible with each other – so the organization will not be able to meet all of the expectations. Instead, it must find a way to select the particular values and expectations to which it will address its corporate social responsibility and its social and environmental reporting.

As indicated by the managerial branch of stakeholder theory, where an organization is motivated to engage in these practices for strategic economic reasons (for example, to maximize shareholder value) then managers will usually choose to address the social, environmental and economic values and expectations of their most economically powerful stakeholders. Conversely where, following the ethical branch of stakeholder theory, an organization's social responsibility and sustainability reporting is motivated by a desire to address the interests of those stakeholders upon whom the organization has the largest impact, it will need to identify and select the interests of those stakeholders upon whom the organization's activities have the largest negative impact. Given that there may be incompatible views among different stakeholders regarding the nature and extent of an organization's impacts, and regarding the priority among different stakeholders' interests, in practice the process of arriving at a consensus set of social, environmental and economic responsibilities is highly problematic.

Unerman and Bennett (2004) addressed this issue. They suggested that while democratically ideal procedures for arriving at a consensus view among all of the stakeholders of any organization regarding that organization's social, environmental and economic responsibilities were probably impossible to fully implement in practice, processes of stakeholder dialogue and debate could move part of the way towards a democratic ideal. The theoretically ideal procedures suggested by Unerman and Bennett draw on some of the theories of the German philosopher Jürgen Habermas (1992), and would require all those potentially affected by an organization's actions to engage in open and honest dialogue with each other (and not just with the organization) about these impacts and the moral acceptability of these impacts. They also require that a person only argues for outcomes which they would consider to be morally acceptable if they were placed in the position of someone negatively affected by that outcome (a requirement that moral positions should only be taken seriously if the person arguing for them believes they should apply universally). A final important requirement is that all stakeholders are prepared to listen to the arguments of others, and are prepared to modify their views in light of stronger arguments.

This 'ideal' democratic debate should then result (in theory) in a broadly accepted consensus view across society regarding the social, environmental and economic responsibilities of any business, and organizations could then direct their social responsibility programmes and policies, and their social and environmental reporting, towards this consensus view. In reality, as indicated above, this 'ideal' situation is unlikely to be realized,[11] but partial implementation of these procedures in practice could result in a move towards a fairer (more democratic) process of determining *for what* an organization is socially and environmentally responsible, and the related accountability duties and practices.

However, only a minority of large companies appear to be actually engaging in dialogue with (some of) their stakeholders. A report by the Institute of Chartered Accountants in England and Wales (2004) discusses a survey by a Swiss organization – Sustainability Asset Management – which found that:

> Of the 800 companies assessed, just 37% have a comprehensive stakeholder dialogue in place. The survey found that, excluding customers and employees, 67% of respondents consider shareholders to be the most relevant for consultation, followed by communities (49%). NGOs, often regarded as a serious risk in view of their potential impact on a company's licence to operate, were considered relevant by only 26%.

This apparent lack of corporate enthusiasm for stakeholder dialogue to identify what issues their stakeholders believe their corporation should be (or is) responsible for is also reflected in the newspaper article in Exhibit 9.4.

Gray *et al.* (1997) provide an alternative view on the role of stakeholders in determining corporate responsibilities. They argue that the model where an organization identifies, and then solicits the views of, a range of its stakeholders places the organization in a position of control over this process. The alternative position, termed the *polyvocal citizenship perspective*, outlined by Gray *et al.* (1997), views the organization as the product of a variety of relationships with different stakeholders, with these stakeholders' views determining the 'reality' (or the nature of the existence) of the organization. As the nature of the organisation's existence, under this perspective, is determined by the stakeholders (very broadly defined), these stakeholders' social values and expectations will automatically be at the core of the organization. However, in practice, the 'entity' tends to be placed at the core of the management of accountability relationships, with managers determining the range of stakeholders to whom they are responsible and accountable.

Irrespective of the procedures used by managers to prioritize and/or select between the competing social, environmental and economic views and interests of different stakeholders, the resulting 'set' of stakeholder expectations will comprise *what* social, environmental and economic issues stakeholders believe an organization is responsible, and therefore accountable, for and thus what issues its social and environmental reporting should address. In the next section, we move on from our discussion of theoretical perspectives regarding mechanisms which

---

Exhibit 9.4 Lack of corporate facilities for stakeholder engagement

Top companies avoid a full and frank exchange

Alison Maitland

Do not expect Shell's corporate web site to convey only glowing words of support for its 'sustainable' energy policies. It is more a case of brickbats and barricades at 'Tell Shell', the open debating forum that is one click away from the home page.

Take the topic 'What is the appropriate role of multinationals in the 21st century?' The question provokes a gush of angry e-mails. 'We will boycott Shell', declares one, castigating the company for its decision, with other western oil groups, to block Chinese expansion into the Caspian Sea.

Scroll down and there is a screed from an anonymous e-mailer on behalf of 'Mother Earth' accusing Shell of 'killing people and planet for profit'.

Hostility of this kind is easy to find on the internet, usually on dedicated anti-corporate websites such as McSpotlight. Most companies, while happy to promote themselves as socially responsible, balk at an uncensored washing of their dirty linen on their own web sites.

Yet is this not what 'stakeholder dialogue' should be about? Is the internet not the ideal place for open debate on issues of trust?

If it is, the message appears to have reached only a handful of companies. The largest nearly all carry social, environmental or ethical information on their web sites. However, it seems many do not expect Joe Public to read the material, let alone want to comment.

Only 36 sites among the FTSE 100 and 17 of the FTSE 250 offer some means of interaction, according to a survey of the UK's biggest companies by CTN, a communications agency, and Futerra, a corporate responsibility consultancy.

While 81 provide a full report, reading these can be hard work. PDF versions of paper reports are common – in one case at an unmanageable 94 pages. Only 14 FTSE 100 websites use Flash animation and only Shell, BP and BT have a forum or bulletin board.

Just two, Royal Bank of Scotland and British American Tobacco, use webcasts. This is in stark contrast to the nearly 90 per cent that use webcasts for their financial reporting, says Richard Coope of CTN.

Only half the FTSE 100 sites and 36 of the FTSE 250 have direct links from their annual report or investor relations pages to their Corporate Social Responsibility sections – surprising, given mounting requirements from investors and government to provide such information. Only 23 of the FTSE 100 make CSR material usable by visually impaired people.

Exhibit 9.4 (*continued*)

CSR is meant to be about engaging with stakeholders. Yet 28 of the FTSE 100 sites give no CSR contact details. Is this a dialogue of the deaf? Very few of the biggest international companies say they have taken action as a result of talking to stakeholders, according to a forthcoming survey of global reporting by the CSR Network consultancy.

How could companies improve their sites? BP, BT Group, J. Sainsbury and Shell top the Futerra/CTN rankings, which are based on a snapshot of sites in March and April and criteria from the Association of Chartered Certified Accountants. The top sites score highly for being a click away from the homepage, easy to navigate, up-to-date, entertaining and interactive.

BT's Betterworld site features independent commentaries on sensitive issues including: 'Does communications technology make life better or worse?' It even runs a competition, although the April teaser 'How many principles are there in the Global Compact?' – was definitely one for CSR nerds.

BP's environmental and social page invites users to create their own site from information including financial results, exploration data, human rights and the environment.

Some of these pioneers could be in danger of going over the top. An FT colleague recently had trouble finding basic corporate data amid all the environmental content on one oil company web site.

But for some, CSR remains a peripheral activity, says Solitaire Townsend, director of Futerra. 'If they are not giving it public profile you have to question how far it's part of the fabric of the company.'

Financial Times, 23 May 2003 p. 14

---

organizations can use to determine *for what* issues their stakeholders hold them responsible and accountable to consider some theoretical perspectives regarding *how* social and environmental reports can be constructed to meet this 'set' of prioritized (or consensus) stakeholder expectations.

Theoretical perspectives on some social and environmental reporting procedures – the *how* stage

Because there is a lack of regulation in the area of social and environmental reporting, as well as an absence of an accepted conceptual framework for social and environmental reporting, there is much variation in *how* this reporting is being done in practice. Some reporting approaches represent quite radical changes from how financial accounting has traditionally been practised. In this section we will examine some theoretical insights into aspects of social and environmental reporting practices. We start by analysing whether the procedures of financial accounting alone could provide suitable mechanisms for capturing and reporting the social and environmental impacts of organizations. If financial accounting practices are unable to effectively capture and report on these social and environmental impacts, then it is necessary to develop other (or additional) social and environmental reporting mechanisms. One very broad mechanism which has been proposed as a method for reporting the social and environmental (in addition to the economic) performance and impact of organizations is *triple bottom line reporting*, and we will discuss the key features and some drawbacks of *triple bottom line reporting* in this section. We will then discuss one of the more influential (and more detailed) sustainability reporting guidelines (the Global Reporting Initiative), which can be regarded as a form of conceptual framework for social and environmental reporting. We complete this section by discussing issues of *social auditing*, which is now being adopted by many large multinational companies as a way of increasing the credibility of their social and environmental reports.

Some possible limitations of traditional financial accounting in capturing and reporting social and environmental performance

Financial accounting is often criticized on the basis that it ignores many of the social and environmental *externalities* caused by the reporting entity. Gray (2005, p. 3) has more profound criticisms of the relationship between financial accounting and sustainability when he argues that:

> Few ideas could be more destructive to the notion of a sustainable planet than a system of economic organisation designed to maximise those things which financial reporting measures. Few notions could be more fundamentally antagonistic to financial reporting and all its cosmetic adjustments than a planet wishing to seek sustainability

Some of the reasons why traditional financial accounting may not be able to effectively reflect the social and environmental impact of organizations could include:

(a) Financial accounting focuses on the information needs of those parties involved in making resource allocation decisions. That is, the focus tends to be restricted to stakeholders with a financial interest in the entity, and the information that is provided consequently tends to be primarily of a financial or economic nature. This has the effect of denying or restricting access to information by people who are impacted in a way that is not financial. But as we appreciate, companies can elect to voluntarily provide social and environmental information. Owen, Shaw and Cooper (2005) show that guidance developed in the UK during the first few years of the 21st century for a new mandatory operating and financial review, to be published alongside the main financial statements, indicated that additional information about social and environmental factors *could* be included in any company's operating and financial review to address the information needs of a wider group than simply those with a financial interest.

(b) One of the cornerstones of financial accounting is the notion of 'materiality' which has tended to preclude the reporting of social and environmental information, given the difficulty associated with quantifying social and environmental costs. 'Materiality' is an issue involving a great deal of professional judgement, and is often judged in terms of the magnitude of the financial value of an item in relation to the size of other accounting metrics (such as turnover, net profit and/or net assets). If something is not judged to be material, it does not need to be disclosed in the financial reports. Unfortunately this has often meant that if something cannot be quantified (as is the case for many social and environmental externalities) it is generally not considered to be material and therefore does not warrant separate disclosure. This obviously implies that materiality may not be a relevant criterion for the disclosure of social and environmental performance data. Social and environmental performance is quite different to financial performance. Yet many accountants have been conditioned through their education and training to adopt the *materiality* criterion to decide whether any information should be disclosed. In a review of British companies, Gray *et al.* (1998) indicate that companies frequently provide little or no information about environmental expenses (however defined) because individually the expenditure is not considered to be *material.*

(c) As highlighted in Gray, Owen and Adams (1996), another issue that arises in financial accounting is that reporting entities frequently discount liabilities, particularly those that will not be settled for many years, to their present value. This tends to make future expenditure less significant in the present period. For example, if our current activities are creating a need for future environmental expenditure of a remedial nature, but that work will not be undertaken for many years, then as a result of discounting we will recognize little or no cost now (which does appear to be at odds with the sustainability agenda). For example, if we were anticipating that our activities would necessitate a clean-up bill of €100 million in 30 years' time to remove some contamination, and if we accept that our normal earnings rate is, say, 10 per cent, then the current expenses to be recognized in our financial statements under generally accepted accounting principles would be €5.73 million. While discounting makes good *economic* sense, Gray, Owen and Adams (1996) argue that it does tend to make the clean-up somewhat trivial (and therefore, not that important) at the current time, perhaps thereby providing little current discouragement for an entity contemplating undertaking activities that will damage the environment, but which will not be remediated for many years.

(d) Financial accounting adopts the 'entity assumption', which requires the organization to be treated as an entity distinct from its owners, other organizations, and other stakeholders. If a transaction or event does not directly impact on the entity, the transaction or event is to be ignored for accounting purposes. This means that the externalities caused by reporting entities will typically be ignored, thereby meaning that performance measures (such as profitability) are incomplete from a broader societal (as opposed to a 'discrete entity') perspective, and accounting reports based on these performance measures fail to reflect all three strands of sustainability discussed earlier in this chapter. Arguably, any moves towards accounting for sustainability would require a modification to, or a move away from, the entity assumption.

(e) A related area in which our traditional financial accounting system generates a rather strange outcome is the treatment of tradable pollution permits. In both the EU and an increasing number of countries outside the EU certain organizations are provided with permits, often free of charge, which allow the holder to release a pre-specified amount of a particular pollutant. If the original recipient of the permit is not going to emit as much as the licence allows, then that party is allowed to sell the permit to another party.[12] As such, what we are finding in some jurisdictions is that particular organizations are treating tradable pollution permits as assets. This may make sense from an 'economic' perspective – but it is questionable whether something that will allow an organization to pollute is an asset from a broader 'societal' perspective.

(f) In financial accounting and reporting, expenses are defined in such a way as to exclude the recognition of any impacts on resources that are not controlled by the entity (such as the environment), unless fines or other cash flows result. For example, under the International Accounting Standards Board's *conceptual framework* (as discussed in Chapter 6), *expenses* for financial reporting purposes are defined as:

> ... decreases in economic benefits during the accounting period in the form of outflows or depletions of assets or incurrences of liabilities that result in decreases in equity, other than those relating to distributions to equity participants. [paragraph 70b]

An understanding of *expenses* therefore requires an understanding of *assets*. Assets are defined as resources '*controlled* by the entity as a result of past events and from which future economic benefits are expected to flow to the entity' (paragraph 49a, emphasis added). The recognition of assets therefore relies upon *control*, and hence environmental resources such as air and water, which are shared and therefore not controlled by the organization, cannot be considered as assets of that organization. Thus their use, or abuse, is not considered as an expense. This is an important limitation of financial accounting and one that must be emphasized. As indicated in Deegan (1996), and using a rather extreme example, under traditional financial accounting if an entity were to destroy the quality of water in its local environs, thereby killing all local sea creatures and coastal vegetation, then to the extent that no fines or other related cash flows were incurred, reported profits would not be directly impacted. No externalities would be recognized, and the reported assets/profits of the organization would not be affected. Adopting conventional financial reporting practices, the performance of such an organization could, depending upon the financial transactions undertaken, be portrayed as being very successful. In this respect Gray and Bebbington (1992, p. 6) provide the following opinion of traditional financial accounting:

> ... there is something profoundly wrong about a system of measurement, a system that makes things visible and which guides corporate and national decisions, that can signal success in the midst of desecration and destruction. [13]

(g) There is also the issue of 'measurability'. For an item to be recorded for financial accounting purposes it must be measurable with reasonable accuracy. Trying to place a value on the externalities caused by an entity often relies on various estimates and 'guesstimates', thereby typically precluding their recognition from the financial accounts on the basis of the potential inaccuracy of the measurement.

Despite the above difficulties, there have been various experimental approaches throughout the world aiming to develop a 'full-cost' approach to profit calculation by placing an economic 'value' on the social and environmental impact of individual organizations. A number of companies have, in the past, experimented with full-cost accounting, including Dow Europe, BSO/Origin (Netherlands), Volvo, Ontario Hydro and IBM. Some academic studies have also developed theoretical approaches in this area (see, for example, Bebbington and Gray, 2001, Gray, 1992). These approaches represent a dramatic departure from conventional accounting.

Nevertheless, the drawbacks with the current state of financial accounting and reporting (which we discussed above) indicate that financial accounting and reporting does not seem to possess suitable mechanisms for capturing and reporting upon the social and environmental impacts of organizations. Financial accounting and reporting alone is therefore unsuitable as a mechanism to provide an account of these social and environmental impacts and to meet stakeholders' information needs and expectations. Consequently, other mechanisms need to be employed to provide a suitable social and environmental account to these stakeholders. One broad mechanism which has been discussed widely in the business world as a way to provide a desirable balance of information about the social and environmental, in addition to the economic, performance of organizations is *triple bottom line reporting.*

Triple bottom line reporting

Triple bottom line reporting is based on the triple bottom line approach to business sustainability discussed earlier in this chapter, where a balance is sought between economic, social and environmental sustainability. Advocates of triple bottom line reporting argue that, if properly implemented, it should provide information to enable others to assess how sustainable an organization's or a community's operations are. The perspective taken is that for an organization (or a community) to be sustainable (a long-run perspective) it must be financially secure (as evidenced by such measures as profitability); it must minimize (or ideally eliminate) its negative environmental impacts; and it must act in conformity with societal expectations. Triple bottom line reporting therefore provides a very broad answer to the question of *how* an organization should report upon its social, environmental *and* economic impacts (or performance).

Brown, Dillard and Marshall (2005) demonstrate that while there has been much discussion of triple bottom line reporting, there have been few concrete proposals to realize this reporting model. Among the problems they highlight with implementing the triple bottom line reporting model in practice are: firstly, that while use of the bottom line metaphor has been useful in capturing the attention of managers for issues of social and environmental impact, this metaphor is severely restricting as the term 'bottom line' conveys the impression of something which can be measured in a single number. The economic profit figure is the summation, in a common currency,[14] of all the income and expenses figures over a period of time (or, in conceptual framework terms, the difference between the summation of all the assets and liabilities at one year end and the summation of these figures at the next year end). Brown, Dillard and Marshall (2005) demonstrate that it is highly problematic, and probably impossible in practice, to reduce all environmental impacts, or all social impacts, to a common currency. Indeed, most reports that have claimed to be based on a triple bottom line approach have tended to report on social and environmental impacts using a combination of narrative reports and a number of different metrics. If neither social nor environmental factors can be reduced to a single currency, then it is not possible to equate trade-offs between these factors. Such a trade-off between 'maximizing' economic, social and environmental performance appears to be a key element (or requirement) of the triple bottom line.

Secondly, the economic bottom line is commonly understood among managers as being a metric which should be maximized. Brown, Dillard and Marshall (2005) argue that it is difficult to apply this objective of maximization to nature. While there could be agreement on maximizing a factor such as biodiversity, there is no commonly accepted understanding of what this might mean, and how it could be measured. Even more problematic is knowing which social metric should be maximized. Thus, attempting to equate the notion (and management) of the bottom lines of social and environmental with the more conventional economic bottom line is not possible in practice. Therefore attempting to report upon, or manage, all three bottom lines in a common manner is not appropriate.

Thirdly, *if* it is not possible to adopt metrics which treat each of the bottom lines equally, then the notion of three separate bottom lines might give the impression that the economic, social and environmental are not interconnected. For reasons explained earlier in this chapter, this would be a fundamental misconception, and from a social and environmental sustainability viewpoint could be highly damaging. Brown, Dillard and Marshall (2005) believe that due to these problems in the triple bottom line concept, management and reporting on the triple bottom line is likely to result in a focus on the economic bottom line to the detriment of social and environmental sustainability.

Despite these difficulties with implementing the triple bottom line reporting concept in practice, Gray (2005) argues that it could provide a structure which pioneering organizations could then use to help develop innovative sustainability reports – although Gray does appear somewhat sceptical regarding the actual potential of triple bottom line reporting in practice: ' ... it would take a vivid imagination to envisage what a world of *substantive* [triple bottom line] reporting might look like' (p. 20, emphasis in original).

It therefore appears that the process of triple bottom line reporting is, at present, not very helpful in providing guidance to organizations regarding the details of *how* to produce a sustainability report which will address the specific information needs of their stakeholders. Perhaps what is required to provide more useful guidance is a conceptual framework for social and environmental reporting. The Global Reporting Initiative, which we discuss next, could possibly be considered to be one example of a move towards a conceptual framework for social and environmental reporting.

The Global Reporting Initiative – a conceptual framework for social and environmental reporting?

Despite (or perhaps because of) the deficiencies in the ability of traditional financial reporting (and triple bottom line reporting) to capture and reflect the social and environmental impacts of organizational activities, many organizations have developed a variety of practices which seek to report on these broader impacts. The inclusion of particular items for disclosure tends to be based on particular managers' perceptions of the information needs of particular stakeholder groups

(Solomon and Lewis, 2002), while much reliance also tends to be placed on what is acknowledged as best reporting practice (as perhaps evidenced by an entity winning a reporting award for its disclosures).

As an attempt to codify *best reporting practice*, several bodies have been active in developing social and environmental reporting guidelines. At an international level, one source of reporting guidance that has taken a dominant position in the social and environmental reporting domain is the Global Reporting Initiative's Sustainability Reporting Guidelines (commonly referred to as the GRI).[15] These guidelines are generally accepted as representing current 'best practice' reporting, and comprise 97 separate indicators (which are continually evolving, so might not remain at 97 for long). Fifty are designated as 'core' indicators that are deemed to be of relevance to most organizations. The remaining 47 indicators are deemed to be 'additional' and therefore are only expected to be used depending upon the characteristics of an organization. Whilst the GRI guidelines are argued by many to have brought about improvements to sustainability reporting, it must be acknowledged that, not being mandatory, many companies are selective about what indicators they choose to use in their reporting. However, such companies might still indicate that they are using the GRI guidelines and therefore gain the 'legitimacy' that is associated with using such guidelines. As Sustainability (2002, p. 17) notes:

> The GRI Guidelines themselves allow companies partially off the hook. A company can be GRI compliant whilst looking at the least impactful aspect of their business. Consider the case of McDonalds whose inaugural GRI-based report, released earlier in 2002, makes only passing mention of agriculture issues, where an enormous proportion of McDonalds impact lies .... Alan Willis, one former GRI Steering Committee member and Verification Working Group participant urges: 'GRI needs to be increasingly vigilant of company abuse of the guidelines or process – claiming their reporting is "In Accordance" when its not; incomplete, inaccurate, misleading or inappropriate.'

The GRI Guidelines could be used as a basis for mandatory reporting if mandatory social and environmental (and sustainability) reporting was to be introduced within a particular jurisdiction. For example, the King Report on Corporate Governance for South Africa, which was endorsed in 2002 by the Johannesburg Stock Exchange, makes reference to the GRI Guidelines.

The GRI provides a number of categories for disclosing environmental performance information, together with related performance indicators. The key categories of disclosure relate to:

◆ types and quantities of materials used together with information about wastes;

◆ energy consumption;

◆ water consumption;

◆ biodiversity issues;

◆ emissions, effluents and wastes;

◆ supplier-related environment issues;

◆ significant environmental impacts of products and services;

◆ legal compliance;

◆ significant environmental impacts of transportation;

◆ total environmental expenditures.

Given the apparent importance of the GRI to current developments in social and environmental performance reporting, it is worth considering the development of the GRI in some depth.

The multi-stakeholder Global Reporting Initiative was established in 1997. Its mission is to promote:

> ... international harmonization in the reporting of relevant and credible corporate environmental, social and economic performance information to enhance responsible decision-making. The GRI pursues this mission through a multi-stakeholder process of open dialogue and collaboration in the design and implementation of widely applicable sustainability reporting guidelines. (Global Reporting Initiative, 1999)

The GRI was originally convened by United States-based organization Coalition for Environmentally Responsible Economies (a non-profit non-government organization based in Boston) in partnership with the United Nations Environmental Program (whose website is at www.unep.org) with subsequent inputs from ACCA (United Kingdom); Tellus Institute; World Business Council for Sustainable Development; World Resources Institute; Canadian Institute of Chartered Accountants; Institute of Social and Ethical Accountability (United Kingdom); Council on Economic Priorities (United States); and other organizations and corporate bodies from around the world. Given its representation, the initiative is clearly 'global' in nature.

GRI released draft guidelines in March 1999. This first draft was open to comment, with the consultation period for the first draft closing at the end of 1999. Revised guidelines were then released in June 2000. A subsequent revision was undertaken and a revised set of guidelines was released in 2002 (the guidelines are available on GRI's website). The 2002 guidelines comprise four parts, these being:

◆ using the GRI Guidelines (what are they, who should use them, etc.);

◆ reporting principles and practices (underlying reporting principles, qualitative characteristics, classification of reporting elements, ratio indicators, reporting policies);

◆ report content;

◆ glossary and annexes.

The 'Report content' section is the main part of the document, and describes five components which might be found in a sustainability report. These are:

1 **Vision and strategy** – description of the reporting organization's strategy with regard to sustainability, including a statement from the chief executive officer.

2 **Profile** – overview of the reporting organization's structure and operations and of the scope of the report.

3 **Governance structure and management systems** – description of organizational structure, policies and management systems, including stakeholder engagement efforts.

4 **GRI content index** – a table supplied by the reporting organization identifying where the information listed in Part C of the GRI guidelines is located within the organization's report.

5 **Performance indicators** – measures of the impact or effect of the reporting organization divided into integrated, economic, environmental and social performance indicators.

From an accounting perspective, it is generally accepted that information should be comparable across time and between entities. The attribute of comparability is also something that has been promoted in the GRI guidelines. Other qualitative characteristics that are promoted in the GRI include: transparency, inclusiveness, auditability, relevance, completeness, sustainability context, accuracy, neutrality, reliability, clarity, timeliness, and verifiability. These are similar to the qualitative characteristics commonly suggested in financial reporting conceptual frameworks. As stated in the June 2002 guidelines, the guidelines are expected to continually evolve across time, and a revised set of GRI guidelines is due to be published in 2006.

One of the other areas covered by the 2002 GRI guidelines is 'the use of assurance processes as a means of enhancing the credibility and quality of their sustainability reports' (Global Reporting Initiative, 2002, p. 76). Assurance, or audit, of information contained in sustainability reports is an increasingly common practice, and we will now discuss aspects of social and environmental auditing.

Social audit (or assurance)

Closely linked to social and environmental accounting is the practice of social and environmental auditing, or 'independent' attestation (or verification) of the social and environmental reporting information. According to Elkington (1997, p. 88) the purpose of social and environmental auditing (commonly referred to simply as *social audit*) is for an organization to assess its performance in relation to society's requirements and expectations. The results of a social audit, or the statement of assurance, often form the basis of an entity's publicly released social accounts (thereby increasing the apparent transparency of the organization), and the outcomes of social audits can be considered as an important part of the ongoing dialogue with various stakeholder groups.

In its guidance standard on social and environmental reporting assurance, The Institute of Social and Ethical Accountability define assurance as:

> an evaluation method that uses a specified set of principles and standards to assess the quality of a Reporting Organisation's subject matter, such as Reports, and the organisation's underlying systems, processes and competencies that underpin its performance. Assurance includes the communication of the results of this evaluation to provide credibility to the subject matter for its users. (ISEA, 2003, p. 5)

The Institute of Social and Ethical Accountability's website (ISEA, 2005a) outlines three key principles underlying social audit, and these give a good flavour of the broad issues an ideal social audit should cover:

> **Materiality:** does the sustainability report provide an account covering all the areas of performance, that stakeholders need to judge the organisation's sustainability performance?
>
> **Completeness:** is the information complete and accurate enough to assess and understand the organisation's performance in all these areas?
>
> **Responsiveness:** has the organisation responded coherently and consistently to stakeholders' concerns and interests?

Despite this guidance regarding the ideal components of a social audit, not all social audits provide these types of information. Owen and O'Dwyer (2005) demonstrate that there are two distinct approaches to social audit, and these tend to be broadly related to the type of organization that conducts the social audit on behalf of a reporting organization. One of the types of organization that commonly conducts social audits are the large multinational accountancy practices which also conduct financial audits; the other type are social/environmental consultancies.

In comparing the social audit practices of these two different types of providers of social audits, Owen and O'Dwyer (2005) found that the social audits provided by accounting firms tended 'to adopt a cautious approach that largely focuses on the issue of consistency of information appearing in the organisation's report with underlying data sets' (p. 225), and mostly failed to comment on whether the social and/or environmental information in the report presented a 'true and fair view' of the underlying social and/or environmental performance or whether this information was complete. Conversely, social audits provided by social/environmental consultancies did tend to express an opinion regarding the 'completeness, fairness and overall balance' (p. 225) of the social and/or environmental information reported, and also provided 'more in the way of commentary on [social and environmental] systems, reporting and performance weaknesses' (pp. 225–226). However, despite the apparently higher level of assurance provided by the 'consultant auditors', Owen and O'Dwyer (2005) caution that the perceived independence of these auditors might be compromised in comparison to the 'accountant auditors' given that the former tend to also provide social and environmental management consultancy to the firms they then audit.

From the organization's perspective, once activities such as social audits are undertaken they can act as a catalyst for the organization and, importantly, for senior management to embrace new values. A 'sustainable organization' needs to ensure that it complies with community expectations. As such, activities such as social audits make good long-term business sense. It also appears that some organizations are undertaking social audits as a means of gaining (or regaining) some legitimacy from the perspective of their stakeholders. Undertaking a social audit, particularly if the audit is undertaken by a credible, independent party, should act to increase the perceived transparency and legitimacy of the organization. Exhibit 9.5 provides an example of some of the benefits to organizational legitimacy that can arise from conducting a social audit.

Exhibit 9.5 Implementing social audits as a possible means of establishing corporate legitimacy

When companies take a good look at themselves
More businesses are seeking a social audit, but what exactly can you expect from this lengthy process and do its benefits always outweigh its costs?

Paul Gosling

Social audits have been commissioned by some of the UK's largest and most successful companies, including Shell, Diageo and Camelot. But it is less clear whether for SMEs the resource costs involved are too great to justify, despite the valuable management information obtained through social auditing.

Henry Stewart, chief executive of Happy Computers, an IT training company with 40 staff and a £2m turnover, is convinced that its social audit nine years ago helped to set it on the right track, not just in achieving the social aims his business is committed to, but also in contributing to the bottom line. 'It was actually incredibly useful,' recalls Stewart. 'But it was also incredibly time consuming for a small business.'

... Social auditing is a system of reviewing a company's operations, to examine its social impacts and to compare outcomes against any social objectives the organisation may have. This makes it a highly suitable process for charities and social enterprises, businesses which trade to achieve social purposes, but also for large companies which have suffered reputational damage which they are keen to correct. One of the core

---

Exhibit 9.5 (*continued*)

elements of a social audit is to survey various stakeholders 'from staff to customers, sub-contractors to shareholders' to establish how the organisation is regarded. The audited body itself will often collate a large amount of information from them.

When Happy had its social audit, the results led to fundamental changes in the way the company operated and was marketed. 'It was very helpful,' says Stewart. 'We have definite social objectives. The audit told us how the market saw us. This had a major effect on our direction. One conclusion was that we did not need to hide our social objectives. Previously we had three brochures: one each for charities, the public sector and for the commercial world. The social audit told us that one of the reasons corporate bodies liked us was our commitment to support charities and that we would get more business if we marketed that fact.'

Since then, Happy has ended what Stewart calls the approach of 'social responsibility by stealth' and has been comfortable to say that it pays the wages each year of two or three staff to go to African countries for two to four weeks to provide free IT training to local people.

Maria Sillanp of AccountAbility, which sets down standards for social auditing, says that the widespread acceptance of the principle of corporate social responsibility (CSR) has led to much greater interest in social auditing. 'Increasingly the expectation is that CSR should lead to social auditing,' she says. 'And in the corporate space, increasingly it does.'

She says benefits from social auditing will typically include improved risk awareness particularly of emerging risks, better risk management processes and greater recognition of market opportunities. But their full value will not be felt if companies fail to use adequately the huge amounts of information gathered for social reporting to change their management processes.

Many SMEs have now become aware of these potential gains and are interested in conducting social audits, says Sillanp. But she concedes that the amount of information collated involves a heavy commitment. 'It can be very resource intensive,' she says. 'After two or three cycles, an organisation can be fatigued.'

The Independent on Sunday, 24 April 2005

In this section we have examined theoretical perspectives on four areas related to *how* organizations can provide information to meet the identified needs and expectations of their stakeholders. As this is a book about accounting theory rather than accounting practice, our discussion has largely focused on exploring these theoretical perspectives, rather than providing a detailed explanation of how to produce a social and environmental report in practice. We started by analysing whether financial accounting practices alone were suitable for capturing and reporting upon the social and environmental impact of organizations' activities, and concluded they were not suitable. We then discussed the proposition of triple bottom line reporting, and the problems with (and some argue the theoretical impossibility of) implementing effective triple bottom line reporting in practice. This was followed by an examination of the reporting mechanisms suggested in the Global Reporting Initiative Sustainability Reporting Guidelines, and we concluded this section by discussing issues related to social audit.

Chapter summary

This chapter has reviewed various issues associated with corporate social and environmental reporting. Since around the early 1990s many organizations throughout the world have been providing an increasing amount of information about their social and environmental performance in a variety of reports. Concerns associated with sustainability (which relates to economic, social and environmental performance issues) have increased since the early 1990s and the evolution of corporate social and environmental performance reporting appears to be related to these concerns, as developments in reporting are probably a reflection of changing community expectations about the performance and responsibilities of business. In examining various theoretical issues associated with social and environmental reporting, we structured our discussion to follow the *why – who – for what – how* stages of the sustainability reporting process.

In the *why* stage we explored various aspects of the motivations for organizations to engage in corporate social responsibility, and social and environmental reporting. When a firm voluntarily discloses information publicly about its social and environmental performance this may imply that the managers are acknowledging that they are accountable to a broad group of stakeholders in relation to not only their financial performance, but also their social and environmental performance. However, as this chapter indicates, not all people consider that managers have social responsibilities to a broad group of stakeholders. Some researchers believe that the prime responsibility of managers is to shareholders alone, and within these confines, to maximizing shareholder (financial) value. However, this narrow perspective of corporate responsibility seems to be becoming less widely accepted, as concepts of an interrelated triple bottom line of social, environmental and economic sustainability become more widely accepted.

For the *who* (or *to whom*) stage, we examined the range of stakeholders different organizations are likely to wish to address in their social and environmental reporting strategies. This range of stakeholders is likely to be directly related to an organization's motives for engaging in social and environmental reporting. It will be very broad for organizations which follow the ethical branch of stakeholder theory by seeking to minimize their negative social and environmental impact upon all those who are affected by these impacts (and will include future generations). Conversely, organizations following the managerial branch of stakeholder theory will tend to focus on the demands and expectations of a narrower range of stakeholders – those with the most power over the organization.

Having addressed issues relating to the identification of stakeholders to whom an organization's social and environmental reporting will be directed, we then explored some theoretical perspectives regarding the mechanisms which organizations may use to identify *what* information these stakeholders need, or *for what* issues these stakeholders believe the organization is socially and environmentally responsible and accountable. We firstly drew on several studies which demonstrated that stakeholders do appear to make use of information about the social and environmental performance of organizations, and we were thus able to conclude that stakeholders do want some social and environmental performance information (so the answer to the *accountable for what* question is not '*accountable for no social or environmental issues*'). We then analysed theoretical perspectives on processes of stakeholder dialogue, which can be used by organizations to develop an understanding of what social and environmental information is likely to be demanded by their stakeholders. We demonstrated the difficulties involved in seeking to reach an acceptable consensus view among a wide range of stakeholders regarding the social, environmental and economic responsibilities of an organization – and the consequent accountability duties related to these responsibilities.

Finally, in the *how* stage, we reviewed theoretical perspectives on some of the processes involved in the production of social and environmental reports, including the limitations of conventional financial reporting for capturing and reflecting the social and environmental impact of an organization's policies and practices, the potential and drawbacks of the *triple bottom line reporting* model, key aspects of the *Global Reporting Initiative*, and some issues related to social auditing. Evidence shows that the practice of social accounting and social auditing, which was promoted in the 1970s, has re-emerged as a major issue in corporate accountability and reporting in the 21st century.

Questions

9.1   What has the environment to do with accounting?

9.2   What is accountability and what is its relationship to:
(a) accounting?
(b) an organization's responsibilities?

9.3   What is sustainable development?

9.4   Are 'economic rationality' (as defined by economists) and 'sustainability' mutually inconsistent?

9.5   What is an externality, and why do financial accounting practices typically ignore externalities?

9.6   What is a social audit and why would a profit-seeking entity bother with one?

9.7   Why do you think the European Union called for a 'redefinition of accounting concepts, rules, conventions and methodology so as to ensure that the consumption and use of environmental resources are accounted for as part of the full cost of production and reflected in market prices' (European Commission, 1992, Vol. II, Section 7.4, p. 67)?

9.8   What is triple bottom line reporting, and what has it to do with sustainable development?

9.9   Of what relevance to the accounting profession is sustainable development?

9.10   Why do you think that the accounting profession has generally not released any accounting standards pertaining to the disclosure of environmental information?

9.11   Collison (2003, p. 861) states that: 'Attention to the interests of shareholders above all other groups is implicit in much of what is taught to accounting and finance students. The very construction of a profit and loss account ... is a continual, and usually unstated, reminder that the interests of only one group of stakeholders should be maximised. Indeed it may be very difficult for accounting and finance students to even conceive of another way in which affairs could be ordered ... even at the algebraic level, let alone the moral.'
(a) Do you agree or disagree with Collison, and why?
(b) If 'profit' maximization is biased towards maximizing the interests of only one stakeholder group, would you expect that over time there will be less emphasis on profits, and more emphasis on other performance indicators? Why? What might be some of the alternative measures of performance?
(c) Would Collison's comments provide a justification for moves towards profit measures that incorporate 'full costs' (that is, that consider the externalities of business)?

9.12 How would the following theories explain corporate social responsibility reporting:
   (a) Positive Accounting Theory?
   (b) legitimacy theory?
   (c) stakeholder theory?
   (d) institutional theory?

9.13 In publicly released reports a number of organizations are referring to their 'public licence to operate'. What do you think they mean by this, and is there a theoretical perspective that can explain what this term means?

9.14 Consider how the concept of sustainable development, as it applies to business entities, compares to the accountant's notion of a 'going concern'. Do you believe that they are similar, or are they quite different?

9.15 Read Exhibit 9.6 below and answer the following questions:
   After considering the implications (externalities) associated with the promotion of tobacco use by cigarette companies, if the allegations made against the tobacco companies were true, what would be the implications for these companies' reported results if:
   (a) conventional financial accounting practices were employed?
   (b) triple bottom line reporting was employed?

Exhibit 9.6 A view on safety versus profit

Tobacco industry deliberately misled smokers on health risks, court told

Demetri Sevastopulo

The tobacco industry engaged in a massive 50-year fraud to deceive consumers about the risks from smoking, the US Justice Department said yesterday at the start of a landmark trial. In opening arguments, government lawyers said that tobacco companies deliberately misled the public about the harmful effects of smoking while privately acknowledging the dangers.

The government wants the tobacco companies to forfeit $280bn (€228bn, £156bn) of past profits. It claims the industry marketed cigarettes to young people, manipulated nicotine levels in cigarettes and funded studies that cast doubt on whether smoking causes lung cancer and other diseases.

The industry denies fraud and says it has already changed many of the marketing practices the government criticises.

Government lawyers produced internal company documents suggesting tobacco executives understood the risks of smoking but continued to say

Exhibit 9.6 (*continued*)

publicly that there was insufficient evidence to reach that conclusion. Frank Marine, a government lawyer, provided details of a 1953 meeting of top industry executives which, he argued, represented the first step in 'one of the most elaborate public relations schemes in history.'

The companies argue the meeting was not secret because they had told the government it would take place. The government counters that the companies hid its true intention, which it alleges was to form an industry-wide alliance to obscure the issue of the dangers of smoking.

The suit is being brought under the 1970 Racketeer-Influenced and Corrupt Organizations (Rico) Act, which was designed to crack down on organised crime. The defendants – Philip Morris, RJ Reynolds, Brown & Williamson, Lorillard, Liggett and British American Tobacco – have challenged the government's legal authority to seek a $280bn penalty. An appeals court is expected to decide that issue in November.

The industry is also opposing restrictions on cigarette marketing sought by the government, saying they mirror those imposed by the 1998 Master Settlement Agreement. Under that deal, tobacco companies agreed to pay $264bn to settle claims with the 50 US states.

The companies are expected to argue there was no concerted effort to mislead consumers. The industry cites, for example, the requirement that packets of cigarettes carry health warnings since 1966 – two years after the US surgeon-general concluded that smoking caused cancer – as evidence that it could not have deceived consumers.

Financial Times, 22 September 2004, p. 8

Notes

1 Some practitioners and academics argue that the issue of *what* a social and environmental report should address has to be the first (not the third) stage in the social and environmental reporting process, because only having ascertained what a reporting process should address is it then possible to identify relevant stakeholders. However, a close reading of the arguments of these practitioners and academics usually reveals that the types of issues they cover with their '*what*' questions are similar, or identical, to the issues we referred to above as the first stage '*why*' questions. These practitioners and academics therefore sometimes have two levels of '*what*' questions – a macro/philosophical level question asking what are the broad reasons for undertaking social and environmental reporting, and micro level questions asking what are the detailed issues that should be covered in a social and environmental report if it is to meet stakeholders' information needs. To avoid the confusion that could arise in using the term '*what*' to refer to two different stages in the social and environmental reporting process, we will apply this term only to the third stage where detailed questions arise regarding the information needs of identified stakeholders.

2   As we have stressed throughout this book, and in particular within Chapter 1, whether we elect to accept that a particular theory provides an explanation of a particular phenomenon will be dependent upon whether we are prepared to accept the underlying assumptions of the theory in question.

3   As indicated in Chapter 8, the social contract is a concept used to represent the multitude of implicit and explicit expectations that society has about how an organization should conduct its business. It is assumed that society allows an organization to continue operations to the extent that it generally meets society's expectations. These expectations will change over time and different individuals (including the organization's managers) will have different perspectives about what these expectations actually encompass at a given point in time. Hence, to all intents and purposes it is not possible to provide any form of accurate depiction of what specifically are the terms of the social contract – nevertheless, it is arguably a useful construct to describe the relationship between an organization and the society in which it operates.

4   As such, it is probably not a theory that provides a great deal of hope in terms of moves towards sustainable development – moves which, if we accept the Brundtland Report definition of sustainability discussed later in this chapter, would require current generations to consider forgoing consumption to ensure that future generations' needs are met. Sacrificing current consumption for the benefit of future generations, and Positive Accounting Theory's central assumption of self-interest, could be deemed to be mutually inconsistent.

5   According to Clarkson (1995, p. 103), 'Friedman chose to interpret social issues and social responsibilities to mean non-business issues and non-business responsibilities. He, like so many neo-classical economists, separated business from society, which enabled him to maintain that "the business of business is business". By placing the two abstractions of business and society into separate compartments, Friedman was able to deny the necessity, or even the validity, of the concept of corporate social responsibility, decrying it as a fundamentally subversive doctrine'.

6   There is an ethical issue here in that the higher priced goods will thereafter only be available to the more wealthy. That is, the supply of those goods with a high 'environmental price' will be restricted to the wealthier people.

7   Some people would argue that an actual example of largely unrestrained profit maximization leading to a breakdown in many social systems occurred in Russia during the 1990s – in the period of 'cowboy capitalism' following the collapse of the Soviet Union, when a small proportion of the population became very wealthy while vast numbers had little to eat.

8   Stakeholders have been defined in various ways. For our purposes we broadly define stakeholders as parties impacted by, or having an impact upon, the organization in question. This is also consistent with definitions provided by Freeman (1984) and Gray, Owen and Adams (1996).

9   These views are, however, often 'represented' by a variety of campaign groups.

10   ISEA's website is www.AccountAbility.org.uk.

11   For example, in the case analysed by O'Dwyer (2005, p. 286) 'several stakeholders complained they had little opportunity to engage in dialogue with each other. It was widely claimed that stakeholders needed to learn from each other across the organization as opposed to merely enabling the board to learn from them and then isolate them'.

12   Details of the EU emissions trading scheme, which became operational on 1 January 2005, can be found at: www.europa.eu.int/comm/environment/climat/emission.htm.

13   Motivated by their concern about the limitations of traditional financial accounting, Gray and Bebbington have sought to develop alternative methods of accounting – methods that embrace the sustainability agenda. See, for example, Gray and Bebbington (2001).

14   This notion of economic profit being a summation of economic factors in *a common currency* does, however, need to allow for the effects of changing prices – which we discussed in Chapter 5.

15   See www.globalreporting.org for details of the GRI reporting guidelines.

References

Accounting Standards Steering Committee (1975) 'The Corporate Report', London: Institute of Chartered Accountants in England & Wales.

Adams, C. A. (2002) 'Internal organisational factors influencing corporate social and ethical reporting', *Accounting, Auditing & Accountability Journal*, 15 (2), pp. 223–50.

Adams, C. A. (2004) 'The ethical, social and environmental reporting-performance portrayal gap', *Accounting, Auditing & Accountability Journal*, 17 (5), pp. 731–57.

Adams, C. A. & Harte, G. (1998) 'The changing portrayal of the employment of women in British banks' and retail companies' corporate annual reports', *Accounting, Organizations & Society*, 23 (8), pp. 781–812.

Adams, C. A. & McPhail, K. (2004) 'Reporting and the politics of difference: (Non)disclosure on ethnic minorities', *ABACUS*, 40 (3), pp. 405–35.

Anderson, J. C. & Frankle, A. W. (1980) 'Voluntary social reporting: An Iso-beta portfolio analysis', *The Accounting Review*, 55 (3), pp. 405–35.

Bebbington, J. & Gray, R. (2001) 'An account of sustainability: Failure, success and a reconceptualisation', *Critical Perspectives on Accounting*, 12 (5), pp. 557–87.

Beck, U. (1992) *Risk Society: Towards a New Modernity*, London: SAGE Publications Ltd.

Beck, U. (1994) 'The reinvention of politics: towards a theory of reflexive modernization', in Beck, U., Giddens, A. & Lash, S. (eds) *Reflexive Modernization: Politics, Tradition and Aesthetics in the Modern Social Order*, Cambridge: Polity Press, pp. 1–55.

Beck, U. (1999) *World Risk Society*, Cambridge: Polity Press.

Beck, U. (2000) 'Risk society revisited: theory, politics and research programmes', in Adam, B., Beck, U. & van Loon, J. (eds) *The Risk Society and Beyond: Critical Issues for Social Theory*, London: SAGE Publications Ltd, pp. 211–29.

Belkaoui, A. R. (1976) 'The impact of the disclosure of environmental effects of organizational behavior on the market', *Financial Management* (Winter), pp. 26–31.

Benston, G. J. (1982) 'Accounting and corporate accountability', *Accounting, Organizations and Society*, 6 (2), pp. 87–105.

Blacconiere, W. G. & Patten, D. M. (1994) 'Environmental disclosures, regulatory costs and changes in firm value', *Journal of Accounting and Economics*, 18, pp. 357–77.

Brady, A. (2003) 'Forecasting the impact of sustainability issues on the reputation of large multinational corporations', Cambridge: Judge Institute of Management, University of Cambridge.

Brown, D., Dillard, J. F. & Marshall, R. S. (2005) 'Triple bottom line: A business metaphor for a social construct', Paper presented at Critical Perspectives on Accounting Conference, Baruch College, City University of New York, 28–30 May 2005.

Buhr, N. (1998) 'Environmental performance, legislation and annual report disclosure: the case of acid rain and Falconbridge', *Accounting, Auditing and Accountability Journal*, 11 (2), pp. 163–90.

Campbell, D. J. (2000) 'Legitimacy theory or managerial construction? Corporate social disclosure in Marks and Spencer Plc corporate reports, 1969–1997', *Accounting Forum*, 24 (1), pp. 80–100.

Clarkson, M. (1995) 'A stakeholder framework for analyzing and evaluating corporate social performance', *Academy of Management Review*, 20 (1), pp. 92–118.

Collison, D. J. (2003) 'Corporate propaganda: Its implications for accounting and accountability', *Accounting, Auditing & Accountability Journal*, 16 (5), pp. 853–86.

Deegan, C. (1996) 'A review of mandated environmental reporting requirements for Australian corporations together with an analysis of contemporary Australian and overseas environmental reporting practices', *Environmental and Planning Law Journal*, **13** (2), pp. 120–32.

Deegan, C. M. & Rankin, M. (1997) 'The materiality of environmental information to users of accounting reports', *Accounting, Auditing and Accountability Journal*, **10** (4), pp. 562–83.

Dillard, J. F., Brown, D. & Marshall, R. S. (2005) 'An environmentally enlightened accounting', *Accounting Forum*, **29** (1), pp. 77–101.

Donaldson, T. (1982) *Corporations and Morality*, Englewood Cliffs: Prentice-Hall.

Elkington, J. (1997) *Cannibals with Forks: The Triple Bottom Line of 21st Century Business*, Oxford: Capstone.

Environmental Accounting and Auditing Reporter (2000) 'First standard for building corporate accountability and trust', *Vol. 5, No. 1.*

Ernst & Young (2002) 'Corporate social responsibility: A survey of global companies', Melbourne: Ernst & Young.

European Commission (1992) 'Towards sustainability: A community programme of policy and action in relation to the environment and sustainable development', Brussels: European Commission.

Freedman, M. & Patten, D. M. (2004) 'Evidence on the pernicious effect of financial report environmental disclosure', *Accounting Forum*, **28** (1), pp. 27–41.

Freeman, R. (1984) *Strategic Management: A Stakeholder Approach*, Marshall, MA: Pitman.

Friedman, M. (1962) *Capitalism and Freedom*, Chicago: University of Chicago Press.

Georgakopoulos, G. & Thomson, I. (2005) 'Organic salmon farming: risk perceptions, decision heuristics and the absence of environmental accounting', *Accounting Forum*, **29** (1), pp. 49–75.

Giddens, A., (1990) *The Consequences of Modernity*, paperback edn, Cambridge: Polity Press.

Giddens, A. (1991) *Modernity and Self-identity*, paperback edn, Cambridge: Polity Press.

Giddens, A. (1994) 'Living in a post-traditional society', in Beck, U., Giddens, A. & Lash, S. (eds) *Reflexive Modernization: Politics, Tradition and Aesthetics in the Modern Social Order*, Cambridge: Polity Press, pp. 56–109.

Global Reporting Initiative (1999) 'GRI Vision and Mission Statements', *http://www.global reporting.org/about/mission.asp*, accessed: 11 July 2005.

Global Reporting Initiative (2002) 'Sustainability Reporting Guidelines', Boston, MA: Global Reporting Initiative.

Gray, R. (1992) 'Accounting and environmentalism: An exploration of the challenge of gently accounting for accountability, transparency and sustainability', *Accounting, Organizations and Society*, **17** (5), pp. 399–426.

Gray, R. (2005) 'Social, environmental and sustainability reporting and organisational value creation? Whose value? Whose creation?' Paper presented at European Accounting Association annual congress – Symposium on New Models of Business Reporting, Gothenburg, 18–20 May.

Gray, R. & Bebbington, J. (1992) 'Can the grey men go green?' Discussion Paper, Centre for Social and Environmental Accounting Research, University of Dundee.

Gray, R. & Bebbington, J. (2001) *Accounting for the Environment*, London: Sage Publications Ltd.

Gray, R., Bebbington, J., Collison, D., Kouhy, R., Lyon, B., Reid, C., Russell, A. & Stevenson, L. (1998) *The Valuation of Assets and Liabilities: Environmental Law and the Impact of the Environmental Agenda for Business*, Edinburgh: Institute of Chartered Accountants in Scotland.

Gray, R., Dey, C., Owen, D., Evans, R. & Zadek, S. (1997) 'Struggling with the praxis of social accounting: stakeholders, accountability, audits and procedures', *Accounting, Auditing and Accountability Journal*, **10** (3), pp. 325–64.

Gray, R., Owen, D. & Adams, C. (1996) *Accounting and Accountability: Changes and challenges in Corporate Social and Environmental Reporting*, London: Prentice-Hall.

Greene, D. (2002) 'Socially responsible investment in Australia 2002: Benchmarking survey conducted for the Ethical Investment Association', Sydney: Ethical Investment Association.

Guthrie, J. & Parker, L. D. (1989) 'Corporate social reporting: a rebuttal of legitimacy theory', *Accounting & Business Research*, **19** (76), pp. 343–52.

Habermas, J. (1992) *Moral Consciousness and Communicative Action*, Cambridge: Polity Press.

Hogner, R. H. (1982) 'Corporate social reporting: Eight decades of development at US Steel', *Research in Corporate Performance and Policy*, **4**, pp. 243–50.

Hutton, W. (1996) *The State We're In*, London: Vintage.

ICAEW (2004) *Sustainability: The role of acountants*, London: Institute of Chartered Accountants in England & Wales.

Ingram, R. W. (1978) 'Investigation of the information content of certain social responsibility disclosures', *Journal of Accounting Research*, **16** (2), pp. 270–85.

ISEA (2003) 'Assurance Standard AA1000', London: Institute of Social and Ethical Accountability.

ISEA (2005a) 'AA1000 Series: Assurance Standard', *http://www.accountability.org.uk/aa1000/default.asp?pageid = 52*, accessed: 11 June 2005.

ISEA (2005b) 'Accountability: AA1000 Series', *http://www.accountability.org.uk/aa1000/default.asp*, accessed: 8 June 2005.

Jaggi, B. & Freedman, M. (1982) 'An analysis of the information content of pollution disclosures', *Financial Review*, **19** (5), pp. 142–52.

Lewis, L. & Unerman, J. (1999) 'Ethical relativism: a reason for differences in corporate social reporting?' *Critical Perspectives on Accounting*, **10** (4), pp. 521–47.

Lorraine, N. H. J., Collison, D. J. & Power, D. M. (2004) 'An analysis of the stock market impact of environmental performance information', *Accounting Forum*, **28** (1), pp. 7–26.

Mathews, M. R. (1993) *Socially Responsible Accounting*, London: Chapman and Hall.

Neimark, M. K. (1992) *The Hidden Dimensions of Annual Reports: Sixty Years of Social Conflict at General Motors*, New York, NY: Markus Wiener Publishing Inc.

O'Dwyer, B. (2003) 'Conceptions of corporate social responsibility: the nature of managerial capture', *Accounting, Auditing and Accountability Journal*, **16** (4), pp. 523–57.

O'Dwyer, B. (2005) 'The construction of a social account: a case study in an overseas aid agency', *Accounting, Organizations and Society*, **30** (3), pp. 279–96.

Owen, D. & O'Dwyer, B. (2005) 'Assurance statement practice in environmental, social and sustainability reporting: A critical evaluation', *British Accounting Review*, **37** (2), pp. 205–29.

Owen, D., Shaw, K. & Cooper, S. (2005) 'The Operating and Financial Review: A catalyst for improved corporate social and environmental disclosure?' London: ACCA.

Shane, P. & Spicer, B. (1983) 'Market response to environmental information produced outside the firm', *The Accounting Review*, **58** (3), pp. 521–38.

Solomon, A. & Lewis, L. (2002) 'Incentives and disincentives for corporate environmental disclosure', *Business Strategy and the Environment*, **11** (3), pp. 154–69.

Solomon, J. F. & Solomon, A. (2005) 'Private social, ethical and environmental disclosure', *Accounting, Auditing & Accountability Journal*, **Forthcoming**.

Sustainability Ltd and United Nations Environmental Programme (2002) 'Trust us: The global reporters 2002 survey of corporate sustainability reporting', London: Sustainability Ltd/UNEP.

Tinker, A. & Neimark, M. (1987) 'The role of annual reports in gender and class contradictions at General Motors: 1917–1976', *Accounting, Organizations and Society*, **12** (1), pp. 71–88.

Tinker, A. & Neimark, M. (1988) 'The struggle over meaning in accounting and corporate research: A comparative evaluation of conservative and critical historiography',

Accounting, Auditing & Accountability Journal, **1** (1), pp. 55–74.

Unerman, J. (2000a) 'An investigation into the development of accounting for social, environmental and ethical accountability: A century of corporate social disclosures at Shell', Unpublished PhD thesis, Sheffield University Management School, University of Sheffield.

Unerman, J. (2000b) 'Reflections on quantification in corporate social reporting content analysis', *Accounting, Auditing & Accountability Journal,* **13** (5), pp. 667–80.

Unerman, J. & Bennett, M. (2004) 'Increased stakeholder dialogue and the internet: towards greater corporate accountability or reinforcing capitalist hegemony?' *Accounting, Organizations and Society,* **29** (7), pp. 685–707.

Unerman, J. & O'Dwyer, B. (2004) 'Theorising corporate social responsibility/corporate social disclosures as a risk discourse', Paper presented at International Congress on Social and Environmental Accounting, University of Dundee.

Venetoulis, J., Chazan, D. & Gaudet, C. (2004) 'Ecological footprint of nations', Oakland, CA: Redefining Progress.

World Commission on Environment and Development (1987) *Our Common Future (The Brundtland Report),* Oxford: Oxford University Press.

CHAPTER 10

Reactions of capital markets to financial reporting

Learning Objectives

Upon completing this chapter readers should:

- understand the role of capital market research in assessing the information content of accounting disclosures;
- understand the assumptions of market efficiency adopted in capital market research;
- understand the difference between capital market research that looks at the *information content* of accounting disclosures, and capital market research that uses share price data as a *benchmark* for evaluating accounting disclosures;
- be able to explain why unexpected accounting earnings and abnormal share price returns are expected to be related;
- be able to outline the major results of capital market research into financial accounting and disclosure.

Opening issues

Assume that there are five companies from the same industry with the same balance sheet date, 31 December. All five companies are to make earnings announcements for the financial year (the announcements being made in February), but the earnings announcements are spread over two weeks, with no two companies announcing their earnings on the same date.

(a) Would you expect the earnings announcements made by each company to impact on their share prices, and if so, why?

(b) If it is found that the share prices of some entities change more around the date of the earnings announcement than others, what might have caused this price–effect differential?

(c) Would you expect the share prices of larger companies, or smaller companies, to be relatively more impacted by an earnings announcement?

(d) Once the first company in the sample of five makes its earnings announcement, would you expect this announcement to impact on the prices of shares in the other four companies? Why?

Introduction

In some of the previous chapters we have considered various normative prescriptions pertaining to how accounting *should* be undertaken. For example, Chapter 5 discussed theories that had been developed to prescribe how accounting *should* be undertaken in times of rising prices (for example, general price level accounting, current cost accounting, and continuously contemporary accounting). Chapter 6 considered the role of conceptual frameworks in providing prescription (such frameworks can tell us what the objective of accounting is; what qualitative characteristics accounting information *should* possess; how elements of accounting *should* be defined and recognized; and how assets and liabilities *should* be measured). Parts of Chapter 9 provided an insight into various approaches adopted to disclose information about an organization's social and environmental performance (which has indeed become an area of accounting research that has grown rapidly in recent years).

While the above-mentioned chapters provided a great deal of prescription, they tended not to provide any theoretical arguments as to the *motivations* for managers to make the disclosures. This void was filled by Chapters 7, 8 and parts of Chapter 9, which provided different theoretical perspectives about what drove management to make the disclosures. Chapter 7 discussed Positive Accounting Theory and it indicated that where management had a choice in selecting a particular approach to accounting, both *efficiency* arguments and *opportunistic* arguments could be advanced to explain and predict management's accounting choices. Chapter 8 provided alternative explanations of management's behaviour. It showed that the choice of a particular accounting method might be made to restore the *legitimacy* of an organization (from legitimacy theory), or because such disclosure was necessary to retain the support of powerful stakeholders (from stakeholder theory), or because the accounting method had been adopted by other organizations (institutional theory).

While the above material provided a perspective of what motivates managers to provide particular accounting information, the material did not consider the further issue of how individuals, or groups of individuals in aggregate, react to accounting disclosures. This chapter and Chapter 11 provide material that addresses this issue.

This chapter and Chapter 11 examine the impact of financial accounting and disclosure decisions on the users of financial reports. Specifically, we look at research that focuses on the impact of alternative accounting and disclosure choices on the investment decisions of financial statement users such as share market investors, financial analysts, bank lending officers, and auditors.

Reported profit depends on many financial accounting decisions. Managers have much scope in selecting between alternative accounting methods and accounting assumptions. For example, they will choose between expensing or capitalizing particular costs; they will choose between alternative accounting methods such as straight-line or reducing balance depreciation; they will exercise discretion in relation to accounting estimates such as the useful life of assets to be depreciated; and so on. Further, decisions must be made in relation to how much information to disclose, the medium for disclosure, and, in some circumstances, whether to recognize particular items in the financial statements, or merely disclose them in the footnotes to the statements.

Financial reporting decisions impact on the information provided to users of financial reports. This in turn may have implications for the decisions that users make. There are two ways to assess the impacts of financial reporting decisions:

◆ determine the impact of the information on the decisions of individual information users (behavioural research); and

◆ determine what impact the release of information has on share prices (capital market research).

In this chapter we consider capital market research (which considers reactions at an *aggregate* or *market* level). In Chapter 11 we review behavioural research undertaken at the *individual* level.

An overview of capital market research

Capital market research explores the role of accounting and other financial information in equity markets. This type of research involves examining statistical relations between financial information, and share prices or returns. Reactions of investors are evidenced by their capital market transactions. Favourable reactions to information are presumed to be evidenced by a price increase in the particular security, whereas unfavourable reactions to information are evidenced by a price decrease. No price change around the time of the release of information implies no reaction to the information (the release does not provide anything that is *new*).

Conclusions about the market's reaction to particular information releases or events are generally based on evidence from a large number of companies, with data spanning several years. This type of research is often used to examine equity market reactions to announcements of company information, and to assess the relevance of alternative accounting and disclosure choices for investors. If security prices change around the time of the release of particular information, and assuming that the information and not some other event caused the price change, then it is considered that the information was relevant and useful for investment decision making.

In contrast to behavioural research (considered in Chapter 11) which analyses *individual* responses to financial reporting, capital market research assesses the *aggregate* effect of financial reporting, particularly the reporting of accounting earnings, on investors. By analysing share price reactions to financial information releases, the sum of individual investor decisions is captured in aggregate. But when considering such research, a possible question that comes to mind is why have so many research studies been undertaken that focus on the market's response to accounting earnings announcements? Brown (1994, p. 24) provides one answer to this issue. He argues:

> Four reasons are that, according to the Financial Accounting Standards Board, infor-
> mation about earnings and its components is the primary purpose of financial reporting;
> earnings are oriented towards the interests of shareholders who are an important group
> of financial statement users; earnings is the number most analysed and forecast by
> security analysts; and reliable data on earnings were readily available.

Another important difference between capital market and behavioural research is that capital market research considers only investors, while behavioural research is often used to examine decision making by other types of financial statement users such as bank managers, loan officers or auditors.

Capital market research relies on the underlying assumption that equity markets are efficient. Market efficiency is defined in accordance with the efficient market hypothesis (EMH) as a market that adjusts rapidly to fully impound information into share prices when the information is released (Fama *et al.*, 1969). Capital market research in accounting assumes that equity markets are *semi-strong form efficient*. That is, that all publicly available information, including that available in financial statements and other financial disclosures, is rapidly and fully impounded into share prices in an unbiased manner as it is released. Relevant information is not ignored by the market.

Semi-strong form efficiency is the most relevant for capital market research in accounting, since it relates to the use of *publicly available* information. Other hypotheses about market efficiency are the *weak-form efficiency* perspective, and the *strong-form efficiency* perspective. The *weak form* of market efficiency assumes that existing security prices simply reflect information about past prices and trading volumes. The *strong form* of market efficiency assumes that security prices, on average, reflect all information known to anyone at that point in time (including information not publicly available). According to Watts and Zimmerman (1986, p. 19) the available evidence is generally consistent with the semi-strong form of the EMH.[1]

The view that markets are efficient does not imply that share prices will always provide an accurate prediction of the value of future cash flows. Market predictions are sometimes proved in hindsight to be wrong, thus necessitating subsequent adjustments. As Hendriksen and Van Breda (1992, p. 177) state:

> It needs to be stressed that market efficiency does not imply clairvoyance on the part of the market. All it implies is that the market reflects the best guesses of all its participants, based on the knowledge available at the time. New information appears all the time that proves the market was incorrect. In fact, by definition, the market will not react until it learns something that it did not know the day before. One cannot prove the market inefficient, therefore, by looking back, using the benefits of hindsight and pointing to places where the market was incorrect. Market efficiency simply asserts that prices are appropriately set based on current knowledge; practical evidence shows that with hindsight the market is always incorrect.

The assumption of market efficiency is central to capital market research. But why is the assumption of information efficiency so important for capital market research in accounting? Simply put, unless such an assumption of efficiency is accepted, it is hard to justify efforts to link security price movements to information releases. A great deal of capital market research considers the relationship between share prices and information releases. The reason for looking at this relationship is that share prices in an efficient market are deemed to be based on expectations about future earnings. If particular information leads to a price change, then the assumption is that the information was *useful* and caused investors to revise their expectations about the future earnings of the organization in question. That is, share prices and returns are used as benchmarks against which the usefulness of financial information is assessed. If we do not assume market efficiency, then there is an inability to explain how or why share prices change around the date of information releases. If share markets are not semi-strong form efficient, they do not provide accurate benchmarks against which to assess alternative financial reporting choices. Overall, market inefficiency would render capital market research results to be at best less convincing, and at worst extremely unreliable, depending on the extent of inefficiency present.

Assumptions about market efficiency in turn have implications for accounting. If markets are efficient, they will use information from various sources when predicting future earnings, and hence when determining current share prices. If accounting information does not impact on share prices then, assuming semi-strong form efficiency, it would be deemed not to provide any information over and above that currently available. At the extreme, accounting's survival would be threatened.[2]

A share price reaction to the release of financial information is taken to indicate that the announcement has 'information content', while a high association between financial information and share prices or returns over an extended period of time indicates that the information provided by the accounting system reflects information that is being used by the capital market (and this information will come from a multitude of sources). Each of these roles for accounting information in equity markets is explored in the following sections. While the 'information content' of many types of financial information can be assessed using capital market research, the bulk of this work has focused on earnings as the primary measure of the financial accounting system. For example, one issue that has been the subject of many research papers is whether earnings announcements cause a movement in share price. This focus is reflected in the following discussion.

The information content of earnings

Many research papers have investigated capital market reactions to earnings announcements. That is, when a company announces its earnings for the year (or half-year), what is the impact, if any, on its share price? Assuming that capital markets are semi-strong form efficient (they react swiftly and in an unbiased manner to *publicly available* information), a movement in share price is considered to indicate that the new information in the public earnings announcement has been incorporated into the security's price through the activities of investors in the market. It was *useful* in reassessing the future cash flows of the entity.

A number of studies have shown information about earnings to be linked to changes in the price of securities. But, why would we expect accounting earnings and share prices to be related? Modern finance theory proposes that a share price can be determined as the sum of expected future cash flows from dividends, discounted to their present value using a rate of return commensurate with the company's level of risk. Further, dividends are a function of accounting earnings, since they can generally only be paid out of past and current earnings. It follows therefore that if cash flows are related to (a function of) accounting earnings, then the price of a share in company i, which we can denote as (P_i), can be viewed as the sum of expected future earnings per share $(\overline{E})$, discounted to their present value using a risk-adjusted discount rate (k_i).[3] That is, for company i today:

$$P_i = \sum_{t=1}^{\infty} \overline{E}_t / (1 + k_i)^t \tag{10.1}$$

Equation 10.1 shows that a relation exists between share price and expected future earnings. In general, companies with higher expected future earnings will have higher share prices. These expectations are formed, at least in part, on the basis of historical earnings for the company. However, all currently available information (for example, media releases, analysts' reports, production statistics, market surveys, etc.) are considered when predicting future earnings. Any revisions to expectations about future earnings per share, including those resulting from new information contained in announcements of current earnings, will be reflected in a change in share price.

Revisions to expectations about future earnings per share will result only from *new* information, since under the maintained assumption of a semi-strong form efficient market, price is assumed to already reflect all *publicly known* information, including expectations about current earnings. Therefore, only the unexpected component of current earnings announcements constitutes new information. That is, unexpected earnings, rather than total earnings, are expected to be associated with a change in share price. For example, if CMR Company announces annual earnings of €11 million when only €10.5 million was expected, unexpected earnings are equal to €0.5 million. Any share price reaction will be to these unexpected earnings rather than to total annual earnings of €11 million, since investors already anticipated most of this.

Such a change in share price results in a return to investors (R_{it}), since returns are a function of capital gains or losses, in addition to dividends received (D_{it}). Thus, for an investment in firm i for one holding period $(t-1$ to $t)$ the return would be:[4]

$$R_{it} = \frac{(P_{it} - P_{it-1}) + D_{it}}{P_{it-1}} \tag{10.2}$$

The length of time over which returns are calculated (the return period) depends on the particular research focus, but is generally not less than one day, or longer than one year. In return periods where no dividend is paid, returns can simply be calculated as a percentage change in share price. This is generally the case when returns are calculated on a daily basis. For example, if CMR Company's share price moved from €5.42 to €5.56 during the day when earnings were announced, the daily return (R_{CMR}) is equal to $(€5.56 - €5.42)/€5.42$ or 2.6 per cent.

Given that returns are a function of changes in share prices (from Equation 10.2), and share price can be expressed as a function of expected future earnings (from Equation 10.1), returns are related to changes in expected future earnings. This relation is often referred to as the earnings/return relation. For CMR Company, the unexpected announcement of an additional €0.5 million of earnings has resulted in a return to investors of approximately 2.6 per cent, as indicated in the above calculation. This positive return indicates that investors expect future earnings to be higher than originally expected.

Of course, not all share returns are due to investors trading on information about individual companies. Share prices tend to change on a daily basis due to things that affect the whole market, or sectors of it. We can call these 'systematic changes'. For example, the publication of new (and unexpected) statistics about factors likely to affect the whole economy to some extent – such as rates of inflation, levels of unemployment, or the general level of consumer or business confidence – and daily returns for individual companies largely reflect this.

The market model (see Fama, 1976, for details about its early development), which is derived from the capital asset pricing model (CAPM), is used to separate out firm-specific share price movements from market-wide movements.[5] The CAPM explains how a market should decide the appropriate return on a share, given its riskiness. It predicts a linear relationship between expected returns and systematic risk, where systematic risk is the riskiness of an asset when it is held as part of a thoroughly diversified portfolio. Systematic risk is the non-diversifiable or unavoidable risk that investors are compensated for through increased returns. The market model is expressed as:

$$R_{it} = \alpha_{it} + \beta_{it} R_{mt} + \mu_{it} \tag{10.3}$$

where R_{it} is the return for company i during period t, calculated in accordance with Equation 10.2; R_{mt} is the return for the entire market during period t (as would be approximated by the average return generated from a very large diversified portfolio of securities); and β_{it} is company i's level of systematic risk, which indicates how sensitive the returns of firm i's securities are, relative to market-wide (systematic) movements.[6] α_{it} is a constant specific to firm i, while μ_{it} is an error term that provides an indication of how the return on a security relates or moves with respect to specific events.

For the market model it is assumed that the variations in returns on individual securities are largely due to market-wide factors. As a portfolio of investments increases in diversity, the non-systematic risk of the diversified portfolio (measured by $\alpha_{it} + \mu_{it}$) tends to disappear, thereby leaving only returns that are due to market-wide movements (that is, $\beta_{it} R_{mt}$). The market model makes a number of assumptions, including that investors are risk averse and that investors have homogeneous expectations (they think alike).

Equation 10.3 shows that total or actual returns can be divided into normal (or expected) returns, given market-wide price movements ($\alpha_{it} + \beta_{it} R_{mt}$), and abnormal (or unexpected) returns due to firm-specific share price movements (μ_{it}).[7] Normal returns are expected to vary from company to company, depending on their level of systematic risk in relation to the market, while abnormal returns are expected to vary from company to company, depending on whether there is new information about the company that causes investors to revise expectations about future earnings.

The market model is used to control for share price movements due to market-wide events, allowing the researcher to focus on share price movements due to firm-specific news. For example, part of the 2.6 per cent return earned by CMR Company upon announcing its annual earnings may be due to an overall rise in the market on the announcement day. A researcher analysing the impact of the earnings announcement would control for the impact of this rise in the market by deducting it from CMR Company's return. Assuming $\alpha_{CMR} = 0$, $\beta_{CMR} = 1$, and $R_m = 1$ per cent, this calculation would leave an abnormal return (μ_{CMR}) of 1.6 per cent.[8] It is abnormal returns, or firm-specific share price movements, that are analysed by researchers to determine the information effects of company announcements.

Capital market research into the earnings/return relation analyses firm-specific price movements (abnormal returns) at the time of earnings announcements. These abnormal returns are used as an indicator of the information content of the announcement. That is, how much, if any, *new* information has been released to the capital markets. If there is no price reaction, it is assumed that the announcement contained no new information. That is, the information was already known or anticipated by market participants.

Results of capital market research into financial reporting

Capital market research has been a major focus of financial accounting research over the past 35 years. The research has investigated the information content of earnings as well as many other accounting and disclosure items. Results of this research are useful for both practising accountants and finance professionals such as security analysts. Knowledge of these results is considered to be particularly useful in relation to making financial reporting decisions. More informed choices between accounting and disclosure alternatives can be made if the expected impacts on share prices are anticipated when making financial reporting decisions. A summary comprising some of the more important capital market research results follows.

Historical cost income is used by investors

Ball and Brown (1968), in the first major capital market research publication in accounting, investigated the usefulness of accounting earnings under a historical cost model. Prior to their research, there was a widely held view that historical cost accounting methods resulted in 'meaningless' information that was not useful for investors and other users of financial statements.[9] Ball and Brown saw the need for empirical evidence about whether accounting earnings, calculated using historical cost accounting principles, provide useful information to investors. They state (p. 159):

> If, as the evidence indicates, security prices do in fact adjust rapidly to new information as it becomes available, then changes in security prices will reflect the flow of information

to the market. An observed revision of stock prices associated with the release of the income report would thus provide evidence that the information reflected in income numbers is useful.

Using data for 261 US companies, they tested whether firms with unexpected increases in accounting earnings had positive abnormal returns, and firms with unexpected decreases in accounting earnings had negative abnormal returns (on average). Unexpected earnings were calculated (quite simplistically) as the difference between current earnings and previous year earnings. That is, they assumed that this year's earnings were expected to be the same as last year's earnings. Monthly share price data were used, with the market model being used to calculate abnormal returns for each company. Cumulative abnormal returns (CARs) were

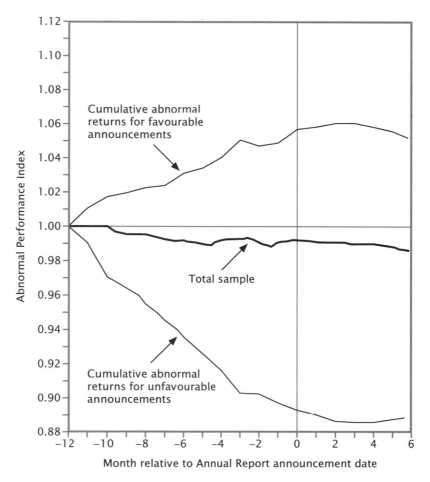

Figure 10.1 Movements in cumulative abnormal returns before and after the announcement of earnings
Source: Ball and Brown (1968)

then calculated for each of (a) the full sample of companies, (b) firms with unexpected increases in earnings (favourable announcements), and (c) firms with unexpected decreases in earnings (unfavourable announcements), by summing the average abnormal returns for each of these groups over time.

They found evidence to suggest that the information contained in the annual report is used in investment decision making, despite the limitations of the historical cost accounting system. This result is evidenced by the CARs during the month of the earnings announcements (month 0). As can be seen from Figure 10.1, firms with unexpected increases in earnings (favourable announcements), represented by the top line in the chart, had positive abnormal returns, while firms with unexpected decreases in earnings (unfavourable announcements), represented by the bottom line in the chart, had negative abnormal returns during the announcement month (on average). Since Ball and Brown's early study, this research has been replicated many times using more sophisticated data and research methods. The results appear to confirm the usefulness of historical cost income to investors. This is not to say that the historical cost accounting system is the 'most useful', since a present value or current cost accounting system may be more useful, but it gives some credence to the continued use of historical costs.

Prior to an earnings release, investors obtain much of the information they need from other sources

In addition to confirming the usefulness of the historical cost accounting model, Ball and Brown found that most of the information contained in earnings announcements (85–90 per cent) is anticipated by investors. The gradual slope in the lines (which represent the cumulative abnormal returns) prior to the earnings announcements (which were made at time 0) in Figure 10.1 provide evidence of this. Anticipation of earnings changes by investors indicates that investors obtain much of the information useful for investment decision making from sources other than annual earnings announcements (perhaps from media releases, analysts' releases, information about the industry's production and sales trends, and so on). This is not surprising given that alternative sources of information such as conference calls to analysts, and press releases, are generally more timely than the annual report, which tends to be issued several weeks after balance sheet date and less frequently than many alternative sources of information. Therefore, we can never expect to produce accounting statements that will tell investors everything they may want to know. That is, provision of *all* relevant information to investors is not a good basis for regulation or practice. When making financial reporting decisions, it is important to remember that, while accounting appears to be an important source of information for the stock market, it is not the only source of information.

In finishing our discussion of Ball and Brown (1968) it is perhaps worth noting that this paper is generally accepted as the most cited academic accounting article.

It certainly represented quite a change from previous accounting research, which was predominantly normative. Reflecting on the significance of Ball and Brown (1968), Brown (1994, p. 24) states:

> A number of reasons have been given to explain the paper's major impact on the accounting literature since 1968:
>
> ◆ It was cast in the mould of a traditional experiment: hypothesis, data collection, data analysis, conclusion.
> ◆ It expressed a view that ran counter to the critics of GAAP (these critics arguing that historical cost accounting information was meaningless and useless).
> ◆ It was an early plea for 'empirical research'.
> ◆ It emphasized the use of data to test a belief.
> ◆ It adopted an information perspective.
> ◆ It contained the basic elements of a research design that became a model for future research: the semi-strong form of the EMH was a maintained hypothesis, so the focus was on market behaviour around an announcement date; earnings predictions were modelled to identify the news in, or what was new about, the earnings report; GAAP earnings were compared with a primary version of operating cash flows; and abnormal returns were measured by the Market Model and the CAPM.
> ◆ It was a particularly robust experiment, in the sense that it has been replicated for firms with different fiscal years, in different countries, and at different times.
> ◆ It gave rise to many papers in related areas.

As Chapter 7 indicates, Watts and Zimmerman (1986) credit the development of Positive Accounting Theory, at least in part, to the early experimental approach adopted by Ball and Brown (1968).

The information content of earnings announcements depends on the extent of alternative sources of information

Research indicates that the information content of earnings varies between countries and between companies within a country. For example, Brown (1970) found that when compared to US markets, the Australian market has slower adjustments during the year, with larger adjustments at the earnings announcement date. This result implies that annual reports were a more important source of information for the Australian capital markets than they were for US capital markets because there were fewer alternative sources of information for Australian companies. This difference in the extent of alternative sources of information is partly due to Australian regulations that required only semi-annual rather than quarterly reporting, and is also a function of differences in average firm sizes between the two countries. Smaller firms tend to have fewer alternative sources of information than larger firms, and are less likely to be followed by security analysts. This difference in the extent of alternative sources of information between smaller and larger firms causes differences in the usefulness of earnings announcements, with these being more useful for smaller than larger Australian firms. Therefore, the extent of alternative sources of information should be considered when making financial reporting decisions. (We return to the issue of size later in this chapter.)

The capital market impact of unexpected changes in earnings depends on whether the change is expected to be permanent or temporary

Following Ball and Brown's finding that the *direction* of unexpected earnings changes is positively related to the *direction* of abnormal returns, further research was conducted into the relation between the *magnitude* of the unexpected change in earnings, or earnings per share, and the *magnitude* of the abnormal returns. This relationship is often referred to as the *earnings response coefficient*. The results show that this is not a one-to-one relationship. Indeed, some research has shown that the average abnormal return associated with a 1 per cent unexpected change in earnings is only 0.1 to 0.15 per cent (Beaver *et al.*, 1980). This relationship varies, depending on whether the change in earnings is expected to be permanent or temporary. Permanent increases are expected to result in increased dividends, and therefore future cash flows, and this implies a change in the value of the company. On the other hand, temporary increases are discounted or ignored, since they are not expected to have the same impact on expected future dividends (Easton and Zmijewski, 1989). While some earnings changes such as those due to one-off restructuring charges are obviously temporary, it is more difficult to determine whether other earnings changes are likely to persist.

Earnings persistence depends on the relative magnitudes of cash and accruals components of current earnings

The accrual system of accounting differs from the cash basis of accounting owing to differences in when cash flows are recognized in the financial statements. Under the accrual system, some items are recognized before the cash flows are received or paid (for example, credit sales and purchases), while others are recognized on a periodic basis (for example, the cost of a fixed asset is recognized over its useful life through periodic depreciation charges). Therefore, the accrual process involves adjusting the timing of when the cash inflows and outflows of a firm are recognized to achieve a matching of revenues and expenses. Earnings, the summary performance measure of the accrual system, has fewer timing and mismatching problems than performance measures based on unadjusted cash flows (for example, cash flows from operations). However, application of the accrual system can be a subjective rather than an objective process, and depending upon the choices made, many different earnings figures can be achieved. For example, if the reducing balance method of depreciation is chosen over the straight-line method, reported profits will initially be lower, owing to a greater depreciation expense. However, reported earnings will be higher in the later years of the asset's life due to lower depreciation expense. Sloan (1996) undertook a study to see if share prices behave as if investors simply 'fixate' on reported earnings without considering how those numbers have actually been determined (that is, what methods of accounting have been employed). According to Sloan (1996, p. 291):

> A meaningful test of whether stock prices fully reflect available information requires the specification of an alternative 'naïve' expectation model, against which to test the null of market efficiency. The naïve model employed in this study is that investors 'fixate' on earnings and fail to distinguish between the accrual and cash flow component of current earnings. This naïve earnings expectation model is consistent with the functional fixation hypothesis, which has received empirical support in capital market, behavioral and experimental research. [10]

Sloan provides evidence that firms with large accruals relative to their actual cash flows are unlikely to have persistently high earnings, since the accruals reverse over time, reducing future earnings. However, share prices are found to act as if investors simply 'fixate' on reported earnings, thereby failing to take account of the relative magnitudes of the cash and accrual components of current earnings (fixation implying a degree of market inefficiency). In concluding his paper, Sloan (p. 314) states:

> This paper investigates whether stock prices reflect information about future earnings contained in the accrual and cash flow components of current earnings. The persistence of earnings performance is shown to depend on the relative magnitudes of the cash and accrual components of earnings. However, stock prices act as if investors fail to identify correctly the different properties of these two components of earnings.

Hence, while earnings can be managed up through various discretionary accruals, this cannot be done indefinitely, and earnings will eventually be lower as the accruals subsequently reverse. Likewise, while it may be possible to increase share prices through reporting higher earnings, this effect will be reversed when lower earnings are reported in the future. Although the lower earnings are due to the reversal of accruals, evidence indicates that the market *fixates* on the lower reported earnings, and share prices therefore fall as the accruals subsequently reverse. Notions of market efficiency, such as the functional fixation perspective, have been hotly contested in the accounting literature.

The earnings announcements of other firms in the same industry have information content

When a company announces its annual earnings, this generally results in abnormal returns for not only the company concerned, but also for other companies in the same industry (Foster, 1981). That is, there is information content for similar firms as well as for the announcing firm. This phenomenon, known as 'information transfer', reduces the surprise (unknown) element in earnings announcements of other firms in the industry who choose to announce their earnings later. The direction of the capital market reaction is related to whether the news contained in the announcement reflects a change in conditions for the entire industry, or changes in relative market share within the industry. Because information is gained from the announcements of similar firms, information releases about sales and earnings changes result in price reactions for other firms in an industry, as well as the firm making the announcement (Freeman and Tse, 1992). Therefore, in forming expectations about how information releases, such as earnings announcements, might affect share prices, it is important to consider the timing of information releases relative to those of similar firms, since information about a company can be gained from the information releases of similar companies.

Firth (1976) investigated the 'information transfer' issue. He sought to 'investigate the impact of a company's results being publicly announced on the share price behaviour of competing firms' (p. 298). His results indicated that when 'good news' was released about accounting earnings, the share prices of the non-announcing firms in the same industry reacted quickly (the same day) by showing a statistically significant increase. Interestingly there seemed to be no abnormal returns in the days before the announcement (limited anticipation) or the days after the announcement. That is, most of the adjustment appeared to occur fairly immediately. Similar results were found with respect to 'bad news' earnings announcements. The share prices of non-disclosing firms in the industry tended to fall on the day of the 'bad news' earnings announcement.

If the announcement of earnings by one company impacts on the share prices of other companies in the same industry, there would be an expectation that if a number of companies are about to release earnings information, then all other things being equal, the largest share price reactions might be generated by the entity that makes the first release. By the time the last entity releases its earnings announcements for a particular year end, it could be expected that a great deal of this information would already have been impounded in share prices and hence the last announcement would have relatively little impact on share prices. This expectation was confirmed by Clinch and Sinclair (1987). In summarizing their findings they state (p. 105):

> The directional association between daily price changes for announcing and non-announcing firms and the magnitude of the price change diminishes for subsequent announcing firms in the same industry over the reporting period.

We can relate the view that announcements by one company can impact on share prices of another company to a recent newspaper article relating to consumer product companies. Exhibit 10.1 shows that when two large consumer product companies released profit warnings, this seemed to cause share price reactions in the shares of other companies in the sector. This is consistent with the results reported above.

Exhibit 10.1 An illustration of the 'information transfer' effect

Colgate, Unilever warn on profits: Consumer products sector hit as household names highlight pressure to cut costs and keep sales

Lauren Foster and Adam Jones

Unilever and Colgate-Palmolive yesterday delivered profit warnings that knocked shares across the consumer products sector and highlighted the intense competition in an industry trying to please price-conscious retailers and consumers.

Unilever, the maker of Dove soap and Knorr soup, saw its shares fall five per cent to 459 1/2p after it said that it would not report the promised double-digit growth in underlying earnings per share this year. It now expects only low single-digit growth.

Colgate shares fell more than 10 per cent after it warned third- and fourth-quarter earnings would be lower than expected as increased marketing spending outweighed growth in volumes and market share and higher raw material costs offset its cost-cutting programme.

As well as competition from rival manufacturers, consumer goods multi-nationals have also had to cope with pricing pressure from powerful retail customers such as Wal-Mart, as well as a reluctance among many consumers to pay extra for brands.

Unilever's profit warning was a blow for Niall FitzGerald, its co-chairman, who steps down at the end of this month after 37 years with the company.

It is also another failure for the company's ambitious Path to Growth restructuring, which is coming to the end of its five-year life. The Path to Growth leading brands' sales target of 5–6 per cent annual growth had already been abandoned.

Unilever said that the poor summer weather in northern Europe had hit sales of ice cream and 'ready-to-drink' tea.

The market for toiletries and cleaning products became tougher in western Europe, with many consumers reluctant to pay extra for branded goods. Sales of its leading brands are expected to fall in the third quarter.

Patrick Cescau, Mr FitzGerald's successor, said he did not see a need for radical structural change, such as splitting the company into a stand-alone food business and another business selling toiletries.

Exhibit 10.1 (*continued*)

He said: 'The challenge we are facing at the moment is one of under-performance and operation.'

Unilever also pledged to increase the amount of money it spent on marketing its brands. Last month the Financial Times reported that some investors feared the company was endangering its brands by spending too little on advertising and promotions to avoid a profit warning.

Reuben Mark, Colgate chairman and chief executive, also highlighted the need for high marketing budgets.

He said: 'We are confident that we are taking the right measures to accelerate our growth and profitability for 2005 and beyond.

'It is vital that we maintain the aggressive commercial spending to build market share and blunt competitive efforts.'

He said Colgate expected earnings of 57–59 cents a share for the third and fourth quarters – well below consensus forecasts.

Analysts expected earnings of 67 cents a share for the third quarter, and 68 cents a share for the fourth quarter, according to Thomson First Call.

Colgate is locked in a fierce battle with Procter & Gamble for leadership of the US toothpaste and tooth-whitening markets. Its shares were down 11.4 per cent at $48.15 in late afternoon trade.

Financial Times, 21 September 2004, p. 1

Earnings forecasts have information content

Announcements of earnings forecasts by both management and security analysts are associated with share returns. That is, not only do announcements of actual earnings appear to cause share prices to change, but announcements of expected earnings also appear to cause price changes. Similar to earnings announcements, earnings forecasts are associated with market returns in terms of both direction and magnitude (Imhoff and Lobo, 1984; Penman, 1980). These results are not surprising since earnings forecasts are expected to contain *new* information that can be used in the prediction of future earnings. Forecasts of expected future earnings appear to be an effective way of communicating information to the share market. Also, bad news forecasts about lower than anticipated future earnings may be useful for avoiding potential shareholder lawsuits (Skinner, 1997).

Earnings forecasts have also been explored in terms of the 'information transfer' phenomenon discussed above. Baginski (1987) generated results that showed that the share prices of firms within the same industry that did not provide an earnings forecast were positively correlated with the change in earnings expectation indicated by earnings forecasts released by managers of other firms within the same industry.

Exhibit 10.2 provides an example of where it appears that a profit forecast led to a decrease in share price, consistent with some of the research results reported above. However, what must be remembered in research that looks at market reactions around particular events is that it is possible that share prices might actually be reacting to other unknown (by the researcher) contemporaneous events.

Exhibit 10.2 Profit forecasts and their potential influence on share price

You can't rush an artist: why Coldplay's struggle is bad for EMI

Jane Martinson and Alexis Petridis

For the first time in years, tomorrow night's Brit awards, the annual love-in for the British music industry, should make the home crowd proud. Not only are the nominations dominated by British talent such as Franz Ferdinand and Keane, but the industry is showing signs of recovery after years in the doldrums.

Imagine the disappointment, then, among executives of EMI, when it put out a profits warning yesterday that sales would be 8–9% lower in the year to the end of March. Analysts, who had expected sales to hold steady from the company, cut their profits forecasts by about £30m to £138m. The profits warning prompted a 16% decline in the company's share price yesterday, wiping £320m from its stock market value.

Yet the story behind EMI's announcement was all the more puzzling. There were no signs of a wider malaise, no indications that internet down-loading – the threat that induces cold sweats in industry executives – was exacting a price.

The explanation was much more simple, and traditional: over the weekend, executives had been told by Coldplay that the top-selling band's third album would not be ready for release until after EMI's financial year ended in March. To compound the problem, the next release from Gorillaz, the cartoon-inspired act founded by former Blur star Damon Albarn, will also be later than expected.

Several industry executives said yesterday's surprise announcement showed that EMI and its new finance director, who started from satellite group Sky last week, were 'putting artists first'.

The very idea would probably come as a shock to the Sex Pistols, who turned their lyrical fury on the company when it withdrew their contract after they appeared to become a little too punk for their own good.

Exhibit 10.2 (*continued*)

In their catharsis-heavy song EMI, Johnny Rotten sang: 'There's unlimited supply/And there is no reason why/I tell you it was all a frame/They only did it 'cos of fame/Who?/EMI EMI EMI'.

The fact remains, however, that there is very little a record company can do when artists refuse to be rushed by financial imperative. As one executive, who refused to be named, said: 'These people don't read [EMI's] fiscal calendar before they go to bed.'

But they do bring in huge amounts of money. From the Beatles to U2 and through to Coldplay, the biggest bands in a record company's stable have always lived by a different set of rules to its promising newcomers.

And, although Gorillaz have failed to make a Coldplay-sized dent in the global music market, they have chalked up sales of more than 1m in the US – quite an achievement for a British act.

Chris Martin, the lead singer of Coldplay, otherwise known as Mr Gwyneth Paltrow, has described the making of their third album as 'one of the most difficult experiences of my life'. After the band's second album, A Rush of Blood to the Head, sold 10m copies, Coldplay could also be facing the 'tall poppy' syndrome that has previously affected artists including Alanis Morrissette and David Gray: releasing a follow-up album which appears a failure because it does not match the mammoth sales of its predecessor.

The pressure is compounded further by the fact that Coldplay has spawned imitators – including Keane, Snow Patrol and Athlete, the EMI-signed band whose Tourist is currently number one in the album chart – whose commercial success has not been matched by critical acclaim. As for the Gorillaz album's delay, one rumoured reason is that Albarn has concurrently been making an album in Lagos with Tony Allen, formerly the drummer in Fela Kuti's band.

About half of the downturn was due to weak sales since the start of the year.

Even EMI blamed the difficulty of timing success in a notoriously volatile market rather than the market itself. Alain Levy, chairman and chief executive of EMI Music, said: 'Creating and marketing music is not an exact science.' Five years after illegal downloading helped push the industry into recession, UK album sales rose by 2.6% by volume in 2004, according to the Official Chart company. Pressure on pricing, mainly due to online competition, meant that the value of those sales rose by only 1%, but they were still the best for years.

With sales globally expected to be flat last year, the UK music market is the only one in the world bigger than it was five years ago.

Exhibit 10.2 (*continued*)

The singles market – decimated by illegal downloading – showed signs of recovery at the end of last year once legal downloads were included.

The UK contributes about 19% of EMI's sales so it is still dependent on a global market that is still struggling to return to life, particularly in continental Europe.

The industry pick-up comes on the back of a wave of successful new acts last year. Four of the top five best-selling albums were signed in the UK with three of those – the Scissor Sisters, Keane and Katie Melua – unknown in 2003.

Last year was not entirely gloomy for EMI. The British R&B singer Jamelia proved an unlikely success in a market dominated by US artists, while greatest hits albums by Robbie Williams and Kylie Minogue sold strongly.

However, it was not a vintage one for new artists. Despite having their single Walkie Talkie Man featured in a TV advertising campaign, there were few takers for the New Zealand-based pop-punk band Steriogram.

The first solo album from Melissa Auf Der Maur, the former bass player for Smashing Pumpkins, and Courtney Love's Hole met with a strong press response, but underwhelming sales.

The crowd at tomorrow night's Brits may be too absorbed by the music to worry about the balancing of books. But EMI executives will be hoping that Chris Martin and Damon Albarn are not.

Copyright Guardian Newspapers Limited, 8 February 2005

There are benefits associated with the voluntary disclosure of information

The disclosure of additional information, over and above that required by accounting regulations, has benefits in the capital markets. Voluntary disclosures include those contained within the annual report, as well as those made via other media such as press releases and conference calls to security analysts. For example, Lang and Lundholm (1996) show that firms with more informative disclosure policies have a larger analyst following and more accurate analyst earnings forecasts. They suggest that potential benefits to disclosure include increased investor following and reduced information asymmetry. Further, Botosan (1997) shows that increased voluntary disclosure within the annual report is associated with reduced costs of equity capital, particularly for firms with low analyst following. For these low-analyst firms, disclosure of forecast information and key non-financial statistics is particularly important, while for firms with a high analyst following, disclosure of historical summary information is beneficial. Therefore, these potential benefits of increased disclosure should perhaps not be ignored when deciding the extent of voluntary disclosure.

Recognition is perceived differently to mere footnote disclosure

Recognizing an item by recording it in the financial statements and including its numerical amount in the financial statement's totals is perceived differently to merely disclosing the amount in footnotes to the statements. For example, Aboody (1996) finds that where firms in the US oil and gas industry recognize a write-down in their financial statements, the negative pricing effect is significant, whereas when firms in the same industry merely disclose such a write-down in footnotes, the pricing effect is not significant. In other words, the market perceives recognized write-downs to be more indicative of a value decrement than disclosed write-downs. Further, Cotter and Zimmer (1999) show that mere disclosure of current values of land and buildings indicates that the amount is less certain when compared to current values that are recognized in the balance sheet via an asset revaluation. These results indicate that investors place greater reliance on recognized amounts than on disclosed amounts. Therefore, while it is not necessary to recognize information in the balance sheet for it to be useful, since merely disclosing the information in the footnotes conveys the information to investors, disclosed information is perceived to be less reliable than recognized information.

Size

There is evidence that the relationship between earnings announcements and share price movements is inversely related to the size of an entity. That is, earnings announcements have been found generally to have a greater impact on the share prices of smaller firms relative to larger firms. This is explained on the basis that with larger firms there is generally more information available in the marketplace and therefore greater likelihood that projections about earnings have already been impounded in the share price. The earnings announcement for larger firms would have a relatively limited unexpected component. For example, research has shown that the relationship between the information content in earnings announcements and changes in share prices tends to be more significant for smaller firms. That is, in general, larger firms' earnings announcements have relatively less information content (for example, Collins *et al.*, 1987; Freeman, 1987). This is consistent with the EMH and is explained by the fact that larger firms tend to have more information being circulated about them as well as attracting more attention from such parties as security analysts. Hence, on average, earnings announcements for larger firms tend to be more anticipated and hence already impounded in the share price prior to the earnings announcement.

Grant (1980) also explored this issue. He investigated the information content of earnings announcements of securities traded on the New York Stock Exchange, as well as securities traded on what is known as the Over The Counter Market (OTC). Firms traded on the OTC are typically smaller than firms traded on the New York Stock Exchange. Consistent with the perceived size effect, the prices of securities traded on the OTC were more responsive to earnings announcements than were the prices of securities traded on the New York Stock Exchange.

Do current share prices anticipate future accounting earnings announcements?

The previous discussion in this chapter has provided evidence that accounting earnings announcements, because of their potential information content, can have some impact on share prices. That is, prices change in relation to information as it becomes available. However, this impact seems to be more significant for smaller firms. As we saw, this is explained on the basis that there tends to be more information available for larger firms (for example, through analysts paying particular attention to the larger firms). Hence, as firm size increases, the general perspective taken is that share prices incorporate information from a wider number of sources (including, perhaps, numerous forecasts of the larger entity's earnings) and therefore there is relatively less unexpected information when earnings are ultimately announced. Therefore, for larger firms, we might actually be able to argue that share prices *anticipate* future earnings announcements with some degree of accuracy. As Brown (1994, p. 105) states, if we take the perspective that share prices anticipate earnings announcements, then we are effectively 'looking back the other way' from traditional perspectives that assume that earnings announcements actually drive share price changes.

A more recent focus in capital market research investigates how well accounting information, such as annual earnings, captures information that is relevant to investors. This is a different focus from research considered previously in this chapter. Rather than determining whether earnings announcements *provide* information to investors, this alternative form of research seeks to determine whether earnings announcements *reflect* information that has already been used by investors in decision making. That is, this research views market prices, and hence returns, as leading accounting earnings, while 'information content' research (the previous focus of this chapter) views earnings as leading (or driving) market returns. Both perspectives have merit, since the earnings announcement is likely to contain some information about a firm's activities that was not previously known to investors, as well as information that investors have already determined (or anticipated) from alternative sources.

In considering why share prices convey information about future accounting earnings, Brown (1994, p. 106) argues:

> In a world of rational expectations, events that affect future distributions to shareholders will be reflected in today's share price, whereas accounting standards often require that the recognition of those events be deferred until some future accounting period.

Share prices and returns (changes in prices plus dividends) are considered by some researchers to provide useful benchmarks for determining whether accounting information is relevant for investor decision making. Share prices are deemed to represent a benchmark measure of *firm value* (per share), while share returns represent a benchmark measure of *firm performance* (per share). These benchmarks are in turn used to compare the usefulness of alternative accounting and disclosure methods. For example, this methodology is used to answer questions such as: are cash flows from operations a better measure of a firm's performance than earnings calculated using the accruals system? Each of these accounting measures of performance is compared to the market benchmark measure of performance (returns) to determine which accounting measure best *reflects* the market's assessment of company performance. This type of capital market research also assumes that the market is efficient, and acknowledges that financial statements are not the only source of information available to the markets, such that security prices reflect information that is generally available from a multitude of sources. In particular, it assumes that investors and financial analysts actively seek out relevant information when making investment decisions or recommendations, rather than awaiting the release of the annual report. Further, this area of the research allows researchers to consider questions about balance sheet measures. For example, are disclosures about current values of assets value-relevant? That is, are they associated with, or linked to, the current market value of the company? Again, there is an assumption that market values reflect all publicly available information, including, but not limited to, information contained in financial statements.

This area of the research is based on a theoretical framework that is derived from the premise that market values and book values are both measures of a firm's value (stock of wealth), even though book value measures wealth with some error. That is, at any point in time, the market value of a company's equity (MV_{it}) is equal to the book value of shareholders' equity (BV_{it}) plus some error (ε_{it}):

$$MV_{it} = BV_{it} + \varepsilon_{it} \tag{10.4}$$

This error is due to the conservative nature of the accounting system. Book value is generally expected to be lower than market value for a number of reasons. First, not all assets and liabilities are recognized in the financial statements. For example, human resources, customer satisfaction levels, and internally generated goodwill are not included in the balance sheet, nor are their values amortized to the profit and loss account (income statement).[11] Second, some assets are recognized at less than their full value. For example, fixed assets, that have not been revalued, and inventory are generally recorded at less than their expected sale prices.

If markets are assumed to be efficient, market value provides a benchmark measure against which alternative measures of book value can be assessed. As we see shortly, there is a great deal of research that evaluates the output of the accounting system on the basis of how the accounting information relates or compares to current market prices of the firm's securities.[12]

If market value and book value of a company are considered as 'stocks' of wealth, then changes in each of these measures of wealth between two points in time can be considered as 'flows' of wealth. Just as market and book measures of stocks of wealth equate with error, market and book measures of flows of wealth (changes in value) can be equated, albeit with some degree of error:

$$\Delta MV_{it} = \Delta BV_{it} + \varepsilon'_{it} \tag{10.5}$$

Change in market value (ΔMV_{it}) is simply the difference in the market capitalisation of a company between two points in time ($t-1$ to t). On a 'per share' basis, it can be expressed as the change in the price of one share.

$$\Delta MV_{it}/\text{no. of shares} = P_{it} - P_{it-1} \tag{10.6}$$

Change in book value (ΔBV_{it}) is the difference between opening and closing total shareholders' equity. However, if we assume that there have been no additional capital contributions during the period, ΔBV_{it} can also be measured by considering the change in retained earnings for the period. On a per share basis, this is measured as earnings per share (E_{it}) less dividends paid per share (D_{it}):

$$\Delta BV_{it}/\text{no. of shares} = E_{it} - D_{it} \tag{10.7}$$

This formula is based on the concept of 'clean surplus' earnings, which assumes that all increases in book value pass through the statement of financial performance. Clean surplus earnings does not always hold in practice, since items such as asset revaluation increments are credited directly to owners' equity. However, the assumption of clean surplus is useful for simplifying our analysis. Substituting Equations 10.6 and 10.7 into Equation 10.5 gives:

$$P_{it} - P_{it-1} = E_{it} - D_{it} + \varepsilon'_{it} \tag{10.8}$$

That is, there is a theoretical relationship between change in price and change in retained earnings for the period. With a small amount of manipulation, this equation can be expressed to relate returns to earnings (the return/earnings relation). First, adding dividends to both sides of the equation, and dividing through by beginning of period price, gives:

$$\frac{(P_{it} - P_{it-1}) + D_{it}}{P_{it-1}} = E_{it}/P_{it-1} + \varepsilon''_{it} \tag{10.9}$$

Since the left-hand side of the equation, $((P_{it} - P_{it-1}) + D_{it})/P_{it-1}$, is equal to returns (Equation 10.2), we are left with an equation relating returns to earnings:

$$R_{it} = E_{it}/P_{it-1} + \varepsilon''_{it} \tag{10.10}$$

Equation 10.10 shows that we should expect returns (R_{it}) and earnings per share divided by beginning of period price (E_{it}/P_{it-1}) to be related.

In short, this perspective says that if market value is related to book value, returns should be related to accounting earnings per share, divided by price at the beginning of the accounting period. This analysis provides an underlying reason why we should expect returns to be related to earnings over time. However, it is interesting to note that it is *total earnings per share* rather than *unexpected earnings per share* that this theoretical framework proposes should be associated with returns. This is in contrast to research that assesses the 'information content' of earnings announcements by analysing the association between unexpected earnings per share and abnormal returns at the time of the announcement. We will see that there has been a number of studies that evaluate reported earnings on the basis of how closely the movements in reported earnings (or EPS) relate to changes in share prices.[13]

Beaver, Lambert and Morse (1980) was an early paper that sought to investigate how efficiently data about share prices enable a researcher to estimate future accounting earnings. Accepting that share price is the capitalized value of future earnings, they regressed the annual percentage change in share price on the percentage change in annual EPS. Consistent with Equation 10.10, they found that share prices and related returns were related to accounting earnings, but they also found that share prices in year t were positively associated with accounting earnings in year $t+1$ (share prices led accounting earnings). It was accepted that share price movements provided an indication of future movements in accounting earnings. Because of various information sources, prices appeared to anticipate future accounting earnings. These findings were also supported in a later study by Beaver, Lambert and Ryan (1987) who regressed changes in security prices on the percentage changes in earnings.

In previous discussion we showed that research indicates that share prices of larger firms do not adjust as much to earnings announcements as do the share prices of smaller firms. This was explained on the basis that there is more information available and analysed in relation to larger firms, and hence information about earnings is already impounded in the share price. That is, 'for larger firms, there is a broader and richer information set, and there are more market traders and more analysts seeking information' (Brown, 1994, p. 110).

Now if we adopt the position taken in this section of the chapter that share prices can actually anticipate earnings announcements ('looking back the other way'), as indicated in Beaver, Lambert and Morse (1980) and Beaver, Lambert and Ryan

(1987), then perhaps share prices anticipate accounting earnings more efficiently in the case of larger firms. Collins, Kothari and Rayburn (1987) found evidence to support this view – *size does matter*, with the share prices being a better indicator of future earnings in larger companies.

As noted above, there have been a number of studies using stock market valuations as a basis for evaluating accounting information. In Equation 10.10 we indicated that, theoretically, market returns should be related to earnings. Dechow (1994) investigates how well accounting earnings reflect market returns. She also considers whether another measure of performance, based on cash flows, relates better to returns than earnings based on the accrual accounting system. According to Dechow (p. 12):

> This paper assumes that stock markets are efficient in the sense that stock prices unbiasedly reflect all publicly available information concerning firms' expected future cash flows. Therefore, stock price performance is used as a benchmark to assess whether earnings or realised cash flows better summarise this information.

According to Dechow, earnings are predicted to be a more useful measure of firm performance than cash flows because they are predicted to have fewer timing and matching problems. In her conclusions, she states (p. 35):

> This paper hypothesizes that one role of accounting accruals is to provide a measure of short-term performance that more closely reflects expected cash flows than do realized cash flows. The results are consistent with this prediction. First, over short measurement intervals earnings are more strongly associated with stock returns than realized cash flows. In addition, the ability of realized cash flows to measure firm performance improves relative to earnings as the measurement interval is lengthened. Second, earnings have a higher association with stock returns than do realized cash flows in firms experiencing large changes in their working capital requirements and their investment and financing activities. Under these conditions, realized cash flows have more severe timing and matching problems and are less able to reflect firm performance.

Using the market value of a firm's securities as a benchmark, a number of studies have also attempted to determine which asset valuation approaches provide accounting figures that best reflect the valuation the market places on the firm. The perspective taken is that book values that relate more closely to market values (determined through a review of share prices) provide more relevant information than other accounting valuation approaches. Barth, Beaver and Landsman (1996) undertook a study that investigated whether fair value estimates of a bank's financial instruments (as required in the US by SFAS No. 107) seem to provide a better explanation of bank share prices relative to values determined on the basis of historical cost accounting. Their findings indicate that SFAS No. 107 disclosures 'provide significant explanatory power for bank share prices beyond that provided by book values' (p. 535), thereby providing evidence that such values are the values that are relevant to investors.

Easton, Eddey and Harris (1993) investigate whether revaluations of assets result in an alignment between information reflected in annual reports and information implicit in share prices and returns. Again, share price data are used as the 'benchmark' against which accounting data is assessed. According to Easton *et al.* (p. 16):

> Prices are used to assess the extent to which the financial statements, including asset revaluations, reflect the state of the firm at a point in time, while returns are used to assess the summary of change in financial state that is provided in the financial statements.

They found that the revaluation of assets generally resulted in better alignment of market and book values. In concluding their paper, they state (p. 36):

> Our analyses support the conclusion that book values including asset revaluation reserves are more aligned with the market value of the firm than book values excluding asset revaluation. That is, asset revaluation reserves as reported under Australian GAAP help to provide a better summary of the current state of the firm. Thus, allowing or requiring firms to revalue assets upward should be carefully considered by organizations such as the UK Accounting Standards Board, the Japanese Ministry of Finance, and the International Accounting Standards Committee as they debate the merits of various proposed changes in asset revaluation practice.

Consistent with a view that market prices already seem to reflect the current values of an entity's assets, as indicated in the research discussed above, it is interesting to note that asset revaluations do not appear to provide information to investors over and above historical cost accounting information. That is, some studies have indicated that the provision of current cost data in financial statements does not have information content (Brown and Finn, 1980). These results suggest that investors are able to estimate current value information prior to it being disclosed in the financial statements. Therefore, while the provision of current value information does not provide new information to investors, it appears to reflect the information used by investors in making their investment decisions.

Chapter summary

In concluding our discussion on capital market research we can see that this research has investigated a number of issues. Central to the research are assumptions about the efficiency of the capital market. In the 'information content' studies considered in the earlier part of this chapter we saw that researchers investigated share market reactions to the releases of information, often specifically the release of accounting information. The view taken was that the accounting disclosures often revealed new information and in a market that was deemed to be informationally efficient with regard to acting upon new information, share prices react to this information.

In the latter part of this chapter we considered studies that investigated whether accounting disclosures reflected, or perhaps confirmed, information already impounded in share prices. The perspective taken was that in an informationally efficient capital market, market prices of shares will reflect information from a multitude of sources. If the accounting information did not reflect the information already impounded in share prices, then some researchers would argue that accounting data that do not relate to share prices, and changes therein, are somewhat deficient. The idea is that market prices reflect information from many sources and if the accumulated data provide a particular signal, the accounting disclosures should also provide similar signals. As we noted, this approach implies that the market has it 'right' when determining share prices, and hence returns. In practice, the market cannot be expected always to get it 'right'.

Because much knowledge about the performance of an entity will be gained from sources other than accounting, it is perhaps reasonable to expect that accounting information should relate (not perfectly) to expectations held by capital market participants, as reflected in share prices. However, because there will arguably always be some unexpected information released when accounting results are made public, we might expect that not all accounting disclosures will be of a confirmatory nature. Some information in the accounting releases will be new, and in a market that is assumed to be information efficient, some price revisions are to be expected.

Many share price studies have investigated the market's reaction to particular disclosures. Often, if no reaction is found, it is deemed that the information is not useful and therefore entities should not go to the trouble and expense involved in making such disclosures. This form of argument has been used to criticize accounting regulators for mandating particular disclosure requirements. What must be recognized, however, is that capital market research investigates the aggregate reaction of one group of stakeholders, the investors. While the share market is an important user of accounting information, provision of information to the share market is not the only function of the accounting system. Accounting information is also used for monitoring purposes (Jensen and Meckling, 1976; Watts and Zimmerman, 1990) and, hence, financial statements play an important role in relation to the contracting process (see Chapter 7). Financial statements provide a relatively low cost way of measuring managers' performance and monitoring compliance with contract terms, thereby helping to reduce agency costs. Further, financial statement information can be used to satisfy people's 'rights to know', that is, to fulfil the duty of accountability (see Chapter 8 for an overview of the notion of accountability). Therefore, while investors are important users of financial statements, it would be foolish to focus solely on the investor-information role of financial reporting, to the exclusion of considerations about the monitoring/accountability role.

Questions

10.1 What is the role of capital market research?

10.2 What assumptions about market efficiency are typically adopted in capital market research? What do we mean by market efficiency?

10.3 What would be the implications for capital market research if it was generally accepted that capital markets were not efficient in assimilating information?

10.4 If an organization releases its earnings figures for the year and there is no share price reaction, how would capital market researchers possibly explain this finding?

10.5 What, if any, effect would the size of an entity have on the likelihood that the capital market will react to the disclosure of accounting information?

10.6 Would you expect an earnings announcement by one firm within an industry to impact on the share prices of other firms in the industry? Why?

10.7 Researchers such as Chambers and Sterling have made numerous claims that historical cost information is *meaningless* and *useless*. Are the results of capital market research consistent with this perspective?

10.8 Some recent capital market research investigates whether accounting information reflects the valuations that have already been made by the market (as reflected in share prices). In a sense, it assumes that the market has it 'right' and that a 'good' accounting approach is one that provides accounting numbers that relate to, or confirm, the market prices/returns. If we assume that the market has it 'right', then what exactly is the role of financial accounting?

10.9 Review Exhibit 10.1 (newspaper article entitled 'Colgate, Unilever warn on profits ... '). Explain the reason for the change in the prices of Colgate's and Unilever's shares. Also, what might have caused the price changes in the shares in the other consumer product companies?

10.10 In this chapter we have emphasized that the capital market appears to respond to information from many sources, including, but not limited to, accounting. As an illustration of how non-accounting information appears to impact on share prices consider Exhibit 10.3. Why do you think the market reacted the way it did to the announcement, and do you think that the announcement implies market efficiency or inefficiency?

Exhibit 10.3 An illustration of how non-accounting information may impact upon share prices.

Appearance by new chief lifts Swiss Aviation

Haig Simonian

The first public appearance by Christoph Franz as the new chief executive of Swiss International Airlines was marked yesterday by a 10 per cent rally in its share price.

Mr Franz, a former board member of the Deutsche Bahn railways group, gave no indication of his plans for Swiss, which is struggling to regain profitability.

The rise in the price of the illiquid stock came in spite of the fact that Mr Franz was pushed out of Deutsche Bahn last year after a public outcry over a controversial new fare system.

In a brief news conference at Zurich airport, the surprise successor to Andre Dose, the Swiss boss who stepped down unexpectedly last month, said he would spend his first two months getting to know the company and its staff. Although he will join Swiss at the beginning of next month, Mr Franz will not formally take up the chief executive role until July 1.

The appointment of Mr Franz, who played a part in the restructuring of Lufthansa, the German airline, in the early 1990s, came far sooner than expected. It was made possible by the fact that, since leaving Deutsche Bahn, he has been working as an independent transport industry 'adviser'.

Analysts said his quick appointment would help to build confidence in Swiss, in spite of continuing uncertainties about its viability.

Pieter Bouw, the Swiss chairman who took on the additional jobs of chief executive following Mr Dose's departure, said Mr Franz's selection had been a unanimous decision by the airline's four-member nomination committee. An initial list of 12 candidates had been whittled down to a shortlist of six, the company said.

Mr Franz, a 43-year-old German, has had extensive transport industry experience. As an additional advantage in multilingual Switzerland, he yesterday displayed fluent French alongside his native German.

Financial Times, 21 April 2004, p. 32

10.11 Review Exhibit 10.2 (newspaper article entitled 'You can't rush an artist: why Coldplay's struggle is bad for EMI'). In an efficient capital market, why would a profit forecast lead to a revision in EMI's share price?

10.12 Read Exhibit 10.4 and, relying upon some of the capital market studies we have considered in this chapter, explain why the share prices of the pharmaceutical companies might have reacted in the way they did.

Exhibit 10.4 Market reactions to drug marketing ruling

Market reactions to drug marketing ruling

Rachel Stevenson

SHARES IN the pharmaceutical sector received a shot in the arm yesterday after an American drug authority panel ruled that controversial painkillers could stay on sale.

AstraZeneca, GlaxoSmithKline and Shire Pharmaceuticals all saw their share prices soar following a Food and Drug Administration (FDA) advisory panel recommendation on Friday that Vioxx, Merck's controversial painkiller, can return to shelves and drugs of the same class can stay on sale.

The FDA said Vioxx, which was pulled from the market in September on concerns it doubled the risk of heart attacks and strokes, was safe to market, albeit with heightened safety warnings, because the benefits of the drug outweighed the risks. Pfizer's rival painkillers, Celebrex and Bextra, which have also been under threat because of elevated risks of heart problems, were also given clearance to stay on sale.

GlaxoSmithKline, which is developing a painkiller in the same class as Vioxx, saw its shares rise 4.4 per cent, closing 54p up at 1,295p. It is due to meet with FDA officials to discuss developments on its drug shortly.

AstraZeneca also rose more than 4 per cent to close at 2,162p and Shire bounced up 3.4 per cent to 581p. Shire saw its shares tumble 16 per cent last week after its key hyperactivity and attention deficit disorder drug was withdrawn in Canada after fears for its safety. The three companies were yesterday's highest risers in the FTSE 100.

There had been fears that the FDA would introduce much tighter safety regulations, causing many more drug withdrawals and a slower rate of approvals on new treatments. Adrian Howd, an analyst at ABN Amro, said: 'This was a relief rally after the FDA showed some common sense with regard to drug safety. All drugs carry risks and some side effects will always be found ... but the FDA appears to have seen the balance between safety and the rewards from drugs.'

The panel found that the key component of the drugs, called Cox-2 inhibitors, did increase risks of heart problems and should carry the strongest possible warnings, but the drugs would help patients who have struggled to find other treatments that work.

The Independent, 22 February 2005

Notes

1 Brown (1994, p. 14) notes that 'few if any investors would seriously accept the *strong form*, although many would accept the *semi-strong form* as their working hypothesis'.

2 Once we relax notions of efficiency, and once we consider broader issues about corporate accountability to stakeholders other than investors, threats to accounting's survival tend to dissipate.

3 The risk-adjusted discount rate chosen should be commensurate with the level of uncertainty associated with the expected earnings stream.

4 Where price at the end of the holding period (P_{it}) is adjusted for any capitalization changes such as rights issues, or bonus issues.

5 For further information on the development of the CAPM, reference can be made to Sharpe (1964) or Lintner (1965).

6 For example, if the returns of firm i's securities are expected to fluctuate in period t at the same rate as a very large diversified portfolio of securities, then beta (β_{it}) would be approximately 1. If the returns of the individual are twice as sensitive or volatile as general market movements (indicating that the returns on the undiversified security are more risky than the returns on a very large diversified portfolio) then beta would be approximately 2, and so on.

7 Normal returns can also be thought of as the level of return to investors that is expected simply as a reward for investing and bearing risk. Abnormal returns are the realized rate of return, less the expected normal rate of return (calculated by reference to the market model).

8 When returns are calculated on a daily basis, the assumption that $\alpha = 0$, $\beta_{it} = 1$ is not unrealistic.

9 For example, see Chambers (1965) and Sterling (1975).

10 According to Watts and Zimmerman (1986, p. 160), 'the hypothesis of functional fixation maintains that individual investors interpret earnings numbers in the same way, regardless of the accounting procedures used to calculate them. If all investors acted in this way, there would be a mechanical relation between earnings and stock prices, and the stock market would not discriminate between efficient and less efficient firms'.

11 As another example, the appointment of a very reputable managing director would be value-relevant because it is an action that could be expected to lead to improved company performance, cash flows, and hence share value. However, such an appointment would not generally be reflected in the financial statements themselves.

12 This research assumes, perhaps somewhat simplistically, that the market has it 'right' in its determination of the firm's value. Thereafter, accounting figures are compared with the market's 'benchmark'. Clearly, the benchmark figure of valuation might over- or under-value the entity relative to the value that would be placed on it if all private and public information was known and 'appropriately' used. As noted earlier in this chapter, market predictions are sometimes, in hindsight, proved to be wrong, thus necessitating subsequent adjustments.

13 Again, this research assumes, perhaps somewhat simplistically, that the market has determined the 'right' valuation of the organisation.

References

Aboody, D. (1996) 'Recognition versus disclosure in the oil and gas industry', *Journal of Accounting Research* (Supplement), pp. 21–32.

Baginski, S. P. (1987) 'Intra-industry information transfers associated with management forecasts of earnings', *Journal of Accounting Research*, **25** (2), pp. 196–216.

Ball, R. & Brown, P. (1968) 'An empirical evaluation of accounting income numbers', *Journal of Accounting Research*, **6** (2), pp. 159–78.

Barth, M., Beaver, W. & Landsman, W. (1996) 'Value-relevance of banks' fair value disclosures under SFAS 107', *The Accounting Review*, **71** (4), pp. 513–37.

Beaver, W. H., Lambert, R. & Morse, D. (1980) 'The information content of security prices', *Journal of Accounting and Economics*, **2** (1), pp. 3–38.

Beaver, W. H., Lambert, R. A. & Ryan, S. G. (1987) 'The information content of security prices: A second look', *Journal of Accounting and Economics*, **9** (2), pp. 139–57.

Botosan, C. A. (1997) 'Disclosure level and the cost of equity capital', *The Accounting Review*, **72** (3), pp. 323–50.

Brown, P. (1970) 'The impact of the annual net profit report on the stock market', *Australian Accountant* (July), pp. 273–83.

Brown, P. (1994) 'Capital markets-based research in accounting: An introduction', *Coopers and Lybrand Research Methodology Monograph No. 2*, Melbourne: Coopers and Lybrand.

Brown, P. & Finn, F. (1980) 'Asset revaluations and stock prices: Alternative explanations of a study by Sharpe and Walker', in Ball, R. (ed.) *Share Markets and Portfolio Theory*, St Lucia: University of Queensland Press.

Chambers, R. (1965) 'Why bother with postulates?' *Journal of Accounting Research*, **1** (1).

Clinch, G. J. & Sinclair, N. A. (1987) 'Intra-industry information releases: A recursive systems approach', *Journal of Accounting and Economics*, **9** (1), pp. 89–106.

Collins, D., Kothari, S. & Rayburn, J. (1987) 'Firm size and information content of prices with respect to earnings', *Journal of Accounting and Economics*, **9** (2), pp. 111–38.

Cotter, J. & Zimmer, I. (1999) 'Why do some firms recognize whereas others merely disclose asset revaluations?' Unpublished working paper, Universities of Queensland and Southern Queensland.

Dechow, P. (1994) 'Accounting earnings and cash flows as measures of firm performance: The role of accounting accruals', *Journal of Accounting and Economics*, **18**, pp. 3–24.

Easton, P. D., Eddey, P. & Harris, T. S. (1993) 'An investigation of revaluations of tangible long-lived assets', *Journal of Accounting Research*, **31** (Supplement), pp. 1–38.

Easton, P. D. & Zmijewski, M. E. (1989) 'Cross-sectional variation in the stock market response to accounting earnings announcements', *Journal of Accounting and Economics*, **11** (2), pp. 117–41.

Fama, E. F. (1976) *Foundations of Finance*, New York: Basic Books.

Fama, E. F., Fisher, L., Jensen, M. C. & Roll, R. (1969) 'The adjustment of stock prices to new information', *International Economic Review*, **10** (1), pp. 1–21.

Firth, M. (1976) 'The impact of earnings announcements on the share price behavior of similar type firms', *Economic Journal*, **96**, pp. 296–306.

Foster, G. J. (1981) 'Intra-industry information transfers associated with earnings releases', *Journal of Accounting and Economics*, **3** (4), pp. 201–32.

Freeman, R. & Tse, S. (1992) 'Intercompany information transfers', *Journal of Accounting and Economics* (June/September), pp. 509–23.

Freeman, R. N. (1987) 'The association between accounting earnings and security returns for large and small firms', *Journal of Accounting and Economics*, **9** (2), pp. 195–228.

Grant, E. B. (1980) 'Market implications of differential amounts of interim information', *Journal of Accounting Research*, **18** (1), pp. 255–68.

Hendriksen, E. S. & Van Breda, M. F. (1992) *Accounting Theory*, 5th edn, Homewood: Irwin.

Imhoff, E. A. & Lobo, G. J. (1984) 'Information content of analysts' forecast revisions', *Journal of Accounting Research*, **22** (2), pp. 541–54.

Jensen, M. C. & Meckling, W. H. (1976) 'Theory of the firm: Managerial behavior, agency costs and ownership structure', *Journal of Financial Economics*, **3** (October), pp. 305–60.

Lang, M. H. & Lundholm, R. J. (1996) 'Corporate disclosure policy and analyst behavior', *The Accounting Review*, **71** (4), pp. 467–92.

Lintner, J. (1965) 'The valuation of risk assets and the selection of risky investments in stock portfolios and capital budgets', *Review of Economics and Statistics*, **47**, pp. 13–37.

Penman, S. H. (1980) 'An empirical investigation of the voluntary disclosure of corporate earnings forecasts', *Journal of Accounting Research*, **18** (1), pp. 132–60.

Sharpe, W. F. (1964) 'Capital asset prices: A review of market equilibrium under conditions of risk', *Journal of Finance*, **19**, pp. 425–42.

Skinner, D. J. (1997) 'Earnings disclosures and stockholder lawsuits', *Journal of Accounting and Economics*, **23**, pp. 249–82.

Sloan, R. G. (1996) 'Do stock prices fully reflect information in accruals and cash flows about future earnings?' *The Accounting Review*, **71** (3), pp. 289–316.

Sterling, R. (1975) 'Towards a science of accounting', *Financial Analysts Journal*.

Watts, R. L. & Zimmerman, J. L. (1986) *Positive Accounting Theory*, Englewood Cliffs, New Jersey: Prentice-Hall Inc.

Watts, R. L. & Zimmerman, J. L. (1990) 'Positive accounting theory: A ten year perspective', *The Accounting Review*, **65** (1), pp. 259–85.

CHAPTER 11

Reactions of individuals to financial reporting: An examination of behavioural research

Learning Objectives

Upon completing this chapter readers should understand:

- how behavioural research differs from capital market research;
- how different accounting-related variables can be manipulated in behavioural research;
- how the results of behavioural research can be of relevance to corporations and the accounting profession for anticipating individual reactions to accounting disclosures;
- how the results of behavioural research can form the basis for developing ways to more efficiently use accounting-related data;
- the limitations of behavioural research.

Opening issues

The accounting profession often considers introducing new regulations relating to the disclosure of new items of information, or specifically requiring information to be disclosed in a particular format. A concern that often arises is how or whether various categories of financial statement users will react to the new disclosures which are potentially going to be mandated, particularly given that new disclosure requirements typically impose costs on those entities required to make the disclosures. How can behavioural research be used to assist the concerns of accounting regulators about financial statement users' reactions to the proposed requirements?

Introduction

In Chapter 10 we considered capital market research. Capital market research considers the *aggregate behaviour* of investors in the capital market. This aggregate behaviour is typically observed by looking at movements in share prices around the time of particular events, such as when earnings announcements are made.

In this chapter we consider decision making at the *individual level.* The research, which we refer to as behavioural research, involves performing studies to see how a variety of financial statement user groups (not just investors, as is the case in capital market research) react to a variety of accounting information, often presented in different forms, and in different contexts. By generating knowledge about how different categories of financial statement users (for example, investors, research analysts, auditors, bankers, loan officers, and so on) react to particular accounting disclosures, corporations and the accounting profession will be better placed to *anticipate* how different individuals will react to particular information.

Apart from the anticipatory implications associated with behavioural research, results of analysis of the decision-making processes of individuals can also provide the basis for developing procedures to improve future decision making.

An overview of behavioural research

In Chapter 10 we considered research that investigated the aggregate reaction of the capital market to various accounting disclosures. In this chapter we turn to a different approach to research which considers how *individuals* react to various accounting disclosures. Research that considers how individuals react or behave when provided with particular items of information can be classified as *behavioural research.* According to Libby (1975, p. 2), research that attempts to describe individual behaviour is often grounded in a branch of psychology called *behavioural decision theory*, which has its roots in cognitive psychology, economics and statistics. According to Libby (1975, p. 2):

> The goal of much of this work is to describe actual decision behavior, evaluate its quality, and develop and test theories of the underlying psychological processes which produce the behavior. In addition, these descriptions reveal flaws in the behavior and often suggest remedies for these deficiencies.

Behavioural research was first embraced by accounting researchers in the 1960s (Maines, 1995) but became particularly popular in the 1970s when embraced by researchers such as Ashton and Libby. It has been used to investigate a variety of decision-making processes such as the valuation of market shares by individual analysts, the lending decisions of loan officers, the assessment of bankruptcy by bankers or auditors, and the assessment of risk by auditors.

Some of the various published behavioural research studies have been undertaken in a laboratory setting where a group of individuals are assigned a number of simple or complex tasks (which may or may not be reflective of 'real-life' decisions), while other research has been conducted in the individual's own workplace.[1] Behavioural research can have a number of aims. Some research has been undertaken to *understand* underlying decision-making processes, while other research has been conducted to *improve* decision making. Some research manipulates the amount and types of information provided to particular subjects to assess how such differences impact on any final decisions, while other research provides all subjects with the same information and attempts to derive a model to explain how decisions by a particular category of decision maker appear to be made (for example, decisions by auditors, stockbrokers, bankers or lending officers).

The Brunswik Lens Model

In explaining behavioural research, a number of researchers have found it useful to relate their work to a model developed by Brunswik, this being the Brunswik Lens Model (Brunswik, 1952). Libby (1981, p. 6) provides a simplistic representation of the Lens Model. See Figure 11.1.

Libby (1981, p. 5) illustrates the application of the Brunswik Lens Model to the decision by graduate schools to admit students. As indicated in Figure 11.1, the criterion event is the students' future success, denoted by $ (on the left-hand side of the model). Given that this event will take place in the future, the decisions made by admissions officers within particular schools must be based on a number of factors or environmental 'cues' (pieces of information), which can be probabilistically related to the particular event under consideration (in this case, student success). A number of cues can be used, for example GMAT scores, grade point averages in prior studies, quality of the undergraduate school attended, recommendations or references from various people, whether the individual participates in extra-curricular activities, and answers to particular subjective questions.[2] As Libby indicates, none of these individual cues, or combinations of cues, can be expected to provide a perfect indication of the future success of the student, but some may be linked, with some degree of probability, to success. As Libby explains, in effect, perspectives about the environment (the issue in question in this case being student success) are generated (observed) through a 'lens' of imperfect cues. The relationships between these imperfect cues and the judgement about success are represented by broken lines.[3]

There would also be an expectation that some of the cues will be interrelated. For example the GMAT score might be expected to be correlated with grade point averages, as well as quality of school attended. Such interrelationships are represented by the broken lines linking the various cues, as indicated in Figure 11.1. To determine the weighting (or importance) of the various cues (independent variables) to the criterion event of success (the dependent variable which could

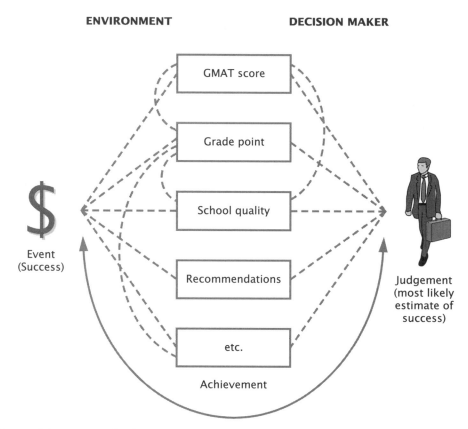

ENVIRONMENT   **DECISION MAKER**

Figure 11.1 A simple diagrammatic representation of the Brunswik Lens
Model (after Libby, 1981, p. 5)

simplistically be categorized as either success or failure in this case), as well as the
correlations between the cues, various advanced statistical modelling approaches
are applied. One model might be developed that provides a linear representation of
the assessors' weightings of the various cues. This then provides a model of how the
assessors actually went about their job of assessing applications. Knowledge of this
model may be useful to a number of parties. For example, intending students would
know what factors (cues) are particularly important to the assessors and hence the
students may then know what factors to concentrate on. From the assessors'
perspective it might be interesting for them to see how as a group they appear to
be making their judgements. This might not be obvious until such a model is
developed.

A model could also be developed that looks at the relationship between the actual
outcome (student success or failure) and the various items of information available.
That is, a model could also be developed by looking in the reverse direction from
the event (the left-hand side) back to the cues (that is, not involving individuals

making judgements). Obviously, such analysis could only be undertaken when a measure of actual success or failure can be obtained.

Libby (1981) provides an insight into the general applicability of the Lens Model to various decision-making scenarios. As he states (p. 6):

> This structure is very general and can be applied to almost any decision-making scheme. Again, consider a simplified commercial lending decision in which the principal task of the loan officer is to predict loan default. Loan default–non default is mainly a function of the future cash flows which will be available to the customer to service the debt. The customer provides a number of cues, some of which are probabilistically related to future cash flows. These include indicators of liquidity, leverage, and profitability drawn from financial statements, management evaluations resulting from interviews, plant visits, discussions with other knowledgeable parties, and outside credit ratings. No individual cue or combinations of cues is a perfect predictor of future cash flows, and there is overlap in the information (e.g., credit ratings are closely associated with profitability and liquidity measures). In making this judgement, the loan officer combines these cues into a prediction of future cash flows. Even if the banker's judgemental policy is highly stable over time, some inconsistencies are likely to arise, which will result in a probabilistic relationship between the cues and the final judgement. At the end of the term of each loan, the officer's prediction of cash flows can be compared with the actual event, and any resulting losses can be computed to measure achievement. While this example is highly simplified, it illustrates the generality of the framework and its importance for accountants. The model's principal concern with information-processing achievements in an uncertain world coincides with accountants' interest in improving the decisions made by users of accounting information and their more recent attention to the quality of their own decisions.

In applying the Lens Model it is common for researchers to mathematically model both the left-hand and right-hand sides of the lens. For example, on the right-hand side of the model we are interested in providing a model (typically linear) of how the individual uses cues to make an ultimate decision about the issue under investigation. This is often the major goal of much behavioural research. This can be undertaken by considering how each particular cue individually relates to the ultimate decision (univariate analysis), or how the entire set of cues relates to the ultimate decision or judgement (multivariate analysis). If statistical regression is undertaken as part of the multivariate analysis, the decision maker's response might be summarized or modelled as follows:[4]

$$\hat{Y}_s = a_s + B_{1s}X_1 + B_{2s}X_2 + \dots B_{ks}X_k \tag{11.1}$$

where:

$\hat{Y}_s$ is the model's prediction of the judgement (for example, that the student succeeds or fails) based on the individual's judgements or predictions;

$X_1, X_2, \dots X_k$ represent the set of cues (for example, the GMAT score, grade point average, etc.) for cue number 1 through to cue number k;

B_1, B_2, ... B_k represent the weighting in the model given to each of the cues, based on the responses of the subjects.

If a cue contributes nothing to the prediction, it will be given a zero weighting. Because the model will need to be generated from many observations and because models such as the above assume that individual cues contribute to the decision in a linear manner, it is clear that the model will not explain or predict with total accuracy the actual judgements made by particular individuals – but as we would appreciate, it is not expected to – it is a model of individual behaviour. As Libby states (1981, p. 22):

> It is important to note that the algebraic models resulting from these studies simply indicate the functional relationship between the cues and the judgement. These, like all models, are abstractions and do not purport to represent 'real' mental processes.

Some researchers also model the left-hand side of the lens model (often referred to as the environmental side) which looks at the relationship between the *actual phenomenon* under consideration and the particular *cues* provided. Without relying on judgements provided by individuals, this equation can be used to predict a particular environmental event.[5] The model can be represented as follows:

$$\hat{Y}_e = a_e + B_{1e}X_1 + B_{2e}X_2 + ... B_{ke}X_k \qquad (11.2)$$

where:

> $\hat{Y}_e$ is the model's prediction of the environmental event under consideration (for example, student succeeds or fails);
> X_1, X_2, ... X_k represent the set of cues (for example, the GMAT score, grade point average, etc.) for cue number 1 through to cue number k;
> B_1, B_2, ... B_k represent the weighting in the model given to each of the cues, based on the modelling of the relationship between the actual event and the available cues.

Researchers often compare the results of the model derived from studying the decision-making processes of individuals (Equation 11.1) with the results of the model provided by considering the relationship of the actual environmental event and the various cues (Equation 11.2). As we will see below, other issues focused on by researchers include how different individuals or groups weight particular cues, the consistency of the weighting, what issues associated with the presentation format of the cues might influence factor usage and weighting, and so on.

We can use the Lens Model to categorize a great deal of the behavioural research that has been undertaken over the last 20 to 30 years. The Lens Model explicitly considers *inputs* (uses of various cues), the *decision process*, and *outputs* (ultimate decisions). Libby (1981, p. 8) provides a summary of the type of issues that can be considered when undertaking research about how individuals process information when making a decision. These issues include:

At the *input* level (that is, issues pertaining to the cues):

♦ scaling characteristics of individual cues (for example, whether the presentation of the cues as nominal, ordinal, discrete, continuous, deterministic or probabilistic influences whether the cues are used in making a decision);

♦ method of presentation (for example, does the presentational format appear to impact on the use of the cue(s));

♦ context (for example, do perceived rewards, social setting, and so on, seem to impact on the use of the various cues).

At the level of *processing* the information:

♦ characteristics of the person making the judgement (for example, whether the demographics, attitudes of the judge, or the level of prior experience or interest impact on the decision that is made);

♦ characteristics of the decision rule (for example, how the individuals weight the cues; whether the judgements are stable over time; whether the judges use any simplifying heuristics when presented with potentially complex data).

At the *output* or decision level:

♦ qualities of the judgement (whether the response is accurate, quick, reliable; whether it incorporates particular biases; whether the judgements are consistent over time; whether there is consensus between the various judges);

♦ self-insight (whether the judge is aware of how they appear to weight various factors, etc.).

The use of particular information items and the implications of different forms of presentation

At the *input* level, the issues of how and whether particular cues (information items) are used in decision making are particularly relevant to the accounting profession. If it is shown that users of financial statements do not use particular information items (cues), it could be deemed that such information is not *material* and hence does not require disclosure, or associated disclosure regulation. The accounting profession would also be particularly interested in whether form of disclosure (for example, whether an item is provided in the balance sheet, in a supplementary financial statement, or in a footnote) impacts on users' decisions. We now consider a limited number of papers that have considered such issues.[6]

In relation to the use of particular items of accounting information, Pankoff and Virgil (1970) investigated financial analysts' predictions of financial returns on particular shares. They found that the analysts acquired earnings and sales information (often through purchasing such information) more often than other types of information. In another study of financial analysts' information demands (cue usage) Mear and Firth (1987) also found that analysts believed that sales growth and profitability were particularly important for estimating returns on particular securities.

From time to time accounting professions throughout the world consider whether they should require reporting entities to provide additional information as a supplement to existing financial information. One particular instance of this was the accounting profession's move in the 1980s to require supplementary current cost financial information to be disclosed in corporate annual reports. Clearly, research can be useful in providing an insight into how and whether current cost information would actually be used by readers of annual reports.[7] Such research includes that undertaken by Heintz (1973) and McIntyre (1973). These studies examined how three forms of disclosure impact on investment decisions. Subjects were provided with either historical cost information (only); current cost information (only); or both current cost and historical cost information. The results generally questioned the provision of current cost information, as the subjects did not appear to alter their decisions as a result of being provided with current cost information. Such results obviously challenged the accounting profession's move to require supplementary current cost information.[8]

Behavioural research has also been undertaken in human resource accounting, an area that has been typically neglected by the accounting profession. In related research, both Elias (1972) and Hendricks (1976) found that the disclosure of information on costs incurred in relation to recruiting, training and personnel development had an impact on subjects' decisions about acquiring shares in particular sample companies. We could imagine that such results, particularly if replicated across a number of studies, would potentially act as a stimulus for the accounting profession to put such issues on their agenda for consideration. In the absence of this type of research, the accounting profession might be ignorant of the fact that people would actually use such information if it were provided.

In relation to the *format of presentation* some studies have found that different presentation formats seem to impact on users' decisions. For example, some researchers have investigated how the presentation of particular graphics, such as the inclusion of bar charts, line graphs, pie charts and tables, impact on the decisions of different user groups (Davis, 1989; DeSanctis and Jarvenpaa, 1989). In a famous piece of research, Moriarity (1979) examined whether the accuracy of subjects' (students and accounting practitioners) judgements pertaining to potential bankruptcy of merchandising firms was impacted by whether they were given a number of financial ratios, or whether they were provided with a series of schematic faces (referred to as *Chernoff faces*, see Chernoff and Rizvi, 1975), where the faces themselves were constructed on the basis of the various ratios. Depending on the ratios, different facial features were provided (for example, mouth shape, angle of the eyebrow, nose length, represented changes in ratios). The findings of the research indicated that the students and accountants using the faces outperformed those using ratios in predicting bankruptcy. Further, the subjects using the faces were able to outperform models of bankruptcy that had been developed by other researchers (for example, Altman, 1968). The potential implications of this research are interesting. On the basis of the results, companies perhaps should provide numerous cartoon-like faces in their annual reports if they want to assist people in their decision-making processes (perhaps the accounting profession might release an accounting standard on drawing faces?). However, to date, the disclosure of faces in annual reports is not an approach adopted by corporate management.

Another disclosure issue that has been addressed is whether subjects will make different decisions depending upon whether particular information is incorporated within the financial statements themselves, or included in footnotes only. One study that investigated this issue was Wilkins and Zimmer (1983). They studied the decisions of bank lending officers and how their decisions were influenced by whether information about leases was incorporated in the financial statements, or simply provided in the footnotes. They found that from the loan officers' perspective the format of disclosure did not impact on their assessment of the entity's ability to repay a debt. Again, such evidence should be of potential interest to the accounting profession when deciding whether to mandate adoption of particular accounting methods within the financial statements, or simply within the footnotes to those accounts.[9]

Research has also investigated whether the disclosure of segmental information will impact on the decisions of particular individuals. For example, Stallman (1969) found that providing information about industry segments reduced the subjects' reliance on past share prices when making choices to select particular securities. Doupnik and Rolfe (1989) found that subjects were more confident in making assessments about future prices of an entity's shares when they were also provided with information about geographical performance.

Decision-making processes and the use of heuristics

In relation to research that considers the *processes* involved in making a judgement (the middle part of the Lens Model), a number of studies have considered issues associated with how the various cues (information items) are weighted. As an example of such research Schultz and Gustavson (1978) used actuaries as subjects (who were deemed to be experts) to develop a model to measure the litigation risk of accounting firms. They found that cues deemed to be important (relatively more weighted) were the number of accountants employed within the firm, the extent to which the work of the accountants was rotated among themselves, the size and financial condition of the clients, and the percentage of 'write-up' work performed.[10]

Another issue that has been considered is *consistency*. For example, do the individuals make the same judgements over time? Ashton (1974) investigated this issue. Ashton used 63 practising auditors in a study that required the auditors to assess the internal control system associated with an organization's payroll. In undertaking the assessment the subjects were required to do the task twice, the second time being between 6 and 13 weeks after the first time. The findings indicated that the subjects were very consistent in their weightings over time and that the weightings between the various subjects were quite consistent. Further, the cue that was weighted the most was 'separation of duties'.

When considering how individuals make decisions, researchers have also found evidence that decision makers often appear to employ simplifying heuristics when making a decision.[11] Tversky and Kahneman (1974) identified three main heuristics often employed in decision making: representativeness, anchoring and adjustment, and availability. We can briefly consider them.

According to Maines (1995, p. 83), individuals who use the *representativeness heuristic* assess the likelihood of items belonging to a category by considering how similar the item is to the typical member of this category. For example, the probability that a certain person is an accountant would be assessed by how closely he or she resembles the image of a typical accountant. The fact that there may be few or many accountants is ignored. An implication of this bias is that individuals typically ignore the base rate of the population in question. In some cases this bias has the effect of overstating the number of cases placed within a particular category. For example, in bankruptcy prediction studies, this bias may lead to an overstatement in the prediction of bankrupt firms as the base rate of real bankrupt firms is typically quite low.

The *anchoring and adjustment* heuristic indicates that individuals often make an initial judgement or estimate (perhaps based on past experience or through partial computation of the various factors involved) and then only partially adjust their view as a result of access to additional information. That is, they 'anchor' on a particular view and then will not move sufficiently in the light of additional information or changing circumstances. Joyce and Biddle (1981) undertook research that sought to provide evidence of this heuristic being used by auditors when they assess internal control systems. They found that new information (obtained through various substantive testing) was used by auditors to revise their assessments about the quality of internal controls, and that no evidence could be found of anchoring and adjustment. However, results of anchoring and adjustment were found when Kinney and Ueker (1982) investigated similar tasks. Other research to support the use of this heuristic is provided in Biggs and Wild (1985) and Butler (1986).

The *availability heuristic* relates to whether recollections of related occurrence and events can easily come to mind. That is, the probability judgements regarding the occurrence of an event are influenced by the ease with which the particular type of event can be recalled (Maines, 1995, p. 100). For example, in assessing the likelihood of a plane crash, a subject might overstate the probability as a result of remembering a number of highly publicized crashes. The actual base rates of such an occurrence are ignored. In a study of this heuristic, Moser (1989) found that when subjects were required to make an assessment about whether the earnings of a company would increase, their assessments were influenced by the order of the information provided to them.

We have briefly considered a number of heuristics, or rules of thumb, that might be employed in decision making. But, *so what*? Why would it be useful to know about such heuristics? First, if the heuristic results in inappropriate decisions being made (for example, lending funds to organizations that are not creditworthy, or accepting that internal controls are functioning soundly when they are not) then this behavioural tendency should be highlighted so that remedial action (perhaps training) can be undertaken.[12] Secondly, perhaps the heuristic employed by particular experts are efficient relative to costly data gathering and processing. If this is the case then perhaps novices should be encouraged to adopt the rule of thumb.

Issues of decision accuracy

When looking at the actual *output* of the decision-making process (the decision or judgement) some research has considered how *accurate* the predictions are relative to the actual environmental outcomes. For example, Libby (1975) investigated the accuracy with which loan officers predict business failure. The results showed that loan officers were able to predict bankruptcies fairly regularly, with their various answers also being relatively consistent among them.

In a similar study, Zimmer (1980) investigated how accurate bankers and accounting students were in predicting bankruptcy when provided with a number of accounting-related cues. The results showed that bankruptcies were typically correctly predicted. Also, a composite model of bankruptcy prediction generated from pooling all the bankers' responses typically outperformed the judgements of individuals.[13] A particularly interesting finding was that the students with limited experience performed nearly as well as the bankers.

Research has also considered the potential improvements to decision making that might result from combining the decisions of multiple decision makers. As noted above, Zimmer (1980) found that the composite model developed by combining the judgements of the different subjects was able to outperform judgements and models derived from individual subjects. Such findings are also presented in Libby (1976). Further, evidence indicates that decision makers working together in an interactive team can also outperform individuals working alone. Chalos (1985) found this result when reviewing the bankruptcy predictions of interacting loan officers, relative to predictions provided by loan officers working independently. Such results were subsequently explained by Chalos and Pickard (1985) as being due to the greater consistency in decision making that happens when groups, as opposed to individuals, are involved in making decisions. Again, these findings have implications for how organizations might make decisions in practice. Perhaps when major loans are being made, and assuming that these results are perceived as being reliable, banks should consider requiring approvals to be based on committee decisions.

Protocol analysis

Another approach to researching the decision-making processes at the individual level that we can also briefly consider now is research undertaken using *verbal protocol analysis*. This form of analysis usually requires subjects to think aloud (that is, to verbalize their thought processes) while they are making decisions or judgements. The subjects' comments are taped and then transcribed for further coding and analysis.[14] This form of research has tended to be more popular in auditing than in other financial accounting areas. One of the first studies using this method was Biggs and Mock (1983) who reviewed judgements being made by auditors when assessing internal controls. Other auditing-based studies to use verbal protocol analysis include Biggs, Mock and Watkins (1989), and Bedard and Biggs (1991).

According to Trotman (1996) there are a number of advantages and disadvantages in the use of protocol analysis. In relation to some possible advantages he states (p. 56):

> One of the main advantages of verbal protocol analysis is the ability to examine the process by which judgements are made. Understanding how judgements are made is an important start in improving those judgements. Second, verbal protocols are particularly useful in examining information search. The sequence in which information is obtained can be traced and the amount of time a subject devotes to particular cues can be determined. Third, verbal protocol can be useful in theory development. For example, Biggs, Mock and Watkins (1989) suggest the need to 'begin gathering data about how auditors make analytical review judgements in realistic settings and attempt to build a new theory from the results'. (p. 16)

In relation to some of the potential disadvantages or limitations that arise from using verbal protocol analysis Trotman states (p. 56):

> Consistent with all other methods of studying auditor judgements, verbal protocol studies have a number of limitations. First, it has been noted that the process of

verbalising can have an effect on the auditors' decision process (Boritz, 1986). Second there is an incompleteness argument (Klersy and Mock, 1989) which suggests that a considerable portion of the information utilised by the subjects may not be verbalised. Third, some have described the process as epiphenomenal, that is, subjects provide verbalisations which parallel but are independent of the actual thought process. Fourth, there has been some criticism of the coding methods. For example, Libby (1981) notes that the choice of coding categories, the choice of phrases that serve as the unit of analysis, and the assignment of each phrase to categories are highly subjective. Libby suggests the need for comparisons using competing coding schemes. Finally, there are significant difficulties in communicating the results to the reader, given the large quantity of data and possibly large individual variations in decision processes.

Trotman has provided a number of limitations in relation to protocol analysis which, as he indicates, can also be applied to behavioural research in general. In concluding our discussion on behavioural research, we further consider some of these limitations.

Limitations of behavioural research

First, as we have already seen in some of the material presented in this chapter, many of the studies that review similar issues generate conflicting results. This clearly has implications for whether the research can confidently provide guidance in particular areas. Unfortunately it is often difficult or impossible to determine what causes the inconsistencies in the various results because typically a number of variables differ between the studies (for example, the issue of concern, the realism of the setting, the experience and background of the subjects, the incentives provided, and so on). Further, within studies, differences in judgements between the subjects are frequently not explored to any extent, meaning that some unknown but potentially important decision-making factor remains unknown.

Another perceived limitation relates to the settings in which the research is undertaken. These settings are quite often very different from real-world settings, with obvious implications for the generalizability of the findings. In the 'real world' there would typically be real incentives and ongoing implications from making particular decisions – this usually cannot be replicated in a laboratory setting.[15] Further, there will be no real accountability for the decisions being made.

Related to the above point is the realism of the cues provided to the subjects. It is very difficult to replicate the various cues that would typically be available in the workplace. Also knowing that the results on a particular judgement are being carefully scrutinized could clearly be expected to have an effect on the decision-making processes being employed.

A number of studies also use students as surrogates for auditors, lending officers, and so on. This has also been seen as a limitation because such people perhaps have limited training in the area and have not had the same background experiences as the parties for whom they are acting as proxies (there has been some research that shows that students do make judgements comparable to those of particular experts. However, such findings are not universal).

A final criticism that we can raise is the typically small number of subjects used in experiments and, again, whether results based on relatively small samples can be expected to apply to the larger population.

What still appears to be lacking in this area of research is a theory as to why people rely upon particular items of information, adopt simplifying heuristics in some situations, and so on. For example, much of the research tells us that some decision makers were consistent in their judgements, while others were not, or that particular groups seemed to adopt a particular heuristic. But we are still not sure *why* they did this. Perhaps theory will develop in this area.

Chapter summary

In this chapter we considered how individuals use information to make decisions. More specifically we considered how individuals use accounting information to make a variety of judgements. Research pertaining to individual decision making (behavioural research) has shed a great deal of light on how various groups of individuals such as auditors, lending officers, bankers, and so on, make decisions. We found that financial statement users often employ simplifying heuristics when making particular judgements. The perspective taken is that if we know how individuals appear to make decisions, we can *anticipate* how they will react to particular accounting disclosures and forms of disclosures. This could be particularly relevant to the accounting profession when contemplating the introduction of a new accounting requirement. Knowledge of how financial statement users make decisions could also provide the basis for making suggestions about how decision making can be improved (for example, it might be found that a certain category of financial statement users are inappropriately adopting particular heuristics, possibly unknowingly, that could lead to potentially costly implications).

Questions

11.1   Contrast behavioural research with capital market research.

11.2   How and why would the accounting profession use the results of behavioural research in accounting?

11.3   How and why would the management of individual reporting entities be interested in the results of behavioural research in accounting?

11.4   Briefly explain the Brunswik Lens Model and its relevance to explaining the various facets of the decision-making process.

11.5   What is a 'heuristic' and why could it be beneficial for a group of financial statement users to be informed that they are applying a particular heuristic?

11.6   What is the point of modelling the decision making processes of different financial statement user groups (that is, for example, identifying how they appear to weight particular cues when making judgements)?

11.7   If the results of behavioural research indicate that a particular accounting-related information item (cue) is not used by individuals when making decisions, should this be grounds for the accounting profession to conclude that such information is not material and therefore does not warrant the related development of mandatory disclosure requirements? Explain your answer.

11.8   There have been a number of behavioural studies in financial accounting and auditing that have generated conflicting results. What are some possible reasons for the disparity in results?

11.9   What is 'protocol analysis' and what are some of its strengths and weaknesses?

11.10 What are some general strengths and limitations of behavioural research?

Notes

1 A laboratory setting would constitute a setting different to where the subjects would normally undertake their work and where the researcher is relatively more able to control certain variables relating to the decision-making task than would otherwise be possible.

2 As we show later, in an accounting study such as the prediction of bankruptcy, the 'cues' might be information about various accounting ratios.

3 Libby (1981, p. 5) notes also that relative reliance on various cues is likely to change over time as a result of fatigue, special circumstances, learning, and so on.

4 We have elected to provide only a brief overview of this modelling. For further insight, interested readers are referred to Libby (1981, pp. 19–21) and Trotman (1996, pp. 33–6).

5 For example, Altman (1968) developed a bankruptcy prediction model by forming equations that related a particular environmental event (bankruptcy) with particular financial variables (derived from financial statements). Representative of modelling the left-hand side of the 'lens', no use was made of decisions of individual judges or experts.

6 The overview of research provided in this chapter is certainly not comprehensive. Rather, the intention is to provide an insight into some of the different research that has been undertaken in this area. For those readers desiring a more comprehensive insight, reference could be made to Libby (1981); Ashton (1982); Ashton and Ashton, (1995); Trotman (1996).

7 Also, behavioural research relating to reactions to particular disclosures can be done in advance of an accounting requirement being introduced. On the basis of the behavioural research findings, accounting regulators might determine that there is no point in progressing a particular issue past its initial stages of development. This can be contrasted with capital market research which relies on historical share price data; data which capture how the market actually

reacted to the implementation or formal proposal of the particular requirement.

8 In Chapter 7 we discussed research that investigated the incentives for managers to lobby in support of, and/or to potentially adopt a general price level accounting (which like current cost accounting, adjusts historical cost accounting information to take account of rising prices). Specifically we considered Watts and Zimmerman (1978). This research applied economic-based theory to explain lobbying positions of individuals. It did not directly involve any human subjects in the experimentation. Other research has considered how capital markets react to current cost information by investigating share price changes around the time of the information disclosure (for example, Lobo and Song, 1989). What is being emphasized here is that there is a variety of approaches that can be taken to investigate particular phenomena.

9 Consistent with a great deal of behavioural research, the results of Wilkins and Zimmer were contradicted by other research. For example, Sami and Schwartz (1992) provided evidence that loan officers' judgements about an entity's ability to repay a debt were influenced by whether information about pension liabilities was included in the financial statements or in the footnotes. However, because this research relates to pension liabilities, it is not clear whether the results contradict a general notion that users can equate information provided by way of footnote disclosure with information provided by financial statement disclosure, or whether the differences in the respective studies' results were due to the fact that one study considered pension liabilities, while the other study considered lease liabilities.

10 Another approach to gathering such information would simply be to send out questionnaires asking respondents to rank the importance of various items of information in terms of the various decisions they make. Of course this would be much simpler than a process involving the actual modelling of decision making which typically occurs in Lens Model-type research.

11 A heuristic can be defined as a simplifying 'rule of thumb'. That is, rather than fully considering all the potentially relevant factors, a simplifying rule may be employed which takes a lot less time but nevertheless generates a fairly acceptable (and cost effective) prediction or solution.

12 For example, Kida (1984) provides evidence that auditors when undertaking particular tasks often initially formulate a hypothesis to explain a certain event (for example, the reduction in bad debt write-offs) and then seek information to confirm this hypothesis (hypothesis-confirming strategies). Clearly, such information gathering is not objective and could expose the auditors to certain risks. Knowledge of this behavioural tendency would therefore be useful.

13 As the composite model out-predicted the individuals, there could be a case to make the model available to the lending officers, particularly the inexperienced bankers. The model could provide a low-cost approach to screening loan applications at the initial stages of the application.

14 This form of data collection can sometimes lead to many hundreds of pages of typed quotes which can tend to become quite unmanageable. There are a number of computer packages available to organize transcribed data into a more manageable form. One such package is NUD*IST which stands for non-numerical, unstructured, data indexing, searching and theorising. Another package is NVivo.

15 Interestingly, at one meeting of professional accountants held in Sydney some time ago (attended by one of the authors of this text) some researchers made use of the assembled attendees to undertake an experiment related to interactive judgements and their impact on bankruptcy prediction tasks. In an attempt to provide an 'incentive' (perhaps in an effort to increase the 'realism' of the task) at the commencement of the task the subjects were told that each member of the 'winning team' was to be provided with a bottle of whisky. Clearly this is an imperfect incentive and might actually introduce other unwanted factors into the analysis. For example, people with a 'drinking problem' might find this a tremendous incentive and really try hard to win. Others might be fairly indifferent, whereas others, perhaps with a religious objection to alcohol, might actually make judgements that guarantee that they and their team-mates will not 'win'.

References

Altman, E. I. (1968) 'Financial ratios, discriminant analysis and the prediction of corporate bankruptcy', *Journal of Finance*, **23** (4), pp. 589–609.

Ashton, A. H. & Ashton, R. H. (eds) (1995) *Judgement and Decision-Making Research in Accounting and Auditing*, Cambridge: Cambridge University Press.

Ashton, R. H. (1974) 'An experimental study of internal control judgements', *Journal of Accounting Research*, **12**, pp. 143–57.

Ashton, R. H. (1982) 'Human information processing in accounting', *American Accounting Association Studies in Accounting Research No. 17*, Florida: American Accounting Association.

Bedard, J. C. & Biggs, S. F. (1991) 'Pattern recognition, hypothesis generation, and auditor performance in an analytical review task', *The Accounting Review*, **66** (3), pp. 622–42.

Biggs, S. F. & Mock, T. J. (1983) 'An investigation of auditor decision processes in the evaluation of internal controls and audit scope decisions', *Journal of Accounting Research*, **21** (1), pp. 234–55.

Biggs, S. F., Mock, T. J., & Watkins, P. R. (1989) 'Analytical review procedures and processes in auditing', *Audit Research Monograph No. 14*, The Canadian Certified Accountants' Research Foundation.

Biggs, S. F. & Wild, J. J. (1985) 'An investigation of auditor judgement in analytical review', *The Accounting Review*, **60** (4), pp. 607–33.

Boritz, J. E. (1986) 'The effect of research on audit planning and review judgements', *Journal of Accounting Research*, **24** (2), pp. 335–48.

Brunswik, E. (1952) *The Conceptual Framework of Psychology*, Chicago: University of Chicago Press.

Butler, S. (1986) 'Anchoring in the judgmental evaluation of audit samples', *The Accounting Review*, **61** (1), pp. 101–11.

Chalos, P. (1985) 'Financial distress: A comparative study of individual, model and committee assessments', *Journal of Accounting Research*, **23**, pp. 527–43.

Chalos, P. & Pickard, S. (1985) 'Information choice and cue use: an experiment in group information processing', *Journal of Applied Psychology*, **70**, pp. 634–41.

Chernoff, H. & Rizvi, M. (1975) 'Effect of classification error on random permutations of features in representing multivariate data by faces', *Journal of the American Statistical Association*, **70**, pp. 548–54.

Davis, L. (1989) 'Report format and the decision makers task: An experimental investigation', *Accounting, Organizations and Society*, **14**, pp. 495–508.

DeSanctis, G. & Jarvenpaa, S. (1989) 'Graphical presentation of accounting data for financial forecasting: An experimental investigation', *Accounting, Organizations and Society*, **14**, pp. 509–25.

Doupnik, T. & Rolfe, R. (1989) 'The relevance of aggregation of geographic area data in the assessment of foreign investment risk', *Advances in Accounting*, Vol. 7, Greenwich CT: JAI Press.

Elias, N. (1972) 'The effects of human asset statements on the investment decision: An experiment', *Journal of Accounting Research*, **10**, pp. 215–33.

Heintz, J. A. (1973) 'Price-level restated financial statements and investment decision making', *The Accounting Review*, **48**, pp. 679–89.

Hendricks, J. (1976) 'The impact of human resource accounting information on stock investment decisions: An empirical study', *The Accounting Review*, **51**, pp. 292–305.

Joyce, E. J. & Biddle, G. C. (1981) 'Anchoring and adjustment in probabilistic inference in auditing', *Journal of Accounting Research*, **19**, pp. 120–45.

Kida, T. (1984) 'The impact of hypothesis testing strategies on auditors' use of judgement data', *Journal of Accounting Research*, **22**, pp. 332–40.

Kinney, W. R. & Ueker, W. C. (1982) 'Mitigating the consequences of anchoring in auditor judgements', *The Accounting Review*, **57**, pp. 55–69.

Klersy, G. F. & Mock, T. J. (1989) 'Verbal protocol research in auditing', *Accounting, Organizations and Society*, **14** (2), pp. 133–51.

Libby, R. (1975) 'Accounting ratios and the prediction of failure: Some behavioral evidence', *Journal of Accounting Research*, **13** (1), pp. 150–61.

Libby, R. (1976) 'Man versus model of man: The need for a non-linear model', *Organizational Behavior and Human Performance*, **16**, pp. 13–26.

Libby, R. (1981) *Accounting and human information processing: Theory and applications*, Englewood Cliffs: Prentice-Hall.

Lobo, G. & Song, I. (1989) 'The incremental information in SFAS 33 income disclosures over historical cost income and its cash and accrual components', *Accounting Review*, **64** (2), pp. 329–43.

Maines, L. A. (1995) 'Judgment and decision-making research in financial accounting: A review and analysis', in Ashton, R. H. & Ashton, A. H. (eds) *Judgment and Decision-making Research in Accounting and Auditing*, Cambridge: Cambridge Press.

McIntyre, E. (1973) 'Current cost financial statements and common stock investment decisions', *The Accounting Review*, **48**, pp. 575–85.

Mear, R. & Firth, M. (1987) 'Assessing the accuracy of financial analyst security return predictions', *Accounting, Organizations and Society*, **12**, pp. 331–40.

Moriarity, S. (1979) 'Communicating financial information through multidimensional graphics', *Journal of Accounting Research*, **17**, pp. 205–24.

Moser, D. (1989) 'The effects of output interference, availability, and accounting information on investors predictive judgements', *The Accounting Review*, **64** (3), pp. 433–44.

Pankoff, L. & Virgil, R. (1970) 'Some preliminary findings from a laboratory experiment on the usefulness of financial accounting information to security analysts', *Journal of Accounting Research*, **8**, pp. 1–48.

Sami, H. & Schwartz, B. (1992) 'Alternative pension liability disclosure and the effect on credit evaluation: An experiment', *Behavioral Research in Accounting*, **4**, pp. 49–62.

Schultz, J. J. & Gustavson, S. G. (1978) 'Actuaries' perceptions of variables affecting the independent auditor's legal liability', *The Accounting Review*, **53**, pp. 626–41.

Stallman, J. (1969) 'Toward experimental criteria for judging disclosure improvements', *Journal of Accounting Research*, **7**, pp. 29–43.

Trotman, K. T. (1996) 'Research methods for judgement and decision making studies in auditing', *Coopers and Lybrand Research Methodology Monograph No. 3*, Melbourne: Coopers and Lybrand.

Tversky, A. & Kahneman, D. (1974) 'Judgment under uncertainty: Heuristics and biases', *Science*, **185**, pp. 1124–31.

Watts, R. & Zimmerman, J. (1978) 'Towards a positive theory of the determination of accounting standards', *Accounting Review*, **53** (1), pp. 112–34.

Wilkins, T. & Zimmer, I. (1983) 'The effect of leasing and different methods of accounting for leases on credit evaluation', *The Accounting Review*, **63**, pp. 747–64.

Zimmer, I. (1980) 'A lens study of the prediction of corporate failure by bank loan officers', *Journal of Accounting Research*, **18**. (2), pp. 629–36.

CHAPTER 12

Critical perspectives of accounting

Learning Objectives

Upon completing this chapter readers should:

◆ have gained an insight into particular perspectives that challenge conventional opinions about the role of accounting within society;

◆ understand the basis of arguments that suggest that financial accounting tends to support the positions of individuals who hold power, wealth and social status, while undermining the positions of others;

◆ understand that the disclosure (or non-disclosure) of information can be construed to be an important strategy to promote and legitimize particular social orders, and maintain the power and wealth of elites.

Opening issues

As we saw in Chapter 6, conceptual framework projects promote approaches to financial accounting that are built on qualitative characteristics such as *neutrality* and *representational faithfulness*. How do arguments regarding the unequal distribution of power between different social groups challenge these assumptions of the *neutrality* and *objectivity* of financial reports?

Introduction

In previous chapters we explored numerous issues, including how accounting may be used to: assist in decision making (Chapters 5 and 6); reduce agency and political costs (Chapter 7); maintain or assist in bringing legitimacy to an organization

(Chapter 8); and satisfy the information demands of particular stakeholders (Chapter 8). We also considered how the practice of accounting could be modified to take into account some social and environmental aspects of an organization's operations (Chapter 9), as well as considering how accounting disclosures might impact on share prices (Chapter 10). In this chapter we provide an overview of an alternative perspective on the role of accounting. This perspective, which is often called the *critical perspective*, explicitly considers how the practice of accounting tends to support particular economic and social structures, and reinforces unequal distributions of power and wealth across society.

The view promoted by researchers operating from a *critical perspective* is that accounting, far from being a practice that provides a *neutral* or *unbiased* representation of underlying economic facts, actually provides the means of maintaining the powerful positions of some sectors of the community (those currently in *power*, and with *wealth*) while holding back the position and interests of those without wealth. These theorists challenge any perspectives which suggest that various *rights* and *privileges* are spread throughout society[1] – instead they argue that most rights, opportunities and associated power reside in a small (but perhaps well defined) *elite*.

This chapter considers various (critical) arguments about the role of the State (government); the role of accounting research; and the role of accounting practice in sustaining particular social orders that are already in place – social orders that some researchers argue function on the basis of inequities, where some individuals (with capital, or wealth) prosper at the expense of those without capital and where accounting is therefore regarded as one of the tools used by those with (more) capital to help subjugate those without (or with considerably less) capital. We will see that researchers adopting a critical perspective often do not provide direct solutions to particular inequities, but rather seek to highlight the inequities which they perceive to exist in society and the role which they argue accounting plays in sustaining and legitimizing those perceived inequities.

The critical perspective defined

Under the heading (or umbrella) of *critical accounting theory*, there are several different specific perspectives on critical accounting. Therefore, a single critical perspective is not easy to define. In broad terms, critical accounting theory is used to refer to an approach to accounting research that goes beyond questioning whether particular methods of accounting should be employed, and instead focuses on the role of accounting in sustaining the privileged positions of those in control of particular resources (capital) while undermining or restraining the voice of those without capital. Tinker (2005, p. 101), who is one of the founders of the critical accounting movement, has offered one definition of critical accounting research as encompassing:

> ... all forms of social praxis that are evaluative, and aim to engender progressive change within the conceptual, institutional, practical, and political territories of accounting.

Social praxis

A key element of this definition is the notion of 'social praxis', as distinct from the investigation (for example in other branches of accounting theory and research) of social (accounting) practice. [2] *Praxis* within critical accounting research is generally understood to refer to the assumption that there is a two-way (and possibly circular) relationship between theories and practices, whereby theory influences social practices while social practices influence theory. One implication of this relationship between theory and practice is that when social conditions (and practices) change, theories based on these conditions need also to change. This should not be a new concept to you, as in many parts of this book we have discussed accounting theories which evolved to suit (or reflect) business practices.

The other key implication of the two-way relationship between theory and practice embodied in the term *praxis*, and possibly the more important implication from the perspective of critical accounting, is that development of different theoretical perspectives can bring about (needed) changes in social practices and structures (such as the distribution of wealth and power). Again, this should not be a novel concept to you as we have discussed several normative theories of accounting earlier in this book – theories which seek to prescribe how accounting *should* be practised.

What is different about the relationship between theory and practice as embodied in the term *praxis* (as used in critical accounting research) is the explicit notion of a two-way relationship. Each of the theoretical perspectives we studied earlier in this book rely on a one-way relationship whereby either theory determines practice *or* practice determines theory.

What is also different is the focal point of changes in practice implied in the term *praxis*. While the normative theories we examined earlier in this book sought to develop and then implement specific accounting practices which they argued were (in some way) superior to existing practices, the focus of the changes in practice embodied in the term *praxis* are usually at the broader level of society rather than specific technical accounting practices within that society.

More specifically, a critical accounting understanding and use of the term praxis is usually informed by a Marxist-inspired approach 'whose central concern [is] to study and influence the role of free creative activity in changing and shaping ethical, social, political, and economic life along humanistic socialist lines' (De George, 1995, p. 713), and this is why we argue that the role of theory in changing social practices is probably more important to many critical accounting scholars than the role of changed social practices in altering theories. Tinker (2005, p. 101) argues that this approach to critical accounting both 'promises a rich synthesis of new forms of praxis', and requires that critical accounting scholars 'who participate [in critical accounting research] must do so from committed, partisan, passionate, and sometimes militant positions'.

Insights into the partisan nature of accounting

While we have argued earlier in this book that all research is likely to be influenced to some extent by the (possibly subconscious) biases of the researchers involved, this explicit promotion of partisan research in critical accounting studies might upset and worry researchers who adopt other approaches. However, it could be considered simply more honest in that it is making explicit that all research in social sciences relies on the subjective (and therefore biased) interpretations of the researchers involved. Within critical accounting research, these explicit biases usually range from moderate socialism to more extreme anti-capitalist positions, which could be regarded as threatening by accounting researchers (and students and practitioners) who have prospered under the capitalist system. We return to this point later in the chapter.

Researchers within the critical accounting area, whom we call *critical accounting theorists*, therefore seek to highlight, through critical analysis, the key role of account-ing in society. The perspective they provide challenges the view that accounting can be construed as being objective or neutral, and these researchers often seek to provide evidence to support this view. Accounting is seen as a means of constructing or legit-imizing particular social structures. As Hopper *et al.* (1995, p. 528) state:

> ... in communicating reality accountants simultaneously construct it (Hines, 1988) and accounting is a social practice within political struggles and not merely a market practice guided by equilibrium in an efficient market.

This view is supported by Baker and Bettner (1997, p. 305). They state:

> Critical researchers have convincingly and repeatedly argued that accounting does not produce an objective representation of economic 'reality', but rather provides a highly contested and partisan representation of the economic and social world. As such, the underlying substance of accounting cannot be obtained through an ever more sophis-ticated elaboration of quantitative methods. Accounting's essence can be best captured through an understanding of its impacts on individuals, organisations and societies. Hence it is important for accounting research to adopt a critical perspective.

As noted at the beginning of this section, the term 'critical accounting' is a very broad term that captures a variety of different perspectives about accounting. However, what these perspectives have in common is that they seek to highlight, oppose and change the perceived role of accounting in supporting the privileged positions of some people in society. As Hopper *et al.* (1995, p. 535) state:

> Critical theory is an umbrella term for a wide variety of theoretical approaches perhaps more united in what they oppose than what they agree upon.

A Marxist critique of accounting

One of the main branches, and probably the founding branch, of critical accounting theory is (as indicated above in discussing the term 'social praxis') grounded in a Marxist-informed critique of capitalism. Within this Marxist critique, owners of capital are regarded as having (unfairly) accumulated their wealth by the historical exploitation and expropriation (over several centuries) of the value created by workers (or labour); workers are seen as feeling alienated both from society and from the products they produce, as their lives are largely controlled by external and impersonal markets rather than by their own free choices;[3] and capitalism is also regarded as fundamentally structurally flawed.

To give an example of one such fundamental structural flaw, a key Marxist argument is that one effective way for individual businesses to increase profits (or economic returns to capital) over a long period of history has been to increase the level of mechanization in a factory or office process, and thereby replace the productive capacity of some workers (labour) – who have to be paid and cannot work 24 hours per day – with the productive capacity of additional machinery (capital – which ultimately has been paid for by accumulating the value created by labour and expropriated over the years by capital). The costs of usage of this machinery (such as depreciation, repairs and the opportunity cost of capital invested in the machinery) were historically often considerably lower than the cost of the labour displaced by the machinery, and the machinery could also be 'worked' for long periods with minimal stoppage (rest) periods. While such mechanization might have been in the economic interests of the owners of one business, Marxists argued that there was a fundamental contradiction in the drive of all owners of all businesses to increase the returns to capital through ever greater mechanization. This fundamental flaw in the structure of the capitalist system is that for capital to earn returns, not only do costs need to be minimized but also revenues need to be maximized. While the actions of one or two factory owners in replacing some labour with capital might not affect the market for their goods, and therefore makes economic sense for these business owners individually, Marxists historically argued that if all business owners acted in this way then, as the total amount paid to labour overall would decline, total buying capacity in the consumer markets overall would decline. At some point, the reduction in resources available to consumers to purchase the end-products of the production process would, it was argued, be greater than the increase in productive capacity from mechanization and would therefore lead to a reduction (or collapse) in demand, and thereby threaten the overall prosperity of capital.

Marxist theorists argue that as the capitalist system operates in a manner which alienates workers (and the working class), and is riddled with inherent structural contradictions (such as the one discussed in the last paragraph), it is fundamentally unstable. This inherent instability will, it is argued, manifest itself in different symptoms in different eras, such as unemployment, inflation, economic depression.

While action might be taken by governments and businesses to address the negative symptoms (or outcomes) of the instability of capitalism that manifest themselves in a particular era, Marxists regard this as treating a symptom (such as policies against unemployment in one era, anti-inflation policies in another era) rather than addressing the common cause of all these symptoms – the structural instability of the capitalist system itself. Furthermore, 'successfully' treating the current negative symptom of the inherent instability of capitalism will not, it is argued, prevent the inevitability of new symptoms (whose precise nature is unforeseen and largely unforeseeable) arising in future periods. Policies to address these symptoms are therefore regarded as acting at a relatively superficial level and, rather like pharmaceutical products which treat the symptoms rather than the underlying causes of a disease, will do little in the long term to cure what Marxists regard as the deeper malaise of capitalism.

Many of these symptoms, and/or the social unrest caused by these symptoms, are regarded by Marxist scholars as threatening to undermine the power and wealth of capital (to quote Marx: 'capitalism produces its own gravediggers' (Marx and Engels, 1967, p. 94, as cited in Tinker, 2005, p. 122)). Therefore, the privileges, power and wealth of capital are regarded by Marxists as being unstable, and owners of capital will take action to defend their privileges, power and wealth.

Critical accounting theorists regard accounting as a powerful tool in both enhancing the power and wealth of capital, and in helping to protect this power and wealth from threats arising from the structural instability of capitalism. As, following Tinker's (2005) arguments outlined earlier in this chapter, many critical accounting researchers tend to be opponents of many aspects of the capitalist system and of accounting, they seek to expose the role of accounting in supporting unequal distributions of power and wealth across society, and some seek to subvert this role of accounting. This aim also tends to be shared by several of the critical accounting researchers who do not adopt a pure Marxist perspective.

As Gray, Owen and Adams (1996, p. 63) state, a major concern of the critical (or 'radical' theorists) is that:

> ... the very way in which society is ordered, the distribution of wealth, the power of corporations, the language of economics and business and so on, are so fundamentally flawed that nothing less than radical structural change has any hope of emancipating human and non-human life. The social, economic and political systems are seen as being fundamentally inimical.

Given that the practice of accounting is in the hands of reporting entities, such as large corporations, and accounting regulation is in the hands of government and associated regulatory bodies (which are viewed as being linked to, or under substantial influence from, large corporations and therefore as having a vested interest in maintaining the *status quo*), accounting information will, it is argued, never act to do anything but support our current social system, complete with all its perceived problems and inequities.

Critical accounting research versus social and environmental accounting research

One of the key areas in which our current social system is perceived by large numbers of people (and not just Marxist scholars) to produce many problems and inequities is in the area of the social and environmental impact of business. We discussed many issues in this area, and their relationship to accounting theory and practice, in Chapters 8 and 9. In this section of this chapter on critical accounting theory, we consider how critical accounting research differs from and/or complements social and environmental accounting research, as it might be considered that both are seeking substantial changes in social practices.

The critical perspective adopted by many critical accounting researchers is grounded in political economy theory, which we also considered in Chapter 8. More specifically, critical accounting research tends to be grounded in 'classical' political economy theory. As Chapter 8 indicates, the 'political economy' has been defined by Gray, Owen and Adams (1996, p. 47) as the 'social, political and economic framework within which human life takes place'. The view is that *society*, *politics* and *economics* are inseparable, and economic issues cannot meaningfully be investigated in the absence of considerations about the political, social and institutional framework in which economic activity takes place. Relating these arguments specifically to accounting, Guthrie and Parker (1990, p. 166) state:

> The political economy perspective perceives accounting reports as social, political, and economic documents. They serve as a tool for constructing, sustaining and legitimising economic and political arrangements, institutions and ideological themes which contribute to the organisation's private interests.

As Chapter 8 also indicates, political economy theory has been divided into two broad streams that Gray, Owen and Adams (1996, p. 47) and others have classified as 'classical' and 'bourgeois' political economy. The 'bourgeois' political economy perspective does not explore structural inequities, sectional interests, class struggles and the like.[4] It accepts the way society is currently structured as 'a given'. Many critical theorists consider that research which simply accepts the existing nature and structure of society without challenge effectively supports that (undesirable) society (Hopper and Powell, 1985). By accepting a pluralist conception of society it thereby tends to ignore struggles and inequities within society (Puxty, 1991). Prominent critical researchers such as Tinker, Puxty, Lehman, Hopper and Cooper have therefore often considered it necessary to challenge the works of researchers who they regard as researching within the bourgeois stream of political economy, such as Gray, Owen, Maunders, Mathews and Parker (these researchers, plus a number of others, have researched numerous issues associated with corporate social responsibility reporting); individuals who have for many years been promoting the need for organizations to be more accountable for their social and environmental performance (that is, to provide more information in relation to whether the corporations are meeting community expectations in their social and environmental performance). As Gray, Owen and Adams (1996, p. 63) state, critical theorists believe that:

> Corporate social reporting (CSR) will be controlled by the reporting corporations and a State which has a vested interest in keeping things more or less as they are. CSR has little radical content. Furthermore, CSR may do more harm than good because it gives the impression of concern and change but, in fact, will do no more than allow the system to 'capture' the radical elements of, for example, socialism, environmentalism or feminism and thus emasculate them.

Critical theorists argue that any such emasculation of these movements, which seek to protect and advance the interests of groups or entities often regarded as negatively affected by capitalism, will have the effect of protecting the capitalist system from 'threats' these movements pose to the power and wealth of capital.[5]

Thus, while to many of us calls for greater disclosure of social responsibility information would seem to be a move in the right direction, some critical theorists argue that such efforts are wasted unless they are accompanied by fundamental changes in how society is structured. They would tend to argue that the disclosure of corporate social responsibility information only acts to legitimize, and not challenge, those providing the information. Cooper and Sherer (1984), for example, argue that attempts to resolve technical issues (such as how to account for environmental externalities) without consideration of inequities in the existing social and political environment may result in an imperfect and incomplete resolution, owing to the acceptance of current institutions and practices – which are seen to be part of the problem itself.

Reflecting on some of the views of critical theorists about the deficiencies of social and environmental accounting research, Owen, Gray and Bebbington (1997, p. 181) note:

> Early radical critique of the social accounting movement emanated from a socialist, largely Marxist, perspective. For writers such as Tinker et al. (1991) and Puxty (1986, 1991) society is characterised by social conflict. In Tinker et al.'s (1991) analysis, the social accounting movement, particularly as represented in the work of Gray et al. (1988, 1987), fails to examine the basic contradictions and antinomies of the social system under investigation and is therefore, at best, irrelevant, and, at worst, malign, in implicitly adopting a stance of 'political quietism' that simply benefits the already powerful (i.e. the capitalist class). Thus, for example, Puxty writing in 1986 suggested the irrelevance of social accounting, in noting that 'more radical critics of capitalist society have been more concerned with the broader issues of accountancy and accountants within that society than particular (almost parochial) issues such as social accounting which appears to be ... rearranging the deck chairs on the Titanic'. (p. 107)

> However, by 1991, Puxty had taken his critique a stage further in arguing that by leaving basic social structures intact, social accounting can even lead to legitimation 'since the powerful can point to their existence as evidence of their openness in listening to criticism, it paves the way for ... the extension of power'. (p. 37)

As accounting is deemed to sustain particular social structures, the introduction of new forms of accounting (for example, experimental methods relating to accounting for social costs) will only help sustain that social system. Reflecting on the critical theorists' perception of the ongoing research being undertaken to explore how to account for the social and environmental implications of business, Gray, Owen and Adams (1996, p. 63) state that some critical theorists consider that by undertaking such research:

> ... one is using the very process (current economics and accounting) that caused the problem (environmental crisis) to try to solve the problem. This is known as the process of 'juridification' and it is well established that one is unlikely to solve a problem by applying more of the thing which caused the problem.

Although the above discussion indicates substantial disagreements (or even antagonisms) from some critical accounting researchers towards social and environmental accounting research, in recent years several social and environmental accounting researchers have made attempts to address the concerns expressed by these critical accounting researchers.[6] For example, Bailey, Harte and Sugden (2000), Boyce (2000), Lehman (1999, 2001), O'Dwyer (2005) and Unerman and Bennett (2004) are just some of the social and environmental accounting research studies that have touched upon issues and implications of differential power between organizations and different groups of stakeholders in accountability relationships. Furthermore, one of the foremost (if not *the* foremost) social and environmental accounting scholars, Rob Gray, recently wrote a joint paper (Tinker and Gray, 2003) with one of the foremost critical accounting scholars, Tony Tinker (who, as can be seen from the above discussion, was a long-standing critic of aspects of Rob Gray's work) in which it was recognized that many academically driven environmental and sustainability initiatives – including those in the area of social and environmental accountability – had been 'captured' by the corporate world and subverted to serve the needs of (and deflect some of the threats to) continued capital accumulation by rich and powerful companies – while enabling these corporations to continue operating in an environmentally and socially damaging manner.

Having briefly explored the relationship between critical accounting research and social and environmental accounting research, we now turn to an examination of the impact of critical accounting research on accounting and business practices and on so-called 'mainstream' accounting research, including a discussion of some possible reasons for the marginalization that many critical accounting scholars believe they experience.

Possible impact of critical accounting research on social practice

As previously stated, the critical perspective tends to be grounded in a 'classical' political economy perspective, and as such explicitly considers structural conflict, inequity and the role of the State at the heart of the analysis.

By adopting a research (and arguably, ideological) perspective that is grounded in 'classical' political economy theory, critical accounting researchers can highlight particular issues that might not otherwise be addressed. According to Cooper and Sherer (1984, p. 208):

> Social welfare is likely to be improved if accounting practices are recognised as being consistently partial; that the strategic outcomes of accounting practices consistently (if not invariably) favour specific interests in society and disadvantage others. Therefore, we are arguing that there already exists an established, if implicit, conceptual framework for accounting practice. A political economy of accounting emphasises the infrastructure, the fundamental relations between classes in society. It recognises the institutional environment which supports the existing system of corporate reporting and subjects to critical scrutiny those issues (such as assumed importance of shareholders and securities markets) that are frequently taken for granted in current accounting research.

While a substantial amount of critical research is informed by the work of philosophers such as Karl Marx, not all critical accounting research is based on a pure Marxist critique of capitalism. For example, reference is made by Owen, Gray and Bebbington (1997) to critical researchers who are identified as 'deep ecologists' and 'radical feminists'. The 'deep ecologists' question the trade-off between economic performance and ecological damage – they question the morality of systems that justify the extinction of species on the basis of associated economic benefits. The 'radical feminists' believe that accounting maintains and reinforces masculine traits such as the need for success and competition, and that accounting acts to reduce the relevance of issues such as cooperation, respect, compassion, and so forth.

In adopting positions, and/or pursuing outcomes, which are at variance with the dominant capitalist ideology (whether motivated by a pure Marxist position or, as is the case with many critical accounting researchers, motivated by other philosophical positions), critical theorists provide arguments which are often driven by a desire to create a climate for change in social structures. By arguing for a change in the *status quo* it has been argued that 'critical researchers' are often marginalized to a greater extent than researchers adopting other theoretical or ideological perspectives (Baker and Bettner, 1997). Another possible basis of some of this 'marginalization' is that critical theorists often do not provide solutions to what they see as perceived problems (Sikka and Willmott, 2005). That is, they are often 'critical' without providing direct guidance on how the perceived problems can be solved.[7] For example, Owen, Gray and Bebbington (1997) argue that critical analysis alone is perhaps not enough. As they state (p. 183):

> Restricting one's activities to critique, rather than actively seeking to reform practice, we would suggest, poses a minimal threat to current orthodoxy. Thus Neu and Cooper (1997) are led to observe that: 'while critical accounting scholars have illuminated the partisan functioning of accounting, we have been less successful in transforming accounting (and social) practices'.

Further, Sikka and Willmott (2005, p. 142) state that:

> Marxist traditions must continuously be renewed through lived experiences and opposition to institutions of oppression and exploitation in an effort to enable human beings to live less brutalised and destructive lives. But how are the agents of such change to be galvanized? While there is a role for scholarship and related forms of rarefied intellectual engagement with radical ideas, this activity should not displace principled involvement in the mundane world of practical affairs.

As accountants, we are often trained to provide information to solve particular (predominantly economic) problems, hence 'culturally', many of us might be conditioned against criticism that does not provide a *solution*. Reflecting on the 'attitudes and orientations' of accountants, Cooper and Sherer (1984, p. 222) state:

> A critical approach to accounting, however, starts from the premise that problems in accounting are potentially reflections of problems in and of society and accordingly that the latter should be critically analysed. Thus if a major problem in accounting is identified, say as its overwhelming orientation to investors, then a critical perspective would suggest that this problem is a reflection of society's orientation and to change accounting practice requires both social awareness (e.g. identification of alternative 'accounts' and the roles of accounting in society) and ultimately social change.
>
> Whether critical theory can in practice be applied to accounting research depends on whether researchers can free themselves from the attitudes and orientations which result from their social and educational training and which are reinforced by the beliefs of the accounting profession and the business community. For this socialisation process has produced accounting researchers who may exhibit subconscious bias in the definition of the problem set of accounting and the choice of theories to analyse and solve these problems. The criterion of critical awareness involves recognising the contested nature of the problem set and theories and demystifying the ideological character of those theories.

Critical theorists are often strong in their condemnation of accountants, and this in itself could also provide a basis for some of the marginalization that many believe they experience. Consider the statement of Tinker, Lehman and Neimark (1991, p. 37):

> The enduring nature of this 'Radical Critique' is attributable to the persistence of the underlying social antagonisms, to which it attempts to speak, and the complicity of accountants, which it seeks to elucidate.

More specifically, Sikka and Willmott (2005, p. 138) explain that some of the critical accounting studies in which they have been involved have:

> ... shown that [some accountancy professional associations] have a long history of opposing reforms which arguably would have advanced the accountability of major corporations (Puxty, *et al.*, 1994); that accounting technologies play a major part in the exploitation of workers (Sikka, *et al.*, 1999); and that the accountancy industry is engaged in a ruthless exploitation of citizens (Cousins, *et al.*, 2000). We have also sought to mobilise opinion by holding a mirror to the accountancy trade associations and argue that their claims of ethics, integrity etc are little more than rhetorical garnishes, and that neither their policies nor their actions come anywhere near their self-representations (Cousins, *et al.*, 2000, Mitchell, *et al.*, 1994, Puxty, *et al.*, 1994, Willmott, 1990).

Being informed that we, as accountants, are *complicit* in relation to 'social antagonisms', 'exploitation of workers', or 'a ruthless exploitation of citizens' is not something that is likely to be seen in a favourable light by many accountants and accounting researchers. It is confronting. However, although we might elect not to necessarily agree with what a number of the critical theorists are telling us (perhaps because of some profound ideological differences) it is nevertheless useful, perhaps, to put ourselves under scrutiny from a broader societal perspective. The critical theorists (both Marxists and non-Marxists) encourage such scrutiny.

A critical perspective on Positive Accounting Theory

A review of the academic literature will show that a number of critical theorists have been vocal critics of research that has adopted Positive Accounting Theory as its theoretical basis, as well as being critical of related capital market research (we look more closely at this issue later in this chapter). Positive Accounting Theory focuses on conflicts between what might be construed as 'powerful' groupings within society (for example, owners, managers, debtholders) and does not consider conflicts between these powerful groups and parties that have less ability to impact on the wealth of such powerful parties. Many critical theorists have also been particularly critical of the anti-regulation stance often advocated by Positive Accounting theorists because such a stance further advances the interests of those with power or wealth (for example owners of corporations, because lack of regulation enables the power and wealth of capital to be exercised largely unhindered by anything other than market forces – which operate to the benefit of many powerful businesses) whilst undermining the interests of those who might need some form of regulatory protection. Critical theorists would also argue that in assessing the usefulness of accounting information we really need to look beyond capital market (share price) reactions. The capital market response is driven (obviously) by those with capital. Capital market studies ignore 'other voices'.

We now turn from an examination of the role and possible impact of critical accounting theorists to a consideration, informed by critical accounting theory, of perspectives about the role of the State, accounting research, and ultimately, accounting practice in supporting current social structures (and inequalities). Again, as has been emphasized throughout this book, the views that are presented below are those of a subset of the research community. There will, as we would expect, be other 'subsets' of the research community that challenge such views.

The role of the State in supporting existing social structures

Researchers working within the critical perspective typically see the State (government) as being a vehicle of support for the holders of capital, as well as for the capitalist system as a whole. Under this perspective the government will undertake various actions from time to time to enhance the legitimacy of the social system, and thereby protect and advance the power and wealth of those who own capital, even though it might appear (to less critical eyes) that the government was acting in the interests of particular disadvantaged groups. For instance, a government might impose mandatory disclosure requirements for corporations in terms of the disclosure of information about how the corporations attend to the needs of certain minorities, or the disabled. Arnold (1990) would argue, however, that such disclosures (which, on average, really do not cause excessive inconvenience for companies) are really implemented to pacify the challenges, for example by and/or on behalf of particular minorities, that may be made against the capitalist system in which corporations are given many rights and powers. Relating this perspective to the development of various securities acts throughout the world, Merino and Neimark (1982, p. 49) contend that 'the securities acts were designed to maintain the ideological, social, and economic status quo while restoring confidence in the existing system and its institutions'.

It is generally accepted that to make informed decisions, an individual or groups of individuals must have access to information. Restricting the flow of information, or the availability of specific types of information, can restrict the ability of other parties to make informed choices. Hence, restricting available information is one strategy that can be employed to assist in the maintenance of particular organizations and social structures. Puxty (1986, p. 87) promotes this view by arguing that:

> ... financial information is legislated by the governing body of society (the state) which is closely linked to the interests of the dominant power group in society (Miliband, 1969, 1983, Offe and Ronge, 1978) and regulated either by agencies of that state or by institutions such as exist within societies like the United Kingdom, United States, and Australia that are linked to the needs of the dominant power group in partnership with the state apparatus (albeit a partnership that is potentially fraught with conflict).

Hence we are left with a view that government does not operate in the public interest, but in the interests of those groups that are already *well off* and *powerful*.[8]

Apart from the State and the accounting profession, researchers and research institutions have also been implicated as assisting in the promotion of particular (inequitable) social structures. We now consider some of the arguments that have been advanced to support this view.

The role of accounting research in supporting existing social structures

Rather than thinking of accounting researchers as being relatively *inert* with respect to their impact on parties outside their discipline, numerous critical theorists see many accounting researchers as providing research results and perspectives that help to legitimize and maintain particular political ideologies. Again, this is a different perspective than most of us would be used to.

Accounting research and support for deregulation of accounting

As an example, in the late 1970s and in the 1980s there were moves by particular governments around the world towards deregulation. This was particularly the case in the US and the UK. Around this time, researchers working within the positive accounting framework, and researchers who embraced the efficient market hypothesis, came to prominence.[9] These researchers typically took an anti-regulation stance, a stance that matched the views of the government of the time. Coincidentally, perhaps, such research, which supported calls for deregulation, tended to attract considerable government-sourced research funding.[10] As Hopper *et al.* (1995, p. 518) state:

> Academic debates do not exist in a vacuum. It is not enough for a paradigm to be intellectually convincing for its acceptance, it must also be congruent with prevailing powerful beliefs within society more generally. The history of ideas is littered with research that was mocked but which subsequently became the dominant paradigm when other social concerns, ideologies and beliefs became prevalent. The story of PAT [Positive Accounting Theory] can be told in such terms. Its rise was not just due to its addressal of academic threats and concerns at the time of its inception but it was also in tandem with and connected to the right wing political ideologies dominant in the 1980s.

Mouck (1992) also adopts a position that argues that the rise of Positive Accounting Theory was made possible because it was consistent with the political views of those in power (that is, the State). He argues that:

> ... the credibility of Watts and Zimmerman's rhetoric of revolt against government regulation of corporate accountability was conditioned, to a large extent, by the widespread, ultra-conservative movement toward deregulation that was taking place in society at large .... I would argue that accountants have been willing to accept the PAT [Positive Accounting Theory] story, which is built on Chicago's version of laissez faire economics, because the rhetoric of the story was very much attuned to the Reagan era revolt against government interference in economic affairs.

Consistent with the development of Positive Accounting Theory, in the late 1970s a great deal of accounting research sought to highlight the economic consequences of new accounting regulations. This perspective (which we considered in Chapters 2 and 3) argues that the implementation of new accounting regulations can have many unwanted economic implications, and hence, before a new requirement, such as an accounting standard, is mandated, careful consideration is warranted. Economic consequences analysis often provided a rationale for not implementing accounting regulation. Critical researchers have argued that it was the economic implications for shareholders (for example, through changes in share prices) and managers (for example, through reductions in salary or loss of employment) that were the focus of attention by those who researched the economic consequences of accounting regulation. As Cooper and Sherer (1984, pp. 215, 217) argue:

> It seems unfortunate, however, that the 'rise of economic consequences' (Zeff, 1978) seems to have been motivated, at least in the United States, by a desire of large corporations to counter attempts to change the existing reporting systems and levels of disclosure. To date, it would seem that accounting researchers have generally reiterated the complaints of investors and businessmen about the consequences of changes in required accounting practice. Studies using ECA (economic consequences analysis) have almost invariably evaluated the consequences of accounting reports solely in terms of the behaviors and interest of the shareholder and/or corporate manager class (Selto and Neumann, 1981).
>
> More fundamentally, studies adopting the ECA approach have focused their attention on a very limited subset of the total economy, namely, the impact on the shareholder or manager class. The effects of accounting reports directly on other users, e.g., governments and unions, and indirectly on 'non-users', e.g. consumers, employees, and taxpayers, have been ignored. The basis of such a decision can, at best, be that any such effects are either secondary and/or lacking in economic significance. Thus, these studies have made an implicit value statement that the needs of the shareholder and manager class are of primary importance and the concentration on those needs is sufficient for an understanding of the role of accounting reports in society. Unless the insignificance of the effects on other users and 'non-users' is demonstrated rather than merely assumed, the conclusion from this research cannot be generalised for the economy as a whole and these studies are insufficient for making accounting prescriptions intended to improve overall social welfare.

Apart from indicating that economic consequences research focused predominantly on the economic implications for managers and shareholders, Cooper and Sherer (1984) also note that major studies that adopted this paradigm were funded by the US Securities Exchange Commission and the US Financial Accounting Standards Board. It was considered that the interests of these bodies were aligned with the 'shareholder and manager class', rather than society as a whole.

In a similar vein, Thompson (1978) and Burchell et al. (1980) suggest that the research efforts into inflation accounting in the 1960s and 1970s were not actually motivated by the rate of inflation *per se*. Instead, they argue that the research had been motivated by a desire to alleviate the shifts in real wealth away from owners (in the form of lower real profits and dividends) and towards higher wages.

If research gains prominence because it supports particular political beliefs of those in power, then we might assume that as the views of those in 'power' change, so will the focus of research. During the 1990s many governments around the world tended to move away from deregulation. Reflecting on this, Hopper *et al.* (1995, p. 540) noted:

> The environment is continually being reconstituted within changing economic, political conditions. Accordingly, the ability of PAT [Positive Accounting Theory] to resonate with the prevailing discursive climate may be subject to challenge ... . Following the removal of the Republican government in the USA, this particular period and form of conservative reform may have ended. In the USA President Clinton is adopting a more interventionist strategy and in the UK, the Major regime claims to espouse an alternative 'caring society', albeit with market forces, in contrast to the harsher face of Thatcherism. In the 1990s a new set of values may be emerging which do not emphasise so greatly the efficiency and effectiveness of unregulated markets, for example, ecology, health care in the USA, gender issues. The ability of PAT to resonate with this changed environment may be brought into question, for example, the consecutive failure of some business enterprises and the stock market crash of 1987 augmented the call for more regulation.

A critical accounting interpretation of increased accounting regulation post-Enron

Despite the election of what many consider to be a highly pro-business and anti-regulation Republican President (George W. Bush) and government in the USA at the beginning of the 21st century, and the re-election of this President and government at the end of 2004, few governments (including the US government) have reversed this 1990s trend against deregulation of accounting. Although the Bush government initially made moves towards greater deregulation of accounting, this policy direction was reversed following public revelations about the large scale accounting failures (or abuses) at Enron, WorldCom and several other large US corporations in 2001 and 2002, and the apparent complicity of Enron's auditor (Andersen) in some of these failed and damaging accounting practices. Despite any existing governmental desire there may have been to further empower large corporations by deregulating accounting practices, Unerman and O'Dwyer (2004) argue that these highly publicized accounting failures led to a considerable reduction of trust placed by many investors and workers in both accounting practices and, more importantly, in the reliability of capital markets as a medium for investment. One reaction of many governments throughout the world to these corporate and accounting failures was to increase regulation of accounting and corporate governance, in an attempt to rebuild trust in the reliability of both accounting information and in the capital markets which are supposedly dependent on the claimed reliability of this accounting information. From a critical perspective, this increase in regulation would be regarded as serving the needs of large corporations (rather than protecting investors) as it was aimed at sustaining investor trust in the capital markets upon which large corporations rely.

The damaging impact of accounting failures at Enron, followed by highly publicized accounting failures over a relatively short period of time at several other large corporations – both in north America and in Europe (for example: Parmalat in Italy, Ahold in the Netherlands and Addeco in Switzerland) could be regarded by critical accounting scholars as just another symptom of the inherent instability of the capitalist system (as discussed earlier in this chapter). These researchers would tend to argue that any actions taken to prevent a reoccurrence of this latest symptom of the structural conflicts inherent in capitalism (accounting failures) misses the point that it is the capitalist system itself which is flawed, and the only way to prevent other (different) failures emerging in the future is to replace the - capitalist system with a different system in which the weak (employees, the environment, many sections of society) are not exploited by the powerful (large corporations and the governments they support). Several researchers have indeed examined the early 21st century accounting failures at Enron (and other large corporations), and/or the regulatory reaction to these failures, from a variety of critical perspectives (see, for example, Arnold and de Lange, 2004; Baker, 2003; Briloff, 2004; Craig and Amernic, 2004; Froud *et al.*, 2004; Fuerman, 2004; O'Connell, 2004; Williams, 2004).

A critical accounting view on the active role of academic and non-academic discourse in protecting capitalism

In another area, some critical theorists have implicated the editors of accounting journals in ensuring that accounting research does not challenge the interests of dominant groups in society, arguing that these editors will reject research that does not have 'complementarity with themes prevailing in the social milieu' (Mouck, 1992). In relation to the role of accounting journals, Tinker, Lehman and Neimark (1991, p. 44) state:

> Accounting literature represents the world in a manner conducive to the changing needs of capital accumulation. Journals such as Accounting Review, adjudicate in secondary conflicts by filtering research, scholarship (and untenured scholars) in a manner conducive to this primary purpose. The hostility of this journal to even the tamest 'deviants' is well known.[11]

Other research in critical accounting demonstrates that it is not just academic discourse which is biased in a manner designed to support the interests of capitalism. For example, Collison (2003) characterizes as propaganda many of the justifications which are given by organizations operating in the corporate sector in support of existing business and accounting practices, where subjective values (biased in the direction of furthering the power and wealth of capital) are portrayed as objective facts. He argues (p. 853) that:

> The effect of this use of propaganda ... is to buttress the hegemony of discourse ... in which the contestable values that are often implicit in the practices and terminology of accounting and finance are treated as though they are uncontentious ... [and that propa-

ganda is] a tool that can be used by powerful interests, often covertly, to support and proselytise a prevailing ideology.

Developing this theme of accounting being used as a tool to 'objectify' subjective views, we now move our analysis to the critical theorists' perceptions of the role of accounting practice in supporting existing social structures.

The role of accounting practice in supporting existing social structures

As we know, the qualitative attributes of *objectivity*, *neutrality* and *representational faithfulness* are promoted in various conceptual framework projects throughout the world as being 'ideals' to which external financial accounts should aspire. There is a view promoted by the profession that accounting can and should provide an objective representation of the underlying economic facts.[12]

However, a number of critical theorists see a different role for conceptual frameworks; a role that involves *legitimizing* the accounting profession, as well as the financial reports produced by reporting entities. Hines (1991, p. 328) states:

> CFs presume, legitimise and reproduce the assumptions of an objective world and as such they play a part in constituting the social world ... CFs provide social legitimacy to the accounting profession. Since the objectivity assumption is the central premise of our society ... a fundamental form of social power accrues to those who are able to trade on the objectivity assumption. Legitimacy is achieved by tapping into this central proposition because accounts generated around this proposition are perceived as 'normal'. It is perhaps not surprising or anomalous then that CF projects continue to be undertaken which rely on information qualities such as 'representational faithfulness', 'neutrality', 'reliability', etc., which presume a concrete, objective world, even though past CFs have not succeeded in generating Accounting Standards which achieve these qualities. The very talk, predicated on the assumption of an objective world to which accountants have privileged access via their 'measurement expertise', serves to construct a perceived legitimacy for the profession's power and autonomy.

The role of accounting statements in creating a selective 'reality'

Hines (1988) argues that accountants impose their own views about which performance characteristics are important and thereby require emphasis (for example, 'profits'). Accountants also decide which attributes of organization performance are not important, and therefore are not worthy of measurement or disclosure. Through the practice of accounting, attention will be directed to the particular measures the (apparently objective) accountant has emphasized and in turn these measures will become a means of differentiating 'good' organizations from 'bad' organizations. Hines argues that in *communicating reality*, accountants simultaneously *construct reality*. Accounting provides a selective visibility for particular issues within an organization that dictates which financial issues are 'significant' (Carpenter and Feroz, 1992). Cooper, Hayes and Wolf (1981, p. 182) also adopt this perspective in stating:

> Accounting systems encourage imitation and coercion by defining the problematic (by choosing which variables are measured and reported) and they help to fashion solutions (by choosing which variables are to be treated as controllable). Of course, the way accounting systems are used is highly significant, but nevertheless the structure and elements of accounting systems help to create the appropriate and acceptable ways of acting, organizing and talking about issues in organisations. Accounting systems are a significant component of the power system in an organisation.

In exploring the role of accounting reports in 'constructing' particular 'realities', Macintosh and Baker (2002) and Macintosh (2001) draw on developments in literary theory, and argue that accounting reports can be viewed as a form of literary texts/documents. They demonstrate that in literary theory the 'expressive realism' notion that a text is an objective reflection of an underlying reality (that a novel, for example, 'acts like a mirror to reflect reality' (Macintosh and Baker, 2002, p. 189)) has long been regarded as highly problematic, and they draw on these criticisms from literary theory to demonstrate how similar assumptions of accounting reports objectively reflecting an external economic reality are equally problematic:

> ... the common-sense view of accounting assumes that the financial reality of an enterprise is 'out-there' prior to its capture in accounting reports. The proper way of ascertaining this reality is thought to be with objective and verifiable measurement processes. This realist correspondence view of the accounting assumes the financial reality of a corporation exists independently of accountants, auditors, and accounting reports. Yet accounting runs up against the same problem that undermined expressive realism [in literary theory]. Different equally qualified professional accountants come up with different financial statements for identical transactions and events. (Macintosh and Baker, 2002, p. 192)

Macintosh (2001) and Macintosh and Baker (2002) then use different paradigms in literary theory to analyse and explain the subjectivity of accounting reports, and the partial views of reality constructed by these reports. They argue that any accounting report will tend to present selective and biased information in a manner designed to lead to the construction of a single view of the underlying reality, with this view being the one that most favours management and providers of capital. These academics then argue, based on post-structuralist literary theory, for accounting reports to change so they contain a sufficient variety of information to enable different users of accounts to see a variety of sometimes contradictory views of the reality underlying the business, rather than accounting information being selectively presented in an objectified manner to 'force' a single partisan view of the business.

The power of accountants through a false image of neutrality

For those people who have not previously considered accountants in the same light as do the critical theorists, there may be some form of bewilderment. How can accountants have so much power? In part, some arguments for this issue have been provided in the discussion above. The accounting profession is portrayed (through such vehicles as conceptual frameworks) as being objective and neutral – that is, free from any form of bias. Such characteristics (if true) are apparently beyond reproach. In fact, accountants are perceived as so *objective* and *neutral* that they have a reputation for being very *dull*. But if we are to believe the critical theorists, this 'dullness' is a façade that perhaps hides a great deal of social power.[13] As Carpenter and Feroz (1992, p. 618) state:

> ... accounting may be viewed as a means of legitimising the current social and political structure of the organisation. Hopwood (1983) further suggests that the legitimising force of accounting derives in part from the apparently dull, unobtrusive, and routine nature of accounting procedures, which generate an aura of objectivity and legitimacy in the eyes of financial statement users. Far from being dull and routine, accounting and accountants can and do take sides in social conflicts.

Tinker, Merino and Niemark (1982, p. 184), argue:

> This image of the accountant – often as a disinterested, innocuous 'historian' – stems from a desire to deny the responsibility that accountants bear for shaping subjective expectations which, in turn, affect decisions about resource allocation and the distribution of income between and within social classes. The attachment to historical facts provides a veneer of pseudo-objectivity that allows accountants to claim that they merely record – not partake in – social conflicts.

Earlier in this chapter (as well as in Chapter 3) we considered research that investigated the economic consequences of accounting requirements. Once a profession starts considering the economic consequences of particular accounting standards, it is difficult to perceive that the accounting standards, and therefore accounting, can really be considered as truly objective and neutral.

A critical accounting perspective of accounting and legitimation

Moving on to another aspect of how critical accounting researchers believe that accounting practices 'silently' and 'stealthily' reinforce capitalist power, among the other theoretical perspectives we considered earlier in this book is legitimacy theory (which we discussed in Chapter 8). We explained how organizations often use documents, such as annual reports, to legitimize the ongoing existence of the entity. While these disclosures were explained in terms of a desire by the corporation to appear to be acting in terms of the 'social contract' (which may or may not be the case), some critical theorists see the legitimation motive as potentially quite harmful, particularly if it legitimizes activities that are not in the interests of particular classes within society. As Puxty (1991, p. 39) states:

> I do not accept that I see legitimation as innocuous. It seems to me that the legitimation can be very harmful indeed, insofar as it acts as a barrier to enlightenment and hence progress.

In considering the use of social and environmental disclosures to legitimize corporate behaviour, Deegan, Rankin and Tobin (2002, p. 334) state:

> Legitimising disclosures mean that the organisation is responding to particular concerns that have arisen in relation to their operations. The implication is that unless concerns are aroused (and importantly, the managers *perceive* the existence of such concerns) then unregulated disclosures could be quite minimal. Disclosure decisions driven by the desire to be legitimate are not the same as disclosure policies driven by a management view that the community has a *right-to-know* about certain aspects of an organisation's operations. One motivation relates to survival, whereas the other motivation relates to responsibility.

Deegan, Rankin and Tobin (2002, p. 335) further state:

> Legitimising disclosures are linked to corporate survival. In jurisdictions where there are limited regulatory requirements to provide social and environmental information, management appear to provide information when they are coerced into doing so. Conversely, where there is limited concern, there will be limited disclosures. The evidence suggests that higher levels of disclosure will only occur when community concerns are aroused, or alternatively, until such time that specific regulation is introduced to eliminate managements' disclosure discretion. However, if corporate legitimising activities are successful then perhaps public pressure for government to introduce disclosure legislation will be low and managers will be able to retain control of their social and environmental reporting practices.

Consistent with the above discussion, according to Guthrie and Parker (1990, p. 166), the political economy perspective adopted by critical theorists emphasizes the role of accounting reports in maintaining (or legitimizing) particular social arrangements. As they state:

> The political economy perspective perceives accounting reports as social, political, and economic documents. They serve as a tool for constructing, sustaining, and legitimising economic and political arrangements, institutions, and ideological themes which contribute to the corporation's private interests.

The role of accounting in legitimizing the capitalist system

Given the role of these reports in 'constructing, sustaining, and legitimising economic and political arrangements, institutions, and ideological themes which contribute to the corporation's private interests' (Guthrie and Parker, 1990, p. 166), the classical political economy perspective views one of the key roles of accounting reports as being to legitimize the capitalist system as a whole, and protect this system from threats arising as a result of the outcomes of the structural conflict inherent in the capitalist system (as discussed earlier in the chapter). This, for example, is part of the reason why many critical accounting scholars are opposed to much research into corporate social reporting practices, as we high-lighted earlier in this chapter.

A major critical accounting empirical study, examining the role which dis-closures in annual reports played in protecting (and legitimizing) the capitalist system as a whole from the outcomes of social conflict, analysed the annual reports of the US-based car multinational General Motors over the period 1917 to 1976. This empirical material was analysed in a series of papers (Neimark, 1983; Neimark and Tinker, 1986; Tinker *et al.*, 1991; Tinker and Neimark, 1987; Tinker and Neimark, 1988) which demonstrated that the focus of voluntary, discursive, material in the annual reports tended to change to address the changing challenges to capitalism arising from the structural instability of capitalism. For example, in times when the (claimed) symptoms of this structural instability were weaknesses in overall consumer demand, the annual reports focused on giving the impression that increased consumption – such as regularly buying a new car – was an ideal social norm. At other times, when the symptoms of the structural instability of capitalism was labour militancy, the focus of the core messages in the annual report switched to a demonstration that workers were better off if they acted in cooperation rather than in conflict with managers.

The argument in these studies seems to be that while successful articulation of these management viewpoints might benefit General Motors economically, through maintaining the support of economically powerful stakeholders, they also benefited the capitalist system as a whole because, for example, developing a norm of consumption in times of weakened overall economic demand should result in greater demand for the products of many businesses. If many other businesses also used their annual reports, in conjunction with messages in many other media such as advertising, newspaper articles etc., at this point in history to help reinforce a consistent message about the social desirability of consumption, this would help protect and advance the power and wealth of many businesses by increasing overall consumer demand. As Tinker, Lehman and Neimark (1991, p. 39) state:

> The General Motors studies (Neimark, 1983, Neimark and Tinker, 1986, Tinker and Neimark, 1987, Tinker and Neimark, 1988) focus on the various ways the company uses its annual reports as an ideological weapon, and the social circumstances that govern one use rather than another ... [they uncover] the conflictual and antagonistic situations that embroiled GM over that period, and the way the firm's reports were used to modify and ameliorate these conflicts ... This is not to argue that annual reports have a dramatic impact on business and political decision making. Rather, like other ideological materials (party political statements, advertising, public relations 'fluff', religious dogma) it is the repetition of the mundane and particularly the censoring of other points of view that make these reports most effective.

Chapter summary

This chapter provides an overview of research that has been undertaken by people who have been classified as working within the critical perspective of accounting. These researchers are very critical of current accounting practices. They argue that existing financial accounting practices support the current economic and social structures – structures that unfairly benefit some people at the expense of others. The view that financial accounting practices are neutral and objective (as promoted in various conceptual framework projects) is challenged.

The critical perspective of accounting covers many different specific perspectives, of which we have only had space to explore a few of the major ones in this chapter. However, at a broad level, much critical accounting research is grounded in classical political economy theory in which conflict, inequity and the role of the State are central to the analysis. While the research positions of many critical accounting scholars are informed by a Marxist critique of capitalism, there are many other critical accounting researchers whose critiques of the role of accounting in sustaining inequities in society are not based on Marxist philosophy. A common theme among most Marxist (and some non-Marxist) critical accounting theorists are calls for fundamental changes in how society is structured as, without this restructuring, they believe that any changes or modifications to accounting practices will have no effect in making society more equitable for all. Critical theorists also argue that governments (the State) tend to put in place mechanisms and regulations to support existing social structures. Many accounting researchers are also believed to be supporters of particular political ideologies with the results of their research being influential in supporting those people with privileged access to scarce capital.

Although this chapter is relatively brief, the aim has been to provide an insight into a point of view that traditionally has not received a great deal of attention in accounting education or in accounting journals. Perhaps, as the critical theorists would argue, this lack of attention is due to the fact that this branch of the accounting literature challenges so many of the views and values held not only by accountants, but by many others within society. The literature can indeed be quite confronting. It does, however, provide a different perspective on the role of accountants, and one that we should not immediately dismiss. If the literature causes us to be critical of our own position as accountants within society, well and good. As a concluding quote, we can reflect on the following statement by Baker and Bettner (1997, p. 293):

Accounting's capacity to create and control social reality translates into empowerment for those who use it. Such power resides in organisations and institutions, where it is used to instill values, sustain legitimizing myths, mask conflict and promote self-perpetuating social orders. Throughout society, the influence of accounting permeates fundamental issues concerning wealth distribution, social justice, political ideology and environmental degradation. Contrary to public opinion, accounting is not a static reflection of economic reality, but rather is a highly partisan activity.

Questions

12.1 What is a *critical perspective* of accounting?

12.2 What are some of the fundamental differences between the research undertaken by *critical theorists*, relative to the work undertaken by other accounting researchers?

12.3 From a critical perspective, what is the role of a conceptual framework project?

12.4 From a critical perspective, can financial reports ever be considered objective or neutral? Explain your answer.

12.5 If it is accepted that there are many inequities within society, would critical theorists argue that introducing more accounting, or *improved* methods of accounting, would or could help, or would they argue that such a strategy will only compound existing problems? Explain your answer. Do you agree with the position taken by the critical theorists? Why?

12.6 Critical theorists would challenge the work of authors whose work is grounded within Positive Accounting Theory. What is the basis of their opposition?

12.7 Critical theorists would challenge the work of authors whose work is grounded within legitimacy theory. What is the basis of their opposition?

12.8 If accounting is deemed to be complicit in sustaining social inequities, how would critical theorists argue that accounting can be 'fixed'?

12.9 Tinker, Merino and Neimark (1982) argue that 'the social allegiances and biases of accounting are rarely apparent; usually, they are 'masked' pretensions of objectivity and independence'. Explain the basis of this argument.

12.10 Cooper and Sherer (1984) argue that 'accounting researchers should be explicit about the normative elements of any framework adopted by them. All research is normative in the sense that it contains the researcher's value judgements about how society should be organized. However, very few accounting researchers make their value judgements explicit'. Do you agree or disagree with this claim? Why?

12.11 Explain the importance in critical accounting theory of assumptions regarding the distribution of power in society. How do these assumptions differ from those adopted in other theoretical perspectives?

Notes

1 The assumption that there is a spread of rights and privileges across different groups within society is commonly referred to as pluralism.

2 The Oxford English Dictionary (2nd edition, 1989) contains several definitions of the word 'praxis', including 'The practice or exercise of a technical subject or art, as distinct from the theory of it' and 'Habitual action, accepted practice, custom'. However, as will become clear from the discussion in the next few paragraphs, the word 'praxis' in most critical accounting research is used in a very specific manner which accords with the following definition from the Oxford English Dictionary: 'A term used ... to denote the willed action by which a theory or philosophy (esp. a Marxist one) becomes a social actuality'.

3 In this Marxist perspective on workers' feelings of alienation, ' ... the market-place ... purports to be a sphere of individual freedom, but is in fact a sphere of collective slavery to inhuman and destructive forces' (Wood, 1995, p. 525)

4 Legitimacy theory and stakeholder theory, which were both examined in Chapter 8, are embedded within a 'bourgeois' political economy perspective.

5 Included in the Oxford English Dictionary's (2nd edition, 1989) definition of *emasculation* is: 'The depriving of force, vigour ...; making weak'.

6 However, there does not seem to have been much of a reciprocal movement by some critical accounting researchers towards recognizing the potential impact that some social and environmental accounting research may have had in reducing a variety of negative social and environmental externalities of some businesses. This lack of movement by some critical accounting researchers is implied, for example, in a statement by Tony Tinker (2005, p. 124, footnote 18) that in selecting areas of accounting research for one of his latest critiques based on a Marxist approach to critical accounting 'Environmental research is another candidate, however as far as 'the cannon' is concerned I have little to add to the 1991 critique (Tinker *et al.*, 1991)'.

7 From a research perspective it has also been argued that critical theorists have been marginalized because they do not tend to use mathematical modelling and statistical analysis – both of which have become (to many researchers, as well as to a number of editors of accounting journals) part of accepted accounting research. As Hopper *et al.* (1995, p. 532) state: 'Critical researchers emphasise the social embeddedness of accounting practice, consequently, they tend to neglect mathematical modelling, preferring detailed historical and ethnological studies of structures and processes which help identify societal linkages to show that accounting is not merely a technically rational service activity but plays a vital role in effecting wealth transfers at micro-organizational and macro-societal levels (Chua, 1986).'

8 Contrast this with the view provided by public interest theory – a theory of regulation described in Chapter 3 and in which it is argued that government puts in place rules and regulations for the benefit of society generally.

9 According to Tinker, Merino and Neimark (1982), researchers within the positive accounting and efficient markets paradigm adopted 'a neoconservative ideological bias that encourages us to take the 'free' market and implicit institutional apparatus as given'. We discussed Positive Accounting Theory and the efficient markets hypothesis in Chapters 7 and 10 respectively.

10 Consistent with this perspective, in 1979, Milton Friedman, a leading advocate of deregulation, became a senior adviser to President Reagan.

11 In recent years, however, it does appear that more research of a critical nature is being published within some leading accounting journals. One journal that has been in existence for a number of years (edited by David Cooper and Tony Tinker) and which publishes various 'critical' papers is *Critical Perspectives on Accounting*. According to the journal (as per its Instructions to Authors), it 'aims to provide a forum for a growing number of accounting researchers and practitioners who realize that conventional

theory and practice is ill-suited to the challenges of the modern environment, and that accounting practices and corporate behaviour are inextricably connected with many allocative, social and ecological problems of our era. From such concerns, a new literature is emerging that seeks to reformulate corporate, social and political activity, and the theoretical and practical means by which we apprehend and affect that activity'.

12 This is consistent with the argument provided by Solomons (1978) that to increase the usefulness of accounting reports they should be as objective as cartography. That is, just as an area can be objectively 'mapped', so can the financial position and performance of an organization.

13 We are again back to the position that we introduced in Chapter 2 – accountants are indeed very powerful individuals.

References

Arnold, B. & de Lange, P. (2004) 'Enron: an examination of agency problems', *Critical Perspectives on Accounting*, **15** (6–7), pp. 751–65.

Arnold, P. (1990) 'The state and political theory in corporate social disclosure research: A response to Guthrie and Parker', *Advances in Public Interest Accounting*, **3**, pp. 177–81.

Bailey, D., Harte, G. & Sugden, R. (2000) 'Corporate disclosure and the deregulation of international investment', *Accounting, Auditing & Accountability Journal*, **13** (2), pp. 197–218.

Baker, C. & Bettner, M. (1997) 'Interpretive and critical research in accounting: A commentary on its absence from mainstream accounting research', *Critical Perspectives on Accounting*, **8** (1), pp. 293–310.

Baker, R. C. (2003) 'Investigating Enron as a public private partnership', *Accounting, Auditing & Accountability Journal*, **16** (3), pp. 446–66.

Boyce, G. (2000) 'Public discourse and decision making: exploring possibilities for financial, social and environmental accounting', *Accounting, Auditing & Accountability Journal*, **13** (1), pp. 27–64.

Briloff, A. (2004) 'Accounting scholars in the groves of academe In Pari Delicto', *Critical Perspectives on Accounting*, **15** (6–7), pp. 787–96.

Burchell, S., Clubb, C., Hopwood, A., Hughes, J. & Naphapiet, J. (1980) 'The roles of accounting in organisations and society', *Accounting, Organizations & Society*, **5** (1), pp. 5–28.

Carpenter, V. & Feroz, E. (1992) 'GAAP as a symbol of legitimacy: New York State's decision to adopt generally accepted accounting principles', *Accounting, Organizations and Society*, **17** (7), pp. 613–43.

Chua, W. F. (1986) 'Radical developments in accounting thought', *The Accounting Review*, **LXI** (4).

Collison, D. J. (2003) 'Corporate propaganda: Its implications for accounting and accountability', *Accounting, Auditing & Accountability Journal*, **16** (5), pp. 853–86.

Cooper, D., Hayes, D. & Wolf, F. (1981) 'Accounting in organized anarchies', *Accounting, Organizations & Society*, **6**, pp. 175–91.

Cooper, D. J. & Sherer, M. J. (1984) 'The value of corporate accounting reports – arguments for a political economy of accounting', *Accounting, Organizations and Society*, **9** (3/4), pp. 207–32.

Cousins, J., Mitchell, A., Sikka, P., Cooper, C. & Arnold, P. (2000) *Insolvent abuse: Regulating the insolvency industry*, Basildon: Association for Accountancy and Business Affairs.

Craig, R. J. & Amernic, J. H. (2004) 'Enron discourse: the rhetoric of a resilient capitalism', *Critical Perspectives on Accounting*, **15** (6–7), pp. 813–52.

De George, R. (1995) 'Praxis', in Honderich, T. (ed.) *The Oxford Companion to Philosophy*, Oxford: Oxford University Press, pp. 713.

Deegan, C., Rankin, M. & Tobin, J. (2002) 'An examination of the corporate social and environmental disclosures of BHP from

1983–1997', *Accounting, Auditing & Accountability Journal*, **15** (3), pp. 312–43.

Froud, J., Johal, S., Papazian, V. & Williams, K. (2004) 'The temptation of Houston: a case study of financialisation', *Critical Perspectives on Accounting*, **15** (6–7), pp. 885–909.

Fuerman, R. D. (2004) 'Accountable accountants', *Critical Perspectives on Accounting*, **15** (6–7), pp. 911–26.

Gray, R., Owen, D. & Adams, C. (1996) *Accounting and Accountability: Changes and Challenges in Corporate Social and Environmental Reporting*, London: Prentice-Hall.

Gray, R., Owen, D. & Maunders, K. (1988) 'Corporate social reporting: emerging trends in accountability and the social contract', *Accounting, Auditing and Accountability Journal*, **1** (1), pp. 6–20.

Gray, R., Owen, D. & Maunders, K. T. (1987) *Corporate Social Reporting: Accounting and Accountability*, Hemel Hempstead: Prentice-Hall.

Guthrie, J. & Parker, L. (1990) 'Corporate social disclosure practice: A comparative international analysis', *Advances in Public Interest Accounting*, **3**, pp. 159–75.

Hines, R. (1988) 'Financial accounting: In communicating reality, we construct reality', *Accounting, Organizations and Society*, **13** (3), pp. 251–62.

Hines, R. (1991) 'The FASB's conceptual framework, financial accounting and the maintenance of the social world', *Accounting, Organizations and Society*, **16** (4), pp. 313–51.

Hopper, T., Annisette, M., Dastoor, N., Uddin, S. & Wickramasinghe, D. (1995) 'Some challenges and alternatives to positive accounting research', in Jones, S., Romano, C. & Ratnatunga, J. (eds) *Accounting Theory: A Contemporary Review*, Australia: Harcourt Brace and Company.

Hopper, T. & Powell, A. (1985) 'Making sense of research into the organisational and social aspects of management accounting: A review of its underlying assumptions', *Journal of Management Studies*, pp. 429–65.

Hopwood, A. G. (1983) 'On trying to study accounting in the context in which it operates', *Accounting, Organizations & Society*, **8** (2/3), pp. 287–305.

Lehman, G. (1999) 'Disclosing new worlds: a role for social and environmental accounting and auditing', *Accounting, Organizations & Society*, **24** (3), pp. 217–42.

Lehman, G. (2001) 'Reclaiming the public sphere: Problems and prospects for corporate social and environmental accounting', *Critical Perspectives on Accounting*, **12**, pp. 713–33.

Macintosh, N. B. (2001) *Accounting, Accountants and Accountability*, London: Routledge.

Macintosh, N. B. & Baker, R. C. (2002) 'A literary theory perspective on accounting: Towards heteroglossic accounting reports', *Accounting, Auditing & Accountability Journal*, **15** (2), pp. 184–222.

Marx, K. & Engels, F. (1967) *The Communist Manifesto*, Harmondsworth: Penguin.

Merino, B. & Neimark, M. (1982) 'Disclosure regulation and public policy: A socio-historical appraisal', *Journal of Accounting and Public Policy*, **1**, pp. 33–57.

Miliband, E. (1969) *The State in Capitalist Society*: Weidenfeld & Nicholson.

Miliband, E. (1983) 'State power and class interest', *New Left Review* (March), pp. 57–68.

Mitchell, A., Puxty, A., Sikka, P. & Willmott, H. (1994) 'Ethical statements as smokescreens for sectional interests: The case of the UK accountancy profession', *Journal of Business Ethics*, **13** (1), pp. 39–51.

Mouck, T. (1992) 'The rhetoric of science and the rhetoric of revolt in the story of positive accounting theory', *Accounting, Auditing and Accountability Journal*, **5** (1), pp. 35–56.

Neimark, M. (1983) 'The social constructions of annual reports: A radical approach to corporate control', Unpublished Doctoral Dissertation, New York University.

Neimark, M. & Tinker, A. (1986) 'The social construction of management control systems', *Accounting, Organizations & Society*, **11** (3), pp. 369–96.

Neu, D. & Cooper, D. (1997) 'Accounting interventions', Paper presented at Fifth Interdisciplinary Perspectives on Accounting Conference, University of Manchester.

O'Connell, B. T. (2004) 'Enron. Con: "He that filches from me my good name. makes me poor indeed" ', *Critical Perspectives on Accounting*, 15 (6–7), pp. 733–49.

O'Dwyer, B. (2005) 'The construction of a social account: a case study in an overseas aid agency', *Accounting, Organizations and Society*, 30 (3), pp. 279–96.

Offe, C. & Ronge, V. (1978) 'Theses on the theory of the state', in Giddens, A. & Held, D. (eds) *Class, Power and Conflict*, London: Edward Arnold, pp. 32–9.

Owen, D., Gray, R. & Bebbington, J. (1997) 'Green accounting: Cosmetic irrelevance or radical agenda for change?' *Asia-Pacific Journal of Accounting*, 4 (2), pp. 175–98.

Puxty, A. (1986) 'Social accounting as immanent legitimation: A critique of a technist ideology', *Advances in Public Interest Accounting*, 4, pp. 95–112.

Puxty, A. (1991) 'Social accountability and universal pragmatics', *Advances in Public Interest Accounting*, 4, pp. 35–46.

Puxty, A., Sikka, P. & Willmott, H. (1994) '(Re)Forming the circle: Education, ethics and accountancy practices', *Accounting Education*, 3 (1), pp. 77–92.

Selto, F. & Neumann, B. (1981) 'A further guide to research on the economic consequences of accounting information', *Accounting and Business Research*, 11 (44), pp. 317–22.

Sikka, P., Wearing, B. & Nayak, A. (1999) *No accounting for exploitation*, Basildon: Association for Accountancy and Business Affairs.

Sikka, P. & Willmott, H. (2005) 'The withering of tolerance and communication in interdisciplinary accounting studies', *Accounting, Auditing & Accountability Journal*, 18 (1), pp. 136–46.

Solomons, D. (1978) 'The politicization of accounting', *Journal of Accountancy*, 146 (5), pp. 65–72.

Thompson, G. (1978) 'Capitalist profit calculation and inflation accounting', *Economy and Society*, pp. 395–429.

Tinker, A. & Gray, R. (2003) 'Beyond a critique of pure reason: From policy to politics and praxis in environmental and social research', *Accounting, Auditing & Accountability Journal*, 16 (5), pp. 727–61.

Tinker, A., Lehman, C. & Neimark, M. (1991) 'Falling down the hole in the middle of the road: Political quietism in corporate social reporting', *Accounting, Auditing and Accountability Journal*, 4 (1), pp. 28–54.

Tinker, A. & Neimark, M. (1987) 'The role of annual reports in gender and class contradictions at General Motors: 1917–1976', *Accounting, Organizations and Society*, 12 (1), pp. 71–88.

Tinker, A. & Neimark, M. (1988) 'The struggle over meaning in accounting and corporate research: A comparative evaluation of conservative and critical historiography', *Accounting, Auditing & Accountability Journal*, 1 (1), pp. 55–74.

Tinker, A. M., Merino, B. D. & Neimark, M. D. (1982) 'The normative origins of positive theories: Ideology and accounting thought', *Accounting, Organizations and Society*, 7 (2), pp. 167–200.

Tinker, T. (2005) 'The withering of criticism: A review of professional, Foucauldian, ethnographic, and epistemic studies in accounting', *Accounting, Auditing & Accountability Journal*, 18 (1), pp. 100–35.

Unerman, J. & Bennett, M. (2004) 'Increased stakeholder dialogue and the internet: towards greater corporate accountability or reinforcing capitalist hegemony?' *Accounting, Organizations and Society*, 29 (7), pp. 685–707.

Unerman, J. & O'Dwyer, B. (2004) 'Enron, WorldCom, Andersen *et al.*: A challenge to modernity', *Critical Perspectives on Accounting*, 15 (6–7), pp. 971–93.

Williams, P. F. (2004) 'You reap what you sow: the ethical discourse of professional accounting', *Critical Perspectives on Accounting*, 15 (6–7), pp. 995–1001.

Willmott, H. (1990) 'Serving the public interest', in Cooper, D. J. & Hopper, T. M. (eds) *Critical Accounts*, London: Macmillan.

Wood, A. (1995) 'Marx, Karl Heinrich', in Honderich, T. (ed.) *The Oxford Companion to Philosophy*, Oxford: Oxford University Press, pp. 523–26.

Zeff, S. A. (1978) 'The rise of economic consequences', *Journal of Accountancy*, **146** (6), pp. 56–63.

Index